THE HAPPINESS PHILOSOPHERS

The Happiness Philosophers

THE LIVES AND WORKS OF
THE GREAT UTILITARIANS

Bart Schultz

PRINCETON UNIVERSITY PRESS

PRINCETON & OXFORD

Published by Princeton University Press,
41 William Street, Princeton, New Jersey 08540

In the United Kingdom: Princeton University Press,
6 Oxford Street, Woodstock, Oxfordshire OX20 1TR

press.princeton.edu

Jacket art: "Marigold," by Morris & Co., 1873.
Hand block-printed paper, 73 ¼ × 22 ½ in. (186.06 × 57.15 cm.).
Photo © Museum Associates / LACMA
Jacket design by Andrea Guinn

ISBN 978-0-691-15477-0
Library of Congress Control Number 2017932289

British Library Cataloging-in-Publication Data is available

This book has been composed in Miller

Printed on acid-free paper. ∞

Printed in the United States of America

10 9 8 7 6 5 4 3 2 1

For Madeleine

Wise and Imaginative, Brave and Strong, Smart and Centered,
And always Kind

CONTENTS

AFTER THE VICE PRESIDENT of the United States Aaron Burr killed his political rival Alexander Hamilton in a duel, on July 11, 1804, his reputation grew steadily more radioactive, until some years later he was forced to leave the country that he had long served. Traveling Europe between 1808 and 1812 as a largely friendless object of controversy, Burr found something of a refuge with two of the great utilitarians, William Godwin and Jeremy Bentham, figures who never went out of their way to avoid controversy when they could instead productively cause it.

Burr had long admired Godwin's famous (and alas, late) wife, Mary Wollstonecraft, author of the 1792 *Vindication of the Rights of Woman* and one of the world's first great feminists. Burr believed in equality for women and used to have Wollstonecraft's picture hanging over his mantel. Godwin, living in London with his family, welcomed Burr's company. Burr, for his part, was delighted to be received by one of the most amazing literary families in history, and he developed a special affection for the daughter of Godwin and Wollstonecraft, Mary, who would in short order run off with and then marry the scandalous, brilliant atheist poet Percy Bysshe Shelley and write the horror classic *Frankenstein*. As Charlotte Gordon has observed, even at age thirteen Mary was impressive. One evening, the children persuaded Burr

> to listen to eight-year-old William deliver a speech that Mary had written, entitled 'The Influence of Government on the Character of the People'. Fanny served tea while Burr admired a singing performance by Jane . . . .
>
> Burr praised the tea and the song, but he reserved his greatest praise for the speech and the speechwriter. Even at thirteen, Mary knew that she was the one who had taken the laurels. She had won Burr's attention with her pen. Her father had taught her that writing was her legacy, that she was the daughter of Wollstonecraft and Godwin, the child of philosophers.[1]

When Burr was not at home with the Godwins, or traveling around Europe, he might well be found at home with Bentham, enjoying the run of Bentham's library. Burr stayed with Bentham, using his mailing address, during his time of European exile, and he introduced the freethinking Irish artist Amelia Curran to him in 1811. Curran painted Bentham's portrait and spent much time with him at Queen's Square Place. She apparently grew quite close to Bentham, who took the place in her heart that Burr had previously occupied. Bentham and Burr were reconciled, but what became of the relationship with Curran remains unknown, though she did become close friends with Percy and Mary Shelley, painting several portraits of the poet.

Burr did however proclaim himself Bentham's disciple.[2]

Did Burr also meet the precocious young John Stuart Mill, whose father was one of Bentham's disciples and consulted Bentham on the education of his children?

The great classical utilitarians lived and worked in just such amazing, absorbing webs of people and places. Mary Wollstonecraft, William Godwin, Aaron Burr, Mary Shelley, Percy Bysshe Shelley, Amelia Curran, Jeremy Bentham, John Stuart Mill—such are the fascinating figures featured in this book, which seeks to bring to life the history of classical utilitarianism in a way worthy of its founders, who ought to be as controversial now as they were then. Their struggles continue, not least their struggles to guarantee a decent education for all and an end to needless suffering. Oddly enough, and despite the passing of centuries, no one today really knows with any finality what is living and what is dead in the classical utilitarianism of Godwin, Bentham, Mill, and Sidgwick, the main characters featured in this book. Their defenses of the claim that the greatest happiness, or pleasure, of the greatest number is the ultimate moral standard remain both rich, historically contextualized resources and a set of ongoing research projects, with the history informing the research and vice versa. The more one probes, the more one needs to probe—the strange only leads to the stranger, to more possibilities. But even in our broken world, the possibilities are very promising.

ACKNOWLEDGMENTS

THE ACKNOWLEDGMENTS SECTION of my book *Henry Sidgwick, Eye of the Universe*, is nine pages long, and much as I would like to repeat all of those expressions of gratitude again and again, I must content myself here with a simple declaration that they still stand—if anything, my indebtedness has grown with time. But there are a few people and places that I must mention here, their contributions to this book being so conspicuous. Among philosophical colleagues, two reviewers for Princeton University have been extremely helpful. One has remained anonymous, but one has been revealed as Roger Crisp, whose extensive commentary is evident on nearly every page of what follows. My Princeton editor, Rob Tempio, has been absolutely wonderful, and his encouragement was crucial in bringing this book to completion. His colleagues Ali Parrington and Eva Jaunzems have also been most supportive, and Maria denBoer did an excellent job of compiling an index. Others who have provided vitally important, encouraging critical feedback on all or part of this work (or certain earlier publications incorporated herein) include: Philip Schofield, the late Derek Parfit, Peter Singer, Kasia de Lazari-Radek, Fred Rosen, Rob Shaver, Anthony Skelton, Brad Hooker, Mariko Nakano-Okuno, Martha Nussbaum, J. B. Schneewind, John Skorupski, Alan Ryan, Georgios Varouxakis, Robert Cord, Jim Crimmins, Thomas Hurka, Placido Bucolo, Hortense Geninet, Alan Gauld, Francesca Mangion, Bill Mandler, Simon Cook, Frank Turner, Tom Holt, Timuel D. Black, and the late Terence Moore.

While I was in the process of correcting the proofs for this book, I received the devastating news that Derek Parfit had died. My first major publication in philosophy was devoted to Parfit's arguments about personal identity, and it was through Parfit, and the late Brian Barry, that I first came to be absorbed in Sidgwick studies. No philosopher has meant more to me than Parfit, and virtually every line of this book, and of my previous books, was written with him in mind. His always generous, always insightful comments on my work, including chapter four of this book, meant more to me than I can say.

I would also like to record my debt to Danielle Allen, whose creation, the University of Chicago Civic Knowledge Project (CKP), has given me a new perspective on philosophy over the course of the last decade, as I have served as its Executive Director. A similar acknowledgement is owed my colleagues on the Board of the Philosophy Learning and Teaching Organization (PLATO). In addition, I would like to thank Sir Richard McAlpine, for generously allowing me to visit Stone Gappe and taking the time to discuss its history with me. Also, Paul and Lucy Irven were extraordinarily gracious and hospitable, when I unexpectedly dropped in on them, upon determining that their Skipton residence (along with the adjoining Cross Keys pub and a power station) was once part of the Old Grammar School and the likely birthplace of Henry Sidgwick. Sidgwick's great niece, Ann Baer, now over one hundred years old, has as always been a wonderful friend and extremely helpful during my visits with her, as has her nephew Andrew Belsey. Naturally, there are also all those libraries that I love so dearly: at Cambridge University, the Wren Library, Trinity College (my favorite library of all), the University Library, Newnham College Library, and King's College Library; at Oxford, the Bodleian Library; the British Library and the Lambeth Palace Library; the Bentham Project at University College London, and all the others listed in *Henry Sidgwick, Eye of the Universe*. My grateful acknowledgments to all of them, and to their wonderful librarians, for facilitating my research and allowing the use of their materials. The various presses that have given me permission to reproduce material are acknowledged in the relevant notes, but a special thanks goes to Cambridge University Press, the publisher of two of my previous books, as well as of the journal *Utilitas*, an indispensable source for anyone working on utilitarianism.

Finally but foremost, my family—without the love and support (and candid criticism) of my wife Marty and my daughter Madeleine (and all the companion animals, real or imagined, inhabiting our home), my life and work would be unimaginable.

THE HAPPINESS PHILOSOPHERS

Introduction

A philosophy is the expression of a man's intimate character.

—WILLIAM JAMES

But even as we as a nation have embraced education as critical to economic growth and opportunity, we should remember that colleges and universities are about a great deal more than measurable utility. Unlike perhaps any other institutions in the world, they embrace the long view and nurture the kind of critical perspectives that look far beyond the present.

—DREW GILPIN FAUST, PRESIDENT OF HARVARD UNIVERSITY

THE WORD "UTILITARIAN" is not apt to strike the right chord in the world's moral consciousness. Today, as in the nineteenth century, it can all too easily conjure up visions of soulless manager drones addicted to "efficient" administration in the least imaginative and most dehumanizing sense, or of those who would destroy a many-sided liberal education in the name of the immediately practical, useful, and vocational. The defenders of the humanities, including the presidents of Harvard and Columbia and their peers, have tended to define themselves by their opposition to instrumental or "utilitarian" approaches to education, which, it is implied, will prioritize "economic growth and opportunity" and miss the big issue: how over the long haul to cultivate individuals who can think critically, empathize with others, imagine better worlds, and actively engage in meaningful democratic citizenship. These, in their view, are the invaluable intangibles that cost-benefit-minded, bean-counting, Dickensian utilitarian functionaries cannot even conceptualize much less defend. The iron-cage of administrative rationality—perhaps with a panoptical observation tower or its security state equivalent—that is all that the utilitarians can offer. And they do not even see it as a problem.[1]

Yet philosophical utilitarianism is and has always been something quite different. The great classical utilitarians, William Godwin, Jeremy Bentham,

John Stuart Mill, and Henry Sidgwick, were certainly not lacking in either imagination or liberal education, and their visions, when defended with some fidelity, are more likely to inspire such influential activists as the philosopher Peter Singer, a founding father of the animal liberation and effective altruism movements, than serve the purposes of managerial "leadership," whether capitalist or state socialist. This book aims to show how and why this is so. It offers, to adapt some titular words from E. M. Forster, "two cheers for utilitarianism."

It offers only two cheers because some of the criticisms of utilitarianism are very serious. But then, two cheers may be about the best that any developed ethical and political theory can hope for, and at any rate, my aim in this work is primarily to foster a better sense of what the great utilitarians were really like, of what they really stood for, when they are considered from all sides. The hope is to revisit and repurpose classical utilitarianism in ways that will bring out some important aspects of it that have tended to be neglected or underestimated by both the critics and the professed friends of utilitarianism, including many economists of the last century. Although certain forms of utilitarianism would appear to have been flourishing in recent decades, the great roots of these perspectives always seem capable of generating new growth.[2] Perhaps the history explored in this book, selective and strategic though it may be, can help facilitate further growth, but simply sparking some greater and more intelligent curiosity about this cast of characters, their lives and works, is hope enough.

Philosophical utilitarianism would seem to be an ism with a sharp point: that the supreme ethical and political principle, the normative bottom line so to speak, demands maximizing total happiness for all sentient creatures living and yet to be. Is this supreme principle true? Possibly—it could turn out that there are decisive objective reasons for it.[3] But at the least, there are certainly lots of more or less powerful arguments in its defense, and it remains a live philosophical option, albeit one with much competition. Putting happiness first in this way is, philosophically and historically, a matter both of revealing how pervasive and inescapable the concern with happiness already is, demonstrating how it undergirds and defines such familiar moral duties as veracity and promise keeping, and of creatively experimenting with possibilities for understanding and advancing happiness in new and more effective ways. As John Stuart Mill recognized, in words adopted by some recent feminist philosophers, it calls for "experiments in living." And with the classical utilitarians, the experiments were exceptionally creative and wide-ranging, imaginative in the extreme. The sharp point tore through the crust of convention and custom and opened up new worlds of possibility. Virginia Woolf, in her marvelous account of Wollstonecraft and Godwin, quoted Godwin's observation, "Ours is not an idle happiness, a paradise of selfish and transitory pleasures," and noted: "No, it too was an experiment, as Mary's life had been an experiment from the start, an attempt to make human conventions conform more closely to human needs."[4]

Described in this way, utilitarianism has little in common with the prosaic, visionless notion of the "merely utilitarian," in the sense of a narrowly or mundanely functional or efficient option. No such limited horizon confined the thought and character of the great English-language utilitarian philosophers, whose influence ran its course from the period just before the French Revolution through the Victorian era. Happiness, for them, was more of a cosmic calling, the path to world progress, and whatever was deemed "utilitarian" had to be useful for that larger and inspiring end, the global minimization of pointless suffering and the global maximization of positive well-being or happiness. It invokes, ultimately, the point of view of universal benevolence. And it is more accurately charged with being too demanding ethically than with being too accommodating of narrow practicality, material interests, self-interestedness, and the like.[5]

Apparently, the very word "utilitarian" came to Bentham in a dream. According to James Crimmins:

> Jeremy Bentham (1748–1832) coined the term 'utilitarian' in the summer of 1781, when he recorded a dream in which he 'was the founder of a sect; of course a personage of great sanctity and importance. It was called the sect of the *utilitarians*.' The dream turns on Bentham's hopes for *An Introduction to the Principles of Morals and Legislation* . . . printed the previous year (but not published until 1789), 'my driest of all dry metaphysics,' parts of which he had read to the company of guests at the country seat of his patron, the reformist Whig the Earl of Shelburne, who served as Prime Minister 1782–1783 and became Marquis of Lansdowne in 1784. In Bentham's telling of the dream he writes, 'there came to me a great man named L. [Shelburne] and he said unto me, what shall I do to . . . save the nation? I said unto him—take up my book, & follow me.' With the noble lord in tow, he then encountered King George III and instructed his 'apostle,' Shelburne, to give the king 'a page of my book that he may read mark learn and inwardly digest it.'[6]

As the years passed, Bentham would dream less of nobles and kings and more of democracy as the utilitarian vehicle for saving the nation and, in fact, the world. But the grandeur and ambition of his vision remained.

Such is the great irony of the legacy of utilitarianism: its name has long been an obstacle to its message. This irony has been compounded by the infatuation, in recent decades, with work in the area of "happiness studies," an offshoot in many respects of the "positive psychology" movement that emphasizes the positive side of human nature, or what the well-being of fully functioning, self-actualizing, super-healthy psychological types seems to involve. Alas, the cascade of recent books on happiness has, with few exceptions (such as Richard Layard's), not been matched by a serious interest in utilitarianism, one of the most historically significant philosophical frameworks for thinking about happiness. Aristotle and ancient eudaimonism have received far more attention in this area than Godwin and Bentham and their successors.[7] The growth industry of happiness studies has largely developed apart from the recent renaissance in utilitarian philosophizing and has owed surprisingly little to it, despite the transformation of utilitarianism into, potentially, one of the most relevant and radically progressive philosophies of our time, sparking vital new work in environmental philosophy, population ethics, global poverty reduction, and more.[8] No such critical edge has marked the "Happiness Industry," as work in happiness studies has been aptly labeled.

Thus, this book is about that other utilitarianism, which is in truth genuine utilitarianism, though it is scarcely recognizable in the pervasive caricatures floated by everyone from Dickens to Marx to Foucault. One thought behind this assemblage of biographical/philosophical sketches is that an introduction to the actual personalities behind utilitarianism might help challenge the dismissive caricatures of this tradition. The great classical utilitarians were fascinating people, brilliant and complex, and as intrinsically interesting as great artists. Inspired, weird, provocative and controversial, they were neither as complacent nor as naïve as their followers—or their critics.

What is more, the ancient concern with philosophy as the art of living or a way of life, and with philosophers as exemplars of philosophies in their actual lived lives, has much to recommend it. The lives of the individuals in question are profoundly interesting as exemplars of the varieties of philosophical experience, to tweak a title from William James. Whatever his factual failings, the tales that Diogenes Laertius tells in his *Lives of the Eminent Philosophers* about Socrates, Plato, Aristotle and so many other philosophers do make them come alive as persons. Although far too many contemporary academic philosophers take an excessively narrow approach, focusing solely on writings rather than persons and dismissing as ad hominem argument a central element of much of the philosophical tradition, there are always powerful critics around ready to challenge that prejudice. As James Miller explains in his engaging work *Examined Lives: from Socrates to Nietzsche*:

> Such a principled disregard of ad hominem evidence is a characteristically modern prejudice of professional philosophers. For most Greek and Roman thinkers from Plato to Augustine, theorizing was but one mode of living life philosophically. To Socrates and the countless classical philosophers who tried to follow in his footsteps, the primary point was not to ratify a certain set of propositions (even when the ability to define terms and analyze arguments was a constitutive component of a school's teaching), but rather to explore 'the kind of person, the sort of self' that one could elaborate as a result of taking the quest for wisdom seriously. [9]

Or as Socrates put it, "If I don't reveal my views in a formal account, I do so by my conduct. Don't you think that actions are more reliable evidence than words?"

That so many previous generations have studied philosophy through such works as those of Diogenes Laertius, Seneca, Plutarch, Montaigne, and Nietzsche, for example, whose accounts of philosophical lives are so often interwoven with ennobling myth, should be taken as an indication that current academic opinion on what is or is not "philosophy" might be more reflective of the institutional imperatives and limits of academe than of the larger historical practices of philosophy. This book reflects the belief that one needs the works *and* the lives, the words *and* the deeds, in order fully to harvest the contributions of the great philosophers, who can be so much more than their books. Nor, as we shall see, is such an approach unfitting for the great utilitarians, for they were deeply indebted to the ancients and offered up their own visions of utilitarianism as a way of life, a way of life often obsessed with the question of *parrhesia* (frank speaking). Mill, for example, was profoundly influenced by the ancient Greek view of philosophy, and was a forceful proponent of the method of interrogating both lives and works, reading a philosopher's works not separately, but as a whole interwoven with the life.[10]

That is, this book is meant to do for the great utilitarians something of what Miller and so many others[11] have done for Socrates, Plato, et al., and it is in that way rather different from the various stock histories of utilitarianism.[12] Curiously, Miller avoids the utilitarians altogether, limiting his account of the moderns to Montaigne, Descartes, Rousseau, Kant, Emerson, and Nietzsche. But as I hope to show, the utilitarians may furnish some of the very best material on the significance of philosophical lives. Just how their lives realized or failed to realize their visions—often quite different visions—of advancing happiness by utilitarian standards is a subject full of surprises, particularly for those wedded to the stock conceptions of utilitarianism. And surely we can learn a lot about the utilitarian legacy by carefully considering what the very philosophers who made utilitarianism famous took to be its practical implications for their most important and personal decisions. If we take their writings seriously, why not take their lives seriously as well, especially when it comes to problems about which their more theoretical works leave us wondering? That their lives were often their best work is particularly evident from the company they kept—as we may see through the examples of Godwin and Mary Wollstonecraft, or Mill and Harriet Taylor. Indeed, the lives are but strands in larger webs of shared lived experience that call to us from the past, asking to be remembered. The friendships and the loves, the children and the young people, the comrades and the mentors, the vulnerabilities as well as the strengths make up much of the story of how these people became who they were. The relevant historical contexts are rich and various, and much is missed when they are condensed and constrained in the current academic fashion.

On this score, it is worth stressing that the great utilitarians represent a special chapter in gender and LGBTQ studies, in the history of constructions of gender and sexuality. Their writings and their lives were often astonishingly insightful, subversive, and transgressive, challenging in unprecedented ways the distortions caused by patriarchal power, homophobia, religious prejudice, etc. There really is nothing like Bentham on same sex relations in the entire history of philosophy, at least up until recent decades.[13]

Perhaps by viewing utilitarianism in this way, it will be possible to better appreciate its complexities and variations, and the ways in which more reductive treatments of this legacy, often as one or another form of ideology, fail to do it justice. This view animated my earlier work, *Henry Sidgwick, Eye of the Universe*, and it shapes the present book, though this is more of a sketchbook and less a detailed portrait. My purpose here is simply to review and pull together some recent, suggestive scholarly developments in dealing with the history of utilitarianism, developments that taken together display the utilitarian legacy in a different and often better light.[14] Again, the point is not to pronounce, in any final, decisive way, on the truth or justifiability of utilitarianism, sympathetic though the portraits will often be. Utilitarianism must change its shape as the times change, and some of the challenges now confronting it (and every other plausible ethical approach) could scarcely have been envisioned during its classical era. But there are still many lessons to learn from that era, and it would be idle to deny that a rather Godwinian hope and method, for life writing as a consciousness raising agent of social change, pervades this work as a whole. Contra various radical critics, the utilitarian legacy harbors some powerful resources for penetrating the perverse psychological and ideological effects of severe inequality, and for envisioning a compelling ethic for dealing with the problems of future generations. The cruel effects of inequality and racial and gender injustice, the harsh failures of such social institutions as prisons and schools, the invisibility of so much suffering, and mistreatment of populations yet to be—utilitarianism may yet help to solve these problems.

Moreover, some of the big and more familiar philosophically charged themes of classical utilitarianism simply do need to be explicated more accurately and researched more thoroughly. The interplay of egoism and benevolence, self and other, often reflects a subtle strategy rather than a conceptual blunder, and a vision of the progress of happiness that has distributive elements built into it in ways that are both defensible and largely ignored by utilitarianism's many critics. Even such powerful recent works as de Lazari-Radek and Singer's *The Point of View of the Universe: Sidgwick and Contemporary Ethics* do not fully capture all the resources of the utilitarian legacy.[15]

Indeed, it is singularly curious that the great "secular" utilitarians had so much to say about the religious side of humanity, about which they could be deeply insightful as well as scathing. Their reformism in ethics and politics was typically bound up with reformism in religion, aimed at the powerful established churches especially. But in the case of the individuals described in what follows, utilitarianism was not only radically reformist in conventional religious terms, but also mixed with a keen interest in the uncanny, the strange, and the occult, with magic, ghosts, necromancy, romanticism, and "intimations of immortality." However dismal the normal business of political economy may be, the great utilitarians couched it in the larger business of getting a grip on life, on the cosmos and one's place in it. It was a quest that carried them into far stranger places than one would ever guess from either their critics or their admirers. They had probing things to say about God and the afterlife, theism and pantheism, the longing for immortality, and the supernatural. If there was a "utilitarian character," it was a character decidedly given not only to a sympathetic opposition to needless suffering, but also to opening up and critically examining religious experience, including some of its weirder dimensions. We would do well to remember that the great pragmatist William James dedicated his extraordinarily wide-ranging *Varieties of Religious Experience* to none other than John Stuart Mill.

Relatedly, it is also important to remember throughout what follows, that there are many possible metaphysical routes to a utilitarian moral theory. The springs feeding a utilitarian outlook have run from such diverse sources as immaterialism (William Godwin), Platonism (G. E. Moore), Absolute Idealism (T.L.S. Sprigge), and a Buddhist conception of the self (Derek Parfit). The naturalism of, say, Mill is but one option, however familiar; although utilitarianism is often thought of as part of a comprehensive philosophical and/or religious doctrine, it can, in some cases, yield something more like an overlapping consensus between different comprehensive doctrines.

There are a great many more issues, philosophical and methodological, that loom here. Some think that philosophical biography is flourishing; others worry that biography as a genre and in general is doomed. For my part, philosophical biography is still a work in progress, and biography as a genre is also changing and in need of change. Whether the present experiment will much advance these improvements remains to be seen. Whether it is even biography in any familiar sense is hard to say. As in *Henry Sidgwick, Eye of the Universe*, the works and lives herein considered are often cast in the light of Edward Said's brilliant critique of Orientalism, or of theoretical frameworks derived from critical race theory, postcolonial studies, etc.[16] To be sure, it is strange that so many academic philosophical works on, say, Mill, could bracket his extensive involvement with the East India Company or his writings on colonization in much the same way that conservative textualists have read, say, Jane Austin, without acknowledging the historical, political, and economic contexts that seep into her fiction. Although the great classical utilitarians were not of one mind about matters of race or imperialism, and in retrospect their views compare favorably with more orthodox ethical and political traditions,[17] that is no reason to erase from history the parts that current philosophers find embarrassing or offensive. Efforts to reconstruct for present purposes the classical utilitarian perspective—or efforts to reconstruct Kantianism, Thomism, Aristotelianism, etc.—must be alert to just what it is, historically, that is being reconstructed. If the critics of utilitarianism fail through ignorant and alarmist hyperbole, the "friends" of utilitarianism often fail as well, through ignorant "charity in interpretation," when really, the truth will do. All too often, what passes for the history of philosophy is ennobling myth, disguised as a righteous fixation on the better arguments.

To call such narrowness a blind spot scarcely does justice to the problem, a problem that plagues much of academic philosophy, which in some parts of the world, such as the United Kingdom and the United States, is in a state of open crisis because of the sexism and racism of its academic practices.[18] Efforts to reconstruct and reinvigorate utilitarianism need to take place on a wider front, and with an honest confrontation with both past and present problems of power and prejudice.[19] The history of philosophy need not be an exercise in evasion and hypocrisy.

These larger debates provide the backdrop for what follows, and my hope is that these personal impressions offered from some historical distance will prove engaging and illuminating enough, perhaps even felicific enough, to render them valuable both in themselves and as contributions to a wider and more diverse practice of philosophy. The future of happiness may depend on it.

CHAPTER ONE

The Adventures of
William Godwin

In April 1788, when he was thirty-two, William Godwin began a journal.
He maintained it for the next forty-eight years, making his final entry on
26 March 1836, less than two weeks before his death at the age of eight-one.
For most of those forty-eight years Godwin followed, so far as he could, the
same daily routine: before breakfast he read from one of the Greek or Latin
classics; in the morning he read and wrote; in the afternoons he became
sociable and sought out one or more of his many London friends, with
whom he enjoyed arguing, dining, and going to the theatre. His journal
reflects this orderly life. Each of the thirty-two, soft-bound notebooks is
of uniform size and shape; each one has been neatly divided into days
and weeks in red ink. The entries themselves (in black ink) are brief and
matter-of-fact. Godwin records what he has read, what he has written, and
the people he has seen. Occasionally he is cryptic: he writes in Latin or
French, or employs a form of personal code. The journal is at once highly
informative and profoundly reticent.

—STEPHEN HEBRON AND ELIZABETH C. DENLINGER,
SHELLEY'S GHOST: RESHAPING THE IMAGE
OF A LITERARY FAMILY[1]

Introduction and Early Life

What was Godwin reticent about in his journal? His life knew the extremes
of fame and obscurity, but both poles could be problematic, and much of his
inner life remains a mystery. What should not be mysterious, however, is the
vital role that he played in the development of philosophical utilitarianism.
Although Bentham is usually given star billing as the first great classical utilitarian, both utilitarians and their critics have on important counts drawn even

more heavily from the works of Godwin. Godwin's puzzle cases and illustrations are familiar to every student of ethics, even though he often does not receive the credit for them.

Thus an infamous moral dilemma often used to condemn utilitarianism goes as follows. Two people are trapped inside a burning building, a palace. One of them is a famous benefactor of humanity, the great Archbishop Fénelon. The other is an obscure individual of no repute, his chambermaid. Only one can be saved—who should it be?

Godwin harbored little doubt that it should be the Archbishop, a benefactor to thousands:

> Supposing I had been myself the chambermaid. I ought to have chosen to die rather than that Fénelon should have died. The life of Fénelon was really preferable to that of the chambermaid. But understanding is the faculty that perceives the truth of this and similar propositions; and justice is the principle that regulates my conduct accordingly. It would have been just in the chambermaid to have preferred the archbishop to herself. To have done otherwise would have been a breach of justice.
>
> Supposing the chambermaid had been my wife, my mother or my benefactor. That would not alter the truth of the proposition. The life of Fénelon would still be more valuable than that of the chambermaid and justice—pure, unadulterated justice—would still have preferred that which was most valuable. Justice would have taught me to save the life of Fénelon at the expense of the other. What magic is there in the pronoun 'my' to overturn the decisions of everlasting truth? My wife or my mother may be a fool or a prostitute, malicious, lying, or dishonest. If they be, of what consequence is it that they are mine?[2]

Critics have found this a monstrous extreme of impartiality, and its author a "monster " or, in De Quincy's words, a "ghoul, or bloodless vampire," a case of waking reason producing nightmares.

Of course, Godwin was no friend of conventional marriage and family, even under normal, non-emergency circumstances, deeming the institution a most perversely unjust form of private property law and an obstacle to human happiness and free love. He would in due course come to be regarded as another terror produced by the French Revolution, but not before putting on the map an influential perfectionistic and anarchistic form of utilitarianism, and giving to the world his and Mary Wollstonecraft's daughter, Mary, who would marry the poet Percy Bysshe Shelley and write the horror classic *Frankenstein*. This was a family of both Reason and Romanticism, a family circle that would spin everything—from utilitarianism to anarchism to atheism to feminism to Gothic horror to children's literature—into an endless fabric of treatises, novels, poems, stories, fables, letters, plays, syllabi, and manifestos. Godwin represented the shock of the new even to those identified with utilitarianism.

Recall that although British utilitarianism came to be identified as a largely secular philosophy, its first influential form was theological. William Paley (1743–1805) was an Anglican clergyman whose *Principles of Moral and Political Philosophy* (1785)—a key text in the curriculum at Cambridge University—helped the utilitarian perspective achieve wide influence.[3] On some counts, Paley was a reformer: he opposed slavery and the slave trade, and championed poor relief and progressive taxation. Still, he was always searching for the concordance of existing religious moral practices and institutions with the greatest happiness. Paley took moral obligation to mean being obliged (commanded or even threatened), and thus anticipated the later utilitarian reliance on external sanctions, rewards, and punishments. The difference was in his reliance on God's commands, with the prospect of heaven or hell, rather than on the visible or invisible hands of social institutions. And for Paley, if the hand of God was invisible, God's handiwork was nonetheless highly visible, not only in scripture, but also in the order of the natural world. In various theological works, he elaborated in classic fashion the argument from Design, which held that nature itself bespoke intelligent design, just as finding a watch in the wilderness would.

It was Paley's fame that spurred both Jeremy Bentham and William Godwin to publicly defend a secular version of utilitarianism, taking the doctrine off its conventional religious foundations. Although Bentham's seminal *Introduction to the Principles of Morals and Legislation* appeared in 1789, its impact was slow at first, and very much in the shadow of Godwin's colossally successful philosophical work of 1793, *An Enquiry Concerning Political Justice, and Its Influence on General Virtue and Happiness,* which was followed in 1794 by his colossally successful novel *Things as They Are, or the Adventures of Caleb Williams.* Thus, although Bentham was the slightly senior figure, it makes sense to begin the story of the great English utilitarians with Godwin, whose name was by far the greater in that formative era. This is, to be sure, a somewhat provocative move, but as will become clear, it is Godwin who better represents utilitarianism in all its tensions and complexities. As Peter Marshall, one of Godwin's best biographers put it:

> Because of his influence on British institutions Bentham has been remembered most, but Hazlitt was undoubtedly right when he observed that Godwin was 'the first *whole-length* broacher of the doctrine of *Utility'.* [Francis Place, the radical tailor] moreover was in a good position to know that the abuse showered on *Political Justice* was 'mainly caused by its propagating utilitarian doctrines'. It is Godwin's transformation of Christian ethics into an original system of utilitarianism which earns him not only an important place in the history of ethics but makes him an innovating moralist highly relevant to the modern world.[4]

Born on March 3rd, 1756, at Wisbech, Cambridgeshire, William Godwin was the son of a Dissenting Protestant minister—who was also the son of a Dissenting minister—who found it difficult to get along with or maintain his congregations. The Dissenters were Calvinists tolerated despite their rejection of the Church of England, though they were banned from the universities and from public office. They formed a permanent oppositional religious group, a mostly prosperous middle-class one, deeply committed to the right of private judgment. A dwindling congregation in Wisbech had the family soon moving to Debenham, in Suffolk, to a congregation that had run through seventeen ministers in sixteen years. Thanks to an Arian schism, Godwin senior's tenure was also short, and in 1760 the family moved to Guestwick, near Norwich, where, thanks to the death of the paternal grandfather, they achieved a certain security. Still, as Mark Philp has noted:

> Godwin's upbringing was rather gloomy. He was not a robust child and his aunt "instructed me to compose myself in sleep, with a temper as if I were never again to wake in this sublunary world." ["Autobiography," in *Collected Novels and Memoirs* (*CNM*), 1992, I, 12.] At five he was reading *The Pilgrim's Progress* with her, together with James Janeway's *Account of the Conversion, holy and exemplary lives and joyful deaths of several young children* (1671–2), and hymns, catechisms and prayers written by Dr. Isaac Watts. One of Godwin's earliest memories was of composing a poem entitled 'I wish to be a minister' (*CNM* I, 15), and a favourite childhood entertainment was to preach sermons in the kitchen on Sunday afternoons.[5]

His mother was warmer, his father colder, and a succession of deeply religious teachers—a Mrs. Gedge, followed by a Mr. Akers who ran a school Godwin attended—apparently insured that Godwin's religious enthusiasms never flagged; he in due course went off to prepare for the ministry with one Samuel Newton, minister of an independent congregation in Norwich, who was under the influence of the strange, very extreme Calvinist Robert Sandeman (1718–1771). Like Godwin's father and grandfather, Sandeman also held that redemption was a matter not of faith or good works, but of right judgment, and he found even most Calvinists deficient in this department. Godwin came to detest Newton for his cruelty and use of caning, leaving him in mid-1770 to go off to become a bookseller before finding his way to the more liberal Hoxton Academy. But the core Sandemanian outlook remained with him in some form all of his life, an outlook that enjoined, on New Testament grounds, not only the rational apprehension of the truth, but also brotherly love, the sharing of wealth, and the equality of the sexes. The right judgment of the individual, truth perceived and proclaimed, so dear to his father, grandfather, and to the Sandemanians, was Godwin's North Star from the beginning of his voyage through to its end. But there was a constellation around it of other points of belief fixed at an early age. As Peter Marshall notes:

> On leaving Newton's intellectual and emotional hothouse, Godwin en-
> tered at the age of seventeen the Dissenting Academy at Hoxton, one
> of the best centres of higher education in eighteenth-century England.
> Godwin received here a thorough grounding in Locke's psychology
> which saw the mind as a blank sheet, in Newtonian sciences which
> pictured the universe as a machine governed by natural laws, and in
> Hutcheson's ethics which upheld benevolence and utility as the corner-
> stones of virtue. The academy was extremely favourable to free enquiry,
> and Godwin formed in his own time a belief in determinism, or in the
> philosophical language of the day, 'necessity'... and in idealism or 'im-
> materialism' (i.e. the external world is created by the mind). These be-
> liefs subsequently underwent no fundamental change.... Godwin was
> a Tory and a Sandemanian when he entered Hoxton Academy. Being
> cautious about accepting new ideas and fearful of eternal punishment,
> he left five years later with his beliefs intact.[6]

Following in the family tradition, and despite his father's warnings about his excessive pride as a child, Godwin, still set on becoming a minister, failed to find a congenial congregation: "Three times he tried to become a minis-ter, and three times he was rejected by rural congregations. They no doubt disliked his learned sermons and pricklish manner."[7] Thanks to those rural congregations, to the ferment of the times, and to a well-read artisan trades-man, Godwin would in the end lose his Calvinism and Tory conservatism and embark on the unsteady career of a writer. At age 26, while waiting for one of his congregations to reject him,

> [a]n artisan put into his hands the works of D'Holbach, Helvetius and
> Rousseau, the most subversive philosophers of the French Enlighten-
> ment whose banned works were causing an uproar on the other side of
> the Channel.... Godwin read in Rousseau that man is naturally good
> but corrupted by institutions, that the foundation of private property
> was the beginning of the downfall of humanity, and that man was born
> free, and everywhere he is in chains. From Helvetius and D'Holbach, he
> learned that all men are equal and society should be formed for human
> happiness. When he closed the covers of their books, his whole world
> view had changed.[8]

The artisan tradesman in question, to whom history owes a great debt, was Frederick Norman, and his timely reading list added to other forces in God-win's life—his growing sympathies for the Whigs during the controversies over the American Revolution, and an enhanced appreciation for Roman historians and Jonathan Swift that conduced to republicanism—to produce a remarkable conversion, both to the views of Socinus, who denied Christ's divinity and the doctrine of original sin, and to a much needed change in career aspirations. Godwin moved to London, hoping to make it as a writer and teacher.

Success did not come quickly, to put it mildly. In 1783 he published a remarkably progressive tract, *An Account of the Seminary*, which was a prospectus for a school that he intended to open in Epsom, one that would offer a wide range of foreign and classical language instruction for a small cohort of pupils. For Godwin, "our moral dispositions and character depend very much, perhaps entirely, upon education."[9] The plan was excellent, but not the recruitment: no students showed up.

But Godwin did write at a furious pace, producing his first book (a life of the Tory politician William Pitt), lots of pamphlets on behalf of the Whig cause, and a string of forgettable novels. He was, to a considerable degree, doing political reporting for the Dissenting community through his contributions to the *New Annual Register*, journalistic work that paid the bills. Perhaps most interestingly, a selection of his sermons, the 1784 *Sketches of History*, shows him softening to the views of Satan in Milton's *Paradise Lost*. For Godwin, it was understandable that Satan should rebel against such a tyrannical God, and after his fall continue to rebel, because, as Godwin put it in *Political Justice*, "he saw no sufficient reason for that extreme inequality of rank and power which the creator assumed." Having reached such a juncture, his next step was scarcely surprising: "His friendship with the radical playwright Thomas Holcroft further persuaded him to become an atheist and confirmed the evils of marriage and government."[10] Although Godwin did not remain an out-and-out atheist for long, he neither returned to genuine religious orthodoxy nor to belief in a personal God, but only to a form of cosmic optimism that saw a mysterious power in the universe moving it in the direction of perfection. His "arc of the moral universe," however, bent toward a form of justice not usually associated with the utilitarian legacy.

The Spirit of the Age

Godwin had, in fact, reached many of the ideals of the French Revolution in advance of the event, and was well positioned to give English utilitarian thinking a very different cast from that favored by Paley. When 1789 came, there was never any question about which side Godwin was on. Indeed, he even helped with the publication of Tom Paine's *Rights of Man*. When Burke famously responded in his classic of reactionary prejudice, *Reflections on the Revolution in France*, Godwin conceived the idea of writing a major work that would transcend pamphleteering and make the principles of justice clear once and for all, and he persuaded his publisher to support him in the endeavor, which would yield his immortal—for many, immoral—work, *Political Justice*, an overnight sensation that made him, in Hazlitt's words, "as a sun in the firmament of reputation." As his famous daughter Mary would later sum it up: the idea that "no vice could exist with perfect freedom" was "the very basis of his system, the very keystone of the arch of justice, by which he desired to knit together the whole human family."[11] In Godwin's words, "Once annihilate the quackery of government, and the most homebred understanding might be strong enough to detect the artifices of the state juggler that would mislead him." Government stood in the way of genuine society and sociability, of mutual aid, as Peter Kropotkin would later call it, and of individual growth. And it often did so in sinister, indirect ways, seeping into people's souls and creating "mind-forg'd manacles," including an unhealthy awe of the great and powerful. Godwin would take Adam Smith's vision of social progress through freedom and the "euthanasia" of government to a new level, showing, in effect, how Smith had failed to address the full scope of social power and domination.

Godwin's aim was to "treat in a methodical and elementary way of the principles of science," in this case the science of politics. And in his helpful (and quite consistent) "Summary of Principles, Established and Reasoned Upon in the Following Work," which first appeared in the third edition, the very first principle is the highly utilitarian "The true object of moral and political disquisition, is pleasure or happiness."[12] After distinguishing between the primary and secondary pleasures (the "pleasures of intellectual feeling, the pleasures of sympathy, and the pleasures of self-approbation") and indicating that the latter are "more exquisite" than the former, he states, "The most desirable state of man, is that, in which he has access to all these sources of pleasure, and is in possession of a happiness the most varied and uninterrupted," which is a state of "high civilization." And more specifically, justice, which is the "true standard of the conduct of one man towards another," is "a principle which proposes to itself the production of the greatest sum of pleasure or happiness." It requires that "I should put myself in the place of an impartial spectator of human concerns, and divest myself of retrospect to my own predilections."[13] The impartial, moral point of view led straight to utilitarianism, which in Godwin's hands seemingly called on people to take the impartial, moral point of view at a great many turns.

But again, as the body of the work demonstrates, the road to high civilization is more blocked than built by government, which thwarts "individual independence." "Government, as it was forced upon mankind by their vices, so has it commonly been the creature of their ignorance and mistake," and although intended to "suppress injustice," it "offers new occasions and temptations for the commission of it." Monarchy was the worst form of government, but even more representative regimes were simply tools of the wealthy and powerful, generating only an illusion of consensus and, through the machinations of party politics and such devices as the secret ballot, generating a love of lies rather than a love of truth. Thus, "the most desirable state of mankind, is that which maintains general security, with the smallest encroachment upon individual independence."[14] Government and law are nothing but coercion, reflecting the "venal compact" of tyrants rather than the appeal to reason, and Godwin's depiction of their complex, obfuscatory support of class interests is as harsh as Bentham's indictment of "sinister interests." And like Bentham, he has no patience with doctrines of "natural rights" or social contractarian views of political legitimacy. If Godwin allowed that "I am entitled to the produce of my labour on the basis of the right of private judgement" and "my neighbor has a right to my assistance if he is in need," this was because of the beneficial consequences involved, not because of any inalienable natural rights or revered social institutions: "The idea of property, or permanent empire, in those things which might be applied to our personal use, and still more in the produce of our industry, unavoidably suggests the idea of some species of law or practice by which it is guaranteed. Without this, property could not exist. Yet we have endeavoured to show, that the maintenance of these two kinds of property is highly beneficial." Furthermore:

> The most destructive of all excesses, is that, where one man shall dictate to another, or undertake to compel him to do, or refrain from doing, anything . . . otherwise than with his own consent. Hence it follows that the distribution of wealth in every community, must be left to depend upon the sentiments of the individuals of that community. If in any society wealth be estimated at its true value, and accumulation and monopoly be regarded as the seals of mischief, injustice and dishonor, instead of being treated as titles to attention and deference, in that society the accommodations of human life will tend to their level, and the inequality of conditions will be destroyed. A revolution of opinions is the only means of attaining to this inestimable benefit. Every attempt to effect this purpose by means of regulation, will probably be found ill conceived and abortive. Be this as it will, every attempt to correct the distribution of wealth by individual violence is certainly to be regarded as hostile to the first principles of public security.[15]

Indeed, whether the matter was one of social contract or simply keeping a promise or honoring a legal contract, the last word came with the individual's judgment of the best consequences. Every case was a "rule to itself," and the dead hand of the past should never be allowed to strangle future possibilities. Promises and contracts were only to be made on the understanding that they would have no force should felicific calculations run against the keeping of them, a point that applied to the marriage contract as well: "[M]arriage is an affair of property, and the worst of all properties. So long as two human beings are forbidden by positive institution to follow the dictates of their own mind, prejudice is alive and vigorous. So long as I seek to engross one woman to myself, and to prohibit my neighbor from proving his superior desert and reaping the fruits of it, I am guilty of the most odious of all monopolies."

Godwin admits that "property is the keystone that completes the fabric of political justice. According as our ideas respecting it are crude or correct, they will enlighten us as to the consequences of a *simple form of society without government*, and remove the prejudices that attach us to complexity."[16] And however much he stressed that the change must come from the increasing enlightenment and evolution of humanity, and noncoercively, he also stressed that the change must come and that a high ideal of perfection should light the way. The simple justice of the matter is this:

> I have an hundred loaves in my possession and in the next street there is a poor man expiring with hunger, to whom one of these loaves would be the means of preserving his life. If I withhold this loaf from him, am I not unjust? If I impart it, am I not complying with what justice demands? To whom does the loaf justly belong?
>
> I suppose myself in other respects to be in easy circumstances, and that I do not want this bread as an object of barter or sale, to procure me any of the other necessities of a human being. Our animal wants have long since been defined and are stated to consist of food, clothing and shelter. If justice have any meaning, nothing can be more iniquitous, than for one man to possess superfluities, while there is a human being in existence that is not adequately supplied with these.
>
> Justice does not stop here. Every man is entitled, so far as the general stock will suffice, not only to the means of being, but of well being. It is unjust, if one man labour to the destruction of his health or his life, that another man may abound in luxuries. It is unjust, if one man be deprived of leisure to cultivate his rational powers, while another man contributes not a single effort to add to the common stock.[17]

Of course, Godwin was thoroughly convinced that the change would come, not only without violent revolution, but with the positive aid of the wealthy and privileged: "The rich and great are far from callous to views of general felicity, when such views are brought before them with that evidence and attraction of which they are susceptible."[18] Invincible truth might win them over as well, without resort to violence, secrecy, party machinations, or subversive associations. Indeed, Godwin did not think that England was really ready for full democracy, a view that was only reinforced with age. The effects of an enslaving government ideology were still so powerful and the sincerity of virtuous minds still so weak that the mere mechanisms of democracy would not be sufficient to produce the needed reforms.

Ironically perhaps, many of the most consistent elements of Godwin's philosophy were at odds with what would come to be regarded, albeit much too simplistically, as leading features of classical utilitarianism: empiricist naturalism, psychological egoism (the assumption that human action was largely and by nature narrowly self-interested, or should be treated as such for purposes of legislation), and extensive concern with institutions to insure that a utilitarian result came of partial or self-interested human action. His hedonism, like the younger Mill's, made important distinctions between higher and lower pleasures, and although clearly a determinist despite his immaterialism, his version of "necessity" allowed prominent roles for consciousness, reason, individual judgment, and benevolence (the causation involved concerned mental events). Indeed, his views are far more Socratic in the robust sense of making virtue dependent on knowledge of truth: "Mind is not an aggregate of various faculties contending with each other for the mastery, but on the contrary the will is in all cases correspondent to the last judgment of the understanding. When men shall distinctly and habitually perceive the folly of luxury, and when their neighbours are impressed with a similar disdain, it will be impossible that they should pursue the means of it with the same avidity as before."[19]

What is more, according to Philp, Godwin epitomized "the optimism of events in France at the time he began writing" and "looked forward to a period in which the dominance of mind over matter would be so complete that mental perfectibility would take a physical form, allowing us to control illness and ageing and become immortal." Even sleep and death might be conquered. The road to this perfectibility was, of course, not revolution, but gradual political and cultural reform that would raise consciousness, refine sentiment, and increase anarchy, leaving more and more matters to individual judgment, since "law, private property, marriage and concerts" were but so many forms of "mental enslavement."[20] Godwin was extremely wary of any form of association or cooperation that would incline or encourage people to go along with others rather than think for themselves.

Indeed, Godwin's *Political Justice* was in many ways like an extreme combination of Mill's *Utilitarianism* and *On Liberty*, but with some very novel elements about the extraordinary, liberating power of mental cultivation and biofeedback. And like Mill's work, it has been interpreted as not really or only inconsistently utilitarian—anarchist, undoubtedly, despite the fact that Godwin used the term "anarchy" in the common pejorative sense, and *not* to self-identify. But utilitarian, doubtfully, given his many claims about the perfection of humanity. Thus, Philp has ably and knowledgeably argued that Godwin's utilitarianism could at best be described as "complex utilitarianism," but is probably better described as perfectionism. That is, for Philp, Godwin is clearly not an act utilitarian (calculating the utility of particular individual acts) in the style of Bentham, who having "established the objective nature of this end [utility] . . . is transformed into a besotted systematiser whose primary concern is to devise the most effective institutional structure possible for its fullest realization. His writings thus offer us blueprints, systems, and minute classifications." [21] "Complex utilitarianism," or some form of "ideal, rule and indirect utilitarianism," might better fit Godwin, but "is just too sophisticated for this period." A better alternative account of the coherence of Godwin's views interprets them as an elaborate "perfectionist argument":

> The end for human beings is the development of their rational capacities to the fullest possible extent. But Godwin's commitment to this end cannot be understood as a commitment to the maximization of pleasure. As we become more perfectly rational beings we achieve higher forms of pleasure, but the true end for rational beings, and the reason that Godwin conditions the pursuit of pleasure with ideal, rule and indirect restrictions is the development of a wisdom that can best be characterized as a state of blessedness.[22]

Philp makes a powerful case, and he certainly has a keen eye for the more eccentric sides of Godwin's work. *Political Justice* is indeed one of the most ample funds of bizarre visionary statements ever created, with such passages as:

> The men therefore who exist when the earth shall refuse itself to a more extended population, will cease to propagate, for they will no longer have any motive, either of error or duty, to induce them. In addition to this they will perhaps be immortal. The whole will be a people of men, and not of children. Generation will not succeed generation, nor truth have in a certain degree to recommence her career at the end of every thirty years. There will be no war, no crimes, no administration of justice as it is called, and no government. These latter articles are at no great distance; and it is not impossible that some of the present race of men may live to see them in part accomplished. But beside this, there will be no disease, no anguish, no melancholy and no resentment. Every man will seek with ineffable ardour the good of all.[23]

Godwin himself allows that such claims are "a deviation into the land of conjecture," not crucial to his argument, and there is less of such speculation in the final edition of *Political Justice*. He is more concerned to show how history involves greater and greater perfecting than to describe some final end state of absolute perfection. Still, how, one asks, could one ever think anything like that on nontheological grounds?

The basic answer seems to be that Godwin conceived of mind as rather like an immaterial muscle that could be endlessly buffed. As Philp explains it, in a wonderfully concise summary of Godwin's worldview:

> Our errors arise from the domination of our understanding and will by brute sensation; but because these errors involve us in contradictions and absurdities, we are continually driven to re-evaluate our judgements, actions and objectives. As we do so, our rational capacities gradually improve and gain ascendancy over our brute natures. We come to see the insignificance of the baser pleasures and recognize that

our true happiness lies in the development of our intellectual capacities, the practice of benevolence and the wholehearted pursuit of the common good. It is therefore as a consequence of our increasing rationality and the subjection of our brutish passions to rational control and direction that we are able to emancipate ourselves from government. When people no longer selfishly pursue wealth and power, the accumulation of property and the twin evils of luxury and poverty will cease. . . . The decline of the realm of politics is thus premised on the rise of the realm of morality. But it is an enlarged morality, since it requires the flowering of a full and disinterested benevolence rooted in the increasing ascendancy of truth and reason over what is traditionally conceived of as our irremediably corrupt human nature. This is why Godwin's anarchism cannot be separated from his perfectibilism. Our progressive understanding of truth involves more than a simple liberation from authority, coercion, control and discipline by others. It is also a liberation from non-rational determinants, including our non-rational natures. To achieve progress we must also subject our appetites, passions, needs and so on to rational direction and control. But this process is essentially one of gaining increasing mental control over our physiological natures.[24]

Thus, "private judgment" just keeps getting better and better, and the march of mind and invincible truth—which was, as we shall see, increasingly linked by Godwin to a sensitive cultivation and refinement of the social affections and sympathetic feeling—could potentially yield a race of sleepless immortals who would not even put up with the bondage of being a musician or actor forced to repeat the compositions of others. The duty each owes to the increasing exercise of his or her private judgment and to the Truth with a capital T that it beholds, which as Philp argues, was a Godwinian constant, may have led to what today seem strikingly strange results, but Philp is surely correct in claiming that "Godwin's faith in the brightness of humanity's future was founded upon a moral philosophy and a philosophy of mind and action which, although now largely discredited, was firmly established in the circles in which he lived, talked and worked." [25] For example, Thomas Holcroft, the aforementioned radical playwright who became Godwin's great friend, held the same view, and it was later widely believed that he had held off death from a heart condition through sheer mental effort. Perhaps, as suggested below, with Godwin this was something of a sublimated quest for the philosopher's stone and the elixir of life, the secret of immortality.

At any rate, much of what Godwin conjectured on this score would seem to fit well with the beliefs of those today who hold that health can be highly dependent on one's attitudes and outlook. In some passages worthy of the youth culture of the late nineteenth century (or the 1960s), he celebrates youthful habits and cheerfulness as the best antidote to aging. Moreover, the "true source of cheerfulness is benevolence. . . . But virtue is a charm that never fades. The soul that perpetually overflows with kindness and sympathy, will always be cheerful. The man who is perpetually busied in contemplations of public good, will always be active."[26]

Why, then, is all this supposedly at odds with utilitarianism? Philp sums it up in a more recent piece:

> Godwin's endorsement of both the principle of utility as the sole guide to moral duty and the principle of private judgment as a block on the interference of others, is not without tensions. His consistent doctrine is a combination of these two principles: that it is each individual's duty to produce as much happiness in the world as he is able, and that each person must be guided in acting by the exercise of his private judgment, albeit informed by public discussion. If the resulting doctrine is utilitarian it is a highly distinctive form: it is act-utilitarian in that it discounts reliance on rules (although see Barry's suggestion that his act utilitarianism gives way to motive utilitarianism . . . and see Godwin's invocation of sincerity as a partial rule constraint in the first edition); it is ideal, in that it acknowledges major qualitative differences in the pleasures; and it is indirect, in that we can only promote over-all utility by improving the understanding of our fellow human beings. More troubling to the view that this none the less amounts to utilitarianism is Godwin's insistence on private judgment as a basic constraint, and his associated characterisation of the fully moral agent in terms of the fullest possible development of the individual's intellectual powers and potential. Indeed, Godwin's account of pleasure, in terms of the development of intellect and the exercise of its powers, means that the position looks more like perfectionism than it does a form of hedonistic utilitarianism (what is valued is the ideal as much as the pleasures which are integral to it). Furthermore, it suggests that no distinction can be drawn between the means that we adopt to promote the general good and the character of the general good itself. That is, what promotes the general good is the development of human intellect, but the general good just is the development of the human intellect. If that is true, Godwin's account cannot be utilitarian because it cannot be consequentialist.[27]

Yet it is possible to agree with a great deal of what Philp maintains and still remain convinced that the label "utilitarian" belongs by right as much to Godwin as to Bentham. That he was not a Benthamite utilitarian on many points seems obvious enough, but then neither were Mill or Sidgwick or G. E. Moore (also an "ideal" utilitarian). Godwin was simply convinced, on not altogether unconvincing grounds, that "perfectibilism" and utility were two sides of the same coin. It was as impossible to advance the cause of happiness, in any comprehensive way, without perfectibilism, as it would be to try to advance the cause of health without physiology (and health is also both a means and an end). Intellect and truth, virtue and happiness form one bundle: "Will truth, contracted into some petty sphere and shorn of its beams, acquire additional evidence? Rather let me trust to its omnipotence, to its congeniality with the nature of intellect, to its direct and irresistible tendency to produce liberty, and happiness, and virtue."[28] It is more anachronistic to take a thin, modernized academic version of Benthamism as utilitarianism, and then charge everyone else with being inconsistent or compromised as a utilitarian, than to accept the fact that historically utilitarianism took a rich variety of forms, Benthamism being but one of those, and was more complex historically than Philp allows. That "the development of the human intellect" can be both a means and an end is no problem in itself; the same can be said of many ideal goods, such as friendship, and of many pleasures, such as those of a wine connoisseur. Godwinian utilitarianism seems different because it took a different view of basic human nature and the potentialities of mind, identified the most important pleasures composing happiness in perfectibilist terms, and then drew optimistic "anarchist" conclusions. Godwin just did think that the more perfected the mind, the better the grasp of the truth of utilitarianism.[29] And, at least in the first edition of *Political Justice*, he held, in highly Socratic fashion, that to grasp the truth was to act on the truth; Reason moved and motivated people, and the more people moved and motivated by it, the better.

It might be added, again, that many of the same complexities, e.g., concerning mental development, means and ends, figure prominently in Mill. Consider some passages from his "Inaugural Address at St. Andrews":

> So, at least, it will be if in your early studies you have fixed your eyes upon the ultimate end from which those studies take their chief value— that of making you more effective combatants in the great fight which never ceases to rage between Good and Evil, and more equal to coping with the ever new problems which the changing course of human nature and human society present to be resolved. Aims like these commonly retain the footing which they have once established in the mind; and their presence in our thoughts keeps our higher faculties in exercise, and makes us consider the acquirements and powers which we store up at any time of our lives, as a mental capital, to be freely expended in helping forward any mode which presents itself of making mankind in any respect wiser or better, or placing any portion of human affairs on a more sensible and rational footing than its existing one. There is not one of us who may not qualify himself so to improve the average amount of opportunities, as to leave his fellow creatures some little the better for the use he has known how to make of his

intellect. To make this little greater, let us strive to keep ourselves acquainted with the best thoughts that are brought forth by the original minds of the age. . . . I do not attempt to instigate you by the prospect of direct rewards, either earthly or heavenly; the less we think about being rewarded in either way, the better for us. But there is one reward which will not fail you, and which may be called disinterested, because it is not a consequence, but is inherent in the very fact of deserving it; the deeper and more varied interest you will feel in life: which will give it tenfold its value, and a value which will last to the end. All merely personal objects grow less valuable as we advance in life: this not only endures but increases.[30]

The educated, alert, civilized mind, like the healthy body, is both means and end. Many of the higher pleasures—and many of the lower ones, for that matter—are both means to a happy life and part of a happy life.[31]

And after all, Godwin, like Mill, thought that it was on sound utilitarian grounds that he was so passionately concerned with promoting the political significance of discussion, of the forum, in its best form: "Promoting the best interests of mankind eminently depends upon the freedom of social communication. Let us imagine to ourselves a number of individuals, who, having first stored their minds with reading and reflection, proceed afterwards in candid and unreserved conversation to compare their ideas, to suggest their doubts, to remove their difficulties and to cultivate a collected and striking manner of delivering their sentiments. Let us suppose these men, prepared by mutual intercourse, to go forth to the world, to explain with succinctness and simplicity, and in a manner well calculated to arrest attention, the true principles of society." If "their hearers instigated in their turn to repeat these truths to their companions," then we "have an idea of knowledge as perpetually gaining ground, unaccompanied with peril in the means of its diffusion. Reason will spread itself, and not a brute and unintelligent sympathy."[32]

But these felicific consequences come from "independent and impartial discussion," and can be lost in the "insatiate gulf of noisy assemblies."[33] Educational reform was the key to facilitating the right kind of discussion, to raising the sincere, freethinking, benevolent individuals capable of it. And for Godwin, as for Bentham, iniquitous inequality of educational opportunity was part and parcel of iniquitous inequality in general: "Is it well, that so large a part of the community should be kept in abject penury, rendered stupid with ignorance and disgustful with vice, perpetuated in nakedness and hunger, goaded to the commission of crimes, and made victims to the merciless laws which the rich have instituted to oppress them? Is it sedition to enquire whether this state of things may not be exchanged for a better?"[34] Godwin was if anything even more scathing than Bentham in his condemnation of the educational establishment, including Sunday Schools, Oxbridge, state schools, etc.

This is, of course, not to deny that he favored a great many other reforms as well. He envisioned a system of small voluntary federations, possibly with some noncoercive representative apparatus, that would form to carry out co-operative projects serving the social good. Juries would settle disputes between the federations, but persuasion, exhortation, and education were the key tools, not force. This vision went far beyond republicanism and representative liberal democracy in their usual senses, calling instead for consultation and consensus without the threat of force backing them up and without party politics and such devices as secret ballots. And this held even for dealings with criminals, who in the present system were simply being hardened in their criminality:

> The most common method pursued in depriving the offender of the liberty he has abused is to erect a public jail, in which offenders of every description are thrust together, and left to form among themselves what species of society they can. Various circumstances contribute to imbue them with habits of indolence and vice, and to discourage industry; and no effort is made to remove or soften these circumstances. It cannot be necessary to expatiate upon the atrociousness of this system. Jails are, to a proverb, seminaries of vice; and he must be an uncommon proficient in the passion and the practice of injustice, or a man of sublime virtue, who does not come out of them a much worse man than when he entered.[35]

This passage, as true now as then, is quoted approvingly in Colin Ward's twentieth-century anarchist classic, *Anarchy in Action*.[36] It is small wonder that so many later self-avowed anarchists, from Kropotkin to Ward to Chomsky, would count Godwin as one of their own, given his vision of a truly individualist and voluntary form of communism or communalism. If only people could be cured of the destructive ambition that has them forever seeking greater wealth and luxury, then the truly valuable goods—the means of subsistence and of moral and intellectual growth, and the inexpensive and compossible pleasures—could be had by all equally. In his condemnation of endless material growth and capitalist accumulation, and his devastating critique of the exploitation involved in extensive property rights not grounded in genuine human need and the labor of the individual, Godwin would prove to be an inspiration for not only future anarchists, but for future socialists and radical critics of capitalist oppression across the board. The radical democratic, working-class Chartism movement of the 1840s would invoke his work, as would Marx and Engels.[37]

Godwin well knew what he was saying and how explosive it was. In his original preface, he stated flatly that the "people of England have assiduously been excited to declare their loyalty, and to mark every man as obnoxious who is not ready to sign the Shibboleth of the constitution. Money is raised by voluntary subscription to defray the expense of prosecuting men who shall dare to promulgate heretical opinions, and thus to oppress them at once with the authority of government."[38] Pitt's government, alarmed by the events in France, had grown increasingly repressive, harshly quashing "Jacobinism" at every turn. Godwin (more of a Girondin, not that Pitt cared) only escaped prosecution for treason because his book was deemed too costly to pose much danger of inflaming the masses. But in fact his 1794 novel *Caleb Williams* was meant to be a less costly and more user-friendly introduction to his arguments, and he also bravely pamphleteered for the cause, with such works as *Cursory Structures* (1794), "Letters from Mucius" (1793), and *Considerations on Lord Grenville's and Mr Pitt's Bills, concerning Treasonable and Seditious Practices and Unlawful Assemblies* (1794), which was signed, "By a lover of order." Many of Godwin's friends, including Holcroft and others, from such organizations as the radical (and working-class) Corresponding Society, were being prosecuted and/or imprisoned. Food riots, huge mass meetings in London, and the smashing of King George III's coach window by an angry mob produced a wave of reactionary actions by the Pitt government, effectively crushing free speech for a generation with gag rules, sedition laws, and harassment of one form or another. Otherwise put, in the shorter run, Godwin lost. "Terror," as he noted in the original but unpublished introduction to *Caleb Williams*, was indeed "the order of the day." At least on the political front. There were, of course, other fronts as well.

Love's Reasons

Godwin's turbulent times led to turbulent love.

At a dinner in 1971, he met the great love of his life, Mary Wollstonecraft. He had hoped to talk with Tom Paine, but Paine proved less the conversationalist than expected, and the talk was dominated by Wollstonecraft, the author of the *Vindication of the Rights of Man* (a direct response to Burke) and the *Vindication of the Rights of Woman*, a classic founding text of modern feminism that argued forcefully for the full equality of women as rational beings, not decorative toys. In her words:

> Contending for the rights of women, my main argument is built on this simple principle, that if she be not prepared by education to become the companion of man, she will stop the progress of knowledge and virtue; for truth must be common to all, or it will be inefficacious with respect to its influence on general practice. And how can woman be expected to co-operate unless she know why she ought to be virtuous? Unless freedom strengthen her reason till she comprehend her duty, and see in what manner it is connected with her real good?[39]

Godwin was more irritated than impressed at that first dinner, where he "heard her, very frequently when I wished to hear Paine."[40] And she had at that point acquired "the practice of seeing everything on the gloomy side, and bestowing censure with a plentiful hand," whereas he "had a strong propensity, to favourable construction." Despite a few more encounters, things did not ignite until after a dinner arranged by one Mary Hays on January 8, 1796, when Wollstonecraft, after having seen France first hand and fully established herself as a serious radical feminist critic of marriage, of Rousseau's view of women, of the turn the revolution was taking, and much else besides, found in Godwin something of a soulmate, another who believed that "from the exercise of reason, knowledge and virtue naturally flow."[41] He was, she realized, a most supportive and sympathetic man.

Godwin was not, despite his fame, the most striking of figures. He had a huge head with thinning hair, a heavy brow and a big nose, short legs, and a habit of dress more appropriate to the Dissenting minister that he never was. (Excepting a few dashing yellow coats, this manner of dress stuck with him his whole life, though his youthful slimness did not). Moreover, as "a man, he was somewhat slow of perception, poor in conversation, and pedantic in manner. A sedentary celibate, he had little of Wollstonecraft's experience of love and the world."[42] She, however, "was above the middle height, and well proportioned; her form full; her hair and eyes brown; her features pleasing; her countenance changing and impressive; her voice soft, and, though without great compass, capable of modulation."[43] Godwin would later describe her in somewhat more vivid terms:

> We not unfrequently meet with persons, endowed with the most exquisite and delicious sensibility, whose minds seem almost of too fine a texture to encounter the vicissitudes of human affairs, to whom pleasure is transport, and disappointment is agony indescribable. This character is finely portrayed by the author of the Sorrows of Werter [*sic*]. Mary was in this respect a female Werter. . . . Her whole character seemed to change with a change of fortune. Her sorrows, the depression of her spirits, were forgotten, and she assumed all the simplicity and the vivacity of a youthful mind. She was like a serpent upon a rock, that casts its slough, and appears again with the brilliancy, the sleekness, and the elastic activity of its happiest age. She was playful, full of confidence, kindness and sympathy. Her eyes assumed new luster, and her cheeks new colour and smoothness. Her voice became cheerful; her temper overflowing with universal kindness; and the smile of bewitching tenderness from day to day illuminated her countenance, which all who knew her will so well recollect, and which won, both heart and soul, the affection of almost every one that beheld it.[44]

She had flown in the face of convention often enough, renouncing marriage but having affairs with the married painter Henry Fuseli and the American radical Gilbert Imlay, by whom she had a daughter, Fanny. She had twice attempted suicide as the relationship with Imlay soured. Godwin, after that January dinner, began to fall in love with her, partly through her book, *Letters Written during a Short Residence in Sweden, Norway, and Denmark*, and when she audaciously took the initiative in calling on him, in April, he was receptive to her advance. Wollstonecraft was struggling to emerge from her relationship with Imlay; Godwin was ready to submerge himself in he knew not what. Virginia Woolf has memorably described her initiative and his receptiveness:

> It was in this crisis that she again saw Godwin, the little man with the big head, whom she had met when the French Revolution was making the young men in Somers Town think that a new world was being born. She met him—but that is a euphemism, for in fact Mary Wollstonecraft actually visited him in his own house. Was it the effect of the French Revolution? Was it the blood she had seen spilt on the pavement and the cries of the furious crowd that had rung in her ears that made it seem a matter of no importance whether she put on her cloak and went to visit Godwin in Somers Town, or waited in Judd Street West for Godwin to come to her? And what strange upheaval of human life was it that inspired that curious man, who was so queer a mixture of meanness and magnanimity, of coldness and deep feeling—for the memoir of his wife could not have been written without unusual depth of heart—to hold the view that she did right—that he respected Mary for trampling upon the idiotic convention by which women's lives were tied down? He held the most extraordinary views on many subjects, and upon the relations of the sexes in particular.[45]

In response to some poetical courting on Godwin's part, Wollstonecraft responded, "I want besides to remind you, when you write to me in *verse*, not to choose the easiest task, my perfections, but to dwell on your own feelings—that is to say, give me a bird's-eye view of your heart." She moved to Somers Town, where he now lived, and by July he was writing: "I love your imagination, your delicate epicurism, the malicious leer in your eye, in short everything that constitutes the bewitching tout ensemble of the celebrated Mary." Passionate in ways that previously he had reserved for justice, he declared, "When I make love, it shall be with the eloquent tones of my voice, with dying accents, with speaking glances (through the glass of my spectacles), with all the witching of that irresistible, universal passion. . . . When I make love, it shall be in a storm, as Jupiter made love to Semele, & turned her at once to a cinder."[46] By mid-August they were physical lovers as well, though it was always very much a union of minds, both believing that sensual attraction should start there.[47] By September, she would write to him:

> Let me assure you that you are not only in my heart, but my veins, this morning. I turn from you half abashed—yet you haunt me, and some

look, word or touch thrills through my whole frame—yes, at the very moment when I am laboring to think of something, if not somebody, else. Get ye gone Intruder! Though I am forced to add dear—which is a call back—

When the heart and reason accord there is no flying from volup-tuous sensations, I find, do what a woman can—Can a philosopher do more?[48]

In fact, it is transparently clear that their relationship provided Godwin with that variegated mix of the lower and higher pleasure about which he had previously only theorized, rather too abstractly. Wardle nicely explains: "Each was a stronger and better person for the fusion; each found through it fulfillment—a fulfillment which Mary had long sought in vain and which Godwin had never before known to exist."[49] His gentle, decorous advances to such literary ladies as Elizabeth Inchbald (for whom he cared deeply) and Amelia Alderson were simply not on the order of Godwin and Wollstonecraft. They read each other's drafts, criticizing and apologizing, and exchanged little notes all day long, while each was at work in their own residence, awaiting the evening when they would reunite. Fanny adored Godwin, calling him "Man," and for the first time in Godwin's life, the very real pleasures of domesticity, with an equal, a friend and partner in work, were driven home to him.

But it all moved too quickly. By the end of 1796, Wollstonecraft was pregnant—"Godwin's 'chance-medley system' of contraception, which seems to have been a kind of rhythm method, had clearly failed."[50] Godwin, who really was, as she thought, deep down a most "tender considerate creature," was of course ready to stand by her, despite her declaration, "I can abide by the con-sequences of my own conduct, and do not wish to envolve any one in my dif-ficulties." In fact, she quickly found that she wanted and needed the support, so much so that she suggested that they marry. Both apparently decided that this ammunition being handed to their critics was less unfelicific than the nasti-ness and ostracism attendant upon another illegitimate child, and on March 29, 1797, they ceremoniously entered into that "most odious of all monopolies" at St. Pancras Church in London, with only one witness/guest and a conviction that they could do without all those lines about swearing obedience.

They finally fully moved in together, at house 29, "The "Polygon," and the immediate task confronting them was to explain themselves to their friends and defend themselves against their enemies. A marriage between the two great opponents of marriage was a great temptation to mirth and mockery—"Heigho! What charming things would sublime theories be, if one could make one's practice keep up with them," wrote his lady friend Amelia Alderson, who proceeded to turn on them. To Thomas Wedgwood, son of the famous pottery manufacturer Josiah Wedgwood and one of Godwin's greatest followers, he wrote:

The doctrine of my 'Political Justice' is, that an attachment in some degree permanent, between two persons of opposite sexes is right, but that marriage, as practiced in European countries, is wrong. I still adhere to that opinion. Nothing but a regard for the happiness of the individual which I had no right to injure, could have induced me to submit to an institution which I wish to see abolished, and which I would recommend to my fellow-men, never to practice, but with the greatest caution. Having done what I thought necessary for the peace and respectability of the individual, I hold myself no otherwise bound than I was before the ceremony took place.[51]

As Marshall puts it: "It was at least in keeping with the doctrine of *Political Justice* that general moral rules must give way to the urgency of special circumstances. Besides, as Godwin told another correspondent, every day of his life he was obliged to comply with institutions and customs which he wished to see abolished. Morality, he added, 'is nothing but a balance between opposite Evils. I have to draw between the Evils social & personal, of compliance & noncompliance.'" [52]

At that level, William Godwin and Mary Wollstonecraft femme Godwin, as she signed herself, could take care of themselves. Polemical give and take was hardly anything new to them, and they did have many supporters, including Godwin's mother, who was supportive of him until her death in 1809, many years after the 1772 death of his father. Their love was solid. Despite some occasional and uncharacteristic jealousies, mainly on Wollstonecraft's part, and some all too human squabbling over one thing or another, they really were in each other's veins. She even allowed that a "husband is a convenient part of the furniture of a house, unless he be a clumsy fixture."[53] They were true political and philosophical equals, and made real what for so many others so often remains ideal.

But when their daughter Mary was born, late in the night on August 30, with a midwife attending, things got complicated, and a doctor had to be called in to remove the broken placenta piece by piece, a very painful and very bloody process. The child was fine, and the mother at first appeared to be recovering, until it became evident that septicemia had set in. She died the morning of Sunday, Sept. 10th, her last words devoted to Godwin: "He is the kindest, best man in the world."[54]

Godwin was now truly as much a creature of the heart as of the head, doubting that he "could ever know happiness again." Mary was buried in St. Pancras churchyard, but Godwin was too grief stricken even to attend the funeral. His grief was absolute:

Godwin's first move was to transfer all his books and papers into the room which had been his wife's. He hung Opie's portrait of her which was to remain in his study until he himself died forty years later. He was determined to look after Fanny and the new-born baby, who had been in Maria Reveley's care during their mother's illness, and brought them home. Louisa Jones, a friend of his sister's, came to help and soon became part of the family.

For the time being Godwin rarely went out. His closest friends constantly visited him—Holcroft, the Fenwicks, and Maria Reveley—but they could not dispel his melancholy and anxiety. Seven weeks after the death of his wife, he wrote to one of her friends that he had seen 'one bright ray of light that streaked my day of life only to leave the remainder more gloomy, and, in the truest sense of the word, hopeless'.[55]

He found consolation in going back over his wife's writings and starting work on his biography of her, a work that in many respects stands even higher than *Political Justice* and *Caleb Williams*. It is a work of consciousness-raising truth telling and life writing that in fact explains a very great deal about how Godwin came to his fully mature views, though its honesty about his wife's loves certainly left some people aghast. It was Wollstonecraft who was the "worshipper of domestic life" and best recognized the role personal attachments must play in any serious conception of happiness. As he described her in the *Memoirs of the Author of "A Vindication of the Rights of Woman"*:

> She set a great value on a mutual affection between persons of an opposite sex. She regarded it as the principal solace of human life. It was her maxim 'that the imagination should awaken the senses, and not the senses the imagination.' In other words, that whatever related to the gratification of the senses, ought to arise, in a human being of a pure mind, only as the consequence of an individual affection. She regarded the manners and habits of the majority of our sex in that respect, with strong disapprobation.[56]

Godwin had written to Mary, on June 10, 1797: "You cannot imagine how happy your letter made me. No creature expresses, because no creature feels, the tender affections, so perfectly as you do: &, after all one's philosophy, it must be confessed that the knowledge that there is some one that takes an interest in our happiness something like that which each man feels in his own, is extremely gratifying. We love, as it were, to multiply our consciousness."[57]

Critics, including feminist critics, have maintained that Wollstonecraft's influence on Godwin has been exaggerated, and that he had already become more of a "man of feeling" devoted to the "culture of the heart" when assembling the second, 1796 edition of *Political Justice*, before their romance blossomed. This sensibility, it is claimed, was also manifest in the final chapters of *Caleb Williams*, and it was partly the result of a careful reading of David Hume's *Treatise of Human Nature*, which led Godwin to make his system both more consistently a form of hedonistic utilitarianism and more receptive to the importance of the sentiments (again, the bigger changes occurring in the second edition of *Political Justice*). Hume's account of the affections and the limited circle of human sympathy, and of reason being the slave of the passions, while not leading Godwin to abandon his rational altruism, nonetheless led him to be more accommodating of emotional attachments and the magic in the pronoun "my."[58]

But even if the relationship was not the complete cause of Godwin's altered viewpoint, there can be little doubt that it profoundly reinforced this change and gave Godwin more of a real-world understanding of the meaning of happiness. Moreover, beyond the changes to *Political Justice*, there were the shifts in method evident in other works, a distancing from abstract systematizing toward "an incessant recurrence to experiment and actual observation."[59] He was still very much the reformist, but now it was much clearer to his mind that "the cause of political reform, and the cause of intellectual and literary refinement, are inseparably connected."[60] Rather than resorting to the pamphlet or the treatise, he was more inclined to resort to life writing, to the detailed history of the individual, in his or her full complexity, as the most effective change agent, inspiring people with the spirit of reform. It was the literature of sensibility, and of self-exploration—from Rousseau's *Confessions* to Goethe's *Sorrows of Young Werther*—that moved his pen. He had loved especially that side of Wollstonecraft's writing, preferring the *Letters from Norway* to the *Vindication* (he did not, after all, think much of the notion of natural rights). Whatever the reason, such novels as *St. Leon* (in many respects a Gothic horror story) revealed an altered Godwin, as did *Fleetwood, or The New Man of Feeling*.

He went in fact to some quite unusual extremes in this direction, in such works as the 1809 "Essay on Sepulchres: A Proposal for Erecting Some Memorial of the Illustrious Dead in All Ages on the Spot Where Their Remains Have Been Interred." His hope, somewhat akin to Bentham's plan for Auto-Icons, was to produce something of an "Atlas of Those who Have Lived for the Use of Men Hereafter to be Born." Thomas Laqueur has insightfully described Godwin on this subject:

> Godwin is painfully aware that there exists no more radical rupture than that between the living and the dead body: if its rosy hue could somehow be purchased it 'would be my companion still,' which it— she—painfully is not. The corpse is the great, paradigmatic reminder provided for us by the 'system of the universe' that we are of a degraded nature and of humble origins, that we are mortal. We cast bodies into the ground to mold back into earth as a token of this truth. And yet, strangely, the corpse still remains the person it was, lacking only what seems so little yet so immeasurably great—the breath of life, the 'rosy hue.' He wants to insist that the corpse and the person are not irrevocably sundered, that there is another reality, one grounded in the

emotions, that can challenge the self-evident, acknowledged reality that the dead are really gone; they are no more in this world. . . . As a last resort, Godwin appropriates the remarkable power of the imagination and creates a microcosm of the kinds of stories this book tells. One would have to have an impenetrable heart, he says, not to feel 'a certain sacredness of the grave,' a sensibility as old as writing on the subject of death, and as generative. Based on this intuition—this feeling— Godwin proposes a kind of necromancy: 'the habit of seeing with the intellectual eyes things not visible to the eye of sense,' 'rescuing the illustrious dead from the jaws of the grave,' making 'them pass in review,' querying 'their spirits and recording their answers,' and having 'live intercourse with the illustrious Dead of all ages.' The proposal to erect a small monument, with a name affixed, to the final resting places of the worthy dead—or even the fictional ones like Clarissa—is thus, explicitly, an act of calling them back or willing them into being through an inner voice and the act of building memorials.[61]

As Laqueur shows, Godwin was seeking a secular community of saints, in his effort to make sense of and vindicate the special attachment to the bodies and artifacts of the beloved dead that was so evident in his own life.

Thus, if it was Godwin, more than any other utilitarian, who lent credence to that caricature of the utilitarian as a fanatic of reason, applying the principle of utility at whatever cost to friends, family, and familiar moral rules, it was also Godwin who could learn from experience, including painful personal experience, and grow. Through shifting methods and styles he could make felt in his philosophy the lessons that life taught him. His life presented in microcosm the evolution of utilitarianism on the matter of partial attachments. True, he still believed, as he put it, more softly, in the later editions of *Political Justice*: "A man is of more worth than a beast; because, being possessed of higher faculties, he is capable of a more refined and genuine happiness. In the same manner the illustrious Archbishop of Cambray was of more worth than his valet, and there are few of us that would hesitate to pronounce, if his palace were in flames, and the life of only one of them could be preserved, which of the two ought to be preferred."[62] And true also, he still believed, Reason could do the job as a matter of individual judgment and altruistic action, leaving in doubt what role remained for the state and common-sense moral rules. But now Godwin had second thoughts about special obligations and partial attachments always giving way to impartial utilitarian calculations. In the *Memoirs* of Wollstonecraft, he explained:

> A sound morality requires that "nothing human should be regarded by us with indifference;" but it is impossible we should not feel the strongest interest for those persons whom we know most intimately, and whose welfare and sympathies are united to our own. True wisdom will

recommend to us individual attachments; for with them our minds are more thoroughly maintained in activity and life than they can be under the privation of them, and it is better that man should be a living being, than a stock or a stone. True virtue will sanction this recommendation; since it is the object of virtue to produce happiness; and since the man who lives in the midst of domestic relations, will have many opportunities of conferring pleasure, minute in the details, yet not trivial in the amount, without interfering with the purposes of general benevolence. Nay, by kindling his sensibility, and harmonizing his soul, they may be expected, if he is endowed with a liberal and manly spirit, to render him more prompt in the service of strangers and the public.[63]

This passage, added to the second edition of the *Memoirs*, was also included in Godwin's preface to *St. Leon* and in his response to his former friend, now critic, Dr. Samuel Parr. His response to Parr elaborates in some insightful ways:

For, after all, though I admit that the assiduities we employ for our children ought to be, and must be, the result of private and domestic affections, yet it is not these affections that determine them to be virtuous. They must, as has been already said, be brought to a standard, and tried by a criterion of virtue.

This criterion has been above described, and it is not perhaps of the utmost importance whether we call it utility, or justice, or, more periphrastically, the production of the greatest general good, the greatest public sum of pleasurable sensation. Call it by what name you please, it will still be true that this is the law by which our actions must be tried. I must be attentive to the welfare of my child; because he is one in the great congregation of the family of the whole earth. I must be attentive to the welfare of my child; because I can in many portions of the never-ceasing current of human life, be conferring pleasure and benefit on him, when I cannot be directly employed in conferring benefit on others. I best understand his character and his wants; I possess a greater power of modeling his disposition and influencing his fortune; and, as was observed in *Political Justice*, he is the individual, in the great 'distribution of the class needing superintendence and supply among the class capable of affording them,' whom it falls to my lot to protect and cherish. —I do not require that, when a man is employed in benefiting his child, he should constantly recollect the abstract principle of utility, but I do maintain that his actions in prosecuting that benefit are no further virtuous than in proportion as they square with that principle.[64]

But this passage is really a rather dry rendition of a point that Godwin felt intensely emotional about. In his November 10, 1801 letter to the editor of the *Monthly Magazine*, he responded to a critic as follows:

Really, my friend, I am somewhat at a loss whether to laugh at the impudence of this accusation, or to be indignant at the brutal atrocity and outrageous sentiment of persecution it argues in the man who uttered it. I see that there is a settled and systematical plan in certain persons, to render me an object of aversion and horror to my fellow-men: they think that when they have done this, they will have sufficiently overthrown my arguments. Their project excites in me no terror. As the attack is a personal one, it is only by a retrospect to my individual self that it can be answered.

My character is sufficiently known to you and the friends in whose habitual intercourse I live. Am I a man likely to be inattentive to the feelings, the pleasures, or the interests of those about me? Do I dwell in that sublime and impassive sphere of philosophy, that should teach me to look down with contempt on the little individual concerns of the meanest creature I behold? To come immediately to the point in question, am I, or am I not, a lover of children? My own domestic scene is planned and conducted solely with a view to the improvement and gratification of children. Does my character, as a father, merit reprehensions? Are not my children my favourite companions and most chosen friends?[65]

At an abstract level, Godwin's move here would prove to be the characteristic move for utilitarians (or "complex utilitarians" as Philp calls them), who would commonly defend two-level or indirect forms of utilitarianism allowing that, often enough, it is not utilitarian to have individuals acting directly on the utilitarian principle in their daily decisions.[66] The utilitarian principle should be regarded as a standard to be invoked on reflection under certain special circumstances, not as a maxim or guide expressly invoked in all of one's decisions and actions and at the cost of the very elements of happiness. This though Godwin did think that "the crown of a virtuous character consists in a very frequent and a very energetic recollection of the criterion, by which all his actions are to be tried." As humanity progressed toward ever greater perfection, more and more people would wear such a crown. Some such hope would animate the later utilitarians as well, and it remains ever green.

Some commentators, notably Don Locke in his important work *A Fantasy of Reason: The Life & Thought of William Godwin*, have urged that Godwin's response to Parr represents a fundamental change in his thinking:

Once he had argued that to get a man to do something it was enough to demonstrate that it is right; but now he concedes that what gets a man to do something may be different from what makes it right. Justice or utility is what determines whether my action is moral; but something else is needed, some feeling or emotion, to ensure that the action is performed. And to concede that is, for the author of *Political Justice*, to concede everything; it is to concede that truth will not lead us to justice. Justice may demand that we save Fénelon but a mere man might recognize that fact, and still prefer to save his father. . . . So, humanly speaking we may be incapable of justice, and therefore of political justice.[67]

This is, perhaps, the abstract philosophical version of the notion that Godwin "the great rationalist philosopher of the English Enlightenment was succumbing with his contemporaries to the new cult of sensibility at the end of the eighteenth century."[68]

Yet the change, while real enough in a sense, may not have been either so sharp or so great. At least Godwin himself did not think it so, as he made clear in the later editions of *Political Justice* and in *The Enquirer* (1798), which saw a serious variation in method. They were much less abstractly deductive and more experimental and attuned to experience as "the pole star of truth," while also engaging more extensively with the progressive approach to education that Godwin had long favored, celebrating student-centered growth and the potential of all young people to develop important capabilities, including reasoning capabilities, despite innate temperamental differences. The "true object of education, like that of every other moral process, is the generation of happiness." And what is more:

> Wisdom is not only directly a means to virtue; it is also directly a means to happiness. The man of enlightened understanding and persevering ardour, has many sources of enjoyment which the ignorant man cannot reach; and it may at least be suspected that these sources are more exquisite, more solid, more durable and more constantly accessible, than any which the wise man and the ignorant man possess in common.[69]

Thus Godwin felt that he was expanding and perfecting his system, not abandoning it, though he did allow that he had been too caught up in the contagion that led to the excesses of the French Revolution. The author, with "as ardent a passion for Innovation as ever . . . feels himself more patient and tranquil. He is desirous of assisting others, if possible, in perfecting the melioration of their temper." He is now expanding his investigations into "the humbler walks of private life," and he "ardently desires that those who shall be active in promoting the cause of reform, may be found amiable in their personal manners, and even attached to the cultivation of miscellaneous enquiries. He believes that this will afford the best security, for our preserving kindness and universal philanthropy, in the midst of the operation of our justice."[70] Civility and sensitivity are crucial, since the communication of knowledge must be "without infringing, or with as little as possible violence to, the volition and individual judgement of the person to be instructed. . . . The only possible method in which I can excite a sensitive being to the performance of a voluntary action, is by the exhibition of motive," preferably "intrinsic motives" that "arise from the inherent nature of the thing recommended." For to "be governed by such motives is the pure and genuine condition of a rational being. . . . If a thing be really good, it can be shown to be such."[71]

Thus the change in his views might be construed as amplification and expansion as much as anything. And it would not be out of line to suggest that the imposition of some going form of the "internalism/externalism" distinction on Godwin's notion of reasons—that is, to put it roughly, drawing a sharp contrast between conceiving of moral reasons as inherently motivating and conceiving of them as inert and needing the impetus of external desire—may be as unhelpful as the imposition on him of the "act/rule" distinction.

Even as he mellowed some, or grew more keenly psychological in his investigations, Godwin's radicalism remained potent enough to be seen as part of the dangers spawned by the French Revolution, and from the beginning of the nineteenth century, he was largely off the historical stage, his reputation having waned with that of the revolution, and with the aggressive intolerance of Pitt. Even the later utilitarians tended to disparage him, thinking (wrongly) that he had got the worst of his debates with Thomas Malthus (1766–1834), who had severely criticized his "utopian" view that there was a principle in humanity that would naturally curb excessive population growth. Malthus had criticized Godwin at considerable length in his famous *Essay on the Principle of Population*, though the criticism was mixed with some admiration:

> The system of equality which Mr. Godwin proposes is, on a first view, the most beautiful and engaging of any that has yet appeared. An amelioration of society to be produced merely by reason and conviction gives more promise of permanence than any change effected and maintained by force. The unlimited exercise of private judgement is a doctrine grand and captivating, and has a vast superiority over those systems where every individual is in a manner the slave of the public. The substitution of benevolence, as the masterspring and moving principle of society, instead of self-love, appears at first sight to be a consummation devoutly to be wished. In short, it is impossible to contemplate the whole of this fair picture without emotions of delight and admiration, accompanied with an ardent longing for the period of its accomplishment. But alas! That moment can never arrive. The whole is little better than a dream—a phantom of the imagination. These 'gorgeous palaces' of happiness and immortality, these 'solemn temples' of truth and virtue, will dissolve, 'like the baseless fabric of a vision', when we awaken to real life and contemplate the genuine situation of man on earth.[72]

Godwin in fact had a high regard for Malthus, at least initially, and took him quite seriously, just as he did Bentham. He would write effective responses to him on more than one occasion, not only in his 1820 *Of Population*, and, without being overly utopian in his arguments, rightly point to other factors than famine, disease, and war that could serve to reign in human population growth. He was, in effect, an early champion of the view, now standard in development economics, that at least some forms of progress lead to voluntary population control, and he marshaled a good deal of historical and anthropological evidence to support his case and demolish Malthus's. For better or worse, he was of the mind that "the progressive power of increase in the numbers of mankind, will never outrun the progressive power of improvement which human intellect is enabled to develop in the means of subsistence."[73] And it takes no great feat of historical imagination to think that he would happily have seized on the claim that the emancipation of women would lead to birth control and smaller families. Indeed Francis Place, who would become the common friend and advisor to both Godwin and Bentham, made something very like that point, arguing that contraception would make all the difference.[74]

In any event, dismissive remarks about Godwin's fantasies and waning reputation scarcely capture the magic of the man or the tenor of his vision. Or his resiliency. If his literary reputation was waning because of the nature of the times, he was himself still the most creative and considerate of men. His interest in Fanny and Mary was indicative of his love of children, and of his keen interest in their education. The harsh system that he had endured at the hands of the Sandemanian Samuel Newton had led him early on to progressive views on education, as evidenced in his early and unsuccessful efforts to open a school. This interest remained close to his heart, and the *Examiner* demonstrated how fully developed his ideas were. In fact, on this score, Godwin was in some respects the most progressive and wisest utilitarian of all, especially sensitive to how "it is a miserable vanity that would sacrifice the wholesome and gradual development of the mind to the desire of exhibiting little monsters of curiosity." He became an (anonymous) author of children's books, and went so far as to open up a shop featuring a "choice Collection of School Books; also Cyphering Books, Copy Books, Copper-plate Copies, Quills, Pens, Inkstands, Slates, Blacklead Pencils, Maps and Stationary of all kinds." His various books of fables and history for children were apt to include such morals as: "How happy are children, and the inhabitants of certain nations where no people are rich, that they can live without a continual anxiety about jewels and wealth!"[75] But thanks to his pseudonymous authorship, the books were generally well received and escaped censure from the more orthodox and conservative "Juvenile Libraries." Godwin's pen names were William Scolfield, Edward Baldwin, and Theophilus Marcliffe.

In 1801 Godwin had married again. He met Mary Jane Clairmont, a neighbor with an obscure past, in May of that year, and by December they were wed, with her two illegitimate children, Charles and Mary Jane (later called Claire), also joining the household. In 1803 they would have a son, William Godwin Jr., but it is generally held that the new match produced only a flicker compared to the flame of his first marriage.

Still, it was in collaboration with his new wife that his children's bookshop and publishing house, the Juvenile Library, first opened in 1805. In 1807 they would open a new shop, on Skinner St. in Holborn, where Godwin worked out of sight in an upstairs room, the better not to be known as the hand behind it all. It was an odd fate for the great apostle of sincerity and candor, and as Marshall notes, he was sniffed out by a government agent in 1813, the agent reporting: "The proprietor is *Godwin*, the author of *Political Justice*. There appears to be a regular system through all his publications to supersede all other elementary Books, and to make his Library the resort of Preparatory Schools, that in time the principles of democracy and Theophilanthropy may take place universally."

Arguably, he was somewhat successful in this. Marshall sums it up as follows:

> Godwin's pen and his wife's enterprise thus managed to establish the Juvenile Library as one of the foremost publishers and distributors of children's books. Its list contained more than twenty volumes, with eight booklets in the Copperplate Series. He could be justly proud of them: they were clearly and entertainingly written, handsomely illustrated, well printed and bound, and admirably adapted to children of different ages. They continued to be reprinted long after the firm was forgotten and ensured that Godwin's radical influence reached generations of pupils.[76]

Life was a constant struggle, to be sure, at times a complete crisis, and Godwin had to crank out many other works as well—plays, novels, histories, and on and on (his most memorable work from this period was his excellent *Life of Chaucer*). But for all that, home was often a happy place, and Godwin's life perhaps a happier one than that of the pamphleteering young radical. On one account, "All the family worked hard, learning and studying: we all took the liveliest interest in the great questions of the day—common topics, gossiping, scandal, found no entrance in our circle for we had been brought up by Mr. Godwin to think it was the greatest misfortune to be fond of the world, or worldly pleasure or of luxury or money: and that there was no greater happiness than to think well of those around us, to love them, and to delight in being useful or pleasing to them."[77] Marshall provides this description:

> The children were able to meet some of the best minds of the age. They listened behind the sofa to Coleridge reading his *Ancient Mariner*, they played with Lamb, met Curran, and went on walks with Aaron Burr. Godwin taught the girls Roman, Greek and English history, and they learned French and Italian from tutors. Fanny and Mary drew very well, but as Jane could never draw she learned music and singing instead. Charles knew Latin, Greek, French, mathematics and drawing.

Even the nine-year-old William gave a weekly lecture. In 1812, Burr saw him present, with great gravity and decorum, a lecture written by one of his sisters from a little pulpit on 'The Influence of Governments on the Character of the People.' After the lecture they had tea, and the girls sang and danced an hour.[78]

That last story, also noted in the prologue to this book, is worth rehearsing in more detail. Charlotte Gordon gives this account of it in her remarkable work *Romantic Outlaws: The Extraordinary Lives of Mary Wollstonecraft & Mary Shelley*:

> Skinner Street's central location also made Godwin more accessible to his admirers. Even though he was still considered a notorious radical by many conservatives, political reformers continued to seek Godwin out. Among the most notable was America's third vice president, Aaron Burr. In 1808, Burr had been driven out of the United States by his enemies, only three years after serving as second in command to Thomas Jefferson. During his last year as vice president, Burr had fought a duel and fatally wounded his political rival Alexander Hamilton. Now the fifty-two-year-old was at the low point of his career, and Godwin was one of the few brave enough to befriend him.
>
> A lifelong devotee of Mary Wollstonecraft, Burr believed in the equality of men and women and had encouraged his beloved daughter, Theodosia, to learn Latin, logic, and higher mathematics. But in 1811, tragedy struck: twenty-nine-year-old Theodosia was drowned in a shipwreck off the South Carolina coast. The heartbroken Burr comforted himself by taking a particular interest in the three Godwin girls, nicknaming them "les goddesses." The girls in turn loved Burr. He did not stand on ceremony with them, allowing the girls to call him "Gamp." Sometimes he could be induced to visit them upstairs in the nursery. On one such occasion, they persuaded him to listen to eight-year-old William deliver a speech that Mary had written, entitled 'The Influence of Government on the Character of the People.' Fanny served tea while Burr admired a singing performance by Jane, who, as usual, determined not to be outdone by Mary.
>
> Burr praised the tea and the song, but he reserved his greatest praise for the speech and the speechwriter. Even at thirteen, Mary knew that she was the one who had taken the laurels. She had won Burr's attention with her pen. Her father had taught her that writing was her legacy, that she was the daughter of Wollstonecraft and Godwin, the child of philosophers.[79]

The Godwins had in fact published some of Charles and Mary Lamb's works, and they were very friendly with Burr and the great spirit of the age, Samuel

Taylor Coleridge, whom Godwin had known since the nineties.[80] Coleridge, Robert Southey, and others had planned to build a new Godwinian community, a Pantisocracy, in which property would be held in common, work would be shared and minimized, and government would be equally the work of all. Twelve men and twelve women were to settle on the Susquehanna river in Pennsylvania, at least according to the original plan.

Godwin apparently liked the idea, but the Pantisocracy never actually got off the ground. A lasting relationship with Coleridge did, however. Coleridge even wrote a sonnet "To Godwin":

> O! form'd t' illume a sunless world forlorn,
> As o'er the chill and dusky brow of Night,
> In Finland's wintry skies, the Mimic Morn
> Electric pours a stream of rosy light,
> Pleas'd I have mark'd OPPRESSION, terror-pale,
> Since, thro' the windings of her dark machine,
> Thy steady eye has shot its glances keen—
> And bade th' All-lovely "scenes at distance hail."
> Nor will I not thy holy guidance bless,
> And hymn thee, GODWIN! with an ardent Lay;
> For that thy voice, in Passion's stormy day,
> When wild I roam'd the bleak Heath of Distress,
> Bade the bright form of JUSTICE meet my way—
> And told me, that her name was HAPPINESS.

But what Coleridge admired was Godwin's politics, not his atheism, and their relationship had some serious ups and downs. Indeed, Coleridge felt that he had to meet the challenge posed by Godwin. Yet whatever their conflicts, they had by this point reconciled, and in the end Godwin singled Coleridge out as one of the main influences on him. Henry Crabb Robinson, another of Godwin's keen admirers, records, in a Diary entry from March 1811:

> At C. Lamb's. Found Coleridge and Hazlitt there, and had a half-hour's chat. Coleridge spoke feelingly of Godwin and the unjust treatment he had met with. In apology for Southey's review of Godwin's Life of Chaucer, Coleridge ingeniously observed that persons who are themselves very pure, are sometimes on that account "blunt" in their moral feelings. This I believe to be a very true remark indeed. . . .
>
> Coleridge spoke with severity of those who were once the extravagant admirers of Godwin, and afterwards became his most bitter opponents.[81]

In fact, Godwin's religious views had long ceased to be harshly atheistic, and he could cordially engage and sympathize with Coleridge's views, as another Robinson Diary entry, from February 1812, makes clear:

February 26th A dinner party. Coleridge, Godwin &c. &c. The company rather too numerous. Coleridge by no means the eloquent man he usually is. It was not till ten minutes before he went away that he fell into a declaiming mood "having," as Godwin, said "got upon the indefinites and the infinites," viz. the nature of religious conviction. He contended that the external evidence of Christianity would be weak but for the internal evidence arising out of the necessity of our nature—our want of religion. He made use of one very happy allusion. Speaking of the mingling of subordinate evils with great good, he said, "though the serpent does twine himself round the staff of the god of healing."[82]

Coleridge was the one Godwin chiefly credited for his change of religious views, when their friendship had warmed in 1799:

I ceased to regard the name of Atheist with the same complacency I had done for several preceding years, at the same time retaining the utmost repugnance of understanding for the idea of an intelligent Creator and Governor of the universe, which strikes my mind as the most irrational and ridiculous anthropomorphism. My theism, if such I may be permitted to call it, consists in a reverent and soothing contemplation of all that is beautiful, grand, or mysterious in the system of the universe, and in a certain conscious intercourse and correspondence with the principles of these attributes, without attempting the idle task of developing and defining it—into this train of thinking I was first led by the conversations of S. T. Coleridge.[83]

But it is also, most agree, difficult not to credit Wollstonecraft with having prepared the ground for this concession. Consider Godwin's warm, sympathetic account of her "religion":

Her religion was, in reality, little allied to any system of forms; and, as she has often told me, was founded rather in taste, than in the niceties of polemical discussion. Her mind constitutionally attached itself to the sublime and the amiable. She found an inexpressible delight in the beauties of nature, and in the splendid reveries of the imagination. But nature itself, she thought, would be no better than a vast blank, if the mind of the observer did not supply it with an animating soul. When she walked amidst the wonder of nature, she was accustomed to converse with her God.[84]

And Wollstonecraft had also made her way for a time as an educator, and had composed a piece on "The Education of Daughters." On that subject, too, they were in deep harmony, opposed to corporal punishment and cruelty, in favor of stimulating the imagination and interest in learning. Godwin would recount how Mary, as a young governess, had once had to deal with a rather strict maternal figure who had prohibited her children from reading various books. "These prohibitions had their usual effects; inordinate desire for the things forbidden, and clandestine indulgence. Mary immediately restored the children to their liberty and undertook to govern them by their affections only."[85] Godwin went even further in his *Fables, Ancient and Modern*, claiming:

> If we would benefit a child, we must become in part a child ourselves. We must prattle to him; we must expatiate upon some points; we must introduce quick, unexpected turns, which, if they are not wit, have the effect of wit to children. Above all, we must make our narrations pictures, and render the objects we discourse about, visible to the fancy of the learner.[86]

Godwin manifestly loved children, both his own and in general. While the political climate chilled to freezing, the domestic climate was balmy, and he proved himself to be a thoroughly devoted parent. Though he tried not to show it, Mary was his clear favorite: "She is singularly bold, somewhat imperious, and active of mind. Her desire for knowledge is great, and her perseverance in everything she undertakes almost invincible."[87] And she reciprocated—she was very much her mother's child and her father's girl, not caring much for her stepmother, and she was enjoying a first-rate home schooling, seemingly with the whole Coleridgean clerisy.

And then along came Shelley.

Ruins among the Love

In 1812 matters had gotten singularly rough, financially and otherwise. Godwin had his successes and many supportive friends, but he could never seem to hang on to money or stabilize his finances, and he was forever dependent on the generosity of others, a generosity that in the case of his long-term friend and financial advisor, the radical tailor Francis Place, reached a breaking point in complete exasperation. Time and again he was rescued from bankruptcy only by some last-ditch effort or gift. The financial vicissitudes took their toll, and that was not the end of it.[88]

Many thought that Godwin was not the man he once was. Late in life he would be subject to cataleptic fits, spells of dizziness, fainting, and a very persistent constipation. Heavy, slower than ever, apt to doze off at a dinner unless he was playing the part of the great man, he did not cut the figure of a hero of Romanticism. Indeed, Percy Bysshe Shelley at one point supposed him dead. When corrected, Shelley was overcome with enthusiasm and wrote to Godwin to tell him of his profound admiration for *Political Justice.* The enthusiastic correspondence from this brilliant young admirer, who had been ejected from Oxford for his atheism, at first delighted Godwin. And why not? Shelley explained to him how "your inestimable book on 'Political Justice' . . . opened to my mind fresh & more extensive views, it materially influenced my character, and I rose from its perusal a wiser and a better man.—I was no longer the votary of Romance; till then I had existed in an ideal world; now I found that in this universe of ours was enough to excite the interests of the heart, enough to employ the discussions of Reason."[89]

But Shelley was a more ardent than obedient admirer. An aristocrat who expected a large inheritance, he went about fomenting political rebellion, particularly in Ireland. Godwin had travelled so far down the path leading away from active agitation and toward the effort to free people's minds first that he hardly knew what to do with Shelley, writing to him: "Discussion, reading, enquiry, perpetual communication: these are my favourite methods for the improvement of mankind, but associations, organized societies, I firmly condemn."[90] Hardly knew what to do with him except, that is, to do with him what he did with nearly everyone else: request financial support.

Shelley did help in various ways, though his promises were far greater than his performances. The relationship between master and disciple was tempestuous, to say the least. After March of 1814, things really flew apart. Now going on seventeen, Mary, who had been in Scotland, returned and was reintroduced to Shelley, who was soon writing odes to her: "Upon my heart thy accents sweet / Of peace and pity fell like dew . . ." They had pledged themselves to each other by the grave of her mother. That Shelley was already married seemed to them a matter of little importance. Godwin himself, however, now took a somewhat different view of the institution in question, at least in this particular case. He was flabbergasted, furious, and very far from Reason when Shelley broke the news, and he reacted with every manner of remonstrance and restriction, which, as he of all people should have known, would only strengthen the young couple's resolve. It did, and early in the morning on July 28, 1814, he found Mary's letter, left on his dressing table, informing him that she had eloped with Shelley.

Shelley's wife, Harriet, blamed all this on the influence of *Political Justice*, and she was probably not alone in that thought. The couple had fled to France, and then to Switzerland, taking Claire (Mary Jane) Clairmont with them. They returned in mid-September to a very icy reception. Charles and Fanny played the role of intermediaries in various negotiations, but they too were being drawn into the irrepressible Shelley's orbit, and the Godwins found themselves quite powerless to turn the situation around. The more so as Godwin was forced to continue borrowing money from Shelley in order to avoid ruin. Shelley professed himself still very much Godwin's disciple, and in fact some of his greatest poetry would be devoted to proclaiming the message of *Political Justice*. "Prometheus Unbound," from 1819, is perhaps the best poetic treatment ever given to a philosophy and a philosopher. But for the time being, they mainly confined their discussions to money matters.

As Shelley and his circle continued their experiments, hoping to found a "community of radical spirits," Godwin found that he had another admirer seeking his support for a radical social experiment, none other than Robert Owen (1771–1859), the founder and guiding spirit of New Lanark. Owen shared Godwin's belief in determinism, the role of the environment, and the precedence of nurture over nature, and Godwin often consulted with him during this period, though he found Owen a little too receptive to certain forms of government action, including a national system of education. Still, Owen's great success in his experiment would owe much to Godwin, as would Frances Wright's Nashoba community in Tennessee.

The Shelley circle was far less sober and much more tragic, suicidal, and scandalous. Mary had given birth prematurely to a daughter in 1815, but the infant did not survive. Their son William was born in 1816, but died in 1819, and their daughter Clara, born in 1817, would only survive a year. Both Fanny, Wollstonecraft's daughter with Imlay, and Shelley's wife Harriet committed suicide in 1816. And Claire Clairmont ended up pregnant by another great Romantic poet, none other than Lord Byron. In fact, Mary's novel *Frankenstein, or The Modern Prometheus,* published anonymously but dedicated to her father, had first been conceived during a bleak, sunless, rainy stay near Geneva in June 1816, as a ghost story to entertain a company that included Shelley, Claire, and Byron.[91]

But to Godwin's satisfaction, Shelley and Mary were, following Harriet's death, at last able to marry, which they did in December of 1816. Things were a bit friendlier after that, and Godwin took much pride in Mary's literary work, thinking *Frankenstein* wonderful. He worked very closely with her, as a much interfering editor, on *The Life and Adventures of Castruccio, Prince of Lucca,* a story that, like *Frankenstein,* draws on some of Godwin's favorite themes about destructive ambition. Some of her writings were, however, a bit shocking even for him, especially when they had to do with incest.

Shelley would drown in the Gulf of Spezzia in 1822, and Byron would die in Greece in 1824. Mary would be left with only one child, Percy Florence, born in 1819, and Claire would be left with no one, her child by Byron, Alba (also called Allegra), having died of typhus. Shelley had seemingly gravitated more toward Plato than toward Godwin, in those final years, but the move was not as great as one might suppose, given Godwin's lifelong Socratism and immaterialism. And Shelley's greatest poetry would mainly amount to an extended tribute to his father-in-law, not that his father-in-law had always appreciated it. William St. Clair, in his fascinating, insightful work *The Godwins and the Shelleys: The Biography of a Family,* has observed:

> Godwin told Maria Gisborne that he was eager to read *Prometheus Unbound,* but like others he found the poetry harder going than the Preface. . . . Godwin therefore missed the magnificent ringing speeches

in which the philosophy that he had taught to Shelley was given one of its most vivid and most enduring expressions. But even a cursory glance would have given the main message. *Prometheus Unbound* is a celebration of defiance. The chained but unsubmitting Titan represents suffering humanity at its most noble and at its most effective. It is the Promethean spirit which has brought about every worthwhile human advance. The moral corruption that keeps humanity down among the writhing worms is the institutionalized servility which accustoms them to accept their fate, to perpetuate it, and even to enjoy it.

Aeschylus in his lost drama of *Prometheus Unbound* envisaged an eventual reconciliation between Prometheus and Jupiter, the Champion and the Oppressor—but this was a feeble conclusion, as Shelley could see. Compromise with a cruel and unjust God would be tantamount to submission. Godwin's novels turn on remorse, but as his miseries mounted it was the robust Prometheus of Shelley's myth which increasingly underlay his own life. In his own drama there was going to be no reversal, no triumph, only a long forced retreat until he was overwhelmed. He would however continue to withhold the knee worship, the whining prayers, and the fawning praise which Jupiter demands from the despised slaves who crouch in gratitude round his throne. After two decades of compromise and humiliation, he held hard to the little that was left. Defiance was Godwin's last dignity.[92]

And the defiant Godwin kept on writing and writing, out of necessity. The Juvenile Library, after having moved to the Strand, at last went bankrupt, and Shelley's death was a financial loss as well as a personal one. An enormous work, *History of the Commonwealth*, was a product of this period, as was his extended response to Malthus. A very late novel, *Cloudesley*, begun in 1828, was an unexpected success, (*Deloraine* less so), and a piece of work worthy of the 1960s counterculture, with its theme of love being the key to the universe. But to the end, tragic death haunted him, with his son, William Jr., succumbing to cholera in 1832. He edited for publication his son's unfinished novel, *Transfusion*, adding another touching and insightful memoir of a lost loved one.

Mary's life, too, was often one of enduring loss and isolation. Like her father, she came close to a unique form of ghost seeing or sensing, without the supernatural baggage but yet acknowledging a sense of the uncanny.[93] She could not let go of her dead husband, just as her father could not let go of his dead wife. But her father, while he lived, always did his own quirky best to give her the confidence of independence. In 1823 he wrote to her:

> Do not, I entreat you, be cast down about your worldly circumstances. You certainly contain within yourself the means of your subsistence. Your talents are truly extraordinary. *Frankenstein* is universally known, and, though it can never be a book for vulgar reading, is everywhere

respected. It is the most wonderful work to have been written at twenty years of age that I ever heard of. You are now five-and-twenty, and, most fortunately, you have pursued a course of reading, and cultivated your mind, in a manner the most admirably adapted to make you a great and successful author. If you cannot be independent, who should be?[94]

He even went so far as to add that if "it shall ever happen to you to be placed in sudden and urgent want of a small sum, I entreat you to let me know immediately. We must see what I can do."

St. William

Ironically, just as Godwin was, with *Cloudesley*, in serious danger of becoming the world's first hippie, the political atmosphere started to improve. Various liberalizing reforms culminated in the Reform Act of 1832, which extended voting rights to a large section of the middle class. Godwin may have met Bentham and J. S. Mill for the first time in the early 1830s, in the thick of the changes, which he predictably had reservations about, at least in connection with democratic party politics and the secret ballot.[95] And in the supreme irony, he at last achieved a degree of financial security, thanks to the government that he had so opposed for so long. Grey's Whig ministry decided to support the grand old man with an appointment as Office Keeper and Yeoman Usher of the Receipt of the Exchequer, a position with a salary of £200 per year and free accommodations in New Palace Yard, by the Houses of Parliament. And irony upon irony, he inadvertently helped to burn down Parliament, being out at the theater when the great 1834 fire started. He was supposed to be responsible for maintaining the fire fighting equipment.

When the end came, it was long expected and what Godwin would have wished:

> The man who shocked his readers with the clinical details of Mary Wollstonecraft's death would have wanted the facts to be recorded. From the almost daily mentions of constipation in previous weeks, it seems likely that Godwin may have been suffering from a cancer. But it was the cough that carried him off. After five days of catarrhal fever he took to his bed. Mary Jane and Mary sat at his bedside in turns for the next five nights. 'His thoughts wandered a great deal', Mary noted, 'but not painfully.' Godwin knew he was dangerously ill but he never ruled out the possibility of recovery. He was dozing quietly when a slight rattle called Mary Jane and Mary to his side. It was a little after 7 o'clock on the evening of 7 April 1836.[96]

The works of Godwin's last years are not usually placed on the same level with *Political Justice* and *Caleb Williams*. But three of them, in particular, are extremely rich in Godwinian thought and revelatory of his special talents: *Thoughts on Man* (1831), *Lives of the Necromancers* (1834), and *The Genius of Christianity Unveiled* (which he was working on at the time of his death). *Thoughts* was the first work in decades to appear under his own name, and although meant as an update of *The Enquirer*, setting out again his views about how all people are endowed with some talents needing to be properly cultivated, it was very different in tone. Indeed, the tone of all three works is that of a man so deeply engaged with distancing himself from organized religion and Christianity that he appears to be protesting too much, and taking on more of the concerns and priorities of the religious Other than he realizes. The Godwin of *St. Leon*, the proud literary grandfather of *Frankenstein*, comes to the fore in these works as more than a purely defiant Promethean figure.

To be sure, all of these works profess to be striking great blows for Truth and Reason against the pernicious superstitions in question, and there seems to be no little authorial identification in such passages as:

> What a character would that man make for himself, of whom it was notorious that he consecrated his faculty of speech to the refuting unjust imputations against whomsoever they were directed, to the contradicting all false and malicious reports, and to the bringing forth obscure and unrecognized worth from the shades in which it lay hid! What a world should we live in, if all men were thus prompt and fearless to do justice to all the worth they knew or apprehended to exist! Justice, simple justice, if it extended no farther than barely to the faculty of speech, would in no long time put down all misrepresentation and calumny, bring all that is good and meritorious into honour, and, so to speak, set every man in his true and rightful position.[97]

Such lines echo his younger self in, for example, one of his "Letters from Mucius," which had it that "One upright and intelligent juryman might put a close to that scene of persecution which is the disgrace of Britain." [98]

Thus *The Lives of the Necromancers* is "not a treatise of natural magic. It rather proposes to display the immense wealth of the faculty of imagination, and to shew the extravagances of which the man may be guilty who surrenders himself to its guidance." Although Godwin loves "in the foremost place to contemplate man in all his honours and in all the exaltation of wisdom and virtue," it "will also be occasionally of service to us to look into his obliquities, and distinctly to remark how great and portentous have been his absurdities and his follies."[99]

But the absurdities and follies are so extensive and deeply rooted that Godwin seems embarked on something more like an endless quest than an occasional service. By the end of *Lives*, which is a truly extraordinary biographical romp (praised by Edgar Allen Poe) across an immense historical and literary landscape, depicting everyone from Zoroaster to Socrates, to Merlin, to

Macbeth, to Cornelius Agrippa (who also figures in *Frankenstein*), to Faustus, to Nostradamus, down to his own day, Godwin closes the book more in tears than in triumph: "Let us hail with heart-felt gladness the light which has, though late, broken in upon us, and weep over the calamity of our fore-fathers, who, in addition to the inevitable ills of our sublunary state, were harassed with imaginary terrors, and haunted by suggestions, "[w]hose horrid image did unfix their hair, /And make their seated hearts knock at their ribs, /Against the use of nature."[100] England, he rather sourly notes, was behind France in paying "tribute to the progress of illumination and knowledge; and it was not till the year 1736 that a statute was passed, repealing the law made in the first year of James I, and enacting that no capital prosecution should for the future take place for conjuration, sorcery and enchantment, but restricting the punishment of persons pretending to tell fortunes and discover stolen goods by witchcraft, to that appertaining to a misdemeanor."

What is more, Godwin can evince a good deal of imaginative sympathy for those past, more enchanted ages, when "[m]agic was the order of the day." He even goes so far as to allow: "We are also to consider that, in all operations of a magical nature, there is a wonderful mixture of frankness and *bonhomie* with a strong vein of cunning and craft. Man in every age is full of incongruous and incompatible principles: and, when we shall cease to be inconsistent, we shall cease to be men."[101]

This is a most curious confession for the great proponent of human perfectibility, reinforcing the suggestion that human perfection will end in perfection without the human. And nowhere does Godwin feel the pain of this truth about humanity with more intensity than in the case of Christianity, which, the more he examines it, the more perversely amazing it becomes.

> But if we accurately examine the question, it will be found that there is scarcely the man in existence who truly believes in a future state. The professed devotee strains every nerve, and puts forth his utmost effort, that he may see 'in his mind's eye' the alleged impending condition of the blessed and the cursed; but in vain. The great body of professing Christians acknowledge with their mouths the creed which has been dinned into them; they repeat what has been taught them for truth; but it has scarcely any influence on their actions / and lives. It is a thought laid by on all ordinary occasions, and only brought out at church on Sundays, and fasts and festivals. It is so carefully kept as to be in no danger of becoming familiar. . . . The sort of belief and no belief which is nearly inseparable from the profession of the Christian faith, renders every man in some degree a hypocrite. We profess things which we hardly believe, and most of us, in sacred edifices, and in the face of mankind, lend our countenances and our voice to what obtains with us at best a very doubtful credit. Truth is no longer sacred and inviolable

to our thoughts. We juggle with the powers of our understanding, and 'palter in a double sense.' Each of us becomes, in some sort a double man, and is encumbered with limbs / and articulations which make no proper part of ourselves. Truth is the proper element of the human soul, and frankness its becoming habit. We can never be what under advantageous circumstances we might be expected to become, till our word shall be as sacred as our oath, till ingenuousness is our daily habit, till by self-examination we come to know what we think and what we are, and till we are ready to render to every man an undisguised account of the results of our judgment upon every momentous subject, and the reasons on which our judgment rests for its support.[102]

It is not that Godwin has no feel for the "religious sense." He understands very well indeed how important it is "to the sound and healthy condition of the human mind"—that is, that "we should behold the works of nature with wonder and awe, that we should stand astonished at the symmetry, harmony, subtlety, and beauty of the world around us, is natural and reasonable; and that we should feel how frail and insignificant a part we constitute of the great whole; can alone inspire us with a proper sobriety and humility, and make us sensible of our real state and condition." As he put it to another young would-be disciple, H. B. Rosser:

> I am an adorer of nature. I should pine to death if I did not live in the midst of so majestic a structure as I behold on every side. I am never weary of admiring and reverencing it. All that I see, the earth, the sea, the rivers, the trees, the clouds, animals, and, most of all, man, fills me with love and astonishment. My soul is full to bursting with the mystery of all this, and I love it the better for its mysteriousness. It is too wonderful for me; it is past finding out: but it is beyond expression delicious. This is what I call religion. . . .[103]

He also understands well the particular appeal of Christianity, how the "doctrine of a state of future retribution has been maintained for the purpose of completing our view of the Divine benevolence, and removing all difficulties that arise from the seemingly great proportion of natural and moral evil which presents itself in our present condition of existence." But, in the effort to "render our ideas of the Divine benevolence more uniform and complete," the chief obstacle is the core doctrines of Christianity itself:

> that the gloomy views of a future state were by no means confined to a sect of narrow-minded Christians, but that they received too much countenance from the original and authentic records of the founder of our religion. We are somewhat blinded through Christendom, by our partialities, and the prejudices instilled into us in our education. We hear of the meek and lowly Jesus so much, of his patience and

forbearance, as to cast into shade the tremendous and unsparing de-
nunciations with which his discourses, and those of his apostles, are
plentifully interspersed.[104]

What follows is a great deal of unsparing truth telling directed at Jesus as
much as at St. Paul and others who are usually taken (e.g., by Bentham) as the
harder-edged early Christians. There is, Godwin maintains, "something atro-
cious" in the story of Jesus, in "that gloomy trait in his disposition, which led
him to inculcate, or even induced him to believe in, the doctrine of everlasting
torments."[105]

But Godwin is concerned to set out the "Graces" as well as the "Horrors"
of Christianity, and the story again turns to the curious, divided incoherence
of the views in question. The leading "Grace" of Christianity is of course love,
and on this count:

> It is no matter whether the idea of an intelligent Creator, whose essence
> is love, and who is therefore to be perfect and entirely loved, is the dic-
> tate of the purest and the soundest philosophy. The merit of the prin-
> ciple will remain unaltered. Its characteristic is disinterestedness. It
> stands in direct opposition to the / groveling principle, born in France,
> and which is the curse of modern times, that all human motives are
> ultimately resolvable into self-love. It makes virtue to be really virtue,
> and not a semblance only. It bases the actions of the good man upon a
> just and irrefragable estimate of the value of things, not upon a consid-
> eration in which the best action that ever was performed is made the
> action in the whole world of the most exquisite and deliberate injustice,
> and where the greatest good is most directly postponed to private and
> personal gratification.[106]

Jesus at his best was the Jesus of the parable of the good Samaritan, and Jesus
at his best could surpass even Socrates in his effect:

> Socrates led the men to whom he addressed himself to the conclusions
> he sought by a series of ensnaring questions, by which they were at
> unawares driven to yield to the sentiments he required. He made long
> orations, in which he divided his subjects with a certain degree of ped-
> antry and parade, and pressed his conclusions with scientific and art-
> fully contrived arrangement. By these habits he became in some degree
> allied to the sophists of his country. But the tone of Jesus's discourses
> was of too lofty a character to submit to the shackles of ingenuity. He
> uttered his lessons with a depth of sincerity and a truth of nature, that
> surprised his auditors, and compelled them to exclaim, 'Truly this is
> the Son of God.' It is no doubt in part owing to this, that his religion
> has had so triumphant a career, and that those who have once been
> thoroughly imbued with its principles, have found it so difficult to

disengage themselves from its imposing character, and escape into the liberty in which a truly independent understanding most delights to expatiate.[107]

This, too, is a very strange statement for one who wants to conclude that "[m]en have believed during the successive centuries of the Christian era, because they dared not enquire." Or, more fully:

> The conclusion and moral of the whole of these Discourses may be expressed in the homely proverb, *Hoc age.* . . . It is the wisdom of man to put forth his strength, and apply his energies, to that which he strenuously purposes. Let him suffer no distraction. Let him not relax, either in spirit of intentness, of that at which he aims.
>
> We know what we are; but we know not what we shall be. What is there behind the curtain, beyond the extremest verge of our sublunary life? Probably nothing: neither 'works, nor device, nor knowledge.' But he who gives the reins to his mind, to consider 'in the sleep of death what dreams may come,' can never be fully aware to what an extent he unnerves his 'better part of man.' Let us then resolutely shut the door against 'thick-coming fancies.' Let us shut out the figure of such beings as 'lawless and uncertain thought imagines howling.'[108]

That the author of *Political Justice*, a man never afraid to enter the "land of conjecture" and spin out future possibilities for overcoming death and its daily manifestation, sleep, should in this context so fear the imagination when it is engaged with one of the deepest and most enduring of philosophical questions, is intriguing, to say the least. But the man who contributed so much to literature and inspired so much brilliant poetry was now more emphatic than ever on how

"[i]magination is indeed a marvelous power; but imagination never equaled history, the achievements which man has actually performed. It is in vain that the man of contemplations sits down in his closet; it is in vain that the poet yields the reins to enthusiasm and fancy: there is something in the realities of life, that excites the mind infinitely more, than is in the power of the most exalted reverie."[109]

No doubt the aged Godwin found the control of matter by mind more difficult than he had hoped, particularly with respect to his digestive system. But he also found mind itself less, rather than more, transparent. His final work opens with the wistful confession that

> [t]he motives of our actions are complicated, beyond the power of human skill to unravel them. I would willingly know the truth. Almost all my life it has been my aim, avowed to my own heart, to 'follow truth whithersoever it appeared to lead me.' But who can tell what motives, in the midst of the most diligent search, may lead the enquiries, unawares

to himself, wide of that unbroken direction which he sought to pursue? Vanity, the love of novelty and paradox may insensibly mislead. So may ambition, the desire to be great and to be distinguished. The power of education is immeasurably great. 'After this straitest sect of our religion,' as the apostle says, I was bred a Calvinist. I was destined to the profession of a Christian preacher. And, though at the time that I exercised that profession my aspirations after truth were vehement and continuous, I was for years entangled in the fetters of my profession. Which of us shall discover how subtly our worldly interests or the desire of a fair fame may bias our conclusions? The thought of everlasting damnation is not calculated to leave us cool in drawing impartial inferences.[110]

Applying this lesson to the history that he so hoped to use to excite the Reason might suggest a much more qualified view of its power. No doubt his final works were meant to do for the realm of mind what his earlier work had done for the political sphere—namely, aid Truth on its march by demonstrating what freedom required and could achieve. But the original, unused ending to *Caleb Williams*, which had the hero being poisoned, imprisoned, and driven mad, seems always lurking near the front of the author's mind. In these works Godwin is more haunted than ever by great art in the service of great cynicism, by the thoughts of Horace or the Shakespeare of *Troilus and Cressida*, written "partly with a view to degrade, and hold up to contempt, the heroes of Homer: and he has even disfigured the pure heroic affection which the Greek poet has painted as existing between Achilles and Patroclus with the most odious imputations."[111] Promethean defiance in the name of a broad Optimism about the course of the universe was a struggle to the end, and it apparently did not extend to defiance of the harsh treatment law and opinion accorded to same-sex love, Greek love, as Shakespeare had cast it. It is sad that one of the most creative and innovative utilitarian thinkers ever, who did so much for the cause of sexual equality, should have failed on a matter where one would expect him, rather than Bentham, to be the leading light. But then Bentham on sexuality, as the next chapter will show, is beyond compare.

Mary Shelley had hoped to be buried with her father and mother in the St. Pancras churchyard. But after her death in 1851, it was decided, by Lady Jane Shelley, to bury her in a vault along with her parents (whose bodies were moved from St. Pancras) and the silver casket with the heart of Shelley, in the St. Peter's churchyard in Bournemouth, closer to her estate. Three Godwins and the heart of Romantic hearts.[112]

CHAPTER TWO

Jeremy Bentham's Dream

Shall I seek excuses for introducing these autobiographical sketches?
I think not. They are faithful as pictures; they are interesting as
philosophical studies.

—BENTHAM, QUOTED IN BOWRING,
MEMOIRS AND CORRESPONDENCE

Reading Bentham

Jeremy Bentham usually goes down in history as the great founding father of nontheological utilitarianism, and his claim to the title is impressive, though no better than Godwin's. Yet in many ways, Bentham's reputation is an artifact crafted by later generations of utilitarians, particularly John Stuart Mill, the son of Bentham's leading disciple, James Mill. Mill the younger, whose upbringing was in large part guided by Bentham, designated his own spirits of the age:

> The writers of whom we speak have never been read by the multitude; except for the more slight of their works, their readers have been few: but they have been the teachers of the teachers; there is hardly to be found in England an individual of any importance in the world of mind, who (whatever opinions he may have afterwards adopted) did not first learn to think from one of these two; and though their influences have but begun to diffuse themselves through these intermediate channels over society at large, there is already scarcely a publication of any consequence addressed to the educated classes, which, if these persons had not existed, would not have been different from what it is. These men are, Jeremy Bentham and Samuel Taylor Coleridge—the two great seminal minds of England in their age.[1]

But these two great seminal minds were, on Mill's reckoning, locked in a great seminal conflict, with the Romantic Coleridgean heart pitted against the calculating Benthamite brain. Mill damned Bentham even as he praised him:

> Bentham's contempt, then, of all other schools of thinkers; his determination to create a philosophy wholly out of the materials furnished by his own mind, and by minds like his own; was his first disqualification as a philosopher. His second, was the incompleteness of his own mind as a representative of universal human nature. In many of the most natural and strongest feelings of human nature he had no sympathy; from many of its graver experiences he was altogether cut off; and the faculty by which one mind understands a mind different from itself, and throws itself into the feelings of that other mind, was denied him by his deficiency of Imagination.[2]

This was a charge that would stick—Bentham was no philosopher, and he was the great anti-Romantic, lacking in the most crucial ingredient of the Romantic outlook, imagination. And human sympathy, self-consciousness, and much else besides. "Self-consciousness, the daemon of the men of genius of our time, from Wordsworth to Byron, from Goethe to Chateaubriand, and to which this age owes so much both of its cheerful and its mournful wisdom, never was awakened in him. How much of human nature slumbered in him he knew not, neither can we know."[3] Worse, he was a kind of man-child, more of an exotic plant than Godwin before Wollstonecraft. He had an "undernourished conception of human nature," as a recent edition of Dickens's *Hard Times* has it.[4] He, and/or his devoted disciple Mill senior (whom he first befriended in 1808), supposedly provided the source material for the fact-obsessed Mr. Gradgrind in Dickens's novel, who had no room for poetry or fancy or fun in the educational process. Although the famous opening words from *An Introduction to the Principles of Morals and Legislation* had it that "[n]ature has placed mankind under the governance of two sovereign masters, *pain* and *pleasure*," and it is for them alone to "point out what we ought to do, as well to determine what we shall do," the principle of utility in Benthamite practice seemed to afford little pleasure and much pain.[5]

One of the kindest and most perceptive reconstructions of this take on Bentham is beautifully worded by Martha Nussbaum:

> . . . the childlike nature of Bentham's approach to life, which Mill often stresses, proves valuable: for Bentham understood how powerful pain and pleasure are for children and the child in us. Bentham did not value the emotional elements of the personality in the right way. He simplified them too, lacking all understanding of poetry (as Mill insists) and of love (as we might add). But perhaps it was the very child-like character of Bentham, the man who loved the pleasures of small creatures, who allowed the mice in his study to sit on his lap, that made

him able to see something Aristotle did not see, the need that we all have to be held and comforted, the need to escape a terrible loneliness and deadness.[6]

In other words, at least for Nussbaum, Mill was both right and wrong—something was missing in Bentham, but there was also something there that Mill did not quite get, something that perhaps no one has quite gotten.

This chapter will try, in a rather zigzag fashion, to capture a bit more of the essential Bentham on this score, of Bentham as one of the most curiously sensitive creatures ever to set pen to paper. He belongs more in the company of Godwin than one would ever guess from his minutely detailed blueprints for institutional reform, his endless "codifications."[7] Surprisingly, like Godwin and despite Mill, he cannot really be disentangled from the Romantic movement, despite his infamous remark about the children's game of pushpin being as good as poetry.[8] Bentham, more than any other figure discussed in this book, needs to be made a renewed source of wonder.

Given Mill's indictment, coming from the very man who was raised to be Bentham's true heir, it is perhaps not odd that Bentham still awaits a full first-rate biography.[9] He is often introduced, and sketched, but an up-to-date, truly satisfying, richly-colored portrait of him is not to be had, despite an extremely impressive Bentham Project at University College, London, lovingly devoted to producing excellent scholarly editions of all his works and, in a very innovative program, engaging the public in a great mass effort to transcribe his many as yet untranscribed writings. The work of the Bentham Project is exemplary and provides the best available means for initially framing the life and work of Bentham, which, given the many unknowns, must be approached in a spirit of humility and uncertainty. The Project summarizes and illustrates his life as follows:

> The philosopher and jurist Jeremy Bentham (1748–1832) was born in Spitalfields, London, on 15 February 1748. He proved to be something of a child prodigy: while still a toddler he was discovered sitting at his father's desk reading a multi-volume history of England, and he began to study Latin at the age of three. At twelve, he was sent to Queen's College Oxford, his father, a prosperous attorney, having decided that Jeremy would follow him into the law, and feeling quite sure that his brilliant son would one day be Lord Chancellor of England.
>
> Bentham, however, soon became disillusioned with the law, especially after hearing the lectures of the leading authority of the day, Sir William Blackstone (1723–80). Instead of practising the law, he decided to write about it, and he spent his life criticising the existing law and suggesting ways for its improvement. His father's death in 1792 left him financially independent, and for nearly forty years he lived quietly in Westminster, producing between ten and twenty sheets of manuscript a day, even when he was in his eighties.

Even for those who have never read a line of Bentham, he will always be associated with the doctrine of Utilitarianism and the principle
of 'the greatest happiness of the greatest number'. This, however, was
only his starting point for a radical critique of society, which aimed to
test the usefulness of existing institutions, practices and beliefs against
an objective evaluative standard. He was an outspoken advocate of law
reform, a pugnacious critic of established political doctrines like natural law and contractarianism, and the first to produce a utilitarian justification for democracy. He also had much to say of note on subjects
as diverse as prison reform, religion, poor relief, international law, and
animal welfare. A visionary far ahead of his time, he advocated universal suffrage and the decriminalisation of homosexuality.

By the 1820s Bentham had become a widely respected figure, both
in Britain and in other parts of the world. His ideas were greatly to
influence the reforms of public administration made during the nineteenth century, and his writings are still at the centre of academic debate, especially as regards social policy, legal positivism, and welfare
economics. Research into his work continues at UCL in the Bentham
Project, set up in the early 1960s with the aim of producing the first
scholarly edition of his works and correspondence, a projected total of
some seventy volumes![10]

What follows here is not so much a challenge to this summary account as
an effort to flesh out and cast in a somewhat warmer light the "visionary" Bentham that the Project is doing so much to bring to public awareness. Bentham
the visionary can be very hard to discern in his own best-known writings;
more of the work, and more of the life, might help.

Perhaps it is the sheer mass of Bentham's writings—some twenty million
surviving words—that has frightened away would-be biographers, and the fact
that so many of those words have remained unpublished for so long, acces-
sible only to those willing to try to decipher his often nearly illegible scrawl.
Daunting, too, is the fact that as these writings have come more and more into
the light, it has become all the clearer that on many counts Bentham was even
more extraordinary and visionary than his admirers and critics had supposed.
In fuller and more informed retrospect, the circle around Bentham, including
such incisive intellects as James Mill and George Grote, tends to fade. The
greatest of the "Philosophical Radicals," as the politically charged Benthamites
were called, appears to have ended up far in advance even of his own disciples,
especially on such topics as sexual morality, race, democracy, and imperialism.
It is only in recent years that Bentham has been appreciated for his attacks on
the spread of empire and colonization, and for his extraordinarily enlightened
views on same-sex love. Who knew, circa 1950, that Bentham, the object of
such stinging abuse from Dickens and Marx, would emerge as a hero of gay

studies? Of postcolonial studies? Of the feminist movement? Of animal libera-tion?[11] Mill senior contrived to defend democracy on utilitarian grounds but without extending the vote to women, a critical failure that Bentham himself condemned, and both Mills built careers with the East India Company and condoned aspects of the British Empire that Bentham deemed preposterous. As Peter Cain has cogently argued, Bentham's recently published "Spanish writings" on colonies, "especially those that give a close analysis of the benefits that elites received from colonialism, represent the most acute and innovatory aspects of his thought in this field. When they are added to his better-known economic analyses of colonialism written between the 1780s and early 1800s, and set against the broad currents of liberal and radical questioning of the causes and consequences of empire across two centuries, it would be no exag-geration to say that Bentham made one of the greatest contributions to anti-colonial literature anywhere in the Western world, and one which in some ways was never improved upon in Britain."[12]

Moreover, once one shakes free of Mill's reading of him, Bentham no longer seems happily cast as simply the hermit-like leading light of utilitarianism, the less politically involved theorist who let his activist friends and associates—Mill, Samuel Romilly, Francis Place (who also advised him financially, as he had Godwin), Southwood Smith—do the politicking on behalf of utilitarian-ism. He was far more engaged politically and socially than the image of him as a type of Mycroft Holmes, the brain behind the scenes, would have it. And his political engagements were indeed visionary, however troubling that vi-sion sometimes was. Thus, both philosophically and practically, the standard accounts of the growth of utilitarianism can, in greater historical perspective, seem too Millian in their slant. Consider Graham Wallas's statement, in his *The Life of Francis Place, 1771–1854*:

> In the Utilitarian movement there are two distinct periods divided roughly by the year 1824. Up to that time Bentham had been the active leader of the group; and although Mill and Place were the only two members of the school who were in constant personal intimacy with Bentham himself, Dumont, Brougham, Grote (after 1818), and others would have accepted the name Benthamite. Apart from their writing and thinking, James Mill and Bentham were constantly occupied with practical projects. They used the ordinary methods of committees, subscriptions, and newspaper articles for the direct improvement of schools, and law courts, and political machinery.

In 1823 James Mill's greater son, John Stuart Mill, then seven-teen years old, entered the India Office, and began his independent intellectual life. In the spring of 1824 the *Westminster Review* was founded. From 1824 John Stuart Mill, with the younger generation of Utilitarians—Charles Austin, Eyton Tooke, G. J. Graham, and others—formed the real center of the movement. They wrote books and reviews rather than newspaper articles, and were more really interested in speculative questions than in practical politics or social work.[13]

Although there is some truth to this account, it does not convey all that was lost or left behind in the transition, even though it is embedded in a biography that shows how Place and others in the earlier circle were often pained with the direction taken by the younger Mill, who was charged with becoming "a German metaphysical mystic."[14]

It is of course true that Bentham was first and foremost concerned with, as Ross Harrison has put it, "political or legal reform. His thought, that is, was centrally concerned with the organization of social, or public, institutions; firstly more specifically with the organization and content of the law; latterly with developing a blueprint for a complete administrative state." He did, in the course of this, develop "several more limited plans for the organization of social institutions, for workhouses for the poor, for schools, and above all for the 'mill for grinding rogues honest' . . . the panopticon prison."[15] His work on "private ethics" and many other topics was less of a priority, more of an afterthought or diversion from his main work. But there were many such diversions and they were lengthy. Somehow, Mill did not get that quite right either. Nor did he capture the degree to which there was an extraordinary method to the seeming madness.

Still, it is going too far to claim that the term "classical utilitarianism" is anachronistic or proleptic when applied to Bentham. If his priorities differed from those of, say, Peter Singer, they also differed from those of Godwin, Mill, and Sidgwick, each of whom worked the term "utilitarianism" for his own purposes.[16] And if it is true that Bentham's phases can be, as Stephen Engelmann claims, characterized as "penal law and general jurisprudence early on . . . civil law, political economy, and what we would call public policy in the middle phase . . . and ontology, religion, political reform, and constitutional law late in life," it is also true that, with respect to Bentham's felicific calculus, often enough "it remains unclear what this expansive critical and impartial calculus means for him. It does mean . . . that his were some of the earliest writings calling for female suffrage, and that well before Marx and Darwin he broke with nationalism and humanism in his vision of a continuum of sensitive beings. It also means, however, that in one text . . . we can find condemnation of masturbation, toleration of bestiality, and approval of infanticide as a means of women's self-defense." In his case for "all-comprehensive liberty in consensual sex," Bentham allows "the superiority of same-sex over regular modes (because they do not lead to pregnancy), sex among children as a virtuous substitute of masturbation (which is too available and enervating), and the absurdity of laws against infanticide (which sacrifice the genuine happiness of the aware to the only imputed feelings of the unaware). . . . Sex for Bentham is democratic, even anarchic: 'These are precisely the only pleasures of sense which are as fully and effectually within the reach of the most indigent . . . as within the most affluent classes of mankind: they are equally within the reach of the subject many as of the ruling few.'"[17] However, as will later be shown in detail, Bentham's hedonistic interpretation of happiness, which aligned with his "logic of the will" rather than an Aristotelian "logic of the understanding," had it that "happiness was never fixed, but was changing and developing as societies changed and developed."[18]

Engelmann urges that rather "than react to Bentham's conclusions with approval or disapproval, it might serve us better to know more of his thought. Bentham simply didn't share some fundamental and familiar assumptions about freedom, intervention, and the special dignity of the human subject." He holds that Bentham is primarily useful because we can use his "sometimes troubling consistencies to reflect on what is missing, latent, contradictory, or disturbing in contemporary theory and practice." That is no doubt true, but if left at that, it is also evasive, especially since, as Engelmann himself stresses in a pair of rhetorical questions: "Aren't there many researchers in our universities who tell us that fairness is irrational, or that all goods are commensurable, or that a comprehensive science of human/animal behavior is not only possible but has arrived? And haven't many of us today come to equate freedom with extensive choice under conditions of mutual surveillance, and don't we often look to experts for the latest strategies of pleasure seeking and self-management, while other experts—sometimes the same ones—assure us that there is really no self to manage?"[19] Given such supposedly Benthamite tendencies, perhaps one should acknowledge that enhanced critical awareness of Bentham's "troubling consistencies" might just as well point many of "us" back to his path rather than in a different direction. Avowed Benthamism seems much less anachronistic or proleptic than avowed Aristotelianism, Thomism, virtue ethics, natural law, etc. etc., for better or worse. But avowed Benthamism today can also take some more radical and oppositional turns.

This, to be sure, is not to deny that understanding Bentham in historical context is important and calls for great care. For example, Bentham disliked the word "liberty," which was used in contradictory ways to mean both doing what one pleased without interference and the civil or political liberty created by government. When referring to the latter, he preferred Montesquieu's word "security," which, along with equality, abundance, and subsistence provided "the main aim of legislation concerned with the distribution of property and other entitlements in society." The concern with security, and legitimate expectations, reveals something fundamental about Bentham's perspective on humanity:

> In order to form a clear idea of the whole extent which ought to be given to the principle of security, it is necessary to consider, that man is not like the brutes, limited to the present time, either in enjoyment or

suffering, but that he is susceptible of pleasure and pain by anticipation, and that it is not enough to guard him against an actual loss, but also to guarantee to him, as much as possible, his possessions against further losses. The idea of his security must be prolonged to him throughout the whole view that his imagination can measure.

This disposition to look forward, which has so marked an influence upon the condition of man, may be called expectation—expectation of the future. It is by means of this we are enabled to form a general plan of conduct; it is by means of this, that the successive moments which compose the duration of life are not like insulated and independent points, but become parts of a continuous whole. Expectation is a chain which unites our present and our future existence, and passes beyond ourselves to the generations which follow us. The sensibility of the individual is prolonged through all the links of this chain.[20]

As Rosen notes of this passage, as "with Hume, the maintenance of secure possession of one's life and property was considered the main task of governments, and Bentham was led through the emphasis on security to embrace in part an indirect form of utilitarianism." This interpretation, which owes much to the work of P. J. Kelly, "rejects the view that Bentham was a simple act-utilitarian intent upon the maximization of pleasure and minimization of pain without regard to its distribution or other factors which might affect such a distribution." And other works, such as *Official Aptitude Maximized, Expense Minimized*, also made it clear that the application of the principle of utility would largely involve applying such subprinciples as, in the case of constitutional law, hiring and keeping highly competent public officials. But the *Introduction* is itself misleading on this score, being incomplete in many ways and largely concerned with punishment, and as "a result, the numerous interpretations of Bentham's utilitarianism and conceptions of 'classical' utilitarianism which are mainly based on the early chapters of *IPML* present an erroneous view of how Bentham conceived the operation of the principle of utility."[21] Many of the controversies over act v. rule utilitarianism really are anachronistic, reflecting various rather artificial debates generated in the twentieth century. As Rosen has stressed, in classical utilitarianism "no such contrast is emphasized and utility may be applied to acts, rules, conventions, laws, customs, etc. without discrimination."[22] Indeed, the classical utilitarian standard could be used to judge between these very alternatives simply by calculating the happiness maximizing potential of adopting an act or a rule or a global approach, etc., and the hope was always that this standard would provide a more determinate and objective way of determining what should be done.

But just what Bentham thought should be done remains a source of utter astonishment.

Bentham's Afterlife

To capture something more of the essence of Bentham, who so often goes down as the greatest of the great utilitarians, it might be best to open at the close, with the revealing end of the man whose life had a much steadier upward trajectory than Godwin's. As Engelmann himself makes clear, the later Bentham was in so many ways the better Bentham:

> By 1818 it was clear to Bentham that utility required expansion of the suffrage, representation by population through annual elections, disestablishment of the Church, and the abolition of monarchy and aristocracy—and that fundamental constitutional change was a necessary precondition for political reform. At the same time he was involved in political agitation Bentham was writing new notes into the final year of his life for the introduction to a 'pannomion,' or comprehensive legal code, that might effectively replace existing legal structures. . . . He died at the age of eighty-four on June 6, 1832, one day before the great Reform Act became law: a crucial, if partial, step toward the representative democracy for which he fought in the last years of his life.[23]

And as Schofield adds, by "his death in 1832, he was a republican, admiring the government of the United States of America above all others in existence."[24]

Engelmann and Schofield have gone far to show the consistency in Bentham's views, despite his shifting priorities. The biggest change occurred in the early 1810s, when he became convinced that the ills of society were not historical accidents but the result of a conspiracy of sinister interests, the work of the "ruling few." It was this change in his assessment of the historical facts that drove home to Bentham "that utility required expansion of the suffrage, representation by population through annual elections, disestablishment of the Church, and the abolition of monarchy and aristocracy—and that fundamental constitutional change was a necessary precondition for political reform."[25]

All the more extraordinary, then, that one of his last great efforts would involve an exceedingly weird project for stuffing and displaying the bodies of the deceased great (and others), who could continue to inspire humanity in death as they did in life. Bentham himself would lead the way.

Thus, following his peaceful death from old age, his head, according to one account, resting on the bosom of the editor of his collected works, John Bowring, Bentham, in accordance with his Will, had his body donated to medical science for purposes of dissection, but with the stipulation that his medical friend, follower, and sometimes editor, the Unitarian minister Southwood Smith

> will take my body under his charge and take the requisite and appropriate measures to the disposal and preservation of the several parts of my

bodily frame in the manner expressed in the paper annexed to this my will and at the top of which I have written "Auto Icon" The skeleton he will cause to be put together in such manner as that the whole figure may be seated in a Chair usually occupied by me when living in the attitude in which I am sitting when engaged in thought in the course of time employed in writing I direct that the body thus prepared shall be transferred to my executor [Bowring] He will cause the skeleton to be clad in one of the suits of black occasionally worn by me The Body so clothed together with the Chair and the Staff in my later years borne by me he will take charge of And for containing the whole apparatus he will cause to be prepared an appropriate box or case and will cause to be engraved in conspicuous characters on a plate to be affixed thereon and also on the labels on the glass cases in which the preparations of the soft parts of my body shall be contained.[26]

As James Crimmins notes, the "choice of a black suit for the auto-icon points to a change in taste from 1824, when Bentham expressly forbade black as well as grey!" Moreover, the following additional instructions "annexed to the will under the heading 'Auto-Icon' dated 13 April 1830, were written by Southwood Smith at Bentham's behest and witnessed by Bentham's signature."

The manner in which Mr. Benthams body is to be disposed of after his death The Head is to be prepared according to the specimen which Mr Bentham has seen and approved of The Body is to be used as the means of illustrating a series of lectures to which scientific & literary men are to be invited These lectures are to expound the situation structure & functions of the different organs the arrangement & distribution of the vessels & whatever may illustrate the mechanism by which the actions of the animal economy are performed the object of these lectures being twofold first to communicate curious interesting & highly important knowledge & secondly to show that the primitive horror at dissection originates in ignorance & is kept up by misconception & that the human body when dissected instead of being an object of disgust is as much more beautiful than any other piece of mechanism as it is more curious and wonderful After such lectures have been given those organs which are capable of being preserved for example the heart the kidney &c &c to be prepared in whatever manner may be conceived to render their preservation the most perfect & durable And finally when all the soft parts have been disposed of the bones are to be formed into a skeleton which after the head prepared in the manner already stated has been attached to it is to be dressed in the clothes usually worn by Mr Bentham & in this manner to be perpetually preserved—April 13 1830.[27]

Bentham's instructions were followed as closely as possible, his head being preserved in the manner of the New Zealand Maori, and on a stormy and spooky night a few days after Bentham's death, Southwood Smith delivered a moving eulogy to an audience of friends, followers, and medical students at the Webb Street School of Anatomy and Medicine, in a small circular operating theater with the body of Bentham laid out before him, clothed in a nightshirt. Smith's oration was perhaps the first attempt to do Bentham biographical justice, and the main event that evening was in fact not the dissection itself, but the final rites for which Bentham had hoped, sending a strong and graphic message to humanity to get over the religious superstition and ignorant revulsion that was making the advance of medical science so difficult. Dissection of a body was at the time regarded as a horrific additional disincentive to the crime of murder, making capital punishment in that case all the more fearsome. Shortly after Bentham's example, and perhaps in part because of it, medical dissection was at last divorced from capital punishment and made a legal option for wills.

Bentham's body was indeed soon the object of the appropriate medical research, except for the bits used to create the Auto-Icon, which has been the greatest single conversation piece of utilitarianism ever since. What was Bentham doing? Even the Bentham Project seems hard pressed to keep a straight face when recounting this particular Benthamite project:

> At the end of the South Cloisters of the main building of UCL stands a wooden cabinet, which has been a source of curiosity and perplexity to visitors.
>
> The cabinet contains Bentham's preserved skeleton, dressed in his own clothes, and surmounted by a wax head. . . . Not surprisingly, this peculiar relic has given rise to numerous legends and anecdotes. One of the most commonly recounted is that the Auto-Icon regularly attends meetings of the College Council, and that it is solemnly wheeled into the Council Room to take its place among the present-day members. Its presence, it is claimed, is always recorded in the minutes with the words Jeremy Bentham—present but not voting. Another version of the story asserts that the Auto-Icon does vote, but only on occasions when the votes of the other Council members are equally split. In these cases the Auto-Icon invariably votes for the motion.
>
> Bentham had originally intended that his head should be part of the Auto-Icon, and for ten years before his death (so runs another story) carried around in his pocket the glass eyes which were to adorn it. Unfortunately when the time came to preserve it for posterity, the process went disastrously wrong, robbing the head of most of its facial expression, and leaving it decidedly unattractive. The wax head was therefore substituted, and for some years the real head, with its glass eyes, reposed on the floor of the Auto-Icon, between Bentham's legs. However, it proved an irresistible target for students, especially from King's College London, who stole the head in 1975 and demanded a

ransome of £100 to be paid to the charity Shelter. UCL finally agreed to pay a ransome of £10 and the head was returned. On another occasion, according to legend, the head, again stolen by students, was eventually found in a luggage locker at a Scottish Station (possibly Aberdeen). The last straw (so runs yet another story) came when it was discovered in the front quadrangle being used for football practice, and the head was henceforth placed in secure storage.

Thus, Bentham, with his famous walking stick "Dapple," remains on display to this day, excepting the badly deteriorated head.[28]

Why? Medical dissection is one thing, mummification and public display another, and the purpose of the second of these has been much debated, with some thinking that Bentham was playing a joke on humanity, or was perhaps even being co-opted, in death, for purposes of discrediting utilitarianism. His apparent explanation of his thinking on this score, "Auto-Icon: Or, Farther Uses of the Dead for the Living," has been attacked as inauthentic, tongue in check, and many other things besides. It was, apparently, a further gloss on Southwood Smith's "Uses of the Dead to the Living," which had defended medical dissection in that organ of utilitarianism founded by Bentham and his circle, *The Westminster Review*. But it was less concerned with dissection and more concerned with iconization, the creation of such relics as the Auto-Icon.

Crimmins makes a very compelling case for both the authenticity and seriousness of Bentham's writings on this subject, observing:

> Many people have speculated as to exactly why Bentham chose to have his body preserved in this way, with explanations ranging from a practical joke at the expense of posterity to a sense of overweening self-importance. Perhaps the Auto-Icon may be more plausibly regarded as an attempt to question religious sensibilities about life and death. Yet whatever Bentham's true motives, the Auto-Icon will always be a source of fascination and debate, and will serve as a perpetual reminder of the man whose ideals inspired the institution in which it stands.
>
> Being an atheist and a rigorous utilitarian, Bentham was almost bound at some point in his life to confront the question, 'Of what use can the dead be to the living?' That this question should foster an expansive thesis about the usefulness to be derived from corpses, particularly the remains of those of achievement and intellect, is also typical of Bentham. He had always considered it a part of his utilitarian mission to be a projector of useful proposals, and throughout his life he gave practical effect to his inventive genius in a wide range of areas. In this respect he was truly the great polymath of the age. He slept in a sleeping bag of his own design, mapped out projects for portable houses, a new kind of harpsichord and improvements to the printing of music, and drew up proposals for a school of legislation and a canal

in Central America (to connect the Atlantic and Pacific). He devoted numerous frustrating years to the notorious Panopticon prison plan, introduced improvements to political institutions and constitutions, codes of judicial procedure and civil and penal law (each designed to eliminate delay, expense, complexity, obscurity, and uncertainty, and to enhance the greatest happiness), and offered a bewildering stream of new law proposals on subjects as diverse as inheritance, homosexuality, cruelty to animals, paupers, policing, real property, taxes on law proceedings, and sinecures in church and state. Other Benthamic inventions included numerous statistical manuals, digests, hand-books, and charts which facilitated a scientific approach to health administration. The 'conversation tubes' were a kind of primitive telephone Bentham installed at his London residence in Queen's Square Place and imagined being used in his Panopticon prisons to connect the cells with the central watchtower. Rather more practical were the plans he drafted for a flash pump, 'frigidarium', central hot-air heating system, and document lift—versions of which are all in use today. Bentham's plan for a forgery-proof currency, like so many other schemes, did not fair so well; the Directors of the Bank of England refused to be troubled on the matter, and the manuscripts remained unpublished until the 1950s. Among his enduring legacies are the terms he coined to express and give currency to new ideas, such as 'utilitarian', 'international', and 'codification', and the Oxford English Dictionary bears ample witness to many others.

To be innovative when pondering the utility of his own death, then, was not such a departure for Bentham; but that he should have been thinking along such lines even as a young adult is truly remarkable. His decision to leave his body for medical research, he later recalled, was 'no hasty—no recent determination' but was decided in 1769 on the occasion of his coming of age.[29]

Crimmins is surely right in thinking that Bentham was serious about these efforts, even if they did not have quite the effect anticipated. As previously remarked, Bertrand Russell recalled hearing as a child a humorous jibe to the effect that Bentham recommended making soup of one's dead grandmothers, and there can be little doubt that the wit hit home because of the Auto-Icon project. But, as later sections will show, Bentham's actions here fit quite well with his late-life attacks on religion, especially "Church of Englandism," and they are besides not much weirder than Godwin's notions about the treatment of the dead.[30] As the Bowring memoirs record, Bentham took strong objection to the old nostrum that one should never speak ill of the dead:

This maxim is one of the inventions of despotism: it perpetuates misrepresentation of the ruling few at the expense of the subject many; it employs suppression instead of open lying, for the purpose of deception; it would shield depredation and oppression from exposure; and when it is too late to prevent misdoings by present punishment, would protect the misdoers even against future denunciation and judgment. Aristocracy gets all the benefit of the maxim; for the poor are never honoured with unqualified posthumous praise. And thus the world bestows its foolish confidence on those who always betray it.[31]

What could be more effective than Auto-Iconism at shaking up the established but pernicious practices with respect to the dead? Was that not Bentham's very business, shaking things up, in the most creative ways imaginable?

Crimmins is obviously also right about Bentham's astounding creativity and inventiveness, across an astonishing range of subjects, not simply those having to do with law and legislation. However ironic it may be, he was one of the most imaginative persons who ever lived. Bentham could not touch anything without trying to improve it, and he was perhaps especially odd in being at once both the most imaginative and the most wonkish political and legal philosopher who ever lived, ever ready to go off into a mass of technical details, whether the subject was the penal code or the mummification of great thinkers. And this was apparently his nature at least from the time of his conversion experience, in 1768–69, shortly before he was admitted to the bar, when the principle of utility first struck him as the answer to everything. To understand his seeming eccentricities, one must appreciate how deep his conversion and commitment to this principle really were. With a noted flare, and speaking in the third person, Bentham himself tells the story in the long version of his "Article on Utilitarianism":

> Between the years 1762 and 1769 came out a pamphlet of Dr. Priestly's, written as usual with him *currente calamo* and without any precise method predetermined, but containing at the close of it, it is believed in the very last page, in so many words the phrase 'the greatest happiness of the greatest number', and this was stated in the character of a principle constituting not only a rational foundation, but the only rational foundation, of all enactments in legislation and all rules and precepts destined for the direction of human conduct in private life.
>
> Somehow or other shortly after its publication a copy of this pamphlet found its way into the little circulating library belonging to a little coffee-house called Harper's Coffee-house, attached as it were to Queen's College Oxford, and deriving from the population of the College the whole of its subsistence. It was a corner house having one front towards the High Street, another towards a narrow lane which on that side skirts Queen's College and loses itself in a lane issuing from one of the gates of New College. To this library the subscription was a shilling a quarter, or in the University phrase a shilling a term. Of this subscription the produce was composed to two or three newspapers,

with magazines one or two, and now and then a newly published pamphlet. . . . The year 1768 was the latest of the years in which Mr. Bentham ever made at Oxford a residence of more than a day or two. The occasion of that visit was the giving his vote in his quality of Master of Arts for the University of Oxford on the occasion of a Parliamentary election. . . . This year, 1768 was the latest of all the years on which this pamphlet could have come into his hands.

Be this as it may, it was by that pamphlet and this phrase in it that his principles on the subject of morality, public and private together, were determined. It was from that pamphlet and that page of it that he drew that phrase, the words and import of which have by his writings been so widely diffused over the civilized world. At sight of it he cried out as it were in an inward ecstasy like Archimedes on the discovery of the fundamental principle of Hydrostatics, Eureka.[32]

As the "Shorter Version" of the article also makes clear, the importance of Priestly's formulation of the "greatest happiness of the greatest number" was in "substituting to the equivocal word 'utility' the unequivocal phrase of which happiness is the principal and sole characteristic ingredient."[33] Bentham is clear enough that he was influenced by a great many sources, from the ancients' invocation of utility (e.g., in Horace's *Satires*) to the more recent works of Hume, Hutcheson, Montesquieu, D'Alembert, Helvétius, and Beccaria, all of which had a keen influence on him. But he was also prescient about how misleading the term "utility" could be: "by which approbation was called for by every opinion or operation by which a contribution was made to this or that end, whatsoever might be the nature of that end: instead of its being regarded as the principle by which approbation is called for, for such measures alone as are contributory to human happiness taken in the aggregate, to the maximum of the happiness enjoyed by the aggregate composed of the several members of which the community in question is composed." This was a mistake with very serious implications:

Of this mistake one consequence was that of its being a principle by which disapprobation was called for to the pursuit of pleasure, to every action by means of which pleasure was either at the moment produced, or a probability of seeing it at a true time produced. Whereas in the intention of the originator of it, if such he may be styled, the same sentiment of approbation is called for every action without distinction of which pleasure in any shape, at the moment or any subsequent moment, is produced: such approbation being given on the single condition that by such action, pain or loss of pleasure to a greater amount be not produced. Thus on every occasion happiness is in his view of considering it a subject-matter of account and calculation, of profit and loss, just as money itself is—that precious matter which, but for the happiness which it is contributory to the production of, would be altogether valueless.[34]

Whether or not Bentham's recollection got all the details quite right—Priestly's pamphlet did not have that exact wording, but works by Hutcheson and Beccaria did—this is no doubt how he recalled it all, and the first striking effect of the conversion—"the idea of happiness being in his mind constantly connected with that of utility, and not suspecting that it could fail of being so in any other"—yielded his first, albeit anonymously authored publication, *A Fragment on Government* (which was actually part of a longer work, *A Comment on the Commentaries*). The *Fragment* was an all-out assault on Blackstone, Locke, and the social contractarian view that had had such a powerful influence on English law and politics. Of such doctrine concerning "the original contract" creating political society, Bentham, no more modest than Godwin, recalled that he had "grappled with it and threw it to the ground, from whence it has never since ventured to rear its head—or say from whence no man has since ventured to take it up and give support to it."[35] Or, as he put it in a note written in his own copy of the work: "[T]his was the very first publication by which men at large were invited to break loose from the trammels of authority and ancestor-wisdom on the field of law."[36]

If Bentham could, at a mere twenty-eight years, overthrow the reigning jurisprudence and political philosophy of his country, is it any wonder that he should in due course tackle such matters as religion and the treatment of the dead? Like Godwin, he was consumed in his last years with a renewed interest in the critique of religion. But his scheme seemed to go Godwin one better, leaving no room for the imagination when confronting all the Auto-Icons artfully displayed to remind the living both of the dead individual's strengths— Bentham was to be seated in his writing chair, a model of the serious author at work—and of the dead individual's death. And a very egalitarian afterlife it might perhaps come to be, including both men and women: "If, at common expense poor and rich were Iconized, the beautiful commandment of Jesus would be obeyed; they would indeed 'meet together', they would be placed on the same level." Utilitarianism, in his hands, was about heaven on earth, with Jesus helping the cause.

But this was to be a remarkably well-administered heaven, notable for its architectural innovations.

Worldly Fame, without Pushing

Among the very last things which his hand penned, in a book of memoranda, in which he was accustomed to note down any thought or feeling that passed through his mind, for future revision and use, if susceptible of use, was found the following passage:—'I am a selfish man

as selfish as any man can be. But in me, some how or other, so it happens,
selfishness has taken the shape of benevolence. No other man is there upon
earth, the prospect of whose sufferings would to me be a pleasurable one:
no man is there upon earth, the sight of whose sufferings would not to
me be a more or less painful one: no man upon earth is there, the sight
of whose enjoyments, unless believed by me to be derived from a more
than equivalent suffering endured by some other man, would not be of a
pleasurable nature rather than of a painful one. Such in me is the force of
sympathy!'

—SOUTHWOOD SMITH, "A LECTURE DELIVERED OVER
THE REMAINS OF JEREMY BENTHAM, ESQ.:
IN THE WEBB STREET SCHOOL OF ANATOMY
AND MEDICINE, ON THE 9TH OF JUNE, 1832."

Bentham would certainly seem to differ drastically from Godwin on many counts: the scope of altruism, the natural harmony of interests that freedom could rely upon without the sanctions of codes and institutions, immaterialism, and the notion that some pleasures were simply, qua pleasures, better than others.[37] But on some points they were plainly at one: the personal force of sympathy, and the imperative driving each to a pitch of intellectual honesty, and a devotion to following the argument wherever it led, as innocently as fearlessly.

Of course, thinking was one thing, publishing another. In Godwin's case, that honesty led to fame followed by infamy; in Bentham's, to obscurity followed by fame, with an ever increasing enhancement of his reputation. Bentham, it seems, was shrewdly willing to let rather more of his provocative thoughts remain unpublished during his early life. If he openly attacked the social contract view, and famously, in his *Anarchical Fallacies* (now better and more appropriately known as *Nonsense upon Stilts*, Bentham's title), dismissed talk of natural rights as nonsense—and of natural and "imprescriptible" rights as "nonsense upon stilts"—he did not, early on, go out of his way to attack publicly religion and religious institutions, however little use he found for them. It was only late in life that he would call King George III a "great baby," blast the "sinister interests" by name in an actionable way, and openly side with the democratic movement. Earlier on, he spent more of his time attacking law and lawyers, an activity often as welcome then as it is now, and placed much faith in the reforming potential of enlightened monarchs (as a child and youth, he had been in awe of George II and George III). His best known work to this day, the one usually singled out as the greatest classic of classical utilitarianism, was of course *An Introduction to the Principles of Morals and Legislation* (which was thought out in the 70s and even printed in 1780, though not published until 1789), but it was not at all a plea for radical democracy, and in retrospect rather conspicuously failed to convey many key elements of Bentham's views, even on such central topics as equality, liberty, and security. Bentham had in fact written a companion piece for it, *Of Laws in General* (now properly entitled *Of the Limits of the Penal Branch of Jurisprudence*), largely complete in 1782, but not even published in finished form until 1945.

Bentham was also fortunate enough to have his fame develop more abroad than at home, thanks to the French edition of his writings assembled by the Genevan translator Pierre-Étienne-Louis Dumont, whose translating and editing produced the *Traités de législation civile et pénale* (1802) and other works. Bentham's eventual success owed much to Dumont:

> Dumont records that 3,000 copies of the *Traités* were initially distributed in France, and that it was "frequently quoted in many official compositions relating to civil or criminal codes." Soon after, it was translated into Russian, and later into Spanish, German, Hungarian, Polish, and Portuguese. Other editions of the *Traités* followed. Reportedly, 50,000 copies of Dumont's various recensions were sold in Europe in the early decades of the century and 40,000 in Spanish translation in Latin America alone.[38] (45).

As a result of Dumont's work, Bentham's devoted foreign followers included such figures as Francisco de Paula Santander, vice president of Gran Colombia, who was only kept from making Bentham's work required reading in law schools by a counter-edict from Simón Bolívar himself. And Bentham's help was sought by such figures as José del Valle (who wanted him to draw up a civil code for Guatemala) and Pedro Alcántra de Somellera, a law professor at the University of Buenos Aires.[39] In the United States, he had such followers as "the historian and anti-slave propagandist Richard Hildreth"[40] and, as noted, Aaron Burr, influential but controversial friend of both Bentham and Godwin. He corresponded with James Madison, John Quincy Adams (whom he had met in London), and Andrew Jackson. In fact, as Crimmins has demonstrated, the influence of Bentham in the U.S. was far more important than is commonly recognized, with such popular periodicals as *The Diamond* and *The Yankee* proclaiming on their banners "the greatest happiness for the greatest number."

Indeed, the international fame that Bentham achieved was truly extraordinary, and his influence was felt across the globe—in Russia (where he lived briefly, with his younger brother Samuel), France, Poland, Mexico, Latin and South America, Spain, Portugal, Greece, and many other places as well. Napoleon's minister Talleyrand was counted a friend, and even Napoleon admired the extraordinarily successful *Traités de législation civile et pénale* (1802), despite Bentham having been made an honorary citizen of the French Republic in 1792. He would come to deserve the title "Legislator of the World," bestowed on him by José del Valle for his determined efforts to go beyond piecemeal reform and effect a complete makeover of law, a complete law code or "pannomion" with every law duly rationalized, that could be applied globally.

But clearly, Dumont's Bentham was not the radical republican and democrat so evident in the teens and twenties. The great utilitarian's amazing global celebrity was, as in the case of Dumont and France, grounded on carefully controlled doses of Bentham's writing. Frederick Rosen has explained:

> Bentham's first public declaration of his radical position came only with the appearance of his *Plan of Parliamentary Reform* in 1817. . . . Bentham's reluctance to publish his radical views between 1809 or 1810 and 1817 was based partly on fear of prosecution. During the decade between 1815 and 1825, he developed radical critiques of law . . . [and] religion (*Church of Englandism and Its Catechism Examined* (1818), *Not Paul but Jesus*, published under a pseudonym, Gamaliel Smith, in 1823, and *Analysis of the Influence of Natural Religion on the Temporal Happiness of Mankind,* also published under a pseudonym, Philip Beauchamp, in 1822), and economy in government (*Defense of Economy against the Right Honourable Edmund Burke*, written in 1810 but published in 1817). Bentham often published these against the advice of friends and colleagues, and had to choose radical publishers such as the Hunts, Richard Carlisle, and William Hone who were willing to face prosecution. He also developed a close relationship with Francis Place, whom he met through James Mill in 1812, and with whom he made contact with other writers deeply involved in radical politics, such as John Wade, Thomas Hodgskin, and William Thompson. Place and Bentham also co-operated in a number of radical schemes such as the Parliamentary Candidates Society in 1831.[41]

Although some hold that Bentham flirted with more democratic views at the time of the French Revolution, he clearly did not at that point follow Godwin's example and announce them to the world, and his true conversion only came much later, following on a wave of worldly fame built on a strong but narrower current.

Thus, given that it took him a long lifetime to evolve his views, Bentham should have been the first to admit that the full implications of the greatest happiness principle, for politics and morals, were not always immediately evident. The paradox of that point is of course that he took the principle of utility to be a way of grounding law, politics, and morals on something clear and compelling, rather than on vague talk of natural rights, a moral sense, tradition, etc., the ambiguity of which simply allowed for capture by sinister interests able to exploit it. The judgment of the ruling elites, however glossed in the ancients, was corrupt and self-serving, and served to corrupt language itself. At his most philosophical, Bentham was a philosopher of language and a harbinger of later analytic philosophy, as both Bertrand Russell and W. V. Quine have recognized.[42] And Rosen has noted that "most of Bentham's important writings on logic and language were produced between 1813 and 1815, just as he was writing *Chrestomathia* and involved in the Chrestomathic school." His chief work on ethics, the *Deontology*, was also written at this time, just before he came out as a true Philosophical Radical. The upshot of the more philosophical side of these works was the "theory of fictions,"[43] in which Bentham urged, in good Russellian fashion, that linguistic reform via paraphrase could be used to eliminate from language fictitious entities—such as "natural rights"— terms that are too often taken as referring to something really existing. Such obfuscation was a deliberate tool of the sinister interests. Legal reform thus led him to a more Orwellian concern with fictions and fallacies and the snares of unreformed language, which in turn presaged his own greater clarity and concreteness about the political radicalism of his views. He was fighting fictions and fictitious entities on all fronts, from ghosts to governments.

But how did Bentham himself get to this point? Get, that is, both to the point where the greatest happiness principle would strike him like a thunderbolt, and to the point, nearly fifty years later, where it would move him to become such an original and radical reformer on so many fronts, from language to education to democracy to sexual morality to religion to the care of the dead, moving far in advance of both his global reputation and his intimate circle? If this is what his life looked like at the end, what did it look like at the beginning?

His own words on that subject are often the most striking. In recounting late in life a circumstance that "had much to do with the formation of my character," he explained how when he was boarding at Westminster School, "a boy of the name of Cotton" would return on occasion to stay with his old bedfellow (named Mitford) and tell him stories, with Bentham eagerly eavesdropping:

> While I was lying in bed, I heard from his mouth, stories which excited the liveliest interest in my mind; stories of his own invention; but in which the heroes and heroines were models of kindness and beneficence. They exhibited the quality to which I afterwards gave the name of effective benevolence; and I became enamored of that virtue. I remember forming solemn resolutions, that if ever I possessed the means, I would be an example of that excellence, which appeared so attractive to me. I lost sight of my unconscious instructor in after life; but in my controversies with government on the Panopticon projects, I was thrown into contact with a brother of that Cotton; and Mitford was stationed in the very next seat to him.[44]

But earlier still, there was another formative experience that he would also recall time and again later in life:

> Another book of far higher character was put into my hands. It was Telemachus. In my own imagination, and at the age of six or seven, I identified my own personality with that of the hero, who seemed to me

a model of perfect virtue; and, in my walk of life, whatever it may come to be, why, said I to myself, every now and then, why should I not be Telemachus?[45]

This was, of course, the *Telemachus* of none other than the illustrious Archbishop Fénelon, made all the more famous by Godwin's infamous dilemma. How ironic that Bentham could claim that this "romance may be regarded as the foundation-stone of my whole character; the starting-point from whence my career of life commenced. The first dawning in my mind of the principles of utility, may, I think, be traced to it."[46]

True to form, however, Bentham concluded that he could improve upon his hero, who in his estimation fell rather short of a rival in formulating the best principles of government. The rival had favored a view that "seemed, I say, to border, at least, on the principles of utility; or, in other words, the greatest happiness principle," whereas the hero Telemachus was still too full of "a tissue of vague generalities, by which no clear impression was presented to my mind." Bowring would later hear him "again and again" express "his vexation and disappointment at the poor display made by his favourite, who might, he thought, so much more honourably have won the palm. The goddess of Wisdom, wrapt up, as she was, in the greatcoat of an old man, was much lowered, in his estimation, for not distinguishing and recompensing the wisest of the competitors," namely, the utilitarian rival of Telemachus.[47]

These may seem like strange beginnings for the Bentham of popular caricature—stories of beneficence, a romance based on tales of the son of Odysseus, with no codification in sight. But as Bowring observes, the "impression made on Bentham's mind by the books he read in his childhood, was lasting."[48] And his early reading, which sometimes took place in the limbs of a "lofty elm tree," was a very, very large part of his early life, an early life that was very much colored by his being constantly "talked of and to as a prodigy," and taught "scorn and contempt for other boys." Thus, he "was perpetually placed in a sort of estrangement, by hearing his companions described as dunces; and thus his vanity and pride received constant fuel."[49]

Bentham was a child of affluence, albeit a lonely and sensitive one. His father was Jeremiah Bentham (1712–1792), a prosperous, well-connected, and ambitious London attorney, whose father had also been a Jeremiah Bentham (1685–1741), a prosperous, well-connected, and ambitious London attorney. The father, somewhat severe, had every expectation that Jeremy would follow in this tradition. Bentham's mother was Alicia Woodward Whitehorne, who died at a young age in 1759, when Jeremy was only ten. Of the couple's seven children, only Jeremy and his much younger brother Samuel (1757–1831) had survived childhood.

Bentham was very fond of his mother, who was kind and affectionate, even if she had been a bit of a disappointment to grandfather Jeremiah, who had hoped for a better marriage for his son (she was also a widow, marrying for the second time). Bentham's father would also marry for a second time, in 1766, but the stepmother, Sarah Abbot, was one of the reasons why Bentham preferred to live away from the Queen Square Place home. Relations with the father were sometimes strained and unpleasant as well. Rosen notes:

> Bentham's upbringing and early education was dominated by his father, who sought to develop his talents and produce not only an attorney like himself but also a future lord chancellor of England. Bentham was undeniably precocious, and his intellect was encouraged by his father in a way that resembled the education of John Stuart Mill a generation later. He began to learn Latin at the age of three . . . . Through his father's friendship with William Markham, then headmaster of Westminster School, he was enrolled there at the age of seven in 1755. He became a king's scholar before leaving for Queen's College, Oxford, in 1760 at the age of twelve. He was unhappy at both institutions. Not only was he much younger than the other pupils, he was also small in stature, and physically weak. He had many interests, such as music (he became proficient on the violin, harpsichord, piano, and organ), natural science, and reading, and played battledore (a kind of badminton). But for the most part he was isolated and lonely, living under the crude and often unreasonable authority of his father. In this early period he became thoroughly familiar with the classical authors and the Bible. By the age of ten he could write in both Greek and Latin, and he acquired a reputation at school for writing verses in these languages. He was also known as 'a little philosopher', and, when pushed and prodded by his father, he would reluctantly display his precocity.[50]

According to his own reports, he was physically dwarfish, timid, shy, morbidly afraid of ghosts, goblins, and "the Devil's imp," and prone to nightmares. Books, flowers, and music were his chief comforts, from his childhood through his old age, and such was his love of beauty in these departments that it is very difficult to see how the depiction of him as the great boorish and fact-mongering anti-aesthete could ever have taken hold, at least among those who knew him. Bowring remarks, "[N]ever did he appear more delighted than when speaking of the two spots, Browning Hill and Barking, the country abodes in which his two grandmothers dwelt. He had, through life, the keenest sense of the beauties of nature; and, whenever he could be induced to quit his studies, his enjoyment of fields and flowers was as acute and vivid as that of a happy child."[51] The grandmothers appear to have been his childhood saviors.

The tensions with the father appear to have been at first mostly the result of his great ambitions for his son, and his unwillingness to recognize how sensitive the boy was. On Bentham's recollection:

I never gave him any ground to complain of me. . . . My conduct may indeed have sometimes been a cause of regret and dissatisfaction to him;
but on what ground? My 'weakness and imprudence' in keeping wrapt
up in a napkin the talents which it had pleased God to confer on me—
powers of raising myself to the pinnacle of prosperity. The seals were
mine, would I but muster up confidence and resolution enough to seize
them. He was continually telling me that everything was to be done
by 'pushing;' but all his arguments failed to prevail on me to assume
the requisite energy. 'Pushing,' would he repeat—'pushing' was the one
thing needful; but 'pushing' was not congenial to my character.[52]

Such advice invariably failed to impress Bentham. In the 1760s, when advised
by a friend that "If you mean to rise, catch hold of the skirts of those who are
above you, and care nothing for those beneath you," he "listened coldly to the
advice; was coldly regarded, ever after, by the aspirant; and died, not a judge,
but a philosopher."[53]

But his father and the rest of the family did apparently praise him at every
turn, his father being always given to bragging about his prodigy of a son (and
dismissing other children as dunces) and putting him on display before company. With cause, obviously, at least on the bragging side. Interestingly, as
Rosen has noted, "Bentham's father had numerous interests in the City of London and, for example, was involved for more than fifty years in securing the
future of the Sir John Cass Charity located in Aldgate. At his death a silver cup,
commemorating his father's service, was presented by Bentham to the trustees
in accordance with his father's will."[54] Thus, perhaps in some ways at least,
Bentham did follow in his father's footsteps. But much about the son eluded
the senior Bentham, who seemingly had no clue that his son had a strong aversion to such sports as hunting. His famous sensitivity to the moral standing of
nonhuman animals also appears to have had very early origins:

We had a servant, whose name was Martha: a woman of kindness and
gentleness; and the kindness of her temper ameliorated mine. One day,
while I was a little boy, I went into the kitchen. Some earwigs were running about. I laid hold of them, and put them into the candle. Martha
gave me a sharp rebuke, and asked me, how I should like to be so used
myself? The rebuke was not thrown away.[55]

There were other such early incidents as well, and the young Bentham even
conceived a dislike for fishing, which he deemed cruel and pointless, despite
his occasional engagement in the practice.

Not all the servants were as kindly as Martha, and some of them apparently delighted in exploiting little Jeremy's fears. "When my company became
troublesome, a sure and continually repeated means of exonerating themselves from it, was for the footman to repair to the adjoining subterranean

apartments, invest his shoulders with some strange covering, and, concealing his countenance, stalk in, with a hollow, menacing, and inarticulate tone."[56] Small wonder that he suffered from both day and night terrors, sometimes walking about at night babbling in a nightmarish trance.

Bentham was sixteen when he earned his BA at Oxford, nineteen when he earned his MA, and may have been the youngest graduate Oxbridge had ever seen. According to Bowring, "Jacob Jefferson, who was appointed to be Bentham's tutor, was a morose and gloomy personage, sour and repulsive—a sort of Protestant monk. His only anxiety about his pupil was, to prevent his having any amusement."[57] Indeed, Bentham never had a good word to say about either Westminster School or Oxford, and he seems to have been more inspired by the obscure and unknown Cotton than by any of the faculty. "Generally speaking, the tutors and professors at Oxford offered nothing to win the affections of Bentham. Some of them were profligate; and he was shocked with their profligacy: others were morose; and their moroseness alienated him: but the greatest part of them were insipid; and he had no taste for insipidity."[58]

Worse still, there was the treatment of his hair:

A grievous annoyance to Bentham, at Oxford, was the formal dressing of his hair. 'Mine,' he said, 'was turned up in the shape of a kidney: a quince or a club was against the statutes; a kidney was in accordance with the statutes. I had a fellow-student whose passion it was to dress hair, and he used to employ a part of his mornings in shaping my kidney properly.'[59]

It is intriguing, however, that on the great issue of religious subscription—a torment to Bentham's utilitarian successor Sidgwick—he recorded the following reflections.

The distress of mind which he experienced, when called on to subscribe to the Thirty-nine Articles of the Church of England, he thus forcibly describes:

'Understanding that of such a signature the effect and sole object was the declaring, after reflection, with solemnity and upon record, that the propositions therein contained were, in my opinion, every one of them true; what seemed to me a matter of duty was, to examine them in that view, in order to see whether that were really the case. The examination was unfortunate. In some of them no meaning at all could I find; in others no meaning but one which, in my eyes, was too plainly irreconcilable either to reason or to scripture. Communicating my distress to some of my fellow-collegiates, I found them sharers in it. Upon inquiry it was found, that among the fellows of the college there was one, to whose office it belonged, among other things, to remove all such scruples. We repaired to him with fear and trembling. His answer was cold; and the substance of it was—that it was not for uninformed youths, such as we, to presume to set up our private judgments against a public one, formed by some of the holiest as well as best and wisest men that ever lived. . . . I signed: but by the view I found myself forced to take of the whole business, such an impression was made, as will never depart from me but with life.'[60]

This scar would last a very long time, as his late works on Church of Englandism demonstrate at great and overheated length.

Nor was revulsion against the established religion the only lesson learned at Oxford. Just before the age of sixteen, when already at Lincoln's Inn, Bentham returned to Oxford to attend lectures on jurisprudence by the famous William Blackstone, author of the *Commentaries on the Laws of England*. This made his revulsion complete, encompassing both religion and law, and famously set him on the path of finding his "genius" in the area of legal reform, the odious Oxford behind him.[61]

In 1763 Bentham began his legal studies at Lincoln's Inn at the Inns of Court, and he was admitted to the bar in 1769, though by that point the combined force of his revulsion to Blackstone's lectures and rapture over Priestly's presentation of the principle of the greatest happiness had determined him not to practice law, but to criticize it—indeed, to wage guerrilla warfare against it—despite making Lincoln's Inn his primary residence for many years. It was at Lincoln's Inn that in 1781 he became familiar with William Petty, Earl of Shelburne (later Marquess of Lansdowne), establishing a relationship that would prove to be of considerable importance to his career. Bentham was still a Tory of sorts, but Shelburne (the figure in Bentham's famous dream) was a very influential Whig politician, one who would briefly serve as prime minister in 1782–83. He was friendly with the Pitts and other important political figures, but also unusually interested in ideas and intellectuals, seeking out such figures as Priestly, Richard Price, and Bentham. It was through these connections that Bentham met Dumont, the man who would do so much to make him a global celebrity, and through these connections that the Panopticon scheme almost became a reality.

And it was at the Shelburne estate, Bowood, which Bentham regularly visited, that he emerged as a favorite of "the ladies of the house," who "engaged him at chess and billiards, and shared his devotion to music."[62] It was there that he met Lady Shelburne's niece, Caroline Fox, who, despite being nearly twenty years younger, would ultimately become the object of Bentham's marriage proposal, in 1805, and a deep lifelong love. She was the second great love of Bentham's life, the first having been Mary (Polly) Dunkley, who was only ten years his junior, and with whom he fell deeply in love in the 70s. According to Rosen, "Dunkley, the orphaned daughter of an Essex surgeon, lacked a fortune, and Bentham's father strongly opposed the relationship. For a time

Bentham considered supporting himself by writing, but he abandoned his plan and the relationship eventually ended."[63] On this score, Bentham senior apparently did not want his son to follow in his own footsteps and marry low. But when he tried to marry high, with Caroline Fox, the tables were politely turned, and he was the one rejected as unsuitable. [64]

But there is more to the story. As Schofield explains:

> Bentham needed to make a name for himself—he reckoned that, in order to marry Polly Dunkley, he needed to increase his income, and he could do this by publishing a devastating attack on the leading legal writer of his age. *A Fragment on Government* was, therefore, published anonymously, and gained some degree of attention. Jeremiah, now acting the role of the proud father, let it be known that his son was the author. But once it was discovered that the author was an obscure, briefless barrister, all interest in the work ceased; sales dried up; and Jeremy did not acquire a fortune sufficient to marry Polly.[65]

Although the evidence from Bentham's correspondence is somewhat skimpy, with important letters missing, it appears that Bentham fell in love with Polly in 1774, and that the relationship lasted more than two years, well beyond the point at which Bentham had promised his father that he would break it off. The tensions with his bragging father in this case no doubt reinforced Bentham in his desire for independence.

But what of Caroline Fox, the woman to whom Bentham would propose not once, but twice? She was the sister of Lord Holland and, if Bentham is to be believed, the most endearing individual ever to walk the earth, even if "her face was rather long—and a Fox mouth, with a set of teeth white but too large, 'saved her from being a beauty.'" Bentham described her to his father as a "sprightly good-natured girl, not fourteen, but forward for her age."[66] In a fuller account, related to Bowring in the strictest confidence, he explained:

> He met her at Bowood, when she was very young, and he thirty-four. He was struck with that voluntary playfulness which formed so pleasing a contrast to the aristocratical reserve of most of the females whom he met. . . . One day when Bentham was sitting playing at the spinette . . . a light screen near the instrument was turned over upon him, and a young lady glided away upon feet of feathers.

This was in marked contrast to the "Dignity" that was "the feminine tone of the family."[67] She was, in a word, fun, and Bentham was too. The memory of the fun would remain so sharp that in later life, even "in his playfulness, the introduction of her name, or any circumstance connected with her name, would overpower him with melancholy."[68]

He waited over twenty years before proposing, and when he did, her playfulness was less in evidence as she admonished him to remember his duty to humanity:

It is in your power, however, to make me easy, if you will instantly, without the waste of a single day, return to those occupations from which the world will hereafter derive benefit, and yourself renown. I have enough to answer for already, in having interrupted your tranquility, (God knows how unintentionally,)—let me not be guilty of depriving mankind of your useful labours, of deadening the energy of such a mind as yours. No, I have heard wise people say, and I hope it is true, (though not to the honour of our sex,) that single men achieve the greatest things. Pray, pray, rouse all the powers of your mind—you certainly have weapons to combat this idle passion, which other men, with vacant heads, have not. Let me, as a last request, entreat you to do it, and to devote all the time you can spare from your studies to your friends in Russell Square. There is not a man upon earth who loves you more affectionately than Mr. Romilly—*I know he does*; and his wife's society, you acknowledge, is soothing to you. Do this for my sake, and allow me to hope that, before I have quite reached my grand climacteric, I may again shake hands with you: it would be too painful to think it never could again be so. In the meantime, God bless you, and be assured of the unalterable good wishes and regards of the two spinsters.[69]

This artful but all too direct deployment of the greatest happiness principle against its greatest champion was no doubt the cause of much pain on Bentham's part, but he never really gave up. In 1827, he would write to her, "I am alive: more than two months advanced in my 80th year—more lively than when you presented me, in ceremony, with the flower in the green lane. Since that day, not a single one has passed, (not to speak of nights,) in which you have not engrossed more of my thoughts than I could have wished." Nor, it seems, was it altogether in fun that he also wrote, "I have, for some years past, had a plan for building a harem in my garden, upon the Panopticon principle. The Premiership waits your acceptance."[70]

And yet a third love (beyond of course the principle of utility) deserves mention here. Amelia Curran, who was an Irish artist introduced to Bentham by his friend—and (along with Place) common link to Godwin—Aaron Burr. Burr stayed with Bentham, using his mailing address, during his time of European exile, from 1808 to 1812, and he introduced Amelia to him in 1811. She was to paint Bentham's portrait, and spent much time with him at Queen's Square Place, which he had inherited upon his father's death in 1792. She apparently became quite close to Bentham, who took the place in her heart that Burr had previously occupied, especially while Burr was away in other parts of Europe. Bentham and Burr were reconciled; what became of the relationship with Amelia remains a mystery, though she did become friendly with Mary and Percy Bysshe Shelley, who allowed her to paint some portraits of him, apparently a unique honor.

One cannot help but wonder what schemes of improvement the great projector would have brought to conjugal relations and to the raising of his own children.[71] But it is telling that when it came to love, Bentham was not at all smitten with aristocratic dignity or conventional opinion. A fortuneless orphan, a spirited and fun-loving young girl, and an Irish artist—these were the ones who won his heart and apparently did so precisely in degree to their emancipation from what Mill would call the subjection of women.

In any event, the mere fact that Bentham even had a love life, with serious ups and downs, heartbreaks and rejections, is sufficient to make one doubt Mill's depiction of him as a man who "knew no dejection, no heaviness of heart . . . a boy to the last." And although Bentham himself called Queen's Square Place his Hermitage, and himself the Hermit of it, there is an ever growing body of evidence that he was not such a hermit as all that. He loved his long summer at Shelburne's Bowood in 1781, enjoying being in such an illustrious intellectual circle, even if they did charge him with eating too much. And in due course he would rent his own country home, Ford Abbey, where he would spend half the year from 1814 to 1818. As Catherine Fuller has shown, Bentham's life at Ford Abbey also counters the vision of him as incapable "of any emotional depth, of experiencing pleasure, or of expressing sympathy."[72] In fact, Ford Abbey afforded Bentham all the pleasures that his conception of happiness could ask for. He had his many guests—which included Place, the Romillys, and the entire Mill family, who lived there when Bentham did, otherwise near him in London—walking and jogging around the grounds, playing shuttlecock, listening to and playing music, and taking keen delight in all the flowers and fruits that Bentham, a most earnest horticulturalist, produced. The spacious building and grounds proved remarkably enabling for Bentham, allowing for much experimentation, including that with his famous frigidarium. As many have noted, his cast of mind was really less turgidly legalistic than scientific, even botanical, in its love of identification and classification. Ford Abbey afforded his powers their full scope, and it was in this happy period and place that he took the previously described turn, coming out on so many controversial issues. If the elements of happiness or well-being include social connectedness, health and activity, mindfulness and continued learning or curiosity, and giving, then Bentham was at many points in his life undoubtedly happy, though primarily so late in life.

Prisoners and Paupers

No doubt Bentham's life at Lincoln's Inn, Queen's Square Place, and his other occasional residences (including the Russian village of Zadobrast) was not as sociable and sympathetic as his life at Ford Abbey or Bowood. He was, to be sure, extremely disciplined in his work habits—Bowring claimed that Bentham usually worked at his studies and writing from ten to twelve hours a day—and on some reports he was more introspective and uncomfortable in large company than was his sociable brother Samuel, to whom, however, he was deeply devoted. He was admittedly bashful, and according to Schofield, Bentham "was known to refuse to see visitors who called at his house unannounced, and whom he saw no use in seeing. . . . He had a very particular daily regimen, which included his 'antejentacular circumgyration' or early afternoon jog, reading and answering his correspondence, and, of course, writing his works. His habit was to invite one guest to dinner, when he would be joined by his two amanuenses."[73]

At any rate, it was Samuel's pursuit of a career as a naval architect that had helped plant the idea of the Panopticon prison scheme in Bentham's mind, and that led the two brothers to believe that they might be a big success in Catherine II's Russia. It was in the course of building up Russian connections that Bentham had met Shelburne, and many other worthies as well. Samuel would move to Russia in 1779, not returning until 1791. Bentham followed him in 1785, but only stayed for some twenty months, leaving without the hoped for success.

During these middle years, Bentham certainly knew his share of frustration and heartache, not only in love, but also in work. Again, it is eminently plausible that his many changes of heart in the 1810s reflected his growing frustration with supposedly enlightened monarchs and recognition that the legal reforms he favored could only come about if major democratic political reforms opened the way and obstacles to reform—educational and religious—were cleared away. Both King George III and the Empress Catherine would prove to be less helpful than originally supposed, a story that would repeat itself with many other statesman and leaders. Having tried the powers that be, Bentham had to take his cause to the powers that could and should be, the only powers capable of unseating the sinister interests of Church and State—namely, the people, who, he now judged, were generally the best judges of their own happiness, at least if they were not criminal or indigent. And such shifting beliefs were surely aided and abetted by his friendships with the remarkable Francis Place and James Mill and family.

Even if Bentham was also obsessed with the larger vision of legal reform, the great and chief cause of his mid-life failures and frustrations was his Panopticon scheme for prison reform.[74] Actually, the Panopticon—or "All-seeing" from the Greek—was an architectural scheme of wide application, suitable to be adapted and deployed in reforms in various arenas—education, poverty relief, medical care, and asylums among them. The scheme promised much:

> Morals reformed—health preserved—industry invigorated—instruction
> diffused—public burthens lightened—economy seated, as it were, upon
> a rock—the Gordian knot of the Poor Laws not cut, but untied—all by
> a simple idea in Architecture! . . . A new mode of obtaining power of

mind over mind, in a quantity hitherto without example: and that, to a degree equally without example, secured by whoever chooses to have it so, against abuse.

The plan was in fact set out in a series of letters that Bentham sent from Russia during his time there, letters sent to his father (who supported him with a modest stipend), but which were published together, with two very lengthy postscripts, in 1791. Bentham really had, as Schofield observes, gotten the basic idea from his brother Samuel when they were in Russia together:

> The panopticon . . . was the brainchild of Bentham's brother Samuel, when employed in the 1780s on the estates of Prince Potemkin at Krichev in the Crimea, part of the Russian Empire. He found that, by organizing his workforce in a circular building, with himself at the centre, he could supervise their activities more effectively. Visiting Samuel in the late 1780s and seeing the design, Bentham immediately appreciated its potential. Enshrining the principle of inspection, the panopticon might be adapted as a mental asylum, hospital, school, poor house, factory and, of course, prison. The prison building would be circular, with the cells, occupying several storeys one above the other, placed around the circumference. At the centre of the building would be the inspector's lodge, which would be so constructed that the inspector would always be capable of seeing into the cells, while the prisoners would be unable to see whether they were being watched. The activities of the prisoners would be transparent to the inspector; his actions, insofar as the prisoners were concerned, were hid behind a veil of secrecy. On the other hand, it was a cardinal feature of the design that the activities of the inspector and his officials should be laid open to the general scrutiny of the public, who would be encouraged to visit the prison.[75]

Or, in Bentham's words:

> To say all in one word, it will be found applicable, I think, without exception, to all establishments whatsoever, in which, within a space not too large to be covered or commanded by buildings, a number of persons are meant to be kept under inspection. No matter how different, or even opposite the purpose: whether it be that of *punishing the incorrigible, guarding the insane, reforming the vicious, confining the suspected, employing the idle, maintaining the helpless, curing the sick, instructing the willing* in any branch of industry, or *training the rising race* in the path of *education:* in a word, whether it be applied to the purposes of *perpetual prisons* in the room of death, or *prisons for confinement* before trial, or *penitentiary-houses,* or *houses of correction,* or *work-houses,* or *manufactories,* or *madhouses,* or *hospitals,* or *schools.*[76]

It was this vision of social control, disciplining and controlling via architecture, that led Michel Foucault, in *Discipline and Punish,* to immortalize Bentham as the social theorist above all others who had captured the essence of the modern surveillance state and modern power, power become invisible and used, cruelly, to create, define and control the identities of those subject to it: the "criminal mind," the "sexual deviant," the "psychopathological case," etc.[77] As Schofield has dryly observed, one would never guess from Foucault's account "that the panopticon prison was never built, that standard prison architecture went in a very different direction from that advocated by Bentham, and that Bentham himself did not regard the panopticon as a model for the state."[78]

And of course, as Foucault well knew, Bentham regarded the whole scheme as the humane alternative to the violence of the state being inflicted on criminals at every turn.[79] On the reigning "Bloody Code," hundreds of often relatively minor offenses were subject to the death penalty or to "transportation," which involved having criminals sent to Australia (or New South Wales, as it was called) and was often tantamount to a death sentence. Proposals in 1786 for a resumption of "transportation" and a new penitentiary in Ireland had spurred Bentham to throw himself into the effort to reform the whole system of crime and punishment, work that was, after all, very much in keeping with the humane reformism of Helvétius and Beccaria that had so influenced him. Mere retributive punishment, rather than future-oriented rehabilitation and example, has always been one of the chief objects of utilitarian criticism, whether it comes in the form of mundane systems of criminal justice or Divine eschatological schemes. Punishment merely for retribution, with no felicific effect on future developments, was a mere addition of needless pain to the world. On this, Bentham and Godwin and their successors were entirely at one, and entirely in opposition to much religious morality.

Still, various of Bentham's remarks do seem to lend some credence to Foucault's fears about power taking more sinister forms, as controlling invasions of the psyche. The only adequate response to such concerns is to paint a broader and richer picture of the society that Bentham did envision, and how the state would figure in it. After all, a certain picture does emerge, in the unfolding of Bentham's life, of an ambitious, deeply radical, program for social reform, despite the fact that he defeats most attempts to capture him as an unambiguous advocate of, not only the surveillance state, but also the laissez-faire "night watchman" state, the professionalized bureaucratic state, the imperial state, and so forth. True, he seems to advance a moveable feast of arguments and issues and priorities, such as the need to eliminate perverse incentives, curb sinister interests, make law and other social institutions clear and transparent, and create that security that, to his mind, involved the solid guarantee for various liberties through state action. Again, he was no champion of the view that "liberty" meant a kind of Hobbesian noninterference; civil liberty was structured and underwritten by the state, which needed to provide such oversight as might be necessary to keep some from interfering with others, providing security. But there is an undercurrent to his various schemes that gives them a clearer direction than any such summary suggests, and this amounts to rather more than the familiar "principle of self-preference" and "means-prescribing or junction-of-interests prescribing principle," which of course were simply means to realizing the greatest happiness. Everything was in the name of the principle of utility, or better, the greatest happiness, but happiness could be a very progressive notion.

In midlife he still clung to the view that he had only to enlighten political leaders sufficiently and they would give his plans a try, just as he sought to guide the leaders of the French revolution. Even though the death of his father in 1792 and his consequent inheritance (which included Queen's Square Place) had relieved Bentham of any worries about his own financial security, he was as determined as ever to see the Panopticon realized, whether or not he himself needed the position of "inspector."

It nearly happened. Shelburne, now Landsdowne, sent the Panopticon scheme to Sir John Parnell, chancellor of the Irish Exchequer, who expressed some enthusiasm for it, as did others around the world. Most importantly, in a great irony of history, William Pitt the younger, the persecutor of Godwin and his friends, was in fact a supporter of Bentham and the Panopticon. Bentham had impressed him (and many others) with the model of the structure that he kept in his London home. But somehow, the final deal never got closed:

> Negotiations concerning various locations for the prison ran into numerous difficulties, as few wanted a prison on or near their estates, and the whole idea of public inspection depended on the prison being situated on an accessible and convenient site. For a brief period, when Long offered Bentham the Salisbury estate at Millbank, and Bentham actually acquired the land in November 1799, it seemed that the project would go forward. But Pitt resigned in 1801 without authorizing the prison, and the Addington administration kept Bentham waiting until 1803 before saying that the government was unwilling to fund the project. The Treasury considered panopticon again in 1811–12, when Bentham was still willing to be governor, but in October 1813 he finally gave up hope and accepted £23,000 in compensation.[80]

And turned to philosophy, education, democracy, etc., being less concerned at this point to cultivate the sinister interests that he now recognized as such.

The whole episode is worthy of Dickensian satire, indeed recalls the "circumlocution office" in *Little Dorrit*. Indeed, although it is usually supposed that Dickens had rigidly made up his mind about the Benthamites, he might have been more receptive to Benthamism than the popular wisdom would have it, and may have recognized that many of his targets—for example, the ancient Court of Chancery, blasted in Dickens's *Bleak House*—were also

Bentham's targets.[81] The more so since Bentham's efforts on behalf of the prison scheme became, in the mid-1790s, entangled with his efforts to reform the Poor Laws and institute a scheme for the indigent, a Panopticon Industry House. His work on the poor and indigent is remarkably illuminating of the ways in which he was willing to adapt the workings of the Panopticon to different circumstances, and on this, as on education, his actual views can be better grasped by setting them against their more (supposedly) Dickensian interpretations. For it was not only the character of Mr. Gradgrind in *Hard Times* that has often been read as directed against the utilitarians; what may be the best loved Dickens novel of all, after *A Christmas Carol*, was also aimed at them, at least according to the critics. And as Dickens biographer Michael Slater notes, in his account of Dickens writing *Oliver Twist*:

> Dickens completed what he called his 'glance at the new Poor Law Bill' with an account of Oliver's sufferings at a 'baby-farm.' This was highly topical in early 1837 following a great scandal about child deaths at such an establishment in St. James's, Westminster, to which Cruikshank claimed to have drawn Dickens's attention. Dickens introduced the character of Bumble the parish beadle, who gloriously transcends the beadle figure as already established in popular folklore (and used by Dickens in *Sketches*) and offers a devastating caricature both of the Utilitarian philosophy underlying the New Poor Law and of its often grotesque results in practice. The whole installment is superbly clinched by the now legendary scene of Oliver asking for more.[82]

The scene in question is of course the one in which a young, innocent, and half-starved Oliver Twist asks for a second helping of food, only to be met with outrage, derision, and punishment.

It is true that Bentham's name was associated with the "new" Poor Law that had come into being in the 1830s, replacing the old system (dating back to the reign of Elizabeth I) of local parish relief that offered, in a very inconsistent and unstable way, both indoor relief (workhouses) and outdoor relief (support at home), financed by the "poor rate." The old system was in a state of crisis in the mid-nineties, being both extremely costly and extremely inefficient, and it was at that juncture that Bentham weighed in with his proposals. He was drawn into the controversies by his friend and admirer, the great reformer William Wilberforce, an ally in the Panopticon scheme who was also advising Pitt on the reform of the Poor Laws, and who sent Bentham a draft of a new Poor Bill early in 1796. Bentham sent back many comments on the draft, but was also stimulated to produce a large body of work on the subject.[83]

The first thing to note about his proposals is that, as was so often the case, they were never truly adopted. Indeed, attention-getting though they should have been, they never actually received much attention. Bentham called for nothing less than a system of some 250 "industry houses" spread across the county, each of which could service some 2,000 paupers, adding up to a total of roughly half a million people. The system was projected to grow as it became more successful, within twenty years producing 500 houses serving a million paupers. A joint stock National Charity Company, governed by a central board, would administer this system, appointing governors for each individual institution and collecting revenues from the poor rates, share subscriptions, and the labor of the inmates—revenues that would in due course render the scheme positively profitable. The Company would have a wide range of obligations and powers. If it had to admit anyone who came to it seeking aid, it could also force certain types (orphans, paupers, and vagrants) to be admitted to an appropriate house. Inmates would be apprentices, and they could leave after their work had paid off the costs of keeping them, though minors would be kept until the age of twenty-one, if male, or nineteen, if female.

The National Charity Company scheme does put the companion Panopticon scheme in perspective. Indeed, the Panopticon seems like a modest effort by comparison. Gertrude Himmelfarb has infamously observed how Bentham "while declaring the usury laws an intolerable infringement on free trade, had a penchant for schemes involving a considerable degree of regimentation and for monopolistic establishments of unprecedented size." Poor relief was a case in point, with his scheme for a huge privately run company "with an exclusive contract for the support and employment of over 10 percent of the population of England."[84] This was a kind of *reductio ad absurdum* of the principle of indoor relief. Most alarmingly, Bentham allowed that in "order to apprehend 'suspected depredators' (suspected because they were without visible means of support)," it would be necessary to establish a "Universal Register of names, abodes and occupations." If this seemed like a massive infringement of liberty, Bentham explained, the kind of liberty in question was "doing mischief" and security was more important, even for those being detained: "The persons in question are a sort of forward children—a set of persons not altogether sound in mind, not altogether possessed of that moral sanity without which a man cannot in justice to himself any more than to the community be intrusted with the uncontrolled management of his own conduct and affairs."[85]

But as David Lieberman has perceptively noted, in a more balanced review of Bentham's Poor Law writings:

> Eligibility rules discarded the familiar categories of deserving and undeserving poor: need, rather than desert was the key qualification. Others who did not seek relief—such as vagrants and beggars—would be coercively required to enter and contribute their labor to the company's production. In its full network of responsibilities, the National Charity Company's operations would not only replace the current system of poor laws, but also supplant the better part of established rules

governing settlement, vagrancy, apprenticeship, and employment. Public functions currently undertaken by the parish and the church would instead fall within the orbit of a joint-stock company enterprise.

One obvious and important point of interest in these writings is the "inspection-house" or panopticon architecture Bentham specified for the pauper industry houses. Owing to the deep impact of Michel Foucault's discussion in *Discipline and Punish* (1979), for many scholars Bentham remains above all associated with "panopticonism." Foucault's treatment drew on a very limited set of texts, drawn from Bentham's earliest plan for a panopticon prison. Foucault ignored Bentham's own lengthy revisions and elaborations of the prison project. And the subsequent discussion of "panopticonism" (at least in English) has largely and unfortunately ignored the case of pauper panopticons. As an exercise in inspection-house architecture, "Pauper Management Improved" dwarfed the prison project and demands attention in any consideration of this element of Bentham's thought. Panopticon technology—locating the pauper inmates in a space that placed their conduct at any moment under the "inspection" or surveillance of others—was critical. "Without the benefit of inspection," Bentham maintained, "I would not be responsible for the conduct or condition of a single individual" (p. 105). But in this setting, Bentham made more emphatic than in the prison project both the range of persons whose actions he placed under inspection and the limits of architecture as an instrument of control. With regard to range, Bentham emphasized how much his technologies of inspection were directed at the company managers rather than the pauper inmates alone. The inspection-house design exposed to external view the conduct of the National Charity Company's personnel, and this transparency would provide a powerful restraint against potential abuses. At the same time, architecture served as but one of several technologies needed to secure the plan's goals to ensure reliable performance. As in his later program for the administration of the democratic state, Bentham emphasized how often written records would supplant architecture as the instrument of choice for institutional transparency and systematic inspection. The operations of the National Charity Company were to be equipped with a new system of comprehensive record-keeping. Whereas traditional bookkeeping provided an account of revenues and expenditures, the National Charity Company's required "system of book-keeping will be neither more nor less than the history of the system of management in all its points (p. 541)."[86]

Indeed, as Michael Quinn has also stressed, "Bentham's discussion of poverty involved much more than the minute exposition of a specific plan of reform: it encompassed an investigation of the basic principles on which provision of relief should be grounded, and a sustained comparison of alternative systems of relief."[87] Quinn summarized those principles as follows:

> First, since the aim was to prevent starvation, relief should be limited to 'the necessaries of life.' Second, since laboring for subsistence was mankind's inescapable condition, the indigent too, excepting only those utterly incapable, should be required to labour. Third, since out-allowances, that is cash welfare payments, were incompatible with the efficient extraction of labour, the indigent should be obliged to enter large-scale Industry-Houses, and remain there until the expense of relief was recovered.[88]

In that vein, Bentham himself made it very clear from the start that, with this issue too, the language was in serious need of reform:

> The proper object of the system of laws, known in this country by the name of the *Poor Laws,* is to make provision for the relief not of *poverty* but of *indigence.*
>
> The distinction between poverty and indigence is an article of fundamental and primary importance.
>
> Poverty is the state of everyone who, in order to obtain subsistence, is forced to have recourse to labour.
>
> Indigence is the state of him who, being destitute of property (or at least destitute of the specifies of property necessary to the immediate satisfaction of the particular want by which he happens to be pressed), is at the same time either unable to labour, or unable, even for labour, to procure the supply of which he happens thus to be in want.
>
> Poverty as above defined is the natural, the primitive, the general, and the unchangeable lot of man. The condition of persons whose property has placed them in what are termed *opulent* or *easy circumstances,* that is, who live upon the permanently recurring produce of labour already in store, is but an *exception,* which, under the most equal distribution of the stock thus laid up, could never, for any length of time, be very extensive.
>
> As labour is the source of wealth, so is poverty of labour. Banish poverty, you banish wealth. [89]

Thus, indigence was the issue, and this reform scheme (like the prison scheme) in fact involved what was in key respects a two-way system of transparency, such that those in charge were also subject to careful public inspection—a point that in our own day of unregulated financial markets and official secrecy seems of singular importance. And these are the matters that, as Quinn has pointed out, may well have been the most influential elements of Bentham's writings. One of Bentham's secretaries in his later years, Edwin Chadwick, who had helped edit his poor law writings, became the secretary of the commission "whose report laid the foundation of the 1834 Poor Law Amendment Act." "The Commission's Report contained many features derived directly from those writings; for instance, the definition of poverty as dependence on labour for subsistence; the insistence on the impossibility of relieving poverty, as opposed to indigence; the insistence on a national rather than local system; and, most centrally, the work-house test (i.e. the insistence on indoor-relief for the able-bodied), and the principle of less eligibility."[90]

Which is to say that Bentham was in fact influential on this subject, but quite indirectly and at the more abstract level of conceptualizing the relevant issues and incentives. The particulars of his planned National Charity Company were not realized in the reforms; as remarked, they were not even much noticed. Plausibly, at the more philosophical level, Himmelfarb is right in maintaining that Bentham's notion of pauperism "enlarged the scope of the term by extending it to the considerable number of working poor who would be confined in his industry-houses," whereas the politically successful reformers "deliberately narrowed it precisely to exclude the laboring poor from the compass of the New Poor Law."[91] But that does not capture the dynamic process of reform that he apparently had in mind.

Although Bentham developed his plans for poor law reform well before his radicalization in the 1810s, he apparently continued to cleave to his ideas, and late in life planned to reissue *Pauper Management*. But on some points, his thinking did apparently shift. One great point of pride in Bentham's scheme was that the envisioned system would be not only one of self-supply, with the inmates producing what was needed to cover their own subsistence (and more), but also one in which the economic value of children would be maximized. In fact, children, being cheap to feed, small to house, etc., held great potential as human capital, and their numbers, Bentham urged, should be increased by facilitating early marriage among the apprentices. But with the appearance of Malthus's 1798 *Essay on the Principle of Population*, with its argument that procreation among the poor was rampant and a grave threat to all, Bentham appears to have rethought that part of his program. The connections are not entirely clear, but after 1806, at least, "Bentham endorsed Malthus's principle of population, while rejecting 'moral restraint,' Malthus's pain-imposing solution to population pressure, in favour of pleasure-giving 'unprolific' sex (whether unprolific by birth control or homosexuality)."[92]

But Bentham's thoughts on the subject of children are far more complex and revealing than one would ever guess from the writings of his detractors.

The Visionary

Now, it is at just this point that one can gain a deeper appreciation of Bentham by considering the web of connecting themes that extends between his writings on the Panopticon, the Poor Laws and other topics, particularly those on education, sexuality, and religion. Just as the Panopticon writings are better viewed through the lens of the Poor Law writings, both are better viewed through a wider angle lens that captures Bentham at his most visionary, intimating some of his deeper convictions about human nature and suggesting some of his fonder hopes for humanity.

Plainly, Bentham and the other Philosophical Radicals adopted an associationist psychology that in Enlightenment fashion stressed the power of environmental conditioning, of nurture over nature, such that a more effective educational or socialization process would, its proponents were confident, produce more effectively utilitarian citizens—be they former paupers, criminals, or whatever.[93] The right system could turn "dross" into "sterling," "grind rogues honest," and so on. But for all that, Bentham's thoughts on psychology, child development, and education do point to some more complicating factors, and some additional counters to the (supposed) Dickensian and Foucauldian critiques. In a little-celebrated footnote in his *Outline of a Work Entitled Pauper Management Improved*, Bentham explained the need for a "Child's progress book" or "Calendar of Hebe" (on the model of a Calendar of Flora used by Botanists to trace the growth of vegetation), and he set out the following needed data:

> 1. —Advances independent of instruction—first indication of fear; smiling; recognizing persons; indication of a preference for a particular person; indication of a dislike for a particular person; attention to musical sounds; crowing; appearance of first tooth; appearance of each of the successive teeth; duration and degree of pain and illness in cutting teeth; giving food or toys to others; attempt to imitate sound; laughing; general progress in bodily or intellectual requirements, whether uniform, or by sudden degree.—2. Advances dependent upon instruction:—standing, supported by one arm; standing supporting itself, by resting the hands; token of obedience to will of others; command of natural evacuations; walking, supporting itself by chairs; standing alone; walking alone; pointing out the seat of pain, &c.[94]

Although such thoughts may not represent a breakthrough in the pediatric or child development literature, they do suggest that Bentham had some sense of the need for close observation of children and for recognizing factors that occurred "independent of instruction."

A comparison of Bentham's work on pauper management and his chief work on education, *Chrestomathia* (meaning "conducive to useful learning"), can in some ways specially illuminate the deeper views of the man so often accused of being a man-child himself, incapable of any rounded appreciation of human nature and development. Ultimately, it is Bentham's understanding of the heart of humanity, of what makes for pleasure and pain, happiness and unhappiness, that has to be considered, in order to make sense of his views on utility or what would be productive of happiness. A too quick dismissal of him as reducing the whole of human psychological development to economistic calculation in the crudest of cost/benefit terms cannot capture either his often quite probing analysis of human failings and foibles or the subtlety of the sanctions and educational tactics needed. If money and power were effective rewards, so were prestige and dignity.[95] If learning needed to be useful, it could also be, for that very reason, empowering.

After all, there were progressive features to Bentham's chief educational work. His proposed day school for middle-class students—one was to be housed in the garden of Queen Square Place—in itself reflected an extension of educational opportunity, an effort to provide educational resources that would not be restricted by class, race, religion, or gender. Moreover, he detested cruelty, including the stock forms of corporal punishment routinely used by schoolmasters. His notions of classroom management emphasized the use of spirited competition instead of corporal punishment, the division of students into groups distinguished by ability, the mentoring of younger students by older students, and the effective use of visual aids and other devices to enliven and clarify instruction. If he was obsessed with the micromanagement of schools for useful learning that would lead to employment, he was also clear that "the common end of every person's education is Happiness," and that the larger aims of education included:

> 1. Securing to the possessor a proportionable share of *general respect*. . . . 2. Security against *ennui*, viz. the condition of him who, for want of something in prospect that would afford him pleasure, *knows not what to do with himself*, a malady to which, on *retirement*, men of business are particularly exposed. . . . 3. Security against *inordinate sensuality*, and its mischievous consequences./ 4. Security against *idleness*, and consequent *mischievousness*. . . . 5. Security for admission into, and agreeable intercourse with, *good company: i. e.* company in, or from which, present and harmless pleasure, or future profit or security, or both, may be obtained.[96]

Bentham's interest in this proposed school, which shared some of the design features of the Panopticon prison scheme, was stimulated by his allies Francis Place and Edward Wakefield, whose elaborate schemes for "schools for all" reflected other influences as well. As Southwood Smith noted, the Benthamites were much impressed, in 1813–17, by the work initiated by

> Mr Lancaster and modified and extended by Dr Bell . . . if it were true, as stated by Mr Gray, that since he had introduced this system into his school, his whole class had gained a more extensive knowledge of the Latin language than he had ever known on any former occasion; that *not a single boy* had failed; that it had enabled him *entirely to abolish*

corporal punishment; that it had animated his whole school with one spirit, making them all advance in the intellectual career with the like ardour, and though not with equal success, without *a single failure,* and that Mr Lancaster had put into his hands an instrument which had enabled him to realize his fondest visions in his most sanguine mood;—if such results were obtained by the application of this instrument to the acquisition of Latin and Greek, what, said Mr Bentham, may not be expected from its application to the whole field of knowledge? [97]

Of course, Bentham deemed it a great waste of time and talent to devote most of schooling to "the dead languages." But his emphasis on the useful was, at one level, more an antidote to a curriculum that ignored science and taught subservience than an antidote to poetry. Dickens's satirical portrait of Benthamism in *Hard Times* has the poor, young Sissy Jupe subjected to the suffocating schooling of Mr. Gradgrind and Mr. M'Choakumchild, who dismiss all poetry as idle Fancy—"Facts alone are wanted in life. Plant nothing else, and root out everything else." On such grounds wallpaper representing horses and carpets representing flowers are to be condemned, since "you are not to see anywhere, what you don't see in fact." But Bentham would not have recognized his vision of the aims of education in that deadening scenario. His aim, however problematic the means, was democratic empowerment, not docility; self-respect, not humiliation. The larger issue was well put in a letter from Francis Place to William Allen:

How few are there on whom you can rely for active co-operation in promoting the happiness of the people! Your connection is principally among those whose rank is at the top of the middles class, who, enjoying wealth and leisure, might be expected to possess the disposition to do the greatest service to humanity, with the knowledge necessary to give full effect to their disposition. But is this so? Alas, it is not so, and it cannot be expected to exist in any great quantity as we descend! Why is this? Plainly because of ignorance; people do not see how much is in their power; they doubt their own ability to effect any real and permanent good on a large scale, and they therefore attribute the evils they have no hope of removing to the very constitution of society. They would remove the evils they are constantly obliged to witness, but unable to contemplate the possibility of accomplishing their wishes, they endeavour to get rid of uneasy sensations by trying to forget them, and by continued efforts to free themselves from them they stifle the best feelings of their nature, become morose and disqualify themselves from the performance of any good whatever; or they relieve themselves by the performance of what is vulgarly called charity; they give money, victuals, clothes, &c., and thus by encouraging idleness and extinguishing enterprise, increase the evils they would remove.[98]

Bentham's Chrestomathic school, like his Panopticon prison and National Charity Company, was never realized in any serious way, though Place and Wakefield engaged in heroic efforts to create a system of schools reflecting Bentham's views. If his influence was clearly felt, it was at a higher level, with the construction of University College, London, which reflected his vision of opening up higher education to all, regardless of economic status, religious affiliation, race, gender, or political belief. This was perhaps an apt tribute, and corrective.

For arguably, it was Bentham's obsession with what some would call the "social bases of self-respect" that led him to these conclusions, in his Panopticon, Poor Law, and Chrestomathic works, and in others as well. Achieving happiness was, on his view, extremely difficult for society as a whole. Most people must labor their way through poverty, and the indigent, uneducated, and vulnerable were going to have an especially tough time of it. It would take large scale efforts at social engineering (and effective public administration) to secure their basic necessities, and in doing so give them a stake in a system that otherwise they would have little reason to respect. Much of the country just was badly off, and kept down by ruling elites who had every perverse incentive to continue their predatory practices, masked in an obfuscatory fog about the ancient laws, and marked by corruption, delusion, fictions, and "factious honors." It was not as though the truly disadvantaged had the opportunities to advance, or that such freedom of speech as existed meant much to those with no education or social resources to realize their freedom in any concrete fashion. Destitution and the death penalty awaited them, whether they were deserving or undeserving. As Crimmins has put it, in "contrast with the cesspits of the existing gaols and hulks, and the horrific experiment with the penal colony at Botany Bay, Bentham's prisoners were to be kept clean and their labour made productive and profitable, and serve to develop skills that might be useful to them upon release and assist in their moral reformation." Furthermore, once

the principles that gave shape to the panopticon and the various devices built into its management are understood, the arguments of critics who view it merely as a punitive and repressive institution are less impressive. Bentham did not devise the panopticon as a means of social control, but as a means of minimizing the cost to the public of establishments in which supervision was by definition a requirement. Moreover, his championing of 'the inspection principle' needs to be seen in the context of the development of inspection over the nineteenth century as a tool for the prevention of abuses in establishments like asylums and schools. It was eventually recognized that the legislation introduced by the Factory Acts to end the exploitation of the labour of children could not be properly enforced without a programme of work-place inspection by public officials, a practice universally accepted today in nearly every public place of activity in western societies.[99]

Similar points apply to Panopticism generally, which obviously could involve the use of one scheme, say, the National Charity Company, to help reduce the need for other schemes, say, the Panopticon prisons. And crucially, better educational institutions might help reduce the need for both poor houses and prisons, or at least so Bentham seemed to hope. How, it is only fair to ask, did he envision the potential of his tougher measures turning the times around, and rendering themselves less needful? Was the "ideal republic" of the future all that closely connected to the "ideal republic" of the present? Thomas Peardon, in a classic essay on "Bentham's Ideal Republic," argued that Bentham's *Constitutional Code* (composed between 1820 and 1832) "may be regarded as Bentham's view of the best possible commonwealth—a Utilitarian Utopia" and an essential piece of the Pannomion.[100] But even that work, as extensive as it is, mostly only captures a static, not an evolutionary, picture of Bentham's reformism. Still, as Peardon notes:

> Bentham was hopeful, too, that the influence of sympathy could be increased at the expense of self-regard by wisely contrived political arrangements. Even now, he further concedes, 'In a highly matured state of society, in here and there a highly cultivated and expanded mind, under the stimulus of some extraordinary excitement, a sacrifice of self-regarding interest to social interest, upon a nation scale has not been without example.'[101]

True, "such a phenomenon is less frequent in occurrence than insanity," and self-preference was by far the safer assumption, but even so, the competent public servants with an "aptitude" for the work would have that "moral aptitude" that involved "being in an adequate degree actuated and guided by the desire of securing to the greatest number in question, at all times, the greatest quantity, or say the maximum, of happiness."[102] More such fit public servants would be available as society progressed, and their work would of course be reinforced by publicity and enlightened public opinion, not to mention more artful architectural design, including crescent-shaped government houses that would facilitate the right forms of interaction.

At any rate, the overlap between Bentham's various schemes is striking, and the peculiar details, taken together, can give a rather different, less uniformly disciplinary picture. Thus, in the discussion of education in *Outline of Pauper Management Improved*, Bentham at one point explains his "Talent-cultivation principle":

> Natural talents of any kind, manifesting themselves in an extraordinary degree, to receive appropriate culture. Examples:—Musical habits principally:—viz. an extraordinary fine voice, or an extraordinary good

ear, and thence affection for the pursuit. (In the instance of a natural taste for the arts of *design*, or of strength or comeliness adapted to *dancing*, or other *theatrical exhibitions*, superiority is less manifest, culture is less exceptionable in the eyes of a sever moralist, and the object is of inferior account.)—Advantages:—Comfort and consideration of this part of the pauper community increased.—Importance and desirableness of the condition of a Company's apprentice raised.—For the importance of music, as an assistant to instruction, intellectual, moral, and religious, see . . . .[103]

This is followed by a section on the "Fellow-instruction principle," the same principle figuring in the Chrestomathic schools.

In material that was drafted, but not included in the text as it appeared, Bentham elaborated:

Subjects of instruction, principally such branches of knowledge or art, as exhibit the grounds and reasons of the several branches of economy carried on in the establishment: the general instruction applied all along to the particular processes actually employ'd—These branches are: 1. Reading. 2. Arithmetic (the two necessary inlets to all the rest). 3. Natural history in its several branches. 4. Chemistry. 5. Mechanicks, and 6. Geometry, Land-surveying included: all of them so far, and so far only, as is conducive to the above purpose. Applications of the theological cast will render these subordinate instructions the more suitable to the main purpose of the day. Prints, models or specimens, of the several subject-matters, according to their nature—implements of instruction, all of them addressing themselves to sense—might take place of the uninstructive imitations, toys, and playthings usually put into the hands of children. Imitations have their use, in as far as originals are inaccessible, or can not in equal numbers and for a constancy be subjected to one view. Instructions, such as can be convey'd either by letters or imitative representations, should be digested as much as may be into the form of Tables, printed on but one side of the paper, and matching, though not necessarily equal, in point of size.

Towards the close of the apprenticeship—that is at the approach of the period in which the individual will be committed to his own governance. 7. Of medical knowledge—(e.g., of the sciences explanatory of the structure, functions, and disorders of the human body) enough to give the *rationale* of a set of *prophylactic* instructions: instructions guarding against accidents, practices, and habits immediately or remotely productive of disease. 8. Medical knowledge more at large, as applied to domestic animals. 9. Of moral instruction, what may serve to explain the nature and the mischief of the several sorts of pernicious practices, which he will have been so little exposed either to fall into or to be a sufferer by, during his continuance in these seats of tranquility and innocence.

[10] Music—vocal, and in parts: a preparative to psalmody, a portion of the service of the day.

[11.] For males, say from 14 years of age, military exercise . . . [12] For both sexes, when the season permits, and if the situation affords the means, swimming:—taught as an art as well as practiced as a pastime:—to begin at the earliest ages at which it has been observed to be practiced among savages:—practised latterly with heavy cloaths on, as a lesson of security.

[13.] While those of military age are occupied on military exercise, those of inferior age might be exercised in running or leaping: to which might be added dancing, which is little more than walking, running and leaping in concert and in preconcerted figures—Should the sexes intermingle in the dance? [104]

And there is greater elaboration still on the "[a]dvantages resulting or derivable from musical instruction," music being "an immediate and constant fund of *self-amusement*," an exercise "favourable to *health*," an art "favourable to *intellectual strength*, by the gentle exercise it affords to the mind," and "favourable to *moral health*, by filling up vacancies in the mind, and thereby blocking up the entrance against vitious ideas and desires." It also "ministers naturally to *the faculty of pleasing*" and can even be "rendered subservient to *productive industry*, by giving regularity and quickness to the motions of the workman, and in works performed in concert, by disposing and enabling him to keep time—at any rate by cheering him during the work." And of course, music is recognized as an aid to religion and military strength. Come to that, it "may be made subservient, in the way of communication and retention, to *instruction* of any kind, especially when conjoined with *metre*: —the *multiplication-table*, lately set to a pleasing melody, affords a happy instance of its application to instruction of the driest kind."[105] And the list goes on and on.

This is not exactly the program of young Sissy Jupe, subjected to the suffocating schooling of Mr. Gradgrind and Mr. M'Choakumchild.[106] True, Bentham would discard "Languages, even living; much more dead: Grammar, even English: Mathematics, all the high and difficult branches: Astronomy, unless, in the maritime situations, so much of the practical part as is necessary to navigation: Geography; except so much as is attained by looking at a map: Poetry: Oratory: History: Logic."[107] But somehow, the popular portraits of the dark satanic utilitarian mills of both industry and education leave out the part about everyone singing all the time, confident that they have their share of general respect, can perform productive labor, and have been given the "rudiments of all other intellectual improvements," along with swimming lessons and more. In some cases, the National Charity Company houses would serve as "a seminary for the Choir and the Theatre." And this is not to mention being indulged in the safer forms of sex.

The vision here would seem to import a good deal of the experience, positive and negative, that Bentham himself had when growing up. His enduring love of music and natural beauty shine through, as do his distaste for dead languages and dull instruction. The wonder is that he did not include *Telemachus* in the curriculum as he sought to codify his experiences for the benefit of the world. But the houses would nonetheless be schools of sympathy, not only via the musical cultivation of the inmates, but more broadly, among other things providing a network of lodgings and employment opportunities such that the "self-maintaining poor" might be allowed to maintain better social connections:

> Travelling all over the country, wherever their occasions lead them;— setting out without money, and arriving with money in their pockets. At present this cannot be done, because there is nobody in a condition to give employment at such *short warning*, in large or small *quantities*, as it may happen, to persons *unknown*, coming in any *number*. A man, having money in his pocket, might work or not work, as he chose:—taking the benefit of the diet and lodging at the cheap price of the house, instead of using a public house, under the obligation of paying for expensive food and liquors. Domestic ties would be strengthened, and social affections cherished, by laying open, in this way, to the poor, those opportunities of occasional intercourse, and uninterrupted sympathy, which at present are monopolized by affluence.[108]

Even those who were not at liberty were, if well-behaved, to be allowed to go "to the industry-house nearest to the abode, of any of his near connections, whom he wishes to visit, though it were at the remotest part of South Britain."

It is, however, intriguing that Bentham in these writings had his utilitarian scheme serving both the monarchy and religious practices, rather than disabusing people of them, though some later notes indicate that he was himself on the side of those who sought "the abolition of the monarchical part of the constitution." The astounding, open radicalism of *Plan of Parliamentary Reform* (1817), *Bentham's Radical Reform Bill* (1819), *Church of England and its Catechism Examined* (1818), *Not Paul, but Jesus* (1823), *Analysis of the Influence of Natural Religion on the Temporal Happiness of Mankind* (1822), *Emancipate Your Colonies!* (1830), *Indications respecting Lord Eldon* (1825), etc., etc., is not to be found, at least openly, in the Panopticon or Poor Law writings, and it is difficult not to conclude that here, too, Bentham was advancing a very indirect form of utilitarianism, allowing that, e.g., some forms of religious belief and practice could be felicific under certain circumstances. Of course, it should also be recognized that he certainly allowed that in the role of legislator, considerations of time and place needed to be taken into account; given the relativity of custom, religion, morality, etc., sanctions needed to be tailored to the circumstances, and this despite his hopes for a Pannomion.[109]

But, although the going prejudices had to be accommodated and worked with to a degree, this did not mean that the utilitarian critique of them was stilled. The Panopticon and Poor Law writings do in fact dovetail in some surprising ways with even Bentham's most radical later work, his amazing writings on sexuality, which, in combination with his attacks on religion, make Bertrand Russell look moderate by comparison. The angle on Bentham's work needs to be wider still.

Very Useful Sex

Bentham made himself the spokesman of a silent and invisible minority. First, he rejects the silence taboo. 'It seems rather too much,' he remarks with dry irony, 'to subscribe to men's being hanged to save the indecency of enquiring whether they deserve it.' Then . . . he pleads from a more rational mode of debate, which would scrutinize the purported social evils of forbidden sexual conduct rather than give rise to fervid rhetoric. . . . But, most of all, he insists that we should establish that an act really does cause social harm before we criminalize it.

—LOUIS CROMPTON, *BYRON AND GREEK LOVE*[110]

It is wonderful that nobody has ever yet fancied it to be sinful to scratch where it itches, and that it have never been determined that the only natural way of scratching is with such or such a finger and that it is unnatural to scratch with any other.

—BENTHAM, "OFFENSES AGAINST ONE'S SELF"

Bentham apparently first began writing on matters of sex and sexuality in the mid-1780s as part of his work on a new penal code. In those writings, he was singularly compelling on both his familiar theme of consistency being the rarest of human traits, and various psychological factors that rarely receive much recognition as among his concerns—namely, the "hatred of pleasure and horror of singularity," particularly the latter. He was, surprisingly to some, quite alert to issues of "difference." And in his appreciation of same-sex love as a crucial part of the culture of the ancient Greeks, and the ways in which this undercut claims about its enervating or degenerative effects, he would not be seriously rivaled until John Addington Symonds circulated his pathbreaking "A Problem in Greek Ethics," in 1867, though it might be added that, perceptive as he was of the cultural significance of, say, the Theban Sacred Band, Bentham did not capture all the fine points of Greek man-boy love in the way that Symonds did.[111]

But his interest in these matters developed more fully and even more radically in the mid-1810s, when it was made part and parcel of his extensive critique of religion. The editors of his *Of Sexual Irregularities and Other Writings on Sexual Morality* explain:

> In Bentham's view, the condemnation of sexual practices other than that between one man and one woman, within marriage, for the procreation of children, and more particularly the severe punishment attached under English law to male same-sex relationships, were the products of an asceticism that had its root in the Mosaic law, but which had been incorporated into the Christian religion through the teachings of St Paul. Bentham's purpose in 'Not Paul, but Jesus' was to show that Paul was an impostor, and that he had established his own religion which, in many important respects, including its attitude towards sexual morality and pleasure more generally, was not only distinct from, but opposed to, that of Jesus. Bentham argued that Paul had realized that he had much more to gain, in terms of power, money, and prestige, in abandoning his persecution of the followers of Jesus, and instead becoming their leader; or at least leader of the non-Jewish part of the movement. The essays in the present volume ["Of Sexual Irregularities—Or, Irregularities of the Sexual Appetite," "Sextus," and "General Idea of a Work, Having for One of Its Objects the Defence of the Principle of *Utility*, so Far as Concerns the Liberty of Taste, Against the Conjunct Hostility of the Principle of *Asceticism* and the Principle of *Antipathy;* and for Its Proposed Title, Proposed on the Ground of Expected Popularity, or at Least Protection Against Popular Rage,— Not Paul, But Jesus"] are more directly concerned with arguing that, according to the principle of utility, no consensual mode of sexual gratification should be condemned, but rather that the greatest happiness of the community would be promoted in the most effective way possible by the removal of sanctions—whether religious, political, or moral— from sexual activity, at least insofar as it was undertaken in private. In short, Bentham makes the utilitarian case for sexual liberty.[112]

"Sexual liberty" is putting it a bit too mildly. Bentham was in fact broadminded to an extreme, as Schofield explains in the conclusion to a delightful short work on "Jeremy Bentham: Prophet of Secularism":

> If reason and consistency, in other words the principle of utility, rather than the principle of asceticism, were the guide, argued Bentham, the pleasures of the bed would be treated with the same 'indifference' as the pleasures of the table. Just as with the table, individuals were left free to choose not only the 'crude material' that they ate but 'the mode of cooking, seasoning and serving up', so with the bed they would be left

free to choose: 'with or without a partner—if with a partner, whether with a partner of the same species or with a partner of another species; if of the same species, whether of the correspondent and opposite sex or of the same sex: number of partners, two only or more than two'. In every instance, the 'portions and parts of the body employed' should be left to the free choice of the individuals concerned.[113]

Schofield is quoting from the Bentham manuscripts but one of many such classifications of the options that Bentham wanted to open up. In his work "Sextus," there is a marginal summary that allows "Parties two: one dead" and "Parties two: one not susceptible of life." Another classification in that work considers whether the act involves rape (which is not allowed) or whether the parties are "united in the artificial and pneumatic bonds of the matrimonial contract" (which Bentham held should not be a lifelong contract).[114] But, rape apart, a simple consistency on humanity's part would treat such choices as free differences of taste, like a taste for chocolate over vanilla. Unfortunately, Bentham does not appear to allow, in this context, that such choices ought to be even freer than choices among foods, given the pains involved in food production processes harming nonhuman animals.

Now, as for the religious intolerance of such liberty, the culprit, on Bentham's reading, is clearly Paul. Paul is charged with having imported asceticism and sexual conformity into Christianity (religion being termed by Bentham the "juggernaut"). In Bentham's words, on "this whole field, on which Moses legislates with such diversified minuteness, such impassioned asperity and such unrelenting rigour, Jesus is altogether silent. Jesus, from whose lips not a syllable favourable to ascetic self-denial is, by any one of his biographers, represented as having ever issued. Jesus who, among his disciples, had one to whom he imparted his authority and another in whose bosom his head reclined, and for whom he avowed his love: Jesus who, in the stripling clad in loose attire, found a still faithful adherent, after the rest of them had fled; Jesus, on the whole field of sexual irregularity, preserved an uninterrupted silence."[115]

This line of Benthamism is probably nearly as shocking to many religious sensibilities today as it was when he first set it out. Talk of the "unnatural" is, for Bentham, as empty as talk of natural rights, and scarce "a practice can be named to which, upon the occasion of any condemnation passed upon it, this adjunct has not been applied." The condemnation of sexual pleasures largely reduces to envy and antipathy, when a man witnesses "the contemplation of an enjoyment of which it is out of his power to be a partaker," and to asceticism, when a man without recompense to himself or others "subjects himself to pain in any shape, considered as pain, or avoids receiving pleasure in any shape, considered as pleasure."[116] Contrary to any account of Bentham as an egoist, holding that humans just do, as a matter of fact, always seek to maximize their pleasure and minimize their pain, it is clear that he saw humanity as all too given to the faults of antipathy and asceticism, which needed to be the focus of an all-out assault. This he announced at the beginning of "General Idea":

> The work has for its general object the good of mankind: the greatest happiness of the greatest number:—leading motive of the author, sympathy for the whole human race: this public and social motive, mixt with as little of personal interest as it is possible for it to be mixt with.
>
> In pursuit of this all-comprehensive object, the work has attached itself to two particular objects, in themselves as unconnected with each other as any two can be, but connected by accident. These are—the reclaiming the public mind, 1. From the errors into which it has been led by the principle of asceticism; 2. from the gloomy and antisocial—and, in proportion as they are gloomy and antisocial, pernicious—notions, involved in the Calvinistic and various other modes of the religion of Jesus, and the antipathies that have sprung out of them.[117]

But it is very intriguing that Bentham devotes so much energy, not to dismissing religion *in toto* (though he comes close to that), but to co-opting the founding figure of Christianity, recruiting Jesus for the battle against antipathy and asceticism. There is undoubtedly an element of indirect, even esoteric utilitarian morality at work here, given Bentham's evident hostility to anything smacking of the supernatural and his perfect insouciance in the face of possible non survival in any form of physical death—he in fact had trouble envisioning an afterlife as anything capable of generating happiness, given the absence of the pleasures of food, drink, and sex. But according to Schofield, "the precise nature" of Bentham's skepticism is difficult to make out. "Many have concluded that Bentham must have been an atheist, but there is no direct evidence for this view, in that he refused, as a matter of principle, to express his personal religious views."[118] Apparently, not everything was to be subject to the transparency of the all-seeing eye.

At any rate, the upshot is that in the main religion is among the worst anti-utilitarian forces, and this is in significant measure because of its treatment of sex and sexuality. But what is more, religion is also one of the chief corruptors of education, and much of the need for reform in that area stems from the need to overthrow the force of established religion, which has, in its educational capacities, failed the poor: "Exclusion, and compulsory or seductive proselytism,—exclusion of one part of the community of the poor from the benefits of education—compelling the other part to come within the pale of the church dominion,—such are the two intimately connected, though perfectly distinct, and even contrasted, objects, in the pursuit of which this formulary is made the principle instrument."[119] Bentham had even intended his *Church-of-Englandism* work to be a continuation of his *Chrestomathia*, since its main target "was the system of education sponsored by the Church, and more particularly the schools of the National Society for the Education of the Poor in the Principles of the National Church. The National Society had been founded in 1811 to promote the teaching of the doctrine of the Church of England by means of the 'monitorial' system of education . . . ." But this, of course, was regarded by Bentham as a complete perversion, an appropriation of effective educational techniques to teach preposterous lies through the use of the Catechism, the Bible itself being too subversive (given the utilitarian tendencies of Jesus). Thus:

> Destitute of intellectual instruction, man, even in the bosom of the most civilized country, is often found appearing in no better a charac-ter than that of a savage. Of the Hulks, and the Penal Colonies—not to speak of the home Prisons—the population is, for the most part, com-posed of human beings thus abandoned to ignorance, vice, and wretch-edness. Such, as to the far greater part, appears to be the state of the population under the Church of England.[120]

The system excluded many and corrupted many, wounding by both stigma and indoctrination. The wounds of Bentham's forced Subscription, when at Oxford, had festered rather than healed, and if *Church-of-Englandism* belongs with *Chrestomathia* as his case for education reform, it also belongs with the *Plan of Parliamentary Reform* and *Constitutional Code*, as another compo-nent in his damning indictment of the whole mass of corruption represented by the Establishment. If happiness were to be effectively promoted, in Ben-tham's view, the mass of humanity needed to be able to think critically, and his schemes, not the Establishment's, held out that promise.

Indeed, in one of his most uncompromising works, *The Influence of Natu-ral Religion on the Temporal Happiness of Mankind*, which was expertly as-sembled and edited by George Grote and published under the pseudonym Phillip Beauchamp, Bentham remorselessly exposed the whole, vast range of religion's ill effects:

> Now religion has been shewn to create a number of factitious antipathies—that is, to make men hate a number of practices which they would not have hated had their views been confined simply to the present life. But if men would not naturally have hated these practices, this is a proof that they are not actually hurtful. Religion, therefore, attaches the hatred of mankind to actions not really injurious to them, and thus seduces it from its only legitimate and valuable function, that of deterring individuals from injurious conduct.[121]

And thanks to religion,

> the science of morality has been enveloped in a cloud of perplexity and confusion. Philosophers profess, by means of this science, to interpret

and to reconcile the various applications of approving and disapproving terms. But the practices on which the same epithet of approbation is bestowed, appear so incurably opposite, that it has been found impossible to reduce them to one common principle, or to discover any constituent quality which universally attracts either praise or blame. The intellect has been completely bewildered and baffled in all attempts to explain the foundation of morality, or to find any unerring fingerpost amidst a variety of diverging paths.[122]

As if that were not enough, there is with religion the "noxious" "coincidence and league with the sinister interests of earth—a coincidence so entire, as to secure unity of design on the part of both, without any necessity for special confederation. . . . Prostration and plunder of the community is indeed the common end of both." That is,

> [t]he aristocracy, for instance, possess the disposal of a mass of physical force sufficient to crush any partial resistance, and demand only to be secured against any very general or simultaneous opposition on the part of the community. To make this sure, they are obliged to maintain a strong purchase upon the public mind, and to chain it down to the level of submission—to plant within it feelings which may neutralize all hatred of slavery, and facilitate the business of spoliation. For this purpose the sacerdotal class are most precisely and most happily cut out. By their influence over the moral sentiments, they place implicit submission among the first of all human duties. They infuse the deepest reverence for temporal power, by considering the existing authorities as established and consecrated by the immaterial Autocrat above, and as identified with his divine majesty. The duty of mankind towards the earthly government becomes thus the same as duty to God—that is, an unvarying 'prostration both of the understanding and will.' Besides this direct debasement of the moral faculties for the purpose of assuring non-resistance, the supernatural terrors, and the *extra-experimental* belief, which the priest-hood are so industrious in diffusing, all tend to the very same result. They produce that mistrust, alarm, and insecurity, which disposes a man to bless himself in any little fragment of present enjoyment, while it stifles all aspirations for future improvement and even all ideas of its practicability.[123]

That Bentham could engage in such sustained ideology critique, blasting religion as something rather worse than Marx's "opiate of the masses," and could do so in a way that recognized that no overt "conspiracy" was needed among the ruling elites, given social structural conditions, is a point that cannot be underscored boldly enough. His acute, perceptive account of how the connective tissue of the superstructural institutions of the ruling elites extended across education, religion, morality, law, economics, and more, and involved the systemic effects of mystification and depredation (including the libidinal costs), makes him sound more like a forerunner of Herbert Marcuse than a "leather-tongued oracle of the ordinary bourgeois intelligence of the 19th century." Simply put, for Bentham, the indigent poor (and many others) are cut off from genuine educational opportunity, brainwashed, exploited, and terrorized out of the best forms of happiness readily available to them. He, by contrast, would supply them with the true necessities and the fundamental critical ability to see through their oppressors, even throwing in the means of contraception and sex toys of his own design, albeit with a gentle warning that masturbation was too addictive and might keep one from enjoying sex with others. The rooting out of pernicious religious influences, partly with the help of Jesus, would open the way for democratic reforms ushering in a sexually liberated society that might actually be able to justify its inequalities in the name of happiness. It would in any event have to take seriously, with regard to public policies, another of Bentham's notions—namely, diminishing marginal utility, such that an additional dollar or resource to a poor person represents a much greater increment in happiness than an additional dollar or resource to a member of the ruling elites. As the *Plan of Parliamentary Reform* had it, "all inequality is a source of evil"—the only defensible baseline for applying the utilitarian standard is complete equality, not the status quo. The burden of proof was on the ruling elites, and they would drop under the weight of it. Humanity made more consistent would be humanity made happier and more egalitarian.

On this score, Rosen has forcefully argued, for Bentham:

> If one is a legislator and one's task is to promote happiness in the public sphere, one's concern is not with the perceptions and aggregations of private pleasure, but with the extension of pleasure throughout society. Hence, in its public sense, which is the sense in which Bentham mainly employed it, the principle of utility is concerned with the distribution of happiness and the extent of that distribution.[124]

Maximizing happiness, to Bentham's mind, was like maximizing aptitude among government officials, a task that has distribution built into it, as an effort to extend administrative competence throughout the system. Given social realities, one cannot do this by creating an "aptitude monster," but only by enhancing the aptitude of officials throughout the system. Indeed, for Rosen, "Bentham believed that equality was also a substantive principle to be approximated as closely as possible. Hence, in saying that equal amounts of happiness should be extended to all, he was referring to an equal or near equal outcome."[125]

Needless to say, this interpretation is simply not a stereotypically Dickensian or Marxian or Foucauldian take on Bentham, nor is it in keeping with many of the less provocative, more or less popular accounts of the Benthamite legacy. But the key words are Bentham's own, supported, of course, by his life.

Taken together, the various reflections on Bentham in this chapter might well stimulate many further questions: what were his deepest religious beliefs? What did he really think of those who called themselves his disciples? Did he himself ever practice what he (privately) preached about harmless pleasures and same-sex activities? How, in the end, would he have presented his true priorities, had he been able to do so in an uncensored and perfectly candid way? How, had he been placed in a position of sovereign power, would he have acted? What form of education would he have wanted for his own children (or for John Stuart Mill, had he had him completely in his care)? How would he have depicted the happiest possible life? What degree of perfectibility did he allow, for future humanity? How many people, by his reckoning, could find their selfish impulses satisfied by pursuing the greatest happiness, under better social circumstances? How much overlap could there be, between his views and Godwin's?

Some of these questions may receive better answers as the transcription project continues. Some may remain mysteries forever. But when it comes to what one is tempted to call his critical theory of happiness, it seems possible to formulate some plausible Benthamite responses.

Radical Hedonism

If such was Bentham's vision in the large, could his hedonistic account of happiness and defense of the principle of utility really support it? That may be one of the most fundamental questions, an answer to which might render all the other questions more tractable.

Thus, against a slew of critics who have charged him with incoherently conflating psychological egoism (that people do by nature always seek their own maximal happiness) with the principle of utilitarianism, which calls for promoting the happiness of all, the obvious answer is that it is of course possible for people to find their best interest in serving the interest of all, just as Bentham himself did. More broadly, however, his point is less that such benevolence is impossible—it clearly is not—but that the end of benevolence, the general happiness, is better served by a more indirect approach that relies on narrower and more familiar forms of self-interest, whether this be by the invisible hand of the market or the visible hand of Panoptical institutions and government, the sanctions and incentives artfully arranged. Consider that

> [t]he interest which a member of the community at large, has in the populousness of the community at large, is as nothing, in comparison of the interest thus created; viz. on the part of a member of the company, and still more on the part of an officer of a company's industry-house. This is the only shape which genuine and *efficient* humanity can take. The notion, which insists upon *disinter[est]edness* (i.e. the absence of

the species of motive most to be depended upon) as an indispensable qualification, or even though it were but a recommendation, in the instance of a person bearing a part in the management of such a concern, is a notion respectable in its source, but the most prejudicial in its tendency of any that can be imagined.—Every system of management which has disinter[est]edness, pretended or real, for its foundation, is rotten at the root, susceptible of a momentary prosperity at the outset, but sure to perish at the long run. That principle of action is most to be depended upon, whose influence is most powerful, most constant, most uniform, most lasting, and most general among mankind. Personal interest is that principle: a system of economy built on any other foundation, is built upon a quicksand.[126]

There is no doubt an economistic bent here, but it is less dogmatic a priori psychology than open empirical investigation into when and where which sanctions work. With sanctions, there are both "the thunders of the law" and "the whispers of simple morality," and for Bentham, if the former "prove impotent" it is silly to expect the latter to be influential. But all sanctions, these and others having to do with religion and politics, should be effectively arranged the better to achieve the utilitarian end, rendering the achievement of that end as easy as possible by recognizing that each person is often the best judge of his or her happiness and will, by effectively pursuing that happiness under the right system, in effect be advancing the utilitarian end. Still, as H.L.A. Hart carefully noted, there are some passages where Bentham "seems to treat private ethics as a moral standard requiring the maximization of the general welfare, as if it were simply the principle of utility in its application to the conduct of individuals backed by informal moral pressures." Thus, "Bentham says the question whether to obey bad legislation is a question that 'belongs exclusively to private ethics' and here plainly treats the principle of utility not the pursuit of personal interest as 'guiding a man through these straits.' There are in addition many references to private ethics as concerned to 'prevent' and 'censure' pernicious acts where legal punishment would be inappropriate . . . ."[127]

Hart claims that Bentham may be guilty of some unclarity or inconsistency in the way he puts these matters. But even if that is so, the picture that emerges seems a perfectly familiar indirect or two-level utilitarian one, with the utilitarian standard only being directly deployed as a decision procedure in special circumstances where reliance on other decision procedures will not have the appropriate felicific effect. The question, as with Godwin, is in large part an empirical one, asking just where and when such a critical utilitarian consciousness should kick in and how the needed motives can be made available and institutions rendered as supportive as possible. From the larger perspective of the legislator or moralist, of course, each is to count as one, no one for more than one, as in Bentham's design of the system. But there is no denying that sometimes one must take that point of view in private morality, and the system as a whole should educate and socialize in a way that cultivates the sympathy needed to do so, which is the more necessary given the degree to which utilitarian tendencies remain unconscious and corrupted in so many people:

> By the natural constitution of the human frame, on most occasions of their lives men in general embrace this principle, without thinking of it: if not for the ordering of their own actions, yet for the trying of their own actions, as well as of those of other men. There have been, at the same time, not many, perhaps, even of the most intelligent, who have been disposed to embrace it purely and without reserve. There are even few who have not taken some occasion or other to quarrel with it, either on account of their not understanding always how to apply it or on account of some prejudice or other which they were afraid to examine into, or could not bear to part with. For such is the stuff that man is made of: in principle and in practice, in a right track and in a wrong one, the rarest of all human qualities is consistency.[128]

This verdict on the human frame was one of Bentham's favorite and most consistent themes, and in virtually all of his works he poses the puzzle of just how rational his maximizers really are. Human beings are inconsistent, and curiously defective in that telescopic faculty needed for long-term prudence, as the failure of religious sanctions invoking an afterlife so often demonstrates: "mere remoteness practically annuls the most dreadful of all expectations, without insinuating even the most transient suspicion of ultimate escape. But if distance alone will produce so striking a deduction, how much will its negative effect be heightened, when coupled with uncertainty as to the eventful fulfillment?"[129] Religion aggravates these problems, positively inducing mental disarray and worse. "Fear is the never-failing companion and offspring of ignorance, and the circumstances of human life infallibly give birth to such a communion." There is only one ultimate remedy: "It is only to knowledge that we owe our respite from perpetual suffering; wherever our knowledge fails us and we are reduced to a state of unprotected helplessness, all our sense of security, all anticipations of future ease, must vanish along with it."[130] Knowledge could be very useful indeed.

But Bentham's own consistency was notable, despite many claims to the contrary. Thus, there is no "naturalistic fallacy" or conflation of "ought" and "is" embedded in his account, no misguided attempt at persuasive definition such as might build utilitarianism into the descriptive meaning of the very terms "good," "right," etc., despite the oft-repeated charge that Bentham was conspicuously guilty of such maneuvers. Again, as Hart has observed:

> It is I think impossible to believe that Bentham, who as I have said is so alive to the 'eulogistic' or approval-expressing functions of language even when it is concealed and who elsewhere expressly says of

the word 'ought' that it is used to convey the speaker's approval, could have regarded the words 'good', 'right' and 'ought' as merely having the descriptive meaning which the suggested proof requires. Throughout his work Bentham constantly uses these terms to express approval and to commend actions or legislation and expressly states that considerations of utility are the reasons why actions 'ought' to be done or why it is 'right' to do them. His statement . . . that these terms only have a meaning when used of actions conformable to the principle of utility is I think intended to convey an idea which is central to his whole argument, namely that when so used they raise a rationally settleable issue because only then do they invoke an external standard which reasonable men would accept for the determination of right and wrong. In systems which do not invoke any external standard such expressions remain mere expressions of personal taste and this, as Bentham says . . . makes them 'sounds instead of sense', 'caprice instead of reason' . . . or, as he similarly says elsewhere of the expression 'a right', when it is divorced from the notion of a law which determines the criteria for its application, such terms become 'mere sounds to dispute about'.[131]

Bentham may have been mistaken in believing that the standard of utility was the only such option, but it is uncharitable in the extreme to claim that he did not grasp the normative side of what he was doing as exactly that—normative.

Finally, on Bentham's much maligned hedonism, which has obviously done much of the heavy-lifting in his vision, it would seem that the architect of pleasure had, as we have seen, more concrete particulars in mind than the famous but very abstract account in *An Introduction* suggests. Still, that account is, of course, to be taken seriously, and it is more suggestive than it may seem. When considering the individual, taken as such, Bentham breaks pleasure and pain down according to its intensity, duration, certainty or uncertainty, propinquity or remoteness, fecundity, and purity. When considering a number of persons, he adds to this list "extension," or how far the pleasures/pains extend to others. The whole account is captured in a famous mnemonic ditty that Bentham composed not long after the first edition of *An Introduction*:

> *Intense, long, certain, speedy, fruitful, pure—*
> Such marks in *pleasures* and in *pains* endure,
> Such pleasures seek, if *private* be thy end:
> If it be *public*, wide let them *extend*.
> Such *pains* avoid, whichever be thy view:
> If pains *must* come, let them *extend* to few.[132]

As the following chapters will demonstrate, some such form of hedonism remains an open option, an ongoing research project for explicating the notion of well-being or ultimate good. Considerable reconstruction will be needed, however, to free it from unhelpful distortions, such as a contestable distinction between subjective and. objective and other problematic notions.[133] And of course, as much of this chapter has shown, although Bentham no doubt held that practical reason required the calculation of the pleasures and pains likely to result from actions, rules, institutions, etc., the practical exigencies of law and policy necessitated regular reliance on the more indirect resources of money, security, medical care, education, etc., with their links to pleasure/pain being largely a contingent, empirical matter. He toyed with many possible metrics on this score, and was acutely aware of the difficulties presented by all of them.

But for purposes of concluding this chapter, it is sufficient to emphasize again that, as robust as his conception of the pleasures of the board and the bed may have been, Bentham in fact spelled out a very complex picture of human happiness, allowing that the "several simple pleasures of which human nature is susceptible, seem to be as follows:"

> 1. The pleasures of sense. 2. The pleasures of wealth. 3. The pleasures of skill. 4. The pleasures of amity. 5. The pleasures of a good name. 6. The pleasures of power. 7. The pleasures of piety. 8. The pleasures of benevolence. 9. The pleasures of malevolence. 10. The pleasures of memory. 11. The pleasures of imagination. 12. The pleasures of expectation. 13. The pleasures dependent on association. 14. The pleasures of relief.

Each is in turn broken down into many elements with the pleasures of sense, for example, including:

> 1. The pleasures of the taste or palate; including whatever pleasures are experienced in satisfying the appetites of hunger and thirst. 2. The pleasure of intoxication. 3. The pleasures of the organ of smelling. 4. The pleasures of the touch. 5. The simple pleasures of the ear; independent of association. 6. The simple pleasures of the eye; independent of association. 7. The pleasure of the sexual sense. 8. The pleasure of health: or, the internal pleasurable feeling or flow of spirits (as it is called,) which accompanies a state of full health and vigour; especially at times of moderate bodily exertion. 9. The pleasures of novelty: or, the pleasures derived from the gratification of the appetite of curiosity, by the application of new objects to any of the senses.[134]

Needless to say, there is much further refined classification, and a strong emphasis on how susceptibility to these pleasures and pains differs according to circumstances, with sentient creatures ranging widely in sensibility. In fact, although Bentham often retained the language of simple sensation in his descriptions of pleasures and pains, he advanced far beyond any such reductionistic account and recognized how, in Quinn's words, agents are forever "interpreting the world with the tools made available to them by their particular language, and by the habitual ways in which they put that language together, in a constructivist arena where dominant discourses assert the salience of some connections, and the non-existence or irrelevance of others." Crucially, as Quinn has stressed, the

> socially mediated nature of the vast majority of Bentham's simple plea-
> sures and pains emerges very clearly when we ask how many of them
> depend upon the agent's beliefs about the affective attitudes of other
> sentient beings. At a conservative estimate, the pleasures and pains of
> amity, good name and piety depend absolutely on my belief about the
> degree to which others love me or hate me. In addition, the pleasure of
> power depends on my belief that I can modify the behaviour of others
> in accordance with my will. The extent to which Bentham's enumera-
> tion contains pains and pleasures which depend crucially not only upon
> expectations of future contingencies, but on the agent's beliefs about
> the affective attitudes of others gives the lie to the reductionist critique
> which views his treatment as a monstrous simplification of complex
> psychological processes.[135]

Taking people as they are, one must recognize the full range of pleasures and pains, if only to grasp how the felicific calculus is to work and the difficulties of making it work at all. Bentham was, far more than is commonly recognized, akin to Sidgwick in his belief that although there is no better alternative to the felicific calculus, that "calculus" is riddled with problems, rendering it very rough and uncertain. Clearly, as Crimmins has noted, Bentham was anything but naïve about how challenging this task really was, and may have anticipated Mill as well:

> Clearly, Bentham was aware of the limitations of the mathematical ap-
> proach to summing pleasures and pains. As recent scholars have noted,
> his classification of pleasures included qualitative distinctions not ame-
> nable to strict calculation. It is impossible, for example, to quantify the
> intensity or purity of a pleasure. On the other hand, it is entirely feasi-
> ble for an individual to determine that one pleasure in more intense or
> purer than another he has experienced and to quantify multiple quali-
> ties of pleasures, though Bentham understood that such 'calculations'
> were more impressionistic than mathematical. . . . Viewed in this light,
> the distance between Bentham and the supposed 'revisionism' of Mill's
> distinction between higher and lower pleasures is sharply reduced.[136]

But in determining just how "high" the Benthamite pleasures could or should go, and how that might bear on his more visionary claims for the progress of humanity, it might at this point be best to bring Bentham into comparison with the younger Mill, who did so much to remake utilitarianism in his own image.

CHAPTER THREE

John Stuart Mill and Company

Life with Father

I acquired ... a mental habit to which I attribute all that I have ever done, or ever shall do, in speculation; that of never accepting half-solutions of difficulties as complete ... never allowing obscure corners of a subject to remain unexplored, because they did not appear important; never thinking that I perfectly understood any part of a subject until I understood the whole.

—JOHN STUART MILL, *AUTOBIOGRAPHY*

A memorable champion of the open society, critical thinking, human dignity, and women's equality, John Stuart Mill is surely the most popular and most widely read of the classical utilitarians, with such immortal works as *Utilitarianism, On Liberty,* and *On the Subjection of Women* having become part of the canon of global higher education. Whatever else he did or was, he succeeded, with Harriet Taylor Mill, in framing a vision of a vibrant, individualistic liberalism replete with a healthy public sphere and grounded on the progress of civilization and happiness.[1] Although their vision can today seem rather too individualistic, too fearful of dependency on government or government control, their reformist efforts during a period when, despite the reforms of 1832, the working class and much of the middle class (and all women) could not vote and were often seriously hampered in their progress by the sinister interests of a paternalistic agricultural aristocracy still bent on protecting itself through legislation (including the hated "Corn Laws"), should be appreciated for the emancipatory potential they represented, however unevenly. The means may not have been adequate to the task, but the task was to see that every individual, man or woman, would be provided with the capabilities needed to become his or her own person, leading his or her own life and finding the happiness fitting for humanity.

Like the other great utilitarians, Mill put his own stamp on the creed, and this in ways that have made many doubt whether his creed should still be considered utilitarianism. Yet despite his many worries about Bentham—not all of them warranted, as we have seen—he always remained ready enough to identify with the Benthamite legacy, particularly when it was under attack by the likes of William Whewell, the formidable Master of Trinity College, Cambridge, who stood for Mill as a kind of Master of all the pernicious intuitionist doctrines calling for attack. Thus, in the 1852 essay "Whewell on Moral Philosophy," he would write:

> Dr. Whewell's objections to utility, or the 'greatest happiness,' as the standard of morals, are chiefly contained in his animadversions on Paley and on Bentham. It would be quite open to a defender of the principles of utility, to refuse encumbering himself with a defence of either of those authors. The principle is not bound up with what they have said in its behalf, nor with the degree of felicity which they may have shown in applying it. As for Paley, we resign him without compunction to the tender mercies of Dr. Whewell. It concerns Dr. Whewell more than ourselves to uphold the reputation of a writer, who, whatever principle of morals he professed, seems to have had no object but to insert it as a foundation underneath the existing set of opinions, ethical and political; who, when he had laid down utility as the fundamental axiom, and the recognition of general rules as the condition of its application, took his leave of scientific analysis, and betook himself to picking up utilitarian reasons by the wayside, in proof of all accredited doctrines, and in defence of most tolerated practices. Bentham was a moralist of another stamp. With him, the first use to be made of his ultimate principle, was to erect on it, as a foundation, secondary or middle principles, capable of serving as premises for a body of ethical doctrine not derived from existing opinions, but fitted to be their test. Without such middle principles, an universal principle, either in science or in morals, serves for little but a thesaurus of commonplaces for the discussion of questions, instead of a means of deciding them. If Bentham has been regarded by subsequent adherents of a morality grounded on the 'greatest happiness,' as in a peculiar sense the founder of that system of ethics, it is not because, as Dr. Whewell imagines . . . he either thought himself, or was thought by others to be the 'discoverer of the principle,' but because he was the first who, keeping clear of the direct and indirect influences of all doctrines inconsistent with it, deduced a set of subordinate generalities from utility alone, and by these consistently tested all particular questions. This great service previously to which a scientific doctrine of ethics on the foundation of utility was impossible, has been performed by Bentham (though with a view

to the exigencies of legislation more than to those of morals) in a manner, as far as it goes, eminently meritorious, and so as to indicate clearly the way to complete the scheme.[2]

Mill does go on to rehearse his qualms about Bentham's "want of breadth and comprehension," explaining that it was Bentham's method that "justly earned a position in moral science analogous to that of Bacon in physical," though as with Bacon the method was often applied without sufficient evidence. Nonetheless, there is no mistaking which side Mill took himself to be on. In his own fashion, he was always ready to fight for the cause, whatever the risk to his reputation.

Of course, Mill's literary reputation was vast for much of his own lifetime, with fewer of the serious downs suffered by Godwin, Bentham, and his own father, James Mill, and if anyone could seriously be labeled the "spirit of his age," he was the one. A serious, scholarly, thirty-three volume *Collected Works of John Stuart Mill*, edited by John Robson, was published between 1963 and 1991, and the entire breathtaking work has been made readily available at the Online Library of Liberty, at ll.libertyfund.org/groups/46, in an act of public beneficence that Godwin himself might have found astonishing.[3] Consequently, although there is always more research to be done, recent research on Mill—of which there is much—has not had to confront quite the same obstacles as research on Godwin, Bentham, and Sidgwick. And although the biographies are not exactly plentiful, at least some notable efforts do exist, from those by Alexander Bain and Leslie Stephen, to the substantial work by Michael St. John Packe, down to the more recent ventures by Nicholas Capaldi and Richard Reeves. And this is not to mention the many fine overviews of Mill's work, such as those by Alan Ryan, John Skorupski, and Dale Miller, and the brilliant feminist readings of Mill by Martha Nussbaum, Jo Ellen Jacobs, Wendy Donner, Maria Morales, Elizabeth Anderson, Janice Carlisle, and others who have worked hard to present a sympathetic portrait of Mill's feminism and the role of Harriet Taylor Mill. And of course, there is Mill's own *Autobiography*, a classic that is as revealing in its omissions as in its acts. The father looms very large, while the mother was largely edited out of successive drafts.

Despite this attention, there is still much to worry about in the reception and reconstruction of Mill. In philosophical terms, he has too often been the object of the cheapest of cheap shots, turned into a textbook example of (supposedly) fallacious reasoning on such subjects as the proof of utilitarianism and the theory of the higher pleasures. However, as this chapter will show, although there are certainly many interpretive controversies swirling around Mill's texts, there are highly plausible strategies for making Mill out as a consistent and powerful champion of utilitarianism. Following John Skorupski, it is helpful to think, rather abstractly, of "pure utilitarianism" as holding that "(i) There is a system of agent-neutral final ends (the Good). . . . (ii) There are no complete agent-relative telic reasons. (iii) There are no complete non-telic reasons." This is, of course, simply a slightly technical way of saying that the best action is one that "promotes the most Good" and that "all practical reasons are Good-based, that is, that when spelled out they are instances of the principle of Good." And although Skorupski does not count himself as a pure utilitarian, he forcefully maintains that of "the classical utilitarians, Sidgwick is the only one who is clearly not a pure utilitarian. . . . Mill, on the other hand, is a pure utilitarian: he says that the principle of utility is 'the ultimate principle of teleology' . . . the utility principle is *the* principle of practical reason as such, regulating all its sub-departments (which Mill here [in his *Logic*] describes as 'Morality, Prudence or Policy, and Aesthetics: the right, the Expedient, and the Beautiful or Noble, in human conduct and works')."[4]

Such, then, is the verdict—not an isolated verdict—of one of the leading Mill scholars of the last half century, illustrating how, when one draws on the full range of Mill's writings, including the bits on the Art of Life in his *Logic*, Mill can indeed be cast as a consistent (and consistently high-minded) utilitarian, rather than as a jumble of pure utilitarianism with liberalism, perfectionism, egoism, etc. Skorupski also defends, as later sections will show, the coherence of Mill's hedonism and other components of his utilitarianism. He has his qualms about the Millian perspective, particularly its naturalism and associationism, but like Ryan, Crisp, Miller, and many other Mill scholars, he takes Mill very, very seriously as a philosopher—a utilitarian philosopher.

Thus, compelling defenses of Mill are possible, and needed, though in other areas more critical readings are needed as well, and not only when it comes to his fashioning of the story of utilitarianism. As enlightened as he doubtless was on many subjects, Mill's views on "savages," "backwards peoples," colonization, blacks, the Irish, and India often convey a kind of Orientalism or a subtle (or not so subtle) prejudice that calls for forms of critical cultural and political analysis, as in critical race studies, that have not figured prominently enough in the literature on him.[5] Moreover, as Duncan Bell has urged:

> Recent scholarship on Mill has greatly improved understanding of his arguments about the ethical defensibility of imperial rule, and in particular his account of India, but it has tended to ignore or downplay his extensive writings on colonization. Yet this was a subject that Mill returned to frequently throughout his long and illustrious career. While initially he regarded colonization as a solution to the "social problem" in Britain, he came to believe that its legitimacy resided primarily in the universal benefits—civilization, peace, and prosperity—that it generated for humanity as a whole. In the final years of his life Mill seemed to lose faith in the project. Confronted with the political intransigence and violence of the settlers, yet refusing to give up on the settler empire altogether, his colonial romance gave way to a form of melancholic resignation.[6]

And somehow, work on his relationship with Harriet Taylor Mill, the subject of an extensive literature in itself, still manages to raise more questions than it answers. The same goes for work on his relationship with his father, who, with Taylor Mill, represented the other great influence on his life. In the case of Mill, and by his own critical lights, the extraordinary life and the many works are so deeply and intriguingly entangled that to narrow one's focus is inevitably to distort.

Born in 1773 to James and Isabel Milne, Mill senior had grown up in a severe and religious Scottish household, escaping the modest poverty of his father's shoemaking and farming vocations only through the efforts of his socially ambitious mother, who changed the family name to Mill and insisted that her son devote all his time to reading, and through the good fortune of his benefactors, Sir John and Lady Jane Stuart, who recognized his talents and saw to it that he received a serious education (aimed for the Presbyterian ministry) that included a deep exposure to Greek philosophy at Edinburgh University. It would be James Mill, more than either Bentham or his son, who first effectively combined utilitarianism with a keen admiration for the ancient Greek philosophers, particularly his favorite philosopher, Plato. Although eventually licensed as a preacher, the elder Mill had rather lost all religious orthodoxy and was besides too abstractly intellectual for the role, and in 1802 opted to pursue a career in journalism in London, a career that was moderately successful and relatively conservative until he decided to stake his all on a larger literary and scholarly success, namely, his *History of British India*, which took eleven years to complete, not the four that he had originally supposed. He had married Harriet Burrow in 1805, but his greatest love had been Wilhelmina Stuart, the daughter of his benefactors, for whom he had worked as a tutor from 1790–94. She was, however, too far above him in class, married another aristocrat, and soon thereafter died in childbirth, supposedly using her last breath to call his name.[7]

At any rate, it was from roughly this time to 1817 that the influence, friendship, and support of Bentham (from 1808) proved so crucial, especially given Mill's growing family, with his first child, born on May 20, 1806, being named after his great benefactor. Once the *History* was finally published, in 1817, his name was made and, thanks to both the book and some powerful connections, a position at the East India Company followed (in 1819), a position that ironically proved to be a great blessing to the cause of the Philosophical Radicals. It provided financial security for both Mill senior and Mill junior, demanded little of their time (despite the fact that they were in effect governing India), and exposed them to real-world issues of governance and administration (not that they ever felt compelled to actually visit India).

Thus, the younger Mill was practically born to the part. His father was soon to be taken up by Bentham and converted to utilitarianism, just in time to insure that his first son would, via home schooling, have one of the most remarkable first class educations in history and be bred to become the world's leading utilitarian, albeit one writing from the comfortable, remunerative position at India House that had been secured him by his father when Mill junior was still a teenager. The keys to literary fame were handed to him by his father and Bentham, who brought him into the group that had formed around their organ, *The Westminster Review* (very successfully launched in 1824), though it should be added that he also did his time editing Bentham's manuscripts (the massive, four volume *Rationale of Judicial Evidence*) and proceeded to build his reputation with his weighty *A System of Logic: Ratiocinative and Inductive* (1843) and *Principles of Political Economy* (1848).

If he was early on a fixture of various reading, discussion, and debate societies—the "Society for Mutual Improvement," the "Utilitarian Society," the "Society of Students of Mental Philosophy," and the "London Debating Society"—his pen was his real strength, and he used his fortunate start in life to good advantage to build, in due course, a solid reputation through sound scholarly work, not merely by means of essays and activism as was usual for the Philosophical Radicals (though he certainly did a good deal of that as well, and for much of his youth seemed to entertain Parliamentary aspirations, a goal that would only finally be achieved in 1865).

His father and Bentham had contrived that it would be only after a yearlong sojourn in France—a sojourn that would leave him a lifelong Francophile—that he would first (in 1821) read the creed itself, which happily took the form of Dumont's *Traités*. The effect was as planned. He "became a different being. The feeling rushed upon me, that all previous moralists were superseded, and that here indeed was the commencement of a new era in thought."[8] Much of his education in the broader philosophy of utilitarianism would come from his father's works as well—his *Elements of Political Economy* (1821), various essays (especially the famous "Essay on Government"), *Analysis of the Phenomena of the Human Mind* (1829), and *A Fragment on MacIntosh* (1835). His mother, unlike his grandmother on his father's side, seems not to have been a force in the family, and Mill's remarks about her in the early draft of the *Autobiography* were slighting at best.

Yet as everyone who knows the name John Stuart Mill knows, the conversion soon led to crisis, and the crisis was borne of the childhood, and the child Mill only truly became his own man when he discovered both Romantic poetry and romance itself, in the form of Harriet Taylor (*née* Hardy), the other half without whom he would never have deemed himself whole. All that is to say, his life often looked quite different from the inside. If he credited his father with giving him not only a great deal of time, but also the outlook described in the epigraph to this chapter, he also credited him with having deprived him of the pleasures of childhood, indeed, of childhood itself, and of stunting him in a way that was all too "Benthamite," in the bad sense.

No doubt Mill's home schooling was impressive and intensive, though it is not clear that he was any more a prodigy than Bentham or various others who had received special attention. At any rate, Mill began studying Greek when he was about three, and Greek and arithmetic, along with reading and writing, took up most of his early years, until he began on Latin at about age eight. By the time he was a teenager, he was engaged in much else besides. He gave an extensive description of his studies in a letter to Bentham's brother Samuel, a letter that also indicates how he was helping with the education of his sisters Wilhelmina and Clara (he was the eldest of nine children):

Acton Place, Hoxton

July 30, 1819

My dear Sir,

It is so long since I last had the pleasure of seeing you that I have almost forgotten when it was, but I believe it was in the year 1814, the first year we were at Ford Abbey. I am very much obliged to you for your inquiries with respect to my progress in my studies; and as nearly as I can remember I will endeavour to give an account of them from that year.

In the year 1814, I read Thucydides, and Anacreon, and I believe the Electra of Sophocles, the Phœnissæ of Euripides, and the Plutus and the Clouds of Aristophanes. I also read the Philippics of Demosthenes.

The Latin which I read was only the Oration of Cicero for the Poet Archias, and the (first or last) part of his pleading against Verres. And in Mathematics, I was then reading Euclid; I also began Euler's Algebra, Bonnycastle's principally for the sake of the examples to perform. I read likewise some of West's Geometry.

Æt. 9.—The Greek which I read in the year 1815 was, I think, Homer's Odyssey, Theocritus, some of Pindar, and the two Orations of Æschines, and Demosthenes on the Crown. In Latin I read the six first books, I believe, of Ovid's Metamorphoses, the five first books of Livy, the Bucolics, and the six first books of the Æneid of Virgil, and part of Cicero's Orations. In Mathematics, after finishing the first six books, with the eleventh and twelfth of Euclid, and the Geometry of West, I studied Simpson's Conic Sections and also West's Conic Sections, Mensuration and Spherics; and in Algebra, Kersey's Algebra, and Newton's Universal Arithmetic, in which I performed all the problems without the book, and most of them without any help from the book.

Æt. 10.—In the year 1816 I read the following Greek: Part of Polybius, all Xenophon's Hellenics, The Ajax and the Philoctetes of Sophocles, the Medea of Euripides, and the Frogs of Aristophanes, and a great part of the Anthologia

Græca. In Latin I read all Horace, except the Book of
Epodes; and in Mathematics I read Stewart's Propositiones
Geometricæ, Playfair's [8] Trigonometry at the end of
his Euclid, and an article on geometry in the Edinburgh
Encyclopædia. I also studied Simpson's Algebra.

Æt. 11.—In the year 1817 I read Thucydides a second time,
and I likewise read a great many Orations of Demosthenes
and all Aristotle's Rhetoric, of which I made a synoptic
table. In Latin I read all Lucretius, except the last book,
and Cicero's Letters to Atticus, his Topica, and his treatise,
De Partitione Oratoria. I read in Conic Sections an article
in the Encyclopædia Britannica (in other branches of the
mathematics I studied Euler's Analysis of Infinities and began
Fluxions, on which I read an article in the Encyclopædia
Britannica), and Simpson's Fluxions. In the application
of mathematics I read Keill's Astronomy and Robinson's
Mechanical Philosophy.

Æt. 12.—Last year I read some more of Demosthenes,
and the four first Books of Aristotle's Organon, all which I
tabulated in the same manner as his Rhetoric.

In Latin, I read all the works of Tacitus, except the dialogue
concerning oratory, and a great part of Juvenal, and began
Quintilian. In Mathematics and their application, I read
Emerson's Optics, and a Treatise on Trigonometry by Professor
Wallace, of the Military College, near Bagshot, intended for
the use of the cadets. I likewise re-solved several problems
in various branches of mathematics; and began an article on
Fluxions in the Edinburgh Encyclopædia.

Æt. 13.—This year I read Plato's dialogues called Gorgias
and Protagoras, and his Republic, of which I made an abstract.
I am still reading Quintilian and the article on Fluxions, and
am performing without book the problems in Simpson's Select
Exercises.

Last year I began to learn logic. I have read several Latin
books of Logic: those of Smith, Brerewood, and Du Trieu, and
part of Burgersdicius, as far as I have gone in Aristotle. I have
also read Hobbes' Logic.

I am now learning political economy. I have made a kind
of treatise from what my father has explained to me on that
subject, and I am now reading Mr. Ricardo's work and writing
an abstract of it. I have learnt a little natural philosophy, and,
having had an opportunity of attending a course of lectures
on chemistry, delivered by Mr. Phillips, at the Royal Military

College, Bagshot, I have applied myself particularly to that science, and have read the last edition of Dr. Thomson's system of chemistry.

What English I have read since the year 1814 I cannot tell you, for I cannot remember so long ago. But I recollect that since that time I have read Ferguson's Roman and Mitford's Grecian History. I have also read a great deal of Livy by myself. I have sometimes tried my hand at writing history. I had carried a history of the United Provinces from their revolt from Spain, in the reign of Phillip II., to the accession of the Stadtholder, William III., to the throne of England.

I had likewise begun to write a history of the Roman Government, which I had carried down to the Licinian Laws. I should have begun to learn French before this time, but that my father has for a long time had it in contemplation to go to the Continent, there to reside for some time. But as we are hindered from going by my father's late appointment in the East India House, I shall begin to learn French as soon as my sisters have made progress enough in Latin to learn with me.

I have now and then attempted to write Poetry. The last production of that kind at which I tried my hand was a tragedy. I have now another in view in which I hope to correct the fault of this.

I believe my sister Willie was reading Cornelius Nepos when you saw her. She has since that time read some of Cæsar; almost all Phædrus, all the Catiline and part of the Jugurtha of Sallust, and two plays of Terence; she has read the first, and part of the second book of Lucretius, and is now reading the Eclogues of Virgil.

Clara has begun Latin also. After going through the grammar, she read some of Cornelius Nepos and Cæsar, almost as much as Willie of Sallust, and is now reading Ovid. They are both now tolerably good arithmeticians; they have gone as far as the extraction of the cube root. They are reading the Roman Antiquities and the Greek Mythology, and are translating English into Latin from Mair's Introduction to Latin Syntax. This is to the best of my remembrance a true account of my own and my sisters' progress since the year 1814.

I hope Lady Bentham, and George, and the young ladies are in good health.

Your obedient, humble
servant,
John Stuart Mill[9]

The exposure to Plato was crucial, as Mill explained in the earlier draft of his *Autobiography*:

> There is no author to whom my father thought himself more indebted for his own mental culture, than Plato, and I can say the same of mine. The Socratic method, of which the Platonic dialogues are the chief example, is unsurpassed as a discipline for abstract thought on the most difficult subjects. Nothing in modern life and education, in the smallest degree supplies its place. The close, searching *elenchus* by which the man of vague generalities is absolutely compelled either to express his meaning to himself in definite terms, or to confess that he does not know what he is talking about—the perpetual testing of all general statements by particular instances—the siege in form which is laid to the meaning of large abstract terms, by laying hold of some much larger class-name which includes that and more, and *dividing down* to the thing sought, marking out its limits and definition by a series of accurately drawn distinctions between it and each of the cognate objects which are successively severed from it—all this even at that age took such hold on me that it became part of my own mind; and I have ever felt myself, beyond any modern that I know of except my father and perhaps beyond even him, a pupil of Plato, and cast in the mould of his dialectics.[10]

The emphasis on Greek and Greek literature clearly owed much to his father, who devoted a truly extraordinary amount of attention to his son's education. They would both work at the same table, seated across from one another, the father trying to make headway on his *History of British India*, the son trying to master Greek vocabulary and, in the absence of lexicons, interrupting his father frequently to ask for help. The precise texture of the relationship is curious: Mill senior was quite patient and devoted in some respects, in others less so. In the earlier and somewhat more candid draft of the *Autobiography*, Mill explained how his father, as devoted as he was, could be impatient and angry with him, especially given his weak performances when reading aloud: "[T]hough he reproached me when I read a sentence ill, and *told* me how I ought to have read it, he never *shewed* me: he often mockingly caricatured my bad reading of the sentence, but did not, by reading it himself, instruct me how it ought to be read." In fact, as Mill elaborates, it "was a defect running through his modes of instruction as it did through his modes of thinking that he trusted too much to the intelligibleness of the abstract when not embodied in the concrete."[11] As progressive as his father was, he seems to have lacked the Deweyan touch, though his son would deny that his was "an education of cram. . . . Anything which could be found out by thinking, I never was told, until I had exhausted my efforts to find it out for myself."[12] And, in line with the famous monitorial method, the elder son was entrusted with passing the lessons on to his younger siblings. Still, the slant was on thinking or knowing more than doing (much less feeling), and the young Mill often felt that his father needed to provide a different form of guidance. Mill senior, for his part, was worried by John's inattentiveness, angrily warning him that he might grow up to be an "oddity" and "unfit" for ordinary life, a prophecy that turned out to be somewhat accurate, given his son's notorious ineptness, even as an adult, at such mundane tasks as tying his tie, buttoning his shirt, ordering food, etc., matters that Harriet Taylor would have to take in hand.

Yet the younger Mill made it abundantly clear in his *Autobiography* that his father was his world, devoting more space to him than to any other single figure, even Harriet Taylor. In the final version of the work, he moderated the harsher criticisms of his father, while leaving intact his more supportive statements. It was his father who gave him, among other benefits, his many-sidedness, his love of learning and love of Plato, his grounding in political economy, and much of his utilitarianism, but strangely enough, not his feeling for women's equality, despite the profoundly important role played by his paternal grandmother. The son would claim that, although his father had not been directly involved in starting the *Westminster Review*, he was more truly the voice of the Philosophical Radicals than Bentham. James Mill's associationist psychology, appreciation of Malthus, and other factors were more characteristic of their views, and above all he gave them "an almost unbounded confidence in the efficacy of two things: representative government, and complete freedom of discussion. So complete was my father's reliance on the influence of reason over the minds of mankind, whenever it is allowed to reach them, that he felt as if all would be gained if the whole population were taught to read, if all sorts of opinions were allowed to be addressed to them by word and in writing, and if by means of the suffrage they could nominate a legislature to give effect to the opinions they adopted."[13] Bentham is dismissed—unfairly, to be sure—as more of an eccentric voice behind the scenes, one whose judgment was called into question by both father and son for his designation of Bowring as a favorite, a favorite to some degree displacing Mill senior as Bentham's confidant. Bowring, who became not only Bentham's literary executor but also the first editor of the *Westminster Review*, after James Mill declined Bentham's offer to take that role, would be regularly excoriated in the younger Mill's letters. For example, in an 1843 letter to Macvey Napier, Mill explained that the "reason why I took no notice of Bowring's book was literally that I had not read it. I never attached sufficient value to anything Bowring could say about Bentham, to feel any curiosity on the subject. . . . My experience of the literary estimation in which Bowring is held, & of his reputation for judgment & accuracy, was not such as to make me believe that the loose talk of Bentham, reported by him, would excite general attention, or pass for more than it is worth."[14] Mill was complaining about the use made of Bowring's account of the relations between his father and Bentham.

What, for his part, did James Mill think that he was doing, with his familial educational experiment? He considered himself something of a philosopher of education, writing two influential pieces on the subject, his essay "Schools for All," first published in the *Philanthropist* in 1812, and his article on "Education," which he wrote in 1815 for the *Encyclopedia Britannica*. The first was very much in line with Bentham's attack on the Church of England's appropriation of the Bell and Lancaster methods for purposes of a national society of schools using the Catechism—yes, the poor needed to be educated, but not by the Church of England. And it is clear from both pieces that Mill agreed with the monitorial system that figured so prominently in the systems of Bell, in Madras, and in Lancaster, closer to home. It was this system that held out the potential of a real extension of educational opportunities to the poor.

And both essays reveal a fairly determined utilitarianism, but especially the second, which begins, "The end of Education is to render the individual, as much as possible, an instrument of happiness, first to himself, and next to other beings." Happiness depends partly on the condition of the body, partly on the condition of the mind, and it is the latter that, for Mill, is the distinctive concern of the educator, rather than of the physician. Ironically, when it comes to mind, he holds that "there are several things which we should include under the term *our experience of mind*, to which we should not extend the term *I think*. But there is nothing included under it to which we should not extend the term *I feel*. This is truly, therefore, the generic term."[15]

In practice, Mill's approach was, as previously observed, not quite what one would suppose, given these endorsements of individual happiness and feeling. He would advise Francis Place (who did much to advise and support him) that, in educating his daughter, he must "[a]bove all think of her happiness solely, without one jot of passion being allowed to step into the scale," a remark suggestive of the severe subordination of the ordinary feelings to the prudent long-term pursuit of happiness. Again, as his son noted, "Temperance" was one of the ancient Greek virtues that his father endorsed in the Platonic extreme. For all practical purposes, achieving maximal pleasure for either the individual or humanity demanded something akin to a Platonic ordering of the soul:

> The steady conception of the End must guide us to the Means. Happiness is the end; and we have circumscribed the inquiry, by naming Intelligence, Temperance, and Benevolence, of which the last two parts are Generosity and Justice, as the grand qualities of mind, through which this end is to be attained. The question, then, is how can those early sequences be made to take the place on which the habits, conducive to intelligence, temperance, and benevolence, are founded; and how can those sequences, on which are founded the vices opposite to those virtues, be prevented?[16]

The "sequences" in question are "those sequences among our sensations which have been so frequently experienced as to create a habit of passing from the idea of the one to that of the other"—that is, the sequences of mental associations that Mill took to be the building blocks of the mind. The associationist view, which he absorbed through such figures as Locke, Hume, and Hartley, would be spelled out at great length in his *Analysis of the Phenomena of the Human Mind*, but in its more practical applications, it meant an emphasis on nurture over nature to such a degree that the father was always drumming it into his eldest son that there was absolutely nothing special about him, and that any child could rival his accomplishments if only he had received the right education, in the widest sense, including political socialization.

There are of course a great many questions about the consistency of the senior Mill's views, not the least of which is why he did not extend such egalitarian thinking to the case of women. It is not easy, to say the least, to marry a mechanistic account of the formation of associations and habits with a purposive or teleological account of action aimed at pleasure. As Burston has observed, "Pleasure is an end or goal, and an explanation of behaviour governed by pursuit of pleasure is in these terms. It is an explanation in which the 'cause' of human behaviour lies in an intention or motive, which people are free to have and to pursue as they like. It is sharply different from scientific or mechanistic explanation, for instance in not looking at preceding factors but rather at results or consequences as the explanation of actions."[17] Setting aside the many complexities of the reasons v. causes literature, it can at least be said that there is some difference between what is in effect a simple mental conditioning model and a purposive or rational actor model, and that Mill did not get very far in setting out how the two models could be reconciled, something that his son would come to realize in an all too painful way, as he worked toward a better reconciliation of freedom and necessity, a task that was arguably the greatest challenge to his system.[18]

But it would seem that, as with Bentham, although the generic emphasis on nurture was very important, most of the heavy theoretical lifting was in fact done by a heavily qualified psychological egoism that allowed that people certainly could sometimes act, on principle, for the sake of the general happiness at some cost to their own, but that this would be a shaky basis for designing social and political institutions. But more to the point, it is plain that for James Mill, as for Bentham, people did need to be taught how best to pursue both their own happiness and the general happiness. This was not something that could simply be left to chance socialization, which could be every bit as evil as Bentham claimed.

Sadly, this turned out to be the one big thing that James Mill's home schooling failed to do—teach his son how to effectively pursue his own happiness, much less that of others. To be sure, Mill junior valued, and bent over backwards to make it clear that he valued, many of the educational gifts that his father had bestowed upon him. And his finishing in France, which in part took place while staying with Samuel Bentham, did help round him out, giving him among other things his enduring love of mountains, rural or natural scenery, and France, as well as the model of a strong, independently-minded woman in Lady Bentham. He became, after his reading of Bentham, the great utilitarian hope, something his education had always been designed to achieve, and through his discussion and debating societies and such friends and allies as Charles and John Austin, George Grote, John Roebuck, and George 'John' Graham (the latter two not quite to his father's liking), he took to championing the cause. Despite his distaste for Bowring, he contributed to the *Westminster Review* and other publications, and defended utilitarianism—a term he mistakenly believed had originated in Galt's "Annals of the Parish"—against a wide array of opponents, from Tories and Whigs to Owenites and anyone who dared to criticize Ricardo's economics or its Malthusian premises. Thus, as Richard Reeves has put it, by "his late teens . . . Mill had a creed, comrades and a career."[19]

Le Crise Nécessaire

But they did not sustain him for long. In 1826, when he was twenty, it all came crashing down. At least on the inside:

> It was in the autumn of 1826. I was in a dull state of nerves, such as everybody is occasionally liable to; unsusceptible to enjoyment or pleasurable excitement; one of those moods when what is pleasing at other times, becomes insipid or indifferent; the state, I should think, in which converts to Methodism usually are, when smitten by their first 'conviction of sin.' In this frame of mind it occurred to me to put the question directly to myself, 'Suppose that all your objects in life were realized; that all the changes in institutions and opinions which you are looking forward to, could be completely effected at this very instant: would this be a great joy and happiness to you?' And an irrepressible self-consciousness distinctly answered, 'No!' At this my heart sank within me: the whole foundation on which my life was constructed fell down. All my happiness was to have been found in the continual pursuit of this end. The end had ceased to charm, and how could there ever again be any interest in the means? I seemed to have nothing left to live for.[20]

The "cloud of dejection" did not pass over—"A night's sleep, the sovereign remedy for the smaller vexations of life, had no effect on it." He awoke to "a renewed consciousness of the woeful fact" and indeed for "some months the cloud seemed to grown thicker and thicker," evoking to him Coleridge's lines from "Dejection": "A grief without a pang, void, dark and drear, / A drowsy, stifled, unimpassioned grief, / Which finds no natural outlet or relief / In word, or sigh, or tear." Nothing helped, not even his favorite books, and he became convinced that his "love of mankind, and of excellence for its own sake, had worn itself out."

But he kept all this to himself. Like so many of that age, his troubles struck him as uniquely his own and incapable of eliciting any understanding or sympathy from others, his father least of all. "My education, which was wholly his work, had been conducted without any regard to the possibility of its ending in this result; and I saw no use in giving him the pain of thinking that his plans had failed, when the failure was probably irremediable, and at all events, beyond the power of *his* remedies." After all, his father's associationist psychology was the culprit:

> I had always heard it maintained by my father, and was myself convinced, that the object of education should be to form the strongest possible associations of the salutary class: associations of pleasure with all things beneficial to the great whole, and of pain with all things hurtful to it. This doctrine appeared inexpugnable; but it now seemed to me on retrospect, that my teachers had occupied themselves but superficially with the means of forming and keeping up these salutary associations. They seemed to have trusted altogether to the old familiar instruments, praise and blame, reward and punishment. Now I did not doubt that by these means, begun early and applied unremittingly, intense associations of pain and pleasure, especially of pain, might be created, and might produce desires and aversions capable of lasting undiminished to the end of life. But there must always be something artificial and casual in associations thus produced. The pains and pleasures thus forcibly associated with things, are not connected with them by any natural ties; and it is therefore, I thought, essential to the durability of these associations, that they should have become so intense and inveterate as to be practically indissoluble, before the habitual exercise of the power of analysis had commenced. For I now saw, or thought I saw, what I had always before received with incredulity—that the habit of analysis has a tendency to wear away the feelings: as indeed it has when no other mental habit is cultivated, and the analyzing spirit remains without its natural complements and correctives. The very excellence of analysis (I argued) is that it tends to weaken and undermine whatever is the result of prejudice; that it enables us mentally to separate ideas which have only casually clung together: and no associations whatever could ultimately resist this dissolving force, were it not that we owed to analysis our clearest knowledge of the permanent sequences in nature; the real connexions between Things . . . .[21]

Mill was doubtless right in concluding that teaching the Socratic elenchus or the greatest happiness principle was a task that called for a more sophisticated approach than the methods used to condition a rat to run a maze. Coming to understand the arbitrariness of one's social conditioning, when it is not backed up by insight into intrinsic rewards and punishments, can indeed be very disheartening, especially when it concerns views that one is championing as the salvation of humanity. For that matter, such debunking can be carried even further, as in evolutionary arguments exposing various moral beliefs as explainable in terms of their survival value rather than their truth.[22] Perhaps the larger point here is that the force of the utilitarian principle, as lending meaning to one's life, requires making it one's own in reasoned terms, rather than regarding it as an arbitrary piece of one's psychology, the result of so many mechanical processes of socialization and evolution. To recognize this was to recognize the value of autonomy, of uncoerced, reasoned self-direction.

For Mill's part, he carried on through "the melancholy winter of 1826–7" in his usual ways, but mechanically, from "mere force of habit." He frequently asked himself if he "was bound to go on living when life must be passed in this manner," something he could not envision doing for more than a year. But, as fortune would have it, the darkness broke:

> When, however, not more than half that duration of time had elapsed, a small ray of light broke in upon my gloom. I was reading, accidentally, Marmontel's *Memoirs*, and came to the passage which relates his father's death, the distressed position of the family, and the sudden inspiration by which he, then a mere boy, felt and made them feel that he would be everything to them—would supply the place of all that they had lost. A vivid conception of the scene and its feelings came over me, and I was moved to tears. From this moment my burthen grew lighter. The oppression of the thought that all feeling was dead within me, was gone. I was no longer hopeless: I was not a stock or a stone. I had still, it seemed, some of the material out of which all worth of character, and all capacity for happiness, are made. Relieved from my ever present sense of irremediable wretchedness, I gradually found that the ordinary incidents of life could again give me some pleasure; that I could again find enjoyment, not intense, but sufficient for cheerfulness, in sunshine and sky, in books, in conversation, in public affairs; and that there was, once more, excitement, though of a moderate kind, in exerting myself for my opinions, and for the public good.[23]

Worth underscoring is that Mill's crisis was precipitated by the question he put to himself of whether the realization of the ends of the Philosophical Radicals would "be a great joy and happiness" to himself, not whether it would be a great happiness and joy in general. The crisis was framed in terms of the first aim of his father's philosophy of education, achieving one's own happiness, which of course leaves open the possibility that the two goals are simply incompatible, mirroring the incompatibility of rational egoism and utilitarianism. Or better, that the latter cannot really be rendered effective without the former, without the individual being able to taste the very happiness that he or she is dedicated to promoting on behalf of all sentient creatures. Just as one must be able to form loving attachments in order to fully appreciate the value of love, so too one must have some experience of happiness, some glimpse of the promised land, in order to see the point of promoting it generally. It is not enough merely to have an abstract grasp of the idea.

Paradoxically enough, there was something of a concession to Benthamism in Mill's articulation of his mental crisis—utilitarian self-sacrifice is hard, and the utilitarian result is better guaranteed by an approach that speaks to the individual's happiness. James Mill's "Temperance," when applied to his son's education, was suitable to a Platonic guardian, but not to an ordinary child. A truly utilitarian education, it would seem, needs to carry the student along with the hope that some appropriate share of the general happiness will be his or hers. And what credibility can the utilitarian educator possess whose personality offers no evidence of the very thing that forms the end of the educational enterprise? Bentham himself might, at least in later life, provide a passable example of the happiness sought, but not James Mill, despite his son's best efforts to soften his profile.

Mill himself saw his crisis as a case of the microcosm within the macrocosm: "Though my dejection, honestly looked at, could not be called other than egotistical, produced by the ruin, as I thought, of my fabric of happiness, yet the destiny of mankind in general was ever in my thoughts, and could not be separated from my own. I felt that the flaw in my life, must be a flaw in life itself; that the question was, whether, if the reformers of society and government could succeed in their objects, and every person in the community were free and in a state of physical comfort, the pleasures of life, being no longer kept up by struggle and privation, would cease to be pleasures." That is, if he could see some "better hope than this for human happiness in general" then he might be able to "look on the world with pleasure; content as far as I was myself concerned, with any fair share of the general lot."[24] This intimate entangling of egoism and utilitarianism, such that the former takes on the aspect of one's "fair share" of the general happiness, and the views converge in subtle ways, is in truth one of the leading themes of classical utilitarianism, and one that, as the following chapter will show, would undergo significant further development in the life and work of Henry Sidgwick, Mill's greatest successor.[25] In practice, and possibly in principle, purity promised the convergence of personal and general happiness.

Given the texture of Mill's crisis, it is not all that surprising that so much of the cure came in the form of Romanticism, of Wordsworth and the cultivation of the self, the feeling self. Mill senior's taste in poetry extended only so far as Milton, whose cottage Bentham had generously placed at his disposal.

Mill junior, whose remarkable education had always been at some remove from modern developments, took to the new poetry of his era with all the alacrity that he had brought to the Philosophical Radicals. He defended Wordsworth against all comers, even such old friends as Roebuck, who began to despair of him. He later developed, thanks to Harriet Taylor, a deep passion for Shelley, and even helped establish Tennyson's early reputation, with his remarkable 1835 essay "Tennyson's Poems." If Bentham had been Mill's spirit of the age, now Bentham was set alongside Coleridge, as the essential complement providing the depth of self-cultivation that the age so needed. By his own report he "now began to find meaning in the things which I had read or heard about the importance of poetry and art as instruments of human culture," though this turn took some time to mature, since as with Bentham, the "only one of the imaginative arts in which I had from childhood taken great pleasure, was music."[26]

Music meant a lot. Its "best effect," surpassing "perhaps every other art," "consists in exciting enthusiasm; in winding up to a high pitch those feelings of an elevated kind which are already in the character, but to which this excitement gives a glow and a fervor, which though transitory at its utmost height, is precious for sustaining them at other times." But in his dull state he was "tormented by the thought of the exhaustibility of musical combinations," and he needed a new tonic. He tried Byron, to no effect (Byron was too like him in having "worn out all pleasures,"[27]), but when in autumn of 1828 he picked up Wordsworth's miscellaneous poems, they "proved to be the precise thing for my mental wants at that particular juncture."

What, exactly, did Wordsworth do for him, at this "particular juncture"?

What made Wordsworth's poems a medicine for my state of mind, was that they expressed, not mere outward beauty, but states of feeling, and of thought coloured by feeling, under the excitement of beauty. They seemed to be the very culture of the feelings, which I was in quest of. In them I seemed to draw from a source of inward joy, of sympathetic and imaginative pleasure, which could be shared in by all human beings; which had no connexion with struggle or imperfection, but would be made richer by every improvement in the physical or social condition of mankind. From them I seemed to learn what would be the perennial sources of happiness, when all the greater evils of life shall have been removed. And I felt myself at once better and happier as I came under their influence. There have certainly been, even in our own age, greater poets than Wordsworth; but poetry of deeper and loftier feeling could not have done for me at that time what his did. I needed to be made to feel that there was real, permanent happiness in tranquil contemplation. Wordsworth taught me this, not only without turning away from, but with a greatly increased interest in, the common feelings and common destiny of human beings. And the delight which these poems gave me, proved that with culture of this sort, there was nothing to dread from the most confirmed habit of analysis.[28]

In fact, the coming out of the new Mill took the form of a debate in the Society over the merits of Wordsworth versus Byron, a debate with none other than Roebuck, who dismissed the former as all "flowers and butterflies." It marked the opening of a schism that would grow steadily with the years. And as Mill grew more distanced from his early Philosophical Radical friends, he "fell more and more into friendly intercourse with our Coleridgeian adversaries in the Society, Frederick Maurice and John Sterling, both subsequently so well known, the former by his writings, the latter through the biographies by Hare and Carlyle." Maurice, Mill observed, "was the thinker, Sterling the orator," and it was the passionate Sterling who was destined to become Mill's closest friend, next to Harriet Taylor.[29]

The effect of these shifting allegiances was profound, insuring that Mill would become something of an honorary "Cambridge Apostle." The Apostles discussion group, or, more formally, the Cambridge Conversazione Society, was founded in 1820 by a number of St. John's undergraduates, including George Tomlinson (later bishop of Gibraltar), and it quickly evolved into a secret, select discussion group for Cambridge's best and brightest, drawn primarily from Trinity and King's. It would, in its first one hundred years, include such notable and influential members as Alfred Lord Tennyson, Arthur Hallam, Erasmus Darwin, James Fitzjames Stephen, Henry Sumner Maine, Henry Sidgwick, John Maynard Keynes, Bertrand Russell, and G. E. Moore, but two singularly influential early members were Maurice and Sterling. They were the ones who gave the Apostles the animating spirit of the pursuit of truth that was so vividly described in later years by Sidgwick: "[T]he spirit, I think, remained the same, and gradually this spirit . . . absorbed and dominated me. I can only describe it as the spirit of the pursuit of truth with absolute devotion and unreserve by a group of intimate friends who were perfectly frank with each other, and indulged in any amount of humorous sarcasm and playful banter, and yet each respects the other, and when he discourses tries to learn from him and see what he sees. Absolute candour was the only duty that the tradition of the society enforced. No consistency was demanded with opinions previously held—truth as we saw it then and there was what we had to embrace and maintain, and there were no propositions so well established that an Apostle had not the right to deny or question, if he did so sincerely and not from mere love of paradox."[30]

John Frederick Denison Maurice, Apostle number thirty, was recruited in 1823, but as Arthur Hallam would write to Gladstone, the effect that Maurice "has produced on the minds of many at Cambridge by the single creation of that society, the Apostles, (for the spirit though not the form *was* created by him) is far greater than I can dare to calculate, and will be felt both directly and indirectly in the age that is before us."[31] It was Maurice who was primarily responsible for the "spirit" of which Sidgwick wrote, the spirit of absolute candor and sincerity in the pursuit of truth and willingness to learn from others. As Mill himself appreciated, this was the very Coleridgean spirit that provided an effective counter to Benthamism, as he understood it. Indeed, Maurice was superior to Coleridge himself, since the latter mostly just plagiarized various works of German philosophy. Much of the Romanticism that led Mill to qualify and humanize Benthamism came to him via Maurice, and it was just such an outlook that made Maurice chief of the "Mystics"—the Romantic opponents of the Philosophical Radicals, Whigs, and Tories—who dominated the Saturday evening discussions of the Apostles. The Mystics adored soul-searching dialogue, and they appropriated Coleridge's notion of a "clerisy," an elite set of opinion leaders who could substitute for the traditional clergy and lead the work of spiritual regeneration that society needed. This regeneration was to occur through modern literature, the works of Wordsworth, Shelley, and Keats, rather than via mere political reform. Wordsworth could "make men look within for those things in which they agree, instead of looking without for those in which they differ." As Maurice put it: "Truth, I hold, not to be that which every man troweth, but to be that which lies at the bottom of all men's trowings, that in which these trowings have their only meeting point."[32]

Maurice would hold a series of ecclesiastical and academic positions over the course of his life, returning to Cambridge again, in 1866, as the Knightbridge Professor of Moral Philosophy, when as a very senior Apostle and member of the Grote Club[33] he would have a direct influence on such younger figures as Sidgwick. But his influence was much broader than that of an academic—he became one of the most influential Broad Church theologians of his day and a founding father of Christian Socialism, one who also championed, like Bentham, Mill, and Sidgwick, higher education for women. His attempt to move Anglicanism forward via a very progressive theology that had no place for hell or damnation led Mill to complain that "there was more intellectual power wasted in Maurice than in any other of my contemporaries. . . . Great powers of generalization, rare ingenuity and subtlety, and a wide perception of important and unobvious truths, served him not for putting something better into the place of the worthless heap of received opinions on the great subjects of thought, but for proving to his own mind that the Church of England had known everything from the first."[34]

Still, when it came to what Mill deemed the lasting effects of his crisis, the impact of Maurice, the thinker and channel for the mystic, Coleridgean alternative, is plain:

> The other important change which my opinions at this time underwent, was that I, for the first time, gave its proper place, among the prime necessities of human well-being, to the internal culture of the

individual. I ceased to attach almost exclusive importance to the ordering of outward circumstances, and the training of the human being for speculation and for action. I had now learnt by experience that the passive susceptibilities needed to be cultivated as well as the active capacities, and required to be nourished and enriched as well as guided. I did not, for an instant, lose sight of, or undervalue, that part of the truth which I had seen before; I never turned recreant to intellectual culture, or ceased to consider the power and practice of analysis as an essential condition both of individual and of social improvement. But I thought that it had consequences which required to be corrected, by joining other kinds of cultivation with it. The maintenance of a due balance among the faculties, now seemed to me of primary importance. The cultivation of the feelings became one of the cardinal points in my ethical and philosophical creed. And my thoughts and inclinations turned in an increasing degree towards whatever seemed capable of being instrumental to that object.[35]

The impact was evident, too, in Mill's new recognition that, although "happiness is the test of all rules of conduct, and the end of life," it was an end that "was only to be attained by not making it the direct end. Those only are happy (I thought) who have their minds fixed on some objects other than their own happiness; on the happiness of others, on the improvement of mankind, even on some art or pursuit, followed not as a means, but as an ideal end. Aiming thus at something else, they find happiness by the way." One must, as Carlyle (another friend, and a huge direct influence on Mill) urged, "[l]et your self-consciousness, your scrutiny, your self-interrogation, exhaust themselves on that; and if otherwise fortunately circumstanced you will inhale happiness with the air you breathe, without dwelling on it or thinking about it, without either forestalling it in imagination, or putting it to flight by fatal questioning. This theory now became the basis of my philosophy of life."[36]

In this connection, it should also be noted that the role of poetry in Mill's life and work is illustrative of the inseparability of his life and his work. In a brilliant essay, "Morality, Virtue, and Aesthetics in Mill's Art of Life," Wendy Donner shows how Mill's turbulent poetic therapy had him in short order shifting his allegiances from Wordsworth to Shelley to some middle ground, in an effort to determine the right balance between reason and spontaneous feeling and imagination. There was, of course, no reliance on Wordsworth's nature mysticism or transcendentalism in Mill: "Mill's fluctuating evaluations of the relative merits of Wordsworth versus Shelley move upward and downward in accordance with his corresponding estimations of the contributions of the natural faculties of emotion and reason to the creation of poetry." But the enduring effect of this period, evident even in Mill's late writings, was to highlight the importance of virtue and "aesthetic education," which was what would, Mill hoped, carry humanity forward and improve the content of, help reform, common morality, which was the sphere of rules enforceable by blame and/or punishment. "The capacities to be cultivated are emotional sensibility, sympathetic imagination, empathy, selflessness, and compassion. These capacities are components of moral agency. They are essential for moral conduct as well as the practice of virtues and nobility: 'It brings home to us all those aspects of life which take hold of our nature on its unselfish side, and lead us to identify our joy and grief with the good or ill of the system of which we form part' (*CW* I: 254)." Thus, for Mill, "the unifying theme of the entire period is that in the realm of aesthetic education and experience, the philosopher-poet is the prime model and exemplar, the source of the uplifting and ennobling experiences and inspiration."[37] The aesthetic was the driving force in Mill's Art of Life. It was what made the utilitarian clerisy a clerisy. Such supererogation, such moral heroism, was above and beyond the call of moral duty as it stood, but was nonetheless vital to the progress of civilization.

Now, this perspective was, for Mill, still consistent with hedonism— happiness was a complex, with parts, analogous to health, as Aristotle had famously held. And one desired the parts for their own sake, just as one valued friends for their own sake. But what made them desirable was, ultimately, the pleasure afforded by them. To subtract that would be to subtract such goodness as they have, as parts of happiness or means to it.[38] As he so memorably put it in *Utilitarianism*, "the ultimate end, with reference to and for the sake of which all other things are desirable (whether we are considering our own good or that of other people), is an existence exempt as far as possible from pain, and as rich as possible in enjoyments, both in point of quantity and quality. . . . This, being . . . the end of human action, is necessarily also the standard of morality; which may accordingly be defined as the rules and precepts for human conduct, by the observance of which an existence such as has been described might be, to the greatest extent possible, secured to all mankind; and not to them only, but, so far as the nature of things admits, to the whole sentient creation."[39] True, in advancing happiness, the philosopher-poet has reasons running rather ahead of concern about what calls for moral censure; but then, there is more to the Art of Life than moral censure.

Thus, the lessons Mill learned from his crisis, with the help of his new friends, were somewhat paradoxical, demanding the cultivation of one's feeling self while at the same time freeing that self from a morbid self-consciousness, with analysis trained on the other "ideal ends," and happiness for both self and others coming as a by-product of the pursuit of those ends. Perhaps this was taking utilitarian indirect strategies to a new level, inverting at the psychological level Benthamite reliance on invisible or visible hands at the level of social institutions. It was not the self-conscious and intelligent pursuit of one's own interests that would, under the right conditions, yield the optimal utilitarian social result. One's happiness would come from an intelligent appreciation that one's own interests called for some larger ideal or ideals than one's own small self, and that the general happiness would be best served by cultivating individuals with just such larger concerns, which was the work of the clerisy.[40]

As various discerning commentators have suggested, Mill's construction of the causes and cures of his breakdown reflects, is in fact embedded in, his construction of the views of Bentham and his father. His various direct assessments of Bentham, from his obituary of him in 1832, to his "Remarks on Bentham's Philosophy" in 1833, to his somewhat more moderated "Bentham" of 1838, amount to so many embroiderings on what went wrong with his education and life, and what was needed to repair the damage. Bentham is made out as the villain, and his father is to an astonishing degree exonerated, credited with having given him that interest in learning from others and seeing all sides of a question that, on his reckoning, were conspicuously absent in Bentham. Bentham was "one-eyed," could not learn from others, was cold and mechanical, failed to appreciate the significance of poetry and discussions of taste, had no sense of history or cultural particularity, no appreciation of human honor or dignity, no serious appreciation of how the principle of utility should be understood, no recognition of the importance of "national character" in explaining human action, and so on and on. That his own perspective on Bentham and the "business side" of life might have been limited or skewed seems never to have occurred to Mill. But as the evidence of the previous chapter indicates, Mill may well have missed much.

And he may have hidden or suppressed much. Janice Carlisle has argued forcefully that Mill's *Autobiography* was something of a grief lesson, composed during periods when Mill was worried about his and Harriet's health or grieving her loss, and that in it he actually masked a deeper crisis, which occurred following the death of his father in 1836, a bleak, anxious, sickly period of exhaustion that Mill's friends definitely noticed and that left him with a permanent facial tic, a more or less constant twitching of his left eye. Unable to come to terms with the many parts of his life that derived directly from his father—not least the "principling" or genial nepotistic corruption that led to his position at India House—the *Autobiography* was, as Mill seemed to admit, an attempt to resuscitate his father's reputation when it was in decline, yet another go at giving him proper credit, especially for his work on associationist psychology.[41]

At any rate, through it all, Mill insisted that he was advancing the truer and deeper form of utilitarianism, freeing it from the limitations and aberrations of the Philosophical Radicals, who, as noted, charged him with going over to the side of German Mysticism. No doubt his corrective enthusiasms were a shock to such figures as Place, and no doubt he at moments went somewhat overboard in celebrating even such anti-utilitarian notions as "intuition" (the dogmatic pillar of all the anti-utilitarian forces in both morality and science) in ways that were bound to provoke. But he recovered his balance—or rather, found it for the first time—soon enough, and it is perhaps not so surprising that with the discovery of his feelings came the discovery of love, not simply for humanity at large, but for one representative of it in particular—Harriet Taylor. For Mill, she was the higher pleasures personified. But a full appreciation of her would come only after a good deal of political economy and logic.

The Love of Logic

Although Mill never devoted an essay or a treatise solely to the study of character, it constituted the principal subject of his long career as a writer. Whether he was writing on economics or education, politics or philosophy, whether he was reviewing a work of fiction or formulating a system of logic, his inquiries almost invariably declared their psychological and social orientation and his preoccupation with character, not as a literary concept or phenomenon, but as the central fact of human experience. According to Mill, diverse disciplines join in a common pursuit of this subject. The philosopher, more a psychologist than a theorist of abstract principles, attempts to understand the complexity of human behavior and establish those laws of character that might lead to its reformation.

—JANICE CARLISLE, *JOHN STUART MILL
AND THE WRITING OF CHARACTER*

Mill would claim in his *Autobiography* that his crisis was the only really big turning point in his mental life, the only serious turning of his worldview. And it is true that the ripples spreading out from his conversion to Romantic self-cultivation affected his thoughts in endless ways. Rejecting what he saw as the deductive or a priori rational actor approach of his father, so clearly on display in the latter's "Essay on Government,"[42] he now fell in with the Saint-Simonians and Comte, with their views of different phases of historical progress, from organic periods to transitional or critical ones, from theology to metaphysics to positive knowledge, and so on. Historical and cultural sensitivity and particularity were heralded everywhere, in Carlyle's work on the French Revolution and heroes, in the work of his father's great antagonist Macaulay, and, above all, in Tocqueville's brilliant *Democracy in America*, a work that profoundly affected Mill, despite his resistance to Tocquevillian concerns about the dangers of government "centralization."[43] He was now less the reflexive democrat in the mode of his father, more the ethical socialist who worried about democracy moving too fast in advance of cultural development and civilized education. The tyranny of the majority, so worrisome to Tocqueville, was a very real concern for Mill as well, and the tyranny of a possible ruling elite of Comtean scientist philosophers was not a cure that he found attractive. The progress of civilization was the progress of that general self-cultivation, in freedom, of character that was mirrored in his crisis. It was the advance of a comprehensive liberal individualism, one that would afford the individuals involved the many-sidedness and higher pleasures that Mill celebrated, and as such, it was, to his mind, a refounding of utilitarianism rather than a rejection of it. The "Germano-Coleridge" view had given him, in Skorupski's formulation, the method of "thinking from within":

> Thinking from within requires imaginative understanding of other people and other times, a lesson Mill drew from Coleridge. About other people's ideas, Mill says, Bentham's only question was, were they true? Coleridge, in contrast, patiently asked after their meaning. To pin down the fundamental norms of our thinking calls for careful psychological and historical inquiry into how people think, and also into how they think they should think—what kind of normative attitudes they display in their actions and their reflection. These must be engaged with to be understood. So thinking from within is inherently dialogical. And it always remains corrigible. Both points are significant in Mill's argument for liberty of thought and discussion.[44]

Indeed, for Mill, "character" was simply a matter of making one's life one's own—it was the achievement of an active, self-directed life, largely through dialogue. There was an undeniable element of liberal bootstrapping involved in this notion. As Carlisle put it:

> Ultimately, Mill's associationism was more important as the source of foregone conclusions than as a repository of methods suited to the study of character . . . because Mill could not accept the conclusion inherent in such associationist principles, he tried to use ethology as a way to grant to the individual the opportunity for choice and the power of will that associationism denies. The Irish do not have to remain the lazy, improvident, ill-educated savages that their conditions have made them. The laboring classes can rise above their appetites and choose a life of self-restraint and self-improvement. Women do not always have to remain merely weak, sycophantic witnesses to male power. If nothing else, Mill's unwritten ethology allowed him to recognize and perhaps encouraged his contemporaries to see with him that none of the characteristics customarily accepted by society as the inalterable nature of a group was immune to change.[45]

However unselfconscious Mill may have been about the personal pursuit of happiness, he was quite self-conscious about his role in refounding utilitarianism, though prior to his father's death in 1836, he often had to be rather subtle about just what he was up to. Still, from 1834 until about 1840, Mill worked to insinuate new ideas into the *Westminster Review* and took a leading role in the early development of the *London Review*, which soon swallowed up the former to become the *London and Westminster Review*. In 1837 the journal was taken over by Mill himself (at a loss), when the original owner, Molesworth, tired of the enterprise. Mill had already resolved to "give full scope to my own opinions and modes of thought, and to open the Review widely to all writers who were in sympathy with Progress as I understood it."[46] It was in this context that so much of the work that would shape the future reception of Benthamism was produced, including not only Mill's pieces on Bentham, but his piece on Coleridge and the very telling essay on "Civilization," "into which I threw many of my new opinions, and criticized rather emphatically the mental and moral tendencies of the time, on grounds and in a manner which I certainly had not learnt from him [his father]." [47]

The essay on "Civilization" is indeed illuminating, highlighting in short compass so many of the distinctively Millian themes of his later and better-known works. Addressing chiefly a narrower notion of "civilization" as opposed to barbarism, Mill observes that "by the natural growth of civilization, power passes from individuals to masses, and the weight and importance of an individual, as compared with the mass, sink into greater and greater insignificance."[48] The cost that this exacts on character, on such individual qualities as heroism and spirit (and ability to tolerate pain) is described in terms evoking Carlyle, and the English upper classes, in particular, are treated with some scorn for their want of energy and spirit, not to mention their "effeminacy." The growing insignificance of the individual is, however, yet more corrupting, contributing to "the growth, both in the world of trade and in that of intellect, of quackery, and especially of puffing," though "nobody seems to have remarked, that these are the inevitable fruits of immense competition; of a state of society where any voice, not pitched in an exaggerated key, is lost in the hubbub."[49] In an age of reading, people, Mill charges, now read too quickly and shallowly, with few good indicators of quality. Overall, the age is witnessing "the decay of individual energy, the weakening of the influence of superior minds over the multitude, the growth of charlatanerie, and the diminished efficacy of public opinion as a restraining power."[50] That is, the "evils are, that the individual is lost and becomes impotent in the crowd, and that individual character itself becomes relaxed and enervated."

Still, there are remedies consistent with the direction of civilization: "For the first evil, the remedy is, greater and more perfect combination among individuals; for the second, national institutions of education, and forms of polity, calculated to invigorate the individual character."[51]

Better combination, for example in professional guilds or associations, could help counter the destructive impact of competition on such professions as medicine, and such organizations as the "Society for the Diffusion of Useful Knowledge" might serve as a crude model for a collective guild of authors. But Mill is mostly concerned with "the regeneration of individual character among our lettered and opulent classes, by the adaptation to that purpose of our institutions, and, above all, of our educational institutions," which "is an object of more urgency, and for which more might be immediately accomplished, if the will and the understanding were not alike wanting."[52] To be sure, Mill stresses that he is "at issue equally with the admirers of Oxford and Cambridge, Eton and Westminster, and with the generality of their professed reformers. We regard the system of those institutions, as administered for two centuries past, with sentiments little short of utter abhorrence. But we do not conceive that their vices would be cured by bringing their studies into a closer connexion with what it is the fashion to term 'the business of the world;' by dismissing the logic and classics which are still professedly taught, to substitute modern languages and experimental physics. We would have classics and logic taught far more really and deeply than at present, and we would add to them other studies more alien than any which yet exist to the 'business of the world,' but more germane to the great business of every rational being—the strengthening and enlarging of his own intellect and character."[53]

Here is the theme that Mill would warm to for the rest of his life—better education producing better, more independent thinking, the key component of character. To illustrate the point, he cites in corroboration a passage from the novel *Eustace Conway*: "'You believe' (a clergyman *loquitur*) 'that the University is to prepare youths for a successful career in society: I believe the sole object is to give them that manly character which will enable them to resist the influences of society . . . ; is it wonderful that a puny beggarly feeling should pervade the mass of our young men? That they should scorn all noble achievements, should have no higher standard of action than the world's opinion, and should conceive of no higher reward than to sit down amidst loud cheering, which continues for several moments?"[54]

The author of these lines was none other than that founding spirit of the Apostles, F. D. Maurice, and the remainder of Mill's essay is in fact something of mission statement for the Apostles:

Nothing can be more just or more forcible than the description here given of the objects which University education should aim at: we are at issue with the writer, only on the proposition that these objects ever were attained, or ever could be so, consistently with the principle which has always been the foundation of the English Universities; a principle, unfortunately, by no means confined to them. The difficulty which continues to oppose either such reform of our old academical institutions, or the establishment of such new ones, as shall give us an education capable of forming great minds, is, that in order to do so it is necessary to begin by eradicating the idea which nearly all the upholders and nearly all the impugners of the Universities rootedly entertain, as to the objects not merely of academical education, but of education itself. What is this idea? That the object of education is, not to qualify the pupil for judging what is true or what is right, but to provide that he shall think true what we think true, and right what we think right—that to teach, means to inculcate our own opinions, and that our business is not to make thinkers or inquirers, but disciples. This is the deep-seated error, the inveterate prejudice, which the real reformer of English education has to struggle against. Is it astonishing that great minds are not produced, in a country where the test of a great mind is, agreeing in the opinions of the small minds? . . . . That provided he adhere to these opinions, it matters little whether he receive them from authority or from examination; and worse, that it matters little by what temptations of interest or vanity, by what voluntary or involuntary sophistication with his intellect, and deadening of his noblest feelings, that result is arrived at; that it even matters comparatively little whether to his mind the words are mere words, or the representatives of realities—in which sense he receives the favoured set of propositions, or whether he attaches to them any sense at all. Were ever great minds thus formed? Never.[55]

Mill in this passage is of course working his way to an attack on the requirement of subscription to the Thirty-Nine Articles of the Church of England, but his point is more general. True, a first step in reform must be to "unsectarianize" the universities. But more positively, the "very corner-stone of an education intended to form great minds, must be the recognition of the principle, that the object is to call forth the greatest possible quantity of intellectual *power*, and to inspire the intensest *love of truth*: and this without a particle of regard to the results to which the exercise of that power may lead, even though it should conduct the pupil to opinions diametrically opposite to those of his teachers." The most distinguished minds should be recruited to teach and given the freedom to do so. The classics and history (including literature) will provide models of greatness and nobility, and reminders of "the infinite varieties of human nature." But in "the department of pure intellect, the highest place will belong to logic and the philosophy of mind: the one, the instrument for the cultivation of all sciences; the other, the root from which they all grow." Of course, "the former ought not to be taught as a mere system of technical rules, nor the latter as a set of concatenated abstract propositions. The tendency, so strong everywhere, is strongest of all here, to receive opinions into the mind without any real understanding of them, merely because they seem to follow from certain admitted premises, and to let them lie there as forms of words, lifeless and void of meaning. The pupil must be led to interrogate his own consciousness, to observe and experiment upon himself: of the mind, by any other process, little will he ever know."[56]

But all the other sciences have their place in Mill's encompassing vision, and of course, the "philosophy of morals, of government, of law, of political economy, of poetry and art, should form subjects of systematic instruction, under the most eminent professors who [can] be found; these being chosen, not for the particular doctrines they might happen to profess, but as being those who [are] most likely to send forth pupils qualified in point of disposition and attainments to choose doctrines for themselves." Even religion might be included, if so taught. And all this is trained on "regenerating the character of the higher classes," which, it is hoped, the progress of democracy will advance by putting an end to "every kind of unearned distinction."

The vision is breathtaking, rather elitist, deeply Apostolic, and the set-up for *On Liberty*, the glimmerings of which are unmistakable. Was it really entirely the new Mill? Was it really entirely Mill? Intriguingly, of his father, Mill would allow that he had "frequently observed that he made large allowance in practice for considerations which seemed to have no place in his theory," and even admired Tocqueville's work. His "high appreciation of a book which was at any rate an example of a mode of treating the question of government almost the reverse of his—wholly inductive and analytical, instead of purely ratiocinative—gave me great encouragement," as did his father's approval of "Civilization." It was, after all, an age of transition, and as the next section will demonstrate, Mill was at this time in a very transitional state, bringing Harriet Taylor into his life in the years just before his father's exit from life.

But Mill certainly felt, too, that he had to keep up the side in supporting the Philosophical Radicals, who now for the first time figured in Parliament. Among them was his old friend Roebuck, who took the opportunity to initiate a Parliamentary movement for National Education, as well as for self-government for the colonies. There was still much to admire and support in the forces of Benthamism, even if the hopes for establishing a Radical party were to be disappointed by the somewhat lackluster performances of Buller, Roebuck, et al. As Donald Winch has explained, the "1830s for Mill were a decade of intense involvement in party politics. Denied more overt forms of participation by his position as a civil servant at East India House, he used his journalistic skills to support reform causes and the activities of the large group of radical MPs elected after passage of the Reform Bill in 1832. This activist phase came to an abrupt end in 1839 with the break-up of the Parliamentary radicals and the shattering of any hope of founding a party that could contest political space with Whigs, Tories, and the new extra-Parliamentary forces in British politics represented by the Chartist movement and Cobden's Anti-Corn Law League."[57] At the level of practical politics, then, there was also much continuity, and if Mill was by the end of the thirties thinking of himself more as a writer than a politician, that was something of a grudging admission. For him, the Parliamentary platform was, in an age of organization, one of the best means for making one's voice heard.

Not surprisingly, through it all, Mill was engaged as always with the all important topics of logic (both deductive and inductive) and political economy, returning whenever time allowed to the research that would ultimately yield those great pillars of his reputation, the *System of Logic* and the *Principles of Political Economy*. Both works, substantial as they are, were designed—at least according to Mill's later recollection—to showcase key elements of the new utilitarianism he was championing. And in some cases this meant emphasizing points that were actually more in sync with the old utilitarianism than Mill's Mystic period seemed to allow, such as a deep aversion to sentimentality in political economy (on which subject the spirit of the age, Coleridge, was dismissed as a "driveller") and to intuition in logic. He described the point of the *Logic* in his *Autobiography* accordingly:

> I have never indulged the illusion that the book had made any considerable impression on philosophical opinion. The German, or *a priori* view of human knowledge, and of the knowing faculties, is likely for some time longer (though it may be hoped in a diminishing degree) to predominate among those who occupy themselves with such enquiries, both here and on the Continent. But the *System of Logic* supplies what was much wanted, a text-book of the opposite doctrine—that which derives all knowledge from experience, and all moral and intellectual qualities principally from the direction given to the associations. I make as humble an estimate as anybody of what either an analysis of logical processes, or any possible canons of evidence, can do by themselves, towards guiding or rectifying the operations of the understanding. Combined with other requisites, I certainly do think them of great use; but whatever may be the practical value of a true philosophy of these matters, it is hardly possible to exaggerate the mischiefs of a false one. The notion that truths external to the mind may be known by intuition or consciousness, independently of observation and experience, is, I am persuaded, in these times, the great intellectual support of false doctrines and bad institutions. By the aid of this theory, every inveterate belief and every intense feeling, of which the origin is not remembered, is enabled to dispense with the obligation of justifying itself by reason, and is erected into its own all-sufficient voucher and justification. There never was such an instrument devised for consecrating all deep seated prejudices. And the chief strength of this false philosophy in morals, politics, and religion, lies in the appeal which it is accustomed to make to the evidence of mathematics and of the cognate branches of physical science. To expel it from these, is to drive it from its stronghold: and because this had never been effectually done, the intuitive school, even after what my father had written in his *Analysis of Mind,* had in appearance, and as far as published writings were concerned, on the whole the best of the argument. In attempting to clear up the real nature of the evidence of mathematical and physical truths, the *System of Logic* met the intuition philosophers on ground on which

they had previously been deemed unassailable; and gave its own explanation, from experience and association, of that peculiar character of
what are called necessary truths, which is adduced as proof that their
evidence must come from a deeper source than experience.[58]

There are no kind words for intuition in this work, which Mill would always regard as his most serious effort. Beyond, that is, the praise for William
Whewell for having provided such perfect targets for his attack with *History
of the Inductive Sciences* and *The Philosophy of the Inductive Sciences*, the
foils (and sourcebooks) that Mill had desperately needed. Whewell, whose
philosophical orientation might seem to put him in the company of Maurice,
Julius Hare, and others with an a priori bent, was not one of the Cambridge
Apostles. His spirit was too dogmatic, too hostile, and too lacking the Apostolic spirit of being willing to learn from others, from the band of brothers
whose principles were appreciated as reflections of their personalities and experiences. Whewell, a working class youth who had advanced in status and
now celebrated the system that had allowed him to do so, was in older age no
reformer of the educational system, lacking that spirit of personal growth that
the Apostles and their friends put at the very heart of true education. He was,
therefore, both personally and professionally just the counterpoint that Mill
needed on all fronts, from logic to morals. He was not an Apostle, but he was a
polymath, furnishing the requisite opposition on even more counts than Mill
could count. The famously witty Rev. Sydney Smith quipped of Whewell, *"Science is his forte, and omniscience his foible."*[59]

The battle joined, Mill proved himself to be, as Stefan Collini has observed,
"a good hater."[60] More Public Moralist than Public Intellectual, Mill nonetheless pinned the moral reform and advance of civilization on winning the battle
against intuitionism, even in its stronghold of mathematics. Yet it must be
allowed that the *Logic* does not itself always read like an all-out assault on
the dominant ideology. Mill, especially in the first edition, was at some pains
to urge that he was trying to find common ground, the shared truth behind
the mystery of how one could get from one set of truths to another. The links
between deduction and induction could be tricky. As the *Collected Works* edition has it:

> For Mill there were in logic two sets of rules: the rules of the syllogism
> for deduction, and the four experimental methods for induction. The
> former he considered to be available in the 'common manuals of logic.'
> The latter he considered himself to be formulating explicitly for the
> first time. The question as to how these rules of art can be viewed as
> grounded in the science of valid thinking must be brought under the
> larger question as to how rules of art in general are grounded in sci-
> ence. For Mill, the way in which they are grounded is universally the
> same for all arts in which there are rules. He distinguishes two kinds

of practical reasoning. One is typified in the reasoning of a judge, the other in that of a legislator. The judge's problem is to interpret the law, or to determine whether the particular case before him comes under the intention of the legislator who made the law. Thus the reasoning of the judge is syllogistic, for syllogism or deduction consists in the interpretation of a formula. The legislator's problem, on the other hand, is to find rules. This depends on determining the best means of achieving certain desired ends. It is science alone which can determine these means, for the relation between means and ends is the relation between causes and effects. In this second kind of practical reasoning, art prescribes the end, science provides the theorem which shows how it is to be brought about, and art then converts the theorem into a rule. In this way propositions which assert only what ought to be, or should be done, are grounded on propositions which assert only matters of fact.

The task of finding the rules of logic, whether of deduction or of induction, is of the same type as the legislator's. Knowledge of what ought to be done, as expressed in the rules of art, must be grounded on knowledge of what is the case, as expressed in the theorems of science.[61]

Thus, for Mill, "must" implies "ought," a point that will be important when considering his so-called proof of the principle of utility. People must make inferences, and therefore they ought to do so. Indeed, if there is a fundamental normative principle in Mill rivaling the principle of utility, it is that of generalizing from the particulars of experience.

The famous four methods can be briefly summarized. For Mill, and in his words as he formulates the five "Canons," these methods yield: 1. "If two or more instances of the phenomenon under investigation have only one circumstance in common, the circumstance in which alone all the instances agree, is the cause (or effect) of the given phenomenon." 2. "If an instance in which the phenomenon under investigation occurs, and an instance in which it does not occur, have every circumstance save one in common, that one occurring only in the former; the circumstance in which alone the two instances differ, is the effect, or cause, or a necessary part of the cause, of the phenomenon." 3. "If two or more instances in which the phenomenon occurs have only one circumstance in common, while two or more instances in which it does not occur have nothing in common save the absence of that circumstance; the circumstance in which alone the two sets of instances differ, is the effect, or cause, or a necessary part of the cause, of the phenomenon." 4. (which is not truly an independent method) "Subduct from any phenomenon such part as is known by previous inductions to be the effect of certain antecedents, and the residue of the phenomenon is the effect of the remaining antecedents." And 5. "Whatever phenomenon varies in any manner whenever another phenomenon varies in some particular manner, is either a cause or an effect of that phenomenon, or is connected with it through some fact of causation." As Mill sums it up: "The four methods which it has now been attempted to describe, are the only possible modes of experimental inquiry—of direct induction à posteriori, as distinguished from deduction: at least, I know not, nor am able to imagine, any others. And even of these, the Method of Residues, as we have seen, is not independent of deduction; though, as it also requires specific experience, it may, without impropriety, be included among methods of direct observation and experiment."[62]

These may seem straightforward enough, but still, the *Logic* can be a difficult work to untangle, particularly if one is working with the common notions of contemporary symbolic logic. As various commentators have noted, Mill is more concerned with inference than with formal implication, and though inference is a psychological process, his "psychologism" really amounts only to a kind of naturalism that in many respects he shares with such recent figures as W. V. Quine. Like Quine, Mill holds that all necessity is a matter of language, rather than objective or metaphysical necessity. There is no necessary connection binding subject or substance to property or attribute. The structure of the world is radically contingent. But unlike Quine, Mill tends to think of deductive logic in syllogistic and subject/predicate terms, failing to deal with relations in any satisfactory way. Also, as John Skorupski has observed, there "is no suggestion in Mill that a naturalistic philosophy must eschew intentional states—beliefs, purposes, sentiments, etc. Rather, Mill is a naturalist in the sense that he thinks (i) that beliefs, purposes, sentiments are genuine properties of the human being seen as a natural entity and (ii) that the normative can be grounded in them—nothing *beyond* them is required."[63]

On Mill's account, the meaning of a proposition is a matter of the denotations and connotations of its terms, but the truth of a proposition is a matter of its denotations rather than its connotations, and all propositions are either true or false, either correctly attributing an attribute to a subject or not (e.g., Socrates is mortal, but not Socrates is a fish). Mill denies that deductive or syllogistic logic is genuinely informative—it deals in verbal rather than real propositions, apparent rather than real inferences. He denies that it affords "ampliative" truths, new truths, since the general premises in syllogistic arguments—e.g., All Men are Mortal—are simply shorthand statements of long conjunctions of particulars—e.g., X is mortal, Y is mortal, Z is mortal, etc. Thus, in the case of All Men are Mortal / Socrates is a Man / Therefore Socrates is Mortal, the conclusion really is just a repetition of one bit of the first premise, a move from particular to particular, and begging of the question.

Interestingly, no one was more scornful of Mill's account of deductive logic than his secular (but literal) godson, or *un*godson, Bertrand Russell, whose parents, Lord and Lady Amberly, were among Mill's disciples. As Russell, following Frege, observed:

Everything that Mill has to say in his *Logic* about matters other than inductive inference is perfunctory and conventional. He states, for example, that propositions are formed by putting together two names, one of which is the subject and the other the predicate. This, I am sure, appeared to him an innocuous truism; but it had been, in fact, the source of two thousand years of important error. On the subject of names, with which modern logic has been much concerned, what he has to say is totally inadequate, and is, in fact, not so good as what had been said by Duns Scotus and William of Occam. His famous contention that the syllogism in Barbara is a *petitio principia,* and that the argument is really from particulars to particulars, has a measure of truth in certain cases, but cannot be accepted as a general doctrine. He maintains, for example, that the proposition 'all men are mortal' asserts 'the Duke of Wellington is mortal' even if the person making the assertion has never heard of the Duke of Wellington. This is obviously untenable: a person who knows the meaning of the words 'man' and 'mortal' can understand the statement 'all men are mortal' but can make no inference about a man he has never heard of; whereas, if Mill were right about the Duke of Wellington, a man could not understand this statement unless he knew the catalogue of all the men who ever have existed or ever will exist. His doctrine that inference is from particulars to particulars is correct psychology when applied to what I call 'animal induction,' but is never correct logic. To infer, from the mortality of men in the past, the mortality of those not yet dead, can only be legitimate if there is a *general* principle of induction. Broadly speaking, no general conclusion can be drawn without a general premise, and only a general premise will warrant a general conclusion from an incomplete enumeration of instances. What is more, there are general propositions of which no one can doubt the truth, although not a single instance of them can be given. Take, for example, the following: 'All whole numbers which no one will have thought of before the year A.D. 2000, are greater than a million.' You cannot attempt to give me an instance without contradicting yourself, and you cannot pretend that all the whole numbers have been thought of by someone. [64]

Russell was also among the first to point out that Mill's notion of causation scarcely captures the etiolated notion of causality, if it can be called that, in twentieth-century physics.

At any rate, for Mill, as far as truth is concerned, the real action comes with inductive logic, which he thinks captures the real logic of science—namely, eliminative induction, or the systematic (abductive) effort to eliminate rival causal hypotheses, as in the Canons, though ultimately this is built upon enumerative induction. He advances something like a nomological-deductive or covering law model, in which explanation is a matter of determining the law that best accounts for the phenomenon. But his big differences with the rationalist or intuitionist approach of Whewell come in how he denies that the progressive development of such explanations is in any way a matter of deploying a priori concepts to discover metaphysical necessities, the laws of God, in Whewell's view. Again, Mill emphasizes the radical contingency and relativity (to the perceiver) of knowledge. Even higher-order principles or laws—such as the law that every event has a cause, or that the best hypothesis is available— are but laws of laws and ultimately grounded in the same way, as inductive generalizations, albeit enumerative ones. They may work well enough during periods of normal science, but they can be overthrown during more revolutionary intellectual times. Certainty is simply not to be had.

There are clearly many points on which Mill anticipates later philosophical pragmatists—in his naturalism, embrace of uncertainty but resistance to skepticism, and emphasis on the public sphere and experimental modes of critical thinking that are really but extensions of ordinary or common-sense inference.[65] It is true that at times his account of "experience" seems more reductive or phenomenalist, defining the objects of the external world in terms of the structure of the "permanent possibilities of sensation," as in his most ambitious work of fundamental philosophy, *An Examination of Sir William Hamilton's Philosophy* (1865). But he also uses the term in a more general way, and in his application of his methods to psychology to defend a revised account of associationism, he did make it clear that, as Fred Wilson has put it, "new sorts of mental unity emerge from associational processes and have properties which are not among the properties that appear in the genetic antecedents. Analysis of ideas is still possible, but it is not the simplistic sort of thing, a literal taking apart, that his father would have it be."[66] Mill would in fact edit a new edition of his father's *Analysis of the Phenomena of the Human Mind,* making it clear through his notes that his own version of associationism went further in recognizing how mental parts can combine and fuse. But for all of his efforts, it cannot be said that he succeeded in giving anything like a compelling account of the self and personal identity. This was a matter that he uncharacteristically left wrapped in mystery and enigma. Character, it seems, involving the desire to think for oneself, also had the job of unifying the self out of so many mental sequences. Will, Mill is clear, is not the same as mere desire, and the self that wills is a unified agent. But the self that did the unifying was scarcely explained in Mill's work, a point that later Idealist philosophers would deploy to good effect.

It is worth recapitulating here how aspects of the outlook that went into the *Logic* and these other works (and, for that matter, *The Principles of Political Economy* and all of his other major works) were related to the insights that he felt he had achieved through his crisis. The revision of his father's associationism to better account for agency and self-direction is a case in point. Again, as Wilson has put it, in an especially insightful passage:

> Mill's psychology also includes an account of motivation and action. On this theory, pleasure is the prime motivator, the primary end in itself, and the anticipation of pleasure serves as an immediate cause of bodily motions which in turn bring about that pleasure. Through regular success in attaining pleasure, anticipations of pleasure become associated with the sorts of action that bring about that pleasure. When Mill asserts that people seek pleasure, what he is to be taken to mean is that people seek things other than pleasure but that they seek it because pleasure has become associated with it, and that when the desire is fulfilled they experience the pleasure of satisfied desire. In this sense human welfare consists in satisfied desire. . . . This new account of psychological association and analysis was important in Mill's thinking about ethics. Thus, where his father (and Bentham) had a simple notion that pleasures are all of a piece, and distinctions among them merely quantitative, one bit added to another bit, Mill came to see that there are qualitative distinctions among pleasures: the 'higher' pleasures do result from association but they are different in kind from the 'lower' pleasures out of which they arise, and as a matter of fact turn out to be more satisfying forms of pleasure. So Mill could say, where his father could not, that it is better to be Socrates dissatisfied than a pig satisfied.

It is evident that it was during his mental crisis that Mill came to be clear on the existence of, and importance for personal development, of these higher forms of mental unity in our conscious experience of the world. It was reading Wordsworth, it seems, that gave him this sense that there were forms of human being that were hardly part of his father's scheme of things. These feelings, to be obtained through poetry and human intercourse, were subsequently encouraged through his relationship with Harriet Taylor. These feelings, and their cultivation, came to form an important part of Mill's idea of the good that shaped his thought and his efforts towards social reform and progress.

Given the account of association and of action, it is evident that various means to pleasure will become associated with feelings of pleasure. But on Mill's view, this will not be a mere conjunction; to the contrary, as the association becomes strong enough the two parts will fuse into a new sort of emergent whole. The means will not simply be conjoined to pleasure but will become part of pleasure. And so money, for the miser, becomes not just a means to pleasure but for him part of pleasure, an end in itself.

This account of human action presupposes the acceptance of determinism, which Mill vigorously defends in the *System of Logic*, where he outlines the idea of a naturalistic science of human being. Freedom, Mill argues in Book Six, Ch. 2, which he thought the best in the work, is not the absence of causation but rather the absence of coercion. In fact the whole point of education is to determine the future free actions of the individual: it aims through the associative processes to determine the person's motives and actions. . . . Among the motives that one could acquire is the motive of self-improvement or self-realization. There are irresistible motives; for these we are not as persons responsible. But there are also resistible motives, and these we can shape and determine. . . . The free person is one who is sensitive to good reasons for behaving as he or she does. The second-order ends that lead one to shape one's motives and to develop as an individual became the central feature of Mill's social thinking, and this marks a major break in detail, though, to be sure, not in principle, with the utilitarianism of Bentham and his father. In the *Examination of Hamilton's Philosophy*, Mill vigorously defends the notion of human beings as active in their own self-determination.[67]

Perhaps the operative line in the above account is the one about this marking "a major break in detail, though, to be sure, not in principle, with the utilitarianism of Bentham and his father." For it should be transparently clear that, at least by the time that he was ready to publish his major works, in the 1840s, Mill was struggling to fit the Mystic or Coleridgean or Romantic notions of freedom, self-culture, and personal growth into the naturalistic, deterministic, and associationist worldview that he had inherited from his father and Bentham. Intuitionism, Rationalism, and all forms of a priorism are identified as the opposition, the deeper forces behind the religious, political, and social prejudices reining in progress. Mill evinces no deep sympathy for Kantian or Idealist accounts of noumenal freedom, or for a morality or politics grounded on any such notion. However, as John Skorupski has acutely summed it up:

It is important to remember here that Mill was no more a Humean in epistemology than he was an eighteenth-century *philosophe* in his political thought. His version of naturalistic empiricism was not a rehearsal of Hume, just as Hegel's version of idealism was not a rehearsal of Kant. He did not have an instrumentalist conception of reason. He believed that autonomy as a capacity, or in his words 'moral freedom', was a matter of mastery of the passions by the rational self. He made the German ideal of self-development his own.

Not that Mill succeeded in showing how reason can be naturalized, any more than Hegel succeeded in showing how nature can be an objectification of Reason. We cannot go back to Mill or to Hegel, but the question remains: whether classical liberalism, with its belief in rational

autonomy, and in the historical progress towards it of all human traditions, can flourish in a naturalistic (de Geisted) framework.[68]

Skorupski is as appreciative as anyone of what he calls (alluding to the
Rawlsian "Aristotelian Principle") the "Mill Principle," namely, that "only the
fullest self-development of one's potential gives access to the highest forms
of human happiness."[69] (This could, of course, just as well have been called
the "Godwin Principle"). Indeed, in various works, he has gone far to mount
a sympathetic defense of Millian liberalism, as has Alan Ryan. Yet both to
some degree share the worry voiced by Bertrand Russell, to the effect that the
superstructure of Mill's moral and political views cannot fully be supported by
its foundations. This is, to be sure, of a piece with the standard take on Mill's
syncretic efforts. Supposedly, Mill failed to reconcile the very disparate pieces
of his worldview, failed to reconcile naturalism with Romanticism, determinism with agency, hedonism with perfectionism, utilitarianism with individualistic liberalism, altruism with egoism, utilitarian criticism with common-sense
moral rules, and so forth, much as he tried. By trying, like Locke, to capture
the more persuasive parts of the opposition, he ended up a nest of inconsistencies, however ennobling the various sides of his many-sidedness may have
been. J. B. Schneewind has even argued that Mill's great influence came from
these inconsistent syncretic efforts, in that Mill went further in making utilitarianism respectable, more accommodating of common-sense morality, not
that one would ever guess this from the malign reception of his collaboration
with Harriet Taylor.[70]

More will be said in the next chapter about the enormous controversies
swirling around the contest between naturalism and its alternatives. Again,
one of the great ironies in the history of utilitarianism is that its most formidable philosophical defenses have come from those who ground it on something closer to Whewellian intuitionism rather than Millian naturalism. In the
remainder of this chapter, however, the concern will be more with the moral,
political, and political economical superstructure that Mill built, however un-
steadily, on his naturalistic foundations. Mill himself, as we have seen, thought
the larger worldview was crucial to the defense of utilitarianism and progressive liberalism. And he regarded the final book of his *Logic*, emphasizing the
importance of the science of ethology, as hammering home a key point: "There
is, then, a Philosophia Prima peculiar to Art, as there is one which belongs to
Science. There are not only first principles of Knowledge, but first principles
of Conduct. There must be some standard by which to determine the goodness
or badness, absolute and comparative, of ends, or objects of desire. And whatever that standard is, there can be but one: for if there were several ultimate
principles of conduct, the same conduct might be approved by one of those
principles and condemned by another; and there would be needed some more
general principle, as umpire between them."[71]

But the defense of the principle of utility in this role, as "the ultimate Principle of Teleology" undergirding "the Right, the Expedient, and the Beautiful," would "be out of place, in a work like this," and (in later editions) he refers the reader to his "Utilitarianism."[72] Still, he deems it important to add the following crucial caveat regarding the Art of Life, lest the reader be left with a misleading impression:

> I do not mean to assert that the promotion of happiness should be itself the end of all actions, or even of all rules of action. It is the justification, and ought to be the controller, of all ends, but is not itself the sole end. There are many virtuous actions, and even virtuous modes of action . . . by which happiness in the particular instance is sacrificed, more pain being produced than pleasure. But conduct of which this can be truly asserted, admits of justification only because it can be shown that on the whole more happiness will exist in the world, if feelings are cultivated which will make people, in certain cases, regardless of happiness. I fully admit that this is true: that the cultivation of an ideal nobleness of will and conduct, should be to individual human beings an end, to which the specific pursuit either of their own happiness or of that of others (except so far as included in that idea) should, in any case of conflict, give way. But I hold that the very question, what constitutes this elevation of character, is itself to be decided by a reference to happiness as the standard. The character itself should be, to the individual, a paramount end, simply because the existence of this ideal nobleness of character, or of a near approach to it, in any abundance, would go further than all things else towards making human life happy; both in the comparatively humble sense, of pleasure and freedom from pain, and in the higher meaning, of rendering life, not what it now is almost universally, puerile and insignificant—but such as human beings with highly developed faculties can care to have.[73]

This passage, like the essay "Civilization," points up how closely Mill linked his *Logic* with the views expressed in his most enduringly popular works, *On Liberty, Utilitarianism*, and *The Subjection of Women*. That on his understanding utilitarianism was global, a standard applicable to all departments of conduct, including acts, rules, and institutions, and indirect, involving a happiness in which noble ideals had fused with pleasure and were sought for their own sake, is manifest. Ethology, the science of character formation and development, would develop in tandem with psychology to "determine, from the general laws of mind, combined with the general position of our species in the universe, what actual or possible combinations of circumstances are capable of promoting or preventing" those qualities of interest to us. Of course, this was but a promissory note, and the clerisy had a big task ahead. Much work needed to be done, and many experiments in living. And as mentioned,

Mill was at this time, in the 30s and 40s, engaged in an experiment that would illustrate his character like no other.[74]

The Logic of Love

To the Beloved Memory
Of
Harriet Mill
The Dearly Beloved and Deeply Regretted
Wife of John Stuart Mill
Her Great and Loving Heart
Her Noble Soul
Her Clear Powerful and Original
Comprehensive Intellect
Made Her the Guide and Support
The Instructor in Wisdom
And the Example in Goodness
As She was the Sole Earthly Delight
Of Those who had the Happiness to Belong to Her
As Earnest for the Public Good
As She was Generous and Devoted
To All who Surrounded Her
Her Influence has been Felt
In Many of the Greatest
Improvements of the Age
And will be in Those still to Come
Were There but a few Hearts and Intellects
Like Hers
The Earth would Already Become
The Hoped-For Heaven
She Died
To the Irreparable Loss of Those who Survive her
At Avignon
Nov 3, 1858

Mill's own great experiment in living came in the form of Harriet Taylor. They met in 1830, married in 1851, and were parted cruelly and too soon by Harriet's death in Avignon in 1858, after which Mill would spend half of every year there in order to be close to her grave, which carries the inscription given above. His house there overlooked the cemetery and included furnishings from the very room in l'Hôtel d'Europe where she had died and where Mill had spent the day with her corpse. He would be buried with her upon his own death on May 8, 1873. The story of their love and collaboration is rivaled, in the history of utilitarianism, only by that of Godwin and Wollstonecraft.

It would be a mistake to suppose that the sentiments that Mill had inscribed on her tomb were simply the result of his extreme grief at her passing. In a little diary that he kept in 1854, an experiment in trying to record a decent thought a day, many of the entries strike the same note—e.g., "Even the merely intellectual needs of my nature suffice to make me hope that I may never outlive the companion who is the profoundest and most far-sighted and clear-sighted thinker I have ever known, as well as the most consummate in practical wisdom. I do not wish that I were so much her equal as not to be her pupil, but I would gladly be more capable than I am of thoroughly appreciating and worthily reproducing her admirable thoughts."[75] This utter (and reciprocal) commitment to Harriet Taylor would further alienate Mill from his family and old friends, few of whom saw in her what he saw in her. And this would profoundly affect the framing of Mill's biography. Dale Miller notes:

> There is a tradition of thinking that, in essence, he was psychologically unable to resist her charms. According to Bain, it was commonly held among their contemporaries that "she imbibed all his views, and gave them back in her own form, by which he was flattered and pleased" (1882, 173). Ruth Borchard says that "Accustomed by training and experience to the acceptance of ascetic, masculine values, he was completely overpowered by her intensely feminine atmosphere" (1957, 46). And Laski speculates: "I should guess that she was a comfortable and sympathetic person and that Mill, brought up to fight Austin, Praed, Macaulay and Grote, had never met a really soft cushion before" (op. cit.). Some writers have even advanced the idea that after the death of his domineering father James, Mill felt a need to invent another parental authority in order that he might submit to it (e.g., Trilling 1952, 118; Mazlish 1975, 286–91).[76]

Trying to strike something of a middle course between the friends and foes of Harriet Taylor Mill, Miller ends up striking much the same note at Bain:

> Bain knew Mill extremely well, and even though he says that his friend was under "an extraordinary hallucination as to the personal qualities of his wife," and "outraged all reasonable credibility in describing her matchless genius," he is also adamant not only that Mill "was not such an egoist as to be captivated by the echo of his own opinions" but also that he would only have been stimulated by someone with "independent resources" who had a "good mutual understanding as to the proper conditions of the problem at issue" (1882, 173–4).[77]

The evidence, Miller states, may be insufficient to ever render her anything less than "an essentially contested figure in the history of philosophy."

No doubt the evidence could be better, and the loss of much of the original manuscript material in this case (Taylor Mill's, some of it destroyed during the Second World War) has been problematic. The story has largely been told by those who were hostile to her. As Jo Ellen Jacobs has observed, "Harriet has been labeled

*a 'philosopher in petticoats';
*'one of the meanest and dullest ladies in literary history, a monument of nasty self-regard, as lacking in charm as in grandeur';
*a 'tempestuous' 'shrew';
*'a female autocrat';
*a 'domineering, . . . perverse and selfish, invalid woman';
*a 'vain and vituperative, proud and petulant' masochist;
*a 'very clever, imaginative, passionate, intense, imperious, paranoid, unpleasant woman.'

Harriet has been branded everything short of Wicked Witch of the West by John's biographers and historians of philosophy."[78]

In fact, and very problematically, "Virtually all that has been written about Harriet Taylor Mill focuses on her relationship with John Stuart Mill, and nearly all of these remarks have been vitriolic and uninsightful."[79] It is, in short, astonishing how rarely her own voice ever gets heard in the swirl of acrimony that has enveloped her ever since she became close to Mill.

Jacobs and other recent feminist literary critics, historians, and philosophers have gone far to correct this situation, though it must be owned that there is still much to correct. Although open condemnation of Taylor Mill is much less common these days, polite dismissal or avoidance remain popular means of downplaying her importance. She is scarcely mentioned at all in such works as *The Cambridge Companion to John Stuart Mill*, and she somehow seems to get slighted even by those apparently sympathetic to Mill's feminism. Bertrand Russell, who had an unbounded admiration for *On Liberty* and *The Subjection of Women*, deeming them much more valuable than Mill's *Logic*, could nonetheless explain of Mill that "morals and intellect were perpetually at war in his thought, morals being incarnate in Mrs. Taylor and intellect in his father. If the one was too soft, the other was too harsh." And although he credited her with improving the treatment of socialism in *The Principles of Political Economy*—an influence lamented by Michael St. John Packe—he is only willing to allow that "what Mrs. Taylor did for him in this respect was to enable him to think what his own nature led him to think, as opposed to what he had been taught."[80] Such views are still quite widespread, and even the best of recent biographies of Mill, those of Capaldi and Reeve, though big improvements, suggest that the right interpretation has yet to be framed.

That Taylor Mill was a sharp, creative, radical and independent thinker, the author of *The Enfranchisement of Women* and various works critical of conventional marriage, domestic violence, and other deeply problematic social practices, should be fairly obvious, despite the fact that her *Complete Works* only got published in 1998.[81] And that somehow she and Mill came to think of themselves as achieving their highest happiness through a form of collaborative partnership, the play of mind on mind, is also obvious enough. These facts should form the baseline for any additional assessment of their relationship or its significance. As Jacobs suggests in her introduction to Taylor Mill's *Complete Works*:

> After reading more than 500 pages of her writing collected in this volume, readers will not replace the myth of 'the overbearing shrew who bewitched poor dear John Stuart Mill' with a myth of 'the martyr genius woman who was the source of all the important ideas John published as his own.' The truth lies somewhere in the murky middle. Harriet Taylor Mill was a complex woman who composed a complicated life involving three children; an estranged husband, John Taylor; and a man she loved passionately and with whom she collaborated intellectually, John Stuart Mill. Finding a way to construct such a life took consummate skill in a society that disallowed divorce, prevented married women from maintaining financial independence, and discouraged women from obtaining a liberal arts education.[82]

Indeed. And consequently one can be forgiven for thinking that the combination of the life and the work should lean one more toward the martyred genius side.

Their first meeting may well have been the culmination of various social intrigues. Mill was active socially in London, having joined the new Athenaeum club and various salons, and he had grown closer to the Unitarian circle of the Rev. William Fox (editor of *The Monthly Repository*), a very advanced group that included such members as the feminist Harriet Martineau, the Flowers sisters Sarah and Eliza, and the poet Robert Browning. Of his first meeting with Harriet, in the heady year of 1830, when he was greatly enthused by the revolutionary events in France, Capaldi speculates that:

> Fox had introduced Mill to Harriet supposedly in order to help Harriet find intellectual stimulation that she could not find at home. 'He told her that John Mill was the man among the human race to relieve in a competent manner her dubieties and difficulties.' We do know from Roebuck, who was present, that 'Mrs. Taylor was much taken with Mill.' But there was more to this meeting. Before his meeting with Harriet, Mill had been attracted to Eliza Flower, who was three years older than he. They shared a common passion for music. Mill proposed to Eliza but was refused, allegedly because '[s]he was the spouse of her art, consecrated to its ideal.' What we do know is that Eliza was

in love with the married Fox. It is plausible to suggest that Fox may have arranged the meeting between Mill and Harriet Taylor not only to help Mrs. Taylor but also to distract Mill with another highly attractive person.[83]

The reports do suggest that Mill, at that first meeting, was more interested in talking with Eliza Flower, but that changed quickly. The *Autobiography* claims that "it was years after my introduction to Mrs. Taylor before my acquaintance with her became at all intimate or confidential," but most of Mill's biographers hold that there is evidence to "suggest that the relationship moved beyond that of mere friendship rather more quickly."[84] Among other things, when Harriet explained the new friendship to her husband, he initially forbade her to ever see Mill again, leading to some expressions of heartbreak on both sides. But somehow, for some reason, things were righted, and

> [b]y the autumn of 1832, contact had been re-established. An awkward modus vivendi evolved. Mill was now living with his family in Vicarage Place, Church Street, Kensington, where he would remain until he finally married Harriet twenty years later. However, he was permitted to dine with Harriet at the Taylor's home at least two or three times a week—although only in the company of others—and on these evenings John Taylor would go out to his club. John Taylor bought a country house for Harriet at Keston Heath, Kent, where she spent most of her time; a few years later she relocated to Walton-upon-Thames. Taylor visited her in Kent for the occasional weekend; Mill was there for the majority of the others.[85]

Just why this tolerant arrangement evolved as it did is hard to decipher. On one view, advanced by Jo Ellen Jacobs, Harriet, who had by this point had three children (two sons and her daughter Helen) by John Taylor, was now suffering from syphilis, a condition that kept her from sexual relations with either her husband or John and might well have motivated her husband's acquiescence in her living apart and collaborating in the way that she did. It might also explain some of her physical disabilities, which included periods of partial paralysis, numbing, disequilibrium, etc., in addition to the coughing that came of her tuberculosis. Others think it likely that, as Mill himself claimed, they remained Platonic friends to avoid scandal so long as Harriet was still married to Taylor. Capaldi sees no reason to deny that they consummated their marriage when it was finally possible, not that either had any scruples about extramarital infidelity in and of itself.[86] In any event, the ardor of their correspondence certainly suggests extraordinary passion of some sort. Mill had apparently, in the summer of 1833, written her a very candid note (now lost), to which she responded: "I am glad that you have said it—I am *happy* that you have. . . . Yes, these circumstances do require greater strength than any other—the greatest—that which you have, & which if you had not I should never have loved you and would not love you now."[87]

And it was not long before Mill would be publishing works sounding tones of joint inspiration. Although she had begun writing in 1826 (a work on Caxton and the history of printing), her output increased dramatically in the early 1830s, on topics that were also of interest to Mill. His 1832 article on "Genius" maintained that it, genius, was a matter of originality, autonomy, of the self-direction and independence of thought that made for character and would later figure so famously in *On Liberty*. A piece by her from just before this had condemned conformity in much the same terms. They were apparently already thinking together on the ideas that would later go into *On Liberty*. Mill's "Civilization" also reflected their joint outlook, as much as did his crisis.

It is true that the first formal, fulsome published announcement of their literary collaboration was posthumous, and came in the 1859 dedication to *On Liberty*: "Like all that I have written for many years, it belongs as much to her as to me; but the work as it stands has had, in a very insufficient degree, the inestimable advantage of her revision; some of the most important portions having been reserved for a more careful re-examination, which they are now never destined to receive. Were I but capable of interpreting to the world one half the great thoughts and noble feelings which are buried in her grave, I should be the medium of a greater benefit to it, than is ever likely to arise from anything that I can write, unprompted and unassisted by her all but unrivalled wisdom."[88] But as indicated, their close collaboration seems to have begun very soon after their first meeting, and there was nothing secretive about it, despite Harriet's marriage to Taylor, a wholesale pharmacist whose family had been neighbors to the Mills. Michael St. John Packe, noting that Mill privately "hated his father's house, removed everything of himself that was of any value, and slammed the door behind him," explains:

> With Harriet all this was different, for her society was not imposed but freely chosen. His view of her was not the twisted, stunted view he had of his own family, but a whole view suddenly come upon, and freshen- ingly unfamiliar. Her mind was expanding, reaching eagerly for knowl- edge and for the best ways to apply it. The atmosphere of her coteries was as a lumber room of liberalism, and she was busy sorting. Mill admired the sureness of her grip as she flung aside all that was vague or sentimental, saving out only those things with the hard bright luster of vitality. There was, too, the sharpness of her wit, that now and then would leave him breathless at its point and daring, and its reverse side, the quick flash of anger in defence of her beliefs, not held tentatively as he held his, but jealously possessed as though she lived by them. This incisiveness, this appearance of being constantly embattled, was in vivid contrast to her femininity, to her fragile body, sloping shoulders,

fine white throat, and huge dark eyes, and it delighted him. For even when she talked with greatest earnestness, and he listened solemnly and with attention, he was lapped about by her aura of delicacy, of repose, and of warm intuitive sympathy, the essence of her feminine nature. Over all her excitement, whether playful or intense, brooded the stillness of her dignity, drawing her together, adding balance to her liveliness. Looking at her, with her hair put up in a Greek knob with a few scattered curls coming out beneath the comb, his mind went singing off into the vision of Athenian days that was his heaven.[89]

But Packe continues in a curious vein, explaining, "Not that he consciously saw her as a woman," since he "was too fastidious for a physical approach." Rather, he saw her as "his companion spirit; and companion spirits are traditionally sexless." In Mill's words:

> But the women, of all I have known, who possessed the highest measure of what are considered feminine qualities, have combined with them more of the highest *masculine* qualities than I have ever seen in but one or two men, and those one or two men were also in many respects almost women. I suspect it is the second-rate people of the two sexes that are unlike. The first rate are alike in both—except—no, I do not think I can except anything—but then, in this respect, my position has been and is, what you say every human being's is in many respects, 'a peculiar one.'[90]

The charges that Mill might have been somehow lacking in "manly fiber," and thus easily able to abide a Platonic relationship for so many years, have also been long-standing. To some, he seemed a vaguely androgynous figure, not someone capable of posing a masculine sexual threat. Jacobs put it this way: "Contemporaries of John's mocked his condition and called him undersexed. Carlyle's biographer said of Mill, '[T]hey who ignore [sex] suffer,' and suggested that 'doctors might agree he should marry or take a mistress and quit Mrs. Taylor.' Leslie Stephen quipped that John's feelings 'were . . . as tender as a woman's. They were wanting, not in keenness, but in the massiveness which implies more masculine fibre. . . . . . John's sensuality was not adequate, according to John's contemporaries. To be a real man, John needed sexual intercourse."[91]

John's accounts of what he needed were more apt to emphasize Harriet and the poetry of Shelley than manly fiber, though the language of manliness certainly does figure in his work, especially in condemnation of the upper classes, who in his view lacked manly independence of thought. He was also given, however, to a keen sense of the value of care and caring, as part of the active life of happiness. As the diary has it, in words reminiscent of Godwin's on Wollstonecraft:

What a sense of protection is given by the consciousness of being loved, and what an additional sense, over and above this, by being near the one by whom one is and wishes to be loved the best. I have experience at present of both these things; for I feel as if no really dangerous illness could actually happen to me while I have her to care for me; and yet I feel as if by coming away from her I had parted with a kind of talisman, and was more open to the attacks of the enemy than while I was with her.[92]

Jacobs, in her imaginative reproduction of a diary by Taylor Mill based on the existing evidence, includes two passages that are deeply suggestive of how this collaborative partnership played out the refounding of utilitarianism:

Critics of Bentham accuse him of promoting self-interest, but he does not promote selfishness. The 'Greatest Happiness of the greatest number' is the very opposite of personal selfishness. I certainly agree with Bentham that all creatures desire their own happiness. Yet, in considering others' happiness, we must also consider our own. If we do not count our own interest, we shall not have the strength which wd enable us to do much good even for others. Selflessness is the kind of virtue society tries to instill in women. (Men tend to be hypocrites on this score, since they are allowed some freedom for their own desires, while women wound their wings at every attempt to expand them against their gilded bars.)

After Bentham died, we began talking about the strengths and weaknesses in Bentham's ethics. I wrote a few paragraphs labeled 'Some Uses of the Word Selfish Selfishness & Sentimentality.' I see that some of my ideas appear in John's new article on Bentham. I pointed out the distinction between 'self-interest' and 'selfishness.' John expresses my idea so eloquently when he says that Bentham 'by no means intended by this assertion to impute universal selfishness to mankind. . . . He distinguished two kinds of interests, the self-regarding and the social.' John also writes about the metaphysical shortcomings of Bentham's ideas in ways first drafted by me.

We seem to have stumbled onto a good method of collaboration. First we talk; then sometimes I write a very rough paragraph or two. Then we continue our conversation until John feels ready to write out our ideas.

We are both convinced that we advance intellectually by dialogue—not confrontation of opposing views. We honestly attempt to understand and incorporate the truth of another's position. Likewise, we are improved morally by surrounding ourselves by other honorable people. Or, as John wrote in this article, 'It is by a sort of sympathetic contagion, or inspiration, that a noble mind assimilated other minds to itself; and no one was ever inspired by one whose own inspiration was not sufficient to give him faith in the possibility of making others feel what *he* feels.'[93]

In fact, Taylor Mill's writings do very much support this literary reconstruction, as do Mill's writings. And such an Apostolic dialogical partnership proved
in the 40s to be dynamic in the extreme, with Mill confessing in his diary:

> Whenever I look back at any of my own writings of two or three years
> previous, they seem to me like the writings of some stranger whom I
> have seen and known long ago. I wish that my acquisition of power
> to do better had kept pace with the continual elevation of my stand-
> ing point and change of my bearings towards all the great subjects of
> thought. But the explanation is that I owe the enlargement of my ideas
> and feelings to her influence, and that she could not in the same degree
> give me powers of execution.[94]

What was the direction of the dynamic? It would seem that it ran along the
lines already indicated, but with a decided tilt toward an enhanced emphasis
on socialism and the working class. Taylor Mill was deeply involved with *The
Principles of Political Economy*, and assessments of the nature of her contribution vary depending on one's political orientation. Plausibly, she helped
transform the work over the course of its various editions, rendering it a much
more radical work than Mill would have produced left to his own devices. As
Mill put it, those "parts of my writings and especially of the *Political Economy*
which contemplate possibilities in the future such as, when affirmed by Socialists, have in general been fiercely denied by political economists, would, but
for her, either have been absent, or the suggestions would have been made
much more timidly and in a more qualified form."[95]

To be sure, Mill had been working on the subject of political economy since
before he was even a teenager. His early work on this subject was especially intense, both when he was helping with his father's *Political Economy*, and when
he was engaged with the much-beloved David Ricardo, who at one time was
practically his personal tutor. It is therefore scarcely surprising that Mill's first
true book, written in 1830–31, was *Some Unsettled Questions in Political Economy*, which was not however published until after the success of his *Logic*.
This is to say that he worked on political economy intermittently throughout
his life, returning to the subject again at the very end, with his "Chapters on
Socialism," which Helen Taylor, the daughter who had lived with Harriet and
then with Mill, would publish after his death.

And in this area, the trajectory of his thought is quite clear and consistent,
and considerably indebted to Taylor Mill. By 1846, they were going public as
coauthors on various pieces, and very much working together on the *Principles*. As the *Autobiography* allows:

> The first of my books in which her share was conspicuous was the *Prin-
> ciples of Political Economy*. The *System of Logic* owed little to her except
> in the minuter matters of composition, in which respect my writings,

both great and small, have largely benefitted by her accurate and clear-sighted criticism. The chapter of the *Political Economy* which has had a greater influence on opinion than all the rest, that on "the Probable Future of the Labouring Classes," is entirely due to her: in the first draft of the book, that chapter did not exist. She pointed out the need of such a chapter, and the extreme imperfection of the book without it: she was the cause of my writing it; and the more general part of the chapter, the statement and discussion of the two opposite theories respecting the proper condition of the laboring classes, was wholly an exposition of her thoughts, often in words taken from her own lips. The purely scientific part of the *Political Economy* I did not learn from her; but it was chiefly her influence that gave to the book that general tone by which it is distinguished from all previous expositions of Political Economy that had any pretension to being scientific, and which has made it so useful in conciliating minds which those previous expositions had repelled. This tone consisted chiefly in making the proper distinction between the laws of the production of Wealth, which are real laws of nature, dependent on the properties of objects, and the modes of its Distribution, which, subject to certain conditions, depend on human will. The common run of political economists confuse these together, under the designation of economic laws, which they deem incapable of being defeated or modified by human effort; ascribing the same necessity to things dependent on the unchangeable conditions of our earthly existence, and to those which, being but the necessary consequences of particular social arrangement, are merely coextensive with these. Given certain institutions and customs, wages, profits, and rent will be determined by certain causes; but this class of political economists drop the indispensable presupposition, and argue that these causes must by an inherent necessity, against which no human means can avail, determine the shares which fall, in the division of the produce, to labourers, capitalists, and landlords.[96]

This was surely a very important influence on a matter that was as central to Mill's being (and to utilitarianism) as any. What is more, Mill might for once have been underestimating the impact of Taylor Mill. As Jacobs records, the "original manuscript indicated that Harriet made penciled changes—most accepted, but some rejected by John," and that the results were not only the more radical and provocative parts of the book, but also its feminism:

> *Principles of Political Economy* was recognized as the first book of its kind to attend to women's economic concerns and to view women as autonomous agents. For the first time, a book considered the question of why women's wages are lower than men's. The authors attacked Adam Smith's belief in the division of labor. The efficiency of repetitive

work that Smith argued for was based on men's industrial labor, not on women's work experiences. Harriet and John countered that due to customary training, not to natural ability, women were able and even delighted to move rapidly from one type of work to another. . . . Only by ignoring women's experience do theorists make such errors.[97]

That Taylor Mill could have infused with this significance a work that, however competent, was all too often an unoriginal synthesis of the classical political economy of the Philosophical Radicals, especially Ricardo, is in itself a remarkable achievement, something that continues to make this work stand out. Even later neoclassical economics would have a very difficult time dealing with gender issues, treating households as unified economic actors in a fashion that should have died out with James Mill. That John Stuart and Harriet Taylor Mill worked together to produce the first major treatise in political economy that seriously considered issues of gender is a fact of extraordinary significance.

Moreover, the actual content of Taylor Mill's contribution is still more significant, marking the formulation of a set of socialist concerns of enduring value. Mill would write to her, "I cannot persuade myself that you do not greatly overrate the ease of making people unselfish," but she obviously felt that on this he was still too much under the influence of the Benthamites.[98] The chapter on "The Probable Futurity of the Labouring Classes" comes just after another, "Of the Stationary State," and together these arguably form the most original part of the book, providing the fuel for later reinterpretations of Mill as anticipating some aspects of environmental economics with its critique of growth. Just how far Mill had moved from a crude Malthusian outlook is evident in the following famous passage:

There is room in the world, no doubt, and even in old countries, for a great increase of population, supposing the arts of life to go on improving, and capital to increase. But even if innocuous, I confess I see very little reason for desiring it. The density of population necessary to enable mankind to obtain, in the greatest degree, all the advantages both of co-operation and of social intercourse, has, in all the most populous countries, been attained. A population may be too crowded, though all be amply supplied with food and raiment. It is not good for man to be kept perforce at all times in the presence of his species. A world from which solitude is extirpated, is a very poor ideal. Solitude, in the sense of being often alone, is essential to any depth of meditation or of character; and solitude in the presence of natural beauty and grandeur, is the cradle of thoughts and aspirations which are not only good for the individual, but which society could ill do without. Nor is there much satisfaction in contemplating the world with nothing left to the spontaneous activity of nature; with every rood of land brought into cultivation, which is capable of growing food for human beings; every flowery waste or natural pasture ploughed up, all quadrupeds or birds which are not domesticated for man's use exterminated as rivals for food, every hedgerow or superfluous tree rooted out, and scarcely a place left where a wild shrub or flower could grow without being eradicated as a weed in the name of improved agriculture. If the earth must lose that great portion of its pleasantness which it owes to things that the unlimited increase of wealth and population would extirpate from it, for the mere purpose of enabling it to support a larger, but not a better or a happier population, I sincerely hope, for the sake of posterity, that they will be content to be stationary, long before necessity compels them to it.[99]

Obviously, Mill did not appreciate that there might be a conflict between this view and a "Total View" form of utilitarianism, according to which the principle of utility could rationalize an enormous population increase of lives barely worth living, if that made for more total happiness in the world. His mind was too obsessed with the dangers of overpopulation, the Malthusian dangers of a world with an enormous population of lives not worth living, plagued by famine and disease. To be sure, as with Bentham, natural beauty was one of his deepest sources of pleasure. But as Winch has insightfully argued, "Mill's environmental interests not only predate Wordsworth's influence, they have a deeper and decidedly unromantic provenance as well: they derive directly from the neo-Malthusian anxieties. . . . Reconciling Wordsworth with Malthus—reconciling a romantic ecology with one based squarely on political economy—was not, at first sight, an easy task. But it is not a bad short description of what Mill achieved as an environmentalist."[100]

The following chapter, the one singled out as Harriet Taylor's work, in fact begins with the line that the "observations in the preceding chapter had for their principal object to deprecate a false ideal of human society. Their applicability to the practical purposes of present times, consists in moderating the inordinate importance attached to the mere increase of production, and fixing attention upon improved distribution, and a large remuneration of labour, as the two desiderata. Whether the aggregate produce increases absolutely or not, is a thing in which, after a certain amount has been obtained, neither the legislator nor the philanthropist need feel any strong interest; but, that it should increase relatively to the number of those who share in it, is of the utmost possible importance; and this, (whether the wealth of mankind be stationary, or increasing at the most rapid rate ever known in an old country,) must depend on the opinions and habits of the most numerous class, the class of manual labourers."[101]

The upshot, then, which one would not quite anticipate from earlier parts of the book mainly concerned with economic efficiency, especially in the first edition, is that the fixation on economic growth is lamentable and the crucial question going forward is how the results of production are to be distributed. Moreover, the "working classes have taken their interests into their own hands, and are perpetually showing that they think the interests of their employers not identical with their own, but opposite to them. Some among the higher classes flatter themselves that these tendencies may be counteracted by moral and religious education: but they have let the time go by for giving an education which can serve their purpose." The growth of literacy and dissent and organization have changed everything, such that whatever "advice, exhortation, or guidance is held out to the laboring classes, must henceforth be tendered to them as equals, and accepted by them with their eyes open. The prospect of the future depends on the degree in which they can be made rational beings."[102]

It is important to stress at this juncture that the Millian political economy defended by many of Mill's disciples, such as Henry and Millicent Garrett Fawcett, was profoundly committed to improving the condition of the laboring class, and this in a way that marked an important break from earlier and more Malthusian political economists. The great spectre that hung over the effort, according to so many recent commentators as well as earlier ones, was the grim Malthusian one of workers who multiplied with every improvement in their conditions and thus undid their gains in part by flooding the market with more cheap labor. The narrower, more technical version of this was encapsulated in the Wages-Fund theory, which Mill described and rejected in his "Thornton on Labour and Its Claims":

> The theory rests on what may be called the doctrine of the wages fund. There is supposed to be, at any given instant, a sum of wealth, which is not regarded as unalterable, for it is augmented by saving, and increases with the progress of wealth; but it is reasoned upon as at any given moment a predetermined amount. More than that amount it is assumed that the wages-receiving class cannot possibly divide among them; that amount, and no less, they cannot but obtain. So that, the sum to be divided being fixed, the wages of each depend solely on the divisor, the number of participants. In this doctrine it is by implication affirmed, that the demand for labour not only increases with the cheapness, but increases in exact proportion to it, the same aggregate sum being paid for labour whatever its price may be."[103]

Against any such supposed "law," Mill argues forcefully:

> What is true is, that wages might be so high as to leave no profit to the capitalist, or not enough to compensate him for the anxieties and risks of trade; and in that case labourers would be killing the goose to get at the eggs. And, again, wages might be so low as to diminish the numbers or impair the working powers of the labourers, and in that case

the capitalist also would generally be a loser. But between this and the doctrine, that the money which would come to the labourer by a rise of wages will be of as much use to him in the capitalist's pocket as in his own, there is a considerable difference.

Between the two limits just indicated—the highest wages consistent with keeping up the capital of the country, and increasing it pari passu with the increase of people, and the lowest that will enable the labourers to keep up their numbers with an increase sufficient to provide labourers for the increase of employment—there is an intermediate region within which wages will range higher or lower according to what Adam Smith calls "the higgling of the market." In this higgling, the labourer in an isolated condition, unable to hold out even against a single employer, much more against the tacit combination of employers, will, as a rule, find his wages kept down at the lower limit. Labourers sufficiently organised in Unions may, under favourable circumstances, attain to the higher. This, however, supposes an organisation including all classes of labourers, manufacturing and agricultural, unskilled as well as skilled. When the union is only partial, there is often a nearer limit—that which would destroy, or drive elsewhere, the particular branch of industry in which the rise takes place. Such are the limiting conditions of the strife for wages between the labourers and the capitalists. The superior limit is a difficult question of fact, and in its estimation serious errors may be, and have been, committed. But, having regard to the greatly superior numbers of the labouring class, and the inevitable scantiness of the remuneration afforded by even the highest rate of wages which, in the present state of the arts of production, could possibly become general; whoever does not wish that the labourers may prevail, and that the highest limit, whatever it be, may be attained, must have a standard of morals, and a conception of the most desirable state of society, widely different from those of either Mr. Thornton or the present writer.[104]

The Fawcetts cautiously followed Mill, as did Henry Sidgwick, whose *Principles of Political Economy* was emphatic in rejecting the Malthusian vision.

Still, the progress of the laboring classes was not, for the Mills or their followers, best achieved through the mobilization of collective bargaining power or strikes, or by employing conventional means of poor relief. Rather, they took to theorizing and advocating on behalf of the cooperative movement, a force they adopted nearly as soon as it first appeared on the historical scene in England, with the weavers of the Rochdale Pioneers. As Henry Fawcett put it, following Mill:

During the last few years, the rapid extension of cooperative institutions has excited as much attention as trades-unions and strikes. In the

last chapter we had to refer to much that was unsatisfactory and distressing; we, however, discuss the subject of the present chapter with
unmixed pleasure, because we believe that wherever the principle of co-
operation is carried into practical effect, the labourers enjoy a far more
favourable distribution of wealth, and that this advantage is moreover
secured to them without the slightest suspicion of the least injustice
having been inflicted on any other class.[105]

Citing the Rochdale Pioneers as an outstanding, though not entirely problem
free, example, Fawcett extolled the virtues of the cooperative movement at
length:

The advantages which the working classes derive from a cooperative
store are very apparent. In the first place, it provides them with the
most eligible investment for their savings. This is most important, because the absence of good opportunities for investing small savings
acts most powerfully to increase the improvidence of the poor. Even
the middle and upper classes, whose superior education gives them
prudence and foresight, are very much influenced in the amount they
save by the profit which they believe would be realized on their capital. Hitherto the savings'-bank has been the only investment which, as
a general rule, has been open to the working man. Now the ordinary
English labourer must make many severe sacrifices to save 50£, and if
this amount is placed in the savings'-bank, the labourer obtains an annuity not exceeding thirty shillings a year, as his reward for self-denial
and prudence. If old age or sickness compels him to cease work, his
position is scarcely improved at all by the money which he had saved. If
he had been improvident, and saved nothing, he would have received
parish allowance; but the poor-law guardians perform their duty when
they grant just sufficient relief to enable a man to live; the labourer,
therefore, who possesses an annuity of thirty shillings a year will obtain
from his parish, if he requires relief, thirty shillings a year less than the
man who has recklessly spent everything that he has received. Under
these combined discouragements, it is not surprising that our laboring classes have been extremely improvident. No laboring man, in fact,
has ever had definitely placed before him the prospect that he would
be able himself to employ his savings as capital, and enjoy the profits arising therefrom. Our labourers, therefore, could never be cheered
with the hope of improving their social position, for they must have
seen that at least 99 out of every 100 of those whose parents are hired
labourers, always remain in the same condition. Now it is evident that,
as far as the investment of money is concerned, such cooperative stores
as those we have described afford the laboring classes opportunities for
obtaining profits which they never possessed before. We shall moreover

presently show, that the cooperative principle, when applied to trade and manufactures, enables the labourer to support his industry with his own capital, and in this manner to rise from the mere status of a hired labourer. The figures we have already quoted sufficiently prove the eligible nature of the investment which is provided by a well-managed cooperative store . . . .[106]

Poverty, Fawcett and other Millians urged, could not ultimately be eliminated "as long as the labourer simply works for hire. . . . If the efficiency of labour is to be maintained, and if England is to continue to grow in wealth, happiness, and prosperity, the labourers must participate in the profits yielded by their industry."[107] But poverty could, to a degree the Malthusians never realized, be eliminated.

Of course, the improvement in social intelligence will be achieved through many educational means, including public lectures, Working Men's Colleges, etc. But even so, the chief hope is for an even more comprehensive overcoming of domination and exploitative dependence. "The same reasons which make it no longer necessary that the poor should depend on the rich, make it equally unnecessary that women should depend on men; and the least which justice requires is that law and custom should not enforce dependence (when the correlative protection has become superfluous) by ordaining that a woman, who does not happen to have a provision by inheritance, shall have scarcely any means open to her of gaining a livelihood, except as a wife and mother."[108] And more generally still,

if public spirit, generous sentiments, or true justice and equality are desired, association, not isolation, of interests, is the school in which these excellences are nurtured. The aim of improvement should be not solely to place human beings in a condition in which they will be able to do without one another, but to enable them to work with or for one another in relations not involving dependence. Hitherto there has been no alternative for those who lived by their labour, but that of laboring either each for himself alone, or for a master. But the civilizing and improving influences of association, and the efficiency and economy of production on a large scale, may be obtained without dividing the producers into two parties with hostile interests and feelings, the many who do the work being mere servants under the command of the one who supplies the funds, and having no interest of their own in the enterprise except to earn their wages with as little labour as possible. The speculations and discussions of the last fifty years, and the events of the last thirty, are abundantly conclusive on this point.[109]

The larger solution, that is, lies in the cooperative movement, which calls for an "association of the labourers themselves on terms of equality, collectively owning the capital with which they carry on their operations, and working under managers elected and removable by themselves." The success of this movement to date had been such that "the ideas sown by Socialist writers, of an emancipation of labour to be effected by means of association, throve and fructified; and many working people came to the resolution, not only that they would work for one another, instead of working for a master tradesman or manufacturer, but that they would also free themselves, at whatever cost of labour or privation, from the necessity of paying, out of the produce of their industry, a heavy tribute for the use of capital; that they would extinguish this tax, not by robbing the capitalists of what they or their predecessors had acquired by labour and preserved by economy, but by honestly acquiring capital for themselves."[110]

The revolution would be bloodless, but nonetheless quite real and, in fact, quite productive, since there would be a "vast stimulus given to productive energies, by placing the labourers, as a mass, in a relation to their work which would make it their principle and their interest—at present it is neither—to do the utmost, instead of the least possible." The main dissent from Socialist writers concerns the issue of competition, which can take beneficial forms— "They forget that wherever competition is not, monopoly is; and that monopoly, in all its forms, is the taxation of the industrious for the support of indolence, if not of plunder. They forget, too, that with the exception of competition among labourers, all other competition is for the benefit of the labourers, by cheapening the articles they consume. . . . Besides, if association were universal, there would be no competition between labourer and labourer; and that between association and association would be for the benefit of the consumers, that is, of the associations; of the industrious classes generally." "To be protected against competition is to be protected in idleness, in mental dullness; to be saved the necessity of being as active and as intelligent as other people"—Socialism, contra the Socialists, needs no such protection.

It is a remarkable vision, and gives the *Principles* such verve and uplift as it has. Maurice liked the chapter on the futurity of the working class so much that he wanted to reprint it separately for the Christian Socialists, the influential movement for a spiritual, antimaterialistic form of Socialism based on brotherly love. Millian Socialism was similarly committed to using competition in a way compatible with cooperation and fellow feeling, even if it tended to emphasize self-help on the part of the working class rather than dependence on government aid. In any event, the contrast between these sections and other parts of the book was at its starkest in the first edition, and a more radical sympathy with Socialist concerns grew with every subsequent edition, buoyed by further political developments in Europe, such as the year of revolutions, 1848. But also of note is the concluding chapter, "Of the Grounds and Limits of the *Laisser-Faire* or Non-Interference Principle." The fundamental themes of *On Liberty* are already evident here—albeit somewhat out of place—in such passages as the following:

There is a part of the life of every person who has come to years of discretion, within which the individuality of that person ought to reign uncontrolled either by any other individual or by the public collectively. That there is, or ought to be, some space in human existence thus entrenched around, and sacred from authoritative intrusion, no one who professes the smallest regard to human freedom or dignity will call in question: the point to be determined is, where the limit should be placed; how large a province of human life this reserved territory should include. I apprehend that it ought to include all that part which concerns only the life, whether inward or outward, of the individual, and does not affect the interests of others, or affects them only through the moral influence of example. With respect to the domain of the inward consciousness, the thought and feelings, and as much of external conduct as is personal only, involving no consequences, none at least of a painful or injurious kind, to other people; I hold that it is allowable in all, and in the more thoughtful and cultivated often a duty, to assert and promulgate, with all the force they are capable of, their opinion of what is good or bad, admirable or contemptible, but not to compel others to conform to that opinion; whether the force used is that of extra-legal coercion, or exerts itself by means of the law. [111]

This does not, of course, mean that there are no "large exceptions" to the principle of laissez faire in economics, which is quite distinct from Mill's liberty principle. Consumers can be "incompetent judges" of the commodities in question, as in the case of education: "The uncultivated cannot be competent judges of cultivation." And there are the matters of protecting children, young persons, and lower animals, and the objectionable "contracts in perpetuity," since the "presumption in favour of individual judgement is only legitimate, where the judgment is grounded on actual, and especially on present, personal experience." And there are cases of "delegated management" and where "public intervention may be necessary to give effect to the wishes of the persons interested," which could involve cases of collective action where people are "unable to give effect to it except by concert, which concert again cannot be effectual unless it receives validity and sanction from the law." The determination of the length of the working day is cited as a case in point, and Mill claims that this is an area that has not received enough attention from economists (which is putting it mildly in the context of the popular mobilizations on behalf of the Factory Acts). Also, acts "done for the benefit of others," as in the case of the Poor Laws, since "it will be admitted to be right that human beings should help one another; and the more so, in proportion to the urgency of the need: and none needs help so urgently as one who is starving. The claim to help, therefore, created by destitution, is one of the strongest which can exist; and there is *prima facie* the amplest reason for making the relief of so extreme an exigency as certain to those who require it, as by any arrangement of society it can be made." Government action may also be "necessary in default of private agency," even when the latter would be better, if it existed. Alas, Mill also expands upon the importance of colonization, as another case of acts done for the benefit of others.[112] He had long been overly impressed by Edward Gibbon Wakefield's case for systematic colonization in Australia and New Zealand: "Mill was an early supporter of these colonization ventures and an active adherent to Wakefield's policies for restricting release of unoccupied land in such colonies and using the proceeds of land sales to subsidise immigration."[113] Indeed, colonization involved "the future and permanent interests of civilization itself."

Thus, to be sure, the Mills did also address the issue of poverty in terms redolent of Bentham's writing on the Poor Laws, though with some key differences and much less speculative extravagance, unless their great faith in the cooperative movement be counted as such. Michael Quinn has summarized the three-way contrast between Bentham, Mill, and Malthus as follows:

> It would clearly be absurd to assert that Mill's views on poor relief were derived solely from the twin influences of Bentham and Malthus. However, there are striking similarities and differences between the three thinkers. All three emphasized the danger involved in severing the necessary connection between the investment of labour and the acquisition of substance. Bentham and Mill alike, but emphatically unlike Malthus, consistently supported the maintenance of the right to relief, funded by taxation, and on the same utilitarian ground that the state should assume responsibility for the prevention of avoidable starvation. Malthus and Mill alike, but emphatically unlike the Bentham of the poor law writings, viewed the operation of the principle of population as a clear and present danger, which threatened to wipe out any possibility of progress in the living standards of the poor. For Mill, the tightening of the conditions of relief by means of the workhouse test, the insistence on labour, and the principle of less eligibility, all found both in Bentham's poor law writings and in the New Poor Law of 1834, reconciled the recognition of a right to relief with such progress. For Mill, that reconciliation would be cemented by the adoption of contraceptive methods to prevent excessive growth in population, a view which would have been happily endorsed by Bentham at any time, but especially in circumstances of population pressure.[114]

It is salubrious to keep such points in mind, given the various ways in which Mill, at least, could seem to be somewhat blind to the burning practical relief actions demanded by poverty, such as the poverty of the Irish famine, and exploitation, as in factory work. Reeve has complained that the "social reformers of the age worried about how to get workers more food, money, leisure and health. Mill worried about how to get them more freedom."[115] Thus, for example, the comments on children and child labor in the *Principles* are disappointing. That said, Mill was not unaware of or unsympathetic to the plight of working children:

> To take an example from the peculiar province of political economy; it is right that children, and young persons not yet arrived at maturity, should be protected, so far as the eye and hand of the state can reach, from being over-worked. Labouring for too many hours in the day, or on work beyond their strength, should not be permitted to them, for if permitted it may always be compelled. Freedom of contract, in the case of children, is but another word for freedom of coercion. Education also, the best which circumstances admit of their receiving, is not a thing which parents or relatives, from indifference, jealousy, or avarice, should have it in their power to withhold.[116]

Still, one would never guess, from such passages, that the various mass mobilizations on behalf of the various Factory Acts limiting child labor and the working day were turning England upside down in the 1830s, with the brilliant orator Richard Oastler, the "King of the Factory Children," exposing the textile industry as "Yorkshire Slavery," and John Brown publishing the horrific *A Memoir of Robert Blincoe*, Blincoe supposedly being the original of Oliver Twist. The truth, as Mill's friend Robert Owen had gone to great lengths to demonstrate, was that children were suffering terribly under the factory system, where they were often worked from eleven to thirteen hours a day, standing for much of it. As Frank Podmore observed in his comprehensive biography of Owen, under "such conditions it was inevitable that the health of the children should deteriorate. . . . It need hardly be said that the children had little energy left to take advantage of the educational opportunities which, as the masters one after another explained to the Committee [of Parliament], were freely offered to them. Some of the employers provided an hour's schooling in the evening, for such as chose to attend after thirteen hours' work in the day."[117] Insofar as it is true that the Mills' efforts to avoid paternalism translated, in these cases, into less support for immediate action, even support that would be justified by the standards set out in the *Principles*, that is of course lamentable as well as baffling.

At any rate, without some understanding of the above points, it is difficult to appreciate the views advanced in *On Liberty* or how they reflected the joint work of John and Harriet. John in fact wanted to add a dedication to the *Principles* honoring Harriet's role in it, but John Taylor objected, and the dedication was only included in a limited set of gift copies. But the *Autobiography* presents a famously clear statement of the evolution of their views:

> In those days I had seen little further than the old school of political economists into the possibilities of fundamental improvement in social

arrangements. Private property, as now understood, and inheritance, appeared to me as to them, the *dernier mot* of legislation: and I looked no further than to mitigating the inequalities consequent on these institutions, by getting rid of primogeniture and entails. The notion that it was possible to go further than this in removing the injustice—for injustice it is, whether admitting of a complete remedy or not—involved in the fact that some are born to riches and the vast majority to poverty, I then reckoned chimerical, and only hoped that by universal education, leading to voluntary restraint on population, the portion of the poor might be made more tolerable. In short, I was a democrat, but not the least of a Socialist. We were now much less democrats than I had been, because so long as education continues to be so wretchedly imperfect, we dreaded the ignorance and especially the selfishness and brutality of the mass: but our ideal of ultimate improvement went far beyond Democracy, and would class us decidedly under the general designation of Socialists. While we repudiated with the greatest energy that tyranny of society over the individual which most Socialistic systems are supposed to involve, we yet looked forward to a time when society will no longer be divided into the idle and the industrious; when the rule that they who do not work shall not eat, will be applied not to paupers only, but impartially to all; when the division of the produce of labour, instead of depending, as in so great a degree it now does, on the accident of birth, will be made by concert on an acknowledged principle of justice; and when it will no longer either be, or be thought to be, impossible for human beings to exert themselves strenuously in procuring benefits which are not to be exclusively their own, but to be shared with the society they belong to. The social problem of the future we considered to be how to unite the greatest individual liberty of action, with a common ownership in the raw material of the globe, and an equal participation of all in the benefits of combined labour.[118]

Of course, as noted, it was precisely this influence of Taylor Mill that has, historically, often been lamented, by Michael St. John Packe, Friedrich Hayek, and many others. But in longer and larger retrospect, it would seem that Taylor Mill was the one who moved Mill more in the direction of Godwin, and of Godwin's son-in-law Shelley, to whose poetry she introduced him, and that it was this very shift that led to the most enduringly valuable works associated with his name. No doubt Mill's crisis did in this way help him formulate a political economy that took extreme care not to reduce all human action to self-interest, much less selfishness. That is, he took scrupulous care to specify that the economic was only one department of life, and however important it may be, was not always the most important department—he took pride in being one of the few logicians and political economists who could appreciate that there was much else to life. Much positive change, the progress of civilization no less, was not, past a certain point, entangled with or dependent upon economic growth. The quality of life, the character of happiness, involved much more. It involved the type of friendship reflected in his relationship with Harriet Taylor.

The Remainder

It is an immense defect in a character to be without lightness. A character which is all lightness can excite neither respect nor sympathy. Seriousness must be the font of all characters worth thinking about. But a certain infusion of the laughing philosopher, even in his least popular form—an openness to that view of things which, showing them on the undignified side, makes any exaggerated care about them seem childish and ridiculous—is a prodigious help towards bearing the evils of life, and I should think has saved many a person from going mad. It is also necessary to the completeness even of the intellect itself. The contemptible side of things is part, though but a part, of the truth of them, and to be incapable of seeing and feeling that part with as much force and clearness as any other—to be blind to that aspect of things which was the only one the Cynics chose to look at—is to be able to see things only by halves. There always seems something stunted about the intellect of those who have no humour, however earnest and enthusiastic, and however highly cultivated, they often are.

—JOHN STUART MILL, *DIARY*

Of all the character traits that one might associate with John Stuart Mill, "lightness" would seem to be among the last. If his intensity was not quite that of a Wittgenstein, it was nonetheless such that few of those who knew him would have taken him to be a "laughing philosopher." For all his thirst for many-sidedness, there were many sides of the human experience that were not open to him, perhaps even less open to him than to Bentham. The human costs of ever seeking the higher, the progressive, the improving, the elevated, the advancing forms of individualism and happiness can often provide the materials for a sense of irony and the absurd, a redeeming lightness, but not in Mill's case. It is not merely that, as Skorupski notes, his ideal would obviously fail to impress "Nietzschean perfectionists, communitarians on the left and right, existentialists, religious searchers after transcendence," etc.[119] Such could be as wanting in lightness as Mill. It is rather his failure to capture the undignified part of life much at all, and even when trying to do so, to marry it to something other than contempt. So much went into self-cultivation and growth that there was little left for simple self-acceptance and the common lot of shared Benthamite pleasures, the pleasures of ordinary people whether abroad or at home.

Perhaps this was in part because of the protective and defensive stance that he and Harriet were forced into by the incessant malign rumor and gossip that their unorthodox lifestyle provoked. Mill grew alienated from his family and most of his old friends, the outstanding exception being John Sterling, whose death from tuberculosis in 1844 was a great blow. Taylor Mill's family, the Hardy line, had always been difficult, and scarcely gave any indication of how their remarkable daughter came to be. At any rate, John, Harriet, and Helen, the child who had lived with her when apart from her husband and to whom she was closest, would form their own small but sacred band, more or less constantly set against what they saw as the darker forces of conformity, mediocrity, and cruelty that in their view pervaded both the political and personal worlds surrounding them. And this is not to mention disease, especially the scourge of tuberculosis, which they all lived in fear of (and a diagnosis of which cast a shadow over the *Autobiography*). Lightness and laughter would be hard won, however great Mill's literary reputation.

And after all, the Mills were so keenly aware of the most gruesome forms of the subjection of women, the brutality of domestic violence and the stupidity of the legal system in the face of it. Their joint (publicly joint) writings on such issues are powerful and moving:

> The great majority of the inhabitants of this and of every country— including nearly the whole of one sex, and all the young of both—are, either by law or by circumstances stronger than the law, subject to some one man's arbitrary will. Every now and then the public are revolted by some disclosure of unspeakable atrocities committed against some of these helpless dependents—while, for every such case which excites notice, hundreds, most of them as bad, pass off in the police reports entirely unobserved; and for one that finds its way, even for that brief instant, into light, we may be assured that not hundreds but thousands are constantly going on in the safety of complete obscurity. If, through the accidental presence of some better-hearted person than these poor creatures are usually surrounded by, complaint is made to a magistrate, the neighbors—persons living in the same house—almost invariably testify, without either repentance or shame, that the same brutalities had gone on for years in their sight or hearing, without their stirring a finger to prevent them. The sufferers themselves are either unable to complain, from youth or ignorance, or they dare not. They know too surely the consequences of either failing or succeeding in a complaint, when the law, after inflicting just enough punishment to excite the thirst of vengeance, delivers back the victim to the tyrant.[120]

And again,

> Not only is education by the course of justice the most efficacious, in its own province, of all kinds of popular education, but it is also one on which there needs be no difference of opinion. Churches and political

parties may quarrel about the teaching of doctrines, but not about the punishment of crimes. There is a diversity of opinion about what is morally good, but there ought to be none about what is atrociously wicked. Whatever else may be included in the education of the people, the very first essential of it is to unbrutalise them; and to this end, all kinds of personal brutality should be seen and felt to be things which the law is determined to put down. The Bill of Mr. Fitzroy is a step in the right direction; but, unless its provisions are strengthened, it will be rather an indication of the wish, than a substantial exercise of the power, to repress one of the most odious forms of human wickedness.[121]

The horrific, graphic detailing of these atrocities, of the wounds inflicted on the victims of such violence, make for chilling reading, and shows the outrage that also brought them together contra their countrymen. That they were not weighed down even more heavily by the force of the brutal opposition that they seemingly witnessed everywhere, among both the uneducated and the educated classes of the supposedly "civilized" countries, is itself amazing.

Under such conditions, Taylor Mill's achievement was singularly remarkable. As Jacobs sums it up:

In the 1840s and early 1850s, Harriet co-authored a number of newspaper articles, despite a near-invalid condition caused by consumption and partial paralysis. During this same period, she completed one chapter of *Principles of Political Economy*, the "Enfranchisement of Women" for the *Westminster Review*, and a pamphlet on a domestic violence bill before parliament. Harriet and John shared ideas about women's rights which they wrote jointly. . . . . In the interval between Taylor's death and Harriet's remarriage, she and JSM collaborated on a number of newspaper articles on domestic violence. Harriet also worked with John on the manuscript that would become "On Liberty," as well as his *Autobiography*, both published after her death in 1858.[122]

And this is not to mention the constant dialogue and conversation, the editing and inspiring. Jacobs is right to stress that Taylor Mill had an admirable breadth of knowledge: "She knew French, German, Italian, Greek, and Latin well enough to insert quotes and phrases in these languages into her informal notes to herself as well as her published works. In addition, Harriet's writing includes quotes from philosophers, poets, novelists, essayists, historians, and thinkers from a dozen different centuries and a half a dozen countries. Harriet read voraciously everything from the daily newspapers to Renaissance histories of Venice to novels by Dickens and George Sand. Her knowledge of women's history is humbling."[123] She was also far more practical than Mill, able to deal with the business side of life with a matter of fact efficiency that was quite beyond him.

It is tempting to think that Mill's best work came in his defense of her, in the life that was reflected in such works as *On Liberty* and the *Autobiography*. And this is a judgment that he probably would have endorsed, given his abiding conviction that to truly understand a philosopher, one must read any given work in the light of all the others and the life. That he owed such views to the ancients, to a vision of philosophy as a way of life, is scarcely something that he would have been concerned to deny.[124]

At any rate, they were at last married, on April 21st, 1851, "in Melcombe Regis, Dorset . . . by the registrar. Their witnesses, and only audience, were Helen and Algernon Taylor. 'No one ever was to be more congratulated than I am,' Mill wrote to his little sister Anna."[125] Harriet had been duly attentive to John Taylor during his final illness, and they had waited a decent interval before enjoying whatever form of consummation the marriage offered.

Much of the rest of the story of the Mills has already been told, albeit obliquely. Such works as *On Liberty, The Subjection of Women, Utilitarianism,* and "Chapters on Socialism," as well as "Three Essays on Religion," were still to come, though the story that they tell was already foreshadowed in the *Principles* and in their earlier collaborations, such as the writings on domestic violence, and Taylor Mill's notes on the higher pleasures, the dangers of conformity, self-interest v. selfishness, etc. Needless to say, John and Harriet saw no inconsistency in these various efforts. The utilitarian program simply was best realized by the open society celebrated in *On Liberty* in conjunction with the equality and justice highlighted in *The Subjection of Women* and "Chapters on Socialism." Nor was humanity to be denied such hope for theism as rational argument might allow, in its limitations and indeterminacy, though there was of course no need for recourse to capital R Rationalism or capital I Intuitionism, the great supports of traditionalism, the great bars to progress. Rational hope, however, extends in the main only to harboring some beliefs about the probable design of the universe by some form of intelligence, not to most of the component parts of traditional religion. Thus, "It seems to me not only possible but probable, that in a higher, and, above all, a happier condition of human life, not annihilation but immortality may be the burdensome idea; and that human nature, though pleased with the present, and by no means impatient to quit it, would find comfort and not sadness in the thought that it is not chained through eternity to a conscious existence which it cannot be assured that it will always wish to preserve."[126]

Indeed, it is only by framing these later works in a larger context, both textual and historical, that they can be appreciated in anything like a judicious way. *On Liberty* admittedly does not speak to matters of economic liberty, or to the standard efficiency arguments that fill so much of the *Principles,* but it is often misinterpreted as somehow a brief for laissez faire, despite Mill's express statement in chapter 5 citing legitimate limits to the doctrine of Free Trade:

Trade is a social act. Whoever undertakes to sell any description of goods to the public, does what affects the interest of other persons, and of society in general, and thus his conduct, in principle, comes within the jurisdiction of society: accordingly, it was once held to be the duty of governments, in all cases which were considered of importance, to fix prices, and regulate the processes of manufacture. But it is now recognized, though not till after a long struggle, that both the cheapness and the good quality of commodities are most effectually provided for by leaving the producers and sellers perfectly free, under the sole check of equal freedom to the buyers for supplying themselves elsewhere. This is the so-called doctrine of Free Trade, which rests on grounds different from, though equally solid with, the principle of individual liberty asserted in this Essay. Restrictions on trade, or on production for purposes of trade, are indeed restraints; and all restraint, *qua* restraint, is an evil: but the restraints in question affect only that part of conduct which society is competent to restrain, and are wrong solely because they do not really produce the results which it is desired to produce by them. As the principle of individual liberty is not involved in the doctrine of Free Trade, so neither is it in most of the questions which arise respecting the limits of that doctrine; as for example, what amount of public control is admissible for the prevention of fraud by adulteration; how far sanitary precautions, or arrangements to protect workpeople employed in dangerous occupations, should be enforced on employers. Such questions involve considerations of liberty, only in so far as leaving people to themselves is always better, *ceterus paribus,* than controlling them: but that they may be legitimately controlled for these ends, is in principle undeniable.[127]

This is in no way to deny that the fundamental aim of *On Liberty* is to defend a robust, albeit qualified, anti-paternalism. As the essay famously put it:

The object of this Essay is to assert one very simple principle, as entitled to govern absolutely the dealings of society with the individual in the way of compulsion and control, whether the means used be physical force in the form of legal penalties, or the moral coercion of public opinion. That principle is, that the sole end for which mankind are warranted, individually or collectively, in interfering with the liberty of action of any of their number, is self-protection. That the only purpose for which power can be rightfully exercised over any member of a civilized community, against his will, is to prevent harm to others. His own good, either physical or moral, is not a sufficient warrant. He cannot rightfully be compelled to do or forbear because it will be better for him to do so, because it will make him happier, because, in the opinion of others, to do so would be wise, or even right. These are good reasons for remonstrating with him, or reasoning with him, or persuading him, or entreating him, but not for compelling him, or visiting him with any evil in case he do otherwise. To justify that, the conduct from which it is desired to deter him, must be calculated to produce evil to some one else. The only part of the conduct of any one, for which he is amenable to society, is that which concerns others. In the part which merely concerns himself, his independence is, of right, absolute. Over himself, over his own body and mind, the individual is sovereign.[128]

Of course, immediately following this stirring statement, there is a long list of qualifications: the principle obviously does not apply to children or young people or "those backward states of society in which the race itself may be considered as in its nonage" (for whom "Despotism is a legitimate mode of government"). In fact, the principle of liberty "has no application to any state of things anterior to the time when mankind have become capable of being improved by free and equal discussion." Such exceptions are not, for Mill, to be wondered at. He is not, any more than Bentham, invoking God-given rights, or intuited moral rights and duties, etc. Rather,

I regard utility as the ultimate appeal on all ethical questions; but it must be utility in the largest sense, grounded on the permanent interests of man as a progressive being. Those interests, I contend, authorize the subjection of individual spontaneity to external control, only in respect to those actions of each, which concern the interests of other people. If any one does an act hurtful to others, there is a *prima facie* case for punishing him, by law, or, where legal penalties are not safely applicable, by general disapprobation. There are also many positive acts for the benefit of others, which he may rightfully be compelled to perform; such as, to give evidence in a court of justice; to bear his fair share in the common defence, or in any other joint work necessary to the interest of society of which he enjoys the protection; and to perform certain acts of individual beneficence, such as saving a fellow-creature's life, or interposing to protect the defenceless against ill-usage, things which whenever it is obviously a man's duty to do, he may rightfully be made responsible to society for not doing. A person may cause evil to others not only by his actions but by his inaction, and in either case he is justly accountable to them for the injury. The latter case, it is true, requires a much more cautious exercise of compulsion than the former. To make any one answerable for doing evil to others, is the rule; to make him answerable for not preventing evil, is, comparatively speaking, the exception. Yet there are many cases clear enough and grave enough to justify that exception.[129]

This last point, in particular, would obviously seem to allow a Millian defense of "Good Samaritan" laws requiring good faith efforts to rescue those in grave peril, as in Peter Singer's famous case of the child drowning in a shallow pond—a case that is often taken as a test case for a truly anti-paternalistic policy, but one that the Mills fail.[130]

There is, to be sure, a vast literature on Mill's liberty principle, and there can be little doubt that any defense of it requires much qualification and elaboration, the better to address the differences between harm and offense, to oneself and others.[131] But the point here is simply that the actual scope of the principle was obviously and admittedly taken to be defined by the greatest happiness principle, the ultimate principle of teleology here and in all contexts of human action. Mill may have been wrong about any number of particulars, but for him as for his utilitarian predecessors, this was to be expected, given the empirical calculations involved. At least there were empirical calculations involved, and the issues admitted of resolution through the appropriate research.

Furthermore, the sphere of liberty under discussion is as follows:

> This, then, is the appropriate region of human liberty. It comprises, first, the inward domain of consciousness; demanding liberty of conscience, in the most comprehensive sense; liberty of thought and feeling; absolute freedom of opinion and sentiment on all subjects, practical or speculative, scientific, moral, or theological. The liberty of expressing and publishing opinions may seem to fall under a different principle, since it belongs to that part of the conduct of an individual which concerns other people; but, being almost of as much importance as the liberty of thought itself, and resting in great part on the same reasons, is practically inseparable from it. Secondly, the principle requires liberty of tastes and pursuits; of framing the plan of our life to suit our own character; of doing as we like, subject to such consequences as may follow: without impediment from our fellow-creatures, so long as what we do does not harm them, even though they should think our conduct foolish, perverse, or wrong. Thirdly, from this liberty of each individual, follows the liberty, within the same limits, of combination among individuals; freedom to unite, for any purpose not involving harm to others: the persons combining being supposed to be of full age, and not forced or deceived.[132]

There is, it is worth underscoring, no express mention of freedom of contract, of the trucking, bartering, and trading composing economic liberty. Rather, the work proceeds to advance its famous case for freedom of thought, and for "Individuality, as One of the Elements of Well-Being." The two go hand in glove. Without an open and diverse society, with dialogue flowering at all turns, it is difficult to make one's views truly one's own and achieve self-realization and direction. "Where not the person's own character but the traditions or customs of other people compose the rule of conduct, there is wanting one of the principal ingredients of human happiness, and quite the chief ingredient of individual and social progress."[133] With von Humboldt, the Mills argue, the great end is "the individuality of power and development." As in the language of Mill's crisis, with the reconciliation of egoism and rational benevolence, there is the claim that "in proportion to the development of his individuality, each person becomes more valuable to himself, and is therefore capable of being more valuable to others. There is a greater fullness of life about his own existence, and when there is more life in the units there is more in the mass which is composed of them." Moreover, it can be shown that "these developed human beings are of some use to the undeveloped—to point out to those who do not desire liberty, and would not avail themselves of it, that they may be in some intelligible manner rewarded for allowing other people to make use of it without hindrance."[134]

If the thoughts being given expression here were, the Mills explained, familiar, they were nonetheless also and always threatened. The fear of individuality, the conformity of mediocrity, the herd mentality, etc., etc., were pervasive, as characteristic of society at large as of the society in the small that had made the Mills' relationship so difficult. Society more than ever needed genius, in the sense the Mills had always given to that term. But:

> Persons of genius, it is true, are, and are always likely to be, a small minority; but in order to have them, it is necessary to preserve the soil in which they grow. Genius can only breathe freely in an *atmosphere* of freedom. Persons of genius are, *ex vi termini, more* individual than any other people—less capable, consequently, of fitting themselves, without hurtful compression, into any of the small number of moulds which society provides in order to save its members the trouble of forming their own character. If from timidity they consent to be forced into one of these moulds, and to let all that part of themselves which cannot expand under the pressure remain unexpanded, society will be little the better for their genius. If they are of a strong character, and break their fetters, they become a mark for the society which has not succeeded in reducing them to commonplace, to point at with solemn warning as 'wild,' 'erratic,' and the like; much as if one should complain of the Niagara river for not flowing smoothly between its banks like a Dutch canal.[135]

It is just such passages that can make *The Subjection of Women* seem like so many additional chapters to *On Liberty*, given its remarkable inventory of the "small number of moulds" into which women were being squeezed. Of all the immortal lines to be found in the works of the Mills, perhaps none can match the following:

> All causes, social and natural, combine to make it unlikely that women should be collectively rebellious to the power of men. They are so far in a position different from all other subject classes, that their masters

require something more from them than actual service. Men do not want solely the obedience of women, they want their sentiments. All men, except the most brutish, desire to have, in the woman most nearly connected with them, not a forced slave but a willing one, not a slave merely, but a favourite. They have therefore put everything in practice to enslave their minds. The masters of all other slaves rely, for maintaining obedience, on fear; either fear of themselves, or religious fears. The masters of women wanted more than simple obedience, and they turned the whole force of education to effect their belief that their ideal of character is the very opposite to that of men; not self-will, and government by self-control, but submission, and yielding to the control of others. All the moralities tell them that it is the duty of women, and all the current sentimentalities that it is their nature, to live for others; to make complete abnegation of themselves, and to have no life but in their affections. And by their affections are meant the only ones they are allowed to have—those to the men with whom they are connected, or to the children who constitute an additional and indefeasible tie between them and a man. When we put together three things—first, the natural attraction between opposite sexes; secondly, the wife's entire dependence on the husband, every privilege or pleasure she has being either his gift, or depending entirely on his will; and lastly, that the principal object of human pursuit, consideration, and all objects of social ambition, can in general be sought or obtained by her only through him, it would be a miracle if the object of being attractive to men had not become the polar star of feminine education and formation of character. And, this great means of influence over the minds of women having been acquired, an instinct of selfishness made men avail themselves of it to the utmost as a means of holding women in subjection, by representing to them meekness, submissiveness, and resignation of all individual will into the hands of a man, as an essential part of sexual attractiveness. Can it be doubted that any of the other yokes which mankind have succeeded in breaking, would have subsisted till now if the same means had existed, and had been as sedulously used, to bow down their minds to it?[136]

And, with even more emphasis:

Standing on the ground of common sense and the constitution of the human mind, I deny that any one knows, or can know, the nature of the two sexes, as long as they have only been seen in their present relation to one another. If men had ever been found in society without women, or women without men, or if there had been a society of men and women in which the women were not under the control of the men, something might have been positively known about the mental and moral differences which may be inherent in the nature of each. What is now called the nature of women is an eminently artificial thing—the result of forced repression in some directions, unnatural stimulation in others. It may be asserted without scruple, that no other class of dependents have had their character so entirely distorted from its natural proportions by their relation with their masters; for, if conquered and slave races have been, in some respects, more forcibly repressed, whatever in them has not been crushed down by an iron heel has generally been let alone, and if left with any liberty of development, it has developed itself according to its own laws; but in the case of women, a hot-house and stove cultivation has always been carried on of some of the capabilities of their nature, for the benefit and pleasure of their masters. Then, because certain products of the general vital force sprout luxuriantly and reach a great development in this heated atmosphere and under this active nurture and watering, while other shoots from the same root, which are left outside in the wintry air, with ice purposely heaped all round them, have a stunted growth, and some are burnt off with fire and disappear; men, with that inability to recognize their own work which distinguishes the unanalytic mind, indolently believe that the tree grows of itself in the way they have made it grown, and that it would die if one half of it were not kept in a vapour bath and the other half in the snow.

Of all difficulties which impede the progress of thought, and the formation of well-grounded opinions on life and social arrangements, the greatest is now the unspeakable ignorance and inattention of mankind in respect to the influences which form human character. Whatever any portion of the human species now are, or seem to be, such, it is supposed, they have a natural tendency to be: even when the most elementary knowledge of the circumstances in which they have been placed, clearly points out the causes that made them what they are.[137]

There is no keener analysis in any of Mill's other works of the subtler workings of power than in *The Subjection of Women*, no more perfect harmony with the arguments that he had long shared with his wife and stepdaughter. The most serious ultimate obstacles to the progress of happiness were of this nature, the adaptive preferences and adaptive psychologies of the oppressed, such that what people found desirable and pleasurable could only be described as a warped concession to their unjust social circumstances.[138] There was, certainly, brute violence and intimidation at work in the subjection of women. Terribly so. But that was only one of the more obvious elements of the domination at work, the domination that could keep even the kindest couples from becoming true friends on an equal footing of genuine freedom.

Nor is this to deny the considerable economic forces, including property law, overtly involved in this domination. Here, the arguments of *Subjection* and the arguments of the "Chapters on Socialism" are very much in line: "The idea of property is not some one thing, identical throughout history and incapable of alteration, but is variable like all other creations of the human mind. . . . Society is fully entitled to abrogate or alter any particular right of property which on sufficient consideration it judges to stand in the way of the public good. . . . Assuredly the terrible case which . . . Socialists are able to make out against the present economic order of society, demands a full consideration of all means by which the institution [of private property] may have a chance of being made to work in a manner more beneficial to that large portion of society which at present enjoys the least share of its direct benefits."[139] The growth of the cooperative movement would, as promised in the *Principles*, also aid the cause of the emancipation of women, not least through a critical rethinking of property law. But economic analysis is not enough; it must be tied to a reflexive, critical account of the psychology of power.

It should be tolerably evident how these striking calls for freedom of thought, individuality, complete equality for women, and ever-increasing economic equality were, to the Mills, but the spelling out of the practical import of utilitarianism in its effort to advance human happiness against the forces of religious traditionalism (bolstered by Intuitionism), mediocrity, and conformity. And plausibly, the best case for utilitarianism is precisely this—its role, however rough and ready, in defining the direction of progress. As Mill explains the key point in "Utilitarianism," "utility would enjoin, first, that laws and social arrangements should place the happiness, or (as speaking practically it may be called) the interest, of every individual, as nearly as possible in harmony with the interest of the whole; and secondly, that education and opinion, which have so vast a power over human character, should so use that power as to establish in the mind of every individual an indissoluble association between his own happiness and the good of the whole; especially between his own happiness and the practice of such modes of conduct, negative and positive, as regard for the universal happiness prescribes: so that not only he may be unable to conceive the possibility of happiness to himself, consistently with conduct opposed to the general good, but also that a direct impulse to promote the general good may be in every individual one of the habitual motives of action, and the sentiments connected therewith may fill a large and prominent place in every human being's sentient existence."[140]

The complete realization of such an ideal is, Mill allows, far in the future. Even so, it lights a more immediate path forward:

> Neither is it necessary to the feeling which constitutes this binding force of the utilitarian morality on those who recognize it, to wait for those social influences which would make its obligation felt by mankind at

large. In the comparatively early state of human advancement in which we now live, a person cannot indeed feel that entireness of sympathy with all others, which would make any real discordance in the general direction of their conduct in life impossible; but already a person in whom the social feeling is at all developed, cannot bring himself to think of the rest of his fellow creatures as struggling rivals with him for the means of happiness, whom he must desire to see defeated in their object in order that he may succeed in his. The deeply-rooted conception which every individual even now has of himself as a social being, tends to make him feel it one of his natural wants that there should be harmony between his feelings and aims and those of his fellow creatures. If differences of opinion and of mental culture make it impossible for him to share many of their actual feelings—perhaps make him denounce and defy those feelings—he still needs to be conscious that his real aim and theirs do not conflict; that he is not opposing himself to what they really wish for, namely, their own good, but is, on the contrary, promoting it. This feeling in most individuals is much inferior in strength to their selfish feelings, and is often wanting altogether. But to those who have it, it possesses all the characters of a natural feeling. It does not present itself to their minds as a superstition of education, or a law despotically imposed by the power of society, but as an attribute which it would not be well for them to be without. This conviction is the ultimate sanction of the greatest-happiness morality. This it is which makes any mind, of well-developed feelings, work with, and not against, the outward motives to care for others, afforded by what I have called the external sanctions; and when those sanctions are wanting, or act in an opposite direction, constitutes in itself a powerful internal binding force, in proportion to the sensitiveness and thoughtfulness of the character; since few but those whose mind is a moral blank, could bear to lay out their course of life on the plan of paying no regard to others except so far as their own private interest compels.[141]

How many would, in their reflective moments, deny that it would be better to advance their own happiness in ways advancing rather than retarding the general happiness? However large the self may loom, it is only the psychopath or the sociopath who does not feel the pull of unity to some degree, and the most vivid passages in "Utilitarianism" are those that give expression to this seeming paradox of the growth of individual character providing that fair share of happiness that strengthens the sense of unity that is the emotional fount of utilitarianism. As Mill so compellingly put it, in "The Utility of Religion": "A morality grounded on large and wise views of the good of the whole, neither sacrificing the individual to the aggregate nor the aggregate to the individual, but giving to duty on the one hand and to freedom and spontaneity on the other their proper province, would derive its power in the superior natures from sympathy and benevolence and the passion for ideal excellence; in the inferior, from the same feelings cultivated up to the measure of their capacity, with the superadded force of shame."[142] To truly feel the value of happiness, for oneself and others, is to feel that any forfeiture of it in the individual case is tragic, that there must be a better way, such that the individual is not sacrificed to the aggregate.[143]

Is this vision paradoxical or inconsistent? Could it really be that the course of human happiness through the flourishing of freethinking individuals will be in tandem with an ever growing feeling of unity, such that one's own happiness can increasingly be conceived only as part of the larger whole? That the open society will yield a critique of power and domination keen enough to root out the most pervasive and enduring forms of it? That utilitarian indirection could generate such a powerful reformist impulse, grounded above all on a comprehensive reform of education and the forces of socialization?

Admittedly, relatively few Mill scholars have held that all of these elements could hang together in the way Mill suggested, particularly on the naturalistic grounds that Mill favored, in his characteristic welding together of egoism and benevolence. But too few have identified the most serious flaws in the Millian vision, which mainly lie elsewhere.

Critics

Some of the familiar criticisms of the Millian perspective can be dispatched quickly, in quasi Thomist fashion.

Millian Claim: On Mill's claim that "[i]f the end which the utilitarian doctrine proposes to itself were not, in theory and in practice, acknowledged to be an end, nothing could ever convince any person that it was so. No reason can be given why the general happiness is desirable, except that each person, so far as he believes it to be attainable, desires his own happiness. This, however, being a fact, we have not only all the proof which the case admits of, but all which it is possible to require, that happiness is a good: that each person's happiness is a good to that person, and the general happiness, therefore, a good to the aggregate of all persons."[144]

Defense: As Henry West has argued, Mill "generalizes from the fact that each person desires his or her own happiness to the conclusion that the general happiness is what is desirable for the aggregate of all persons. This has been criticized as a fallacy of composition, but in correspondence Mill makes clear that he does not regard the general happiness as anything but a summation of the happiness of the individuals making up the aggregate. If happiness is the *kind* of thing that is desirable, the instances of it in the consciousness of different individuals can be added to constitute what is desirable for the aggregate. Not all present-day philosophers agree that this kind of addition is possible, but it is now generally accepted as Mill's position." And Mill is, in his account of desiring as involving finding something pleasant, "asking the reader to engage in 'practised self-consciousness and self-observation. . . . Mill's psychology may be mistaken, but there is now a growing consensus that in his 'proof' the author of *A System of Logic* is not committing elementary logical fallacies unworthy of a logician. He is appealing to psychological evidence to move from facts of pleasure and pain and of desires and aversions to judgments of good and bad as ends of action."[145] The argument, in short, is in part epistemic.

This is not to deny that there are various obscurities and ambiguities in Mill's supposed "proof" of utilitarianism. Many have noted how he seems to set up conditions that would make any proof impossible, accepting the claim that first principles cannot be proved in any strict sense, though they are susceptible to "considerations capable of determining the intellect." In practice, outside of the chapter on the proof of utilitarianism, Mill seems, as noted, to follow a strategy much like Sidgwick's demonstration that common-sense morality is in the main not only consistent with utilitarianism, but actually requires it for its systematic completion and coherence.[146] This dialectical strategy of accommodation, and Mill's considered position on rules, will be addressed more fully in the following chapter, in a more extensive analysis of utilitarian indirection. But note should also be made here of how the claims of the *Logic* bear on these matters, particularly in Mill's considered conviction that "must" implies "ought."

Millian Claim: On the supposed inconsistency of the Mills' hedonism and claims about higher pleasures: "If I am asked, what I mean by difference of quality in pleasures, or what makes one pleasure more valuable than another, merely as a pleasure, except its being greater in amount, there is but one possible answer. Of two pleasures, if there be one to which all or almost all who have experience of both give a decided preference, irrespective of any feeling of moral obligation to prefer it, that is the more desirable pleasure. If one of the two is, by those who are competently acquainted with both, placed so far above the other that they prefer it, even though knowing it to be attended with a greater amount of discontent, and would not resign it for any quantity of the other pleasure which their nature is capable of, we are justified in ascribing to the preferred enjoyment a superiority in quality, so far outweighing quantity as to render it, in comparison, of small account."[147]

Defense: From John Skorupski:

> The charge has often been made that this supposed distinction between quality and quantity of pleasure is actually inconsistent with hedonism. Not so. There is no reason in logic why more than one characteristic of pleasures should not be relevant to estimating their value; though if we call those characteristics 'quantity' and 'quality', we need to maintain a careful distinction between the quantity and quality of a pleasure on the one hand and its degree of value on the other (as Mill does in the passage just cited). Activity A can be more valuable pleasure-wise than activity

B, because though it gives less pleasure, the pleasure it gives is of higher quality. All that hedonism requires is that the only things that make a pleasure valuable are its characteristics as a *pleasure*. . . . What often raises readers' hackles here is Mill's elitism: he thinks that only some people are competent to judge the quality, as against the quantity, of pleasure. But this elitism is the direct consequence of the developmental or progressive conception of human beings. One gains access to higher pleasures by cultivation of the feelings—so cultivation is required if one is to be a competent judge. Educating the feelings is neither merely indulging them, on the one hand, nor, on the other, disciplining them by a moral or religious standard external to them. It means working from within their spontaneity, criticizing and strengthening them by their own internal standards. Those internal standards are also the standards by which quality of pleasure is judged. That there are such standards is just another application of Mill's epistemology of 'thinking from within.'[148]

This point gels with those made at the end of the previous chapter concerning Bentham's conception of pleasure, which according to Crimmins actually takes parallel form, since it invokes such qualities of pleasure as purity, intensity, etc., which call for precisely the same form of qualitative assessment.

Something akin to Skorupski's account of Mill's hedonism has also received brilliant treatment by Roger Crisp and Nicholas Sturgeon, both of whom defend Mill's consistency. As Sturgeon notes, Mill actually follows Bentham rather closely in linking the "intensity" of a pleasure to its "quantity," calling in the judgment of competent judges to settle even that. But it should not be supposed that that maneuver translates into "more pleasant" always being equated with intensity. "Mill thinks that there are two kinds of features that can make one pleasure more pleasant, more of a pleasure than another. One of these is greater intensity, which he calls quantity. But the other is something distinct from intensity, and his name for this other feature is 'quality.' He thinks that superior quality in a pleasure, too, can make it more pleasant, more of a pleasure." Or, put more fully, Mill's view is that

> only states of pleasure have positive intrinsic value; that there are two different pleasant-making features of pleasures, their intensity (which he calls quantity) and something else (which he calls quality); and there is only one good-making feature of pleasures, namely their pleasantness. Both quantity and quality come in degrees, and a higher degree of either will make a pleasure more pleasant. There is thus no inconsistency between his professed hedonism and his remarks on quantity and quality.[149]

Again, this is not to deny that Mill and Bentham both interpreted happiness in hedonistic terms, as a surplus of pleasure over pain. Nor, it should be stressed, is it to suggest that they differed over an "internal" v. "external" account of pleasure. That distinction is artificial and unhelpful when applied to hedonism. As de Lazari-Radek and Singer have maintained:

> Hedonism is the view that what is ultimately good is pleasure, understood as desirable consciousness. . . . We saw that one question we can ask about a theory of what is good for someone is whether it accepts the resonance constraint. Internalist theories accept that what is good for someone must resonate with them in some way, by being in accord with what they desire; externalist theories reject this constraint. Because hedonism holds that what is good for people is desirable consciousness, it straddles this divide. For something to be pleasure for a person, it must be something that the person apprehends as desirable, considered merely as a feeling. So the hedonist will not say that it is good for a person to be in a conscious state that she does not take to be desirable, and to this extent hedonism satisfies the resonance constraint and is internalist. On the other hand, hedonism does insist that what is good or bad for you is your states of consciousness, and nothing else, irrespective of whether what you desire is to have certain states of consciousness. . . . To that extent hedonism is externalist. [150]

Millian Claim: That happiness is the only thing desirable for its own sake, but that Mill followed Bentham in endorsing a psychological egoism inconsistent with a utilitarian demand for universal benevolence.

Defense: Recall Bentham's actual views. As Dinwiddy has happily put it, Bentham by 1814 "had come to think that sympathetic feelings, aroused by the consideration of a pleasure or pain being experienced or about to be experienced by another person, were so different from pleasures or pains of an entirely self-regarding kind, that the source of such feelings and of the motives associated with them ought to be classified separately; and he added that 'were it not for the operation of this sanction, no small portion of the good, physical and moral, which has place in human affairs, would be an effect without a cause.' . . . At this juncture, however, the crucial point needs to be made that in Bentham's view the force of the sympathetic sanction and of benevolent motives was not generally very strong." Still, as Bentham put it, "I admit the existence of *philanthropy* . . . I have not far to look for it."[151] Egoism, for Bentham, was also more of a strategy, the best means to advancing aggregate happiness, since each person would be the best judge of his or her own happiness, at least if properly educated, and the advance of the general happiness could best be accomplished by that division of labor that had each taking responsibility for his or her own happiness.

Mill's differences with Bentham on this score were largely a matter of degree, of the degree of their convictions concerning how far humanity could progress in the direction of sympathetic unity. As Brink has argued, in one possible line of defense, "Mill does not endorse psychological egoism. To see this, consider the structure of his proof. Mill claims that the utilitarian must claim that happiness is the one and only thing desirable in itself (IV 2). He claims that the only proof of desirability is desire (IV 3) and proceeds to argue that happiness is the one and only thing desired. He argues that a person does desire his own happiness for its own sake and that, therefore, happiness, as such, is desired by and desirable for its own sake for humanity as a whole (IV 3). He then turns to defend the claim that happiness is the only thing desirable in itself, by arguing that apparent counterexamples (e.g., desires for virtue for its own sake) are not inconsistent with his claim (IV 4–6)." Moreover, against a "sophisticated" psychological egoism holding that everything is still desired as "part of happiness," such that one's "own happiness is a complex whole that can have non-self-regarding parts," "there is room for doubt that Mill is endorsing even a sophisticated psychological egoism. First, he does say that people can develop a purely 'disinterested' desire for virtue itself, 'without looking to any end beyond it' (IV 5). So it's not clear that he thinks one need desire virtue as a part of happiness. Moreover, if the concern with virtue is disinterested, it's hard to see how this involves pursuing one's own interest. Indeed, it's not clear that Mill is here talking about desiring virtue for its constitutive contribution to (a) the agent's own happiness or (b) the general happiness."[152] And again, it should be remembered that the ultimate aim, for both Bentham and Mill, demanded "neither sacrificing the individual to the aggregate nor the aggregate to the individual."

But a better reading of Mill, allowing also for greater continuity between Mill and Bentham, would recognize that when Mill "says about anything else, such as virtue or money, that it is desired as an end, what he means by contrast is that it is desired, not for pleasure to which it is instrumentally conducive, but instead just for the pleasure inherent in it, the pleasure of which it is or has become, as he says, a source. Desiring something as a part of one's happiness is then to be understood as desiring it in this second way, not as instrumentally conducive to pleasure but for the sake of the immediate pleasure of possessing it."[153] The psychological conditioning by which this can happen has already been described, and how Mill claims that it is by this process that the good of others can become part of one's own happiness and valued for its own sake. Thus, Mill can be rendered consistent by allowing that, in Sturgeon's words, he

> has identified a kind of concern that is like genuine benevolence in not being based on an instrumental calculation of external rewards: it is not, for example, a concern to act for another's good because of an expectation of reciprocity or of burnishing one's reputation. But the critics will object that this concern is still unlike what real benevolence or unselfishness would have to be, in depending on a different reward, the pleasure one expects from seeing the good of others promoted or realized. Allow for the moment that this is correct, that a genuinely benevolent

desire, strictly speaking, could not be based on expectation of even this immediate pleasure in the good of others. It still seems, as Mill pictures the situation, that even if the desire isn't benevolent, the *pleasure* certainly is. It is, to repeat, immediate pleasure in the good of others, not based on any calculation of benefit to oneself. (And it will have as its counterpart immediate distress at the unhappiness of others, not based on any calculation of benefit to oneself.) So I think Mill's motivational picture allows for genuinely unselfish, benevolent pleasures.[154]

It would be idle to deny that it does take some exegetical effort on the part of Sturgeon, Crisp, Skorupski and company to bring into focus this portrait of Mill as a consistent, albeit very sophisticated hedonist, and that at a great many points Mill scarcely made his meaning clear. But it would be equally idle to deny that these readings make much better sense of Mill's texts than the readings that insist on Mill's inconsistencies, both in the texts on their own and in connection with those of Bentham. True, the two great masters of humanity, pleasure and pain, turn out to be more complex characters than one would ever suspect from the accounts of the critics, from Carlyle and Whewell to Rawls and Williams. And true, to show Mill's consistency is not to show his correctness, which would take some doing. But it does at least open up some better possibilities for the rethinking of hedonism as a live option in value theory, possibilities that are currently being explored.[155]

There is no end to the list of ungenerous objections to Millian utilitarianism, of course, and one could also include here such objections as his obscurity on the issue of act v. rule utilitarianism (not a distinction that he recognized, or an issue that could be resolved on the basis of his explicit remarks), and the many objections addressed in "Utilitarianism" itself, including all the old nonsense about it having no place for secondary principles or rules of thumb, demanding impossible or constant calculations, being a mundane celebration of the merely useful, a philosophy for swine, etc., etc.[156] There are of course many very real concerns about how to negotiate the tension between the accommodation of ordinary moral rules, particularly those concerning justice, and the radical reform of them. Mill famously argues:

> To have a right, then, is, I conceive, to have something which society ought to defend me in the possession of. If the objector goes on to ask why it ought, I can give him no other reason than general utility. If that expression does not seem to convey a sufficient feeling of the strength of the obligation, nor to account for the peculiar energy of the feeling, it is because there goes to the composition of the sentiment, not a rational only but also an animal element, the thirst for retaliation; and this thirst derives its intensity, as well as its moral justification, from the extraordinarily important and impressive kind of utility which is concerned. The interest involved is that of security, to every one's feelings the most

vital of all interests. Nearly all other earthly benefits are needed by one person, not needed by another; and many of them can, if necessary, be cheerfully foregone, or replaced by something else; but security no human being can possibly do without; on it we depend for all our immunity from evil, and for the whole value of all and every good, beyond the passing moment; since nothing but the gratification of the instant could be of any worth to us, if we could be deprived of everything the next instant by whoever was momentarily stronger than ourselves. Now this most indispensable of all necessaries, after physical nutriment, cannot be had, unless the machinery for providing it is kept unintermittedly in active play. Our notion, therefore, of the claim we have on our fellow-creatures to join in making safe for us the very groundwork of our existence, gathers feelings round it so much more intense than those concerned in any of the more common cases of utility, that the difference in degree (as is often the case in psychology) becomes a real difference in kind. The claim assumes the character of absoluteness, that apparent infinity, and incommensurability with all other considerations, which constitute the distinction between the feeling of right and wrong and that of ordinary expediency and inexpediency. The feelings concerned are so powerful, and we count so positively on finding a responsive feeling in others (all being alike interested), that *ought* and *should* grow into *must,* and recognized indispensability becomes a moral necessity, analogous to physical, and often not inferior to it in binding force.[157]

This line of argument is, as Schneewind has long insisted, the very template of the course that Sidgwick would follow in his famous analysis of common-sense morality, in an effort to show how rather than being at odds with utilitarianism, common-sense moral rules (truth telling, promise keeping, etc.) are grounded in considerations of utility and need the greatest happiness principle to unify and resolve conflicts in ordinary morality. At one level, it is a "debunking argument" that shows how we can account for our feelings and "intuitions" concerning justice, which are not nearly as clear or coherent as the Whewellians claimed. Past a certain point, this is also an assault on those supposed intuitions or considered judgments, since, Mill claims, they are not as final or clear and distinct as the religious moralists would have it. But just where accommodation leaves off and critical reform begins cannot be laid out with any precision, and much will depend on the facts of the matter.

Yet as important as such issues may be, it does seem that the single most important question in relation to Millian utilitarianism concerns the fundamental notion of happiness. Those who would follow the Mills in driving a wedge between their vision and that of the Philosophical Radicals do tend to agree with Taylor Mill about the significance of the higher pleasures. Thus, Brink has recently argued:

Though Mill formulates that doctrine as a modification within hedonism, in fact he conceives of higher pleasures as activities and pursuits that employ our higher, deliberative faculties. Such activities and pursuits are uniquely valuable not because they would be the objects of informed and idealized preference by competent judges. Rather, they would be the objects of idealized preference because they are valuable and appeal to our sense of dignity. This perfectionist reading of the higher pleasures doctrine dovetails nicely with Mill's claims about our happiness as progressive beings in *On Liberty* and elsewhere. In fact, he grounds this perfectionist conception of happiness in our capacities as moral agents, capable of responding to reasons for action, which promises to explain why this conception of happiness should be normative for us. Such an objective conception of happiness may seem elitist, but it is in fact compatible with an attractive form of pluralism and preserves the common assumption that happiness is what matters when we are concerned for anyone for his own sake. Mill's early critics, such as Sidgwick and Green, were right to see that this perfectionist doctrine could not be squared with hedonism, but they were wrong to think that Mill was fundamentally inconsistent. Though his break with his hedonist legacy would have been clearer if he had eschewed talk of pleasure consistently, his higher pleasures doctrine is best interpreted in perfectionist terms, and it is this perfectionist understanding of happiness that accounts for some of the most distinctive and progressive aspects of his utilitarian outlook.[158]

There is much to be said for Brink's account of the Millian conception of happiness as the ultimate good. He is certainly correct in denying that the view can plausibly be cast as a preference or desire satisfaction view; all of Mill's remarks on this issue, such as the claim that the desirable must be desired, are better cast merely as suggestions that desire plays an epistemic role, as providing evidence of the desirable. Mill was as aware as anyone that desires can be stunted and warped, adaptive in perverse ways, such that satisfying them is scarcely a contribution to the person's well-being. His entire vision of progressive society concerns the necessary conditions for cultivating the right kinds of desires and preferences, and for their ongoing critical assessment.

The tougher question is whether there is another, hedonistic ground for arguing for the consistency of this vision. That is, could it be that the Mills were actually presenting a defensible version of hedonism that incorporated various ideal goods, such as friendship, that had to be sought for their own sake?

That, of course, is the very possibility sketched above, in setting out the possible consistency of Mill's account of the higher pleasures, etc. Skorupski has responded to Brink's case in the following way:

What a hedonist is committed to, qua hedonist, is presumably only that the desirability, in its own right, of a pleasure is determined solely by its intrinsic properties *as* a pleasure. So Mill must hold that the quality of a pleasure is just as much an intrinsic property as its intensity. This is not implausible: the intentional content of a pleasure, for example, is an intrinsic, and indeed an essential, property. Whether or not Mill's 'two-dimensional' conception of the desirability of a pleasure is plausible, it is not inconsistent.

But perhaps the point on which Brink places greatest weight is that a close reading of Mill shows that he holds, of a number of activities, that we "take pleasure in these activities because we recognize their value; they are not valuable because they are pleasurable" (p. 56). Among the passages he quotes is the one at *Utilitarianism* II 6 where "Mill explains the fact that competent judges prefer activities that exercise their rational capacities by appeal to their sense of *dignity*" (p. 56).

Whether this explanation of their preferences is consistent with hedonism goes deep into the nature and diversity of value. A key point is that Mill nowhere asserts, as far as I know, that *every* kind of value is to be measured hedonically: the hedonic measure is appropriate in determining how *desirable* a thing is. It does not follow that how *admirable* an activity, or a form of life, etc. is should be measured hedonically. On the contrary, by Mill's naturalistic criterion, one would expect the 'evidence' for how admirable a thing is to be a matter of how much we admire it, not how much we desire it. Pursuing the naturalistic path further, there is then the question of how much, and when, we desire what we admire. It is not a simple matter. Still it is perfectly legitimate for Mill to suggest that an activity that we are proud of is one that, in that respect at least, we desire more than an activity we are ashamed of, for example, because it strikes us as undignified or in general disadmirable. And perhaps it is just a fact about human beings, or at least the ones with developed capacities, that rationality is one of the things they admire. Psychological facts of this kind could underlie the Aristotelian principle. So Mill's appeal to dignity is not inconsistent with hedonism, when that is understood as a doctrine about happiness or about what is desirable, even though to spell it out he would have to venture further than he does into questions about the varieties of value and their grounding in the various sentiments.[159]

Of course, as Skorupski allows, to claim that the Millian conception can be rendered consistent in this way is not to claim that it is true or justifiable. But again, what Skorupski's explanation—and the related but different ones of Crisp and Sturgeon—does allow is that this line of interpretation would capture more of the actual language at issue—and express endorsements of hedonism—and would, as much as Brink's, allow that "[o]n either reading, the features transmitted to Mill's views on democracy and liberty will be similar, and the effect, in comparison to contemporary trends in liberalism, quite distinctive. Either way, Mill stands out as a perfectionist liberal (in a broad sense of perfectionism), with consequent worries about democracy—not as a liberal of the kind now more common, who takes democracy for granted but requires neutrality from the state."

There is perhaps much to be said for this form of hedonism. It is controversial to hold that there is some one particular feeling or feeling tone (or "hedonic gloss") identifiable in every form of pleasurable or desirable consciousness, even more difficult than claiming that there is some one flavor of wine as wine evident in all varieties. And to pursue the analogy, just as one could maintain (however implausibly) that only wine is desirable, that would not in itself eliminate the possibility of various qualities—fruitiness, oak scents, fragrance, etc.—all being qualities that could contribute to making the wine desirable. Again, that, say, dignity is something that humans cannot help but admire, as being one of the central capabilities for being a fully flourishing individual, might, on this construal, be part of the demonstration that dignity is desirable, part of happiness, rather than a strike against it.

The following chapter will indicate some further possible lines of defense of these versions of hedonism, and of hedonism in general, which was not only endorsed by Sidgwick as well, but has now become the value theory of choice among a number of contemporary utilitarians or utilitarian sympathizers, notably Crisp, de Lazari-Radek and Singer. It is on this subject that the renaissance of interest in classical utilitarianism has been particularly striking and helpful, pointing up the poverty of so many of the academic arguments of the last century (in economics and the social sciences generally, as well as in philosophy). At this juncture, however, it would be helpful to assemble some reminders of how the actual Millian applications of any such vision do call out for more critical reflection than they have hitherto received. That the Mills were remarkably advanced "for their time" is obvious; that their views can be adapted and reconstructed to avoid various failings is nearly as obvious. But neither point provides an adequate justification for failing to point out how, for all their brilliance, the Mills played a part in the racism and imperialism of the Victorian era.

The View from Parliament

By the end of Mill's life, his role as un homme politique was the dominant element in his public persona, and the most controversial. In the nineteenth century, Mill's overall standing was damaged by his years as a Member of Parliament. The prevailing judgement at the time was that he would have done better sticking to his books—a view which has only been challenged by Mill scholars in recent years. After his three years as an MP during the historic Parliament of 1865-8, The Times was lamenting Mill's

*'vehement, narrow partisanship' and the 'impetuous eagerness' which
had led him into the position of being 'the apostle of a small and not very
select band of zealots.' Of course The Times was no friend, but even a fairer
observer like Alexander Bain thought that while he was in Parliament his
'idea of ventilating questions that had as yet scarcely any supporters' was
'carried to an extreme.'*

*For Mill, however, his political activities were the natural extension
of his work as an intellectual. Mid-Victorian mainstream opinion
may have been shocked by his 'partisanship' on women, Ireland, rights
to public demonstration and racism; Mill saw them as the natural
political outcrops of his egalitarian, liberal philosophy. His election was
an experiment with the potentially volatile mixture of intellectual and
politician.*

—RICHARD REEVES, *JOHN STUART MILL:
VICTORIAN FIREBRAND*

There was certainly something wonderful and beautiful about Mill's long–
delayed Parliamentary career. Power did not corrupt, though it may have
induced melancholy. He regarded his seat as first and foremost a platform
for presenting his principles in the most forceful way, seemingly without a
thought to reelection. Old political hands, now as then, can point to his abject
failure at getting reelected as a textbook example of the impact of philosophy on politics. Philosophers, however, and Mill chief among them, would not
think this cause for regret any more than the fate of Socrates was cause for
regret. The problem was with the politics, not the principles.

There is much to be said for this perspective. Some of Mill's finest hours
were no doubt when he was ventilating questions to the extreme. As Reeve
shows, it was during "the heady, topsy-turvy politics of 1867" (which would
yield the Second Great Reform expanding the franchise) that Mill

> seized the opportunity to impress his own reforming agenda on the
> public mind. The fact that the Reform Bill was being taken through
> the House by a Conservative government meant he had room to intro-
> duce his 'crotchets', namely women's suffrage and proportional rep-
> resentation. . . . Mill had already presented a petition in support of
> women's votes; now he could press the point. On his sixty-first birth-
> day, he proposed a tiny editorial alteration to the Reform Bill which,
> if accepted, would have triggered a social revolution: the amendment
> simply substituted the word 'person' for 'man' in the legislation. For
> the first time, Women's suffrage was put before the House of Com-
> mons. Mill would later describe the move as 'perhaps the only really
> important public service I performed in the capacity as a Member of
> Parliament.'[160]

That the House of Commons would be treated to a speech by a nervous Mill summarizing (in advance of publication) the arguments of *The Subjection of Women* is sufficient in itself to justify deeming Mill's political career valuable. But in fact, they were treated to many salutary lessons in Millian principle, on everything from reorganizing the government of London to the reform of land tenure in Ireland (very controversial), to taxing coal and resisting deforestation, to the condemnation of Governor Eyre of Jamaica. His support for the death penalty—uncharacteristic for a utilitarian—as a needed measure to curb brutality, as in cases of domestic violence, was also on display. Like his ungodson Bertrand Russell, the years had only heightened his indignation with the system, and he was determined to speak out. It is, in fact, the Parliamentary Mill, speaking against racism, sexism, brutality, corruption, etc. that has done a great deal to enhance his reputation among current-day political philosophers.

All the more reason, then, to take special care that the case for reading Mill be made in ways that take the full measure of the critics, particularly those critics who make a forceful case for reading both Mills as representing certain forms of imperialist and racist thinking. By framing his political career in a more detailed historical way, addressing both the positive and negative interpretations of it, it may be possible to reach a better and more comprehensive judgment on the significance of the Mills and the possible perils embedded in their notion of happiness. As admirable as the Millian feminist arguments may have been, there were some very serious limits to them.

To be sure, there is a valuable and flourishing literature that casts Mill as a multicultural hero. Nussbaum has increasingly incorporated Millian materials in her capabilities approach and feminist work, calling Mill "a vital resource for all who care about the future of women and men, and of the justice that may possibly exist between them." Mill, according to Nussbaum, "shows with daring and clarity how thoroughly the preferences and desires of women have been deformed by male power." And what is more, Mill's critique of male power is strengthened by a conception of happiness that makes it "a richer resource" for "contemporary feminist and, more generally, anti-hierarchical thinking."[161]

The Mill celebrated by Nussbaum has been deployed for purposes of the somewhat more cosmopolitan approach to global justice that Nussbaum at one time championed against those given to excessive love of country or of communitarian particularity. Georgios Varouxakis, in his compelling work *Mill on Nationality*, has driven the point home: "Mill's conception of the relationship between obligations to country and obligations to mankind was close to that of Nussbaum." For both, patriotism is commendable only when it conduces "to the interests of the whole of humanity."[162] Nussbaum's account of patriotism and particular loyalties and attachments generally is indeed at a far remove from old-fashioned communitarian love of country right or wrong.

Even farther when, as sometimes happened, she overstated her opposition to patriotic loyalty, making such loyalty sound wholly derivative of rather than merely subordinate to one's larger duties to humanity. In an important interview, Nussbaum qualified her position, in the familiar Godwinian fashion: "I never said that we should not have a particular love of and attachment to our own nation.... I compared our relation to our country to our relationship with our own children: just as good parents love their own children more, but still, compatibly with that, may and should seek a nation in which all children have decent life-opportunities, so too we may love our own nation more while seeking a world in which all citizens have decent life-opportunities."[163]

Still, Nussbaum did at times suggest that Mill can be cast as a hero of feminist, anti-hierarchical, cosmopolitan thinking, one who adapted for the modern era the valuable bits in Aristotle about happiness as a complex whole, involving activity. She was in effect worrying about an analogue, at the level of the nation, of the old Bernard Williams challenge that the person who puts ethical impartiality above his or her particular love—as the early Godwin seemed to—may have one thought too many. Like many defenders of impartialism, notably Peter Singer, she deemed it more worrisome to have one thought too few—a worry that seems especially apt when it comes to the subject of patriotism, where thoughts are too few to begin with.

But Nussbaum's work on Mill never addressed those critics of Mill who worry that he is an unlikely hero for anti-hierarchical thinking, given the way his application of the higher pleasures doctrine involved various colonialist entanglements. If, however, she has not directly addressed the charges of Mill's ethnocentrism, colonialism, imperialism, racism, etc., Anthony Kwame Appiah has, and in very sharp terms. Mill is in fact the main protagonist of his subtle work *The Ethics of Identity*, a book that counters the charge, common to Uday Mehta, Bhikhu Parikh, and John Gray, that "Mill was an autonomist, and that autonomism is an ethnocentric preference, ruled out by pluralism." Appiah argues that in "fact, Mill is truly ethnocentric precisely where he suspends the requirement of autonomy.... The Mill who says that even the despotism of an Akbar or a Charlemagne can be beneficial for backward societies cannot be accused of foisting an ethic of autonomy upon cultures for whom autonomy is not a value. It is not the smallest of ironies that these critics of Mill accept his arguments at their weakest—and reject them at their strongest."[164]

Appiah continues by invoking Mill versus Carlyle on "the Negro Question"—about which more directly—in support of the conclusion that:

> It hardly needs to be remarked that liberal universalism, or what's sometimes derogated as 'essentialist humanism', did not have the field to itself in the Enlightenment. Among the principal dissenters from such universalism were the early theorists of racial difference, and their

ideas were inevitably enlisted to justify slavery and colonialism, as they later justified genocide. In the history of ideas, then, one should not assume that it's universalism that has the most to answer for, or that ascriptions of diversity should always command our admiration. Let me go further. Our moral modernity consists chiefly of extending the principle of equal respect to those who had previously been outside the compass of sympathy; in that sense, it has consisted in the ability to see similarity where our predecessors saw only difference. The wisdom was hard-won; it should not be lightly set aside.[165]

But as Appiah recognizes, recent decades have witnessed at least a minor flourishing of critical literature in which the younger Mill is cast as grotesquely Eurocentric, complacently and arrogantly imperialistic, and politely racist, arbitrarily confining his liberalism to home turf. These charges are not always made together, though they sometimes are, in works suggesting that Mill's ethnocentric, Eurocentric, and colonialist or imperialist predilections amounted to racist tendencies.

For some critics, Mill's admiration for his father's *History of British India* and his own work with the East India Company are deeply suggestive of his complicity in the growth of the British Empire and in justifications for that growth grounded on racial difference. As Uday Mehta has put it in his influential work, *Liberalism and Empire*: "In India. . . especially following the mutiny of 1857, there was in fact an unmistakable tilt toward the hardening of authoritarian policies and a racializing of political and social attitudes. This was a tilt to which thinkers like J.S. Mill added their prestige and that they justified in their theoretical writings. For example, in *Considerations on Representative Government*, Mill had made clear that in colonies that were not of Britain's 'blood and lineage' any move toward greater representation was not to be countenanced."[166]

Indeed, in a rather too discreet footnote, Mehta suggests that the younger Mill was a "surprising exception" to the generalization that at this historical juncture "race is seldom deployed as an explicit political category in the writings by British liberals." Rather, Mill "invests race with far greater seriousness than most of his liberal contemporaries, who generally view it as a catchall term that loosely designates what might be called cultural difference. Instead Mill elaborates the term through the biological notion of 'blood.' Hence for example in the *Considerations on Representative Government* (chaps. 16, 18) he draws what he takes to be the crucial distinction in terms of readiness for representative institutions by reference to 'those of our blood' and those not of our blood."[167]

For Mehta, Mill and the whole lot of classical utilitarians were as wanting in humility as they were over-brimming with fatuity: "The almost pathological extent to which Bentham made precision the guiding ambition of his science of legislation; the confidence with which James Mill could extol the virtue of 'A Code' for India even if it required an 'absolute government'; the certainty with which J.S. Mill knew that 'there is nothing for [backward people] but implicit obedience to an Akbar or a Charlemagne'—by the nineteenth century these political impulses become verities of liberalism when faced with the unfamiliar. They are the intellectual precursors of Francis Fukuyama's confident projections regarding the 'end of history' and the attitude that typically views regimes like those in Cuba and Iran as being in some provisional interregnum."[168] The unlikely hero of Mehta's book turns out to be Edmund Burke, the last holdout of a humbler form of liberal pluralism before the fanatical onslaught of utilitarian confidence men (never mind that Burke himself was anti-Semitic).

Mehta's line is presented as in some respects a more forceful variant of the arguments of Bhikhu Parekh and John Gray, to the effect that comprehensive Millian liberalism failed badly on the count of sensitivity to culture difference and receptiveness to genuine pluralism. Just as the Calvinists were depicted in *On Liberty* as fundamentally out of sync with the progressive tendencies of civilization, so too the Indians, the black Jamaicans, the Irish, and others were in the rearguard of history, not the vanguard, and might need stern discipline. Come to that, Mill was not all that confident that the English were fit for democracy. Still, the English, even if they were Calvinists, did not bear the burden of different "blood." Mill's elitism took various racialized forms, depending on the context.

Thus, it seems, Mill has been effectively damned for both racistly failing to recognize cultural difference and for recognizing cultural difference in a way that played into racist hands.[169] But in any event, and leaving Burke out of it, his views are suspect. Goldberg, in his important essay "Liberalism's Limits: Carlyle and Mill on 'The Negro Question,'" has put the point with maximal severity:

> Mill's argument for benevolent despotism failed to appreciate that neither colonialism nor despotism is ever benevolent. Benevolence here is the commitment to seek the happiness of others. But the mission of colonialism is exploitation and domination of the colonized generally, and Europeanization at least of those among the colonized whose class position makes it possible economically and educationally. And the mandate of despotism, its conceptual logic, is to assume absolute power to achieve the ruler's self-interested ends. Thus colonial despotism could achieve the happiness of colonized Others only by imposing the measure of Europeanized marks of happiness upon the other, which is to say, to force the other to be less so. Mill's argument necessarily assumed superiority of the despotic, benevolent or not; it presupposed that the mark of progress is (to be) defined by those taking themselves to be superior; and it presumes that the ruled will want to be like the rulers even as the former lack the cultural capital (ever?)

quite to rise to the task. Mill's ambivalence over the inherent inferiority of 'native Negroes', even as he marked the transformation in the terms of racial definition historically from the inescapable determinism of blood and brain size to the marginally escapable reach of cultural determination, has resonated to this day in liberal ambivalence regarding racial matters.[170]

Goldberg is of course referring to Mill's 1850 response to Thomas Carlyle's virulently racist essay "Occasional Discourse on the Negro Question," which was republished in pamphlet form (after Mill's response) with the contemptuous title "Occasional Discourse on the Nigger Question."[171] It would be difficult to find a more baldly racist tract in all of Western history: Carlyle parades every vicious prejudice towards blacks known to humanity, depicting a stereotype of "Quashee," a lazy, laughing, watermelon (or "pumpkin") eating inferior fit only for paternalistic control and direction by "the beneficent whip" of whites, who are superior by birth. Indeed, Carlyle calls for—or at least strongly suggests the desirability of—the reinstitution of slavery, condemning, in his usual way, the cruelties of laissez faire. The entire odious performance is cast in an offensively humorous vein, satirizing a "Universal Abolition of Pain Association."

Goldberg admits, of course, that Carlyle's essay provoked a scathing critical rejoinder from Mill, who remarked of the slave trade, "I have yet to learn that anything more detestable than this has been done by human beings towards human beings in any part of the earth." Mill charged Carlyle with

> the vulgar error of imputing every difference which he finds among human beings to an original difference of nature. As well might it be said, that of two trees, sprung from the same stock, one cannot be taller than another but from greater vigour in the original seeding. Is nothing to be attributed to soil, nothing to climate, nothing to difference of exposure—has no storm swept over the one and not the other, no lightning scathed it, no beast browsed on it, no insects preyed on it, no passing stranger stript off its leaves or its bark? If the trees grew near together, may not the one which, by whatever accident, grew up first, have retarded the other's development by its shade?[172]

Moreover, the "great ethical doctrine" of Carlyle's Discourse "than which a doctrine more damnable, I should think, never was propounded by a professed moral reformer, is, that one kind of human beings are born servants to another kind." Mill identified himself with the "thinking persons" who "either doubt or positively deny" the innate inferiority of blacks. And he had much sport with Carlyle's insane views about work being the be-all and end-all of existence.

Still, Goldberg has serious doubts. "It was Carlyle's call to reinstitute slavery to which Mill principally objected. . . . [His] critical concern with Carlyle's racist sentiment was only secondary and much more understated. Moreover,

not only did Mill not object to colonial domination, he insisted upon it, albeit in 'benevolent' form."[173] And Mill only doubted that blacks were biologi-
cally inferior; he did not, alas, effectively deny Carlyle's claim that blacks were
somehow inferior, so much as recast the inferiority as a historically contingent matter. As Joseph Miller has also observed, "Mill agrees with Carlyle that
blacks generally are less capable than Europeans, comparing blacks to trees
that grew in poor soil or poor climate or that might have suffered from exposure, storms or disease."[174] And in this case, for Goldberg, Mill's defense of
laissez faire, rather than limitation of it, was suspect on racial grounds:

> In objecting to Carlyle's racist hierarchical naturalism ... Mill inscribed
> in its place and in the name of laissez faire and equal opportunity, an
> imputation of the historical inferiority of blacks. Mill implied that this
> assumption of inferiority, because historically produced and contin-
> gent, was not always the case (Egyptians influenced Greeks) and might
> one day be overcome. Yet Mill's superficial bow to what has become
> an Afro-centric cornerstone barely hid beneath the surface the polite
> racism of his Euro-centric history. Contingent racism is still a form of
> racism—not so usual, not so bald, not so vituperative, and polite per-
> haps, but condescending nevertheless even as it is committed to equal
> opportunity. Equal opportunity among those with the unfair, histori-
> cally produced inequities of the colonial condition will simply repro-
> duce those inequities, if not expand them.[175]

Thus, if Carlyle's racism was "bald and vicious," Mill's was merely "polite
and effete." Still, "polite and effete" racism remains racism:

> Mill's erasure in the name of nonracialism rubs out at once the his-
> tory of racist invisibility, domination, and exploitation, replacing
> the memory of an infantilized past with the denial of responsibility
> for radically unequal and only superficially deracialized presents ...
> savages become the permanently unemployable, the uncivilized be-
> come crack heads, the lumpenproletariat the underclass. Distressed
> Needlewomen become sweated labor, poor Irish peasants turn into
> distressed defaulting family farmers and, well, 'Niggers' become
> 'Negroes', or blacks scarcely disguised beneath the seemingly benign
> nomenclature. For every Mill of yesteryear there is today a William
> Bennett or a Gary Becker. . . .[176]

However, Goldberg also supports his case by bringing in Mill on India and
the claims about people of different blood being unfit for representative government. Mill represented "colonialism with a human face. The world was to
be directed by the most developed and capable nations whose self-interests
nevertheless would be mitigated and mediated by the force of utilitarian
reason."

Essentially the same line has been helpfully developed in an essay by Anthony Bogues, "John Stuart Mill and 'The Negro Question': Race, Colonialism,
and the Ladder of Civilization":

> So what we have here in the debate between Mill and Carlyle are the
> following. In one current of English political thought, difference was
> innate, created by nature, and as a consequence there was no chance
> of political and social equality for those who were nonwhite subjects
> of the empire. Another current admitted that the black and colonial
> subjects were indeed inferior but argued that this inferiority was not
> ordained by nature and therefore could be overcome by contact with
> civilization and a process of tutelage. Both currents were united in
> their belief about black inferiority but disagreed on its root causes and
> naturalness. For those who thought that this so-called inferiority could
> be overcome, we should note that the goal was envisioned in terms of
> white normativity. To become fully human and a citizen, the colonial
> and black subject had to master the protocols of Western civilization, to
> become in the words of the nineteenth-century English writer Anthony
> Trollope, a 'Creole Negro.'[177]

These various critiques, then, combine to blast Mill as a racist and nascent neoconservative—like one of those racists, so common in the United
States and Europe, who talk the talk of compassion even while whipping
up support from racist constituencies with carefully encoded sermons about
what makes the country great.[178] On these readings, taken collectively, Mill
is suspect on the count of racism both when urging the spread of representative government and laissez faire and when qualifying their applicability,
both when recognizing difference and when being "blood blind." Goldberg
is incensed both by Mill allowing the English to play Charlemagne in India
and by his supposed call (which was in fact quite qualified) for laissez faire
in Jamaica.

Plainly, on these issues, there is little underlying harmony in Mill studies.
There are extreme defenders of pluralism, such as Parekh and Gray, and there
are the currents represented by Nussbaum and Appiah, who would urge that
the pluralist critique of Mill is losing steam, going the way of communitarian-
ism, identity politics, and other ill-defined movements. Still, even the latter
should allow that Mill had his failings, and if these were not such as to make
him a nascent neocon, they do nonetheless call for concern. Thus, as Jennifer
Pitts has put it, in her admirable work *A Turn to Empire*:

> Mill, for all his radicalism with regard to domestic politics, placed con-
> siderable faith in colonial government as a well-intentioned and legit-
> imate despotism designed for the improvement of its subjects. Both
> his writings on India and his role in the Eyre affair suggest that he

hesitated before a full-scale inquiry into the structure of colonial rule and the repeated abuses that structure invited. He avoided such an inquiry even though he came to acknowledge, late in life, a mistrust of British political judgment on colonial matters.[179]

Pitts provides a very careful analysis of Mill's theoretical and practical work on both India and Jamaica. In the latter case as well as the former, Mill was practically and politically involved; he became the moving force on the Jamaica Committee investigating–or rather, condemning—Governor Eyre's atrocities in response to the Morant Bay Rebellion of 1865, when Eyre brutally repressed the (perfectly justifiable) uprising and judicially murdered such rebel leaders as Paul Bogle and George William Gordon, the latter being a well-to-do mulatto landowner and member of the Assembly who had long been critical of Eyre but was not directly involved in the rebellion.[180] Eyre's ferocity recalled the British response to the Sepoy Rebellion, and Mill's response to it, as Goldberg, Bogues, and Pitts agree, was singularly revealing, suggestive of what he did and did not dissent from in Carlyle, who was a vociferous leader of those defending Eyre, Carlyle's ideal of a hero.

Mill wanted Eyre brought to justice, but that was apparently all he wanted, beyond his usual hopes, now tinged with greater melancholy, for improving the quality of imperial rule.

> [Mill's] belief in the incapacity of non-European subjects for self-rule meant that he failed to argue for—perhaps even to imagine—conditions of accountability to colonial subjects. Until backward peoples were deemed, presumably by European administrators, capable of participating in their own governance, Mill seemed content to rely on colonial administrators themselves for appropriate restraints on the exercise of power. Other than his expressions of mistrust of the local legislature, Mill said little about how progress toward collective self-government in Jamaica might take place. He resorted, as in India, to the tidier and less political solution of administration checked by criminal courts. Mill, that is, tended to regard colonial subjects as objects of administration rather than participants in a political process.[181]

Like Mehta, Pitts allows that Burke was more attuned than Mill to the abuses of colonial rule. But like Goldberg and Bogues, she recognizes how Mill's context was more virulently racist: "Liberal colonial reform itself, and liberal cosmopolitanism, had changed by the mid-nineteenth century. British superiority and the justice of British colonial rule were nearly taken for granted by the bulk of the population by the mid-nineteenth century."[182] Thus, in this context, "Mill's continued opposition to racist argument and his commitment to benevolent and improving colonial government was perhaps the most ambitious posture liberalism could muster. The Eyre trial gives some indication of the constraints on humanitarian discourse more generally in the nineteenth century."[183]

Although Pitts does not label Mill a "polite and effete" racist, she does come quite close: "Both Mill and Tocqueville insisted that claims about biological differences or inequalities were unprovable and morally and politically pernicious. And yet their willingness to see the moral and political standards that governed relations within Europe suspended in dealings with other peoples bore the mark of a discourse increasingly founded on the assumptions about the inequality of different peoples."[184] And after all, fierce as Mill's response to Carlyle was, he did not deny that there might be biological racial differences; he only claimed that scientific knowledge was insufficiently advanced to demonstrate these. This construction has the support of no less a Mill scholar than the late John Robson, who wrote, in his essay "Civilization and Culture," that although Mill had little to say on "race"—the term "national character" being his more common idiom—which he considered an "accident of birth" like sex, he did, like others of his time, tend "to apply it to groups that were indeed genetically loosely interrelated, but distinguished from one another by behaviour and belief." His position was made clear in a letter to Charles Dupont-White, in which Mill emphatically denied that his condemnation of the "vulgar error" of attributing everything to race meant that he attributed no influence to race—"he did not deny, but in fact admits 'pleinement . . . l'influence des races.'"[185]

But mere agnosticism in this context can be deeply troubling, and such worries are not effectively addressed or even acknowledged by such figures as Nussbaum and Appiah. The most forthright defenses of Mill have come from others with some sympathy for the cosmopolitan line, such as Georgios Varouxakis and H. S. Jones. Against Goldberg, Varouxakis has argued that the difference between Carlyle and Mill should be counted as a difference between racist and non-racist: "I think that the two things are separate and that the term 'racism' is not appropriate to describe Mill's attitude; 'Euro-centric' would do."[186] But even so, "Mill's thought was indeed Euro-centric, and, despite his efforts to be open-minded, he did show himself deplorably ignorant and prejudiced about non-European cultures, not least those of the Indian Peninsula. And his belief that a benevolent despotism was a legitimate mode of governing those he called 'barbarians' . . . was paternalistic and based on assumptions that we cannot accept today."[187]

For Varouxakis, to label Mill a type of racist, or even to say, with Parekh that "[f]rom time to time Mill . . . came pretty close to the crude racism of his time," is just too much, given how good he was in the context of his "times," even if we admit that his "open-mindedness did not reach far enough." Varouxakis carefully demonstrates, against Mehta, that what "Mill actually means when he talks of colonists 'of our blood' is their cultural traits, coming from the mother county, the metropolis. He does not use 'blood' literally."[188]

And Jones, for his part, urges that "Varouxakis has definitively refuted the surprisingly resilient belief that Mill had recourse to racial explanations in history and political thought," and condemns Goldberg's case as "curiously slight."[189] Against Goldberg's claims about Mill erasing racial subjectivity, Jones argues:

> Whereas it is largely true at the beginning of the twenty-first century that self-conscious racial subjectivity is a weapon to be used by the oppressed against their current or former oppressors, this was hardly the case in the nineteenth century. Then, race theory was commonly deployed in support of colonial despotism, as the involvement of Carlyle and others in the Governor Eyre controversy demonstrated. J. S. Mill's stance on colonialism may not satisfy our standards of political correctness, but the political bite of his race-blindness was powerfully progressive in its time.[190]

Furthermore, Goldberg's argument for regarding Mill as racist is akin to claims that he was not really a feminist. "The case for regarding Mill as a racist depends on the belief that his 'civilizational perspective' betrayed an unspoken assimilation of 'civilization' to white European civilization: the white European, then, embodied the universal standard of human excellence," much as radical feminists charge him with measuring women by male standards, in effect recognizing their worth as men without penises. Jones stresses in response how Mill "was a consistent believer in the importance of 'nurture' rather than 'nature'" and how he was "unsympathetic to 'equal but different' arguments: that is, arguments for equality founded on the distinctive qualities of the oppressed. Mill tended to believe that oppression made people oppressed, not that it made people good in some distinctive way."[191]

These defenses of Mill have surely gone very far to clarify just how Mill used such key terms as "race," "blood," "national character," etc. But they concede a lot to the critics. As noted, Varouxakis objects to "the rather promiscuous use of the term 'racist' evinced in the writings of many scholars," but he allows that Mill "did show himself deplorably ignorant and prejudiced about non-European cultures, not least those of the Indian Peninsula." Jones allows that Pitts, especially, makes a powerful case: in effect, "the case of the radical emancipationist against the liberal emancipationist," since Mill "did not appreciate the extent to which his understanding of what emancipation must entail was itself rooted in domination." Even if we refrain from calling Mill a racist, we are right to call him arrogantly Eurocentric, too complacently accepting of difference as "inferiority," and blindly paternalistic on the question of subject peoples being allowed to rule themselves, making their own mistakes, etc. And all this in the name of bare historical accuracy, rather than "political correctness," whatever that is supposed to mean. And this is not to mention Mill's avowed receptiveness (acknowledged by Robson) to the possibility that science might in the future make out some significant (biological) racial differences. Apparently, when it comes to arboreal metaphors about stunted growth, Mill's depictions of, say, the Jamaicans were rather more sinister than his depictions of subjected women in England. One can make a case, as Nussbaum does, for Mill as anticipating (at least in the English context) some elements of radical feminism, what with his keen sense of the distortions resulting from power and domination; one cannot make such a case with respect to his account of black Jamaicans.

Furthermore, Varouxakis and Jones do not really bring out just how far Mill's views on, say, the Jamaicans really could have justified a Victorian equivalent of racial profiling.[192] Given the conceptual confusions that swirl around the notion of "race" even in our own day, such that one can find biological essentialists about race casting themselves as anti-racists and anti-biological essentialists cast—not usually by themselves—as racist, one might be forgiven for thinking that on the count of racism, Mill was close enough for imperial government work.[193]

Unfortunately, it cannot be said that Nussbaum and Appiah candidly acknowledge what a close call this matter is, which is especially surprising in Appiah's case, given how perceptive he has been on the long history of black identity politics, even in the nineteenth century. As Appiah notes, the early W.E.B. DuBois held that "people are members of the same race if they share features in virtue of being descended largely from people of the same region. Those features may be physical—hence Afro-Americas are Negroes—or cultural—hence Anglo-Americans are English."[194] Which is to say that DuBois, writing within twenty-five years of Mill's death, used the term "race" in much the way Mill used the term "blood," while seeking "to revalue one pole of the opposition of white to black."

Contra Jones, then, there clearly was an anti-racist, black subjectivity for Mill to ignore.[195] Indeed, he obviously did so when he was fairly confronted to his face (figuratively speaking) by the Jamaicans Paul Bogle and George William Gordon, who, as Thomas Holt argues, effectively used an eclectic blend of Christian and African religious ideas to provide "a vehicle for cultural resistance, giving moral authority to an alternative world-view." As one history of Jamaica puts it:

> Bogle and Gordon, in their last years, defined the central themes of justice and concern for the "many," which widened into a struggle against the monopoly of political power that was taken up by Robert Lowe, Sandy Cox and Bain Alves with their trade unions, Marcus Garvey, Norman Manley in his campaign for universal adult suffrage and Alexander Bustamante in his formation of the labour movement, and led to political independence in 1962.[196]

In short, they were freedom fighters. To understand this, one need only think of the histories portrayed in C.L.R. James, *The Black Jacobins: Toussaint L'Ouverture and the San Domingo Revolution.*

As Bogues notes, during the Morant Bay Rebellion, the rebellious crowds at points confronted those police officers who were black with cries of "Cleave to the black." Of course, the historical situation in the Caribbean and Latin America was very complex; as Holt observes, of the treatment of mulattos and mixed-blood peoples, "they came to occupy a social status not unlike the Jewish and Muslim converts. They were not classified with blacks but as a separate caste, and they filled the interstitial jobs—and some of high status—that American frontier societies with small white settler populations required. In the British West Indies there were legal procedures—if one could pay for them—for having oneself actually declared white by an act of the legislature. In Jamaica in the 1830s the white planters hoped that the brown population could be assimilated to the white side of the racial divide so that they would form a protective bulwark against the soon-to-be-emancipated black slave majority."[197]

(Mill had little to say about the Haitian Revolution, but in his essay in the *Edinburgh Review* he did direct some properly nasty remarks at the apologists for the white slaveholders: "Then all who venture to doubt whether it is perfectly just and humane to aid in reducing one half of the people of Hayti to slavery, and exterminating the other half, are accused of sympathizing exclusively with the blacks. We wonder what the writer would call sympathizing exclusively with the whites. We should have thought that the lives and liberties of a whole nation were an ample sacrifice for the value of a slight, or rather, as the event proved, an imaginary, addition to the security of the property of a few West India planters."[198])

Thus, it is safe to say that even when confronted with a compelling, pragmatic black resistance movement and a possible extension of (genuine) political equality to Jamaican blacks in response, Mill, as Pitts puts it, "sought a solution in the imposition of reforms through the colonial authority."[199] It would seem, then, that to say that he was good for his cultural context is to define his cultural context by (a problematic construction of) English "whiteness," when he himself was actively engaging with the Jamaican situation and an avowedly black liberation movement in a way that can only be described as a failure to appreciate the meaning of the historical moment, a failure in his own effort—and in his own terms—to see all sides of a question.[200]

The point here needs to be underscored: it is not enough to try to exonerate Mill, in the fashion of Varouxakis and Jones, by showing that he was not working with a biological racial essentialism. The racialism involved in racism is never coherent, and although the term "racism" may have gained currency in the early twentieth century and may have many gray areas, there is little reason to resist applying it to earlier periods, when such terms as "blood," etc., seemed to carry a mix of biological and cultural features, just as they sometimes did in more recent times. Indeed, this point is compellingly made by George Fredrickson in his book *Racism: A Short History*. As Fredrickson puts it, "Deterministic cultural particularism can do the work of biological racism quite effectively."[201] With reference to the case of South African apartheid, he observes, "The extent to which Afrikaner nationalism was inspired by nineteenth-century European cultural nationalism also contributed to this avoidance of a pseudoscientific rationale. No better example can be found of how a 'cultural Essentialism' based on nationality can do the work of a racism based squarely on skin color or other physical characteristics."[202]

On Varouxakis' argument, the former regime of South African apartheid ought to be called "Eurocentric" rather than "racist"—which is surely absurd.

At any rate, it is scarcely anachronistic or judgmental to worry about racism in this context; it is more anachronistic and judgmental to insist in advance on accepting the "limits" of the "cultural context," "times," etc. As Fredrickson argues, although we must take care not to make "racism the ideological essence of imperialism," we must, nonetheless, recognize how the "view of colonial rule as a lengthy and problematic apprenticeship for civilized modernity can be viewed as functionally racist to the degree that it justified denying civil and political rights to indigenous populations for the foreseeable future."[203]

Admittedly, of the treatment of Gordon, Mill said some wise things, relevant to our own times: "The great majority of people, especially people in power, are ready to believe almost anything against their political enemies, especially those who have said or published things tending to excite disapprobation of their conduct."[204] But he did not pursue such thoughts to their uncomfortable conclusions. Complain as he might about "the overbearing and insolent disregard of the rights and feelings of inferiors which is the common characteristic of John Bull when he thinks he cannot be resisted," he did not rethink his view of the "inferiors." Not even, strangely enough, when the Sepoy Rebellion in India (labeled the "Indian Mutiny" by the British) spelled the end of India House, Crown control of India, and Mill's retirement. He defended India House to the end.

As all sides really ought to admit, about the best "anti-hierarchical" thought one can find in Mill on this subject comes in an 1866 letter to David Urquhart: "But my eyes were first opened to the moral condition of the English nation (I except in these matters the working classes) by the atrocities perpetrated in the Indian Mutiny & the feelings which supported them at home. Then came the sympathy with the lawless rebellion of the Southern Americans in defence of an institution which is the sum of all lawlessness, as Wesley said it was of all villainy—& finally came this Jamaica business the authors of which from the first day I knew of it I determined that I would do all in my power to bring to justice if there was not another man in Parlt to stand by me."[205] But Mill prefaces this late-in-life explanation with the admission: "You approve of my speech because you see that I am not on this occasion standing up for the negroes, or for liberty, deeply as both are interested in the subject—but for the first necessity of human society, law." Again, his overwhelming concern, throughout the Eyre business, was with the rule of law. As Kinzer, Robson, and Robson insightfully remark, "The moral legitimacy of such imperial rule turned on the intent and capacity of the dominant country to provide the subject people with a government better—in the sense of promoting 'the permanent interests of man as a progressive being'—than they could provide for themselves," but the "men representing the British crown in Jamaica in the autumn of 1865 had disgraced the British Empire and desecrated the principles for which it ought to stand."[206]

Perhaps the best possible construal of Mill's position is judiciously developed by Joseph Miller: "Mill pursues Eyre not simply because Eyre threatens a colonial system whose weaknesses Mill refuses to acknowledge. Rather, Eyre represents a particular vision of colonialism (arbitrary despotism wielded only to the advantage of the colonizer) that is fundamentally at odds with Mill's considered conception of colonialism."[207]

And of course, although he was recalled and his career effectively ended, Eyre never was brought to justice; rather, Mill lost his seat in Parliament in part thanks to his efforts against the former Governor, the Jamaican Assembly was dissolved (by itself, out of fear of black participation), and Crown rule was imposed.[208] That (along with the death threats he received) should have provided Mill with rather more food for thought than it apparently did, though of course he was, at this point in his life, very outspoken about his views and willing to accept the consequences of this forthrightness. Alas, it is pure fantasy to suggest, as some have, that Mill was keeping his better angels under wraps for political purposes, though it is possible that he really let loose only after the failure of Gladstone's Liberal reform efforts, which he had largely supported. In his case, the life is obviously extremely helpful in understanding the work, but it does not serve to exonerate him on questions of race and colonialism.

And what of Harriet Taylor Mill on such questions? Her restored reputation might be helped by the fact that she said less about colonialism than Mill did. And of course, she had died just after Mill's retirement, and well before the events of the sixties. That she and Mill shared a sophisticated view of happiness did not necessarily mean that she had to agree with him about the political applications of it in connection with colonial rule, etc., despite the intimate ways in which the formation of the Millian autonomous character was linked to the progress of civilization and hence to assessments of which parts of the world were progressing, which not. What did she think?

She would, of course, have been all the more remarkable had she pointed the way to a better and more truly emancipatory application of their view of happiness, or seen how there might have been something to be said in favor of Bentham's views on the matter of colonialism, or anticipated to a greater degree the Nussbaum reconstruction of the Millian view, recognizing how women of color might also need experiments in living. But no one has made such a case for her. Her letters and writings do carry some relevant observations, often of a Eurocentric nature—aspersions on "barbaric" Asia and the

Irish, along with an enthusiasm for the Italians—but these are mostly slight, and one cannot help but be struck by her silence on so many global issues. India House is mentioned occasionally, but primarily as Mill's place of employment and without reference to its significance for India. Her thoughts on the Sepoy Rebellion are nowhere to be found. One might argue, as Jane Duran does, that "[a]lthough there is little in Harriet's work that speaks to an awareness of colonialism, and although we know that JSM, in his capacity as a civil servant at East India House, took a dim view of earlier attempts at Indian rebellion, HTM's sensitivity to workers . . . speaks well of her ability to extrapolate from a set of circumstances"[209]—and from this conclude that she might or ought to have been sympathetic to struggles for independence by women elsewhere. But the case is built more on her silences (or missing evidence) than on her actual claims, and one would like to see evidence that she actually wanted Mill to change, say, those lines in *On Liberty* about despotism being justifiable for backward peoples. Although she clearly shared his antipathy to slavery, she is silent on his response to Carlyle on "The Negro Question," despite making any number of critical remarks about Carlyle, Mill's former friend, in other contexts.

For one so given to original thinking about progress and a future realizing utopian hopes and dreams, she in the end seemed too close to Mill in being unable to think ahead on matters of global justice, in part simply because of an insufficient appreciation of what had come before, with the earlier utilitarians. Thus it would fall to the third of the great classical utilitarians, Henry Sidgwick, to seek a better integration of the old and new methods of utilitarian ethics. Mill may have done his work—his dying words, to Helen, the stepdaughter who had tended him so caringly after the death of Harriet, were "You know that I have done my work"—but there was clearly much work still to be done in the cause of utilitarianism.

FIGURE 1. *Thomas Holcroft and William Godwin*, by Sir Thomas Lawrence, pencil with black and red chalk, 1794. © National Portrait Gallery, London. Reproduced courtesy of the National Portrait Gallery, London.

FIGURE 2. *Mary Wollstonecraft*, by John Opie, oil on canvas, circa 1797. © National Portrait Gallery, London. Reproduced courtesy of the National Portrait Gallery, London.

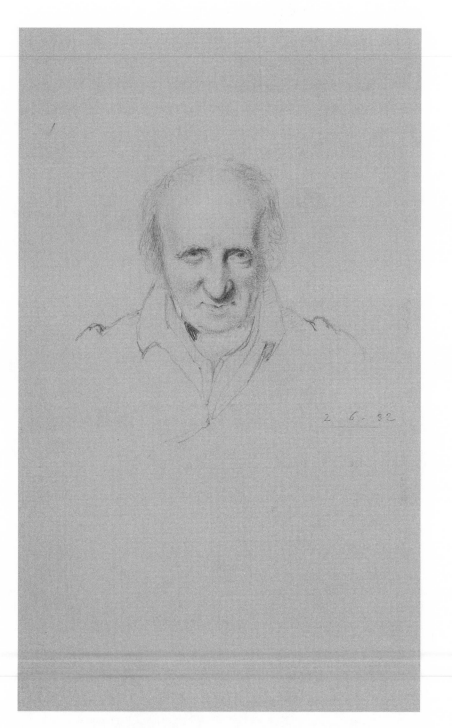

FIGURE 3. *William Godwin*, by William Brockedon, pencil and white and red chalk, 1832. © National Portrait Gallery, London. Reproduced courtesy of the National Portrait Gallery, London.

FIGURE 4. *Jeremy Bentham*, by the Studio of Thomas Frye, oil on canvas, 1760. © National Portrait Gallery, London. Reproduced courtesy of the National Portrait Gallery, London.

FIGURE 5A. Auto-Icon of the Philosopher
and Jurist Jeremy Bentham (1748–
1832), photograph, Bentham Project,
University College London, May 17,
2007. © University College London,
ISD Digital Media, All Rights Reserved.
Reproduced courtesy of the Bentham
Project, University College London.

FIGURE 5B. Jeremy Bentham; Auto-
Icon, photograph, Bentham Project,
University College London, November
3, 2011. © University College London,
ISD Digital Media, All Rights Reserved.
Reproduced courtesy of the Bentham
Project, University College London.

FIGURE 6. *John Stuart Mill*, replica by George Frederic Watts, oil on canvas, 1873. © National Portrait Gallery, London. Reproduced courtesy of the National Portrait Gallery, London.

FIGURE 7. *Harriet Mill*, unknown artist, oil on canvas, circa 1834. © National Portrait Gallery, London. Reproduced courtesy of the National Portrait Gallery, London.

FIGURE 8. *Henry Sidgwick and Eusapia Palladino*, by Eveleen Myers (*née* Tennant), platinum print, circa 1890. © National Portrait Gallery, London. Reproduced courtesy of the National Portrait Gallery, London.

FIGURE 9. *Eleanor ("Nora") Mildred Sidgwick*, by Eveleen Myers (*née* Tennant), platinum print, 1890s. © National Portrait Gallery, London. Reproduced courtesy of the National Portrait Gallery, London.

CHAPTER FOUR

Henry Sidgwick and Beyond

O smile, where are you going? O upturned glance:
new warm receding wave on the sea of the heart . . .
alas, but that is what we *are*. Does the infinite space
we dissolve into, taste of us then?

—RILKE, *DUINO ELEGIES*

*In appearance, in later years, Henry Sidgwick was the only man I have
ever seen who had something of the nobleness of mien, the kindly dignity,
and the unapproachable antiquity of the elders in Blake's designs of the
Book of Job. He wore his massed hair rather long, in ambrosial waves, like
a Greek god. His beard, of fine silky texture and irregular outline, seemed
to flow liquidly from his face rather than to have been applied to it . . .
with him it adorned and amplified his finely chiseled features, his great
brow, and clear-cut nose. He was small of stature, and had very delicate
hands, which he used much in gestures that were elucidatory rather than
emphatic. He often played with his beard, stroking it or lifting it to his
face. His features in repose, with uplifted eyebrows, had a pensive, almost
melancholy air. But this was transfigured in talk by the sweetest and most
childlike of smiles. His voice was soft and high-pitched, and had at times
a note of weariness about it. But he could modulate it very beautifully for
emphasis or emotional effect; while his reciting of poetry was one of the
most thrilling and enchanting things I ever heard.*

—A. C. BENSON, "HENRY SIDGWICK"

Overview—Sidgwick the Man, in Brief

No figure discussed in this book is more paradoxical and provocative than
Henry Sidgwick, whose entire life fell within the reign of Queen Victoria and
entire adult life within the confines of Cambridge University. On the surface

the most respectable and academic of the great utilitarians, his life reveals how much of philosophical importance was concealed by his carefully crafted public persona. Although in some ways the most outrageous thinker of them all, Sidgwick never published explosive attacks on the status quo that could rival the white heatedness of those of Godwin, Bentham, and Mill. But he was in some respects even more subversive than his great predecessors, a philosophical mole of sorts, who sought to do from within the Establishment what the others sought to do mainly from without. With a great reputation for frank speaking, candor, and honesty—the result in part of his 1869 resignation of his Cambridge Fellowship because he could no longer in good conscience subscribe to the Thirty-Nine Articles of the Church of England as was then required—he in fact kept many of his views, including his most philosophically significant views, secret, or at any rate out of the public eye. He did not, for example, want to use his authority to openly undermine popular religious morality, at least until society was in a better position to get on without it. *Parrhesia*, or frank speaking, was for him a defining casuistical problem.[1]

Sidgwick was a strange mix, a philosopher whose life and works could—and this will no doubt sound odd to those who find him a dreary read—run from the mastery of acute, minute, and sobering philosophical analysis to reviews of homoerotic poetry and speculations in parapsychological metaphysics that one has trouble crediting to the same man. Also, his Millian liberalism could run further in the direction of racist imperialism than one would suspect from the adroit evasions in his publications (not to mention his Millian roots), and his warm friendship with and elaborate protective support of some of the most provocative figures in the history of sexuality, such as John Addington Symonds and other notable defenders of Greek or same-sex love, puts him in an orbit beyond even Bentham. The unifying theme of these many sides was best described by Sidgwick himself:

> My aim in what I am about to say now is to give such an account of my life—mainly my inner intellectual life—as shall render the central and fundamental aims that partially at least determined its course when apparently most fitful and erratic, as clear and intelligible as I can. That aim is very simply stated. It has been the solution, or contribution to the solution, of the deepest problems of human life. The peculiarity of my career has been that I have sought light on these problems, and that not casually but systematically and laboriously, from very various sources and by very diverse methods.[2]

He had himself right. His talent for incisive, fine-grained philosophical argument was very real, but always kept in perspective, the larger human perspective concerned with how we are to live. He was decidedly a many-sided Millian character, with an amazing range of interests, from poetry to philosophy to political economy to parapsychology. But his many interests always related back to that basic Socratic problem of how to live one's life. And curiously enough, Sidgwick is at one and the same time the classical utilitarian most celebrated and emulated by recent academic philosophers, and the one most in need of radical reconstruction on such matters as race and imperialism.[3]

To be sure, his was a life of very real achievement. However secret and subversive his views, he would win many honors and in due course become Knightbridge Professor of Moral Philosophy at Cambridge, a position he would hold until he resigned it shortly before his death, from cancer, on August 28, 1900. He was the author of many essays and reviews and of such weighty treatises as *The Elements of Politics* (1891), *The Principles of Political Economy* (1883), and the work that made his reputation, *The Methods of Ethics*, first published in 1874. His *Outlines of the History of Ethics* (1886), which began as an article for the *Encyclopedia Britannica*, remains one of the best short introductions to the subject.[4] Like his great utilitarian predecessors, Sidgwick was profoundly devoted to both political economy and educational reform; he would devote endless hours to his various causes, particularly the reform of Cambridge University and advancing higher education for women, though he also developed considerable expertise on the problems of poverty. And this is not to mention parapsychology, which absorbed much of his life. He cofounded both the Society for Psychical Research and Newnham College, Cambridge, one of England's first colleges for women. His chief collaborator in these efforts was his wife, Eleanor Mildred Balfour (1845–1936), a member of the wealthy and influential Balfour clan whose brother Arthur (a student of Henry's at Cambridge) would become prime minister, and whose uncle was the third Marquess of Salisbury.

Thus, the Sidgwicks were yet another utilitarian power couple, well-known in the circles of privilege and influence. They may in fact have been the most powerful of all, at least potentially, and albeit in a behind-the-scenes fashion. They were friendly with everyone from Tennyson to Gladstone to George Eliot. One of Eleanor's sisters would marry Lord Rayleigh, who won the Nobel Prize for discovering argon, and the Sidgwicks would spend much time at Terling Place, the beautiful Rayleigh estate in Essex (where they are buried), as they would at Whittingehame, the impressive Balfour estate in Scotland.[5] Eleanor was an accomplished mathematician and helped Rayleigh with his research, and her abilities, especially when she became Principal of Newnham, impressed even Bertrand Russell. When the Sidgwicks threw a garden party at Newnham, the political Establishment was there, including the Prince of Wales.

Perhaps most importantly of all, however, Sidgwick would become one of the greatest of the Cambridge Apostles, whose members included such leading lights as Tennyson and Maurice, the friend of John Stuart Mill's. And it was in such contexts, part of the "Platonic revival" of his times, that his most prominent characteristic took shape: his gift for sympathetic conversation.

Family, friends, and students united in celebrating him for his talk, and for a form of reasonableness that was reflective of a remarkably sympathetic nature. As Balfour (who was all three) put it: "Of all the men I have known he was the readiest to consider every controversy and every controversialist on their merits. He never claimed authority; he never sought to impose his views; he never argued for victory; he never evaded an issue."[6] Using his slight stammer to good effect, he was able to draw out the best in his interlocutors, but with a certain witty zest. When Balfour exclaimed that he would follow the Church of England through thick and thin, Sidgwick dryly and stutteringly agreed that he would follow it through thin. But as F. W. Maitland put it, his "irony never hurt, it was so kindly; and, of all known forms of wickedness, 'Sidgwickedness' was the least wicked." Or as his old friend James Bryce explained, his "talk was conversation, not discourse, for though he naturally became the centre of nearly every company in which he found himself, he took no more than his share. It was like the sparkling of a brook whose ripples seem to give out sunshine." A. C. Benson, Sidgwick's nephew, went so far as to say: "He was so sincere, so simple-minded, so unselfish, so sympathetic, so utterly incapable of meanness or baseness, so guileless, so patient, of so crystalline a purity and sweetness of character, that he is one of the few men to whom one could honestly apply in the highest sense the word 'saint.'"[7] There was a remarkable consensus among those who knew him that Sidgwick the man was better than Sidgwick the academic.

The talk that mattered most to Sidgwick, however, was close, deeply philosophical talk with intimate friends. To a remarkable degree, one can best get to know him by the company that he kept; and his closest friends, his intellectual and emotional resources, included (in addition to his wife) such brilliant and controversial figures as Symonds (the erudite cultural historian, poet, and literary critic, author of "A Problem in Greek Ethics" and a great champion of same-sex or "Greek" or "Hellenic" love), and F.W.H. Myers (also sexually controversial, and one of the leading psychical researchers and a breakthrough figure in depth psychology). As with Mill and Sterling, these figures often represented what Sidgwick needed to be truly whole, the missing complement to his more Benthamite half. His most candid confessions were to them, or to other close friends, such as Roden Noel of the famous Gainsborough family or Henry Graham Dakyns, who both were also part of the movement that Symonds represented, a movement that had a great predecessor in Bentham, not that that was known.[8] In the 1890s, Sidgwick would play a leading role in carefully censoring the more explicit parts of Symonds's homoerotic verse and official biography, assembled by Horatio Brown. This he did to avert (successfully) another Oscar Wilde style scandal, when, in the aftermath of the 1885 Criminal Law Amendment Act declaring all forms of male homosexuality illegal, homophobic persecution, especially of such outspoken and frank figures as Wilde, emerged with renewed ferocity.[9]

Of course, there is no denying that Sidgwick was, in academic terms, a brilliant ethical philosopher and a brilliant inspiration to future generations of brilliant ethical philosophers. Nor, as this chapter will demonstrate, should one deny that the current reconstructions and appropriations of many of Sidgwick's positions, in the works of such philosophers as Roger Crisp, Derek Parfit, Rob Shaver, Peter Singer, and Katarzyna de Lazari-Radek, are immensely important and have contributed to a true renaissance of hedonistic and rational intuition-based utilitarianism (or at least rationalistic consequentialism) that few saw coming even in the late twentieth century. And yet, these reconstructions and appropriations do have their limits, and can reflect a narrower conception of "the deepest problems of human life" than Sidgwick's. If ever any classical utilitarian suffered from Cosmic Anxiety, a profound conflict between the outlooks of Cosmic Optimism and Cosmic Pessimism, that utilitarian was Sidgwick.[10] He harbored a deeper, wider-ranging, and more genuine agnosticism than any of his followers, past or present.[11] Unlike Bentham or Mill, he had a religion to lose, and he suffered for it. His claim on us comes from both his ever-intelligent doubt and his astonishing, rare openness to alternative possibilities. Indeed, perhaps his single most important deviation from the classical utilitarian perspectives was this pervasive agnosticism, a deflating of the confidence of his predecessors when it came to thinking that the final answers to the riddles of the universe were in, or nearly so. As Eleanor noted after his death, he never found "the truth he sought."[12]

From Cotton to Crisis to Cosmos—Sidgwick's Ghosts

Like Mill's philosophy, Sidgwick's also had some problematic enabling conditions. Sidgwick was born into a prosperous extended family in Skipton, Yorkshire, in 1838. In *Henry Sidgwick, A Memoir,* compiled by Eleanor and Henry's brother Arthur, the following account is given of the Skipton years:

> Henry Sidgwick was born on May 31, 1838, at Skipton, in the West Riding of Yorkshire. He was the third son, and the fourth child, of the Rev. William Sidgwick, whose father had been established since 1784 as a cotton-spinner at Skipton. The mill, worked by water-power, lay in the grounds behind the castle; and Mr. Sidgwick, who had a country house some miles off, called Stone Gappe, occupied in the winter the gatehouse of the old castle as his private dwelling. Little is known about his origin save that he came from Leeds in 1784, but there was a persistent tradition in the family that they had originally migrated from Dent, a picturesque dale in the far north-west of the county, to the north of Ingleborough, opening out into the larger valley of the Clough at Sedbergh. At Dent there have been for the last four centuries at least, as the parish registers show, "sidesmen" (or small farmers owning their land)

of the name of Sidgwick or Sidgswick. The only one of the clan who was at all widely known was Adam Sedgwick of Cambridge, who held the Professorship of Geology for fifty-five years. Many of this vigorous stock appear in later years to have settled in other places, particularly in the manufacturing towns of the West Riding, and amongst these was William Sidgwick, the cotton-spinner of Skipton. Four of his five sons remained in or near Skipton, engaged in the business; the other (Henry Sidgwick's father), destined for the Church, was sent to Trinity College, Cambridge, where his name appears as the last of the Wranglers in 1829.

After his ordination William Sidgwick the younger undertook parochial work, first at Rampside (near Broughton-in-Furness) in 1833, and in the same year was married to Mary Crofts, the eldest daughter of another Yorkshire family from the East Riding. She with her three brothers and two sisters had been left orphans at a very early age, and the whole charge of these six children was generously undertaken by a bachelor uncle, the Rev. William Carr, who was the fourth in succession of the same family to hold the living of Bolton Abbey. In this beautiful seclusion, with the heather-clad moors above, and the rock-bed stream of the Wharfe flowing through wooded banks not a stone's throw from the parsonage, Henry Sidgwick's mother passed her childhood. Those who knew her in after years observed that while she had many interests and much force both of mind and character, she had no special artistic sensibility either to music or painting; but in regard to scenery she showed all her life the most vivid and discriminating delight. And there can be little doubt that this was largely due to the fact that the sensitive years of early girlhood were passed amid the beauties of Wharfedale.

In the winter of 1834 Mr. and Mrs. Sidgwick, with their eldest son, born at Rampside, moved to another cure at Barnborough, near Doncaster, and two years later to Skipton, Mr. Sidgwick having been appointed to the headmastership of the grammar school, which was then in the old building, a picturesquely situated house at the end of the town, close to the foot of Rumblesmoor. The eldest daughter was born at Barnborough in 1835; and four more children followed in the five years between the move to Skipton in 1836 and their father's death in 1841. In August of the previous year the second boy had died, and the eldest daughter was already failing. The mother tried first Barmouth, and afterwards Tenby, in vain; the child died at Tenby, and in June 1844 the family at last found a settled home in Redland, on the outskirts of Bristol, close to Durdham Down.[13]

Although Mary Sidgwick's family did move on when Henry was quite young, the larger family remained planted in Skipton and nearby Lothersdale, and these locations would be of continuing and considerable significance to Henry for the rest of his life. Strangely enough, however, the significance of this family heritage has largely escaped the attention of the many philosophers who have written about Sidgwick.

Not enough is known about the Sidgwick family's early life in Skipton, but it is clear from reliable sources that the extended family was one of considerable prominence and wealth, friendly with the aristocracy though not of it. As Dawson's *History of Skipton* explains:

> The oldest manufacturing firm in Skipton is that of the Sidgwicks, and the oldest mill is the High Mill, in the Castle Woods, the earliest part of which dates back to the year 1785. A lease was in that year (March 1st) granted by Sackville, Earl of Thanet Island, to Messrs. Peter Garforth, John Blackburn, and John Sidgwick. The Mr. J. Sidgwick here mentioned was brother-in-law to Mr. Garforth, and father of Mr. Wm. Sidgwick [Henry Sidgwick's grandfather], who at that date was twenty years old, and probably when of age became a partner in the firm. In 1806 he was the sole lessee. At this time the High Mill was engaged in spinning cotton yarn, on the old wooden frames. In 1825 the firm consisted of Mr. W. Sidgwick and his sons, Jr. Jno. B. Sidgwick and Mr. Chris. Sidgwick, who after their father's death in 1827 carried on the business until in about six years Mr. C. Sidgwick retired and was succeeded by his brother James. In 1839 the Low Mill was built for weaving and weft spinning, and in 1840 it began to be worked, being at that time conducted by Messrs. J. B. and R. H. Sidgwick. Messrs. J. B. and James Sidgwick, however, continued to work the High Mill, until in 1865 the latter retired, and the firm became Mesrs. J. B. Sidgwick and Co., into whose hands both mills passed.[14]

The details of this family tree need to be set out at greater length, the better to appreciate the family's role in the growth of Lothersdale and Skipton. John Sidgwick, "of Leeds, Bingley and Skipton: sometime of Back o'Shambles, and Kirkgate, Leeds," was born in 1716, married in 1752 (to Sarah Shirtcliffe), and died in 1791. The couple had seven children, but it was William, born August 22, 1765, in Leeds, who actively pursued his father's cotton spinning business in Skipton and first brought the family to Stone Gappe, purchasing it in 1796 (a number of accounts, notably A. C. Benson's, erroneously claim that he built it).[15] He married Anne Benson, who was born in 1774 and would live until 1856, surviving her husband by nearly thirty years. Their children were to play a key role in the growth of Skipton, and of course the Benson family would remain closely connected to the Sidgwicks (Henry's sister Mary in fact ended up marrying Edward White Benson[16]). John Benson Sidgwick, the eldest, was born at Stone Gappe on June 30th, 1800, and went into partnership with his father at an early age. He married Sarah Hannah Greenwood in 1827. His brother Christopher was also born at Stone Gappe, in 1804, and also went into the family business, though he retired from business at age twenty-nine, after only six years, and devoted much of his life and fortune to the construction of Skipton's Christ Church, where he was buried upon his death in 1877. A statue was nearly erected in his honor, but the distinction went instead to the first MP for Skipton, Sir Matthew Wilson.[17] As noted above, his role in the family business was taken over by James Sidgwick, who was born at Stone Gappe in 1812, and who lived mainly at Skipton Castle, where he died in 1890. His parents, particularly his long-lived mother, had also made the Skipton Castle Gatehouse a primary residence. Robert Hodgson Sidgwick, who was born at Stone Gappe in 1816 and married to Mary Jane Ward in 1846, also made a career in the family cotton spinning business, taking over the Low Mill from Christopher and James. Two other children, Edward and Margaret, died in their youth. The third oldest, the Rev. William Sidgwick, was Henry's father.[18]

Clearly, the affluent Sidgwick uncles were important for Henry's later success. He would later refer to his uncle J. B. Sidgwick as the head of the family, writing to his mother in May of 1873: "I had heard of my uncle's death [J. B. Sidgwick's] before you wrote. I was much startled and grieved, having no idea that he was in any danger. I remember well the last time that I saw him at the mill, little thinking that it was the last time. I seem to remember all my childish feelings about him as the Head of the family, and it makes me sad to think that I shall never see his fine impressive old face again . . . ."[19] Charlotte Brontë, who briefly and unsuccessfully served as a governess to the J. B. Sidgwick family at Stone Gappe, would record: "One of the pleasantest afternoons I have spent here—indeed, the only one at all pleasant—was when Mr. Sidgwick walked out with his children, and I had orders to follow a little behind. As he strolled on through his fields with his magnificent Newfoundland dog at his side, he looked very like what a frank, wealthy, Conservative gentleman ought to be. He spoke freely and unaffectedly to the people he met, and though he indulged his children and allowed them to tease himself far too much, he would not suffer them grossly to insult others."[20]

Importantly, the larger Sidgwick family was also a formative influence on Edward White Benson (1829–1896), the future Archbishop of Canterbury, who, as a Rugby schoolmaster in the 1850s, would live with Mary Sidgwick and become young Henry's first serious mentor, later his brother-in-law and philosophical opposite number. After Henry's move to Trinity College, Cambridge, in 1855, he would drift away from the religious influences of his youth, becoming famous for his religious agnosticism, and this made for some difficulties with his uncles and Benson. He would write to his mother in 1866 that "I shall be very glad to meet my Uncle Robert [Sidgwick]. But if by questions of the day you mean theological questions, I cannot say that I am very anxious to talk about them. I have been for some time past rather anxious to *avoid* talking about them more than I can help. If you mean politics or philosophy, I am ready for any amount."[21] But if Henry's mature philosophical outlook was largely utilitarian, and much indebted to the work of Mill, he came to it by working through and then throwing off the influence of Benson, who was for his part much more in line with the outlook of the prosperous uncles, and this for good reason.

The family's intellectual atmosphere is singularly intriguing, particularly in connection with Christopher Sidgwick, who was a great philanthropist and something of a religious intellectual. It has often been noted that the "Factories Acts of 1833 and 1844 stipulated half a day's schooling for five days a week, and said that children of nine to thirteen were not to work more than eight hours a day. Christopher Sidgwick, of Low Mill, built a bungalow school for his child-workers for their half days."[22] However, the story is more complicated, with the Mill school yielding in turn to the Christ Church school. As A. C. Benson explained more fully in his biography of his father, *Edward White Benson, Sometime Archbishop of Canterbury*, who took him on a visit to Skipton in 1874:

> In the afternoon we went to see uncle Christopher: he had retired young from the business; he had been a strong Evangelical, but was a great student and thinker in Theology, and became a very High Churchman. He devoted his fortune to building and endowing Christ Church, Skipton. It was one of the earliest Churches of the Gothic revival, and was described by Archbishop Longley, then Bishop of Ripon, as 'a chaste and beautiful design.' . . . It was furnished with an organ, turned by hand, in order that only the very limited number of tunes that the founder approved of might be sung.
>
> He also built the Church Schools in Water Street; here in old days he kept his books in a house adjoining the school, and came down from the Castle for service at 7 a.m. at Christ Church, and after breakfast retired to the hermitage to read till three,—when he returned to the Castle to dine,—with the intermediate refreshment of a slice of sponge cake, which was kept under a bell-glass on the table, and eaten at the stroke of twelve. He was a man of settled habits. To the end of his life, he had two hats, made after a fashion which he approved in 1840, sent him annually from Lincoln and Bennett. He was fond of *Bradshaw*, and always kept a copy by him, to work out cross-country journeys, which he never took.
>
> After the Board School came to Skipton, he closed his own school, and converted the School-room into his own library. It was here we saw him—I remember a magnificent looking old man, with a somewhat leonine face, dressed like a Quaker, with a swallow-tail coat and frilled shirt-front, sitting in the midst of his books, which lay in some confusion; he talked long and affectionately with my father, but took little notice of us.

He was a great Liturgiologist in days when such things were not well understood; he used to take long walks with Richard Ward, whom he had appointed to Christ Church, discussing the rubrics point by point. My father has told me that his own early taste for ecclesiastical things was mainly derived from him, adding that some of Mr. Christopher's remembered comments were even useful to him in his judgement in the Lincoln case. 'Our business in ritual,' he used to say, 'is to discuss not what we should like, but what is right.' This Christopher carried out in the minutest details in his own Church, such as having a vessel of water by the font, because of the words 'the font which shall then be filled'—'not full,' he used to say, 'but filled.' He would allow no representations of saints in the windows. 'St. John does not say, Little children, keep yourselves from idolatry, but from "idols," that is from representations.' He reserved the first three presentations to the living to himself, but by the speedy death or resignation of the first three incumbents, the patronage passed from his hands; he wrote several tracts on ecclesiastical subjects. He is buried at the east end of the Church which he founded. 'Istius ecclesiae stabilitor' has been cut more recently in the small stone which he ordered to be his only memorial.[23]

Benson also remarks of his father that he "was strongly and deeply imbued with these ecclesiastical tastes, liturgical and antiquarian; and the moment he was brought into contact with a strong high churchman like his cousin Christopher Sidgwick, found himself, even as a boy, in his natural element." Indeed, Benson credited his Sidgwick relatives with providing the guidance he needed after the early loss of his own father.

That Christopher Sidgwick exercised this decisive religious influence on the future Archbishop of Canterbury is surely a point of some significance, testifying to the strong intellectual bent of the Sidgwick family. And at the time of the Benson visit, James Sidgwick—who as A. C. Benson snidely remarked, "led an even less strenuous life"—had also "retired for many years from the High Mills, and had done little since, except read: he did not join much in conversation, but late in the evening was pleased to retail the incautious statements made by members of the party, with corrections. He was something of a cynic, and a high Tory. Being liable to cold, he habitually sat in a kind of porter's chair with a wicker-work hood; he used to walk in the Castle Bailey every morning at eight, but was rarely seen abroad during the rest of the day."[24] In fact, both Christopher and James lived with their mother: "Old Mrs. William Sidgwick, daughter of Christopher Benson of York, my father's great-aunt, lived at Skipton, in the Castle, where my father spent many happy holidays; she was a widow, and with her lived her sons James and Christopher . . . [and] a younger brother, Robert, also lived there till his marriage".

But of course, "John Benson Sidgwick, senior partner in the High Mills, was living in the house his father had built [sic] at Stonegappe, near Cononley, a lonely secluded house in a wooded dingle of the moors." And the future archbishop spent much time there as both a child (when he became known as "the little bishop") and an adult. Margaret Cooper, a daughter of J. B. Sidgwick, recalled in a letter to A. C. Benson:

> One circumstance I recollect perfectly; and have often thought of it since your father was made Archbishop. We were near the fire, which looks as if he had stayed some time with us—William was sitting on my father's right knee, your father on a low stool at his left side—and my father said, 'I wonder which of you two boys I shall see Archbishop of Canterbury.' Then came various questions—'What is Archbishop of Canterbury?' etc. etc. I named this to your father when he was here in 1893, but he did not recollect it, nor did he seem to remember anything of that first visit.[25]

Margaret would also remember a later visit, in 1844, when she was struck by how the future archbishop was "so much more able to discuss matters with my father than was possible to other boys of his age."

Given this context, and the familial sense of great intellectual achievement to come, it is perhaps less surprising that so many members of the Sidgwick and Benson families would go on to achieve academic distinction, or that Henry's father should have become a schoolmaster. Certainly the ambitions were there.

The Rev. William Sidgwick had been sent to Trinity College, Cambridge, and graduated in 1829, after which he toured Europe. Among his friends he counted W. M. Thackeray and Perronet Thompson. The latter would play a minor role in the growth of utilitarianism. This Sidgwick, although not as prominent as his relatives, had a reputation as a dedicated teacher and did serve effectively as master of the fairly remunerative Skipton Grammar School (Ermysted's School) from 1836 until his death from tuberculosis in 1841, and he is on record as having participated in the consecration ceremonies for the new and impressive Christ's Church in Skipton, which his brother had largely funded, though with the other Sidgwicks contributing as well (in the Rev. William's case, no less than £150). His position as headmaster was more challenging than is generally allowed, given that Erymsted's had during the previous decades gone through a series of governance crises brought on by its tangled founding charter. Headmaster Thomas Gartham, who died in office in 1826, had been virtually besieged by opponents among the trustees, to such a degree that he had to lock himself up in the school at times, never venturing out for fear of arrest. The Rev. William Sidgwick inherited the role of headmaster during the very period when earnest reform of the school and its administration was in process, and he apparently contributed much to the reforms that were formally adopted in 1841. A. M. Gibbons's *The Ancient Free Grammar School of Skipton in Craven* explains:

> The school was still to teach Latin to all boys 'according to the capacity and ability of each one'. There had been much argument about this and it would appear that, since the days of Gartham, the revival of the school had only been accomplished by a popular policy of dropping Latin as a compulsory subject and introducing more English, Arithmetic and so on. In consequence the school was, for many boys, only carrying on the sort of instruction that was being given in the National School, which was probably more efficient on the English side and which charged a few pence a week. In other words, the 'Free Grammar School', if it remained free and yet taught no (Latin) grammar, would soon be the resort only of the poorer classes—at least, that seems to be what the Head Master (Wm. Sidgwick) thought when he reported 'If the choice of education were left entirely with the parents, the school in a few years would be filled with none but English scholars many of whom would be sent to obtain the mere elements of English and arithmetic which they might equally obtain at the National School and that thus the intention of the founder would be defeated and the benefits of the institution be engrossed in a great measure by those to whom the saving of a very small weekly payment was an object of much consideration, instead of affording to the Sons of all Classes . . . the benefit of a solid and liberal education'.[26]

Thus it would seem that Henry Sidgwick, the great educational reformer who opposed an undue emphasis on classical languages (and also opposed the exclusion of women from higher education), was often engaging, albeit from a sharply different perspective, with the same issues that had confronted his father. And stranger still, the Rev. William Sidgwick's immediate predecessor, Robert Thomlinson, "was believed to have been frightened to death by the ghost of his predecessor, the Reverend Thomas Gartham, who had died ten years earlier after an unsuccessful three-years' struggle on Thomlinson's part to have him dismissed."[27] One of Henry Sidgwick's major preoccupations throughout his life was tracking down and investigating ghost stories—an obsession that led to his becoming one of the founding fathers of the British Society for Psychical Research. This was an obsession shared by the young Benson, who had founded a "Ghost Society" at Cambridge (a society that Henry would join when he went to Cambridge), and it appears to have been an entrenched part of the Yorkshire culture.[28]

Tellingly, in the reforms of Ermysted's that went into effect in 1841, J. B. Sidgwick was appointed to the new body of trustees organized to manage the school's extensive estates, a role that had previously been one of the perks of the headmasters, leading to both serious remuneration and equally serious conflicts of interest. Moreover, the brothers Christopher and Robert would both serve on the Skipton council, or more accurately, the Skipton Local Board of Health, which was organized in the 1850s to deal with a wide range of civic issues, from sanitation to roads. Thus, the family's economic prominence was translated into a certain political prominence, albeit of a distinctive educational and ecclesiastical philanthropic nature. They were indeed the proverbial pillars of the community, and not only in Skipton. Christopher, moreover, was not the only one to spearhead the construction of a church:

> The building of the Parish Church of Lothersdale was completed in in the year 1838, and consecrated on the 22nd of October by the then Bishop of Ripon, The Right Reverend C. T. Longley. This was the first church to be built and consecrated in Craven for three hundred years. The need of a church at Lothersdale had been felt for many years, and some correspondence had passed between the Vicar of Carleton and the Dean and Chapter of Christ Church, Oxford . . . [but] little was accomplished until John Benson Sidgwick took up residence at Stone Gappe, Lothersdale, following upon the death of his father, William Sidgwick, in 1827. Mr. Sidgwick devoted himself wholeheartedly to the task of creating the Parish of Lothersdale from the Parishes of Carleton and Kildwick, and establishing the Parish Church, as revealed by details contained in documents now in the church chest. The loss to the Parish of Lothersdale, when Mr. Sidgwick left Stone Gappe, in 1847, must have been very great, and it is surprising that no memorial is left to so generous a benefactor. Mr. Sidgwick died at Riddlesden Hall on the 19th of May, 1873, and was buried in Riddlesden churchyard. It was during the period that John Benson Sidgwick was resident at Stone Gappe that Charlotte Brontë was governess to his children and attended the church—for which she made an altar cloth. It is probable that she visited Kildwick Church on many occasions, where she would see the numerous Currer memorials; and it is quite within the realms of possibility that her pen name of Currer Bell was derived from such source.[29]

In sum, although Henry's early residence in Skipton was brief, that area of the country was always the family seat, with the Sidgwicks playing a major economic role there and even living in the gatehouse of Skipton Castle, an imposing medieval fortress, long under the control of the illustrious Clifford family. Their influence in business, religion, and education was crucial, albeit of a very conservative, church-building nature. And in a truly Dickensian touch, William Sidgwick, Henry's grandfather, would even testify before the Parliamentary committee led by Sir Robert Peel to investigate the conditions of child labor in the textile industry, when none other than the utopian socialist Robert Owen was mobilizing support for reform in 1816. The various Factory Acts that followed were not, however, what grandfather Sidgwick was seeking to advance: he did not see any problem with children working fourteen hours a day in the mills, standing for most of that time.[30]

And at a later date, when Henry was still quite young, the family was embroiled in another controversy. In 1842, Yorkshire and Lancashire were the scenes of serious labor disputes and violence, the so-called "plug-drawing" riots of 1842. According to Dawson:

> The rioters obtained the name "plug-drawers" because it was their plan to draw the plugs from the boilers of all the factories they visited, and thus put an end to work. . . . Like a ball of snow the mob increased at every step. The fame of the rioters preceded them to Skipton, and when on the morning of Tuesday, the 16th of August, it became known that this town was to be visited the good folk were thrown into a state of profound alarm. They arrived in the afternoon, to the number of 3,000 persons, including men, women, and children.[31]

The Sidgwick family was perceived as part of the problem by the rioting workers, who were demanding food and an end to steam power employment, and were seeking to build a movement based on such concerns.

> On visiting Mr. Dewhurst's mill, the water was let off from the boiler by the mob, and work was stopped. Mr. W. Sidgwick's (Low) mill was next treated in the same manner, and at the High Mill the plugs were drawn from the boilers, the fires were raked out, and a peremptory order was given that the workmen should be turned away. Here money was demanded of Mr. John Sidgwick, as a condition of the withdrawal of the mob, and was given. The rioters then left; but with the threat that if the mill was worked without their consent they would return and do mischief.[32]

The Riot Act was read and the military called in to disperse the workers, a number of whom were later prosecuted, convicted, and imprisoned for "having at Skipton with force and arms, together with diverse other evil-disposed persons, riotously and tumultuously assembled, to the terror of the Queen's subjects." "The late Mr. C. Sidgwick assisted in the identification of several of the prisoners."[33] One can well imagine the tenor of talk about the state of the world at the Sidgwicks' dinner table at this juncture. At a later date, when the question arose of whether to sell off the historically important Petyt Library (first held in Holy Trinity Church, then at the Old Grammar School) to raise funds to support the poor, Henry's Uncle Robert took action to save the library, though this is perhaps not surprising given the bookishness that so marked the family, even prior to their moving into the academic sphere.

Of course, Henry Sidgwick's immediate family was at some remove from such events. Sidgwick's brothers, William Carr (1834–1919) and Arthur (1840–1920), would become Oxford dons, and his sister Mary, known as Minnie or

Ben (1841–1918), would end up in an oppressive marriage to Benson, who would reside with her at Lambeth Palace at the very center of Victorian social and political life. Yet despite the many family tragedies, such as the marriage to Benson, their younger days would have some share of happiness.

Henry himself was not a terribly robust child. He was not seriously unhealthy, but he was never very vigorous and suffered over the course of his life from hay fever, stuttering, insomnia, depression, impotence, and dyspepsia, with one very serious bout of this last—aggravated, it seems, by a curious abstemiousness that had him drinking only water—as a Cambridge undergraduate, when he seemed near death. As a five year old he was forced on doctor's orders to give up chess because the game was said to "overexcite" him, possibly contributing to his later stammer (though as an adult he continued to enjoy playing). Still, he managed to compensate for his slight and less than athletic propensities later in life, when he took to serious walking, lawn tennis, and garden golf, to which he brought great enthusiasm though very little skill, always wanting to run ahead to see where his ball had gone. Oddly enough, he would also become known for his jogging, fully clothed, and through the middle of Cambridge: "In Cambridge the most characteristic thing about him was that he frequently ran in the street, even in cap and gown. This had its origin in his being told by his doctor to take more exercise, and advised to ride; he pleaded lack of time, but on eliciting the fact that running was better exercise than walking, he determined to put as much exercise as possible into necessary transits."[34]

With William, Henry, the two younger siblings, Arthur and Mary, Aunt Henrietta, and nursemaid Elizabeth (Beth) Cooper (who would serve the family for nearly eighty years), it was a considerable Sidgwick household that in 1844 settled in Redland, on the outskirts of Bristol. Henry would soon prove himself to be precocious, with a fair share of mischief in his character, not to mention early Apostolic tendencies:

> After the move to Redland the boy lived at home for four years under a governess (Miss Green) with Latin lessons from his mother, and then for two years more he went to a day school in Bristol known as the Bishop's College. . . . The younger brother and sister remember chiefly the earlier years, when Henry was the inventive genius of the nursery. Nearly all the games which the three children most relished were either devised by him, or greatly improved by his additions, and amongst them was a special language whereby the children believed they might safely discuss their secrets in the presence of the cold world of elders. The tedium of Sunday, when games (unless constructively religious) were forbidden, was beguiled, under his direction, not only by an extended secular use of the animals of Noah's ark, but for a while by the preaching of actual sermons written with all seriousness, on which the children bestowed remarkable pains.[35]

Such inventiveness and creativity were also evident in later life, in Sidgwick's talent for improvising stories for children (who generally liked him), and in his poetical tendencies. Although he published only a few poems himself, "he had in his early years, like many others, higher hopes and ambitions in this line," and as noted, throughout his life he showed a marked literary bent in his love of poetry and novels.

In 1850, Sidgwick was sent to a school in Blackheath run by the Thucydides scholar H. Dale, where his brother William was also a student. William later recalled "the gaiety and vivacity of his disposition, which made him a general favourite," the "unusual cleverness which he showed from the first in his studies," and his nearly being killed by an accidental blow from a golf club. But the school closed the following year, and after a brief return to the Bristol day school, Henry was off to Rugby—a somewhat surprising development, since his father "had always held the strongest objections to the old public schools, from a rooted belief in their low moral tone."[36] However, Thomas Arnold's reformism had done much for Rugby, transforming it into the very image of a school that could inspire students with a high sense of duty and social responsibility. And Sidgwick would make many lifelong friends there—Henry Graham Dakyns, Charles Bowen, T. H. Green, F. E. Kitchener, Charles Bernard, and C. H. Tawney, among others. He studied primarily under the classical scholars Charles and Thomas Evans, for whom he would always have considerable respect. And according to Bowen, Sidgwick had more of a youth than Mill, and was not wanting in "lightness":

[W]ithin his first few years after leaving school there were but few branches of knowledge and of human interest into which he had not plunged, and in many with good results. Perhaps I should except the world of sport, which he regarded not indeed for a moment with contempt, but with an amused and large-hearted tolerance quite his own. In intellectual matters I should put down, as his first and supreme characteristic, candour. It seemed to me then, as it does now, something morally beautiful and surprising; it dominated and coloured his other great qualities, those of subtlety, memory, boldness, and the tolerance of which I have just spoken was in the next degree his most striking attribute. Perhaps pure laziness was the shortcoming for which he had least sympathy; but he seemed to make, as a very great mind does, allowances for everything; he was considerate and large-hearted because he saw so much.

A younger generation cannot well realize how bright and cheerful a companion he was in early years. In the spring of life he could be versatile and gay with the rest: abundant in quiet humour: not boisterous, as many or most, but full of playful thoughts and ready for the mirthful side of things as well as the serious. He was small and not very strong;

I doubt whether he excelled in any physical game, but he could walk fairly, and I have a delightful recollection of a short knapsack tour that we had together in South Wales.[37]

The decision to allow Henry, and then Arthur, to attend Rugby was apparently the result of Benson's influence. As a young man, Benson had been stunned by the unexpected deaths of his mother and older sister (again, his father had died some years earlier), which had left him in charge of the family, which, he discovered, was quite broke. Mary Sidgwick was one of those[38] who came to the rescue:

> A prevailing wind of melancholy blew through Mrs Sidgwick's soul. Her grief at her husband's death had been deep and suffocating. It would have smothered her entirely had she not maintained such a strong sense of duty, and been of such sound practical character. She was a dignified and handsome woman, yet there was an air of bewilderment about her and a continued note of mournfulness in her speech. Perhaps this is what led Minnie to want so much to please her mother, and make her happy. Two of her six children lay buried, but she had managed successfully to bring up Minnie and three boys, and to give a roof to Henrietta. When Harriet Benson died, even though the families had not been particularly close, she had willingly taken in Edward's sisters, Eleanor and timid little Ada, who hesitated a full year before calling her 'Aunt Mary,' and then only did so in a whisper.[39]

Benson persuaded Mary Sidgwick that Rugby under E. M. Goulburn, Arnold's successor, was an excellent and very high-minded option for her sons. And he would soon join his sisters at the "Blue House" on Newbold Road in Rugby, after taking up a generous offer from Goulburn to join the Rugby staff. Mary Sidgwick had moved the family there in 1853, a move that would allow her sons to live at home while attending the school.

> The Blue House, named for its curiously coloured bricks, was surrounded by a large garden 'agreeably planted with elms.' The household consisted primarily of women—Mama and Minnie, Beth and Aunt Etty, and of course little Ada, nearly Minnie's age and much braver than before, even a touch willful. Eleanor was now married, brother William was off at Oxford, and Henry and Arthur were at school most of the day. The Blue House swished with silk and tinkled politely with teacups. Piano scales faltered across the morning air, occasionally to be joined by Aunty Etty's booming baritone and whooping laugh, or by the whack of cricket bats if the boys were home. With her slightly bewildered look and melancholy voice, armed with her edifying phrases and belief in 'talking people round,' Mrs. Sidgwick drifted through the Blue House keeping the entire vessel afloat.[40]

But Benson's presence did make for some turbulence. He had long and rather perversely had his heart set on marrying Minnie. They were betrothed, in a manner of speaking, when she was not yet a teenager and he still at Cambridge, and after he moved in with the family, he pursued her with all the force of his very forceful personality, fairly crushing the gaiety of a very gay young girl who loved nothing better than a soft chair (or her favorite tree), a good book, and an orange. Her education, at the hands of Benson and her High Church mother and uncles, was a preparation for her future role, but it was joyless and full of reproaches directed at her "thoughtlessness." Benson, as Askwith has put it, "had the Mid-Victorian virtues: intellectual and physical energy, devotion to duty, unswerving rectitude and sincere religious feeling. The qualities he lacked included imagination and the power of putting himself into another's place. He was unceasingly strenuous, vital, dogmatic and domineering and from early on he had armed himself with the triple authority of paterfamilias, schoolmaster and priest."[41]

Henry was apparently initially fairly clueless about all this family intrigue swirling about Minnie, but he certainly felt the force of Benson's muscular brand of Christianity. In his words, "through his talk in home life, his readings aloud, etc., his advice and stimulus abundantly given *tête-à-tête*, his intellectual influence over me was completely maintained." Clearly, Benson represented the authority not only of the Church of England, but of the Sidgwick uncles as well, who had so influenced him. Thus, Henry would counsel his sister, in what was perhaps the worst advice that he ever gave anyone:

> No one knows, my dearest Minnie, I do not think even you could tell, what Edward has been to me—it is not merely that he has been my hero ever since I knew him, and that my hero-worship of him has grown even as my admiration for goodness & beauty & truth has grown—it is not merely that he has come to be as one of ourselves, a sharer of the firm & deep household affection that nothing else can ever resemble—a deeper debt still than these and more than I can tell you now I owe him. There is only one bond that could knit him closer to us, and I need not say what that one is.[42]

Minnie's marriage to Benson would end only with his death in 1896, and although it produced a remarkable family and led to Gladstone calling her "the cleverest woman in Europe," it was suffocating and produced much depression and instability in poor Minnie, though also, eventually, some wonderful sexual experimentation. Remarkably, given her circumstances, she stubbornly insisted throughout her life that love was God, not the other way around.

Henry was rather luckier. Benson's mentorship would fall away fairly quickly, thanks in no small part to the work of the Cambridge Apostles. As he would describe Benson's outlook:

For him, the only hope of effective and complete social reform lay in the increased vitality and increased influence of the Christian Church: useful work might be done by those outside—his recognition of the value of such work was always ample and cordial—but it could only be of limited and partial utility. The healing of the nations could only come from one source; and any social science that failed to recognize this must be proceeding on a wrong track. And the struggle for perfect impartiality of view, which seemed to me an imperative duty, presented itself to him—as I came to understand—as a perverse and futile effort to get rid of the inevitable conditions of intellectual and spiritual life. I remember he once said to me in those years that my generation seemed to be possessed by an insane desire to jump off its own shadow: but the image was not adequate, for in the spiritual region he regarded the effort to get rid of the bias given by early training and unconsciously imbibed tradition, as not only futile but profoundly dangerous.

I do not mean that he failed to do justice to the motives of freethinkers. Even in the sixties—when it was not uncommon for orthodox persons to hint, or even openly say, that no man could fail to admit the overwhelming evidence for Christianity, unless his reason was perverted by carnal appetites or worldly ambitions—I never remember his uttering a word of this kind: and I remember many instance of his cordial recognition of the disinterested aims and moral rectitude of particular free-thinkers. Still, the paralysis of religious life, naturally resulting from the systematic and prolonged maintenance of this attitude of 'unbiassed' inquiry, seemed to him fraught with the gravest spiritual perils; however well-intentioned in its origin, it could hardly fail to be seconded by the baser elements of human nature, the flesh desiring to shake off the yoke of the spirit.[43]

Benson had no taste for the soul-searching discussion of differences on fundamental questions. He had not been an Apostle—his personality was scarcely appropriate—and after providing Henry with his first great role model, he would become for him a measure of respectable orthodoxy by which to gauge how far he had deviated from such. And as A. C. Benson revealed: "I realized early, by some sort of unconscious divination, that there existed a sense of disappointment and even disapproval in my father's mind about my uncle. . . . Thus, though the tie between the two was deep rather than close, my father could never quite banish from his mind the thought that Henry Sidgwick's brilliance and consummate reasonableness might sow the seeds of doubt in the minds of us children. . . . My father had no intention of discussing religious questions with Sidgwick, while Sidgwick had no sort of wish to initiate discussion."[44]

Still, it was with Benson's help that Sidgwick excelled at Rugby, and in 1855 he set off for the alma mater of both his father and Benson: Trinity College, Cambridge. There he excelled in mathematics and, especially, classics, garnering one prize or honor after another: Craven Scholar, Senior Classic, Chancellor's Medalist, and more. But the greatest prize came in 1857, when he was invited to join the Apostles, the intellectual incubator for so many leading lights past and present. Discussion societies would become a crucial part of Sidgwick's life—such societies as the illustrious Metaphysical Society and the Synthetic Society would engage his best philosophical efforts, as would his own "Sidgwick Group" of psychical researchers. But the Apostles, especially in the Mystic form tracing back to Maurice, gave him his first true taste of intellectual freedom, albeit of intellectual freedom in a closely guarded, esoteric form. To give the fuller account, only part of which was quoted in the previous chapter:

> I have noted the great change that took place about the middle of my undergraduate time. Up to that point I cannot remember that I had formed any ambition beyond success in my examinations and the attainment of a Trinity Fellowship; but in the Michaelmas term of my second year an event occurred which had more effect on my intellectual life than any one thing that happened to me afterwards: I became a member of a discussion society—old and possessing historical traditions—which went by the name of 'the Apostles.' A good description of it as it existed in his time is to be found in the late Dean Merivale's autobiography. When I joined the number of members was not large, and there is an exuberant vitality in Merivale's description to which I recall nothing corresponding. But the spirit, I think, remained the same, and gradually this spirit—at least as I apprehended it— absorbed and dominated me. I can only describe it as the spirit of the pursuit of truth with absolute devotion and unreserve by a group of intimate friends who were perfectly frank with each other, and indulged in any amount of humorous sarcasm and playful banter, and yet each respects the other, and when he discourses tries to learn from him and see what he sees. Absolute candour was the only duty that the tradition of the society enforced. No consistency was demanded with opinions previously held—truth as we saw it then and there was what we had to embrace and maintain, and there were no propositions so well established that an Apostle had not the right to deny or question, if he did so sincerely and not from mere love of paradox. The gravest subjects were continually debated, but gravity of treatment, as I have said, was not imposed, though sincerity was. In fact it was rather a point of the apostolic mind to understand how much suggestion and instruction may be derived from what is in form a jest—even in dealing with the gravest matters.

I had at first been reluctant to enter this society when I was asked to join it. I thought that a standing weekly engagement for a whole evening would interfere with my work for my two Triposes. But after I had gradually apprehended the spirit as I have described it, it came to seem to me that no part of my life at Cambridge was so real to me as the Saturday evening on which the apostolic debates were held; and the tie of attachment to the society is much the strongest corporate bond which I have known in life. I think, then, that my admission into this society and the enthusiastic way in which I came to idealise it really determined or revealed that the deepest bent of my nature was towards the life of thought—thought exercised on the central problems of human life.[45]

Arthur would in short order follow his brother Henry to both Trinity and the Apostles, and other members of that era included James Clerk Maxwell, Oscar Browning, and John Jermyn Cowell, with whom Sidgwick was especially close. Benson's influence was no match for the Saturday evening Apostolic meetings over "whales" (anchovy toast), with papers presented and discussed on the hearth rug by luminaries and friends, faculty and students, sharing the very Socratic bond of the Apostolic spirit. The Apostles were the "Real," and the rest of the world merely the "Phenomenal." Members were elected for life, and even after they became "Angels," ceasing to participate on a regular weekly basis, they maintained strong ties to the society and its past and present members—a habit encouraged by the society's annual dinner, at which old and new "Brethren" had a chance to meet. They thus provided a powerful and influential support group, under figures such as Lord Houghton, and they were overwhelmingly leaders in the cause of educational reform, seeking by one means or another to challenge rote learning and pedantry in the name of love of truth. They were the Millian clerisy realized.

It was in this heady context of intimate and profoundly intellectual male bonding that Sidgwick was first led to read Mill and Bentham, to whose ethical and political views he rapidly converted:

> To explain more precisely the 'contrast' of which I have spoken, I will begin by sketching briefly the ideal which, under the influence primarily of J. S. Mill, but partly of Comte seen through Mill's spectacles, gradually became dominant in my mind in the early sixties—I say 'in my mind,' but you will understand that it was largely derived from intercourse with others of my generation, and that at the time it seemed to me the only possible ideal for all adequately enlightened minds. It has two aspects, one social and the other philosophical or theological. What we aimed at from a social point of view was a complete revision of human relations, political, moral and economic, in the light of science directed by comprehensive and impartial sympathy; and an unsparing

reform of whatever, in the judgment of science, was pronounced to be not conducive to the general happiness. This social science must of course have historical knowledge as a basis: but, being science, it must regard the unscientific beliefs, moral or political, of past ages as altogether wrong,—at least in respect of the method of their attainment, and the grounds on which they were accepted. History, in short, was conceived as supplying the material on which we had to work, but not the ideal which we aimed at realizing; except so far as history properly understood showed that the time had come for the scientific treatment of political and moral problems.

As regards theology, those with whom I sympathized had no close agreement in conclusions,—their views varied from pure positivism to the 'Neochristianity' of the Essayists and Reviewers: and my own opinions were for many years unsettled and widely fluctuating. What was fixed and unalterable and accepted by us all was the necessity and duty of examining the evidence for historical Christianity with strict scientific impartiality; placing ourselves as far as possible outside traditional sentiments and opinions, and endeavouring to weigh the pros and cons on all theological questions as a duly instructed rational being from another planet—or let us say from China—would naturally weigh them.

The above account accords well with that affixed to the sixth edition of the *Methods*, in which Sidgwick alludes to the suffocating orthodoxy of both Benson and the formal Cambridge curriculum: "My first adhesion to a definite Ethical system was to the Utilitarianism of Mill: I found in this relief from the apparently external and arbitrary pressure of moral rules which I had been educated to obey, and which presented themselves to me as to some extent doubtful and confused; and sometimes, even when clear, as merely dogmatic, unreasoned, incoherent."[46] He had developed a particular aversion to Whewell, then Master of Trinity, whose *Elements of Morality, including Polity* was required undergraduate reading. Whewell, for all his philosophical sophistication, represented to Sidgwick much the same ethical outlook as his uncles and Benson, but without the familial ties. Like his hero Mill, Sidgwick took Whewell to be the opposing force to progress.

It was thus that Sidgwick was led, by his own account, to identify with the so-called "Academic Liberals," those, such as the contributors to the provocative *Essays and Reviews*, who had taken Mill's indictment of the ancient universities to heart and were out to change things.[47] Sidgwick's reformist activities would prove to be a very large part of his life, and ultimately prove to be wide-ranging and not invariably tied to party loyalty. As an Academic Liberal he tended toward a Millian liberalism, but he never found that perspective to be fully realized in Gladstone, with whom he would break over Home Rule for Ireland, and in later life he would vote more as an independent, sometimes, as will be shown, with the unfortunate racist shadings of the new imperialism of the late Victorian era. But his politics was invariably complex, and if he drifted away from his earlier notions of Academic Liberalism, he was also later on caught up in the Ethical Culture movement, hosting Felix Adler at Cambridge and participating actively in various progressive Ethical Societies. He would serve on a number of government Commissions, and even considered running for office, but opted instead to act in the role of public moralist and well-placed political advisor. Like his utilitarian predecessors, he was keenly interested in issues of poor relief, both theoretically and practically, working with the Cambridge Charity Organization Society. But, also like his utilitarian predecessors, most of his reform efforts revolved around education—in his case, especially the reorganization and professionalization of Cambridge and the expansion of educational opportunities, particularly for women. He was active in the cause of university reorganization generally, in due course serving on the General Board of Studies, the Special Board for Moral Sciences, and the Indian Civil Service Board, and worked tirelessly through such vehicles as correspondence courses, extension lectures, the Cambridge Working Men's College, and the University Day Training College for teachers (initiated by Oscar Browning). On higher education for women, after his 1876 marriage to Eleanor, he had another comrade in the cause, beyond his fellow Apostles. In fact, Eleanor worked with Henry on behalf of both Newnham, where she succeeded Anne Jemima Clough as Principal in 1892, and the Society for Psychical Research, the presidency of which she assumed in 1908. The couple lived, after their marriage, in the imposing house that they had built on Chesterton Road, "Hillside," but when Eleanor took on an official position at Newnham, they would live there. Cambridge was always home.

At any rate, Sidgwick's Cambridge, unlike Benson's, steadily weakened his orthodox Anglican faith and steadily strengthened his Liberal reformist zeal, converting him to utilitarian ethics and Academic Liberalism. Still, as the above passages make clear, it was primarily on matters of ethics and politics and educational reform that he followed Mill, not on theological matters. He continued to struggle with these long after his conversion to utilitarianism, and was in this way never a complete or whole-hearted convert to Millianism, particularly to Millian naturalism, though the more agnostic Mill of the "Essays on Religion" could often sound a Sidgwickian note, allowing for the possibility of reasonable hope, when the evidence proved inconclusive. Indeed, his religious concerns would always shape his life and work, as evidenced by his lifelong interest in psychical research as a possible source of support for the latitudinarian form of theism he found most attractive and important for purposes of philosophical ethics.

Upon graduation Sidgwick was made a Fellow of Trinity and a lecturer in classics (followed by a lectureship in moral philosophy), but the 1860s were his self-described time of "Storm and Stress" when in classic Victorian fashion his religious doubts steadily grew as he struggled with scientific materialism and historical biblical criticism, learning both Hebrew and German the better to engage with the textual historicity of the Bible. His thoughts fluctuated wildly on theological matters, as both historical textual criticism and philosophical analysis led him to regard the Bible as a very problematic text indeed. Little wonder that Benson was reluctant to discuss such matters with him. Instead, he discussed his concerns in long, intimate letters to and discussions with such old friends as Roden Noel and Henry Graham Dakyns, the Rugby friend who became a Clifton schoolmaster forever at work on a new edition of Xenophon. To Dakyns he would write:

> As for our past—you do not think that I have any such thoughts as you suggest. I feel often as unrelated and unadapted to my universe as man can feel: except on the one side of friendship: and there, in my deepest gloom all seems strangely good: and you among the best. And if you might have been more—I know nothing of Might-have-been, and suspect that if I did enquire, the fault would turn out to be my own.
>
> But 'golden news' expect none unless I light perchance on the Secret of the Universe, in which case I will let you know.[48]

As with Mill, crisis would define Sidgwick's life—but these were repeated or ongoing crises of faith and conviction that to his mind were emblematic of the larger crises of the age. Again, there is a depth of angst and anxiety in Sidgwick, an anxiety sparked by the sense that the age was transitioning away from the old moral supports too quickly, before new and better supports had been found, that sets him apart from Godwin, Bentham, and Mill. He may have been the most unmusical of the great utilitarians, with no ear for that art at all, but he was able to sound notes of Nietzschean despair and darkness, of failure and dread, that utilitarianism had never heard before. To survive, he too would rely on poetry, sometimes referring to it as "the wine of life." But the lines always running through his mind were from Tennyson and Clough, and concerned with what if anything could be salvaged from his orthodox religious sensibility.[49] Clough voiced the measured doubt, Tennyson the sober longing to believe: "Yet pull not down my minster towers, that were / So gravely, gloriously wrought; / Perchance I may return with others there / When I have cleared my thought."

Two crises were particularly acute, however—the first the well-known one having to do with his resignation from Cambridge; the second, later and less well-known but even more devastating, having to do with his dashed hopes for finding some empirical proof of the survival of physical death. This second crisis will be described in later sections of this chapter, after explaining just how the *Methods* led to it. Both crises had long gestation periods, and both reveal just what Sidgwick meant when he described his life as devoted to "the deepest problems." And both provide perspectives on the *Methods* that cannot be gleaned from the text itself.

In 1867, by which point Sidgwick had already been struggling with the issue of subscribing to the Thirty-Nine Articles for some years, he sent a draft of his pamphlet on "The Ethics of Conformity and Subscription" to Mill, in what would be their only direct exchange (though they would both belong to the Radical Club). Sidgwick was involved with the Free Christian Union, which was concerned to promote free and open religious inquiry, and his pamphlet eloquently reflected that commitment. Primarily drawn to theism, which allowed for a highly latitudinarian theology emphasizing the justice, or at least non-absurdity, of the universe, he harbored as the result of his biblical studies considerable skepticism when it came to such particular matters as the Trinity, Virgin Birth, or eternal punishment. Try as he might, he could not see his way to believing in something like the Virgin Birth, or that the evidence for "miracles" was the sole possession of the Hebrew-Christian tradition, as opposed to a broader historical and cultural phenomenon calling for something more akin to parapsychological research. His pamphlet was in effect a brief for the type of free and open inquiry that he had absorbed from his beloved Apostles: "I have written a pamphlet . . . on the text 'Let every man be fully persuaded in his own mind.' That is really the gist of the pamphlet—that if the preachers of religion wish to retain their hold over educated men they must show in their utterances on sacred occasions the same sincerity, exactness, unreserve, that men of science show in expounding the laws of nature. I do not think that much good is to be done by saying this, but I want to liberate my soul, and then ever after hold my peace."[50] Put more fully, in the published 1870 version of the pamphlet:

> What theology has to learn from the predominant studies of the age is something very different from advice as to its method or estimates of its utility; it is the imperative necessity of accepting unreservedly the conditions of life under which these studies live and flourish. . . . [W]e only accept authority of a particular sort; the authority, namely, that is formed and maintained by the unconstrained agreement of individual thinkers, each of whom we believe to be seeking truth with single-mindedness and sincerity, and declaring what he has found with scrupulous veracity, and the greatest attainable exactness and precision.[51]

That this statement reflected a deeply Apostolic vision of inquiry, which informed not only his criticisms of the Church of England, but his philosophical work, educational philosophy, parapsychology, and much else besides, should be evident. To his mind, not surprisingly given his own experience, this form of inquiry was the needed antidote to theological orthodoxy: "Theology has gone as far as the moral sense and natural instincts of mankind would allow (and the limit is certainly elastic), in discouraging single-minded inquiry, discouraging exactness of statement, discouraging sincerity of utterance."[52] Its casuistical claims must be brought onto the more "neutral" ground of ethics, and come before the bar "of common sense,—that is, of the mass of well-intentioned, intelligent, and disinterested persons," so that "we can neutralize and dispel at once the special sophistries that tempt, and the singular scruples that beset, an individual thinker shaping his private conduct in solitude."[53] It is noteworthy that neither Sidgwick nor Mill deemed this strategy to be inconsistent with utilitarianism, and that however critical Sidgwick may have been of common-sense morality, he treated it with great respect in certain domains.

Of course, the particular matter at issue was just how unorthodox one might be while still subscribing to the Articles in good faith: "the duty which the persons who form the progressive—or, to use a neutral term, the deviating—element in a religious community owe to the rest of that community; the extent to which, and the manner in which, they ought to give expression and effect to their opinions within the community; and the point at which the higher interests of truth force them to the disruption of old ties and cherished associations." But Sidgwick straightaway allows that this question needs to be addressed with some sensitivity to the changing times:

> It will be as well, therefore, to notice the characteristics of the present state of religious thought, which appear to furnish the fresh conditions that render a fresh inquiry desirable.
>
> The first of these lies in the large strides that we have recently made towards complete civil and social equality of creeds. The secular disadvantages that religious dissidences formerly entailed, have been so rapidly diminishing, that we may look forward confidently to their speedy extinction. We have abolished church rates; we are inaugurating a system of primary education, which is, at any rate, designed to place all sects, as far as possible, on a par; and it is obvious that the ecclesiastical restrictions on the higher education cannot be much longer maintained. A nonconformist is as eligible for any purely civil function, from legislation downwards, as a conformist who is unconnected with the landed aristocracy: indeed, the high-water mark of toleration was indicated at the last general election, by the balanced debate among educated persons as to whether violent and obtrusive atheism should be considered a disqualification for the House of Commons. Moreover, the tone and manner adopted towards dissidents by the adherents, even the ministers, of the establishment, has changed with the changing times,—partly, perhaps, from policy, partly, no doubt, from natural and sincere expansion of sympathy. The effort to unite cordially with Dissenters, wherever such union is possible, has ceased to be the differencing characteristic of one party in the Church of England; and it is but rarely that a conformist dares to avow in public any sentiment but

respect for conscientious nonconformity. Even those who are fighting for the relics of Anglican privilege, have altered the lines of their defence; and instead of sharp, stern monitions of the sin of schism, offer voluble and pathetic appeals to "our common Christianity."[54]

So far, so good. Yet Sidgwick does not then go on to allow that laxity in the matter of subscription to the Thirty-Nine Articles, and correlatively to the Apostles' Creed, is therefore an unproblematic piece of changing popular morality. Quite the contrary—in a telling and revealing statement he explains:

> I will compare two clauses of the Apostles' Creed, preferring these from the peculiar prominence given to that formula in the Anglican services. I may perhaps remark, that I have no personal ground for the distinction which I draw between them, as I am equally unable to assent to either.
>
> The first is the clause affirming a belief in "the Resurrection of the Body." I do not see how these words can, without straining, be understood, except as asserting a belief that bodies, in some sense the same as those which have been buried, will, at a certain time, emerge from the surface of the earth. But, as far as I can ascertain, the majority of even orthodox laity, and many of the clergy, do not believe this; holding, rather, that the soul's life, though continued after death, will continue in some way incomplete until the termination of the present life of humanity on the earth, and that then its vitality will be perfected by its being (in some sense) re-embodied. Now, it seems to me an evil, that men should go on saying one of these things and believing the other. Still, we should all feel that a man was over-scrupulous who declined to perform ministerial functions solely on the ground that he held the latter of these beliefs instead of the former.
>
> I will compare with this the belief that Jesus Christ was born of the Virgin Mary. A man may certainly be a sincere Christian in the strictest sense—that is, he may believe that Jesus was God—without holding this belief. Many persons now take an intermediate view of miracles between accepting and rejecting them *en bloc*. They hold that miracles may occur, and that some recorded in the Gospel undoubtedly did occur; but that also legends may have been mixed up with the evangelical narrations, and that some probably have been. A man who holds this general view is very likely to reject the miraculous conception of Jesus, as the narrative of it has a very legendary aspect, and the evidence which supports it is exceptionally weak. Now, to him, this rejection may appear of no religious importance; it may even seem to him unreasonable that men should make their view of Christ's character and function to depend upon the nature of his conception. Still, to the majority of Christians, the belief is so important—the gulf that divides those who hold it from those who reject it seems so great, that

the confidence of a congregation in the veracity of their minister would
be entirely ruined, if he avowed his disbelief in this doctrine and still
continued to recite the Creed. And it seems to me, that a man who acts
thus, can only justify himself by proving the most grave and urgent
social necessity for his conduct.[55]

Sidgwick is exquisitely tuned to the fine differences between the obligations of clergy and laity, of course, and allows that with the former, especially,
it would be a "serious blow to the spiritual interests of the country, that any
considerable and respectable section of them should be charged with habitual
unveracity and be unable to refute the charge." That is, "just as, by the simple
populace, a lawyer has been roughly called a liar, and a tradesman a rogue, so
to the priesthood has been attributed a disposition to practise solemn imposture. But surely if this esoteric morality is an evil anywhere, it is a disastrous
evil in the profession whose function it is to propagate morality." But the laity
too, himself included, must meet a more stringent standard. For Sidgwick, it
is important to strive to approximate the ideal of a national ministry and a
form of genuine, sincere worship, accomplishing this through "the frank and
firm avowal, on all proper occasions, on the part of the laity, of all serious
and deliberate doctrinal disagreement with any portion of the service." The
course forward should be "by openly relaxing the engagements, not by secretly
tampering with their obligation," especially since no one will "take a strong
interest in grievances by which no one will declare himself aggrieved." He apparently, and not without considerable paradox, wanted the Apostolic attitude
to go public, as it were.

In the event, after prolonged agonizing and the apparent failure to reform
the universities and abolish the subscription requirement, Sidgwick finally and
officially resigned his Assistant Tutorship and Fellowship in late spring of 1869:

As for my resignation and consequent prospects, you are very good to
think about them. Personally I feel no doubt that I have done right. For
long I have had no doubt except what arose from the fact that most
of the persons whose opinion I most regard think differently. But one
must at last act on one's own view. It is my painful conviction that the
prevailing lax subscription is not perfectly conscientious in the case of
many subscribers: and that those who subscribe laxly from the highest motives are responsible for the degradation of moral and religious
feeling that others suffer. It would require very clear and evident gain
of some other kind to induce me to undergo this responsibility. And
such gain I do not see. Even if I make the extreme supposition that
all heretics avow themselves such and are driven away from the universities, some harm would no doubt be done, but not so much as is
supposed. A reaction must come soon and the universities be thrown
open; meanwhile there are plenty of excellent teachers on all subjects
who are genuinely orthodox; and even as regards religious speculation

the passion for truth in young minds would be stimulated by such an event, and they would find plenty of sources for "illumination" even if our rushlights were put out.

All this is, of course, an unpractical supposition. I make it to show myself that I am obeying a sound general rule—I feel very strongly the importance of "providing things honest in the sight of all men." It is surely a great good that one's moral position should be one that simple-minded people can understand. I happen to care very little what men in general think of me individually: but I care very much about what they think of human nature. I dread doing anything to support the plausible suspicion that men in general, even those who profess lofty aspirations, are secretly swayed by material interests.

After all, it is odd to be finding subtle reasons for an act of mere honesty: but I am reduced to that by the refusal of my friends to recognise it as such.[56]

This was a moral act, in the face of an ethical dilemma, and many of the fundamental principles that would be on display in the *Methods,* such as universalizability, were also on display here. As he admitted:

There is nothing in me of prophet or apostle. The great vital, productive, joy-giving qualities that I admire in others I cannot attain to: I can only lay on the altar of humanity as an offering this miserable bit of legal observance.

The worst is that I am forced to condemn others, objectively of course, for not acting in the same way; a moral impulse must be universally-legislative: the notion of "gratifying my own conscience" is to me self-contradictory; the moment I view the step as the gratification of a purely individual impulse the impulse has ceased.

It is curious: the people whom I begin to sympathise with are the orthodox. I begin to feel, during the service of the Church of England, sentimental if not devotional. And, no doubt, I shall probably recover the respect of some of them: though others will think me still more a child of perdition. Yet, alas, they are the men whom I do not sympathise with. Their faces are turned toward the setting sun, "the dear dead light," as Swinburne says; mine toward the rising. Or is mine also westward fixed? Is this Moral Ideal that dominates me a part of the past dispensation, and is harmonious life, and no, however symmetrical, formal abstraction from life, the only ideal of the future?

Even my Positivism is half against me. The effect on society of maintaining the standard of veracity is sometimes so shadowy that I feel as if I was conforming to a mere metaphysical formula.[57]

Happily, Sidgwick was appointed to a Lectureship in the Moral Sciences, and allowed to stay on at Cambridge in that capacity. He should have been appointed to the Knightbridge Professorship earlier in his career, of course, but it does not seem that he suffered, philosophically at least, from having to overcome these obstacles.

Sidgwick's resignation crisis and struggles with the duty of truth-telling would come, ironically, to define his reputation. He was the doubter who was more virtuous, more honest, than the faithful. But however critical he may have been of religious orthodoxy, he was deeply and sympathetically engaged with the social and philosophical attractions of a religious outlook. Indeed, he always kept one or another biblical text in his mind, as a kind of working motto for that period of his life. From 1869 to 1875, the period that saw the completion and publication of the *Methods*, his key text was in fact: "Let every man be fully persuaded in his own mind," Paul, Romans 14:5, and the epigraph of "The Ethics of Conformity and Subscription."

Of course, "fully persuaded" was just not among his many sides. For his part, Mill had commented on the draft: "What ought to be the exceptions . . . to the general duty of truth? This large question has never yet been treated in a way at once rational and comprehensive, partly because people have been afraid to meddle with it, and partly because mankind have never yet generally admitted that the effect which actions tend to produce on human happiness is what constitutes them right or wrong."[58] Sidgwick, Mill urged, should turn his "thoughts to this more comprehensive subject."

Sidgwick did, and the *Methods*, with its famously provocative account of esoteric morality, was the result. However, as the famous story related by Oscar Browning suggested, Sidgwick was less than elated by his great work, commenting dejectedly upon publication of it that the first word was "Ethics" and the last word was "Failure." His sense of failure was really an extension of earlier worries. He always allowed that he found the problem of whether he ought to resign his Fellowship very "difficult, and I may say that it was while struggling with the difficulty thence arising that I went through a good deal of the thought that was ultimately systematised in the *The Methods of Ethics*."[59] But the greater systematizing did not yield the results that he had most hoped to achieve. Ethical duty was left even more problematic after his philosophical investigations than it had been before them, a fact that has not struck Sidgwick's academic admirers as forcibly as it struck him.

Methods *and Method*

Really, in this as in other departments, my tendency is to scepticism, but scepticism of a humble, empirical, and more or less hopeful kind.

—SIDGWICK, *MEMOIR*

Again, of all the classical utilitarians, Sidgwick stands out for the remarkable analytical penetration of his philosophical work, especially in ethics. The "pure white light" of his intelligence, as an admirer called it, could bring a discerning subtlety to any subject on which it shone. Although there was a certain lull in Sidgwick's reputation in the early twentieth century, a long string of philosophical eminences—from C. D. Broad and Brand Blanshard, to William Frankena, R. M. Hare, John Rawls, and J. B. Schneewind, to Peter Singer, Roger Crisp, and Derek Parfit—have applauded Sidgwick's *Methods* as not only his best book, but possibly, as Broad, a later successor to Sidgwick's Cambridge chair, famously put it, "on the whole the best treatise on moral theory that has ever been written, and . . . one of the English philosophical classics."[60] As stressed in earlier chapters, de Lazari-Radek and Singer, in *The Point of View of the Universe,* have argued that progress in philosophical ethics involves nothing less than a return to Sidgwick:

> In this book, we have followed the main lines of Sidgwick's thinking about ethics, and tested his views both against our own reasoning and against the best of the vast body of recent and current philosophical writing on the topics he addresses. The overarching question we have sought to answer is whether Sidgwick's form of utilitarianism can be defended. In most respects we believe it can be. Parfit's claim that, in the long tradition of ethics, "Sidgwick's book contains the largest number of true and important claims" stands up well.[61]

Cogently defending Sidgwick's central claims is obviously no small task, but the philosophical ingenuity that has gone into the rehabilitation of Sidgwick's views can only be described as formidable. De Lazari-Radek and Singer in fact attempt to improve on Sidgwick's position in what they take to be his own terms, defending the ambitious view that the only truly rational option is impartial universal benevolence, reasons from the moral point of view, or as Sidgwick called it, "the Point of View of the Universe." And not only do they accept Sidgwick's Intuitionist or Rationalist account of reason, but they allow that, as Sidgwick maintained, the most defensible account of ultimate Good, of value theory, is the hedonistic one.[62] Hence the previously remarked irony that the most ambitious defenses of the classical utilitarian view place Mill's superstructure on a different, more Whewellian, cognitivist foundation, a move that would have flabbergasted Mill and made him worry about how progressive any such utilitarianism could possibly be, even if its author proclaimed himself a disciple. Sidgwick may have continued to develop Mill's claims about the utilitarian grounding of common-sense morality and the justifications for socialistic intervention in the economy, and no doubt the work he was doing with like-minded educational reformers did make Mill feel much better about what was going on at the ancient universities. But he harbored epistemological and religious concerns that Mill would have found very uncongenial.

The rest of this chapter will return time and again to these reconstructions of Sidgwick, as it tries to set out in greater detail exactly what is being reconstructed and how, and to pick up the arguments concerning intuitionism, hedonism, and distributivism developed in previous chapters. The aim is to do justice to the best interpretations of Sidgwick's views, to the life and works and historical contexts, and to fit him into the narrative developed in previous chapters. Needless to say, this also means capturing the complex and changing times of the late Victorian era. If Sidgwick's philosophical life began with his losing his religion and his engagements with Bentham, Mill, Whewell and other Cambridge Moralists, not to mention Kant, Butler, Plato, and Aristotle, it later evolved into an extended engagement or critical contest with the British Idealists, such figures as T. H. Green (a close friend from his Rugby days), F. H. Bradley (one of his tartest critics), and J.M.E. McTaggart (a Cambridge colleague), all of whom in one form or another championed the fundamental reality of mind rather than matter. He would live long enough to see McTaggart, Russell, and Moore inducted into the Apostles and behaving as young people are apt to do, dismissing him as out of date, the "last of the Benthamites."[63] Of course, both Russell and Moore would shake off their youthful Idealism and develop mature positions that owed an enormous amount to Sidgwick's *Methods*. In Moore's influential *Principia Ethica* (1903), Sidgwick is cited more than any other author.

Still, it is worth stressing at the outset of this discussion of the *Methods* that some of the Idealists actually appreciated Sidgwick's affinities with their concerns, and found even his qualified allegiance to Mill puzzling. Brand Blanshard, who had been greatly influenced by Bradley, would praise Sidgwick on some of these counts from the 1920s on, and conspicuously absent in Blanshard's account is anything like the critiques of Sidgwick by Bradley or F. H. Hayward, a sympathetic early critic who was troubled by how peculiar some of the encomiums to Sidgwick's notion of reason were, given Sidgwick's reputation as a utilitarian:

> Sidgwick's identification of 'Right' with 'Reasonable' and 'Objective'; his view of Rightness as an 'ultimate and unanalysable notion' (however connected subsequently with Hedonism); and his admission that Reason is, in a sense, a motive to the will, are due to the more or less 'unconscious' influence of Kant. Miss Jones appears to think that these are the common-places of every ethical system, and that real divergences only arise when we make the next step in advance. I should rather regard this Rationalistic terminology as somewhat foreign to Hedonism. I do not think that Miss Jones will find, in Sidgwick's Hedonistic predecessors, any such emphasis on Reason (however interpreted).[64]

The "Miss Jones" in question was E. E. Constance Jones, one of Sidgwick's prize students, who became both an impressive philosopher in her own right and one of Sidgwick's literary executors.

Green himself had been puzzled about some of these matters, unable to see how Sidgwick could go so far in his cognitivist account of reason in ethics and yet still defend hedonistic utilitarianism—which was anathema to the early British Idealists—rather than endorsing the self-realization of reason itself. This was something that later Idealists such as Blanshard found less problematic, if still not persuasive.[65] At any rate, Sidgwick was close to the Idealists when it came to thinking that a better, more rational religious perspective needed to be found and that Materialism simply would not do, either as a basis for ethics or a working philosophy for the future. Sidgwick in fact regarded Materialism in much the same way that Mill regarded Intuitionism: as the chief threat to the true progress of civilization. Indeed, Sidgwick shared more with such early non-reductionist pragmatists as William James, whom he knew and admired, than with T. H. Huxley (Darwin's "Bulldog") and his followers. He would, more than any of the earlier utilitarians, seek to do justice to the force and varieties of religious experience. If his best known published works, mostly on ethical and political philosophy and political economy, are in many ways quite reticent about his work on the "deepest" problems, he was nonetheless at the least an agnostic in the truer and deeper sense of the term, as described by Anthony Kenny—that is, someone who was genuinely torn by and struggling with the question of whether religion was a snare and delusion, or something that was in some ways glorious and profoundly important.[66] When the *Methods* is read in the light of such concerns, it presents itself differently, as more of a work in progress.

Now, in the *Methods* Sidgwick mainly considered three methods of ethics—intuitional or common-sense morality (that one ought ultimately to conform to the system of such familiar common-sense duties as truth-telling, promise-keeping, etc.), rational egoism (that one ought ultimately to act to promote one's own good), and utilitarianism (that one ought ultimately to act to promote the good of all, the greatest good). Each method, and by "method" he meant a way of "obtaining reasoned convictions as to what ought to be done," receives what can aptly be called a classic treatment, but the plan of the book can make it hard to follow the thread of Sidgwick's thought, particularly on the more philosophical points having to do with intuitionism. "Intuitionism" confusingly refers to both one of the methods of ethics—either common-sense duties or the more systematic account of them given in such works as those of Whewell and Henry Calderwood—and, in more abstract philosophical form, to the justificatory side of all the methods, particularly when it comes to the fundamental principles they invoke. [67]

Thus, Sidgwick denies that conscience delivers immediate judgments on particular acts, as in "perceptional" or "aesthetic" intuitionism.[68] Rather, "reflective persons, in proportion to their reflectiveness, come to rely rather on abstract universal intuitions relating to classes of cases conceived under general notions." This leads then to intuitional or common-sense morality, which in the *Methods* covers both more deontological views and non-hedonistic teleological ones, on the ground that the latter tend to construe virtue similarly as simply the thing to be done, whatever the consequences. But the process of reflection should not stop there. Without "being disposed to deny that conduct commonly judged to be right is so, we may yet require some deeper explanation *why* it is so." Thus we reach "philosophical intuitionism," which "while accepting the morality of common sense as in the main sound, still attempts to find for it a philosophic basis which it does not itself offer: to get one or more principles more absolutely and undeniably true and evident, from which the current rules might be deduced, either just as they are commonly received or with slight modifications and rectifications."[69]

The ascent to this philosophical intuitionism, which was rehearsed to some extent in "The Ethics of Conformity and Subscription," is especially evident in Book III, where Sidgwick has the utilitarian demonstrating to the dogmatic intuitionist

> that the principles of Truth, Justice, etc. have only a dependent and subordinate validity: arguing either that the principle is really only affirmed by Common-Sense as a general rule admitting of exceptions and qualifications, as in the case of Truth, and that we require some further principle for systematising these exceptions and qualifications; or that the fundamental notion is vague and needs further determination, as in the case of Justice; and further, that the different rules are liable to conflict with each other, and that we require some higher principle to decide the issue thus raised; and again, that the rules are differently formulated by different persons, and that these differences admit of no Intuitional solution, while they show the vagueness and ambiguity of the common moral notions to which the Intuitionist appeals.[70]

This, at least, is a deeply Millian denouement, with common sense revealed as more or less unconsciously reliant upon utilitarian calculation, or shown to presuppose something very like it, since it keeps giving way to certain more abstract formal principles (whose application is less straightforward) as the better candidates for genuinely self-evident truths. In fact, utilitarianism is derived from two more fundamental principles: "the self-evident principle that the good of any one individual is of no more importance, from the point of view (if I may say so) of the Universe, than the good of any other; unless, that is, there are special grounds for believing that more good is likely to be realised in the one case than in the other. And it is evident to me that as a rational being I am bound to aim at good generally,—so far as it is attainable by my efforts,—not at a particular part of it."[71] Sidgwick also defends a universalizability principle (one must be able to will one's maxim to be a universal law) and a principle of rational prudence (or temporal neutrality, such that one should be *ceteris paribus* equally concerned with all parts of one's life), in addition to the utilitarian principle(s) of rational benevolence.

Is the *Methods* therefore a defense of the method of utilitarianism, as best representing the impartial, moral point of view?

Many, including de Lazari-Radek and Singer, have construed it as primarily that, and there can be no denying that Sidgwick had a great impact on the utilitarian agenda and self-identified as utilitarian.[72] But curiously enough, this is something that he often denied as an appropriate description of the *Methods*. His aim, he proclaimed at the beginning of the work, was simply "to expound as clearly and as fully as my limits will allow the different methods of Ethics that I find implicit in our common moral reasoning; to point out their mutual relations; and where they seem to conflict, to define the issue as much as possible." Echoing his views on theological inquiry, he confessed: "I have wished to put aside temporarily the urgent need which we all feel of finding and adopting the true method of determining what we ought to do; and to consider simply what conclusions will be rationally reached if we start with certain ethical premises, and with what degree of certainty and precision."[73]

He was in fact wont to respond to defenders of common sense in a somewhat disarming Hegelian mode, claiming that common-sense morality was his morality as much as anyone's, though he was perhaps more candid in his reply to Calderwood's critical review of the *Methods*, which questioned why he had not simply confined himself "to the consideration of Intuitionism in its most philosophical form." That gambit, he admitted, "would have led me at once to Utilitarianism: because I hold that the only moral intuitions which sound philosophy can accept as ultimately valid are those which at the same time provide the only possible philosophical basis of the Utilitarian creed. I thus necessarily regard Prof. Calderwood's Intuitionism as a phase in the development of the Intuitional method, which comes naturally between the crude thought of Butler's 'plain man' and the Rational Utilitarianism to which I ultimately endeavor to lead my reader." That is, allowing that the morality of common sense is his as well, he must as a philosopher nonetheless

ask myself whether I see clearly and distinctly the self-evidence of any particular maxims of duty, as I see that of the formal principles 'that what is right for me must be right for all persons in precisely similar circumstances' and 'that I ought to prefer the greater good of another to my own lesser good': I have no doubt whatever that I do not. . . . But I could not always have made this distinction; and I believe that the majority of moral persons do not make it: most 'plain men' would probably say, at any rate on the first consideration of the matter, that they saw the obligations of Veracity and Good Faith as clearly and immediately as they saw those of Equity and Rational Benevolence. How then am I to argue with such persons? It will not settle the matter to tell them that they have observed their own mental processes wrongly, and that more careful introspection will show them the non-intuitive character of what they took for intuitions; especially as in many cases I do not believe that the error is one of misobservation. Still less am I inclined to dispute the 'primitiveness' or 'spontaneousness' or 'original-ity' of these apparent intuitions. On the contrary, I hold that here, as in other departments of thought, the primitive spontaneous processes of the mind are mixed with error, which is only to be removed gradu-ally by comprehensive reflection upon the results of these processes. Through such a course of reflection I have endeavored to lead my read-ers in chaps. 2–10 of Book III of my treatise: in the hope that after they have gone through it they may find their original apprehension of the self-evidence of moral maxims importantly modified.[74]

Whether Sidgwick succeeded in this effort has been the subject of much debate. But some of the best textual and contextual commentary on him does take his professed stance very seriously. Thus, J. B. Schneewind's *Sidgwick's Ethics and Victorian Moral Philosophy*, the most penetrating treatment of Sidgwick's ethics produced in the twentieth century, underscored how Sidg-wick's work was shaped by both the utilitarian tradition and its intuitionist and religious opposition (represented in part by the "Cambridge Moralists," Whewell, but also Maurice):

> [I]t is a mistake to view the book as primarily a defence of utilitari-anism. It is true, of course, that a way of supporting utilitarianism is worked out in detail in the *Methods*, and that there are places in it where Sidgwick seems to be saying quite plainly that utilitarianism is the best available ethical theory. From his other writings we know also that he thinks of himself as committed to utilitarianism, and that he as-sumes it in analysing specific moral and political issues. Yet it does not follow that the *Methods* itself should be taken simply as an argument for that position. We must try to understand it in a way that makes sense of its author's own explicit account of it.[75]

Before Schneewind, Blanshard, long an admirer of Sidgwick, agreed that "Sidgwick's acuteness was equaled by his sanity and moral seriousness; and for judicial detachment—the somewhat bleak, but clear, full light in which he sees things—he stands quite alone, so far as I know, in philosophic history. . . . For those who want to know simply what ethical theories make sense and what do not, and who are bored with attempts to make the subject interesting, Sidgwick's book is supreme."[76]

Still, many have disagreed (some vehemently), and charged that the *Methods* fails to capture in an impartial or sufficiently neutral or accurate way the best versions of the views of Aristotle, Kant, Hegel, Whewell, and/ or the Idealist philosophers, and that the best alternative methods are either distorted or neglected out of a bias toward hedonistic utilitarianism, which of course some, such as Singer, think is a healthy bias. And the *Methods* can be effectively explicated precisely through the consideration of these critiques and reconstructions.

One should bear in mind, however, when considering such critiques, that Sidgwick was not claiming that he had in the *Methods* exhaustively treated all possible methods or even all methods that had been of importance historically. Indeed, his most extensive treatments of perfectionism, evolutionism, and Idealism came in other works, and he was singularly appreciative, as his *Outlines* shows, of the rich diversity of historical approaches to ethics, stressing that his own work reflected the distinctively modern, more jural approach to the subject (stressing duty or the moral law), rather than the "attractive" forms of perfectionist egoism characteristic of the ancients. He was in key respects picking up the conversation as he found it, in what he took to be a progressive state of civilization, trying to sort out what could be taken away from the debates between Mill and Whewell. Furthermore, there is invariably an element of risk in following a convergence or reconciliation strategy, seeking to show how the best versions of competing approaches can be harmonized or made to coincide in their results. Just such a strategy has been followed by Parfit, in *On What Matters*, a work that, much like Sidgwick's, invites criticism to the effect that it has not succeeded in addressing the best versions of the views at issue. It is one thing to say that, e.g., Sidgwick just got Kant or Whewell wrong; it is another matter to say that he could have reconstructed their work in better, more charitable ways. The more penetrating criticisms of Sidgwick are of the latter type, as in Donagan's attempts to show that common-sense morality can be rationalized on a more consistently Whewellian or deontological basis.[77]

Yet beyond such rejoinders, it must be recognized, to keep Sidgwick's work in the right perspective, that he was also remarkably critical of past utilitarians and transformed utilitarianism in ways that radically departed from the views of Bentham and the Mills, and, most importantly, that he did not in the end hold that he had succeeded in adequately defending even the best version of utilitarianism, the version Skorupski would describe as "pure." Often described as a non-reductionist, non-naturalist cognitivist in ethics, Sidgwick obviously rejected the empiricism, reductionism, associationism, (supposed) psychological egoism, naturalism, and generally combative antireligious arguments of some of the earlier secular utilitarians. Moreover, his chief emphasis was on the sphere of personal ethics that Bentham and the Mills had relatively neglected, and again, he was profoundly influenced by the Cambridge Moralists, Kant, Clarke, Price, Butler, Plato, and Aristotle, none of whom should be counted as utilitarians. Although, like his utilitarian predecessors, he deemed the metaphysical issue of freedom of the will largely irrelevant to ethics, he argued that it was a fundamental mistake to think that people were psychologically always or mostly caused to act only for their own individual pleasure or good. The earlier utilitarians, he claimed (with very little charity and too much inaccuracy in interpretation), had not succeeded either in providing a fundamental justification for their views or in recognizing the incoherence of promoting the greatest happiness as the ultimate normative standard while taking people to be hopelessly self-interested psychologically. As Sidgwick described it, in a very revealing synopsis of his philosophical development (see Appendix 1 for the full account):

> The two elements of Mill's view which I am accustomed to distinguish as Psychological Hedonism [that each man does seek his own Happiness] and Ethical Hedonism [that each man ought to seek the general Happiness] both attracted me, and I did not at first perceive their incoherence.
>
> Psychological Hedonism—-the law of universal pleasure-seeking—-attracted me by its frank naturalness. Ethical Hedonism, as expounded by Mill, was morally inspiring by its dictate of readiness for absolute self-sacrifice. They appealed to different elements of my nature, but they brought these into apparent harmony: they both used the same words "pleasure", "happiness", and the persuasiveness of Mill's exposition veiled for a time the profound discrepancy between the natural end of action—-private happiness, and the end of duty—-general happiness. Or if a doubt assailed me as to the coincidence of private and general happiness, I was inclined to hold that it ought to be cast to the winds by a generous resolution.
>
> But a sense grew upon me that this method of dealing with the conflict between Interest and Duty, though perhaps proper for practice could not be final for philosophy. For practical men who do not philosophise, the maxim of subordinating self-interest, as commonly conceived, to "altruistic" impulses and sentiments which they feel to be higher and nobler is, I doubt not, a commendable maxim; but it is surely the business of Ethical Philosophy to find and make explicit the rational ground of such action.
>
> I therefore set myself to examine methodically the relation of Interest and Duty. . . . The result was that I concluded that no complete solution of the conflict between my happiness and the general happiness was possible on the basis of mundane experience. This [conclusion I] slowly and reluctantly accepted—-cf. Book ii. chap. v., and last chapter of treatise [Book ii. chap. v. is on "Happiness and Duty", and the concluding chapter is on "The Mutual Relations of the Three Methods"]. This [was] most important to me.[78]

This was, on Sidgwick's own account, the animating ethical dilemma behind the *Methods*, and it was what led him back to Whewell, Butler, Kant, and Aristotle, in search of a reasoned defense of self-sacrifice and an understanding of its relation to common-sense morality. And in this sense, although it is the back story to the *Methods* rather than the explicit story presented in the *Methods*, those who attribute to him a predominant concern to justify the Point of View of the Universe have a point. But more background needs to be considered here, before addressing just how lopsidedly or unfairly utilitarian the book itself might be.

Now, it is evident that Sidgwick's intuitionistic cognitivism, his belief in genuine foundational ethical truth, figures throughout his reconciliation of intuitional morality and utilitarianism. But his is a particularly sophisticated, fallibilistic form of philosophical intuitionism. There are, he holds, four criteria or conditions "the complete fulfillment of which would establish a significant proposition, apparently self-evident, in the highest degree of certainty attainable: and which must be approximately realised by the premises of our reasoning in any inquiry, if that reasoning is to lead us cogently to trustworthy conclusions."[79] 1. The "Cartesian Criterion" demands that the "terms of the proposition must be clear and precise." 2. The "self-evidence of the proposition must be ascertained by careful reflection," which is especially important in ethics because "any strong sentiment, however purely subjective, is apt to transform itself into the semblance of an intuition; and it requires careful contemplation to detect the illusion."[80] 3. The "propositions accepted as self-evident must be mutually consistent," since it "is obvious that any collision between two intuitions is a proof that there is error in one or the other, or in both."[81] And 4., since "it is implied in the very notion of Truth that it is essentially the same for all minds, the denial by another of a proposition that I have affirmed has a tendency to impair my confidence in its validity." This last, already evident in "The Ethics of Conformity and Subscription," adds a social dimension to Sidgwick's epistemology: "The absence of such disagreement must remain an indispensable negative condition of the certainty of our beliefs," for "if I find any of my judgements, intuitive or inferential, in direct conflict with a judgment of some other minds, there must be error somewhere: and if I have no more reason to suspect error in the other mind than in my own, reflective comparison between the two judgments necessarily reduces me temporarily to a state of neutrality."[82]

In other works, notably *Lectures on the Philosophy of Kant* (1905), Sidgwick explained that these conditions (the first two rolled into one) only afforded the best means for reducing the risk of error, rather than establishing indubitable truth. These works have, unfortunately, too often been neglected in the large literature devoted to Sidgwick's epistemology, which has been especially shaped by debates over whether he accorded any epistemic value to common-sense morality. Some, following Rawls, have found in the *Methods* something akin to Rawlsian reflective equilibrium, balancing and granting some weight to considered judgments, including common-sense ones, at all levels of generality. Others, following R. M. Hare and an earlier, non-cognitivist Peter Singer have emphasized Sidgwick's critique of common-sense morality, arguing that it plays no evidentiary role in his argument .[83] Much rides, however, on how tentative, dynamic, and social Sidgwick's epistemology is taken to be, whether one reads him as finding in common sense resources for giving bite to the coherence and consensus conditions, as he apparently did in "The Ethics of Conformity and Subscription," and for filling out a conception of public reason/ethical code, as in such works as *Practical Ethics* (1898). It is in this way that his epistemology can dovetail with more pragmatist or critical theoretical accounts emphasizing the importance of a community of inquiry.

Clearly, for Sidgwick there is, in any given situation, something that it is right to do or that one ought to do. This is the proper sphere of ethics, and the basic concept of morality that figures in this conception is a unique, highly general notion of "ought" or "right" that is irreducible to naturalistic terms and *sui generis*. Moral approbation is "inseparably bound up with the conviction, implicit or explicit, that the conduct approved is 'really' right—that is, that it cannot, without error, be disapproved by any other mind."[84] Subjectivism, emotivism, prescriptivism, expressivism, and other non-cognitivist interpretations of moral judgment misconstrue its nature, the ways in which it is simply not about one's psychological states. As Blanshard put it, summarizing Sidgwick, "I do not call the action right because I feel in a certain way; I feel in this way because I think the action right."[85] With the judgment comes at least some degree of motivation, though not always sufficient motivation, to do the right thing. The familiar recent distinction between internalism and externalism about moral judgment, that is, whether it carries motivational force internally or not, does not easily apply to Sidgwick, though if forced one would have to say that he was a qualified internalist.

Sidgwick was, then, as much concerned to avoid the so-called "naturalistic fallacy" (if there is such a thing) as his student Moore, who in *Principia Ethica* famously challenged all attempts to define "good" in terms of natural properties, since they left an "open question" of whether such and such property really was good. Sidgwick of course tended to emphasize the irreducibility of "ought" or "right," but his account of "ought" versus "good" has led to some controversy, since it seems to be harder to disentangle these than is readily apparent. For Sidgwick, "good" also contained a rational element. Contra interpretations of him as advancing a naturalistic "full-information" account of the good, such that, in his words, "a man's future good on the whole is what he would now desire and seek on the whole if all the consequences of all the different lines of conduct open to him were accurately foreseen and adequately realized in imagination at the present point of time," his account is better read as advancing an objectivist view that allows that some desires, however informed, may be rejected as irrational or unreasonable, as out of harmony with reason.[86]

Sidgwick seems to hold that there is a kind of continuum between rational judgments involving "ought" and those involving "good," with the latter being less tied to immediate action. However, Hurka has raised some important points indicating just how close Sidgwick and Moore actually were:

> After defining the good as what we ought to desire, he [Sidgwick] added that 'since irrational desires cannot always be dismissed at once by voluntary effort,' the definition cannot use 'ought' in 'the strictly ethical sense,' but only in 'the wider sense in which it merely connotes an ideal or standard.' But this raises the question of what this 'wider sense' is, and in particular whether it is at all distinct from Moore's 'good.' If the claim that we 'ought' to have a desire is only the claim that the desire is 'an ideal,' how does it differ from the claim that the desire is good? When 'ought' is stripped of its connection with choice, its distinctive meaning seems to slip away.[87]

Still, Sidgwick's metaethics does seem to be of a more minimal nature—he does not appeal to any special moral faculty or, like Moore in at least some contexts, seemingly posit ontologically a non-natural property of "goodness." With Sidgwick, in fact, one could be forgiven for thinking that the very word "intuition" may often be more trouble than it is worth, since it mostly amounts, as in Crisp and Parfit, to the claim that there are knowable, normative object-given reasons, beliefs justified by their content, for certain acts and desires. That is, Crisp, Parfit, de Lazari-Radek, and Singer all fall in with Sidgwick's effort to defend both a non-reductive and non-naturalistic, but non-metaphysical and non-ontological form of cognitive intuitionism or rationalism. They may— indeed, do—differ over whether it makes sense to parcel out distinct "moral" reasons, but even so they are more in line with each other than not.

Given such an interpretation and defense of Sidgwick's intuitionism, it is also hard to see how one could avoid deploying something like the method of reflective equilibrium in some fashion, when for example comparing one apparent intuition to another, though again, that is a somewhat fraught subject.[88] In any event, as these reconstructions make vividly clear, Sidgwick's treatment of classical utilitarianism was in many respects highly reconstructive, grounding the view on a cognitivist account of moral judgment that, while metaphysically minimal, nonetheless took over much from the earlier intuitionist critics of utilitarianism, albeit with some big exceptions, particularly on the matter of free will. [89]

Pleasures of the Texts

Even on the matter of ethical hedonism, where Sidgwick is often taken as a better, more consistent representative of Benthamism than Mill, his position was in truth highly reconstructive, more in line with Bentham's actual views than he realized. He did claim that the best account of ultimate goodness is a hedonistic one, and that this is an informative, non-tautological claim, though also a more controversial one than many of the others that he defends. It is on this score that critics such as Irwin charge that Sidgwick's hedonistic commitments, and his related criticisms of Green's account of self-realization, problematically presuppose that practical reason simply must be fully clear and determinate in its conclusions.[90] That is, Sidgwick argued, very much in the fashion of Bentham and Mill, that without something like the hedonistic metric it would be impossible to decisively compare, say, one virtue to another. And this was in addition to the larger question of whether one could really recommend making people more virtuous at the expense of their happiness. What if the virtuous life were conjoined to extreme pain, with no compensating good to anyone? As Shaver plausibly argues, in tackling these questions, "Sidgwick works out what it is reasonable to desire, and so attaches moral to natural properties, by the ordinary gamut of philosopher's strategies—appeals to logical coherence, plausibility, and judgment after reflection."[91]

Clearly, as previous chapters have shown, hedonism of one stripe or another, the claim that experienced pleasurable consciousness is the ultimate good, was the common currency of the classical utilitarians, and they cashed out the notion of happiness, and of individual welfare or well-being or Good, in just such terms. But many would agree with Sumner's excellent overview of the subject, which explains that the "equation of well-being with happiness is implicit in the utilitarian tradition—too implicit to count as a developed theory about the nature of welfare . . . it is an assumed conceptual identity."[92] Individual well-being, or prudential value (the good for you), was understood as of a piece with ultimate Good: "In order for my life to be going well for me I must be experiencing it, or its principal ingredients, as pleasant or satisfying."[93] But the line of argument does need greater clarification, as Sumner insists:

> Surely, it will be said, everyone knows that the classical utilitarians were hedonists both in their theory of the good and in their theory of welfare. There is, however, some point to distinguishing the two steps which seem to have led them to their ethical hedonism. The line of thought shared by Bentham, Mill, and Sidgwick yields ethical hedonism (pleasure is the only good) out of welfarism (well-being is the only good) and a view about the nature of welfare (well-being is reducible to pleasure). The exercise of distinguishing these two premises therefore offers the intriguing possibility that, for all their talk about pleasure and pain, what the utilitarians thought ultimately valuable was happiness or well-being. Pleasure and pain came into the picture only because they were believed to be implicated in the nature of well-being. If this hypothesis is correct, then the classical utilitarians were primarily welfarists and only secondarily hedonists.[94]

Sumner's move here marks a thought-provoking effort to reconstruct the utilitarian legacy and bring utilitarianism more in line with the research being done in Happiness Studies. On his view, "happiness" is a subjective albeit cognitive mental state of satisfaction with one's life overall. But insofar as it could provide an account of individual well-being, this life satisfaction would need to be "authentic," such that "the subject's point of view on her life is authoritative for determining when that life is going well *for her*. By connecting welfare with happiness we have interpreted that point of view as an endorsement or affirmation of the conditions of her life. When that endorsement is based on a clear view of those conditions, we have no grounds for questioning or challenging its authority: in this respect, the individual is sovereign over her well-being. But when it is based, wholly or partly, on a misreading of those conditions then its authority is open to question, since it is unclear whether or not she is endorsing her life *as it really is*. Where someone is deceived or deluded about her circumstance, in sectors of her life which clearly matter to her, the question is whether the affirmation she professes is *genuine* or *authentic*."[95] One's affirmations must, for Sumner, be informed and autonomous, not reflective of ignorance, manipulation, adaptive preferences, coercion, etc.

Sumner's account certainly represents a much better, more cogent, appropriation of the notion of happiness as life satisfaction than is common is happiness research, but, as ingenious as it may be, it does carry some serious disadvantages, and other reconstructions of classical utilitarian hedonism seem to capture the legacy in equally persuasive ways. And on the particular matter of Sidgwick's hedonism there has been much heated debate, controversy that needs to be considered in connection with the controversies discussed in the previous chapter.

Thus, Sumner has maintained, in a more problematic reading, that Sidgwick and Mill, by contrast with Bentham,

> seemed to recognize that the mental states we call pleasures are a mixed bag as far as their phenomenal properties are concerned. On their view what pleasures have in common is not something internal to them—their peculiar feeling tone, or whatever—but something about us—the fact that we like them, enjoy them, value them, find them satisfying, seek them, wish to prolong them, and so on.[96]

But Crisp, in the works discussed in the previous chapter, has argued insightfully that the internalism/externalism dualism is misleading here, that the "heterogeneity argument" about pleasures being a "mixed bag" is misguided, and that Sidgwick's writings did not express his better inclinations on the subject, Sidgwick being "at heart an internalist about pleasure."[97]

Crisp's treatment, in his work *The Cosmos of Duty*, of the classical hedonist account of ultimate good is singularly illuminating as both an interpretation of Sidgwick and a tentative defense of what does indeed also deserve to be called the classical view. He carefully explores the many issues and variations, from the synonymic view that "good" means "pleasant" to the externalist accounts interpreting pleasure or pleasurable consciousness in terms of a positive attitude toward or desire for the continuation of the conscious state in question, to internalist or mental-state accounts. Thus, "the difference between internalism and externalism is a difference in what kind of feeling pleasure is. According to internalism, the feeling of pleasure can be characterized without reference to any external attitudes; while according to the more plausible versions of externalism, pleasure is the feeling of having some experience to which some attitude external to it is being taken, such as a desire to sustain that experience." Sidgwick, Crisp rightly claims, resists any synonymic account, but vacillates on extenalist/internalist issues, since he notes for example both the "lack of correlation between strength of attitude and feeling of pleasantness" and the heterogeneity problem that there seems to be "no single phenomenological property common to all pleasurable experiences."98

Now, as noted in the previous chapter, de Lazari-Radek and Singer, in their *Point of View of the Universe*, have tried to challenge a rigid externalism/internalism dichotomy, but still end up defending an interpretation of Sidgwick that incorporates elements of externalism, with pleasure as a state of consciousness apprehended as desirable, but without any one feeling tone or sensation. Their view is set against Crisp's, which insightfully urges that Sidgwick's tergiversations suggest that he "at heart accepts the feeling-tone view of pleasure, but is misled by the heterogeneity argument into developing various externalist accounts, which are open to objections but in the end disappear from his theory."99 But Crisp develops plausible and highly Sidgwickian ways to defend such a position, by avoiding a reduction of pleasure as enjoyment to some mere sensation, and by urging that the former is "a determinable, with particular kinds of enjoyment . . . as determinates," much as seeing in color is a determinable with seeing specific colors as determinates. That is, pleasure "is a feeling-tone, but bodily enjoyment in, say, a massage is as different from a mental enjoyment, such as reading poetry, as seeing red from seeing blue."100 Thus, "the feeling-tone theorist would be best advised not to appeal to an analogy between enjoyment and a special sensation such as sweetness. Enjoyment is better understood as a determinable with particular kinds of enjoyment— that in eating, reading, thinking, and so on—as determinates."101 Seeing red is different from seeing blue, but both involve seeing in color; having sex is a different enjoyment from the joys of reading Sidgwick, but both are enjoyable. There is a common tone or "hedonic gloss."

But as de Lazari-Radek and Singer wonder, does this move simply transfer all the difficulties from "pleasure" to "hedonic gloss"? They reply to Crisp by inquiring:

How is it to be distinguished from other feelings? If we answer this question by saying that it is just a particular kind of feeling, in the way that sweetness is a particular kind of taste, then anyone who thinks that pleasure is intrinsically good needs to explain why just this kind of feeling has intrinsic value. If some people do not desire this kind of feeling, even qua feeling, then hedonistic theories of the good will fail to satisfy what, following Peter Railton, we have called "the resonance requirement"—we will be telling such people that pleasure is good for them, but this will not resonate with anything they desire or value. Obviously, the same problem recurs if we describe the hedonic gloss in terms of certain brain states. If, on the other hand, we say that the hedonic gloss is to be distinguished from other feelings by the fact that we do desire it, qua feeling, we are back to where we started, with pleasure being whatever mental state we desire, qua mental state. These problems remain in need of more work.[102]

No doubt Sidgwick's discussion of hedonism is uncharacteristically obscure on various points, and it is difficult to defend his view in part because it is so difficult to pin it down. But in a very important essay, "Sidgwick on Pleasure," Rob Shaver, while conceding that Sidgwick is unclear on key matters, reconstructs his views in a somewhat different fashion by zeroing in on Sidgwick's deployment of the term "apprehend" in his account of pleasure as "the kind of feeling which, when we experience it, we apprehend as desirable or preferable." After all, a feeling apprehended as desirable may not actually be desirable, as the Stoics claimed. It may "resonate," in some fashion, but not with decisiveness. Thus, "although Sidgwick writes of 'implicit' 'apprehension' or 'judgment,' his view seems best understood as claiming that a pleasure involves a feeling that *appears* desirable qua feeling. This fits his suggestion that the Stoic finds it an illusion that pleasure is desirable. . . . By 'appearance,' I intend a state, different from belief, that give prima facie support for a belief. An appearance may fail to support belief by being judged illusory, or by being outweighed by other evidence, and it can remain even when it fails in either of these ways. Like beliefs, appearances need have no distinctive feel."[103] Indeed, as Shaver notes, on the question of how authoritative individual judgment is here, "I might be wrong about how desirable a feeling is, since that requires unreliable comparisons with feelings not presently felt. Sidgwick stresses that my mood, my current desires, how easy it is to represent the feeling, the opinions of others—each can introduce error (*Methods*, 7th ed., 128, 144–46, 149). But even here I am authoritative in the sense that 'no one is in a position to controvert the preference of the sentient individual' (*Methods*, 7th ed., 128; also 108, 144)."[104]

Shaver mounts a very powerful defense of this interpretation and the advantages of such an account of hedonism, not the least of which is that "Sidgwick's view allows an argument, from the nature of pleasure to its desirability, that one can make even if one does not think that desires give reasons."[105] And a related advantage is how much room this interpretation leaves for the critical correction of one's assessments of how desirable certain feelings actually are: even if the individual might have the last word, it is clear that others with broader experience of feelings apprehended as desirable may be well positioned to push one to critically reconsider one's judgments on this score, as both Bentham and Mill would agree. Kahneman-like concerns about the consistency of an individual's judgments, divergences between immediate reports of pleasurable consciousness and reports dependent on the memory of experiences, are also suggestive of how little scope is left here to "immediacy" in hedonistic judgments—one's own reports of pleasure may not add up in a coherent way.[106] This is not to mention the problems inherent in the social mediation of pleasures and pains.

And even worse difficulties arise when trying—as is crucial—to depict how various pleasures or enjoyments figure in the growth of character and a pleasurable life as a whole, a happy life, which, as Sumner might agree, and as Mill's crisis so poignantly illustrated, was clearly the emphasis of the great utilitarians. Thus, it should by this point be tolerably evident that Godwin, Bentham, and Mill were all concerned to educate people by cultivating character growth in ways conducing to happiness, entwining one's own and that of others, and that they interpreted "happy lives" in hedonistic terms, which were often melded with perfectionistic terms, particularly in Godwin and Mill. But on this score, it is worth addressing, however briefly, just how their position compares to some of the alternative theories of happiness that are now current, including some plausible alternatives to Sumner's positions on both well-being and the utilitarian legacy.

If Daniel Haybron is right, happiness is best thought of in psychological terms as a complex emotional state and mood propensity:

[T]he *emotional state* view departs from hedonism in a different way: instead of identifying happiness with pleasant experience, it identifies happiness with an agent's emotional condition as a whole. This includes nonexperiential aspects of emotions and moods (or perhaps just moods), and excludes pleasures that don't directly involve the individual's emotional state. It might also include a person's *propensity* for experiencing various moods, which can vary over time. Happiness on such a view is more nearly the opposite of depression or anxiety—a broad psychological condition—whereas hedonistic happiness is simply opposed to unpleasantness. For example, a deeply distressed individual might distract herself enough with constant activity to maintain a mostly pleasant existence—broken only by tearful breakdowns during the odd quiet moment—thus perhaps counting as happy on a hedonistic but not emotional state view. The states involved in happiness, on an emotional state view, can range widely, far more so than the ordinary notion of mood or emotion. On one proposal, happiness involves three broad categories of affective state, including "endorsement" states like joy versus sadness, "engagement" states like flow or a sense of vitality, and "attunement" states like tranquility, emotional expansiveness versus compression, and confidence (Haybron 2008). Given the departures from commonsensical notions of being in a "good mood," happiness is characterized in this proposal as "psychic affirmation," or "psychic flourishing" in pronounced forms.[107]

Haybron takes his emotional state theory to be like hedonism in being affect-based,[108] and unlike many other theories of happiness, such as objectivist Aristotelian ones and "life satisfaction" views with their cognitive components. It is a psychological account, and at best only part of what would go into a normative theory of individual well-being or an account of ultimate Good. But even as a psychological account, it points up many of the flaws in empirical research on happiness, which often deploys measures of the wrong concept, life satisfaction (which only loosely tracks emotional states), and at best yields conflicting and question-begging results. De Lazari-Radek and Singer, and many others, have been sufficiently persuaded by Haybron's arguments to relinquish the notion of a hedonistic account of happiness as part of their account of ultimate Good, accepting Haybron's psychological account of it and treating happiness as but one common means to desirable consciousness:

> Still, one might feel that the utilitarian view would be less persuasive if it were stated without reference to happiness. It would at least be helpful if utilitarians could explain why, on their view, happiness is important. Fortunately, Haybron's account of happiness itself provides such an explanation. To be happy, on his view, is to be in a certain emotional state, or set of states, and emotional states have, as he says, 'extremely far-reaching consequences for the character of our lives'. Among these consequences is that emotional states appear to be 'the single most important *determinant* of our hedonic states'. If therefore we combine the classical utilitarian view that the only thing of intrinsic-value is pleasure, with Haybron's view that happiness consists of a set of emotional states that determine how pleasant our experiences are, we reach the conclusion that happiness is instrumentally good, not intrinsically good. Pleasure, in the sense of being in a positive hedonic state, is intrinsically good, and happy people are more likely to experience this positive hedonic state than unhappy people. That is why happiness matters, even if it is not an intrinsic value.[109]

That, it must be said (and as Sumner would insist), is not a step that the classical utilitarians ever thought to take, though it may well be a step in the right direction. [110] The cultivation of character that the great utilitarians called for could just as well proceed by treating happiness in this way, though of course the difficult questions about perfectionistic versus hedonistic value remain. And many other difficult questions as well. Which notion is more fundamental to the classical utilitarian legacy—happiness or pleasure? And how is either best construed?

Even if one wants to resist a move that would have utilitarians dispensing with their key branding, it is hard to deny that both utilitarians and non-utilitarians need to proceed with greater caution in this terrain, as the familiar alternative approaches to happiness and/or well-being and/or ultimate Good—Eudaimonism, objective list, desire satisfaction, life satisfaction, etc.—continue to battle each other to a stalemate, despite overblown claims to the contrary. The issues here are complicated and unresolved, but at the least, in response to any proposed notion of happiness, one must try, if only for the sake of clarity, to:

1. Determine the temporal dimension in question: a. happy moments or present condition or "happy that" some particular thing has happened; b. happy feelings/moods or dispositions; c. happy life or character; or d. some interweaving of these.

2. Determine the big theory at stake: a. Hedonism; b. Eudaimonism or Objective List; c. Desire or Preference Satisfaction; d. Life Satisfaction; e. Emotional Condition; or e. some combination of these or some other alternative (e.g., Schopenhauer's Cosmic Pessimism).

3. Determine the structure of the cognitive/conative/affective components: a. Reports of Pleasures/Pains or Enjoyments/Sufferings; b. Judgments of Life Satisfaction; c. Reports or Expressions of Emotional States or Conditions; d. some combination of the two (as in the mongrel notion of "Subjective Well-Being"); e. Reports/Judgments of Character Traits, Virtues; or f. Reports/Judgments of Positive or Negative Causal Networks or Fragments. Does the theory claim to be on the "subjective" or "objective" side when it comes to happiness, and if so, how so? Is such a dichotomy qualified or rejected? Is the term "subjective" being used simply to indicate the perspective of a conscious subject?

4. Determine the framing of the issue in terms of "happiness" in relation to "well-being" and in relation to "ultimate good"—e.g., Sumner's "authentic happiness" account is an account of well-being;[111] Haybron argues that there is more to well-being, and to value theory in general, than happiness, even authentic happiness, whereas de Lazari-Radek and Singer hold that happiness (as Haybron describes it) is instrumental to ultimate good, hedonistically construed. Ask what kind of "normativity" is at stake?

5. If the Haybron account, determine the specific dimensions and expressions of the emotional conditions, and the character structure of the mood propensities: a. Endorsement (joy v. sadness , cheerfulness v.

irritability); b. Engagement (exuberance/vitality v. listlessness, flow v. boredom/ennui); c. Attunement (peace of mind/tranquility v. anxiety, confidence v. insecurity, uncompression v. compression). Moreover, the criteria or evidence for such conditions and dispositions is highly complex and variable, ranging from facial expressions (e.g., Duchenne smiles) and bodily gestures (e.g., jaunty gait) to neurophysiological evidence of various types to a range of quality of life indicators (rates of suicide, depression, stress and anxiety disorders) to experience sampling techniques to life satisfaction or subjective well-being surveys to personality inventories, to case histories, to anthropological studies, etc. In general, the larger the population being assessed, the cruder and less adequate the measures, and none of the going methods of reporting on world happiness does justice to all of the factors highlighted in the Haybron account.

6. Determine how, with respect to the various conditions, dispositions, and character traits, first-person judgments or reports can be mistaken, misguided, or in various ways "inauthentic." When, e.g., are the judgments/reports warped by adaptive preferences, structures of domination, Kahneman inconsistencies (between the individual's experience sampling results and her/his retrospective assessment), misinformation/ignorance, Davies-style happiness manipulations, built in cognitive/affective Experience Machine mechanisms (consider the "depressive realism" studies), adaptation and satiation mechanisms, psychological defense mechanisms, etc. When might they be vulnerable to evolutionary "debunking" arguments? Why would one even think that one was in a position to report truthfully on one's long-term dispositions or deep character structure?

7. Determine how or to what degree the approach, whether the Haybron theory or a different theory, is dependent on or hostage to ethical, metaethical, or metaphysical claims about such matters as the existence of God, an objective meaning to life, intrinsic value, a real, enduring self, etc., as Brink suggests in his perfectionist reading of Mill. Does it hold that, e.g., true happiness can only come from a. seeing God or the Form of the Good; b. recognizing that justice and other virtues are good for their own sake; c. grasping that life really does have meaning, or that one can choose to give it meaning; d. seeing through the illusions of self; e. seeing that life is suffering; and/or f. escaping from the Experience Machine.[112] Ask how it might be possible to gain something of a reflexive, critical perspective on why one thinks and feels the way one does about happiness, on how cultural context and social structures (including educational and research institutions at all levels) construct, constitute, mediate, and prioritize various conceptions of happiness and techniques for achieving it. E.g.,

could a fixation on mindfulness blind people to the actual problems with educational institutions, the factors that generate stress, anxiety, and depression?[113] Is the obsession with happiness a symptom of deep societal disorder? What would it take, politically and culturally, to be in a position to resist the "Happiness Industry" in the name of happiness? Do we need more actual "experiments in living" under social conditions more conducive to authentic forms of happiness?

The foregoing discussion has obviously bounded into possible reconstructions of classical utilitarian hedonism in terms that they, the great utilitarians, did not fully capture, though Sidgwick went further even than Bentham in detailing the problems with any form of hedonism. If the task of fitting a hedonistic account of ultimate good to a plausible account of the growth of character and the ingredients of a happy life remains a challenging one, particularly given the difficulty of actually spelling out in detail the higher pleasures for which humanity should be striving, that is not a situation that he would have found surprising.

Unfortunately, for his part, Sidgwick seems to have accepted too many of the fallacious objections to Mill's account of the higher pleasures, and he consequently thought that he was defending his version of hedonism against Mill's. But in fact, given Skorupski's interpretation of Mill's argument (presented in the previous chapter), combined with either Crisp's defense of a feeling-tone approach or Shaver's defense of the apprehended-as-desirable account, it is not at all clear how far apart their views really need be. In any event, in his account of the actual content of pleasure, Sidgwick was certainly as high-minded as Godwin and Mill, highlighting the crucial importance of sympathetic pleasures in a happy life:

> I should go further and maintain that, on empirical grounds alone, enlightened self-interest would direct most men to foster and develop their sympathetic susceptibilities to a greater extent than is now commonly attained. The effectiveness of Butler's famous argument against the vulgar antithesis between Self-love and Benevolence is undeniable: and it seems scarcely extravagant to say that, amid all the profuse waste of the means of happiness which men commit, there is no imprudence more flagrant than that of Selfishness in the ordinary sense of the term,—the excessive concentration of attention on the individual's own happiness which renders it impossible for him to feel any strong interest in the pleasures and pains of others.[114]

Intriguingly, as W. J. Mander has shown, Green actually criticized Sidgwick's hedonism (plausibly) for being less definite as a method than the good of self-realization. Some, notably Gadamer and Irwin, have found virtue in the fact that, as Blanshard put it, "in the great mass of ethical discussion in these books [Plato and Aristotle] there is curiously little in the way of definite and solid result regarding the proper method of ethics."[115] But Green, in the conclusion to his *Prolegomena*, seems rather to be suggesting that he has in fact beaten Sidgwick at his own game:

> To most people sufficient direction for their pursuits is afforded by claims so well established in conventional morality that they are intuitively recognized, and that a conscience merely responsive to social disapprobation would reproach us for neglecting them. For all of us it is so in regard to a great part of our lives. But the cases we have been considering are those in which some 'counsel of perfection' is needed, which reference to such claims does not supply, and which has to be derived from reference to a theory of ultimate good. In such cases many questions have to be answered, which intuition cannot answer, before the issue is arrived at to which the theory of ultimate good becomes applicable; but then the cases only occur for persons who have leisure and faculty for dealing with such questions. For them the essential thing is that their theory of the good should afford a really available criterion for estimating those further claims upon them which are not enforced by the sanction of conventional morality, and a criterion which affords no plea to the self-indulgent impulse. Our point has been to show . . . that such a criterion is afforded by the theory of ultimate good as a perfection of the human spirit resting on the will to be perfect (which may be called in short the theory of virtue as an end in itself), but not by the theory of good as consisting in a maximum of possible pleasure.[116]

In other words, when, with Sidgwick, one is reasoning in critical mode, not the everyday serviceable common-sense one, utilitarian calculation is just hopelessly inconclusive—and insufficiently respectful of individual freedom—whereas the perfection of one's capabilities is relatively clear and definite. Green, as much as Sidgwick, was sensitive to the vital importance of having a clear sense of one's duty. He simply differed over which was the more helpful and determinate account of the good for this purpose.

To be sure, Sidgwick knew full well that rational egoism was not a matter of narrow selfishness and could take very high-minded forms, as in Green's Idealism and perfectionism generally. He was quite familiar with the different forms that an ethics of "self-realization" could take, and took such views very seriously as forming a leading alternative to a hedonistic account of the good. But he could never concede that the Idealists had succeeded where hedonism had not—self-realization involved too many different capabilities to be determinate, and there was at least nothing incoherent about the idea of a sum of pleasures. Still, it would seem that he opened up so many complexities and uncertainties in hedonistic calculation that his (impure) form of utilitarianism was in danger of losing its bite. This he would have admitted.

Furthermore, it should be added here that this would also have been much the line that Sidgwick would have taken toward W. D. Ross, A. C. Ewing, and other later defenders of the notion of *prima facie* or *pro tanto* duties—that is, the claim that there are genuinely self-evident duties embedded in common-sense morality, such as promise-keeping, but that these are not absolute, only *prima facie*, that is, holding if other things are equal. Unfortunately, Ross and the others who took this line had nothing of substance to say about how to balance such duties when they conflict, and thus their position tended to collapse into something like perceptional or aesthetic intuitionism. As de Lazari-Radek and Singer argue with reference to Ross's critique of ideal utilitarianism:

> Ross is surely right to point out that consequentialist theorists with more than one intrinsic value are in similar difficulty in telling us how to balance conflicting values as his own theory is in telling us how to decide when there are conflicting prima facie duties. A monistic form of utilitarianism, like hedonistic utilitarianism, is in principle in a better position, because if all the facts were known, we would know which action would produce the greatest net increase in pleasure for all affected, and we would know what we ought to do. In practice, it has to be admitted that we never know this, and there are many situations in which reasonable hedonistic utilitarians can differ about what we ought to do. Nevertheless, monistic utilitarianism at least give us an 'in principle' way of resolving the question, which Ross's theory lacks. If our ability to predict the consequences of our actions improves, utilitarianism will yield more determinate guidance. In contrast, there seems no way of eliminating the indeterminacy that is at the heart of Ross's ethic of prima facie duties.[117]

This seems exactly right, both in terms of the argument and the reconstruction of Sidgwick's position. And it suggests some of the reasons why one might want to resist Hurka's attempt to present Sidgwick as less the last of the classical utilitarians and more the first of the "Sidgwick to Ewing School," upon whose work Ross et al. improved. When addressing such positions, Hurka seems primarily concerned to point up Sidgwick's hypocrisy:

> Though he did not put it this way, his argument about conflicts of duty rested at bottom on the charge that deontologists equivocate between other-things-equal and all-things-considered claims. The unqualified principle 'you ought to keep your promises' makes acts falling under it right only other things equal, since some other principle can make them on balance wrong; it therefore does not yield decisive verdicts. Clear verdicts do follow from a principle that contains exception-clauses and so makes acts falling under it all things considered right, but that principle neither seems self-evident nor is

accepted by all. But Sidgwick's statements of his axioms equivocate just as much between other things equal and all things considered claims. . . . In fact, Sidgwick's axioms are open to the same general objection he made to deontological principles. Only when they are stated as other things equal is it at all plausible to say they appear self-evident and are generally accepted, though even then there can be objections to them. . . . But in that form they cannot ground either egoism or utilitarianism, as Sidgwick needed them to do. To do that they must make all-things-considered claims, but then they are less intuitive and will be widely rejected: many will deny that you should always do only what is best for you, and many will also deny that you should always do what has the best consequences for all. As he said of deontological principles, Sidgwick's axioms may satisfy some conditions in one form and others in a different form, but in no form do they satisfy them all.[118]

Thus, although one of Sidgwick's "main objections to deontological principles turned on the difference between their other-things-equal and all-things-considered forms, his defence of his axioms equivocated on the same point and involved the same ambiguity. In arguing against deontology and for consequentialism he applied, and not just once, a double standard."[119]

But defenders of the alternative, Sidgwickian approach may well deny that their axioms become less compelling when cast in all-things-considered form. The bare fact of disagreement, even serious expert disagreement, has never been treated as putting a stop to this form of intuitional theorizing, nor has conflict with common sense. The consensus of experts is a very long-term concern (one should not be surprised by initial incomprehension and hostility), and common sense, for all its importance, really is a mess. When Sidgwick advanced such axioms as the Axiom of Justice (what is right for oneself must be right for all who are similarly circumstanced), the Axiom of Prudence (smaller present good should not be preferred to larger future good), or the Axiom of Benevolence (the good of others is just as important as one's own good) as an improvement on the less abstract Whewellian axioms concerning promise-keeping, truth-telling, etc. but still only apparently self-evident, that was not a hypocritical lapse into any form of Rossian equivocation so much as a frank admission that the effort to go from apparent self-evidence to true self-evidence at this higher level was still far from complete. Recall, too, this stricture, from "The Ethics of Conformity and Subscription": the best course by way of exceptions to the rule of veracity "is by making our conceptions as clear as possible in respect of the amount of deviation from strict sincerity to be permitted. It is a universal principle of ethics, that if any exceptions are to be admitted to a moral rule, the exceptions should in their turn be made as regular as possible."[120]

On this score, Sidgwickians such as de Lazari-Radek and Singer hope to make an advance, but an advance on Sidgwickian terms, not by turning to Ross. And even those with greater sympathy for Ross, such as Crisp, can allow that "[j]udgement is involved in accepting utilitarianism to start with, but it will also be involved in assessing the implications of the principle in particular cases. . . . What matters is how best to ensure that one's judgements are correct, and Sidgwick, in his discussion of the conditions for highest certainty . . . provides a methodology which is at least as plausible as that of any pluralistic intuitionist."[121]

It should also be stressed, in this detailing of Sidgwick's revisionism, that Sidgwick took hedonistic utilitarianism in directions that no previous secular utilitarian had even imagined. Not only did he pose, apparently for the first time, the problem of future generations and population size, issues that bring out the difference between total and average utilitarianism, and that would be brilliantly developed by Parfit in *Reasons and Persons*.[122] But, notoriously, he also considered, without any invocation of either God's greater wisdom or psychological egoism, how common-sense or everyday morality might have its most felicific effects if largely believed to be true, and acted upon by people who would not in any conscious way be thinking in utilitarian terms:

> Thus, on Utilitarian principles, it may be right to do and privately recommend, under certain circumstances, what it would not be right to advocate openly; it may be right to teach openly to one set of persons what it would be wrong to teach to others; it may be conceivably right to do, if it can be done with comparative secrecy, what it would be wrong to do in the face of the world; and even, if perfect secrecy can be reasonably expected, what it would be wrong to recommend by private advice or example. These conclusions are all of a paradoxical character: there is no doubt that the moral consciousness of a plain man broadly repudiates the general notion of an esoteric morality, differing from the one popularly taught; and it would be commonly agreed that an action which would be bad if done openly is not rendered good by secrecy. We may observe, however, that there are strong utilitarian reasons for maintaining generally this latter common opinion. . . . Thus the Utilitarian conclusion, carefully stated, would seem to be this; that the opinion that secrecy may render an action right which would not otherwise be so should itself be kept comparatively secret; and similarly it seems expedient that the doctrine that esoteric morality is expedient should itself be kept esoteric. . . . A Utilitarian may reasonably desire, on Utilitarian principles, that some of his conclusions should be rejected by mankind generally; or even that the vulgar should keep aloof from his system as a whole, in so far as the inevitable indefiniteness and complexity of its calculations render it likely to lead to bad results in their hands.[123]

Thus, even if one is tempted to say that at some level Sidgwick was an "act" utilitarian rather than a "rule" utilitarian (or a global utilitarian), given his regular use of the word "conduct" in defining the utilitarian principle, and that his notion of method covered in some abstract way the decision-procedures people should deploy at least when thinking critically, he allowed such a degree of possibly justifiable indirect utilitarianism that one can envision a fully Sidgwickian ethical society in which very few people (if any) are consciously invoking the utilitarian standard at any level. Such views might accord well with a few of Sidgwick's own mature practices, but they do not accord with the familiar Kantian insistence on the necessary publicity of fundamental moral principles. Snidely allowing that this perspective allowed Sidgwick a consistent interpretation of the different "levels" of moral thinking, critical versus everyday, Bernard Williams suggested that this was because Sidgwick was a "Government House" utilitarian who identified the different levels with different sets of people, the colonialist rulers and the colonized, respectively.[124] At the extreme, for all humanity knows, the utilitarian standard is God's standard, but the universe is made to accord with it in part by disposing humanity to believe and act on very different terms. As remarked in the previous chapters, the very focal point of utilitarianism—acts, rules, motives, institutions, character—is up for utilitarian assessment, even if Sidgwick did tend to speak in terms of "conduct."

Yet Sidgwick's controversial view about esoteric morality has attracted some forceful defenders. Again, de Lazari-Radek and Singer go straight to the heart of the matter and attack the Kantian and neo-Kantian publicity requirement, seeking instead to justify the indirect and esoteric strategies that Sidgwick elaborated. They demonstrate, among other things, how even such supposedly alternative views as Catholic moral theology admit a "doctrine of 'mental reservation,' which holds that it is permissible to say something that misleads, and yet avoid the sin of lying by mentally adding information that would, if spoken, make the response truthful."[125] Of course, as Sidgwick's stance on subscription suggests, he thought the greater happiness (and the moral authority of organized religion) would be better served by greater clerical and lay transparency. In his more Godwinian moments, he was, paradoxically, openly clear about honest silence being better than obvious oiliness. But as noted, his views were very paradoxical; he resigned his Fellowship, but he certainly did not openly attack the religious views that he wanted to see left behind. As will be shown later in this chapter, his approach to Benson and his uncles was also his approach to the Church of England in general—avoidance.

So, if Sidgwick was less than perfectly impartial in his approach to the methods of ethics, it must at least be conceded that he also came down fairly hard on utilitarian thinking as he found it, in the going caricatures of Bentham et al. On metaethics, moral psychology, "right" v. "good," hedonistic calculation, etc., he reshaped the arguments in dramatic fashion, if not always with a fair regard for his predecessors. But, astonishingly, even after this dramatic makeover, with all the reconstructive philosophical surgery he could manage, Sidgwick confessed his failure to provide an adequate defense of utilitarianism. If he gave classical secular utilitarianism a brilliant makeover, this turned out to be all the more poignant in that despite his best efforts he did not, to his mind, render the view justified. As he put it to Dakyns: "Ethics is losing its interest for me rather, as the insolubility of its fundamental problem is impressed on me. I think the contribution to the *formal* clearness & coherence of our ethical thought which I have to offer is just worth giving: for a few speculatively-minded persons—very few. And as for all practical questions of interest, I feel as if I had now to begin at the beginning and learn the ABC."[126] The "fundamental problem" of ethics was of course the animating problem with which he had begun, the problem of self-sacrifice, rechristened as the "dualism of the practical reason"—such that, unlike intuitional morality, rational egoism could not be reconciled with utilitarianism. Despite all the talk of "ultimately valid" self-evident axioms, the first edition of the *Methods* concluded that "the 'Cosmos' of Duty is thus really reduced to a Chaos, and the prolonged effort of the human intellect to frame a perfect ideal of rational conduct is seen to have been foredoomed to inevitable failure."[127] As Sidgwick put it elsewhere: along with "(a) a fundamental moral conviction that I ought to sacrifice my own happiness, if by so doing I can increase the happiness of others to a greater extent than I diminish my own, I find also (b) a conviction—which it would be paradoxical to call 'moral', but which is none the less fundamental—that it would be irrational to sacrifice any portion of my own happiness unless the sacrifice is to be somehow at some time compensated by an equivalent addition to my own happiness."[128] Each of these convictions has as much clarity and certainty "as the process of introspective can give" and each also finds wide assent "in the common sense of mankind."

According to Sidgwick, his chief debt on this matter was to Joseph Butler. "Butler's express statement of the duality of the regulative principles in human nature constitutes an important step in ethical speculation, since it brings into clear view the most fundamental difference between the ethical thought of modern England and that of the old Greco-Roman world. . . . [I]n Platonism and Stoicism, and in Greek moral philosophy generally, but one regulative and governing faculty is recognized under the name of Reason . . . [whereas] in the modern ethical view, when it has worked itself clear, there are found to be two—Universal Reason and Egoistic Reason, or Conscience and Self-love."[129] As Frankena glossed this passage, the main point "is to say that modern (British) moral philosophers are dualistic in a sense in which the ancients were monistic—in the sense of (all?) holding that there are two governing faculties in each of us, and not just one."[130] Insofar as he did not subsume it under dogmatic intuitionism, Sidgwick regarded classical perfectionism as in large measure but another form of egoism, and regarded distinctively modern ethical theory as marked by Butler's recognition of the duality of "governing faculty" in practical reason, such that "conscience" is a source of justifying reasons for action in addition to reasons of self-love or self-interest. He found in Butler a compelling critique of psychological egoism, of the view that people are necessarily egoistically motivated: "I was led by it to abandon the doctrine of Psychological Hedonism, and to recognise the existence of 'disinterested' or 'extra-regarding' impulses to action . . . as regards what I may call a Psychological basis of Ethics, I found myself much more in agreement with Butler than Mill."[131] And from this source he also derived the "paradox of egoistic hedonism," the insight, also figuring in his great predecessors, that pleasure may not be best achieved by directly aiming at it, which informs his treatment of both egoism and utilitarianism as indirect, as standards of right rather than procedures for everyday decision making.

Many of the same considerations were brought out in early editions of *The Methods* (as in pp. 93–95 of the first edition), though in later editions Sidgwick was increasingly given to excising historical commentary and references, a tactic that has played no inconsiderable role in distorting the reception of him.[132]

No doubt Sidgwick's sweeping characterization of modern moral philosophy requires sweeping qualification, as Crisp has argued.[133] Also, as Frankena noted, really "there is no such thing as *the* modern or even British view about the number of governing faculties found, not even on his own account; he himself describes Hobbes and Spinoza as egoists, that is, as finding, as the Greeks did, that egoistic reason is the sole governing faculty in us." Furthermore, it is obvious that not all of the British moralists "put all of the faculties they regard as operative in us under *reason*," as the well-known examples of Shaftesbury, Hume, and Smith demonstrate.[134] Finally, that Butler held all the views that Sidgwick attributes to him is open to debate—according to Frankena, "ethical dualism, at least in the form in which Sidgwick accepts it, did not work itself entirely clear in Butler and did not do so until Sidgwick himself worked on it, if even then."[135] However, Stephen Darwall, in work deeply indebted to Frankena, suggests that the dualism "is actually closer to Hutcheson's notion that universal benevolence and calm self-love are the two independent 'grand determinations' than to anything in Butler,"[136] or may even derive "ultimately . . . from a contemporary of Locke's, Richard Cumberland."[137]

Whatever Sidgwick's originality, it would seem, from the text of the *Methods*, that he mainly considered two related solutions to the dualism: a weakening of epistemological standards, or a theism postulating the moral government of the universe. On the first, he suggests, in proto-pragmatist fashion, that if "we find that in our supposed knowledge of the world of nature propositions are commonly taken to be universally true, which seem to rest on no other ground than that we have a strong disposition to accept them, and that they are indispensable to the systematic coherence of our beliefs,—it will be more difficult to reject a similarly supported assumption in ethics, without

opening the door to universal skepticism."[138] On the second, he explains that
if "we may assume the existence of such a Being, as God, by the *consensus*
of theologians, is conceived to be, it seems that Utilitarians may legitimately
infer the existence of Divine sanctions to the code of social duty as constructed
on a Utilitarian basis; and such sanctions would, of course, suffice to make it
always every one's interest to promote universal happiness to the best of his
knowledge."[139] But this is put so laconically as to be evasive. One would never
guess, from such guarded remarks, how Sidgwick took the demonstration of
the truth of theism and the moral order of the universe to be a task of the
utmost urgency, a task that, moreover, he would harbor hopes of successfully
completing himself.

Of course, he also considered other efforts to address the dualism, such as
Green's ethics of "self-realization." But he cogently criticized Green for vacil-
lating on the matter of whether one's own perfection could come into conflict
with the common good or perfection of all, which it could do if certain capabilities figuring in one's self-realization were not simply part and parcel of the
common good, but competitive. As David Brink has put it, following Sidgwick,
Green waffled between a notion of perfection involving the exercise of the "full
range of an individual's rational capacities" and one involving "the exercise of
specifically moral capacities connected with the common good." These forms
of perfection are distinct, if not independent, which means that "many sacrifices the perfection of others demands will be genuine, and not all of them will
be fully compensable. And this is enough to raise the spectre that there will be
a kind of dualism of practical reason, not exactly between self and others, but
between self-confined and other-regarding aspects of one's own perfection."[140]
Or, in Sidgwick's words, and more generally: "It is difficult to see why the operation of self-distinguishing consciousness is to obliterate the difference—so far
as natural desire goes—between Own good and Others' good. It would rather
seem to emphasise and intensify it, since a self-distinguishing consciousness
must distinguish itself from other selves."[141]

As with Sidgwick's epistemology, the dualism of practical reason has given
rise to a vast literature. From Idealist efforts to find one's own good in the
common good, to Moore's denial that the notion of "own good" even makes
sense, to Rawls's defense of the reasonable as framing the rational, to Parfit's
attempts to demonstrate that omnipersonal reasons can be stronger than
personal ones, Sidgwick's framing of the "fundamental problem" has been at
the heart of the most important ethical philosophical discussions of the last
century and a half. Even if we reject Sidgwick's language of personal point of
view versus Point of View of the Universe, it is difficult to resist the idea that,
at the least, and in Parfit's words: "When one of our two possible acts would
make things go in some way that would be impartially better, but the other
act would make things go better either for ourselves or for those to whom
we have close ties, we often have sufficient reasons to act in either of these

two ways."[142] Those who would challenge this in the name of the Point of View of the Universe, such as de Lazari-Radek and Singer, admittedly face a considerable challenge. The last section of this chapter will detail promising gambits for dealing with the dualism, though Sidgwick's own rather more cosmic perspective on the issue suggests that philosophical humility is also in order. Sidgwick himself could never shake the conviction that something beyond this world was needed to solve the problem, and that the problem was no mere philosopher's plaything, but a cosmic calamity, not that he wanted to announce that to the world.

The Other Side of the Methods

This is a long interval, but I have been passing through a mental crisis which disinclined me for self-revelation. I have been facing the fact that I am drifting steadily to the conclusion—I have by no means ar-rived at it, but am certainly drifting towards it—that we have not, and are never likely to have, empirical evidence of the existence of the in-dividual after death. Soon, therefore, it will probably be my duty as a reasonable being—and especially as a professional philosopher—to consider on what basis the human individual ought to construct his life under these circumstances. Some fifteen years ago, when I was writ-ing my book on Ethics, I was inclined to hold with Kant that we must *postulate* the continued existence of the soul, in order to effect that harmony of Duty with Happiness which seemed to me indispensable to rational moral life. At any rate I thought I might *provisionally* postu-late it, while setting out on the serious search for empirical evidence. If I decide that this search is a failure, shall I finally and decisively make this postulate? Can I consistently with my whole view of truth and the method of its attainment? And if I answer "no" to each of these ques-tions, have I any ethical system at all? And if not, can I continue to be Professor and absorb myself in the mere erudition of the subject—write "studies" of moralists from Socrates to Bentham—in short, become one of the "many" who, as Lowell says,

> Sought truth, and lavished life's best oil
> Amid the dust of books to find her,
> Content at last for guerdon of their toil
> With the last mantle she hath left behind her.

I am nearly forty-nine, and I do not find a taste for the old clothes of opinions growing on me.

I have mixed up the personal and general questions, because every speculation of this kind ends, with me, in a practical problem, "What is to be done here and now?" That is a question which I must answer;

whereas as to the riddle of the Universe—I never had the presumption to hope that its solution was reserved for me, though I had to try.

The above lines, written in the journal that he regularly sent to Symonds, mark one of Sidgwick's most telling confessions. He took the failure of the *Methods* to overcome the dualism of practical reason as a personal challenge to demonstrate the moral order of the universe, such that one's own true Good and the true Good of all would be harmonized. The failure of the *Methods* might, he hoped, be overcome by the triumph of parapsychology. He even hoped that he would be the one to make the breakthrough. When all seemed for naught, a depression even more devastating than his earlier one descended upon him—his second great crisis. As Myers described the situation:

> Gurney [a key member of the Sidgwick group], up to the time of his death, was quite uncertain on this capital point. He still held that all proved phenomena were possibly explicable by new modes of action between living men alone. Sidgwick often thought this too; and his wife, though more steadily inclining to a belief in survival, was averse to pronouncing herself on the matter. I had therefore often a sense of great solitude, and of an effort beyond my strength;—'striving,'—as Homer says of Odysseus in a line which I should wish graven on some tablet in my memory,—'striving to save my own soul, and my comrades' homeward way.'
>
> It was as late as November, 1887, that these doubts reached their worst intensity. The group who had consulted over *Phantasms of the Living,*—the group whom some regarded as facile in belief,—were certainly then in no credulous mood. Sidgwick's natural skepticism and self-criticism asserted themselves more strongly than ever before. The collapse of Madame Blavatsky's so-called Theosophy,—a mere fabric of fraud,—had rendered all of us severer in our judgment of the human evidence on which our own conclusions depended. Sidgwick urged that all that we had actually proved was consistent with eternal death. He thought it not improbable that this last effort to look beyond the grave would fail; that men would have to content themselves with an agnosticism growing yearly more hopeless,—and had best turn to daily duties and forget the blackness of the end.[143]

Understanding how this crisis came about is difficult. Much was going wrong in Sidgwick's life at this point—he was unhappy with his academic work, with the slow progress of higher education for women, with the recklessness of such friends as Symonds, and in June of 1888, he would be thrown by the possible suicide of Edmund Gurney. But above all, his work on the "deepest problems" seemed to have yielded nothing. To understand this demands an exploration of Sidgwick's parapsychological work (his "psychical research") and the intricate ways in which that project was bound up, not only with his academic philosophical ethics, but with his philosophizing friendships with Symonds and Myers. They were the ones who best understood what he was about when it came to "the deepest problems." That Sidgwick's parapsychological investigations were of apiece with his work on ethics, politics, and religion, and, especially in the late 1880s, similarly frustrating, is made singularly clear in his exchanges with Symonds. After all, it was to Symonds that he had explained that he had "tried *all* methods in turn—all that I found pointed out by any of those who have gone before me; and all in turn have failed—revelational, rational, empirical methods—there is no proof in any of them."[144] And given that Sidgwick was once again worrying that he should resign his position to avoid "solemn imposture," it was appropriate that he should turn to Symonds, who after all had served as his confidante during his crisis in the late sixties. Was being a professor of moral philosophy as hypocritical as swearing belief in the Apostles' Creed?

Sidgwick had first become close to Symonds in 1867, as his crisis of faith was building up to his resignation. At that point, Sidgwick not only contacted Mill, but formed what would be perhaps the defining friendship of his life. He wrote to Symonds shortly after visiting him in London of that year, with that passionate, poetic prose that he had previously reserved for such friends as Dakyns, Noel, and few others:

> My dearest friend I cannot tell you all I feel: I have drunk deep of happiness: I have said to the Augenblick, 'du bist so schön'—I am so glad you say I have done you good: I must have given you my best: my best never comes out except when I am played upon & stirred by affection and subtle sympathy combined: when I do not get this, I become lethargic. Among the 'dim' common populations I seem to change and become common. I am so glad you let me stay with you so long; I might have felt that what of strange, new, delicious rich had come into my life might pass out of it like a dream. I feel now that you are 'not something to be retracted in a certain contingency.'[145]

Symonds would in turn write to their mutual friend Dakyns that "Henry Sidgwick has been with me a week. He is numbered among mine."

Symonds, who was already close to Dakyns and to Arthur Sidgwick, was above all the soulmate whom Sidgwick had long sought, as his struggles in the 1860s wore on and his old Apostolic friends moved on. At that turning point, his mentor Mill gave him direction and his friend Symonds gave him support and set an example, and he took the most forthright action against hypocrisy that he would ever take. Symonds, it seems, was at this point also struggling to break out of a suffocating shell, in his case of the hypocrisy involved in masking his sexual orientation. He had gone through a period of trying to "cure" himself, chiefly through marriage, but his "wolf," as he called it, had now returned, and he suffered a period of deep and devastating depression at Cannes in 1868, to which Sidgwick was witness. Symonds emerged only through honest acceptance of his deeper self, and he wrote the poetry that was to all intents and purposes an effort at coming out. His classic *A Problem in Greek Ethics*, a work that would not see its like until Kenneth Dover's 1978 book on *Greek Homosexuality*, also took shape during this period, and made a profound impression on Sidgwick.[146] Thus, for all their differences, Symonds's casuistry and Sidgwick's shared much, and were hammered out at the same time, together: one could honestly confront and accept one's deepest thoughts and feelings, explore the possibilities with the support of knowing friends, and avoid hypocrisy while also avoiding open confrontation (or scandal), unless it was clearly demanded by the signs of the times, in conjunction with one's social role.

Symonds, a product of Harrow and Benjamin Jowett's Oxford, and the son of a physician who practically personified the medicalization of discourse surrounding sexuality, was early on persuaded that his same-sex attachments reflected an inherent disposition. In due course he became equally convinced that this was not a morbid condition, that the culture of ancient Greece had demonstrated that homosexuality could be a healthy aspect of high cultural life, and that the poetry of Whitman pointed the way to a new synthesis of ancient and modern. He championed a "New Age," with Millian sympathy extended to include that very Hellenic comradeship of Whitman's "Calamus." Sidgwick appreciated him on many levels, and would be a frequent visitor to his homes at Clifton or Davos, where Symonds spent much time out of concern for his problematic health, the result of tuberculosis. The two exchanged journals, journals that would provide the best and most illuminating accounts of their intellectual and emotional struggles, as the passage above indicates. When Sidgwick worked through his crises, it was always in the company of Symonds, whose friendship, as Eleanor allowed, "was one of the things he most valued in life."

But Symonds also served as something of a counterpoint to other forces in Sidgwick's life, including Eleanor and Myers, who were greater enthusiasts for psychical research. Symonds, who at the time of Sidgwick's crisis was suffering terribly from the loss of one of his daughters to tuberculosis, had, even under those conditions, replied:

I do not pretend that I had ever fixed my views of human conduct clearly or hopefully upon the proof of immortality to our ordinary experience. I do not deny that I never had any confidence in the method you were taking to obtain the proof. I will further confess that, had you gained the proof, this result would have enormously aggravated the troubles of my life, by cutting off the possibility of resumption into the personal-unconscious which our present incertitude leaves open to my sanguine hope.

Ethics, I feel, can take care of themselves—that is to say, human beings in social relations will always be able to form codes of conduct, profitable to the organism and coercive of the individual to the service of its uses.[147]

Sidgwick's response that he had tried all methods was not, therefore, really to the point, and he confessed that he found Symonds to be a true puzzle case, challenging everything he thought he knew about the deep rootedness, in common sense and history, of belief in immortality. As his journal to Symonds reveals, Sidgwick had a special respect for Symonds's intellect, and for his very different ethical and religious dispositions, his tough "symmetrical" character. For all his reading of Mill, he found it exceptionally hard to comprehend, face to face, the position of someone like Symonds, who actually longed for the opposite of personal survival of death: "All the activities in which I truly live seem to carry with them the same demand for the 'wages of going on.'"[148] Perhaps the taint of egoism in the Christian hope for happy immortality was just too difficult for Sidgwick to shake, but at any rate, he could not resist testing his convictions against Symonds's insouciant resistance.

And curiously enough, Symonds actually was entangled in some of the work of the psychical researchers, which spoke to many different audiences for many different reasons, as the rest of this section will try to demonstrate. It was Sidgwick's parapsychological inquiries that drew together, in Apostolic fashion, his various circles.

Obviously, the "search for empirical evidence" in the above passage refers to Sidgwick's parapsychological research, his work with the Cambridge "Ghost Society" and as a founder and member (and three-time president) of the British Society for Psychical Research. It is truly amazing just how much time Henry and Eleanor devoted to investigating the claims of mediums, mystics, and those ordinary people who happened to report paranormal happenings, and this often at the cost of their other work. Yet the doings of this society form an amazing chapter in the history of science, as is attested by Alan Gauld's *The Founders of Psychical Research* and Janet Oppenheim's *The Other World*,[149] and the "Sidgwick Group" was a genuinely impressive group, including not only Eleanor's brothers, Arthur and Gerald Balfour, but also the distinguished scientist Lord Rayleigh (who as noted had married Eleanor's sister Evelyn), Myers, Gurney, Oliver Lodge, Richard Hodgson, Frank Podmore (the biographer of Robert Owen), and many others. Somehow, they managed to coexist in a research society that also included a good many "spiritualists" of the William Stainton Moses variety, who were eager to believe in the supernatural whatever the empirical evidence.

Sidgwick's career as a parapsychologist has, in recent decades anyway, been something that his philosophical admirers have preferred to ignore. Indeed, the impression is sometimes given that Sidgwick had no philosophical psychology to speak of, given his lack of interest in "the moral faculty," that he simply did not understand the Kantian position on the ego, and that, unlike Hume, he had little sense of the considerations surrounding atomistic and empiricist accounts of the self and personal identity and how these might bear on ethics.

This is simply mistaken. His minimalism in metaethics was largely an artifact of the *Methods*, and did not translate into minimalism in other areas of metaphysics. Sidgwick had studied Kant, Hume, Hegel, and Idealism in detail, and he was keenly aware of the issues involved in their philosophical accounts of the self—his was very much a self-aware struggle with the limitations of doing ethics, or politics, as a limited, independent concern. He was, as remarked, a vehement opponent of reductionistic, materialistic scientism, a position that he found as dogmatic as the old religious orthodoxies. The effort to situate him within the tradition of British empiricism and associationism only brings out yet again just how eclectic and original he was, how far he carried (supposed) utilitarian moral psychology away from its Benthamite and even Millian roots. He was, in fact, a psychologist (philosophical and para) of considerable repute, and counted among his younger followers such figures as James Ward, who would exercise a powerful influence on British psychology, and who was anything but a reductionist. Whatever one may feel about the particular claims of parapsychology on such things as telepathy, telekinesis, survival of death, etc.—which the Sidgwicks' research often did a great deal to undercut—the issues and models of experimentation and inquiry can hardly be ignored, since they were plainly contiguous with his ethical and philosophical inquiries. Indeed, his reformism, especially in matters of education, was also linked to his ethical and social theories, and perforce drew on his psychological views. And it was in fact this work that drew forth the most revealing philosophical exchanges with those closest to him—Symonds, Myers, and Eleanor.

The work was frustrating beyond belief. Sidgwick found it very difficult to accept the fact that so many of the subjects of his parapsychological researches, apparently people of good, respectable breeding, could be engaged in shameless fraud, and yet this was the conclusion driven home to him time and again. Although he maintained that the object of the society should be to find such compelling evidence for the paranormal that their opponents would have no resort but to accuse them of fraud—a charge that he was confident their respectability could meet—he kept discovering that in this region one simply could not put one's trust in respectable appearances on the part either of the subjects of the research or the researchers themselves. Here his religious and ethical skepticism took on an even more trying form, an exaggerated display in which the comfortable hypocrisy of the Church had been transfigured into the blatant dishonesty of sophisticated and unsophisticated hucksters. What did this say about his society? One can well understand the frustration that Sidgwick vented to Symonds, and to fellow psychical researcher William James, who recognized Sidgwick's "rare mixture of ardor and critical judgment" and the way his "liberal heart" was conjoined to an intellect that managed to act "destructively on almost every particular object of belief that was offered to its acceptance." James reported hearing him say, "the year before his death, that if anyone had told him at the outset that after twenty years he would be in the same identical state of doubt and balance that he started with, he would have deemed the prophecy incredible. It appeared impossible that that amount of handling evidence should bring so little finality of decision."[150]

Indeed, in this department, too, Sidgwick ended up characteristically undercutting whatever Enlightenment ambitions he may have had in a curiously illuminating way. He was not only ultimately unconvinced by the evidence for personal survival of death—which led to the skepticism about the foundations of ethics that caused him such despair. He was also led, in association with such figures as Myers and Symonds, to play a part in the development of depth psychology, the so-called "discovery of the unconscious." Such friends as Dakyns, Browning, Noel, Myers, and Symonds tended to have unorthodox psychological interests and rather pioneering views. This was especially true of Myers and Symonds. The contributions of the psychical researchers in general and Myers in particular are happily sketched in Henri Ellenberger's *The Discovery of the Unconscious*:

> The basis of Myers' thinking was the philosophical question: 'Is the Universe friendly?' A satisfactory answer to this, he thought, could be given only after answering a preliminary question, 'Does man's life have any continuity beyond the grave?' in order to secure further development and fulfillment. The problem of survival after death was thus set in the foreground of parapsychological research. In this context many other problems arose, and Myers believed that a thorough analysis had to be made of the problems of hypnosis and dual personality, as well as the current parapsychological phenomena, before the question of the communication with deceased spirits could be properly approached. He began a critical examination into the entire literature dealing with these topics. . . . Myers was thus not only a parapsychologist, but also one of the great systematizers of the notion of the unconscious mind. In Myers' view, the 'subliminal self' (as he called it) has inferior and superior functions. The inferior functions are shown in those processes of dissociation, described by psychopathologists, and the superior functions are revealed in certain works of genius, which could be understood as the 'subliminal uprush' of rich storehouses of information, sentiment, and reflection that lie beneath the consciousness of the creative thinker. Myers believed that through the superior functions, the human

mind can also occasionally be in communication with the spirits of the deceased. A third function of the unconscious Myers called mytho-poetic function, that is the unconscious tendency to weave fantasies."[151]

Indeed, as an early account by H. Addington Bruce observed, the obsession with the paranormal may actually have interfered with the pursuit of "the important field of investigation opened up by the researches of Myers and Gurney in the subconscious nature of man," the research that could add "appreciably to the Society's present record of solid and valuable achievement."[152]

Myers had been an early student of Sidgwick's, and though initially rather cool towards him, had by 1868 become a warm friend and admirer—"as dear to me as the dearest of brothers," as Sidgwick put it. Myers would often recall how in "a star-light walk . . . I asked him, almost with trembling, whether he thought that when Tradition, Intuition, Metaphysic, had failed to solve the riddle of the Universe, there was still a chance that from any actual observable phenomena—ghosts, spirits, whatsoever there might be—some valid knowledge might be drawn as to a World Unseen. Already, it seemed, he had thought that this was possible; steadily, though in no sanguine fashion, he indicated some last grounds of hope; and from that night onwards I resolved to pursue this quest, if it might be, at his side."[153]

That Myers's quest was pursued very much at Sidgwick's side is made abundantly clear by excerpts from letters included in the *Memoir*. Sidgwick was, predictably enough, always the more skeptical of the two when it came to the claims of spiritualism, and he could not follow Myers in the conviction that communication with the dead had been demonstrated.[154] Still, there is evidence to suggest that Sidgwick, like Symonds and James, was far more receptive to Myers's claims about the unconscious, the subliminal self, and that it was here that he allowed an outlet to and further development of the romanticism that Mill had injected into utilitarianism.[155] His investigations into the God of his uncles and the ordinary experience of civilized life had only convinced him that new methods were required for investigating the "World Unseen," and he had steadily extended his range from interest in cosmology and purported miracles, to interest in the unseen world of the unconscious self. The bond with Myers here was a profound one, "the distant hope that Science might in our age make sufficient progress to open the spiritual gateway which she had been thought to close;—to penetrate by her own slow patience into the vestibule of an Unseen World." For all the disappointment and the souring effects of witnessing so much humbug, they felt that they had no right to abandon the quest: "Its problems were still absolutely unsettled; and it was still possible that at any moment light might come. And the original thesis stood firm—namely, that whether or no it be possible by observation and experiment,—along the paths of science patiently pursued,—to raise the human race into ethical stability,—the Cosmos into intelligible coherence;—at any rate these results are certainly not attainable in any other way. Without fresh facts none of us can get any further."[156]

And it was in precisely this manner that Symonds as well as Myers complemented and deepened Sidgwick's psychological investigations—Symonds himself was deeply impressed with Myers's account of the unconscious and consulted him on dream analysis. Symonds's "best" was primarily manifested in his research into sexuality, in such efforts as his volumes on *A Problem in Greek Ethics* and *A Problem in Modern Ethics*, which he used in his collaboration with Havelock Ellis on the book *Sexual Inversion*.[157] In later years, at least, Symonds would be a keen admirer of Ellis's more original and daring work, and of his creed: "To promote the increase of natural knowledge and to forward the application of scientific methods of investigation to all the problems of life to the best of my ability, in the conviction, which has grown with my growth and strengthened my strength, that there is no alleviation for the sufferings of mankind except veracity of thought and of action, and the resolute facing of the world as it is, when the garment of make-believe, by which pious hands have hidden its uglier features, is stripped off." As Phyllis Grosskurth has observed, Symonds found this project extremely congenial, and was at one with Ellis in praising the homoerotic Whitman, "who described life as it really was rather than as the sham people expected them to make of it."[158] And this unmasking was framed in depth psychological terms, as in part an exploration of the unconscious. Ellis, like Myers, gave an enthusiastic reception to Breuer and Freud's *Studies in Hysteria*. In fact, it was through Myers and the S.P.R. that Freud's work was introduced into England.

Sidgwick, for his part, found all of this utterly enthralling. The "Government House Utilitarian" was himself caught up, with most of his close friends, in Symonds's eroticized rendition of Whitmanian democracy and love of "powerful, uneducated men," all the while being drawn toward a belief in a sexualized unconscious that it would take a new form of science to uncover. True, he was scandalized by Symonds's more overtly homoerotic poetry, and he was forever urging him to censor it, destroy it, or at least refrain from publishing it. It was Sidgwick, too, more than anyone, who effectively ruined Horatio Brown's biography of Symonds—compiled largely from Symonds's own writings—by casting it in such a distorted and censored form that Symonds's agonizing over his "homosexuality" (a term Symonds actually helped put into currency) was made to appear as religious doubt, though Symonds's widow, Brown, and Symonds himself had expressed their faith in "Henry's wisdom" on such matters.[159] Ruin and disgrace—not to mention legal punishment— were all that Sidgwick could see coming of that form of moral honesty and free inquiry, and he took a dim view of publishing *Sexual Inversion* in England, on principle, and perhaps also because another of his closest early friends, the poet Roden Noel, a son of the Earl of Gainsborough and an Apostle elected at the same time as Henry, had contributed his own "case" to the work:

He dreams indifferently about men and women, and has strong sexual feeling for women. Can copulate, but does not insist on this act; there is a tendency to refined voluptuous pleasure. He has been married for many years, and there are several children of the marriage.

He is not particular about the class or age of the men he loves. He feels with regard to older men as a woman does, and likes to be caressed by them. He is immensely vain of his physical beauty; he shuns *paedicatio* and does not much care for the sexual act, but likes long hours of voluptuous communion during which his lover admires him. He feels the beauty of boyhood. At the same time he is much attracted by young girls. He is decidedly feminine in his dress, manner of walking, love of scents, ornaments and fine things. His body is excessively smooth and white, the hips and buttocks rounded. Genital organs normal. His temperament is feminine, especially in vanity, irritability and petty preoccupations. He is much preoccupied with his personal appearance and fond of admiration; on one occasion he was photographed naked as Bacchus. He is physically and morally courageous. He has a genius for poetry and speculation, with a tendency to mysticism.

He feels the discord between his love for men and society, also between it and his love for his wife. He regards it as in part, at least, hereditary and inborn in him.[160]

Still, these were the psychological experiments in living to which Sidgwick was irresistibly drawn, a revolutionary science of the self and its potential for transfiguration.[161] What kind of emotional growth was humanity capable of? How far could it go in doing without religious optimism, without some equivalent for prayer?[162] What was "inborn"? It was in his collaborations with Myers and Symonds and other friends that Sidgwick carried on his investigation into the "deepest problems" of human life, his versions of Mill's "experiments in living." Of course, he refrained from any public attack on religion and was often as cautious about going public with his work in parapsychology as he was about publishing Symonds's poetry. He would work in his quiet, respectable way for the better, more benevolent, less egoistic humanity of the future, hedging his bets by trying to vindicate some form of religion. Perhaps this was an area in which he shared more with Godwin than with Mill, but it was a Godwin recast for the late nineteenth century. [163]

But of course, despite this rich range of interests and audiences, the most important investigation, to Sidgwick's mind, concerned the possible survival of physical death, since this would somehow—he was not terribly clear on how—open up the way to a theistic account of how the universe might be "friendly" in a way that the material world as known scarcely evidenced. In human history, he claimed, the postulate of immortality "is that of the best part of mankind: it has nearly, though not quite, the authority of a belief of

Common Sense."[164] Moreover, as previously noted, he was profoundly convinced that the loss of the most widespread forms of religious faith would be painful for humanity and possibly lead to moral and political chaos.[165] Positive distaste for the prospect of survival, vividly confronting him in the shape of his friend Symonds, was something that he found utterly incomprehensible.

And in the years after first publishing the *Methods*, when he determined to set out on this course of research in earnest, he found another fellow traveler, a somewhat less conflicted spirit in the shape of Eleanor. This was a uniquely appropriate pairing of minds. William James would later describe them, in a vaguely critical tone, as "the incarnation of pure intellect—a very odd appearing couple." Eleanor herself would confess that they were "grey people," not the saints that others saw in them.[166] She was as rarefied a being as Henry, if not more so. According to her biography, she had once explained to a friend that "mathematics especially appealed to her in early youth because she thought a future life would be much more worth living if it included intellectual pursuits."[167] And she too had lost a father at an early age (in 1856) and been raised largely by a forceful mother, Lady Blanche Balfour (née Lady Blanche Gascoigne Cecil), who successfully managed the considerable (10,000-acre) Balfour estate at Whittingehame and taught Eleanor how to do so as well, while also imparting to her that love of mathematics. Like a good effective altruist, though of a religious and aristocratic disposition, she would have her daughter pray every night to determine if she had "omitted any opportunity of doing good or of making others happy." But in 1875, shortly after her devoted mother's death, Eleanor, known as Nora to her friends, decided to take a more independent course and began her collaboration with Lord Rayleigh (on a trip up the Nile), then moved to Cambridge to live in the newly completed Newnham Hall while studying mathematics with Norman Macleod Ferrers. Henry had been busy building Newnham—this was, to his mind, a gratifying form of "positive" work, in contrast to the "negative" resignation of his Fellowship. He had rented, at his own expense, a furnished house at 74 Regent Street for five students and Anne Clough, the first Principal, who were to begin their residence there in 1871. He then mobilized on behalf of what would become Newnham College, generating support for the building of Newnham Hall, which opened in October of 1875 with Eleanor Balfour and twenty-nine other students in residence.

Eleanor's brothers, Arthur and Gerald, were already old Cambridge hands, Arthur having been a treasured student of Sidgwick's in the late sixties, under the newly remodeled Moral Sciences Tripos. Although the Balfours did not suffer from the same loss of religious belief that had moved Henry to study the spirits, they were already deeply involved with his parapsychological researches, and many séances took place at Arthur's London home at 4 Carlton Gardens. The relationship with Eleanor blossomed very quickly, with Henry writing to his mother that although she was "not exactly perfect," it was nonetheless "true that whatever defects she has are purely negative: all that is positive in her is quite good. I cannot even imagine her doing anything wrong."[168] Apparently, no one else could either, something that could not be said of any of Sidgwick's other close friends. She was, it seems, an irresistible vision of intellect and integrity, and they were married on April 4, 1876, setting off on a honeymoon trip to France.

From the start, however, their union was mission driven. Immediately upon their return from their honeymoon, they were back at the investigation of ghost stories, and of course the work on behalf of Newnham, which was never-ending as well. Both lent their respectability to these causes, and both for the most part exercised much greater sobriety of judgment than so many of their comrades in these movements. C. D. Broad, a later admirer of Sidgwick and occupant of the Knightbridge chair, would remark that although one might doubt the value of Sidgwick's work on education for women, there could be no doubt of the value of his psychical research, a judgment that the Sidgwicks themselves would have found comical. For as Gauld has argued, the next quarter of a century saw a tiresome repetition of the same pattern of frustration: "Myers would become enthusiastic about such-and-such a medium; the Sidgwicks would acquiesce far enough to support or participate in an investigation; and everyone would in the end be more or less disappointed. . . . Myers sat, often several times, with practically every famous medium, public or private, of that time; and the Sidgwicks sat with many of them."[169] It was at one of the more hopeful moments, when William Barratt's research on telepathy, or thought transference, seemed especially promising, that the move to found an official Society for Psychical Research at length succeeded, in the early 1880s.[170]

But by the late eighties, as Sidgwick's crisis showed, their confidence was at its nadir. They had investigated so many mediums, ghost stories, etc., and even the infamous (and still extant) Theosophical Society and its founder Madame Blavatsky, without finding anything but fraud, ignorance, and imposture. Such positive results as they could claim could be construed as undercutting the evidence for immortality. If, for example, supposed communications from the "Other Side" were in fact subliminal telepathic communications among the living, then the main quest was compromised. Within the S.P.R., the Sidgwick Group did in fact end up establishing to their satisfaction the reality of telepathic communication among the living, evidence that convinced but dismayed Henry for this very reason.[171] But their best evidence for posthumous survival emerged only in the 1890s, with cases such as that of Leonora Piper, which Henry would concede was "promising" though not conclusive.[172] And by the time of the "cross-correspondence" cases (in which separate messages to different mediums needed to be put together to make sense), the chief founders of the S.P.R., Sidgwick, Gurney, and Myers, were all dead—in fact, were supposedly the personas from the "Other Side" communicating the messages that would convince Eleanor, her brothers, and select others of the reality of personal survival.[173]

And of all the strange things connected with Sidgwick's life and work, this aftermath to his physical life may be the strangest of all, though what it reveals about Eleanor and her brothers is difficult to say. For it was in this context that the decidedly weird and only recently uncovered plan to conceive a new Messiah came about. Augustus Henry Coombe-Tennant (1913–1989) was the earthly child of Gerald Balfour and Winifred Coombe-Tennant (aka the medium "Mrs. Willett"), and the supposed "spirit child" of Gurney. He did not vindicate the great hopes that had been pinned on him, but nonetheless, some today still hold that "from behind the curtain of death . . . came compelling evidence . . . that the group of seven, Myers, Gurney, Sidgwick, William Balfour, Edith Lyttelton, Annie Marshall, and Mary Catherine Lyttelton, still existed, still had an astounding agenda to be pursued, the Story and the Plan."[174]

Put another way, if the S.P.R. has never recovered the respectability that it had during Sidgwick's tenure, that may be in part for good reasons. Archie Roy's book *The Eager Dead*[175] tells the tale of how, after the deaths of Sidgwick and Myers, the surviving members of the Sidgwick Group became convinced, from the so-called cross-correspondence cases,[176] that they were receiving messages from their departed colleagues, and even went so far as to conspire in an Other Worldly Eugenics scheme to give birth to a new Messiah who would bring peace to the world (and of course lay to rest the dualism of practical reason). The supposed mechanics of this effort are not easy to grasp. Roy, in *The Eager Dead*, quotes at length W. H. Salter's summary:

> This group of seven, all dead when the scripts began, is represented as being engaged in one plan of worldwide importance. They are not represented as being the only persons so engaged, but as a group standing in a special relation to the group of automatists, and to the group of interpreters, i.e., G.W. Balfour, J.G. Piddington, Alice Johnson, etc. Many other persons, not named, are said to be acting with them, and friends dying since the scripts began, such as A. W. Verrall & S.H. Butcher, are regarded as additions to the group.
>
> The ultimate purpose of the Plan is to bring about a state of peace between nations and of social justice. This was of course a matter of great interest to Mrs. Willett but there are clear references to it in the quite early M.V. scripts. The allusions are made in various ways, especially through references to the predictions of the '*Pax Augusta*' to be found in "*Vergil's Eclogue*" (4th) and several passages of the *Aeneid* e.g. I 257-VI and VIII.
>
> Before, however, this can come about, two things must happen: first, there are to be wars—note the plural. This is all discussed in

Piddington's paper, in Proceedings XXXIII, which you should read. Second, a breed of human beings fit to live in a world of peace has to be born. This is a matter of 'psychological eugenics' as the scripts call it, in which the pioneer psychological work of Gurney, and the researches in genetics of F.M. Balfour, will be of importance. This is concisely treated by H.V. in a talk she gave [to] the American S.P.R. in 1950; a summary is printed in A.S.P.R. Journal for April 1951 . . . .

A very difficult problem of interpretation is connected with 'psychological eugenics'. Is the Plan intended to produce a race or breed of 'children of the spirit', fitted to introduce the Age of Peace, not of course a race in the national sense, but a number of persons with the requisite gifts of mind and character?

Or has it a more restricted personal aim?

Different passages in the whole body of scripts could be quoted to support either interpretation. The wider aim seems to me to be supported by Vergil's lines 'Romanos, rerum dominos, gentunque togatam' ['Romans, lords of the world, the race that wears the toga'], in early M.V. scripts. Mrs. Willett's scripts, however, favour the more personal view, and point with increasing emphasis, first to Alexander and then to Henry as being of a very special, one might say, unique importance in the Plan. In this view G.W. Balfour, interpreter of her scripts, concurred; but some others, who have read the scripts, J.V. and I, for instance, and I believe Lady Balfour, are not entirely convinced.

I have said nothing about cross-correspondences. There is no doubt that in the main the exposition of them in Proceedings XXI, XXII etc. is correct as far as it goes. In the light of later developments in the scripts, however, they cannot now be regarded as isolated incidents, or as the most important elements in the scripts: but they must be taken *with the whole scriptic context* as being inseparable from the Story and the Plan.[177]

Thus, the idea, apparently, and on the more "personal" interpretation, was that the deceased psychical researchers, especially Gurney and Myers, had pushed Winifred Coombe-Tennant to have another child, such that this: "spiritually designed and influenced infant would be planned by the workers on the other side, including the scientist Francis Maitland Balfour. The child would grow up singularly gifted, to the extent that in some unspecified way he would be able to achieve the gigantic task of reconciling the nations so that they would cooperate in a lasting peace. This peace, they said, would usher in a golden age of prosperity and happiness ."[178]

Augustus Henry was eventually, as an adult, informed that he had been programmed to usher in the Age of Aquarius (or a reinvigorated Age of Empire, as the case may be), but by that time it was fairly clear even to his mother that the "Plan" was not working out. And of course, Henry Sidgwick himself had died, disappointed and agnostic to the end, well before the Plan was hatched; he knew nothing of the cross-correspondence cases, and the work of the Sidgwick Group of psychical researchers had mainly demonstrated, to his mind, how extraordinarily difficult it would be to push any line of argument based on psychical research to the philosophic-religious synthesis that he hoped to achieve.

The image of Eleanor, former Principal of Newnham College, and her brothers, Arthur, former Prime Minister, and Gerald, devoting endless hours to this very strange and very secret "Plan" is disturbing. It is as though they were taking a very American "can do" approach to Heidegger's "only a god can save us now" challenge. The disarming simplicity and too literal Christian format of this Plan ("Unto Us a Child Is Born") as a template for a new religion, was no longer being left to God the Father, but was instead purportedly being engineered by a set of disembodied scientific psychical researchers working on the Other Side, a new ethereal intelligence operation for the Empire. Or as John Gray has put it, the afterlife here featured a familiar set of individuals, all steeped in and communicating in the ideas and images of the classics, the King James Bible, Tennyson etc., such that dying "was only a move from one wing of a great country-house to another, a shift in which nothing was lost."[179] Living, by contrast, was, at least for the surviving loved ones in the know, a matter of devoting long, long hours to trying to decode the ramblings of mediums to piece together the story.

With this retrospective insight, it seems that the company Sidgwick kept was far odder than anyone has ever dreamed, and that Eleanor was perhaps a bit more like Myers than she had seemed to be while Henry was alive. Not even Bernard Williams or Derek Parfit could have conjured up an account of esoteric Government House utilitarianism that featured, on one interpretation, a posthumous utilitarian elite engineering from the Other Side a racial Eugenics scheme to secure "world peace," presumably meaning under the guidance of the British Empire. The politics of the whole affair eludes even Gray, in whose provocative volume, *The Immortalization Commission*, Sidgwick figures prominently. Gray, one of the few academic philosophers to appreciate the philosophical significance of Sidgwick's psychical research, very cleverly juxtaposes the work of Sidgwick and his colleagues in their quest to prove by scientific means the reality of the survival of the human personality beyond physical death, against the work of the Bolshevik scientists who set out to develop the science needed to render physical human beings immortal, preserving Lenin in the process. As he puts it: "The Russian God-builders believed death could be defeated using the power of science. The English psychical researchers believed science could show death was a passage into another life. In both cases the boundaries between science, religion and magic were blurred or non-existent."[180]

These are, of course, quite different things, involving different empires. Indefinitely long physical life versus life on another plane of being, an afterlife on "the Other Side," in "the Other World," perhaps Heaven or Hell or some way station thereto, etc. But for Gray, they represent the same ethical-and-scientific-failing: "Longing for everlasting life, humans show that they remain the death-defined animal. . . . While most people may never give up dreaming of immortality, individuals here and there can loosen the hold of the dream on their lives. If you understand that in wanting to live forever you are trying to preserve a lifeless image of yourself, you may not want to be resurrected or to survive in a post-mortem paradise. What could be more deadly than being unable to die?"[181] To be sure, Gray allows that things have changed somewhat, given the tides of Fundamentalism that have swept through the twentieth century, something that would have depressed Sidgwick yet again. Still, he follows Nietzsche in thinking it better that the clever animals die, a sentiment Symonds shared.

It may be that the Sidgwick Group of psychical researchers does in some ways deserve this historical rebuke, since so many of them, notably Myers and Arthur Balfour, but possibly also the Sidgwicks, were too driven by the mourning of lost loved ones in seeking to make the connection with the Other Side. Sidgwick seems to have been most driven by the more familiar quest that animated such Idealist philosophers as his friend Green (not a fan of parapsychology)—namely, finding an adequate substitute for the religious orthodoxy perceived as being under threat and in decline from the familiar forces of historical biblical criticism and materialist science, etc., a project that, as the next section will show, could be very politically fraught. There is a famous Jungian distinction to be made here, concerning the better or worse ways in which one's mind might turn to the spirits.[182] But it might be better to resist the temptation to be too reductive or dichotomizing on this score: the psychical researchers were complex characters and mixed bags, and the hope of a happy immortality comes in many varieties, then as now.[183]

Marina Warner has nicely captured one key and less reductive point about the Sidgwick Group in her illuminating work *Phantasmagoria*: "These men and women were well-to-do and well-connected; they were also philanthropic and liberal, and their work unexpectedly sustained the original link between paranormal interests and social experiment which turned esoteric quests such as psychic research and Spiritualism into a nursery of emancipatory change in education, politics, women's status, and the approach and enterprise of scientific knowledge itself."[184] It was, in short, a very Apostolic enterprise.

And after all, throughout the entire endeavor, with all of its ups and downs, Sidgwick, at least while he was alive on earth, persevered for at least some plausible philosophical reasons, and remained incapable of believing that the Idealists or any other philosophical or religious school in the ascendance had managed the reconciliation of one's own point of the view and the "Point of

View of the Universe" nearly well enough. He could not, like so many, treat the issue with a distanced equanimity floated by a deep faith that reason would or must somehow prevail. It was only in this context of doubt and dismay that he became a founder and the first president of the British Society for Psychical Research (in 1882). He was sometimes hopeful, but it was an admitted gamble, and he always knew that the work might fail. Again, he knew nothing of the cross-correspondence cases; the work of the Sidgwick Group of psychical researchers had mainly demonstrated, to his mind, how extraordinarily difficult it would be to push any line of argument based on psychical research to the philosophic-religious synthesis that he hoped to achieve, given that the evidence for telepathy might undercut rather than support much of the supposed evidence of survival. Communications from the dead might, for instance, be dismissed as telepathic communications from those who knew the dead, or from the persons on the point of death, etc.

Moreover, the results of this early psychical research were, in fact, even more damaging to Sidgwick's worldview than that. As suggested in *Henry Sidgwick, Eye of the Universe*, the psychical researchers, Myers especially, actually ended up leaving it quite unclear what the human personality that might survive death actually was, for they compiled reams of evidence that testified to the complexities of unconscious processes and the fragmentary nature of the conscious self. Arguably, Sidgwick's psychical research pushed him much farther than he realized toward making the case he glancingly suggested in *The Methods*, in a passage that has much impressed Gray and Parfit:

> I do not see why the Egoistic principle should pass unchallenged any more than the Universalistic. I do not see why the axiom of Prudence should not be questioned, when it conflicts with present inclination, on a ground similar to that on which the Egoistic refuse to admit the axiom of Rational Benevolence. If the Utilitarian has to answer the question, 'Why should I sacrifice my own happiness for the greater happiness of another?' it must surely be possible to ask the Egoist, 'Why should I sacrifice a present pleasure for a greater one in future? Why should I concern myself about my own future feelings any more than about the feelings of other persons? . . . Grant that the Ego is merely a system of coherent phenomena, as Hume and his followers maintain; why, then, should one part of the series of feelings into which the Ego is resolved be concerned with another part of the same series, any more than with any other series?[185]

The proper functioning of the "telescopic faculty," the intertemporal neutrality of self-interest, seemed to go with a metaphysics of personal identity over time as akin to the unity of consciousness at any given time. Why, Parfit and others have asked, did Sidgwick not develop such reflections on the significance of personal identity, addressing the dualism by such means?

A plausible answer is that he did, at least to some extent, but in the context of his psychical research. And the loss of the unity of the self revealed through psychical research was both synchronic and diachronic, in essence a vision of split or multiple personality as only an extreme example of a normal condition in which intrapsychic conflict was modeled as akin to interpersonal conflict. What the evidence the Sidgwick group accumulated really confronted them with was a radical de-throning of the autonomous conscious self. In Myers's words: "[It] is rather sanity which needs to be accounted for; since the moral and physical being of each of us is built up from incoordination and incoherence, and the microcosm of man is but a micro-chaos held in some semblance of order by a law and swaying hand, the wild team in which Phaeton is driving, and which must needs soon plunge into the sea."[186]

Of course, the right language for describing this self, "I", persona, etc., can be very tricky. As Myers put it, in trying to explain how he cast mind as both a multiplicity and a unity: "My contention is, *not* . . . that a man (say Socrates) has within him a conscious and an unconscious self, which lie side by side, but apart, and find expression alternately, but rather that Socrates' mind is capable of concentrating itself round more than one focus, either simultaneously or successively. I do not limit the number of *foci* to *two*."[187]

The general thought is much more than, and much more specific than, the familiar refrain about the introspective and inner, Hamlet-like structure of modernity. It is rather the same note sounded by James at length, albeit in less Idealistic terms. In many ways following on Sidgwick, James appreciated how the "axis of reality runs solely through the egotistic places,—they are strung upon it like so many beads." He was attuned to how "[t]hat unsharable feeling which each one of us has of the pinch of his individual destiny as he privately feels it rolling out on fortune's wheel may be disparaged for its egotism, may be sneered at as unscientific, but it is the one thing that fills up the measure of our concrete actuality, and any would-be existent that should lack such a feeling, or its analogue, would be a piece of reality only half made up." At the same time, he had nothing but praise for Myers on the "subliminal self," quoting him on how "[e]ach of us is in reality an abiding psychical entity far more extensive than he knows." Myers, he held, had revealed "whole systems of underground life."[188] The boundaries of the self may not be watertight, and James, as Sprigge has observed, was, like Myers, not averse to the thought that we are all but parts of some "mother sea of consciousness."[189]

Much of the evidence leading Myers to the conclusions sketched above had to do with automatic writing, which persuaded him (during his physical lifetime) that he had been in touch with his beloved departed, Annie Marshall. But in two significant cases that he juxtaposes in *Human Personality and Its Survival of Bodily Death*, his own with "Clelia" and Sidgwick's experiments with his close friend and fellow Apostle John Jermyn Cowell, the point is simply how surprising and manipulative one's own unconscious can be. As Sidgwick himself put it, "We were continually surprised by evidences of the extent to which his [Cowell's] unconscious self was able to puzzle his conscious mind. As a rule, he knew what he was writing, though he wrote involuntarily; but from time to time he used to form words or conjunctions of letters which we were unable to make out at first, though they had a meaning which we ultimately discovered."[190] And Myers remarks of the Clelia case, "The indisputable evidence for complex subliminal mentation which this case seems to me to furnish lies in the fact that here Mr. A's pen wrote not only unintelligible abbreviations, but absolute anagrams of sentences; anagrams, indeed, of the crudest kind, consisting of mere transpositions of letters, but still *puzzles* which the writer had to set himself to decipher *ab extra*." It was the kind of game playing spiritualists might attribute to trickster spirits, and that Sidgwick's uncles would have attributed to the dark arts.

This was a much richer vein of material than Hume's phenomenalism for casting doubt on the unity of the self, as normally construed, and suggestive of how many selves with their different interests the human personality might harbor (including the uprush of subliminal genius, of a creatively superior subliminal self). It was a vision of deep intrapsychic conflict that certainly spoke to a wide range of Sidgwick's friends, and it anticipated in some ways the rich philosophical literature on personal identity that recent decades have witnessed, which brims with puzzle cases featuring split brains, split selves, etc. But oddly enough, even though Sidgwick had been conducting these experiments as early as the mid-1860s, he made very little use of his research in his philosophical works, including the *Methods*. Although he was very intrigued by Buddhism and the possibilities for a reductionist view of personal identity, he may well have worried, in his usual way, that more selves might also mean more conflicts or divisions within reason, with the dualism becoming a multiplex of practical reason that would be even more intractable.[191] How could fragmentation and unconscious trickster selves solve the problem?

No doubt Sidgwick's academic philosophical reputation has revived in part because he succeeded so well in masking this side of his metaphysical speculation. There is something very odd about this masking, but Sidgwick was undoubtedly a master at it—indeed, was so split up when managing his message in different genres and for different audiences that he was a good case in point of multiple selves, albeit ones that were very finely attuned to what would play as respectability to this audience or that. It was this talent that he deployed on behalf of Symonds, who otherwise surely would have gone the way of Oscar Wilde. Still, to genuinely see what Sidgwick's project was and how it hung together, it is necessary to do a bit more to put these pieces together. After all, he prided himself on the diversity of methods going into his research into "the deepest problems."

Clearly, these depth parapsychological speculations are of great philosophical relevance for thinking about the dualism of practical reason and possible responses to various Idealists in their account of the "True Self," or what one is when one understands and loves.[192] Perhaps the True Self is not so easily recognized, by oneself or others. The Idealists, whether personal or Absolute, were primarily concerned with individual minds as either autonomous wholes themselves or parts of some larger whole, such as the Eternal Consciousness. Sidgwick himself often adopted the language of whole and part, when describing the dualism, and often sounded as convinced as any Idealist of the intuited unity of the self.[193] But with the psychical researchers he pointed to a foundational concern with the unity of any mind, personal or Cosmic, one deeply problematic for any notion, personal Idealist or whatever, of a true "abiding" self finding abiding or unfolding self-realization in the common good. Given these results, a new story about the progression of mind was needed, as Myers realized. This would involve a different form of Idealism from the Idealism of Green, Bradley, and company.[194]

What is more, these remarks hint at the deeper fear stimulated in Sidgwick by the dualism of practical reason, a fear of a great Cosmic unraveling, the loss of unity, of wholeness, of balance, perhaps of the entire moral order of the universe. The loss of not only God and Soul, but Self as well, was a challenge he had never really anticipated. But it is some such fear that makes better sense of Sidgwick's anxieties about the dualism. He could sympathize, but only go so far with Myers, who found solace in the very Idealistic thought that "[t]hat which lies at the root of each of us lies at the root of the Cosmos too. Our struggle is the struggle of the Universe itself; and the very God-head finds fulfillment through our upward-striving souls."[195] From the horizontal effort to bring together the different regions of consciousness and self there would, for Myers, emerge a more vertical spiritual progression, and one that might solve the familiar puzzle of how one can transcend oneself and still be oneself, somehow better realized. Sidgwick, true to form, was less confident and more agnostic, as are Myers's current admirers. But where, then, did that leave him?

The conclusion to the first edition of the *Methods*, when Sidgwick ended his account of the dualism of practical reason with the chilling words "the Cosmos of Duty is thus really reduced to a Chaos," is often cited in this connection, as in the previous section. But also noteworthy is the gloss that he puts on the dualism just before his conclusion in the second edition:

> For, if we find an ultimate and fundamental contradiction in our apparent intuitions of what is Reasonable in conduct, we seem forced to the conclusion that they were not really intuitions after all, and that the apparently intuitive operation of the Practical Reason is essentially illusory. Therefore it is, one may say, a matter of life and death to the Practical Reason that this premise should be somehow obtained. And I cannot fall back on the resource of thinking myself under a moral necessity to regard all my duties *as if they were* commandments of God, although

not entitled to hold speculatively that any such Supreme Being really exists. I am so far from feeling bound to believe for purposes of practice what I see no ground for holding as a speculative truth, that I cannot even conceive the state of mind which these words seem to describe, except as a momentary half-willful irrationality, committed in a violent access of philosophic despair. Still it seems plain that in proportion as man has lived in the exercise of the Practical Reason—as he believed—and feels as an actual force the desire to do what is right and reasonable as such, his demand for this premise will be intense and imperious. Thus we are not surprised to find Socrates—the type for all ages of the man in whom this desire is predominant—declaring with simple conviction that 'if the Rulers of the Universe do not prefer the just man to the unjust, it is better to die than to live'. And we must observe that in the feeling that prompts to such a declaration the desire to rationalize one's own conduct is not the sole, nor perhaps always the most prominent, element. For however difficult it may practically be to do one's duty when it comes into conflict with one's happiness, it often does not seem very difficult, when we are considering the question in the abstract, to decide in favour of duty. When a man passionately refuses to believe that the 'Wages of Virtue' can 'be dust,' it is often less from any private reckoning about his own wages than from a disinterested aversion to a universe so fundamentally irrational that 'Good for the Individual' is *not* ultimately identified with 'Universal Good'.[196]

In this construction of a rational universe in which "Good for the Individual" is identified with "Universal Good," there is something of the older utilitarian line of thought to the effect that the demands of egoism and the demands of benevolence must be made to converge, that no satisfactory future state of general happiness could, as in Parfit's "Repugnant Conclusion," leave out the claims of the individual. Was Sidgwick really wrong in claiming the title "utilitarian" instead of "dualist," when in fact his vision of how the moral government of the world should be organized was so much in line with the secular versions of that convergence to be found in Godwin, Bentham, and Mill? Rational egoism in effect represented the distributionist element built into his conception of the general happiness, and his "impure" utilitarianism, to recall Skorupski's words, may have been more in line with the projects of his great predecessors than abstract accounts of agent-neutral reasons recognize. "Purity" seems to be an artificial, contrived matter that misses the bigger project of getting beyond, in one world or another, Own Good versus Other Good without sacrificing either.

But the point here is that it was this spectre of an unfriendly universe, of a perverse Cosmos and a fragmented self in which reason is schizophrenic or indeterminate, and the "Wages of Virtue" all too often dust, that appears to have most deeply disturbed Sidgwick, that best accounts for the intensity of his anxieties over the dualism, even if he sometimes articulated the issue in drier, more limited terms. His Socratic enterprise of testing common-sense morality ended up threatening to collapse into Aeschylean horror, rather than in an answer to Glaucon's challenge in the *Republic*. He could see how a truly tragic world might at least enable pure sacrifice, moral heroism, but he did not think most people would really be able to embrace such a worldview beyond a certain point. He doubted that he could. The allusions here to "wages" are clearly to Tennyson's poem of that title, the last stanza of which runs:

> The wages of sin is death: if the wages of Virtue be dust,
> Would she have heart to endure for the life of the worm and the fly?
> She desires no isles of the blest, no quiet seats of the just,
> To rest in a golden grove, or to bask in a summer sky;
> Give her the wages of going on, and not to die.[197]

In A. C. Bradley's commentary on Tennyson, this poem is invoked in reference to Tennyson's "In Memoriam" and the following possible explication of Tennyson's attitude floated: "And would it have been just to make him merely that he might die? . . . Or perhaps . . . the idea is rather: To make him such that he thinks himself immortal when he is really not so, would be unjust."[198] Like Tennyson, Sidgwick felt that a belief in immortality was a fixture of common sense, a near universal and very natural belief.[199] Hence the challenge posed by Symonds. It is cruel enough to have no reason to believe in immortality, but it is crueler still to be created with a disposition to delusion. Where would that leave the philosopher?

The third stanza of the prologue to "In Memoriam" signals the key issue:

> Thou wilt not leave us in the dust:
> Thou madest man, he knows not why,
> He thinks he was not made to die;
> And thou has made him: thou art just.[200]

For Sidgwick, ever the Tennysonian, this question of having the heart to endure when the cosmos has turned out to be so productive of cruel delusions about the nature of the self and its duties, and so horribly hopeless with respect to immortality and the moral structure needed to underwrite the righteous, was surely another aspect of his own "disinterested aversion" to an "irrational" universe. He would often sum up his own religious tendencies with reference to "In Memoriam," explaining how his own very human heart, if not his philosophical conscience, could never give up the minimum of faith expressed in the lines:

> No, like a child in doubt and fear:
> But that blind clamour made me wise;
> Then was I as a child that cries,
> But, crying, knows his father near;[201]

All this does suggest that there is rather more going on with Sidgwick's dualism than indicated in the narrower philosophical debates over impersonal v. personal reasons for action, internal v. external reasons for action, objective v. subjective reasons for action, etc.—between, that is, moral rationalism or universal benevolence and rational egoism, which is the way the dualism is constructed in most current accounts of Sidgwick's philosophy. Again, in Parfit's recent reformulation, Sidgwick's better, reconstructed point is primarily that "[w]hen one of our two possible acts would make things go in some way that would be impartially better, but the other act would make things go better either for ourselves or for those to whom we have close ties, we often have sufficient reasons to act in either of these two ways."[202] This is certainly a plausible reconstruction at one level—a level at which Sidgwick would have admired its philosophical clarity—but it leaves Sidgwick's intense fears and anxieties about the dualism a complete mystery, to be dismissed as "sombre overstatements."[203]

The same can be said of de Lazari-Radek and Singer's argument, which has opened up some ingenious new lines of work in this area, work that, it is claimed, is more thoroughly Sidgwickian. As noted, Sidgwick had argued that apparently self-evident claims had to be clear and precise, able to withstand critical reflection, consistent with one another, and able to win a consensus of experts, though in other writings he collapsed the first two into just one condition. De Lazari-Radek and Singer seem less concerned to reject any element of Sidgwick's account than to add to it, such that the significance of evolutionary "debunking" arguments is recognized, and this leads them to reject Sidgwick's Dualism:

> We might have become reasoning beings because that enabled us to solve a variety of problems that would otherwise have hampered our survival, but once we are capable of reasoning, we may be unable to avoid recognizing and discovering some truths that do not aid our survival. That can be said about some complicated truths of mathematics or physics. It can also, as Parfit has suggested, be the case with some of our normative epistemic beliefs; for instance, the belief that when some argument is valid and has true premises, so that this argument's conclusion must be true, these facts give us a decisive reason to believe this conclusion. Parfit argues that this normative claim about what we have decisive reason to believe is not itself evolutionarily advantageous, since to gain that advantage, it would have been sufficient to have the non-normative beliefs that the argument is valid, and has true premises, and that the conclusion must be true. Hence this and other normative epistemic beliefs are not open to a debunking argument. This may also hold for some of our moral beliefs. One such moral truth could be Sidgwick's axiom of universal benevolence: 'each one is morally bound to regard the good of any other individual as much as his

own, except in so far as he judges it to be less, when impartially viewed, or less certainly knowable or attainable by him'.[204]

Thus, if, with Sharon Street,[205] one holds that in many cases "it is more scientifically plausible to explain human evaluative attitudes as having evolved because they help us to survive and to have surviving offspring, than because they are true," one can debunk many of the beliefs competing with the Axiom of Universal Benevolence, such as those purportedly justifying partial or personal reasons for action. If Benevolence is not debunked, and if it can in fact be accounted for straightforwardly as a result of reason coming as a unity or package, such that either "we have a capacity to reason that includes the capacity to do advanced physics and mathematics and to grasp objective moral truths, or we have a much more limited capacity to reason that lacks not only these abilities, but others that confer an overriding evolutionary advantage [then, if] reason is a unity of this kind, having the package would have been more conducive to survival and reproduction than not having it."[206]

That Singer, in particular, should in this way have developed defenses, not only of Sidgwickian hedonism, but also of Sidgwickian metaethical cognitivism (against his former commitment to Hare's prescriptivism), and have used these to advance a form of utilitarianism that, he holds, is more consistently utilitarian than Sidgwick's own position and in that way in line with Sidgwick's deeper tendencies, is illustrative of the increasingly important role that Sidgwick's work is playing in cutting edge ethical theory. Whether the principle of Universal Benevolence really has the ability to withstand evolutionary debunking arguments, and whether such arguments can really be made compelling in the first place, are open questions.[207] Less open, however, is the question of whether Sidgwick himself would not have found such gambits too narrow and irrelevant to his deeper worries about the broader religious significance of the dualism of practical reason. Sidgwick's larger philosophical self manifestly harbored that deeply Tennysonian sense of the costs of skepticism that on many counts was closer in spirit to the sensibilities of the Idealists, both early and late, than to those of his utilitarian forefathers, and de Lazari-Radek and Singer seem closer to Bentham on religious issues than to Sidgwick. As Gauld has neatly put it, if "Clough was the poet of Sidgwick's retreat from Christianity, Tennyson—though he never followed Sidgwick down the road, or blind alley, that led to the dualism—was the poet who best reflected his prolonged endeavour to remain a theist, and a believer in some relatively benign form of after-life."[208] Tennyson, it should be noted, became an honorary member of the Society for Psychical Research, whose quest for a wider, non-materialistic conception of mind or spirit that could be gleaned through rigorous empirical research was deeply appealing to him.

To be sure, the Idealists were more buffered by a conviction of Reason's wholeness and ultimate harmony, even if this was worked out through some form of historical progression. But Sidgwick nonetheless shared with them a sense that reason, practical and theoretical, needed to heal and unify itself, and to fill the void left by the receding religious consciousness. If Sidgwick could not follow them in their metaphysics, and picked apart Green's claims for a "spiritual principle" in nature, for an Eternal Consciousness of which individual minds are but parts, etc., his project nonetheless shared their sense that practical reason needed to be harmonized—and this not merely by well-designed social institutions—leaving no fundamental conflict between "Own Good" and "Other Good." This was no mere fetishizing of determinateness in ethics. It was a concern about just how tragic the Cosmos might really be, with the recognition of that tragedy seemingly coming just as the civilizational mission of the European world was in vital need of defense, not deflation, a point to be revisited at the end of this chapter.

And illuminatingly, it was Blanshard who so insightfully stressed this very point, in his description of Sidgwick's dualism:

> For even if self-sacrifice were sometimes clearly called for by reason, was it just that a person should be penalized for being rational? He could not see that a world so ordered could be just. Was it just that a person who sacrificed his good for that of others should lose that good forever, should never be compensated for that loss? That surely would be unjust and reflects its injustice upon the creator who so arranged things. And since ordinary life did not supply such compensation, it must occur, if at all, in another life.[209]

The issue is not merely to determine what normative reasons one ultimately has, but to determine whether the structure of those reasons could be consistent with theism and/or cosmic justice. How hard on the human heart and its hopes will the reasons that we have turn out to be? And what hopes can one reasonably harbor? Although Sidgwick was not apt to confuse a poet with a philosopher, he did use poetry—indeed, almost invariably used poetry—to convey his deepest philosophical concerns, as in those Tennysonian lines: "He thinks he was not made to die; / And thou has made him: thou art just."[210]

These questions are simply not addressed, or addressed in anything like Sidgwick's way, in the work of de Lazari-Radek and Singer, Crisp, Parfit et al.

Given the stakes, it is all the more amazing, then, that even during periods when he got his hopes up,[211] Sidgwick was always the voice of restraint and doubt in the business of parapsychology, never, as Eleanor admitted, persuaded that he had found "the truth he sought." He was indeed very, very skeptical, a tough critic, not just with respect to evidence accumulated through psychical research, but also with respect to the ambitious projections of more social theoretical prophets—Hegel, Marx, Comte, Spencer, and so on. Myers too, for that matter. And that is precisely why it is very difficult to imagine him treating "the Plan" for a new Messiah any differently, given his reservations about entering the "illimitable cloudland" of utopian thinking, much though he might warm to that in certain significant others. As the cross-correspondences themselves suggest, even his supposed spirit was skeptical, communicating such messages as "We no more solve the riddle of death by dying than we solve the problem of living by being born. . . . The solution to the Great Problem I could not give you—I am still very far away from it and the abiding knowledge of the inherent truth and beauty into which all the inevitable uglinesses of Existence finally resolve themselves will be yours in due time."[212] That is the kind of thing the ghost of Sidgwick would say.

Obviously, Sidgwick's second crisis had a different result from his first crisis. He did not resign his position, and ultimately, he did not give up all hope, though he dragged on in a pretty bleak and sleepless state until the nineties, when with Eleanor he moved out of Hillside and into Newnham. Matters brightened somewhat for the S.P.R. in the nineties, and that helped, but even so, Sidgwick stayed the course that he had set himself long before. As he put it to an old friend:

> In fact, the reason why I keep strict silence now for many years with regard to theology is that while I cannot myself discover adequate rational basis for the Christian hope of happy immortality, it seems to be that the general loss of such a hope, from the minds of average human beings as now constituted, would be an evil of which I cannot pretend to measure the extent. I am not prepared to say that the dissolution of the existing social order would follow, but I think the danger of such dissolution would be seriously increased, and that the evil would certainly be very great.[213]

Caught between the "Great Either-Or" of "Pessimism or Faith," Sidgwick regarded his position as "an inevitable point in the process of thought," but it was one he took "as a soldier takes a post of difficulty," and he could not assume the responsibility of drawing others to it.[214] He was not sure—he was never sure, of course—that the subject of ethics was sufficiently like science and unlike theology to render his academic position legitimate, even if he did not have to swear belief in the Thirty-Nine Articles. But as usual, he at least allowed himself the hope that "a considerable improvement in average human beings in this respect of sympathy is likely to increase the mundane happiness for men generally, and to render the hope of future happiness less needed to sustain them in the trials of life."[215] Symonds was more or less out, despite Sidgwick's efforts, and Sidgwick was more or less in, despite Symonds's. And compared to "The Plan," Symonds's efforts to advance a more homoerotic Whitmanian culture of comradeship seem quite sane.

Education for Growth

Given the material presented in the previous section, many may wonder whether Eleanor was to Henry what Harriet was to John Stuart or Mary

Wollstonecraft to William. The paradox of Eleanor and "The Plan" is palpable. She was a truly brilliant woman who deployed her talents and standing on behalf of many admirable causes, Newnham College being the outstanding example. But given the battering that her intellectual reputation has taken because of her work in parapsychology, it is difficult to appreciate her in all of her complexity.

At some level, of course, the Sidgwicks were the embodiment of the Millian notion of high-minded, highly intellectualized marital friendship—indeed, they went beyond the Mills in being the very model of a mutually active, professional academic couple, with in fact a less than predictable assortment of feminine/masculine gender traits. Needless to say, neither cared for the "frivolous and doll-like women," the hothouse plants, that *The Subjection of Women* had lamented. Although earlier on, they had both harbored various doubts about what women might ultimately prove themselves capable of, and about what degree of political equality they ought to be given, those doubts had rapidly diminished once they began active work on behalf of women's higher education. Women, they allowed, had demonstrated their capacity for even the most "masculine" intellectual work (such as mathematics, not to mention political reformism). Philippa Garrett Fawcett, born in 1868 and the only child of their very Millian friends Millicent Garrett and Henry Fawcett, would become both a lecturer at Newnham and one of Newnham's most famous early success stories. In 1890 , when women were allowed to sit for the Tripos, though not officially classed, she triumphed in the Mathematical Tripos, beating out even the official Senior Wrangler and demonstrating to the critics with some finality that women were indeed capable of abstract thought. Part of an anonymous poem in her honor runs: "Hail the triumph of the corset / Hail the fair Phillipa Fawcett / Victress in the fray / crown her queen of Hydrostatics / And the other Mathematics / Wreathe her brow with bay."[216]

The Fawcetts were both deeply Millian political economists, and Millicent Garrett was a leading activist in the cause of women's suffrage. Her copy of Mill's *The Subjection of Women,* presented to her by Mill himself, was one of her most precious possessions. And one of her proudest hours concerned Henry Sidgwick and the founding of Newnham, which she deemed a deeply Millian cause:

> As I am writing now of the early days of Newnham, I cannot forbear mentioning what I have always regarded as an honour, viz. that Professor Henry Sidgwick, the real founder of Newnham, asked me and my husband to lend our drawing-room for the first meeting ever held in Cambridge in its support. So far as I can remember, this must have been in 1870. We were then occupying a furnished house which possessed a drawing-room of suitable size for such an occasion. I therefore recognize that the birth of Newnham under my roof was more or less

accidental; nevertheless, such is human folly, I go on being proud and
pleased about it. I know that Philippa was a little baby girl at the time,
but was old enough to be brought in at the tea-drinking stage at the end
of the proceedings and to toddle about in her white frock and blue sash
among the guests. [217]

Indeed, to consider another example, Eleanor and her allies were not
overly impressed by the very masculinized profession of political economy.
Alfred Marshall, who goes down in history as one of the greatest figures in
economics and the founder of the so-called "Cambridge School" of economics,
once confessed:

> As regards the informal instruction and advice given 'at home', I do not
> admit women to my ordinary 'at home' . . . but make occasional special
> appointments for them. I adopt this course partly because of the dif-
> ficulty of getting men and women to open their minds freely in one
> another's presence, and partly because I find the questions asked by
> women generally relate to lectures or book works and/or else to practi-
> cal problems such as poor relief. Whilst men who have attended fewer
> lectures and read fewer books and are perhaps likely to obtain less
> marks in examinations, are more apt to ask questions showing mental
> initiative and giving promise of original work in the future.[218]

Marshall, who had early on been a supporter of Newnham and women's
higher education, had turned against the Sidgwicks in the 1880s, and apparently at this point, in 1896, could no longer entertain the idea that such
differences were the result of societal sexism in shaping gender roles. He
had, paradoxically, a low estimate of women's potential, despite being married to Newnham graduate Mary Paley, whose promising academic career he
quashed.

Such challenges from a former ally called out the best in Eleanor, who was
at this point firmly established as Newnham's principal:

> I may perhaps remind Professor Marshall that the whole course of the
> movement for the academic education of women is strewn with the
> wrecks of hasty generalizations as to the limits of women's intellectual
> powers. When the work here began, many smiled at the notion that
> women, except one or two here and there, could be capable of taking
> University honours at all. When they had achieved distinction in some
> of the newer Triposes, it was still confidently affirmed that the highest
> places in the time-honoured Mathematical and Classical examinations
> were beyond their reach. When at length a woman obtained the posi-
> tion of Senior Wrangler, it was prophesied that, at any rate, the second
> part of the Mathematical Tripos would reveal the inexorable limitations
> of the feminine intellect. Then, when this last prophecy has shared the

fate of its predecessors, it is discovered that the domestic qualities of women specially fit them for Tripos examinations of all kinds, but not for vigorous mental work afterwards. With this experience, while admiring the pertinacity and versatility of our opponents, we may be pardoned for distrusting their insight and foresight; and in any case we hope that the University will not hesitate to allow women who satisfy its intellectual tests unrestricted opportunities for cultivating whatever faculties they possess for receiving, transmitting, and advancing knowledge.[219]

That Eleanor could so annihilate one of the founding fathers of modern mathematical economics is wonderful, to be sure. By this point, the Sidgwicks no longer felt that there was anything terribly experimental about equality for women. As Janet Oppenheim has demonstrated, if she, Eleanor "thought that most women would find their greatest joy in marriage, she denounced the notion that marriage was the only career worth having and warmly sympathized with the need felt by many women for 'the kind of happiness which can only come from work' and from 'the habit of reasonable self-dependence in thought and study'. . . . The most rewarding life for a woman, she believed, necessarily combined 'intellectual autonomy with emotional bonds to friends and family.'"[220]

Thus, if Eleanor "never discounted the legitimacy of family claims on a woman's time, she always balanced her gospel of self-renunciation for others with a paean to the joys of nurturing one's own mental garden." She harbored no doubts about women being able to enter into the true spirit of the university, "the love of knowledge for its own sake and apart from its examination and professional value." "Among such women," she wrote,

> will be found a few who will add to our literary stores, and a few who will help in advancing knowledge by reflection, observation, experiment, or research, or—more humbly—by rendering accessible the work of others. Those who advance knowledge will not probably be many—there are not many among men—but the others if they have been really interested will not have wasted their time; and will have received a training which will directly or indirectly help them in any work they may undertake, and they will form part of the audience—the cultivated, interested and intelligent public—without which scientific progress and literary production is well nigh impossible.[221]

For both Sidgwicks, the true university was ultimately a model of Millian (or Apostolic) friendship, affording "the sense of membership of a worthy community, with a high and noble function in which every member can take part," along with "the habit of reasonable self-dependence in thought and study." Institutions of higher education, for Eleanor, must "never cease to aim at producing that intellectual grasp and width of view which Mill regarded as their chief object," even if this had to be done by teaching people "in connection with their prospective careers."

Henry, for his part, had also come a long way on the subject, allowing that

> [i]n refusing to treat sex alone as a ground of disfranchisement, the Legislature would simply recognize in our political constitution what the best reflection shows to be an established fact of our social and industrial organization. . . . So long as the responsibility is thrown on women, unmarried or widows, of earning their own livelihood in any way that industrial competition allows, their claims to have the ordinary constitutional protection again any encroachments on the part of other sections of the community is *prima facie* undeniable.[222]

And in the nineties, he would also advance some of his most Millian endorsements of the value of higher education, for women and in general. Sidgwick's views on education and culture have not received nearly as much attention as his ethical work. But they merit careful consideration, given the way in which he resembled Mill and Dewey in being a true philosopher-educator. Judicious and balanced in his call for the inclusion of both older humanistic and modern scientific elements in any form of education worthy of the name, his vision would inspire the later educational reformism of both Russell and Dewey, along with that of many others. As he put it, in one of his most thoughtful essays, "The Pursuit of Culture," which was included in his collection on *Practical Ethics*:

> [S]ince the most essential function of the mind is to think and know, a man of cultivated mind must be essentially concerned for knowledge: but it is not knowledge merely that gives culture. A man may be learned and yet lack culture: for he may be a pedant, and the characteristic of a pedant is that he has knowledge without culture. So again, a load of facts retained in the memory, a mass of reasonings got up merely for examination, these are not, they do not give culture. It is the love of knowledge, the ardour of scientific curiosity, driving us continually to absorb new facts and ideas, to make them our own and fit them into the living and growing system of our thought; and the trained faculty of doing this, the alert and supple intelligence exercised and continually developed in doing this,—it is in these that culture essentially lies.[223]

As with Mill, the Socratic and Apostolic spirit was set against mere cram, and it was certainly not narrowly "useful" in some small-minded sense. The education of the whole person meant change and growth and happiness. And hope. It is worth again recalling Mill's words, from his "Inaugural Address at St. Andrews":

If we wish men to practice virtue, it is worth while trying to make them love virtue, and feel it an object in itself, and not a tax paid for leave to pursue other objects. It is worth training them to feel, not only actual wrong or actual meanness, but the absence of noble aims and endeavours, as not merely blamable but also degrading: to have a feeling of the miserable smallness of mere self in the face of this great universe, of the collective mass of our fellow creatures, in the face of past history and of the indefinite future—the poorness and insignificance of human life if it is to be all spent in making things comfortable for ourselves and our kin, and raising ourselves and them a step or two on the social ladder. Thus feeling, we learn to respect ourselves only so far as we feel capable of nobler objects: and if unfortunately those by whom we are surrounded do not share our aspirations, perhaps disapprove the conduct to which we are prompted by them—to sustain ourselves by the ideal sympathy of the great characters in history, or even in fiction, and by the contemplation of an idealized posterity: shall I add, of ideal perfection embodied in a Divine Being? Now, of this elevated tone of mind the great source of inspiration is poetry, and all literature so far as it is poetical and artistic.[224]

This was the real work that Henry and Eleanor sought to advance. And Newnham reflected that vision, with its beautiful Queen Anne architecture, well-rounded liberal arts education (including sports), and, most controversially, absence of a chapel. The Sidgwicks wanted Newnham to be positively better than the rest of Cambridge, with fewer retrograde requirements and pointless restrictions. The "Previous Examination" in Greek and Latin was, for Sidgwick, a pointless obstacle. One student recalled:

> Our lives were so excitingly novel. We worked, some of us, ten hours a day, and there were so many College societies and preoccupations that there was little time or energy for anything else. There were the Political, Debating, Sharp practice societies, the Historical, Classical, Scientific societies, The Browning, Shakespeare and other Literary societies, the Sunday Society, the Musical Society and many others. Those were recognized by authority, and there were many not recognized and indeed concealed from authority. (I remember my special contributions was a secret society called the L.S.D. And the letters hadn't the significance they have now. . . . They merely meant 'Leaving Sunday Dinner'. A small group of us signed off for Sunday dinners and we hired a room in Grantchester Street. . . . Each of us had in turn to provide a meal for the group. And there I may add we used to make our own cigarettes after a fashion.) For athletics there were tennis, hockey, cricket, fives, boating and the fire brigade. Life was never dull.[225]

What would Henry's church-building uncles have said about all that? But this appears to have been another subject that he avoided discussing with them.

The work on behalf of such opportunities was, however, nearly as frustrating as psychical research in that the Sidgwicks and their supporters, while feeling justifiable pride in the creation of Newnham (and other efforts, such as Girton), found it difficult to anticipate or credit the stupidity and entrenched prejudice that would always stall their efforts. After the burning hopefulness of the sixties and seventies, the eighties and nineties witnessed, along with the triumphs, an entrenched opposition to full educational equality for women such that "[w]omen were not awarded degrees on an equal basis to men at Cambridge until 1948, partly because if women had degrees they would also have the privileges that came them, i.e. equal status, voting rights and a share in the governance of the institution."[226] The Marshalls of the place were always too powerful to allow the changes that the Sidgwicks hoped to see. In the nineties, jeering students would burn an effigy of a woman in bloomers outside the University Senate, which resoundingly defeated a vote for full equality. Henry, it seems, was wrong when in the 1870s he predicted progress because "all the jokes have been made." And given their experience of hidebound Cambridge prejudice, one can almost forgive Eleanor for thinking that the world needed nothing less than a new Messiah, though it really should have been a woman.

Interestingly, the involvement with Newnham and women's higher education overlapped at points with their psychological and parapsychological interests, since so much of the opposition now was taking a familiar medicalized form: "Much of the opposition now came from the medical profession and the scientists who stressed the physiological and psychological differences between men and women."[227] But the Sidgwicks wanted to fight this fight in the open, pitting better science against the pseudoscience used to buttress social prejudice. Their success with women had in effect marked another of the successful experiments in living that Mill had called for, and a new sense of the psychological frontiers that could be explored on behalf of the progressive interests of humanity. As in the battle against materialism, or against the pathologizing of same-sex love, the problem was to prevent the authority of science from being misused, though of course there was still plenty of unthinking bigotry to contend with as well. The anti-Millian, antifeminist old Apostle James Fitzjames Stephen, Sidgwick mocked,

is unexpectedly checked by the consideration that any minute examination of the differences between men and women is—not exactly indecent, but—'unpleasant in the direction of indecorum'. We should be sorry to encourage any remarks calculated to raise a blush in the cheek of a Queen's Counsel: but as the only conceivable ground for subjecting women, as a class, to special disabilities, must lie in the differences between them and men, it is obviously impossible to decide on the justice . . . of those disabilities, without a careful examination of these differences. And in fact Mr Stephen's sudden delicacy does not suffice to hinder him from deciding the question with his usual rough

dogmatism: it only renders his discussion of it more than usually narrow and commonplace.[228]

But this was the good fight, and the Sidgwicks were always ready to fight
it. They could get discouraged, but they never considered abandoning the effort, as they often did with psychical research. And despite the loss of such
old friends as Symonds and Noel, and of the formidable Benson, the nineties brought Sidgwick into a better state of mind, especially once they had
relocated to Newnham. Henry liked being surrounded by youth, and he liked
working as "an appendage" to the Principal, who, he allowed, would be missed
at Cambridge more than he would be, should they ever leave. But although
he fantasized about leaving, about being really free to express himself openly,
without the burdens of his role, that was not in his future. Still, he loved wan-
dering the grounds of Newnham, chewing on his beard in meditation and admiring the masses of yellow flowers that were his favorites. [229] He was always
on hand to help Eleanor with the socializing, telling a favorite story or reading
a favorite poet. He worried that the students who came to Newnham were too
independent to "submit to maternal governance," but really, he would not have
had it any other way, and they considerably brightened his life.

To read the Sidgwicks on Newnham and higher education for women is to
read them at their Millian best, when they could bring remarkable insight into
the workings of prejudice and oppression, the misuses of science, and the demands of social justice. And if it was an experiment in living on a small scale,
it nonetheless did suggest to them the possibilities for change.

But like the Mills, the Sidgwicks could be conflicted and compromised in
ways that read much more painfully. And this is especially the case in Henry's
work in politics and political economy. Like all the great utilitarians, he did
his time with political economy, and his professional credentials as both an
economist and political scientist were impeccable, although the professional
organizations now associated with these disciplines were only beginning to
take shape in his era. He was an active member of the section of the British
Association concerned with political economy and economics, and his book
The Elements of Politics, first published in 1891, became a staple of political
science at Cambridge and elsewhere. He is rightly thought of as one of the
founding fathers of the "Cambridge School" of economics, one whose contributions should be classed with those of Alfred Marshall and A. C. Pigou.[230]

Economics and Politics

Sidgwick's reputation as an economist has often suffered from an invidious
comparison with Marshall, his Cambridge colleague and rival. Marshall,
however obnoxious and bigoted, was no doubt a brilliant economic thinker
and a relentless discipline builder, the man who basically established modern

economics as an independent academic discipline at Cambridge. But as "University politicians" he and Sidgwick were often at odds with each other, and not only over women's equality, since Sidgwick on other points resisted his efforts, believing that economics should remain integrated with the study of politics. Almost immediately upon his appointment as professor in late 1884, Marshall, in a famous incident, confronted Sidgwick and ridiculed him for his "mania" for "over-regulation" and his "failure to attract men on a large scale," the way Green had at Oxford. Marshall claimed that Sidgwick was hampering his efforts, despite his greater knowledge of economics. Sidgwick reflected on the charges, but came to a very characteristic conclusion:

> [F]eeling that the deepest truth I have to tell is by no means 'good tidings,' I naturally shrink from exercising on others the personal influence which would make men [resemble] me, as much as men more optimistic and prophetic naturally aim at exercising such influences. Hence as a teacher I naturally desire to limit my teaching to those whose bent or deliberate choice it is to search after ultimate truth; if such come to me, I try to tell them all I know; if others come with vaguer aims, I wish if possible to train their faculties without guiding their judgements. I would not if I could, and I could not if I would, say anything which would make philosophy—my philosophy—popular.[231]

Sidgwick had actually known Marshall for a long time—since the 1860s—and had in fact helped his career. He had in effect tutored Marshall in philosophy, stimulated his interest in educational reform, fostered their mutual interest in political economy, and helped call attention to the importance of Marshall's early work, privately circulating some of it. But by the 1880s and 90s, relations between the two men were often quite strained.[232]

Sidgwick had in fact long been a student of political economy, from before he had ever met Marshall. "Mill's influence," he explained, led him "as a matter of duty" to "study political economy thoroughly, and give no little thought to practical questions, social and political."[233] In the early 1860s, he was absorbed in the study of Mill's classic *Principles of Political Economy*, and much influenced by Mill's Cambridge disciples, the Fawcetts. From the late 1870s on, he regularly published works in this field, producing his own *Principles of Political Economy* in 1883, heading the political economy section of the British Association, contributing to *Palgrave*, and serving on various government commissions concerned with economic questions (he developed considerable expertise devising intricate taxation schemes). His work as an academic and policy advisor put him in touch with (directly or indirectly) many of the leading economists of the day—not only such Cambridge colleagues as Marshall, J. N. Keynes (a former student and close friend), and Herbert Foxwell, but also such figures as F. Y. Edgeworth (one of his leading disciples, in fact), Leon Walras, N. Senior, J. E. Cairnes, and W. S. Jevons (a particularly profound influence). He was even familiar with the work of Karl Marx, at a time when few trained economists even knew who Marx was. Moreover, he was long involved with both the practical and theoretical work of the Cambridge Charity Organization Society, developing a sophisticated, eclectic approach to the issue of poor relief, another point of continuity with Bentham and Mill.

Like Mill, Marshall, and many economists down to the present, Sidgwick drew a careful distinction between the descriptive side (the science) of economic analysis and the normative or policy side (the art), which especially concerns the proper role of government intervention in the market system to improve "either the social production of wealth or its distribution."[234] He was also steeped in the great methodological debates over the historical or inductive versus the analytic or deductive approaches to the subject, and his balanced efforts to combine the two—and strengthen comparative studies as well—considerably distance his work from older Benthamite defenses of laissez faire. For Sidgwick, as for Marshall, "economic man" is simply an abstraction that may be useful for explaining or predicting some aspects of the behavior of people under certain historical circumstances and in certain situations. Both the science and art of economic analysis need to recognize the limitations of the assumption that people always act out of self-interest and happily so. Indeed, he put it rather heatedly in his "The Scope and Method of Economic Science":

> There is indeed a kind of political economy which flourishes in proud independence of facts; and undertakes to settle all practical problems of Governmental interference or private philanthropy by simple deduction from one or two general assumptions—of which the chief is the assumption of the universally beneficent and harmonious operation of self-interest well let alone. This kind of political economy is sometimes called 'orthodox,' though it has the characteristic unusual in orthodox doctrines of being repudiated by the majority of accredited teachers of the subject. But whether orthodox or not, I must be allowed to disclaim all connection with it; the more completely this survival of the *a priori* politics of the eighteenth century can be banished to the remotest available planet, the better it will be, in my opinion, for the progress of economic science.[235]

Sidgwick's position certainly reflected the more sophisticated, more historical, and even more socialistic views of the later Mill, who as noted had been deeply influenced by Harriet Taylor, the Romantic movement, and Macaulay's withering criticisms of the apriorism of Benthamism—that is, of the (supposed) Benthamite attempt to deduce the best form of law and government from the assumption of universal self-interest. Sidgwick followed Mill in emphasizing that political economy needed to pay attention to the complexity and historical variety of human motivation and character, as well as to the condition of the working class. Perhaps characteristically, however, Sidgwick appreciated the paradox involved in the successful application of the historical method:

> [I]t may be worth while to point out to the more aggressive 'histori-
> cists' that the more the historian establishes the independence of his
> own study, by bringing into clear view the great differences between
> the economic conditions with which we are familiar and those of earlier
> ages, the more, *prima facie*, he tends to establish the corresponding
> independence of the economic science which, pursued with a view to
> practice, is primarily concerned to understand the present.[236]

This is not to applaud the increasing individualism and self-interested behavior of the modern world, which worried Sidgwick even more than it worried the Mills. Like Mill and Taylor, he and Eleanor hoped that the future
would bring a growth in human sympathy and moral motivation. He even
hoped that individuals would come to be motivated to work by their concern
to do their bit for the common good, to make their contribution to society;
"ethical" socialism, though not necessarily governmental socialism, was for
him a very attractive development.

But with respect to his contributions to the "science" of economics, there
has long been some controversy over how successful Sidgwick was in going
beyond Mill and appreciating the "marginalist revolution" taking place around
him. Phyllis Deane, for example, argued that "the *Principles* owed more to
the classical tradition of J. S. Mill than to what contemporaries were then
calling the 'new political economy' of Jevons and Marshall."[237] And Howey,
in an influential work, insisted that economists "must add something to and
take something away from hedonism, as ordinarily construed, before it becomes marginal utility economics. Jevons and Gossen could make the transformation; Sidgwick never could."[238] On the other side, however, Sidgwick's
economic work has been praised by more than one Nobel Prize winner, including George Stigler. Stigler, after remarking on how the work of Cournot
and Dupuit on monopoly and oligopoly "began to enter English economics,
in particular through Edgeworth, Sidgwick, and Marshall," confessed that he
was "coming to admire Henry Sidgwick almost as much as the other two. His
Principles . . . has two chapters (bk. II, ch. IX and X) which are among the
best in the history of microeconomics, dealing with the theories of human
capital and noncompetitive behavior."[239] Elements of the Chicago School of
Economics, particularly of law and economics, have been intriguingly traced
back to Sidgwick by Steven Medema, who has also helpfully brought out the
impact of Sidgwick's religious concerns on his economic approach.[240]

For his part, Sidgwick at least claimed that he was part of the new movement, describing himself as a disciple of Jevons: "As Jevons had admirably explained, the variations in the relative market values of different articles express

and correspond to variations in the comparative estimates formed by people in general, not of the *total* utilities of the amounts purchased of such articles, but of their *final* utilities; the utilities, that is, of the last portions purchased."[241] But he did claim that the differences with the older, Millian school had been exaggerated, and he continued, despite his considerable mathematical expertise, to do economics in a qualitative mode. Even so, he showed considerable acumen in setting out and conceptually clarifying the fundamental concepts of economics (wealth, value, labor, money, efficiency, etc.), in bringing out the difficulties involved in cross-cultural and trans-historical comparisons of wealth, and in analyzing the various cases of market failure, from monopoly to collective action problems to negative externalities. Indeed, his accounts of market failure and the possible remedies—the "art" of political economy— have received somewhat more recognition.

Even Marshall praised this side of Sidgwick's work, calling the relevant section of the *Principles* the best thing of its kind "in any language."[242] It is the received wisdom that Marshall's hand-picked successor at Cambridge, A. C. Pigou, produced a form of welfare economics that largely recapitulated Sidgwick's contributions, though contemporary hedonists, such as Singer and Kahneman, tend to be more impressed with the formalization of Sidgwick's hedonism developed by Edgeworth, whose work was forbiddingly technical, as well as eccentric.[243]

The form of Sidgwick's *Principles of Political Economy*, with its careful conceptual clarifications and distinction between normative and descriptive arguments, and its successive qualifications to individualistic, free market accounts of both, would prove to be characteristic, figuring in many of his essays and in such works as *The Elements of Politics*. As in the case of the *Methods*, the structure of these works has often made it difficult to see precisely where Sidgwick comes down on many issues. Typically, he begins with a robust statement of the "individualistic principle," as, for example, in the *Elements*:

> What one sane adult is legally compelled to render to others should be merely the negative service of non-interference, except so far as he has voluntarily undertaken to render positive services; provided that we include in the notion of non-interference the obligation of remedying or compensating for mischief intentionally or carelessly caused by his acts—or preventing mischief that would otherwise result from previous acts. This principle for determining the nature and limits of governmental interference is currently known as 'Individualism' . . . the requirement that one sane adult, apart from contract or claim to reparation, shall contribute positively by money or services to the support of others I shall call 'socialistic'.[244]

He then typically goes on to explain how any such principle reflects various psychological and sociological presuppositions—for example, that sane adults are the best judges of their own interests—and that these are only approximate generalizations and subject to crucial limitations. The psychological assumption that "every one can best take care of his own interest" and the sociological one that "the common welfare is best attained by each pursuing exclusively his own welfare and that of his family in a thoroughly alert and intelligent manner"—both essential to the case for laissez faire—end up being very heavily qualified and subject to so many exceptions that it is scarcely evident what Sidgwick means when he calls individualism "in the main sound." It comes off at least as badly as the common-sense morality that he claimed as his own. The list of qualifications covers everything from education, defense, childcare, poor relief, public works, collective bargaining, environmental protections, and more. An unfortunate—but alas, very revealing—note adds that the "protection of inferior races of men will be considered in a subsequent chapter."[245]

These qualifications and limitations then invariably involve a discussion of the case for socialism and/or communism, a subject that Sidgwick addressed at length in many works. His main objection to socialistic interference was the all too familiar one that too much of it would lead to splendidly equal destitution, and that for people as presently constituted economic incentives were needed to spur them to produce. But again, he hoped that "human nature" would change, growing more sympathetic and more amenable to ethical socialism, leaving the door open to the possibility of legitimating greater governmental interference with the market. Indeed, in his political theoretical work, he admittedly simply assumed the utilitarian criterion as the normative bottom line, rather than arguing for it against rational egoism. Unfortunately, as he also stressed in many different works, no one could confidently predict the direction of civilization. Although in his more historical works, notably *The Development of European Polity*, Sidgwick assembled evidence to suggest that a continued growth in federalism and large-scale state organizations was likely, it was a very carefully hedged conclusion and cast against a broad critique of the social sciences. Much as he admired the sweep and ambition of such pioneers of sociology as Spencer and Comte (whose emphasis on the "consensus of experts" was appropriated for his epistemological work), he regarded their "sciences" of the laws of human development as absurdly over-blown, yielding wildly different predictions about the future course of humanity. He sincerely hoped that a more cosmopolitan attitude would be the wave of the future, and that the growth of international law and cooperation would decrease the likelihood of war, but he could not convince himself that social science—with the partial exception of economics—was beyond its infancy when it came to predicting things to come.[246] And much, much more work needed to be done by way of psychological experiments in living.

Thus, although the Idealist D. G. Ritchie—who was in fact quite sympathetic to utilitarian ethical theory—famously charged that with Sidgwick utilitarianism had grown "tame and sleek" and lost its reforming zeal, others, notably F. A. Hayek, held that he had in effect paved the way for the "New Liberalism" and even Fabian socialism that soon overtook British politics, legitimating a far greater degree of state intervention. Woodrow Wilson, the future president of the United States, admired Sidgwick's *Elements*, but perceptively found the more abstract, analytic side of his work oddly "colorless" and in need of historical content. At the least, Sidgwick's work in politics and political theory, like his work in economics, does reveal how far he was from "orthodox"—which is to say, "caricatural"—Benthamism; he even criticized at length the Austinian theory of sovereignty—which analyzed law in terms of authoritative command and habitual obedience.

No doubt Sidgwick's personal commitment to utilitarianism informed his economic views, especially when it came to the "art" of political economy, which concerned the normative considerations that came to be called "welfare economics." Roger Backhouse has argued that Sidgwick's emphasis on method, attentiveness to empirical evidence, and the balancing of analytical and historical analysis marked important points of overlap with Marshall on the descriptive side as well, and it is clearly true that the two men influenced each other.[247] Whatever differences there were in their conceptions of mathematicizing their Millian inheritance, neither Sidgwick nor Marshall was enthusiastic about mere exercises in formal modeling. Sidgwick's "Economic Method" of 1879 is sharp in its point:

> Indeed, what economist affects to foretell, by any method whatever, "the exact rates at which goods of every kind will be sold"? Mr. Leslie lays great stress on the "failure of deductive economists," as represented by the late Mr. MacCulloch, to recognise duly the local inequalities of wages in England. But who now takes MacCulloch for a sure guide? Or who is so "deductive" as to ignore a point that has been enforced and illustrated for half a generation in all the successive editions of Professor Fawcett's manual?[248]

He was even more emphatic in a March 16, 1881 letter to Foxwell, explaining that he hated "the error of presenting economic doctrine as a mere tissue of barren abstractions and confident but imperfectly verified Generalisations."[249]

In arguing for the significance of Sidgwick's contribution to the Cambridge School, and for the value of his careful discussion of terms, Backhouse convincingly develops the claim that the "fundamental part of Sidgwick's argument was a distinction between two senses in which the term 'wealth' was used. The first was as the sum of goods produced, valued at market prices. The second was as the sum of individuals' utilities—what we would now term welfare." This "separation of two concepts of wealth made it possible, arguably for the first time, to conceive of welfare economics as something distinct from economics in general," marking a departure from the classical tradition and greatly compromising the definiteness of comparisons of utilities. Wealth maximization and welfare maximization were, in short, not equivalent. Analogous arguments are evident in Sidgwick's scrupulous and skeptical account of the possibilities for comparing wealth in cross-cultural or trans-historical contexts (an area Marshall treated in terms of consumer surplus). Sidgwick explained how these two types of wealth could differ, as in the case of those goods for which no price was paid. People value such goods, but, their price being zero, they are not counted as "wealth" under the first definition. Such unpurchased utilities, not measured by exchange values, when conjoined to a belief in declining marginal utility, allowed that, as Backhouse puts it, "if the marginal utility of a particular good were higher for one person than for another, total utility could be raised by redistributing goods to those who valued them most. This would leave wealth at market prices unchanged." According to Backhouse and others, the radical, redistributivist potential implications of such views were evaded by both Sidgwick and Marshall: "Marshall is much more aware of the quantitative side of the problem than is Sidgwick . . . but no nearer a way to thinking quantitatively about how to achieve the best use of resources. They share both a philosophical viewpoint that inclines them towards egalitarianism and a conservatism that will not risk any interference with incentives, lest output be reduced."[250]

Sidgwick surely was, as Backhouse suggests, too impressed by alarmist claims that, incentives being crucial to production, communism would lead to splendidly equal destitution; there can be no doubt about his calling for extreme caution in developing socialistic reforms, whatever sympathies he may have harbored for, say, Henry George's claim that the community was the rightful owner of increases in land values. Indeed, as Backhouse has long insisted, it was Pigou, rather than Marshall, who most openly reflected the "radical side" of Sidgwick's welfare economics.

But one plump paradox in Sidgwick's role concerns the way in which Pigou, Marshall's hand-picked successor and the author of *The Economics of Welfare*, could be so much more Sidgwickian in his approach. The paradox is seemingly heightened by the supposed way in which Sidgwick, on Steven Medema's account, forms a "bridge between Bentham and Becker," as though Sidgwick were a pivotal figure in both twentieth-century welfare economics and the Chicago School that overthrew it, in the work of Frank Knight, Coase, and so many others. But Medema, who has done much excellent research on Coase and his predecessors, has produced a major and most welcome appreciation of the significance of Sidgwick in economic history that succeeds in demonstrating just how fertile the Sidgwickian influence was, even if in the end it seems closer to Pigou than to Coase.

In his insightful work *The Hesitant Hand: Taming Self-Interest in the History of Economic Ideas*, Medema has developed at some length his sophisticated narrative of Sidgwick's historical role:

The theory of market failure brought analytical refinement to a centuries-old concern with the impact of self-interested behavior on economic activity, and . . . we attempt to shed some light on the transition from the fairly non-interventionist approach of the classical tradition to the more interventionist orientation that came to characterize neoclassical welfare theory and public economics. The argument here is that this transition occurred via a two-stage process, in which John Stuart Mill and Henry Sidgwick were central players. The first step involved the elaboration of a greatly expanded theory of the failure of the system of natural liberty—akin to what we today call 'market failure'—as against the classical success story. Mill was instrumental in this expansion, and it continued at the hands of Sidgwick. The second stage involved the move to a much more markedly positive assessment of the possibilities of corrective policy actions undertaken by the state than we find in the classical tradition, and it was here that Sidgwick took center stage. All of this fed into Pigovian welfare theory, the market failure aspect of which, at least, came to dominate professional discourse.[251]

As Medema rightly insists, one corollary of the marginalist revolution was a more refined and systematic account of market failure, and in this Sidgwick led the way, ascribing "an even greater set of failings to the system of natural liberty than did Mill" and expressing "a great deal more optimism about the efficacy of government intervention."[252]

Medema does, to be sure, note Sidgwick's many worries about the potential dangers of government intervention—corruption and catering to special interests, waste, problems with regulation and supervision, the costs in taxes, and the want of appropriate incentives among government workers. But as he also observes, "Sidgwick suggested optimism—that in the long run 'moral and political progress [in society] may be expected to *diminish* the extent and severity of the shortcomings associated with government intervention.'"[253]

Medema's account is compelling and accords quite well with the account of Sidgwick's economic contribution given by Donald Winch in his rich, more historically contextualized work, *Wealth and Life: Essays on the Intellectual History of Political Economy in Britain, 1848–1915*. Winch notes how, although both Sidgwick and Marshall stressed the role of education in helping to overcome poverty and economic inequality, Sidgwick appears to have gone beyond both Mill and Marshall in setting out on full display the various areas of market failure, the limits of laissez faire, and the limitations of economic analysis in general, whether descriptive or normative. Sidgwick was, in Winch's view, being more categorical than Mill ever was when he wrote: "It seems to me quite possible that a considerable extension of the industrial functions of government might be on the whole advantageous, without any Utopian degree of moral or political improvement in human society."[254]

Both Medema and Winch demonstrate, in their different ways, how both the *Elements* and the *Principles* take the laissez-faire principle of individualism—again, that "what one sane adult is legally compelled to render to others should be merely the negative service of non-interference, except so far as he has voluntarily undertaken to render positive services"—only as a unifying thread, on which to string a very long list of needed qualifications and exceptions: education, childcare, poor relief, disease control, countering depravity, public works or goods (the famous lighthouse example, but also pure research and defense), environmental regulations, collective bargaining, treatment of future generations, and others. Sidgwick always highlighted two extreme cases that are especially effective at pointing up the limitations of economic individualism in situations where rational actor assumptions manifestly fail to apply—the "humane treatment of lunatics, and the prevention of cruelty to the inferior animals." Such restrictions hardly aim at securing the freedom of the lunatics or the animals, but are rather "a one-sided restraint of the freedom of action of men with a view to the greatest happiness of the aggregate of sentient beings." The same points apply to, for example, the treatment of children, another area in which paternalism and/or maternalism is clearly required. Like most utilitarians, Sidgwick recognized that the good of all sentient creatures and of future generations should count in the utilitarian calculus, though it was plain that the good of the mentally ill, nonhuman animals, and future generations was scarcely going to be covered merely by protecting the libertarian rights of presently existing people.

And on that sticky question of children, the labor of whom had been such an issue for his grandfather and uncles, it is intriguing that Sidgwick would, in his *Elements of Politics*, provide the following, somewhat evasive, somewhat meliorizing take on the issue:

> So far I have chiefly had in view the executive or administrative work of government, together with the financial business which this entails. But perhaps the most important question that belongs to the present chapter—and one of the most important questions in the whole discussion of the structure of government—relates to the extent to which Legislation should be allowed to be localised. We have seen before that some power of laying down general rules, to be obeyed by others besides the servants of government, cannot without inconvenience be denied to the central executive: and in the same way the local executive work that we have been considering will naturally involve some exercise of legislative functions. Thus we may assume that local governments will have a limited power of making general regulations for the common use of streets, bridges, parks, and other public property, of which the use is necessarily confined in the main to the inhabitants of certain localities, and of which, therefore, as we have already seen, the expense

may properly be localised. So again the sanitary intervention of government and protective measures against noxious plants and insects, and against destructive floods, will usually involve a certain amount of general coercive regulation. But the peculiar interest that a man's neighbours have in his right behaviour is obviously not restricted to his observance of such rules as these. Even as regards the fundamental rights of personal security, property, and contract, it is indefinitely more important to a Yorkshireman that they should be properly defined and protected in Yorkshire, than that they should be properly defined and protected in Kent. Nay, further, it is to be expected that differences of physical conditions and industrial development—if not of race and political history—will render the special needs of Yorkshiremen in respect of protection from mutual mischief, enforced co-operation for common benefit, or regulated use of natural resources, somewhat different from the special needs of Kentishmen; thus Yorkshire may require factory acts, but be indifferent to the regulation of hop-picking, or compulsory insurance against fruit disease, which may be prominent objects of concern in Kent. Hence localised legislation will tend to be more fully and closely adapted to these varying requirements than centralised legislation is likely to be.[255]

Although Sidgwick was not explicitly personal in such remarks, one does get the sense that he was struggling with his family's history, albeit with his usual masking abstractions.

As the above passage suggests, Sidgwick was never dogmatic about such matters, especially when treating the exceptions that arose even in purer cases, "in a society composed—solely or mainly—of 'economic men,'" when markets failed in their own terms at the efficient production of material wealth. Again, as Winch notes, he included here "the accepted range of public goods such as lighthouses, bridges, and harbours, and went on to deal with other topics that would furnish the heartland of what later became known as 'welfare economics', those examples of market failure attributable to externalities, neighbourhood effects, and indivisibilities. Prominent among the examples chosen by Sidgwick were those connected with the natural environment (afforestation and flood or disease control); conservation (regulation of fishing and hunting where voluntary agreement was like to break down), and public utilities (natural monopolies, activities that promised only long-term social returns but were unremunerative to private agencies); and cases such as roads where collection of tolls could detract from their utility to the public."[256] But he was also eloquent on the benefits of protecting "infant industries" and on other forms of protectionism. Of course, in keeping with a utilitarian outlook on such matters, which requires that the contingent facts of the particular case rather than any abstract principle of natural rights or duties must determine the best course, Sidgwick allowed that not all such failures called for or could be resolved by government intervention, only that such divergences of private and public interests meant that government involvement must be treated "as not merely a temporary resource, but not improbably a normal element of the organization of industry."[257]

Here again, the wording was telling, characteristic, and indicative of the deeper drift of Sidgwick's arguments. True, as Ronald Coase has pointed out, in his classic essay on "The Lighthouse in Economics," Sidgwick's phrasing in the case of the lighthouse example of a public good was much more circumspect than that of later economic writers (for example, Paul Samuelson). As Sidgwick put it: "It may easily happen that the benefits of a well-placed lighthouse must be largely enjoyed by ships on which no toll could be conveniently imposed." On Coase's gloss, "this does not say that there may not be circumstances in which the benefits of the lighthouse are largely enjoyed by ships on which a toll could be conveniently laid and it implies that, in these circumstances, it would be desirable to impose a toll."[258] But as Backhouse, Medema, and Winch allow, Sidgwick could be more forceful. In his presidential address to the British Association, he proclaimed: "The absolute right of the individual to unlimited industrial freedom is now only maintained by a scanty and dwindling handful of doctrinaires, whom the progress of economic science has left stranded on the crude generalizations of an earlier period."[259] And however much Sidgwick's critics may have complained that it was difficult to catch the drift of his arguments given all the qualifications heaped on, the recent scholarship cited above has made it much clearer just what that drift was. As Medema sums it up, his

> *Principles of Political Economy* reveals an extensive list of divergences between private and social interests, both where laissez-faire's wealth-maximizing results are not in society's best interest because there are "extra-economic considerations" that are more important than wealth, and where laissez-faire does not even generate the wealth-maximizing result. . . . He was concerned that orthodox political economy had "often produced a blind confidence in the economic harmony resulting from natural liberty," to the point where it even seemed to neglect to note the opposition between the monopolists' interests and those of the community.[260]

And Sidgwick made it plain enough in his practical work that he believed there were few reasons to oppose taxes on luxury goods, or efforts to develop a more eclectic and effective model of poor relief, possibly introducing some of the statist elements found in the German model.

Again, Sidgwick was ultimately persuaded that the growth of federalism and large-scale state organizations would continue, though he doubted that the social sciences were anywhere near to discovering actual laws of historical development. He could see the point of the radical positions of Marx, William Morris, and George Bernard Shaw, even if in the end he found them intellectually wanting, as speculative and inexact as the positions of Auguste Comte and Herbert Spencer. He was a gradualist, not a revolutionary, but he was a gradualist who entertained some remarkably radical possibilities for the future.

Of special importance for a comparison with Mill is chapter X of the *Principles*, the "investigation of the conditions under which self-interest will prompt to combination, and of the extent of gain which the persons combining may realize." It provocatively argues—in line with the late Mill—that in many ordinary cases "it is possible for a combination of workmen to secure, either temporarily or permanently, a rise in wages" without such gain having "any manifest tendency to be counterbalanced by future loss," it being only the bankrupt "Wages-Fund Theory" that would suggest otherwise. More generally, and skeptically, it is

> only in a partial and subordinate way that Economic Science can offer assistance in dealing with the practical problem presented to Boards of Conciliation or Courts of Arbitration when they attempt to avert or close a controversy between employers and employed in any industry as to the rate of wages. Economic science cannot profess to determine the normal division of the difference remaining, when from the net produce available for wages and profits in any branch of production we subtract the minimum shares which it is the interest of employers and employed respectively to take rather than abandon the business and seek employment for their labour and capital elsewhere[261]

The spectre of the more Malthusian early utilitarian political economy has thus clearly been banished, and the horizons for labor opened, though Sidgwick, very much like Mill and Fawcett, feared strife between labor and capital and hoped that new forms of economic organization, such as the cooperative movement, might reduce the risk of violent class conflict without requiring state intervention:

> And many who are not socialists, regarding the stimulus and direction of energy given by the existing individualistic system as quite indispensable to human society as at present constituted, yet feel the moral need of some means of developing in the members of a modern industrial community a fuller consciousness of their industrial work as a social function, only rightly performed when done with a cordial regard to the welfare of the whole society,—or at least that part of it to which the work is immediately useful. From this point of view great interest attaches to the development of what is called, in a special sense, "cooperation," by which the conflict of interests—either between producers and consumers, or between different sets of workers engaged in

the same productive industry—has been more or less subordinated to the consciousness of associative effort for a common good. Any experiment of this kind that is economically successful is to be welcomed as a means of education in public spirit, no less than for its more material advantages.[262]

But of course Sidgwick was rather soberer about the possibilities afforded by the cooperative movement. In "The Economic Lessons of Socialism," he famously put it that

> while the earlier Socialists were much disposed to experiment, their experiments were mostly such palpable failures that their only effect was to harden the orthodox economist in his prejudices as well as his sound conclusions. It is true that the success of the artisans' co-operative stores—and, in a much more limited degree, of attempts at co-operative production—may be partly set to the account of Socialism; as, without the impulse given by Owen to the co-operative movement, the venture of the Rochdale Pioneers would probably never have been made. But the successes of these co-operative stores, though they have taught us something worth knowing, have not taught the lesson that Socialists have desired to teach: they have not demonstrated the great capitalist or great employer to be superfluous, but only that competition does not tend to the most economical supply of the services of the ordinarily humble and struggling retail tradesmen of the poor.
>
> The tendency of the later school has been to discourage all voluntary essays in Socialism: on the pretext that no instructive experience can be gained except through the action of the State. From a scientific point of view this attitude is to be regretted, but I can quite understand that it is politic in those who aim at producing an immediate and far-reaching movement in a Socialistic direction: since a study of the broad results of previous experiments of the kind certainly does not tend to encourage such a movement. At any rate it seems at present that if we are to derive important economic instruction from Socialistic experimentation, the *corpus vile* will have to be a West-European nation. One nation will probably be found sufficient: and I trust that we shall all agree to yield the post of honour to Germany, in this branch of the pursuit of knowledge.[263]

Thus, Sidgwick brought his trademark skepticism to bear on the cooperative movement as well, and his attitude was suggestive of the changing times. Much as he admired the movement, he could not share the Fawcetts' or the Mills' extreme enthusiasm for it, nor could he shake the belief that the currents of history were rendering its role less significant and that the task ahead would demand the exploration of more statist alternatives.

Yet here it is worth stressing again that, whatever his anxieties about economic socialism, Sidgwick was openly enthusiastic about ethical socialism, the possibility of humanity growing more altruistic and compassionate, and coming to regard their labor as their contribution to the common good. He was under no illusions whatsoever, not only about the market failing to reflect claims of desert or merit, but also about the limitations of that abstraction, "economic man," since historical and cultural or national context could dramatically alter the possibilities for moving beyond economic individualism, though again, in some areas this emphasis on "national character" lent itself to the racist and imperialistic tendencies of the British Empire.[264] It is noteworthy that Sidgwick's drift toward racism may have been in significant part a result of his absorption in the work of Jevons, who held that a "man of lower race, a negro for instance, enjoys possession less, and loathes labour more; his exertions, therefore, soon stop."[265] Such views on matters of race, more extreme than Mill's, would increasingly reverberate through late nineteenth-century political economy, finding expression in Sidgwick's admirer Edgeworth, who would insist that "[c]apacity for pleasure is a property of evolution, an essential attribute of civilization," with "civilization" being determined in part by race.[266]

Even so, Sidgwick found himself quite alienated from the jingoist, militarist political rhetoric of the 1890s. He feared the growth of a materialistic, Machiavellian form of self-interested power politics, whether domestically or globally. Against the ruder and cruder forms of self-interest—aggravated by a practical reason in chaos—he sought a continued moral and political evolution, led by the European powers, toward a greater federalism and cosmopolitanism that would generate the institutional mechanisms and political morality needed to avoid war and avert other forms of strife. Ethical socialism, the fostering of humanity's sympathetic and cooperative tendencies, was the road he favored in all regions, and education, in a broad sense, remained the vehicle of reform to which he would ever return. He never indicated that he would continue his work on this posthumously.

So far, so Millian. Still, it must be allowed that Sidgwick's political writings did not achieve the Mills' inspiring tone, and that, for all of his indebtedness to *On Liberty*, *Considerations on Representative Government*, etc., he tended to highlight rather different concerns—concerns that often reflected his views on the dualism of practical reason. Like the later Mill, he harbored many suspicions about the wisdom of democracy and championed the need for a cultural "clerisy" or vanguard of educated opinion, often sounding a note not unlike that of Walter Lippmann in the twentieth century, stressing how an educated elite should benevolently shape public opinion. He much admired the work of his friend James Bryce, author of *The American Commonwealth*, which pointed up both the vitality and the dangers of the U.S. political system. But he devoted comparatively little effort to proclaiming the benefits of freedom of conscience and speech, was quite critical of Mill's schemes for proportional representation, and worried at length about how "to correct the erroneous and short-sighted views of self-interest, representing it as divergent from duty, which certainly appear to be widely prevalent in the most advanced societies, at least among irreligious persons." In fact, for the government to supply teachers of this view might even be "indirectly individualistic in its aim, since to diffuse the conviction that it is every one's interest to do what is right would obviously be a valuable protection against mutual wrong," though it would probably detract from the credibility of such teachers if they were salaried employees of the state.[267] The more sinister aspects of Sidgwick's worries about what he termed the "lower classes" and the "lower races," and the ways in which his work intertwined with a variety of late Victorian imperialistic projects, including those of his colleague Sir John Seeley, his brother-in-law Arthur Balfour, and his old friend Charles Henry Pearson, will be addressed in the next section.

What Sidgwick's political writings do so effectively highlight, however, is the crucial role of education in his practical and theoretical work, something that seems a clear parallel to and continuation of the projects of Mill and the earlier utilitarians. Insofar as his more academic research carried a practical political point, this concerned the need for expanding and improving educational opportunities for all. Thus his feminism was focused on higher education for women and the foundation of Newnham College, and his many attempts to improve the curriculum of Cambridge University (by including Bentham, modern literature, physiology and other new subjects) were correlated with efforts to expand its audience and impact.[268] And beyond formal educational institutions, Sidgwick was simply indefatigable in promoting and participating in discussion societies, ever aiming at the elusive "consensus of experts" that his epistemology called for. If, towards the end of his life, his participation in such vehicles as the "Ethical Societies" reflected some despair over the possibility of achieving such a consensus on the "deepest problems," and instead involved an effort to set such problems aside in the hope of agreeing on the practical upshot of ethical questions, this was scarcely his characteristic attitude.[269]

Civilization and Crisis

At this point, it is perhaps best to pick up the story of the Sidgwicks with the issues of racism, colonization, and imperialism raised in the final sections of the previous chapter. For as in the case of the reconstructions and rehabilitations of Millian views (for example, in Nussbaum's work), progress can only be made through an honest confrontation with the more problematic applications and interpretations of the philosophical views at issue.

However "good for his times" some aspects of Sidgwick's work might seem, his agnosticism about hereditary racial differences, which was much like Mill's, clearly had an even more problematic side, the more so given that, unlike Mill, Sidgwick in his correspondence sometimes used the "N word"— "nigger"—and this in an alarmingly offhand way. Indeed, despite ample opportunity to blast "bald and vicious" forms of racism of the Carlylean type—as in the case of his review of Charles Henry Pearson's book, *National Life and Character*—Sidgwick never did so, preferring instead to politely sidestep such issues. As much as the Idealists issuing forth from Benjamin Jowett's Oxford, Sidgwick was a creature of the culture of imperialism, and Eleanor does not, for her part, appear to have pulled against that tendency, though like Harriet Taylor Mill, she rarely went on record with her views.

Although Sidgwick does not, in any of his major (or minor) works, actually comment on Mill versus Carlyle, his line is extremely close to Mill's—while conceding that historically things are not so simple and that the Egyptians and other nonwhites played important roles in cultural advance, he nonetheless allows that future science might demonstrate significant racial differences, that "savages" are "inferior," even if it is a contingent inferiority, and that "civilized" Europeans, to whom we owe constitutional government, are for the foreseeable future to be the judges and schoolmasters of the world. In an extremely Millian fashion, he recognizes how the rights of subjected peoples must be protected from the abuses of colonial governments. Indeed, on that count, Sidgwick might be construed as rather better than Mill, even the later, melancholy Mill, bringing to his work a much keener sense of the ferocious cruelty and bigotry that marked the history of colonialism and that promised to mark growing British imperialism. Mill's late-in-life mistrust of British political judgment on such matters was in fact developed and systematized by Sidgwick, who dealt with the subject far more extensively in such works as *The Elements of Politics*, his last major work, first published in 1891. He was every bit as cosmopolitan as Mill, looking to a future in which duty to humanity would increasingly trump love of country. But he was perhaps rather soberer than Mill when it came to recognizing the obstacles to this cosmopolitanism, which he thought would need to be led by the "Concert of Europe." On this count, at least, some might actually defend the superiority of the late Victorian Sidgwick against the mid-Victorian Mill, though neither came close to the anti-colonialist and anti-imperialist Bentham.

But on the other side, there are some very problematic passages in the *Elements*, passages in which Sidgwick sounds rather more like the defenders of Eyre than like a good Millian. Towards the end of his section on "Principles of External Policy," Sidgwick discusses "special restrictions on freedom of contract" in a singularly disturbing way:

> [If] such contracts are left unrestricted, there is some risk that the inferior race may be brought too completely into the power of private employers. This point is of course peculiarly important in the case of

colonies in which the superior race cannot or will not undertake the main part of the manual work required: in this case the demand of the capitalist employer for a steady supply of reliable labour led modern civilization in its earlier stage back to the institution of slavery in an extreme form: and prompts even now to longing aspirations after some system of compulsory labour, which shall have the economic advantages of slavery without its evils. But I know no ground for thinking that such a system can be devised: and should accordingly deprecate any attempt to approximate to it. I do not therefore infer—as some have inferred—that contracts of long duration ought to be prohibited altogether; but only that they ought to be carefully supervised and closely watched. The need for this vigilance arises equally–it may be even greater—when the labourers in question are not natives, but aliens belonging to a lower grade of civilization; at the same time there are strong economic reasons for introducing labour from abroad in colonies of this class, where the natives are either not sufficiently numerous or wanting in industrial capacity.[270]

The plausible suspicion that Sidgwick was here referring to the Jamaican case, as construed by Mill, is strengthened by a footnote a couple of pages earlier that reads: "In our own empire, the South African colonies form, from this point of view, a series of links intermediate between Australia and New Zealand which are clearly colonies of settlement, and the West Indian islands which are clearly not." "Colonies of settlement" are those in which "the manual labour can be and will be supplied by the civilized race," the other colonies, only loosely so called, being those "in which it can only supply capital and superior kinds of labour." Moreover, Sidgwick does emphasize that

the protection of the lives and property of the settlers will require effective prosecution and exemplary punishment of crimes against them: at the same time, it will be the imperative duty of Government to keep such punishment within the limits of strict justice. The difficult task of fulfilling this double obligation is likely to be better performed if those charged with it are not hampered by pedantic adhesion to the forms of civilized judicial procedure: what is important is that substantial justice should be done in such a manner as to impress the intellect of the aborigines with the relation between offence and punishment.[271]

For all of Sidgwick's Millian tendencies, these passages certainly lend themselves to a far from Millian reading. The Morant Bay rebellion was set off precisely in reaction to reassurances in the "Queen's Letter" that "[t]he prosperity of the labouring classes, as well as of all other classes, depends, in Jamaica, and in other countries, upon their working for wages, not uncertainly, or capriciously, but steadily and continuously, at the times when their labour is wanted, and for so long as it is wanted."[272] This only served to evoke memories of slavery and fears of an attempt to reinstitute it by other means. And of course, the defenders of Eyre were the very ones who complained vociferously about how unfair it was to insist on "pedantic adhesion to the forms of civilized judicial procedure" in the case of a rebellion by those whose labor was needed but not forthcoming, these rebels being equally identifiable by race. Such racism was not all that polite and ought to be recognized as such.

Moreover, such openness to the case for Eyre appears to have been a long-standing Sidgwickian position. At the very time when Mill was working for the Jamaica Committee, when Sidgwick was supposedly a younger and more radically Millian figure, Sidgwick confided to his mother that although all of his friends (this would have included such figures as T. H. Green and A. V. Dicey) were joining the committee, he could not make up his mind on the matter.[273] There is in fact no record of his having departed from that agnostic stance. Rather, he was apt to complain, at that time, about Mill's influence waning because of the public displays of his radicalism. And in his own defense, he might well have been able to invoke Mill's own (earlier) words, from *The Principles of Political Economy*:

> To civilize a savage, he must be inspired with new wants and desires, even if not of a very elevated kind, provided that their gratification can be a motive to steady and regular bodily and mental exertion. If the negroes of Jamaica and Demerara, after their emancipation had contented themselves, as it was predicted they would do, with the necessaries of life, and abandoned all labour beyond the little which in a tropical climate, with a thin population and abundance of the richest land, is sufficient to support existence, they would have sunk into a condition more barbarous, though less unhappy, than their previous state of slavery. The motive which was most relied on for inducing them to work was their love of fine clothes and personal ornaments. No one will stand up for this taste as worthy of being cultivated, and in most societies its indulgence tends to impoverish rather than to enrich; but in the state of mind of the negroes it might have been the only incentive that could make them voluntarily undergo systematic labour, and so acquire or maintain habits of voluntary industry which may be converted to more valuable ends. In England, it is not the desire of wealth that needs to be taught, but the use of wealth, and appreciation of the objects of desire which wealth cannot purchase, or for attaining which it is not required. Every real improvement in the character of the English, whether it consist in giving them higher aspirations, or only a juster estimate of the value of their present objects of desire, must necessarily moderate the ardour of their devotion to the pursuit of wealth.[274]

Here again the somewhat paradoxical point—that the Jamaicans supposedly need a more stringent materialistic work ethic to bring them to the civilizational level of the English, who need to get over their materialistic work ethic—suggests how far from innocent Mill's use of the notions of civilization and barbarism really was. Sidgwick would have had a case for claiming that the older Mill's criticisms of Carlyle obscured their potential points of agreement. And after all, Mill and Sidgwick were as convinced as Carlyle that, in Hall's words, "colonization could provide a key to a better world," however much they differed from him in the grounds for such convictions.[275]

Of course, it can be argued that, like Mill, Sidgwick "did a great deal to defend some of the accomplishments of other historical civilizations, that he thought nurture far more important than nature in determining human differences, and that he was mainly impressed by European achievements in science and constitutional government." But this, as remarked earlier, does not do justice to the forms of nineteenth-century racism, which often did blend biological and ethnic notions in conceptions of race as deployed in assessing the capacity for self-government. To again cite Fredrickson:

> Nativists seeking to restrict immigration from eastern and southern Europe stressed an association between a capacity for self-government and Anglo-Saxon, Anglo-American, or Nordic (not simply white or European) ancestry. Hence the United States was not immune from its own variety of ethnic nationalism. But what the right kind of people inherited from their ancestors was the capacity to be liberal or democratic in the manner prescribed by the Enlightenment and the founding fathers. In Germany, *volkisch* nationalism was explicitly promoted as antithetical to liberalism and the heritage of the Enlightenment, and it had relatively weak opposition from those who sought to make the national project a prototype for humanity as a whole or even a large segment of it.[276]

In short, an emphasis on certain European civilizational contributions to self-government is not, in this context, all that reassuring, since such a construction often served quite obviously racist purposes.

If Sidgwick's notions of race, civilization, etc., seem worrisome in this respect, it should be noted again that the Millian notion of "blood" was no more or less incoherent, and in both cases, their agnosticism about the determinants of "nature" got washed out at the practical political level, where the "character" of the "savages"—the stunted trees, whose growth had been "retarded"—was immutable enough for purposes of maintaining colonial rule and de facto racial segregation and domination. More theorizing went into the problem of who was fit for manual labor than how to grant self-rule. This form of racism was perfectly consistent with support for abolitionism, the cause of the North in the American Civil War.

Thus, when it comes to matters of race and imperialism, there are deeply problematic sides to both Mill and Sidgwick, and the leaders of the resistance in Jamaica and other countries would and could have effectively labeled them as racist in the equivalent terminology of the day.[277]

But it is importantly illustrative of how the times were changing that one cannot quite find in Mill the type of perspective that one finds in, say, the work of Sidgwick's friend Charles Henry Pearson. Born in 1830, Pearson, who had studied at King's College, London, under F. D. Maurice, and at Oriel College, Oxford, would go on to become education minister in Victoria, Australia, and a stalwart of the Liberal Party in general. He was brought to Cambridge by Sidgwick just at the time of the latter's resignation, when the changes in the curriculum meant that Sidgwick would no longer have to teach history as part of the Moral Sciences. They would work together closely for two years and correspond for many years afterward, and Sidgwick even came to think and hope that in the mid-1870s Pearson would receive a professorship in history. Sidgwick thought very highly of him, and in a telling review, which appeared in the *National Review* in 1894, he warmly praised Pearson's *National Life and Character*:

> I will begin by remarking that prophecies are not always put forward, even by the most highly educated prophets, as based on a scientific grasp of the laws of social evolution. Indeed, in the most impressive book of a prophetic nature which has appeared in England for many years—I mean Pearson's *National Life and Character*—the prophecies are not announced with any such pretensions; they always rest on a simply empirical basis, and only distinguish themselves from the common run of such forecasts by the remarkably wide and full knowledge of relevant historical facts which the writer shows, and the masterly skill with which the facts are selected and grouped. His predictions are almost always interesting and sometimes, I think, reach a degree of probability sufficient to give them a real practical value.[278]

The distressing thing about this encomium is that Pearson's book was concerned to make such arguments as the following, in which Mill's worries about the loss of cultural vitality get transmuted into a Nietzschean mode, not that one would ever guess it from Sidgwick's review:

> Summing up, then, we seem to find that we are slowly but demonstrably approaching what we may regard as the age of reason or of a sublimated humanity; and that this will give us a great deal that we are expecting from it—well-ordered polities, security to labour, education, freedom from gross superstitions, improved health and longer life, the destruction of privilege in society and of caprice in family life, better guarantees for the peace of the world, and enforced regard for life and

property when war unfortunately breaks out. It is possible to conceive the administration of the most advanced states so equitable and efficient that no one will even desire seriously to disturb it. On the other hand, it seems reasonable to assume that religion will gradually pass into a recognition of ethical precepts and a graceful habit of morality; that the mind will occupy itself less and less with works of genius, and more and more with trivial results and ephemeral discussions; that husband and wife, parents and children, will come to mean less to one another; that romantic feeling will die out in consequence; that the old will increase on the young; that two great incentives to effort, the desire to use power for noble ends, and the desire to be highly esteemed, will come to promise less to capable men as the field of human energy is crowded; and generally that the world will be left without deep convictions or enthusiasm, without the regenerating influence of the ardour for political reform and the fervor of pious faith which have quickened men for centuries past as nothing else has quickened them, with a passion purifying the soul. It would clearly be unreasonable to murmur at changes that express the realization by the world of its highest thought, whether the issue be good or bad. The etiolated religion which it seems likely we shall subside upon; the complicated but on the whole satisfactory State mechanism, that will prescribe education, limit industry, and direct enjoyment, will become, when they are once arrived at, natural and satisfactory. The decline of the higher classes as an influence in society, the organization of the inferior races throughout the Tropical Zone, are the natural result of principles that we cannot disown if we would. It would be impossible for a conservatively-minded monarch to reconstruct the nobility of the eighteenth century in the twentieth; and even now no practical statesman could dream of arresting Chinese power or Hindoo or negro expansion by wholesale massacres. The world is becoming too fibreless, too weak, too good to contemplate or to carry out great changes which imply lamentable suffering. It trusts more and more to experience, less and less to insight and will.[279]

The tone here may be reminiscent of Carlyle on heroism, but Pearson was an admirer of Nietzsche and Ibsen, and he fretted endlessly about the fate of a society of weak men, a society that "has no purpose beyond supplying the day's needs, and amusing the day's vacuity." What has such a society "to do with the terrible burden of personality"? But there "seems no reason why men of this kind should not perpetuate the race, increasing and multiplying till every rod of earth maintains its man, and the savour of vacant lives will go up to God from every home."

There are Millian thoughts in such lines, about a stationary state of society, character development, and ethology, but they have been adapted to a more explicitly racist purpose. For Pearson, the human predicament has everything to do with race:

> Even during historical times, so-called, the world has mostly been peopled by races, either like the negro very little raised above the level of brutes, or at best, like the lower-caste Hindoo and the Chinaman, of such secondary intelligence as to have added nothing permanent to our stock of ideas. At this moment, though the civilized and progressive races have till quite recently been increasing upon the inferior types, and though the lowest forms of all are being exterminated, there seems, as we have seen, good warrant for assuming that the advantage has already passed to the lower forms of humanity, and indeed it appears to be a well-ascertained law that the races which care little for comfort and decency are bound to tide over bad times better than their superiors, and that the classes which reach the highest standard are proportionally short-lived. Nay, so profusely is life given to excess of what we can account the efficient use made of it, so many purposeless generations seem to pass away before humanity is in travail of a prophet or a thinker, that some inquirers have actually defined the method of creation as a law of waste.[280]

Pearson is willing to console his readers with invocations of the Norse "twilight of the gods" as the possible future, when, although there may be a "temporary eclipse of the higher powers," even the losing struggle is a kind of vindication. As the Nietzschean thought continues:

> We are so accustomed to the fierce rapture of struggle and victory, to that rough training of necessity by which the weak are destroyed, to revolutions of the political order, transferences of power and wealth, and discoveries in science, that we can hardly conceive a quiet old age of humanity, in which it may care only for sunshine and food and quiet, and expect nothing great from the toil of hand or thought. . . . It is now more than probable that our science, our civilization, our great and real advance in the practice of government are only bringing us nearer to the day when the lower races will predominate in the world, when the higher races will lose their noblest elements, when we shall ask nothing from the day but to live, nor from the future but that we may not deteriorate. Even so, there will still remain to us ourselves. Simply to do our work in life, and to abide the issue, if we stand erect before the eternal calm as cheerfully as our father faced the eternal unrest, may be nobler training for our souls than the faith in progress.[281]

Pearson's passionate racism can make Sidgwick's concern with colonization and manual labor look singularly suspicious, as though his doubts about progress and faith in federation and the "Concert of Europe" might have

reflected an all-too-conservative faith in a saving remnant of civilization holding out again the peril of the "lower races." After all, his views on the difficulty
of determining what made for scientific and cultural change and development
certainly left a very wide field for alternative explanations, such as Pearson's.
And it is all too clear what Pearson has in mind, given his account of the attitudes that he deems overly complacent:

> No one, of course, assumes that the Aryan race—to use a convenient
> term—can stamp out or starve out all their rivals on the face of the
> earth. It is self-evident that the Chinese, the Japanese, the Hindoos,
> if we may apply this general term to the various natives of India, and
> the African negro, are too numerous and sturdy to be extirpated. It is
> against the fashion of modern humanity to wish that they should suffer
> decrease or oppression. What is assumed is that the first three of these
> races will remain stationary within their present limits, while the negro
> will contribute an industrial population to the states which England
> and Germany will build up along the Congo or the Zambesi. The white
> man in these parts of the world is to be the planter, the mine-owner, the
> manufacturer, the merchant, and the leading employee under all these,
> contributing energy and capital to the new countries, while the negro
> is to be the field-hand, the common miner, and the factory operative.
> Here and there, in exceptional districts, the white man will predomi-
> nate in numbers, but everywhere he will govern and direct in virtue of
> a higher intelligence and more resolute will.[282]

Pearson is insistent that the "character of a race determines its vitality
more than climate," and he strikes a pessimistic, alarmist note, arguing that
the day will come when the globe is "girdled with a continuous zone of the
black and yellow races, no longer too weak for aggression or under tutelage,
but independent, or practically so. . . . The citizens of these countries will then
be taken up into the social relations of the white races, will throng the English
turf, or the salons of Paris, and will be admitted to intermarriage. It is idle to
say, that if all this should come to pass our pride of place will not be humili-
ated." As Pearson elaborates on this vision, those who had been struggling "for
supremacy in a world which we thought of as destined to belong to the Aryan
races and to the Christian faith" will wake up to find themselves "elbowed
and hustled, and perhaps even thrust aside by peoples whom we looked down
upon as servile, and thought of as bound always to minister to our needs."
Against the "solitary consolation" that the changes were "inevitable," he con-
fesses that "in some of us the feeling of caste is so strong that we are not sorry
to think we shall have passed away before that day arrives."[283]

It is not surprising that in Australia Pearson fanned fears of "the Yellow
Peril," the Chinese workers who could swamp the white laborers of the country, or that he cited with approval the racist American laws restricting Chinese

immigration. As Sidgwick put it, Pearson seemed to envision, and fear, how "the human world would gradually become mainly yellow, with a black band round the tropics, and perhaps an aristocratic film of white on the surface!"[284]

In his contribution to *Charles Henry Pearson: Memorials by Himself, His Wife, and His Friends*, Sidgwick makes it all too clear not only that he knew Pearson very well and thought very highly of him, but also that he had long known of his most provocative views: "Though I had much interesting talk with him on these subjects, the impression derived there from has become, in the main blended with or obliterated by the impression derived . . . from his remarkable book on "National Life and Character" . . . [as] many of the startling conclusions of that book were certainly held by him at the earlier date, though his tendency to pessimistic forecast seemed to me to have grown stronger in the interval."[285] Of the book, Sidgwick had written to Pearson: "I am much obliged to you for sending me your book which I am reading with much interest. When I find myself too depressed by it, I console myself by thinking that sociology is not yet an exact science, so that the powers of prediction possessed by the wisest intellect are limited. / I am glad to see that the reviews are giving you justice—so far as I see them."[286] Sidgwick's own review primarily objected to the underdeveloped state of the social sciences.

Whatever Millian agnosticism Sidgwick may have shared concerning innate racial differences, his agnosticism was apparently broad enough to credit in the strongest terms Pearson's claims about race and national character, and the possibility that greater knowledge in this area would provide deep cause for concern about the direction of civilization. The sweeping optimism of Comtean Positivism, or even of a Herbert Spencer or a Marx, never captured Sidgwick, and his anxieties about the future of civilization and its possible degeneration were often inflected with Pearsonian thoughts. After all, he did allow that if evidence of racial "debasement" from interracial marriage were forthcoming, then segregation should be maintained, as it should also be in cases where the "inferior races" supplied most of the manual labor. And he harbored too few doubts that "[c]ivilised nations, so long as they are independent, have to fight; and, in performance of their legitimate business—for it is their legitimate business on utilitarian principles—of civilizing the world, they have to commit acts which cannot but be regarded as aggressive by the savage nations whom it is their business to educate and absorb."[287] Such views were also given voice by his brother-in-law Arthur Balfour. Balfour worried publicly that if cultural advance in Europe "is some day exhausted, who can believe that there remains any external source from which it can be renewed? Where are the untried races competent to construct out of the ruined fragments of our civilization a new and better habitation for the spirit of man?" His answer was: "They do not exist; and if the world is again to be buried under a barbaric flood, it will not be like that which fertilized, though it first destroyed, the western provinces of Rome, but like that which in Asia submerged forever the last traces of Hellenic culture."[288] Power and prejudice, it seems, came with severe anxiety attacks and no little depression. And that this was part of what animated the Sidgwicks' work in education would be difficult to deny; possibly it animated "The Plan" as well.

The Serious Problem

What emerges from the previous two chapters is this: neither the Sidgwicks nor the Mills had anything like the science of ethology (or sociology and psychology) that they clearly needed, except to some degree in the cases of sex and gender. Although it is true that both had extensive psychological interests in the structure of character—Mill in associationism, Sidgwick in parapsychology—and developed some very sophisticated twists on the research they analyzed, each was ultimately left with little more than a promissory note that a viable account of character formation and identity might be forthcoming in the future. And the redemption of that promissory note would be crucial to redeeming the hedonism that they favored. Like Godwin, they were looking ahead to a long period of social experimentation, much of which would take place with family and community relations. And although they were properly agnostic in some areas, in others their agnosticism was but a reflection of racial and ethnic or civilizational prejudice.

In the case of the Sidgwicks, however, there was a far more anxious view of the fate of civilization. Their potential for pessimism about the progress of humanity went far beyond Mill's, and could lend itself in a supportive way to the exceedingly weird efforts of the Sidgwick Group, which grew even weirder following Henry's death.[289] That such pillars of the political establishment should find their highest calling in "The Plan" suggests a perspective on civilization and politics that betrays some desperate anxieties. Godwin's memorials and Bentham's Auto-Iconism look sane by comparison. And the dualism of practical reason was part and parcel of the death of God—and of reason—that boded ill for a humanity confronting the "barbarism" of the "savage races." For Sidgwick, "dissolution of the existing social order" was a serious threat and cause for anxiety, not a philosopher's academic puzzle case.

Consequently, perhaps some will argue that after Henry's death, Eleanor was thinking along lines he might have found congenial. He obviously had been very concerned about the decline of the religious outlook and was very sympathetic to the call for enthusiastic and inspiring ethical teachers and, in effect, a new, less superstitious, more rational religion, the better to overcome the social conflict and Machiavellianism too prevalent in the modern world. He had, after all, initially been quite enthusiastic about the Theosophical Society, until, at his behest, the S.P.R. investigated and debunked it. There is also a rather literal esotericism about the whole scheme that makes the abstract defense of esoteric morality in the *Methods* seem eerily relevant, as though this were one way to pursue that line of thought that would have come quite naturally to Sidgwick and his circle. Sensitive mediumship and its interpretation might, like refined utilitarian calculation, be the province of the few. And certainly, there was considerably Orientalism at work in the prejudices of the psychical researchers, who would disproportionately discount evidence from "Orientals" and others they dismissed as of a lower civilizational level.

It is intriguing that Sidgwick's later biblical textual mottos were, from 1875 to 1890, "But this one thing I do forgetting those things which are behind, and reaching forth unto those things that are before, I press toward the mark for the prize of the high calling of God in Christ Jesus" (Paul, Phillipians 3.13–14) and "Gather up the fragments that remain, that nothing be lost" (John 6.12). The last refers to the aftermath of the miracle of the loaves and fishes, and suggests that he had high expectations for psychical research.

Still, at least in the published works of the Sidgwick who is taken to have died in 1900, there is a much more resolutely critical stance running through his work. However obvious it may be from his psychical research that Sidgwick was profoundly critical of a materialist metaphysics, and engaged sympathetically with a complex depth psychological account of the self and personal identity that shared much with that of his greatly admired friends Myers, Symonds, and James—and this much in the fashion of recent defenders of parapsychology—his academic philosophical work tended to be more committed to elaborate and very acute critiques of Spencer's evolutionism, Kantian transcendentalism, Hegelianism, the Idealism of Green and Bradley, and so on. In an illustrative case, against Green's fundamental tactic for establishing a spiritual principle in nature, he argued that the "argument seems to me unthinkable, because, as Green has emphatically declared, I cannot even conceive the manifold things out of the relations: and therefore I cannot even raise the question whether, if I could so conceive them, I should see them to require something other than themselves to bring them into relations."290 Sidgwick suggested that Green would never "seriously trouble himself with Materialism," and was not therefore a source for truly effective anti-materialist arguments.

This is not to deny that his hope really was that future generations would also represent a or would see a continued evolution in human nature, with a Millian—even Godwinian—growth of the sympathetic capabilities that would reduce social conflict and support high-minded forms of ethical socialism and cooperativism, such that people would be more motivated to do their part for society rather than merely advance their own interests in any narrow sense. It is only to admit that, as he himself complained, he was "condemned to criticize." And his political philosophy admittedly assumed the utilitarian criterion as the normative bottom line, rather than arguing for it against rational egoism or other positions, which makes the political valence of Sidgwick's work hard to gauge. Suspicious of democracy and warm to the need for a cultural "clerisy" or vanguard of educated opinion, Sidgwick in his politics tended more to reflect, albeit somewhat obliquely, the anxieties that found expression in the dualism of practical reason, as in that concern with how to supply teachers or public moralists "to correct the erroneous and short-sighted views of self-interest, representing it as divergent from duty, which certainly appear to be widely prevalent in the most advanced societies, at least among irreligious persons."[291]

But Sidgwick was also insightful enough to worry that the failure of ethical philosophy and philosophy in general indicated that his civilization as a whole was in something akin to the position of the hypocritical clergy, who when accused of "solemn imposture" would be unable to refute the charge. If he was a "Government House" utilitarian of some sort, he was not a very confident one, even when he was no longer in despair over the failures of psychical research. As his contributions to the Cambridge and London Ethical Societies demonstrate, he also harbored doubts about just how those public moralists might be able to perform their function, how they would find the common ethical ground or public reason that could render them effective; the philosophical elite might not be as all-seeing as he had hoped:

> If we are to frame an ideal of good life for all, and to show how a unity of moral spirit and principle may manifest itself through the diversity of actions and forbearances, efforts and endurances, which the diversity of social functions render necessary—we can only do this by a comprehensive and varied knowledge of the actual opportunities and limitations. The actual needs and temptations, the actually constraining customs and habits, desires and fears, of all the different species of that 'general man' who, as Browning says, 'receives life in parts to live in a whole.' And this knowledge a philosopher—whose personal experience is often very limited—cannot adequately attain unless he earnestly avails himself of opportunities of learning from the experience of men of other callings. But, secondly, even supposing him to have used these opportunities to the full, the philosopher's practical judgment on particular problems of duty is liable to be untrustworthy, unless it is aided and controlled by the practical judgment of others who are not philosophers.[292]

If only the Sidgwicks had pursued the thought beyond their own familiar racial and ethnic comfort zones. But then, Anglo-American philosophy still invites some such critique, and the practical and experimental deployment of Experience Machines remains an armchair exercise.

Yet at least in this somewhat limited sense, in the end, education and ethics were always at the heart of Sidgwick's work, and Eleanor's, even when proclaiming their common failures as they tackled, in the strangest of ways, the "deepest problems" of human life. If they rendered the utilitarian project more problematic on some fronts, they also left it more healthily reflective and self-doubting on others. Happiness, pleasure and pain, the growth of character or self-cultivation, the reconciliation of one's own Good with the Good of all, indeed, virtually all the core concerns of the great utilitarians— these had now become open-ended research projects, best pursued by bold experiments in living underwritten by a fearless, open, and many-sided liberal education. As they had in the past, the philosopher-poets looked to the future.

Appendix 1

The two elements of Mill's view which I am accustomed to distinguish as Psychological Hedonism [that each man does seek his own Happiness] and Ethical Hedonism [that each man ought to seek the general Happiness] both attracted me, and I did not at first perceive their incoherence.

Psychological Hedonism—-the law of universal pleasure-seeking—-attracted me by its frank naturalness. Ethical Hedonism, as expounded by Mill, was morally inspiring by its dictate of readiness for absolute self-sacrifice. They appealed to different elements of my nature, but they brought these into apparent harmony: they both used the same words "pleasure," "happiness," and the persuasiveness of Mill's exposition veiled for a time the profound discrepancy between the natural end of action—-private happiness, and the end of duty—-general happiness. Or if a doubt assailed me as to the coincidence of private and general happiness, I was inclined to hold that it ought to be cast to the winds by a generous resolution.

But a sense grew upon me that this method of dealing with the conflict between Interest and Duty, though perhaps proper for practice could not be final for philosophy. For practical men who do not philosophise, the maxim of subordinating self-interest, as commonly conceived, to "altruistic" impulses and sentiments which they feel to be higher and nobler is, I doubt not, a commendable maxim; but it is surely the business of Ethical Philosophy to find and make explicit the rational ground of such action.

I therefore set myself to examine methodically the relation of Interest and Duty.

This involved a careful study of Egoistic Method, to get the relation of Interest and Duty clear. Let us suppose that my own Interest is paramount. What really is my Interest, how far can acts conducive to it be known, how far does the result correspond with Duty (or Wellbeing of Mankind)? This investigation led me to feel very strongly *this* opposition, rather than that which Mill and the earlier Utilitarians felt between so-called Intuitions or Moral Sense Perceptions, and Hedonism, whether Epicurean or Utilitarian. Hence the arrangement of my book-ii., iii., iv. [Book ii. Egoism, Book iii. Intuitionism, Book iv. Utilitarianism].

The result was that I concluded that no complete solution of the conflict between my happiness and the general happiness was possible on the basis of mundane experience. This [conclusion I] slowly and reluctantly accepted—-cf. Book ii. chap. v., and last chapter of treatise [Book ii. chap. v. is on "Happiness and Duty", and the concluding chapter is on "The Mutual Relations of the Three Methods"]. This [was] most important to me.

In consequence of this perception, moral choice of the general happiness or acquiescence in self-interest as ultimate, became practically necessary. But on what ground?

I put aside Mill's phrases that such sacrifice was "heroic": that it was not "well" with me unless I was in a disposition to make it. I put to him in my mind the dilemma:—-Either it is for my own happiness or it is not. If not, why [should I do it]? It was no use to say that if I was a moral hero I should have formed a habit of willing actions beneficial to others which would remain in force, even with my own pleasure in the other scale. I knew that at any rate I was not the kind of moral hero who does this without reason; from *blind* habit. Nor did I even wish to be that kind of hero: for it seemed to me that that kind of hero, however admirable, was certainly not a philosopher. I must somehow see that it was right for me to sacrifice my happiness for the good of the whole of which I am a part.

Thus, in spite of my early aversion to Intuitional Ethics, derived from the study of Whewell, and in spite of my attitude of discipleship to Mill, I was forced to recognise the need of a fundamental ethical intuition.

The utilitarian method—-which I had learnt from Mill—-could not, it seemed to me, be made coherent and harmonious without this fundamental intuition.

In this state of mind I read Kant's Ethics again: I had before read it somewhat unintelligently, under the influence of Mill's view as to its "grotesque failure". I now read it more receptively and was impressed with the truth and importance of its fundamental principle:—-*Act from a principle or maxim that you can will to be a universal law*—-cf. Book iii. chap. i. §3 [of *The Methods of Ethics*]. It threw the "golden rule" of the gospel ("Do unto others as ye would that others should do unto you") into a form that commended itself to my reason.

Kant's resting of morality on Freedom did not indeed commend itself to me, though I did not at first see, what I now seem to see clearly, that it involves the fundamental confusion of using "freedom" in two distinct senses—-"freedom" that is realised only when we do right, when reason triumphs over inclination, and "freedom" that is realised equally when we choose to do wrong, and which is apparently implied in the notion of ill-desert. What commended itself to me, in short, was Kant's ethical principle rather than its metaphysical basis. This I briefly explain in Book iii. chap. i. §3 [of *The Methods of Ethics*]. I shall go into it at more length when we come to Kant.

That whatever is right for me must be right for all persons in similar circumstances—which was the form in which I accepted the Kantian maxim—seemed to me certainly fundamental, certainly true, and not without practical importance.

But the fundamental principle seemed to me inadequate for the construction of a system of duties; and the more I reflected on it the more inadequate it appeared.

On reflection it did not seem to me really to meet the difficulty which had led me from Mill to Kant: it did not settle finally the subordination of Self-Interest to Duty.

For the Rational Egoist—-a man who had learnt from Hobbes that Self-preservation is the first law of Nature and Self-interest the only rational basis of social morality—-and in fact, its actual basis, so far as it is effective—-such a thinker might accept the Kantian principle and remain an Egoist.

He might say, "I quite admit that when the painful necessity comes for another man to choose between his own happiness and the general happiness, he must as a reasonable being prefer his own, *i.e.* it is right for him to do this on my principle. No doubt, as I probably do not sympathise with him in particular any more than with other persons, I as a disengaged spectator should like him to sacrifice himself to the general good: but I do not expect him to do it, any more than I should do it myself in his place."

It did not seem to me that this reasoning could be effectively confuted. No doubt it was, from the point of view of the universe, reasonable to prefer the greater good to the lesser, even though the lesser good was the private happiness of the agent. Still, it seemed to me also undeniably reasonable for the individual to prefer his own. The rationality of self-regard seemed to me as undeniable as the rationality of self-sacrifice. I could not give up this conviction, though neither of my masters, neither Kant nor Mill, seemed willing to admit it: in different ways, each in his own way, they refused to admit it.

I was, therefore, [if] I may so say, a disciple on the loose, in search of a master—or, if the term "master" be too strong, at any rate I sought for sympathy and support, in the conviction which I had attained in spite of the opposite opinions of the thinkers from whom I had learnt most.

It was at this point then that the influence of Butler came in. For the stage at which I had thus arrived in search of an ethical creed, at once led me to understand Butler, and to find the support and intellectual sympathy that I required in his view.

I say to understand him, for hitherto I had misunderstood him, as I believe most people then misunderstood, and perhaps still misunderstand, him. He had been presented to me as an advocate of the authority of Conscience; and his argument, put summarily, seemed to be that because reflection on our impulses showed us Conscience claiming authority therefore we ought to obey it. Well, I had no doubt that my conscience claimed authority, though it was a more utilitarian conscience than Butler's: for, through all this search for principles I still adhered for practical purposes to the doctrine I had learnt from Mill, *i.e.* I still held to the maxim of aiming at the general happiness as the supreme directive rule of conduct, and I thought I could answer the objections that Butler brought against this view (in the "Dissertation on Virtue" at the end of the *Analogy*). My difficulty was, as I have said, that this claim of conscience, whether utilitarian or not, had to be harmonised with the claim of Rational Self-love; and that I vaguely supposed Butler to avoid or override [the latter claim].

But reading him at this stage with more care, I found in him, with pleasure and surprise, a view very similar to that which had developed itself in my own mind in struggling to assimilate Mill and Kant. I found he expressly admitted that "interest, my own happiness, is a manifest obligation", and that "Reasonable Self-love" [is "one of the two chief or superior principles in the nature of man"]. That is, he recognised a "Dualism of the Governing Faculty"—or as I prefer to say "Dualism of the Practical Reason," since the 'authority' on which Butler laid stress must present itself to my mind as the authority of reason, before I can admit it.

Of this more presently: what I now wish to make clear is that it was on this side—if I may so say—-that I entered into Butler's system and came under the influence of his powerful and cautious intellect. But the effect of his influence carried me a further step away from Mill: for I was led by it to abandon the doctrine of Psychological Hedonism, and to recognise the existence of "disinterested" or "extra-regarding" impulses to action, [impulses] not directed towards the agent's pleasure [cf. chap iv. of Book i. of *The Methods of Ethics*]. In fact as regards what I may call a Psychological basis of Ethics, I found myself much more in agreement with Butler than Mill.

And this led me to reconsider my relation to Intuitional Ethics. The strength and vehemence of Butler's condemnation of pure Utilitarianism, in so cautious a writer, naturally impressed me much. And I had myself become, as I had to admit to myself, an Intuitionist to a certain extent. For the supreme rule of aiming at the general happiness, as I had come to see, must rest on a fundamental moral intuition, if I was to recognise it as binding at all. And in reading the writings of the earlier English Intuitionists, More and Clarke, I found the axiom I required for my Utilitarianism [that a rational agent is bound to aim at Universal Happiness], in one form or another, holding a prominent place (cf. *History of Ethics*, pp. 172, 181).

I had then, theoretically as well as practically, accepted this fundamental moral intuition; and there was also the Kantian principle, which I recognised as irresistibly valid, though not adequate to give complete guidance.—-I was then an "intuitional" moralist to this extent: and if so, why not further? The orthodox moralists such as Whewell (then in vogue) said that there was a whole intelligible system of intuitions: but how were they to be learnt? I could not accept Butler's view as to the sufficiency of a plain man's conscience: for it appeared to me that plain men agreed rather verbally than really.

In this state of mind I had to read Aristotle again; and a light seemed to dawn upon me as to the meaning and drift of his procedure—-especially in Books ii., iii., iv. of the *Ethics*—-(cf. *History of Ethics*, chap. ii. §9, p. 58, read to end of section).

What he gave us there was the Common Sense Morality of Greece, reduced to consistency by careful comparison: given not as something external to him but as what "we"—-he and others—-think, ascertained by reflection. And was not this really the Socratic induction, elicited by interrogation? Might I not imitate this: do the same for our morality here and now, in the same manner of impartial reflection on current opinion?

Indeed ought I not to do this before deciding on the question whether I had or had not a system of moral intuitions? At any rate the result would be useful, whatever conclusion I came to.

So this was the part of my book first written (Book iii., chaps. i—xi.), and a certain imitation of Aristotle's manner was very marked in it at first, and though I have tried to remove it where it seemed to me affected or pedantic, it still remains to some extent.

But the result of the examination was to bring out with fresh force and vividness the difference between the maxims of Common Sense Morality (even the strongest and strictest, *e.g.* Veracity and Good Faith) and the intuitions which I had already attained, i.e. the Kantian Principle (of which I now saw the only certain element in Justice—-"treat similar cases similarly"—-to be a particular application), and the Fundamental Principle of Utilitarianism. And this latter was in perfect harmony with the Kantian Principle. I certainly could will it to be a universal law that men should act in such a way as to promote universal happiness; in fact it was the only law that it was perfectly clear to me that I could thus decisively will, from a universal point of view.

I was then a Utilitarian again, but on an Intuitional basis.

But further, the reflection on Common Sense Morality which I had gone through, had continually brought home to me its character as a system of rules tending to the promotion of general happiness (cf. [*Methods of Ethics*] pp. 470, 471).

Also the previous reflection on hedonistic method for Book ii. had shown me its weaknesses. What was then to be done? [The] conservative attitude [to be observed] towards Common Sense [is] given in chapter v. of Book iv.: "Adhere generally, deviate and attempt reform only in exceptional cases in which,—notwithstanding the roughness of hedonistic method,—-the argument against Common Sense is decisive."

In this state of mind I published my book: I tried to say what I had found: that the opposition between Utilitarianism and Intuitionism was due to a misunderstanding. There was indeed a fundamental opposition between the individual's interest and either morality, which I could not solve by any method I had yet found trustworthy, without the assumption of the moral government of the world: so far I agreed with both Butler and Kant.

But I could find no real opposition between Intuitionism and Utilitarianism. . . . The Utilitarianism of Mill and Bentham seemed to me to want a basis: that basis could only be supplied by a fundamental intuition; on the other hand the best examination I could make of the Morality of Common Sense showed me no clear and self-evident principles except such as were perfectly consistent with Utilitarianism.

Still, investigation of the Utilitarian method led me to see defects [in it]: the merely empirical examination of the consequences of actions is unsatisfactory, and being thus conscious of the practical imperfection in many cases of the guidance of the Utilitarian calculus, I remained anxious to treat with respect, and make use of, the guidance afforded by Common Sense in these cases, on the ground of the general presumption which evolution afforded that moral sentiments and opinions would point to conduct conducive to general happiness; though I could not admit this presumption as a ground for overruling a strong probability of the opposite, derived from utilitarian calculations.

CONFRONTING THE WORST can reveal the best. In the end, the lives and works of the great utilitarians can continue to inspire us, even given our candid awareness of all their warty complexity and compromised historical circumstances. Decorous academic evasion of charged issues only compromises our efforts to learn from the "illustrious dead"; it does not strengthen them.

This book has not been overly obsessed with rehearsing the familiar (and too often tedious, misguided, and inconclusive) objections to utilitarianism, such as John Rawls's famous claim, in *A Theory of Justice*, that utilitarianism ignores the differences between persons. Or at least, it has not rehearsed them in the familiar ways—the larger objective has been to open up doubts and possibilities for different readings of the classical utilitarians, both positive and negative, and to do so in what is now a relatively unfamiliar way, though my approach is in fact highly indebted to Godwin and Mill. They, and the others considered here, were not ones to separate the reasons—or the pleasures and pains—from the persons, but were forever engaged in tackling both together, in often breathtaking visions of a future of maximally happy beings who had through education and personal growth in a many-sided and comprehensive fashion achieved their utilitarian potential. Their practice often revealed their preaching, or better, their philosophizing. If, in certain important contexts, some of them failed to heed the better thinking of their own philosophical inheritance, their errors, injustices, and eccentricities may for all that also provide important lessons for the present, when the problems of racism, empire, prejudice, inequality, domination, supernaturalism, religious bigotry, fragmented selves, and sinister interests remain in troubling profusion. Truth and reconciliation, not evasion, mark the arc of justice, in philosophy as in politics.

There are always grave risks attached to the exercise of original thought and creative imagination, of philosophy and poetry as the great utilitarians exemplified them. That they sparked as much good as they did, advanced the reforms that they did, and provided the very instruments for the critique of their own ethical and political failings in the way that they did, must be considered grounds for rescuing them from the "enormous condescension of posterity," as E. P. Thompson put it in that famous expression that he never applied to the utilitarians. Arguably, if today we were to follow the lead of the great utilitarians, a decent education for all would be more of a priority, and the world would be less cruel. If the leading colleges and universities of our world were to follow the recommendations of Mill and Sidgwick, they would be much more humanities oriented than they are. They would be more keenly alert to the need for the ongoing exploration of creative experiments in living, of fostering personal growth as well as active and reflective citizens, and of the dangers posed by pressures to conform to massive structures of institutional power, corporate or governmental. The fusion of egoism and benevolence, self and other, and the fostering of sympathetic unity with fellow creatures would be a much greater priority than it is. The "empathy deficit" resulting from the technological innovations of recent decades would be confronted for what it is, a severe challenge to human recognition and sociability.[1] The value of meaningful dialogue and a robust public sphere would be more forcefully advanced. And disconnection from the natural world—and the human one— would be cause for even more anxious worry than it is. Economic measures of growth and efficiency would be exposed for the deeply prejudiced measures that they are, for failing, for example, to consider or count the well-being of nonhuman animals and future generations in calculations of optimality.[2] And economics and the other social sciences would be challenged to do more to eliminate poverty, reduce crime and punitive incarceration, and promote the equality of women. Philosophy itself would be more relevant, more diverse, more interdisciplinary—and far less gendered.

Of course, one challenge to any such perspective might be to this effect:

> The humanist core of 'Man'—namely the universal powers of reason, self-regulating moral inclinations and a set of preferred discursive and spiritual values—asserts an ideal of mental and bodily perfection. Together, they spell out a political ontology that combines belief in human uniqueness with enduring faith in a teleologically ordained view of rational progress through scientific and cultural development manifested in European history. This model not only set standards for individuals but also for whole supranational cultures, including a certain idea of Europe. The imperial humanism that underpinned it developed into a civilizational model, which, in turn, has shaped the idea that the West coincided uniquely with the universalizing powers of self-reflexive reason. That self-aggrandizing vision has been consolidated amidst chronic economic and political crisis. It still assumes Europe to be much more than a geopolitical location. As an expression of universal consciousness, Europe transcends its specificity and posits the conspicuous power of that transcendence as its most distinctive characteristic. It becomes a universal attribute of humanity that can invest its special character in any suitable object. The old rationale for colonialism endorsed this variety of assumption of hierarchy. It endures in contemporary projections of inter-civilizational strife and in the firmly militarized varieties of economic development in which they culminate.[3]

That such forms of imperial humanism are both a past and a present danger is all too true. Legitimate concerns about oppressive and ideologically inflected forms of universalism and humanism cannot be ignored. As Emanuel Chukwudi Eze has warned, the pursuit "of objectivity in both the physical and the moral sciences regarding race is predicated on a capacity for an ethics of critique. But this is an ethics menaced from several sides by false universalism."[4]

The story told in this book is different in important respects. The historical direction of utilitarianism had it becoming more entangled in imperialistic politics at precisely the point when it lost its foundational philosophical confidence, when it was forced to confront the incoherence of its own accounts of such fundamental notions as reason, pleasure and pain, and happiness. Sidgwick was right to worry; he revealed the "solemn imposture" of philosophers as well as parsons. He hungered after determinateness, but found only difficulties.

And his doubts have endured. The greater the research into these matters, the greater the bafflement. It is hard to read current work on, say, pain research without concluding that we are still very far indeed from fully understanding, much less appropriating for purposes of public policy, the complex mechanisms of pain and pleasure.[5] And if the previously described exchanges between Rossians like Hurka and Crisp and anti-Rossians like de Lazari-Radek and Singer are any indication, the issue of evolutionary debunking arguments will continue to generate rather than settle key ethical problems for many years to come. And this is not even to mention the contested terrain of happiness.

If the interpretations advanced in this book are apt, the great utilitarians helped sow the seeds of such doubts. They were the great precursors to the critical pragmatism of James and Dewey, figures who lend themselves to appropriation by the very critical projects represented in the work from which the above passage about imperial humanism was taken. Again, as Eze maintains, the

> postmodern pragmatist and postcolonial philosopher share commitments to certain projects: the clarification of values, especially values relevant to questions of social suffering. These sufferings often result from factors such as poverty and class division, racism and sexism, and colonial exploitation. Rather than merely developing analytical virtuosity, value pragmatism and postcolonial criticism can help to re-anchor the idea of philosophy and the practices of philosophical life in larger forms of social freedom and in conceptions of political liberty.[6]

As Sidgwick recognized, philosophy needed to work with a richer set of sources, a wider range of experiences. Philosophically, the Empire was built on sand, and the utilitarians pointed it out, even when embedded in the colonialist and imperialist practices that defined their lives. The legal profession, East India House, the cotton-spinning mills—these were admittedly the enabling institutions for the great utilitarians. But from those institutions they pushed towards something better, steadily if not always successfully, and they raised questions about the fate of human and nonhuman happiness that still call out for answers. We cannot justly or with any finality pronounce on their positions until we have better answers to those questions, and in seeking such answers, the great utilitarians still offer much guidance.

Prologue

1. See "Mary Godwin: Childhood and New Family," pp. 34–35, from *Romantic Outlaws: The Extraordinary Lives of Mary Wollstonecraft & Mary Shelley* by Charlotte Gordon, copyright © 2015 by Charlotte Gordon. Used by permission of Random House, an imprint and division of Penguin Random House LLC. All rights reserved. Any third party use of this material, outside of this publication, is prohibited. Interested parties must apply directly to Penguin Random House LLC for permission.

2. For an engaging account, see Vidal, *Burr* (New York: Vintage Books, 1973), p. 395.

Introduction

1. And this is not to mention all the other indictments, some of a more philosophical nature: that utilitarianism is and has always been mere capitalist ideology or a prop for imperialism, is wobbly at best on human rights, reduces the value of human excellence or perfection to swinish pleasure, would in fact literally support the pleasures of swine over those of humans should they be greater, would have us endlessly multiply creatures capable of adding, however minutely, to the stock of global happiness, would justify harvesting the organs of one healthy person in order to save others in need, etc. etc. As a child, Bertrand Russell, the secular godson of John Stuart Mill, was even warned that utilitarianism would have one make soup of one's dead grandmother (see "The Harm That Good Men Do," in his *Skeptical Essays* [London: Allen & Unwin, 1928], chap. 9).

2. To cite some examples, consider the dramatic shifts in Peter Singer's views, as reflected in his work with Katarzyna de Lazari-Radek, *The Point of View of the Universe: Sidgwick and Contemporary Ethics* (New York: Oxford University Press, 2014) and the book symposium devoted to it in *Etica & Politica* XVIII, No. 1 (Spring 2016), with the reply to critics, http://www2.units.it/etica/2016_1/SINGER-DE%20LAZARI%20RADEK.pdf. Over the course of his career, Singer has moved ever closer to the views of Henry Sidgwick (see chapter 4), ultimately accepting both Sidgwick's cognitivist metaethics and hedonistic account of the good. Nobel Prize–winning economist/psychologist Daniel Kahneman has also revisited classical utilitarian hedonism; see *Thinking, Fast and Slow* (New York: Farrar, Straus and Giroux, 2013). As Daniel Hausman has argued, and as later chapters will demonstrate, such reconstructions are sorely needed, both in welfare economics and more generally—see *Preference, Value, Choice, and Welfare* (New York: Cambridge University Press, 2011). But such economistic mining of classical utilitarianism is only a start, and it is a mistake to think that utilitarianism belongs in some special way to the province of economics, influential though that constituency has been.

3. For a provocative but insightful recent overview, see Roger Crisp, "Taking Stock of Utilitarianism," *Utilitas* 26(3) (September 2014), pp. 231–49. And for a short but very informative historical review, see Julia Driver, "The History of Utilitarianism," *Stanford Encyclopedia of Philosophy* (September 22, 2014), http://plato.stanford.edu/entries /utilitarianism-history/. For more extensive overviews, see Krister Bykvist, *Utilitarianism: A Guide for the Perplexed* (London: Continuum, 2010); Tim Mulgan, *Understanding Utilitarianism* (London: Routledge, 2014); Ben Eggleston and Dale E. Miller, eds., *The Cambridge Companion to Utilitarianism* (New York: Cambridge University Press, 2014);

and James Crimmins, ed., *The Bloomsbury Encyclopedia of Utilitarianism* (London: Bloomsbury Academic, 2013).

4. Virginia Woolf, "Mary Wollstonecraft," in *The Second Common Reader, Annotated Edition* (London: Harvest Books, 2003), pp. 156–63.

5. Though as the following chapters will explain, the apparent clarity of the utilitarian demand quickly dissolves in a sea of distinctions and controversies—for example, over acts, rules, or motives as the appropriate foci of utilitarian calculation, over the coherence of indirect or two-level forms of utilitarian reasoning, over the interpretation of such key notions as happiness and pleasure, and so on.

6. James Crimmins, "Bentham and Utilitarianism in the Early Nineteenth Century," in B. Eggleston and D. Miller, eds., *The Cambridge Companion to Utilitarianism* (New York: Cambridge University Press, 2014), p. 38.

7. See the perfunctory references to utilitarianism in *The Oxford Handbook of Happiness*, S. David, I. Boniwell, and A. Conley Ayers, eds. (New York: Oxford University Press, 2013). One of the happy partial exceptions here is philosopher Daniel Haybron's work *The Pursuit of Unhappiness: The Elusive Psychology of Well-Being* (Oxford: Oxford University Press, 2008), which will be discussed in later chapters. Lest there be any puzzle about the politics running through the present book, it should be admitted that my sympathies are very much in line with such works as William Davies, *The Happiness Industry: How the Government and Big Business Sold Us Well-Being* (New York: Verso, 2015). Utilitarianism requires a genuinely critical theory of happiness. Put another way, this book tries to show, controversially, how the classical utilitarians often do not fit the "eclipse of reason" critique of modernity as described by, for example, Martin Jay in *Reason after Its Eclipse: On Late Critical Theory* (Madison: University of Wisconsin Press, 2016).

8. Again, the works of Singer, both early and late, are exemplary in this respect. The impact of such works as *Animal Liberation* (New York: Harper Perennial Modern Classics, Reissue edition, 2009, originally published in 1975) and *The Life You Can Save* (New York: Random House Trade Paperbacks, Reprint edition, 2010, expanding arguments originally made by Singer in the early 1970s) has been extraordinary, leading to such developments as People for the Ethical Treatment of Animals and the effective altruism movement— see, for example, http://www.thelifeyoucansave.org/. Like Bentham, Singer questioned why the sufferings and enjoyments of nonhuman animals, sentience in general, should not count when calculating the greatest happiness; like Godwin, he questioned why individual people should not do more to aid others. In his famous illustrative case, it seems clear that one ought to rescue a small child drowning in a shallow pond, if one can do so with only minor risks and costs, such as muddying one's shoes. But, Singer asks, why not do the same in the parallel case of saving the lives of those suffering from extreme poverty, wherever they may be? Indeed, why not do the most good that you can do?

9. James Miller, *Examined Lives: From Socrates to Nietzsche* (New York: Farrar, Straus, and Giroux, 2011), p. 7. This work is deeply reflective of the perspectives of Nietzsche and Foucault.

10. See chapter 3, below. It is no exaggeration to say that most of the subjects of this book would find its approach very congenial.

11. And of course there are many, many others—Danielle Allen's *Why Plato Wrote* (London: Wiley-Blackwell, 2012), Sarah Bakewell's *At the Existentialist Café*, Alexander Nehamas's *The Art of Living*, Pierre Hadot's *Philosophy as a Way of Life*, Elizabeth Anderson's "Journeys of a Feminist Pragmatist," and John Stuhr's *Pragmatic Fashions: Pluralism, Relativism, Democracy, and the Absurd*, to name but a few. It is no accident that many feminist philosophers have been sympathetic to this approach.

12. Which are surprisingly few in number. Halevy's *The Growth of Philosophical Radicalism*, Leslie Stephen's *The English Utilitarians*, Albee's *A History of English*

Utilitarianism are classic works with no recent rivals, not even the *Cambridge Companion to Utilitarianism* (New York: Cambridge University Press, 2014). Much of the detailed historical knowledge of the movement comes from biographies of its leading figures, and even these are relatively sparse. Still, as will become clear, there is a great deal of important, excellent and inspiring historical work in this area—for example, J. B. Schneewind's classic *Sidgwick's Ethics and Victorian Moral Philosophy* (Oxford: Clarendon Press, 1977), which covers an extraordinary range of relevant material, even though the main object of the work is Sidgwick's *Methods of Ethics*.

13. See Schultz, *Henry Sidgwick, Eye of the Universe* (New York: Cambridge University Press, 2004), for one of the more extensive treatments of this subject. The writings of Martha Nussbaum and other feminist philosophers have also been singularly important here— see, for example, her *Sex and Social Justice* (New York: Oxford University Press, 2000), *Women and Human Development: The Capabilities Approach* (New York: Cambridge University Press, 2001), and *Philosophical Interventions: Reviews 1986–2011* (New York: Oxford University Press, 2011). My own work is deeply indebted to Nussbaum's, though my readings of the great utilitarians render them much more imaginative and literary than one would suppose, from her criticisms of utilitarianism in such works as *Love's Knowledge* (New York: Oxford University Press, 1990).

14. Thus, in this book, I will be somewhat more reliant on the archival research of others, especially the specialists in the areas of Godwin studies and Bentham studies.

15. De Lazari-Radek and Singer, *The Point of View of the Universe*. See also my review of this work in the *Notre Dame Philosophical Reviews*, http://ndpr.nd.edu/news/49215-he -point-of-view-of-the-universe-sidgwick-and-contemporary-ethics/, and my e-book, "A More Reasonable Ghost: Further Reflections on Henry Sidgwick and the Irrationality of the Universe," *Rounded Globe* (February 15, 2016), https://roundedglobe.com/html/34a3e7ff -778f-48d5-bca0-ed4e10132715/en/A%20More%20Reasonable%20Ghost:%20Further %20Reflections%20on%20Henry%20Sidgwick%20and%20the%20Irrationality%20of %20the%20Universe/.

16. See especially Said's great work, *Culture and Imperialism* (New York: Vintage, 1994). My own work on this subject is deeply indebted to Said, and to many others, notably those featured in the wonderful collections *Philosophers on Race*, Julie K. Ward and Tommy L. Lott, eds. (London: Blackwell Publishers, 2002) and Rosi Braidotti and Paul Gilroy, eds., *Conflicting Humanities* (London: Bloomsbury Academic, 2016). See also Bart Schultz and Georgios Varouxakis, eds., *Utilitarianism and Empire* (Lanham, MD: Lexington Books, 2005).

17. Kathleen Blake, in her rich work *Pleasures of Benthamism: Victorian Literature, Utility, Political Economy* (New York: Oxford University Press, 2009), sounds a similar note, lamenting the remarkable (and remarkably unfair) disparaging of utilitarianism common in departments of English language and literature, and effectively pointing up how such figures as Dickens were in fact highly utilitarian in their reformist orientation. As later chapters will show, the utilitarians were quite at one with Dickens in condemning the form of education represented by the character of the cruel Yorkshire schoolmaster Squeers in *Nicholas Nickleby*.

18. See, for example, http://www.apaonline.org/?page=diversity_resources and, more pointedly, https://feministphilosophers.wordpress.com/2011/06/01/how-few-blacks-are -there-in-philosophy/.

19. It is very curious, to me, that although much of my academic work on utilitarianism, including a large section of *Henry Sidgwick, Eye of the Universe*, has been concerned with problems of racism and imperialism, very few reviewers have addressed that aspect of it at any length. But much of my written work and academic teaching (and community work) addresses how academic philosophy and philosophers have dealt with issues of race

and racism. See, for example, my "On Not Seeing in Philosophy," http://blog.apaonline
.org/2016/09/29/on-not-seeing-in-philosophy/, and my "The New Chicago School of
Philosophy," https://roundedglobe.com/html/3fa819cb-df93-4e3b-bab7-cf2e7d4f8a08
/en/The%20New%20Chicago%20School%20of%20Philosophy/. See, for background,
Paul C. Taylor, *Race: A Philosophical Introduction* (London: Polity, 2nd edition 2013).

Chapter 1

1. Stephen Hebron and Elizabeth C. Denlinger, *Shelley's Ghost: Reshaping the Image of a Literary Family* (Oxford: Bodleian Library, 2010), p. 27.

2. *Political Justice*, first edition, pp. 49–50. Most references to *Political Justice* are to the two volume edition included in Mark Philp's great edition of Godwin's works, *The Political and Philosophical Works of William Godwin*, 7 volumes (London: Pickering & Chatto, 1993) and *The Collected Novels and Memoirs of William Godwin*, eight volumes (London: Pickering & Chatto, 1992).

3. Some, such as Sidgwick, have urged that the essence of modern utilitarianism can be traced back to Richard Cumberland's 1672 work *On Natural Laws*. And there is at least a vestige of that view in what has been called the "contemplative utilitarianism" of Adam Smith, which allows that from a God's-eye point of view one can see the evolution of civilization as moving in a utilitarian direction—see T. D. Campbell and I. S. Ross, "The Utilitarianism of Adam Smith's Policy Advice," *Journal of the History of Ideas* 42 (1981), pp. 73–92. But Smith and his great friend Hume were at best proto-utilitarians, as will be explained in the following chapter.

4. Peter H. Marshall, *William Godwin* (New Haven: Yale University Press, 1984), p. 398. What follows in this chapter is deeply indebted to Marshall's splendid biography (to be republished, with corrections, by PM Press) and to others of his works, notably *Demanding the Impossible: A History of Anarchism* (Oakland: PM Press, 2010) and his edition of *The Anarchist Writings of William Godwin* (London: Freedom Press, 1986). In the quoted passage he is referring to William Hazlitt (1778–1830) and Francis Place (1771–1854). Both were friends of Godwin; Hazlitt was an important literary figure, and Place, the "radical tailor," was an important political activist, a member of the Corresponding Society and a leading "Philosophical Radical," bridging the work of Godwin, Bentham, and Mill, though it appears that the latter two may have helped alienate him from Godwin circa 1817.

5. Mark Philp, "Godwin, William," entry in the *Stanford Encyclopedia of Philosophy*, at http://plato.stanford.edu/entries/godwin/. This chapter is also greatly indebted to Philp's extensive work on Godwin, including his *Godwin's Political Justice* (Ithaca: Cornell University Press, 1986) and his great edition of Godwin's works, cited above.

6. Marshall, ed., *Anarchist Writings*, p. 14.

7. Ibid.

8. Ibid., pp. 14–15.

9. Quoted in Marshall, *Godwin*, p. 194.

10. Ibid.

11. Ibid., p. 195.

12. *Political Justice*, third edition, p. 8.

13. Ibid.

14. Ibid., p. 9.

15. Ibid., p. 314.

16. *Political Justice*, first edition, p. 421.

17. Ibid., pp. 422–23.

18. Ibid., p. 470.

19. Ibid., p. 474.

20. Philp, "William Godwin."

21. Philp, *Political Justice*, p. 83.

22. Ibid., p. 96. As Roger Crisp has suggested to me, the tensions with a perfectionist reading of Godwin only make the comparison to Mill all the more appropriate, given such perfectionist interpretations of Mill as David Brink's *Mill's Progressive Principles* (New York: Oxford University Press, 2013).

23. *Political Justice*, first edition, p. 465.

24. Ibid., pp. 4–5.

25. Ibid., p. 98.

26. *Political Justice*, first edition, pp. 461-462.

27. Philp, "William Godwin."

28. *Political Justice*, first edition, p. 142.

29. It is curious that Marshall can think it perfectly obvious that Godwin is an act utilitarian, such that each act ought to maximize happiness, while Philp can think it perfectly obvious that he is not. Admittedly, trying to fit Godwin's sometimes shifting views into something like the act v. rule utilitarian box (judging the utility of particular acts rather than of rules generally adhered to) can be difficult, especially since, as this passage indicates, the utility of motives is also a factor. And in fact, all the great utilitarians were indirect utilitarians to some degree.

30. Mill, "Inaugural Address Delivered to the University of St. Andrews, Feb. 1st, 1867," (London: Longmans, Green, Reader, and Dyer, 1867), pp. 47–48.

31. Adam Phillips, *Unforbidden Pleasures* (New York: Farrar, Straus and Giroux, 2016), nicely highlights, from a liberal psychoanalytic perspective, the fecundity of pleasures, a theme that will loom large in the following chapters.

32. *Political Justice*, first edition, p. 121.

33. Ibid., p. 122.

34. Ibid., p. 265.

35. Ibid., p. 403.

36. Colin Ward (1924–2010) was one of the most persuasive of recent anarchist thinkers and activists, and he furnishes wonderful proof that many of Godwin's ideas remain highly relevant to our world. See his *Anarchy in Action* (London: Freedom Press, 1973) and Chris Wilbert and Damian White, eds., *Autonomy, Solidarity, and Possibility: The Colin Ward Reader* (London: AK Press, 2011).

37. Though obviously Godwin would have found the various forms of later state socialism as oppressive as capitalism. Both would have been found wanting—as they obviously are—by the utilitarian standard.

38. *Political Justice*, first edition, p. v.

39. Mary Wollstonecraft, *The Vindications: The Rights of Men, and The Rights of Woman*, D. L. Macdonald and K. Scherf, eds. (Peterborough, Ontario: Broadview Press, 1997), p. 102.

40. William Godwin, *Memoirs of the Author of "A Vindication of the Rights of Woman,"* P. Clemit and G. L. Walker, eds. (Peterborough, Ontario: Broadview Press, 2001), p. 80. The editors' introduction to this fine edition has been particularly helpful, especially since, as Godwin came to admit, some of his sources may not have been completely reliable. A fascinating, lively recent tribute is Bee Rowlatt's *In Search of Mary: The Mother of All Journeys* (Richmond: Alma Books, 2015). But on Wollstonecraft, the works of Janet Todd are absolutely indispensable; see her *Mary Wollstonecraft, A Revolutionary Life* (New York: Columbia University Press, 2002) and *The Collected Letters of Mary Wollstonecraft* (New York: Columbia University Press, 2004). I am much indebted to Todd's work.

41. Quoted in Marshall, *Godwin*, p. 178.

42. Ibid., p. 179.

43. Ibid.

44. Godwin, *Memoirs*, p. 88.

45. Virginia Woolf, "Mary Wollstonecraft," in *The Second Common Reader, Annotated Edition* (London: Harvest Books, 2003), pp. 156–63.

46. William Godwin and Mary Wollstonecraft, *Godwin & Mary*, R. M. Wardle, ed. (Lawrence: Bison Books, 1977), pp. 4–5, p. 8.

47. Remarkably, Godwin kept a very careful, if coded, record of their sexual encounters, using dashes and dots to indicate intercourse. This document is reproduced in William St. Clair, *The Godwins and the Shelleys* (Baltimore: The Johns Hopkins University Press, 1989), pp. 497–503. I am much indebted to St. Clair's excellent work.

48. Ibid., p. 33. But see also, Todd, *Wollstonecraft*, chaps. 33–34.

49. Ibid., p. 7.

50. Marshall, *Godwin*, p. 185.

51. Quoted in Marshall, *Godwin*, p. 186.

52. Ibid.

53. Godwin and Wollstonecraft, *Godwin and Mary*, p. 83.

54. And as Woolf noted, "she has her revenge. Many millions have died and been forgotten in the hundred and thirty years that have passed since she was buried; and yet as we read her letters and listen to her arguments and consider her experiments, above all, that most fruitful experiment, her relation with Godwin, and realise the high-handed and hot-blooded manner in which she cut her way to the quick of life, one form of immortality is hers undoubtedly: she is alive and active, she argues and experiments, we hear her voice and trace her influence even now among the living." Woolf, *Second Commonplace Book*, p. 163.

55. Marshall, *Godwin*, p. 191.

56. Godwin, *Memoirs*, p. 79.

57. Godwin and Wollstonecraft, *Godwin and Mary*, p. 89.

58. It should be noted that Godwin's expression has captured the imagination of many philosophers. A famous review by Alasdair MacIntyre of Bernard Williams's book *Moral Luck* was titled "Review: The Magic in the Pronoun 'My'." *Ethics* 94, No. 1 (Oct., 1983), pp. 113–25.

59. Godwin, *Memoirs*, p. 15.

60. Ibid.

61. Thomas Laqueur, *The Work of the Dead: A Cultural History of Mortal Remains* (Princeton: Princeton University Press, 2016), pp. 51–52. Copyright © 2015 by Princeton University Press. Reprinted by permission.

62. *Political Justice*, p. 74.

63. Godwin, *Memoirs*, p. 208.

64. William Godwin, "Thoughts Occasioned by the Perusal of Dr. Parr's Spital Sermon," in *Political and Philosophical Writings of William Godwin*, vol. II, *Political Writings*, M. Philp, ed. (London: Pickering & Chatto, 1993), p. 183.

65. Godwin, "To the Editor of the Monthly Magazine," in *Political and Philosophical Writings of William Godwin*, vol. II, *Political Writings*, M. Philp, ed. (London: Pickering & Chatto, 1993), p. 212. It is worth noting that even in the first edition of *Political Justice* Godwin had expressed some doubts about the value of Fénelon's *Telemachus*, noting that on the matter of secrecy, "Fénelon with all his ability has fallen into the most palpable inconsistency upon the subject" (PJ1: 139).

66. A classic formulation of this approach is R. M. Hare's *Moral Thinking: Its Levels, Method and Point* (Oxford: Clarendon Press, 1980). Hare cited Godwin in his account of the distinction, as did Peter Singer in his appropriation of it; see Singer, *One World: The Ethics of Globalization* (New Haven: Yale University Press, 2004). As later chapters will further demonstrate, the literature on this issue is endless. And some recent utilitarians

hold that the distinction has been abused; see Amia Srinivasan's "Stop the Robot Apocalypse," a review of William MacAskill's *Doing Good Better*, at http://www.lrb.co.uk/v37/n18/amia-srinivasan/stop-the-robot-apocalypse: "A more pressing objection to utilitarianism is not that it demands too much, but that it demands the wrong things, the things that constitute us as humans: our personal attachments, loyalties and identifications. On the utilitarian view, a pound spent without maximal effect is a pound spent immorally. Luxuries are naturally ruled out, but so is spending on worthwhile causes to which you might feel some personal affinity. Here MacAskill agrees: to choose to donate to a relatively cost-ineffective charity just because it's close to your heart—the local soup kitchen, or a seeing-eye dog charity in honour of a blind relative (it costs £32,400 to train one seeing-eye dog and its owner)—is wrong. How far should the effective altruist go with this logic? If you're faced with the choice between spending a few hours consoling a bereaved friend or earning some money to donate to an effective charity, the utilitarian calculus will tell you to do the latter. If effective altruists really are committed to doing the most good, they should say the same."

67. Don Locke, *A Fantasy of Reason: The Life & Thought of William Godwin* (London: Routledge & Kegan Paul, 1980), p. 200.

68. Marshall, *Godwin*, p. 210.

69. Godwin, *The Enquirer: Reflections on Education, Manners and Literature in a Series of Essays* (New York: Augustus M. Kelley, 1965), pp. 2–3.

70. Ibid., p. x.

71. Ibid., pp. 76–77.

72. Thomas Malthus, *An Essay on the Principle of Population*, D. Winch, ed. (Cambridge: Cambridge University Press, 1992), p. 56.

73. Godwin, *Enquiry Concerning Population*, in *Political and Philosophical Writings of William Godwin*, vol. II, *Political Writings*, M. Philp, ed. (London: Pickering & Chatto, 1993), p. 295.

74. On the fascinating figure of Place, Graham Wallas's *The Life of Francis Place* (London: Longmans, Green & Co., 1908) remains highly valuable. There is a fine (rather sympathetic) treatment of Malthus in Robert Mayhew's *Malthus: The Life and Legacies of an Untimely Prophet* (Cambridge, MA: The Belknap Press of Harvard University Press, 2014), a work that nicely reviews the Malthus/Godwin controversy and the role that Shelley also played in carrying it on, though Place and other lesser-known Godwinians are not brought into the picture.

75. Marshall, Godwin, pp. 266–68.

76. Ibid., p. 289.

77. Quoted in ibid., p. 293.

78. Ibid., p. 293.

79. Charlotte Gordon, *Romantic Outlaws: The Extraordinary Lives of Mary Wollstonecraft & Mary Shelley* (New York: Random House, 2015), pp. 34–35. Copyright © 2015 by Charlotte Gordon. Used by permission of Random House, an imprint and division of Penguin Random House LLC. All rights reserved. Any third party use of this material, outside of this publication, is prohibited. Interested parties must apply directly to Penguin Random House LLC for permission.

80. It is worth noting that Hazlitt's popular 1825 book, *The Spirit of the Age*, had celebrated Godwin himself as such.

81. Henry Crabb Robinson, *Diary, Reminiscences and Correspondence of Henry Crabb Robinson, Barrister at Law*, T. Sadler, ed. (Kessinger Publishing, 2006), p. 208.

82. Ibid., p. 238.

83. Marshall, Godwin, pp. 238–39.

84. Godwin, *Memoirs*, p. 56.

85. Ibid., p. 65.

86. Quoted in Marshall, *Godwin*, p. 267.

87. Ibid., p. 294.

88. Such circumstances have rendered Godwin subject to conservative attacks down to the present day. In his review essay "Mary Shelley Among the Radicals" (*National Review*, April 15, 2016), M. D. Aeschliman writes "Mary's obnoxiously domineering father constantly preyed on Shelley and numerous others for money. As C. P. Snow pointed out in a review of a biography of Godwin, he was a world-class leech, living to age 80 and getting loans of about £400 a year, and 'his income from all sources, while protesting indigence, was well over 1000 Pounds a year. In the 1820s that would have been substantial for a successful professional man.' No one knew where all the money went. Like Shelley and Byron, Godwin was inordinately vain in a megalomaniacal, messianic way, and endlessly loaded guilt on Mary about the indispensability of his writings to the progress of the world." See http://www.nationalreview.com/article/434151/mary-shelley-and-delusions-free-love.

89. Quoted in Marshall, *Godwin*, p. 296.

90. Quoted in Marshall, *Godwin*, p. 297.

91. The company also included Byron's personal physician, John William Polidori, who composed *The Vampyre*, picking up on an idea of Byron's—see Polidori, *The Vampyre and Ernestus Berchtold; or, The Modern Oedipus*, D. L. Macdonald and K. Scherf, eds. (Peterborough, ON: Broadview Editions, 2008). It is possible, as Aeschliman suggests, that of this brilliant company, Mary Shelley was the wisest: "Mary Shelley understood, even as a very young woman, intuitively and imaginatively rather than discursively, that power without goodness is dangerous, that knowledge without ethics is 'a cancer in the universe.' On December 20, 1830, a few months before the second edition of Frankenstein was published, the English essayist Charles Lamb wrote to his friend the poet George Dyer: 'Alas! Can we ring the bells backwards? Can we unlearn the arts that pretend to civilize, and then burn the world? There is a march of science; but who shall beat the drums for its retreat?' 'Can we unlearn the arts that pretend to civilize, and then burn the world?' It is an eloquent, profoundly relevant conception and question, which Mary Shelley's precocious novel helps us to understand and meditate on. Two hundred years after the young woman's imaginative apprehension was written down on the shores of Lake Geneva, we ignore the novel, and the question, at our peril." http://www.nationalreview.com/article/434151/mary-shelley-and-delusions-free-love.

92. William St. Clair, *The Godwins and the Shelleys* (Baltimore: The Johns Hopkins University Press, 1989), pp. 453–54.

93. Percy Shelley had of course been given to strange fits and visions; see, for example, Susan Wolfson and Ronald Levao, eds., *The Annotated Frankenstein* (Cambridge, MA: Harvard University/Belknap Press, 2012), which provides a wealth of detail about that strange summer near Geneva.

94. Quoted in Jane Shelley and Percy Bysshe Shelley, *Shelley Memorials from Authentic Sources to Which is Added an Essay on Christianity* (London: Smith, Elder and Co., 1859), p. 218.

95. There is some controversy about this point. Marshall states that "Godwin met Bentham for the first time at James Northcote's on 6 July 1831," (p. 374), but in a fuller account by Philip Schofield, "Godwin and Bentham's Circle," *The Bodleian Library Record*, vol. 24 (1) (2011), little is made of that meeting and the evidence for previous meetings is carefully reviewed and found to be ambiguous, though it seems safe to conclude that there was surprisingly little direct contact between the two. Bentham appears to have regarded Godwin as bringing a "tinge of melancholy" to every book he touched, and of putting the term "justice" center stage when he should have used "utility." At any rate, Schofield concludes that "[i]n terms of bringing Godwin within the fold of Philosophical Radicalism, more

significant than Bentham's attitude, may have been that of James Mill, insofar as it was the latter who was the more active recruiter to the ranks of the emerging political party. Mill may, indeed, have been influenced by Place, whose personal hostility towards Godwin came to a head after Bentham, Mill, and Place had spent some time together at Ford Abbey in the summer of 1817. It may, moreover, have been the case that Bentham was able to connect with established society, both because of his own privileged social background and his insistence on the relationship of theory to practice, in a way that Godwin was never quite able to do. Godwin's diary suggests that, as Bentham made his circle and his brand of radicalism more relevant to the practical politics of an increasingly democratic age, Godwin himself remained on the periphery" (p. 63). Intriguingly, Godwin may have visited Bentham's Auto-Icon when it was being kept at Southwood Smith's house, though he may have tried calling when Smith was not at home. As for Place, the break with Godwin probably came earlier. According to Wallas's biography, some harsh words were exchanged in 1814, when Place "makes a calculation showing that Godwin muddled away £1500 a year during the ten years 1804–1814, 'notwithstanding he had for the last four or five years paid no rent for the house he lived in, which was worth £200 a year.' Place's own loss from his connection with this prince of spongers was something under £400" (p. 60). On his side, Godwin would complain that God, like Bentham, sits "perched on top of his Panopticon, to spy into all our weaknesses." (Quoted in Blamires, *The French Revolution and the Creation of Benthamism* [New York: Palgrave Macmillan, 2008], p. 26).

96. Marshall, *Godwin*, p. 487. As St. Clair also records, in August of 1834, Godwin "looked through the journal which he had kept continuously since 1788. There were now thirty-two volumes, the entry for each day beautifully written and meticulously punctuated with scarcely a smudge or a correction. . . . He read about his early liberation from religion, his period of rational confidence, of the rights of woman, the discovery of feeling, of love, and of poetry, the struggles to conserve his diminishing integrity, the years with Shelley and their aftermath, the deaths of friends and of family, and a final tranquility. Godwin's life was the cultural history of his times" (p. 486). These remarkable manuscripts are now part of the Abinger archive in Oxford's Bodleian Library.

97. Godwin, *Thoughts on Man, His Nature, Productions, and Discoveries, Interspersed with some Particulars respecting the Author* (London: Effingham Wilson, Royal Exchange, 1831, British Library Historical Collection), p. 304.

98. In Godwin, *Caleb Williams*, G. Handwerk and A. A. Markley, eds. (Peterborough, Ontario: Broadview Press, 2000), p. 503.

99. Godwin, *Lives of the Necromancers, or, An Account of the Most Eminent Persons in Successive Ages, Who have claimed for Themselves, or to Whom has been imputed by Others, the Exercise of Magical Power* (London: Frederick J. Mason, 1834, Cambridge Library Collection), pp. xii-xiii.

100. Ibid., p. 465.

101. Ibid., p. 72.

102. Godwin, *The Genius of Christianity Unveiled in a Series of Essays*, in *Political Writings and Philosophical Writings of William Godwin*, vol. 7, *Religious Writings*, M. Philp, ed. (London: Pickering & Chatto, 1993), p. 108.

103. Quoted in C. Kegan Paul, *William Godwin, His Friends and Contemporaries* (London: Henry S. King & Co., 1876), vol. II, p. 264.

104. Godwin, *Genius*, p. 103.

105. Ibid., p. 207.

106. Ibid., p. 209.

107. Ibid., p. 210.

108. Ibid., p. 233.

109. Godwin, *Thoughts*, p. 470.

110. Godwin, *Genius*, p. 96. Godwin continues: "But with all this my readers have little to do. The purpose of this book is argument."

111. Godwin, *Thoughts*, p. 70.

112. Hebron and Denlinger, *Shelley's Ghost*, and Jane Shelley and Percy Bysshe Shelley, *Shelley Memorials from Authentic Sources* are both wonderful sources of information about the arduous work Mary Shelley confronted, what with inheriting both her husband's and her father's papers. Godwin had named her his literary executor, and, knowing his desire for posthumous fame, she had taken her duties to his archive very seriously. But a planned memoir was never completed, and in the end she resisted the course that, as with her husband, would have involved reviving the old scandals. She had to consider the fate of her son, Percy Florence, who in 1848 married Jane St. John, who in turn became the guardian of the family archives. Godwin himself was, at the end, content to be judged by his works, the "most faultless of which" was, he suggested, his *Thoughts on Man*. He seemed less sure that the study of his life and character would, as he had supposed in his memoir of Mary Wollstonecraft, enhance his reputation and inspire the living. The fear of unknown motives, of a benefactor to humanity's love of posthumous fame being exposed as too egotistic, may have undermined his confidence. In this too he perhaps anticipated what philosophy would become.

Chapter 2

1. Mill, "Bentham," in *Dissertations and Discussions, Political, Philosophical, and Historical* (New York: Haskell House Publishers, 1973), vol. 1, pp. 330–31. See also his "Remarks on Bentham's Philosophy," CW X, which is rather better (see J. Robson, ed., *The Collected Works of John Stuart Mill*, vols. I–XXXIII [Toronto: University of Toronto Press, 1963–99], herein referred to as CW; *The Collected Works* is now published by Routledge). Much more will be said about the relationship between Bentham and the Mills in the next chapter.

2. Ibid., p. 353.

3. Ibid., p. 355.

4. Dickens, *Hard Times*, ed. G. Smith (London: Norton, 1994), p. 317. This work is commonly taken as one of the most relentless attacks on utilitarianism ever, with its wicked depiction of the Benthamites as so many Mr. Gradgrinds, obsessed with facts at the expense of all that makes life worth living. But in some respects, as will be explained below, it is also profoundly misleading, given how close Dickens was to utilitarian reformism. See, especially, Kathleen Blake, *Pleasures of Benthamism: Victorian Literature, Utility, Political Economy*, which persuasively argues that Dickens, Bentham, and Mill were on the same page when it came to the importance of a decent education, even for Sissy Jupe.

5. Bentham, *An Introduction to the Principles of Morals and Legislation*, J. H. Burns and H. L. A. Hart, eds., with a new Introduction by F. Rosen (Oxford: Oxford University Press, 1970, 1982, 1996), p. 11. This remarkable edition of Bentham's best-known book is a classic in itself, and remains extremely valuable as a guide to the interpretation of Bentham's work (though this is alas not the case with Hart's edition of *Of Laws in General*, which has been re-edited and published as *Of the Limits of the Penal Branch of Jurisprudence*). The charge that the early utilitarians were in practice pleasure averse also had a prominent advocate in the younger Mill, who wrote of his father, "His standard of morals was Epicurean, inasmuch as it was Utilitarian. . . . But he had . . . scarcely any belief in pleasure. . . . He thought human life a poor thing at best, after the freshness of youth and of unsatisfied curiosity had gone by." J. S. Mill, *Autobiography*, p. 48.

6. Martha Nussbaum, "Mill on Happiness: The Enduring Value of a Complex Critique," in B. Schultz and G. Varouxakis, eds. *Utilitarianism and Empire* (Lanham: Lexington

Books, 2005), p. 119. My account of J. S. Mill, especially, will owe much to Nussbaum's work on him.

7. Though again, see Schofield, "Godwin and Bentham's Circle" on how limited their direct contact actually was.

8. A remark that is often misunderstood, since Bentham meant for purposes of government policy. Mill, who made this remark of Bentham's so infamous, did not indicate that it was buried in the *Rationale of Reward* and concerned the comparative importance of different pleasures for purposes of the state. But Bentham did famously crack that the difference between poetry and prose was simply that in prose all the lines end at the right hand margin.

9. His own autobiographical/biographical accounts, for example in vol. X of the Bowring edition of Bentham's work (which was detested by J. S. Mill), are not always reliable, though the much maligned Bowring volumes still remain the richest resource in this area, along with Southwood Smith's eulogy (London: Effingham Wilson, 1832) and the 1905 biography by C. M. Atkinson, *Jeremy Bentham, His Life and Work* (London: Methuen and Co., 1905). Leslie Stephens, *The English Utilitarians*, vol. 1: *Bentham* (Bristol: Thoemmes, 1991 reprint of 1900 edition) also remains useful, and of more recent works, Frederick Rosen's "Bentham, Jeremy," in the *Oxford Dictionary of National Biography* (Oxford: Oxford University Press, 2014–14) is especially helpful, along, of course, with the volumes of correspondence published as part of *The Collected Works of Jeremy Bentham*.

10. University College London Bentham Project, at http://www.ucl.ac.uk/Bentham -Project/who. As Philip Schofield has explained, "The discrepancy in the date of birth is because 4 February is Old Style and 15 February New Style. Given that the calendar changed in 1751, 4 February is technically correct, though I think many people were already using New Style before then" (private communication). It is worth noting that Frederick Rosen and other Bentham scholars often specify the Old Style birth date, which has Bentham "born on 4 February 1748 in Church Lane, Houndsditch, London. . . . He was baptized on 14 February at St. Botolph's, Aldgate." F. Rosen, "Bentham, Jeremy," *Oxford Dictionary of National Biography*, at http://www.oxforddnb.com/index/2/101002153/. I am quite indebted to Rosen's work on utilitarianism, particularly his *Classical Utilitarianism from Hume to Mill* (New York: Routledge, 2003), which congenially aims to "correct a number of misleading views of classical utilitarianism common among philosophers, legal and political theorists, historians of economic thought, and intellectual historians." (p. x). And the influence of Schofield's brilliant Bentham scholarship is evident throughout this chapter. It should also be noted that the Bentham Project website is of course always undergoing revision, and my quotations are from the website as it stood at the time this chapter was written. Recent additions include a Panopticon game and other innovations.

11. A profoundly important and influential work on the many dimensions of Bentham's radicalism is Lea Campos Boralevi's *Bentham and the Oppressed* (New York: Walter de Gruyter, 1984). As Boralevi demonstrates, on topic after topic—feminism, sexual nonconformism, Jews, the indigent, native peoples, slaves, and nonhuman animals—Bentham was so far in advance of his time that one can only wonder whether he was even of it. He did have his blind spots and personal prejudices, especially when it came to various Jewish communities, and he could compromise for the sake of expediency, as he did with women's suffrage in his *Constitutional Code*. But even then he seemed to be aware of his limitations as limitations, personal prejudices, or compromises that should not affect the utilitarian effort to help the oppressed, whoever they might be. And it was in a piece on the Polish Jews that Bentham used "for the first time (at least in English) the term 'capitalist.'" (p. 89).

12. Peter Cain, "Bentham and the Development of the British Critique of Colonialism," *Utilitas* 23, No. 1 (March 2011), pp. 1–24. See also Jennifer Pitts, "'Great and Distant Crimes': Empire in Bentham's Thought," in S. Engelmann, ed., *Jeremy Bentham, Selected Writings* (New Haven: Yale University Press, 2011), pp. 478–99. Although, as Pitts notes,

Bentham may have, under the influence of Edward Gibbon Wakefield's ardent colonialism, softened some on colonies very late in life (after a lifetime of opposition), the younger Mill's portrait of him (and Mill's own work) quite missed "Bentham's lively sense of irony and self-mockery, his healthy disgust for existing political and legal systems, and his suspicion of those who presume the superiority of their own tastes and judgments" (p. 479). Bentham would have loved Michael Lewis's *The Big Short: Inside the Doomsday Machine* (New York: W. W. Norton, 2010), exposing the venality and stupidity of those sinister interests at the top of the financial world. See also the essays in B. Schultz and G. Varouxakis, eds., *Utilitarianism and Empire* (Lanham, MD: Lexington Books, 2005).

13. Wallas, *Francis Place*, pp. 85–86. Wallas does note that "[o]ne service which all Bentham's disciples were allowed to perform was the writing of Bentham's later books," and this despite the fact that, as Mill explained to Place, "There is no one thing upon which he plumes himself so much as his style, and he would not alter it if all the world were to preach to him till Domesday" (p. 83, p. 85).

14. Ibid., p. 91. It is important, however, that Mill senior was especially close to Bentham earlier on, while completing his *History of British India*, and that after the publication of that work in 1818 and Mill's subsequent employment at the East India House, Bentham saw less of him and more of Place, who had been introduced to Mill by Edward Wakefield around 1808, the formative period for the Philosophical Radicals. Mill senior and Place were certainly Bentham's leading disciples, and by 1817 Bentham was considering making Place his literary executor.

15. Ross Harrison, *Bentham* (London: Routledge & Kegan Paul, 1983), p. 4.

16. A point that is, plainly, a chief theme of this book.

17. Stephen Engelmann, "Introduction," in *Jeremy Bentham, Selected Writings*, p. 3 and p. 5.

18. Rosen, in Bentham, *An Introduction*, p. lxiv. But as Philip Schofield has pointed out to me, the "logic of the will is concerned with the formal relationships between such notions as command, prohibition, and permission, and related to the respective power relationships of the persons involved, e.g. a superior issues commands to an inferior, whereas an inferior makes pleas to a superior" (private communication).

19. Ibid., pp. 3–4. Engelmann hopes that Bentham studies is now in a "postrevisionist" phase, but this seems to amount to little more than a reluctance to engage with the obvious ethical questions and arguments posed by any attempt to take Bentham seriously. Such problems are also raised in an acute way by William Davies in his book *The Happiness Industry: How the Government and Big Business Sold Us Well-Being* (London: Verso, 2015). Although much of Davies's critique is well aimed, the sections on Bentham appear to miss how Bentham would criticize the opportunistic and exploitative use of measures of happiness to support a corrupt corporate agenda.

20. Quoted in Bentham, *An Introduction*, p. xxxvi.

21. Ibid. See also the important work of Kelly, *Utilitarianism and Distributive Justice, Jeremy Bentham and the Civil Law* (Oxford: Oxford University Press, 1990), which provides a powerful defense of the interpretation of Bentham as an indirect utilitarian emphasizing how the pursuit of the greatest happiness is often best done via indirect strategies that have people deploying different decision procedures in various contexts. Also, the recent symposium on Bentham and indirect legislation in *History of European Ideas*, http://www.tandfonline.com/toc/rhei20/43/1?nav=tocList.

22. Rosen, *Classical Utilitarianism*, p. 7. This view is sometimes described as "global utilitarianism," though that construction can also be misleading if it fails to capture the determinacy the classical utilitarians sought. Rosen's interpretation of Bentham as combining aggregation and distribution is extremely controversial and rejected by other Bentham

scholars, notably Schofield, who insists that "Bentham sees it [the principle of utility] as an aggregative principle, and equality is subordinate to it—in other words, equality is a sub-end of the principle of utility because, thanks to diminishing marginal utility, an equal distribution will produce the greatest total welfare—assuming that there are no pre-existing expectations involved (which there usually are)" (private communication).

23. Engelmann, "Introduction," p. 5.

24. Philip Schofield, *Bentham: A Guide for the Perplexed* (London: Continuum Books, 2009), p. 13. This was a very great change from his attitudes circa 1776, when he was emphatically not an admirer of the United States (the political philosophy of which he mocked) and still more of a Tory. Again, I am very greatly indebted to Schofield's wonderful Bentham scholarship, both this work and his more extensive study *Utility and Democracy: the Political Thought of Jeremy Bentham* (Oxford: Oxford University Press, 2006).

25. Engelmann, "Introduction," pp. 4–5.

26. Quoted in James Crimmins, "Introduction," Jeremy Bentham's Auto-Icon and Related Writings (Bristol: Thoemmes, 2002), http://www.utilitarian.net/bentham/about /2002.htm. This is an excellent piece on the subject, providing extensive background on the legal and medical context in which dissection was such an important issue. Bentham had long stipulated in his Will that his body would be used for medical dissection.

27. Ibid.

28. University College London Bentham Project, at https://www.ucl.ac.uk/Bentham -Project/who/autoicon. And I am proud to report that I am among the fortunate few to have dined with Bentham. His Auto-Icon was brought out for a memorable dinner at UCL, as part of a conference celebrating the 200th birthday of John Stuart Mill. But not the head, which, on an earlier occasion, H.L.A. Hart described to me as "deeply repellent."

29. Crimmins, "Introduction," http://www.utilitarian.net/bentham/about/2002.htm.

30. Indeed, considered in the context of the histories recounted in Laqueur's *The Work of the Dead*, they seem appropriately ingenious but scarcely comical. Laqueur devotes some space to Bentham and rightly notes how tormented he was by the subject of ghosts (see p. 65). More broadly, "Science, Bentham thought, would free mankind from superstition, groundless terrors, and 'word magic'; it would abolish the whole category of fictions—'as ifs'—that terrorize us" (p. 66).

31. Bentham, *The Works of Jeremy Bentham*, vol. X: *Memoirs and Correspondence*, J. Bowring, ed. (Edinburgh: William Tait, 1843), pp. 586–87.

32. Bentham, "Article on Utilitarianism, Long Version," in *The Collected Works of Jeremy Bentham: Deontology, Together with a Table of the Springs of Action and Article on Utilitarianism* (Oxford: Clarendon Press, 1983), pp. 291–92.

33. Ibid., p. 326.

34. Ibid., pp. 296–97.

35. Ibid., p. 293.

36. Bentham, *A Fragment on Government*, R. Harrison, ed. (Cambridge: Cambridge University Press, 1988), p. vi.

37. Though as indicated in the previous chapter, my sympathies are with Marshall: "Godwin's utilitarianism differed from that of Helvétius and Bentham in upholding the reality of altruism, the natural harmony of interests, and the moral importance of intentions. Unlike them, he further advocated the restraint of certain desires and made a qualitative distinction between pleasures. Yet these were innovations rather than departures from the utilitarian ethic, and he made a consistent attempt to subordinate his principles to the criteria of 'utility, pleasure, or happiness.'" Marshall, *Godwin*, p. 398. But this statement calls for some qualification, given Bentham's indirect utilitarianism (a controversial interpretation) and evident belief in the complexity of human motives, about which more below.

38. J. Crimmins, "Bentham and Utilitarianism," in *The Cambridge Companion to Utilitarianism*, eds. B. Eggleston and D. Miller (New York: Cambridge University Press, 2014), p. 45.

39. Special mention should also made of Bentham's attachment to Venezuelan General Francisco Gabriel de Miranda (1750–1816), the "Spanish soldier, friend of U.S. presidents, paramour of Catherine the Great, French revolutionary general in the Belgian campaigns, perennial thorn in the side of British Prime Minister William Pitt, and fomenter of revolution in Spanish America," who was also one of Bentham's chief hopes for change in the Americas. See Karen Racine, *Francisco de Miranda: A Transatlantic Life in the Age of Revolution* (Lanham, MD: Rowman & Littlefield, 2002); also, Cain, "Bentham and the Development of the British Critique of Colonialism," which highlights the anti-colonialist radicalism of Bentham's writings on the Spanish colonies.

40. Ibid., p. 47. Crimmins has done more than anyone to unearth the importance of utilitarianism in the United States from the founding through to the First World War. See his and M. Spencer's magisterial, edited collection *Utilitarians and Their Critics in America, 1789-1914* (Bristol: Thoemmes Continuum, 2005).

41. Rosen, "Bentham, Jeremy," in the *Oxford Dictionary of National Biography*, http://www.oxforddnb.com/view/printable/2153.

42. See Quine's delightful essay "Five Milestones of Empiricism," in *Theories and Things* (Cambridge, MA: Belknap Press, 1986). Russell often invoked Bentham, but perhaps his most interesting treatment of the Philosophical Radicals was in his *Freedom and Organization, 1814-1914* (London: Routledge, new edition 2001). See also his trenchant essay "The Harm That Good Men Do," in his *Sceptical Essays*, which includes the story about Bentham's supposed soup recipe.

43. Though according to Schofield, this expression is unfortunate: the "conflation of fiction and fictitious entity is a plague in Bentham scholarship. A fiction is a falsehood or a lie, whereas the name of a fictitious entity is the name of an abstraction. Fallacies, on the other hand, are false arguments (fictions assert false facts)" (private communication).

44. Bentham, *Memoirs*, p. 27–28.

45. Ibid., p. 10.

46. Ibid. This is perhaps the strongest point in favor of Godwin's claim that the Archbishop was a great benefactor of humanity.

47. It is difficult, on the basis of the text of *Telemachus*, to determine exactly what Bentham found so inspiring in the rivals. In the relevant scene, the nearest approximation would seem to involve the sage from Lesbos, who in response to the question, Who is the most wretched of all men? answered: "Of all men he is the most unhappy who thinks himself so; for misery arises not so much from what we suffer, as from our lack of patience, which adds to it greatly." (Fénelon, *Telemachus, Son of Ulysses*, P. Riley, ed. [New York: Cambridge University Press, 1994], p. 68.) This would at least comport with Bentham's fixed views about the significance of human foresight.

48. Bentham, *Memoirs*, p. 21.

49. Ibid., p. 26.

50. Rosen, "Bentham, Jeremy," p. 2.

51. Bentham, *Memoirs*, p. 8. Bowring's work includes the story of Bentham being introduced by the Duke of Leeds as a "little philosopher," which led to the following exchange (p. 30):

> "A philosopher!" said the doctor; "Can you screw your head off and on?"
> "No, sir!" said [Bentham].
> "Oh, then, you are no philosopher."

52. Ibid., p. 4.

53. Ibid., p. 47.

54. F. Rosen, "Jeremy Bentham," in the *Oxford Dictionary of National Biography*, http://www.oxforddnb.com/view/printable/2153.

55. Ibid., p. 17. As some of Bentham's most oft-quoted lines from the *Introduction* put it: "The day may come, when the rest of the animal creation may acquire those rights which never could have been withholden from them but by the hand of tyranny. The French have already discovered that the blackness of skin is no reason why a human being should be abandoned without redress to the caprice of a tormentor. It may come one day to be recognized, that the number of legs, the villosity of the skin, or the termination of the os sacrum, are reasons equally insufficient for abandoning a sensitive being to the same fate . . . the question is not, Can they reason? nor, Can they talk? but, Can they suffer?"

56. Bentham, Memoirs, p. 19.

57. Ibid., p. 37.

58. Ibid., p. 29.

59. Ibid., p. 39.

60. Ibid., p. 37. These exact words appear in his *Church-of-Englandism and Its Catechism Examined*. See *The Collected Works of Jeremy Bentham: Church-of-Englandism and Its Catechism Examined*, J. Crimmins and C. Fuller, eds. (Oxford: Clarendon Press, 2011), pp. 35–36.

61. His father had once challenged him, in company, to define "genius," and his humiliating failure to do so on the spot had led to considerable soul searching on his part and in due course the conviction that if he had a genius for anything, it was for legislation. He would, as Schofield observes, later go on to define "genius" as the ability to invent.

62. Atkinson, *Bentham*, p. 49.

63. Ibid., p. 4.

64. Though the relationship was a strange one, with Bentham proposing not once, but twice, and this at long intervals (1805 and 1828), long after the initial friendship and time together at Shelburne's estate in the 1780s. An American follower of Bentham, John L. O'Sullivan, was so struck by Bentham's lifelong love of Fox, that he would write: "Disappointed in his love, he gave to his race, he gave to the cause of truth, he gave to a sublime philanthropy and an expansive political philosophy, those mental energies, and those deep and deathless affections of the heart, which were thus debarred from the natural vent their first young impulse had sought. Have we not here the key to Bentham's whole life and character?" Sullivan, "Early Life of Jeremy Bentham," in J. Crimmins and M. G. Spencer, eds., *Utilitarians and Their Critics in America, 1789–1914*, p. 15.

65. Schofield, *Bentham*, pp. 4–5.

66. Atkinson, *Bentham*, pp. 49–50.

67. Bentham, *Memoirs*, p. 557.

68. Ibid., p. 419.

69. Ibid., p. 420.

70. Ibid., p. 558. Cf. CW XII on the author of this letter, and vol. VII on Bowring's missing reply.

71. Gore Vidal uncharacteristically missed this bit of intrigue in his historical novel *Burr* (New York: Vintage Books, 1973). But there is much about the Bentham/Burr relationship that remains uninvestigated, despite Burr himself having declared in his journal: "I will never again believe in anything I read in a book (excepting Jeremy Bentham's)" (*The Private Journal of Aaron Burr*, W. Bixby, ed. [Rochester: BiblioLife, reprint of 1903 edition], p. 283). Unfortunately, the whereabouts of Curran's portrait of Bentham are unknown. According to the Bentham Project, all of their representations of Bentham are included in *The Old Radical: Representations of Jeremy Bentham*, ed. C. Fuller (London: The Bentham Project, University College London, 1998), an excellent illustrated introduction to Bentham.

72. See her engaging work "'It is a Theatre of Great Felicity to a Number of People': Bentham at Ford Abbey," http://discovery.ucl.ac.uk/1323723/1/007%20Fuller%202004 .pdf. Bentham had rented a number of different country residences over the years, but none that rivaled Ford Abbey. And George Wheatley's priceless account of his 1831 visit to Queen's Square Place is now available at http://www.ucl.ac.uk/Bentham-Project /publications/wheatley/wheatley.html.

73. Schofield, "Godwin and Bentham's Circle," p. 59.

74. The fullest account of this remains Janet Semple, *Bentham's Prison* (Oxford: Oxford University Press, 1993), but see also her "Foucault and Bentham: A Defense of Panopticism," in *Utilitas* IV (1992), pp. 105–20, and Miran Bozovic, ed., *The Panopticon Writings* (New York: Verso, 2011).

75. Schofield, *Bentham*, p. 11.

76. Bentham, *Selected Writings*, p. 284.

77. See M. Foucault, *Discipline and Punish*, A. Sheridan, trans. (New York: Vintage Books, 2nd ed. 1995), but also many of Foucault's other works on power, sexuality, psychopathology, etc.

78. Schofield, *Bentham*, p. 70. Some prisons, notably Stateville Prison in Joliet Illinois, in the U. S., did incorporate elements of the Panopticon architecture, though in more limited ways.

79. It is hard to resist the thought that Bentham's ideas on punishment owed something to his childhood discomfort at being paraded and asked to perform in company by his father.

80. Rosen, "Bentham," p. 11.

81. Again, the insightful work by Kathleen Blake, *Pleasures of Benthamism: Victorian Literature, Utility, Political Economy*, does a splendid job of bringing out the common bonds between the utilitarians and Dickens (and other supposed critics of Bentham). In their attacks on the corruptions of law and government, they were often working on the same side: "Thus Chancery is as far as possible from panoptical. It is a centuries-old establishment, aristocratic, quasi-ecclesiastic, time-wasting, uneconomical, uncomprehensive in view, closed to inspection, and self-serving at the expense of those it serves. Chancery was, in fact, a prime target of Benthamite-spearheaded legal reform through the Chancery Commission Report of 1826, the Court of Chancery Act of 1850, the Chancery Procedure Acts of 1852, and the Judicature Act of 1873, which integrated the equity with the common-law system" (p. 11).

82. Slater, *Charles Dickens* (New Haven: Yale University Press, 2009), p. 94.

83. See *The Collected Works of Jeremy Bentham: Writings on the Poor Laws*, vols. I and II, M. Quinn, ed. (Oxford: Clarendon Press, 2001 and 2010).

84. Himmelfarb, *The Idea of Poverty: England in the Early Industrial Age* (New York: Viking Books, 1985), pp. 78–79. And Charles Bahmueller's, *The National Charity Company: Jeremy Bentham's Silent Revolution* (Berkeley: University of California Press, 1981) remains a helpful, though very critical, work.

85. Ibid. p. 81.

86. Lieberman, Review of *The Collected Works of Jeremy Bentham: Writings on the Poor Laws*, Humanities and Social Sciences H-Net online, at http://www.h-net.org/reviews /showrev.php?id=31179. This line of argument is common to Lieberman, Blake, and Crimmins, and it has been defended at great length and very effectively by Cyprian Blamires in *The French Revolution and the Creation of Benthamism* (London: Palgrave Macmillan, 2008). On this view, Bentham certainly deserves credit as an architect of modernity, but not in the way that Foucault claimed. As Blake put it, "Emphasizing one-way surveillance, Foucault focuses on the overseer who remains unseen. He notes only briefly that the overseer can also be seen, not by the prisoners but by prison inspectors and the general public.

In Bentham this is a major feature. It insures openness to official and public scrutiny of an institution that by its panoptic sight-lines reveals all its practices at a glance. . . . In his calculation of pleasures and pains Bentham gives full weight to the moral sanction. This operates through people's concern for what others think of them, and there is a parallel here with Adam Smith on the impartial spectator. Thus officials are as interested as other people are in how they are seen, and this makes oversight a powerful force for influencing and controlling those in power" (pp. 5–6).

87. Quinn, "Editorial Introduction," *Writings on the Poor Laws*, vol. I, p. xiii.

88. Quinn, "Poor Laws," in J. Crimmins, ed., *The Bloomsbury Encyclopedia of Utilitarianism* (London: Bloomsbury Academic, 2013), p. 430.

89. Bentham, *Writings on the Poor Laws*, vol. I, p. 3.

90. Quinn, "Poor Laws," p. 431.

91. Himmelfarb, *The Idea of Poverty*, p. 85.

92. Quinn, "Poor Laws," p. 431. He also endorsed Place's cogent critique of Malthus, which called for a heavier reliance on contraception.

93. The great psychological work of the earlier utilitarian movement is usually taken to be James Mill's *Analysis of the Phenomena of the Human Mind*, originally published in 1829.

94. Bentham, *Writings on the Poor Laws*, vol. II, p. 627f.

95. This side of Bentham is almost entirely missed in Davies, *The Happiness Industry*, which instead seizes on some of Bentham's speculations about such matters as pulse rate as possibly an objective measure of happiness.

96. Bentham, *The Collected Works of Jeremy Bentham: Chrestomathia*, M. J. Smith and W. H. Burston, eds. (Oxford: Clarendon Press, 1983), pp. 8–10.

97. Ibid, p. ii.

98. Quoted in Walls, *Francis Place*, pp. 102–103.

99. Crimmins, "Panopticon," in J. Crimmins, ed., *The Bloomsbury Encyclopedia of Utilitarianism*, p. 396. It should be stressed that Bentham came to oppose solitary confinement as a punishment and insisted that the inmates be well fed. He even sketched out a Panopticon cookbook to help with that latter aim; see *Jeremy Bentham's Prison Cooking: A Collection of Utilitarian Recipes*, with special contributions by Chef Fergus Henderson, Food Historian Dr. Annie Gray, and the Co-Ordinator of Transcribe Bentham, Dr. Tim Causer (London: UCL Centre for Publishing, 2015) for both his recipes and an excellent introduction to the Panopticon scheme. It might also be kept in mind that the current U.S. "prison-industrial complex" is in actuality in large part a set of disciplinary institutions dealing much more harshly with the poor, especially the poor of color; see Michelle Alexander, *The New Jim Crow* (New York: The New Press, 2012). Bentham's schemes look good in comparison; as is clear from Alexander's work and such movements as Black Lives Matter, the prison-industrial complex and the police and security forces connected to it remain in serious need of effective public oversight. See also James Kilgore, *Understanding Mass Incarceration* (New York: The New Press, 2015).

100. T. Peardon, "Bentham's Ideal Republic," *The Canadian Journal of Economics and Political Science* 17, no. 2 (May 1951), p. 184.

101. Ibid., p. p. 186.

102. Ibid., p. 197.

103. Bentham, *Writings on the Poor Laws*, vol. II, p. 527.

104. Ibid., p. 673.

105. Bentham, *Writings on the Poor Laws*, vol. II, p. 675–76.

106. Dickens, *Hard Times*, pp. 3, 6. In line with Blake's argument, in *Pleasures of Benthamism*, it ought to be stressed that the brutal, half-blind Yorkshire schoolmaster Mr. Squeers in Dickens's *Nicholas Nickleby* is a telling example of the educational practices that both Dickens and Bentham sought to abolish. The Dickens character was probably

based on an actual Yorkshire schoolmaster, and the Yorkshire schools really were, as Mark Ford has explained, "barbarically cruel places in which the boys were starved, flogged and taught little or nothing. Inadequate sanitation and overcrowded living conditions allowed diseases to spread as rapidly as in the poorest slums." See Dickens, *Nicholas Nickleby*, M. Ford, ed. (New York: Penguin Books, 1999), p. xv.

107. Bentham, *Writings on the Poor Laws*, vol. II, p. 677.

108. Ibid., p. 608.

109. See Pitts, "'Great and Distant Crimes.'"

110. All writing on the subject of Bentham and sexuality owes an immense debt to Louis Crompton, both *Byron and Greek Love: Homophobia in 19th-Century England* (Swaffham: The Gay Men's Press, 1998) and his edited publication of Bentham's "Offenses Against One's Self: Paederasty," *The Journal of Homosexuality* 3, no. 4 (Summer 1978), and 4, no. 1 (Fall 1978).

111. For more on the pivotal role played by Symonds on the nature of ancient Greek sexuality, see my *Henry Sidgwick, Eye of the Universe*, especially chaps. 1 and 6. See also Bart Schultz et al., *Strange Audacious Life*, unpublished manuscript. As these works show, Bentham did not provide enough detail on how the legitimate forms of same-sex male love in many regions of ancient Greece prohibited submissive postures. They might also suggest that, on various points, the scholarly discussions of Bentham on sexuality have to date been insufficiently informed by the better social constructionist histories of sexuality, which, inspired in part by Foucault, bring out the importance of the categories of sexual identity that emerged in late nineteenth-century medical and psychiatric discourse. In important respects, Bentham was writing in a period without the notion of a "homosexual identity," as it was construed a century later.

112. Bentham, *The Collected Works of Jeremy Bentham: Of Sexual Irregularities and Other Writings on Sexual Morality*, P. Schofield, C. Pease-Watkin, and M. Quinn, eds. (Oxford: Clarendon Press, 2014), pp. xi–xii. This work, valuable as it is, is still incomplete, and does not capture the full range of Bentham's writing on these subjects. More of the relevant material will appear in the appropriate volumes of the *Collected Works*.

113. Schofield, "Jeremy Bentham: Prophet of Secularism" (London: South Place Ethical Society, 2012), pp. 20–21.

114. "Sextus" is included in Bentham, *Of Sexual Irregularities*, p. 56.

115. Ibid., pp. 14–15.

116. Ibid., pp. 10, 16.

117. Ibid., p. 119.

118. Schofield, *Bentham*, p. 2.

119. Bentham, *The Collected Works of Jeremy Bentham: Church-of-Englandism and Its Catechism Examined*, J. Crimmins and C. Fuller, eds. (Oxford: Clarendon Press, 2011), p. 88.

120. Ibid., pp. xi, 93.

121. Bentham, *The Influence of Natural Religion on the Temporal Happiness of Mankind*, D. McKown, ed. (Amherst: Prometheus Books, 2003), p. 113. According to Schofield, this work owes a great deal to Grote, though the ideas, especially in the first part, do seem to be Bentham's.

122. Ibid., p. 116.

123. Ibid., pp. 164, 162–63. And as Peardon put it, Bentham saw how everything, with the ruling elites, "co-operated to surround them with an air of false glamour—'a sort of clouded majesty'—through which they appear to the people supremely competent, benevolent, and even sacred. Criticism becomes a violation of good taste, of that 'decorum' which Bentham rightly recognized as one of the props of the English social and political system" (p. 189). In this too, Bentham is developing a point stressed by Smith, especially in his *Theory of Moral Sentiments*, which laments the human tendency to bow to the high and mighty.

124. Rosen, *Classical Utilitarianism*, p. 228.

125. Ibid., p. 229. Again, this is an especially controversial interpretation.

126. Bentham, *Writings on the Poor Laws*, vol. II, pp. 517–18.

127. Hart, "Bentham's Principle of Utility," in Bentham, *An Introduction*, p. xcv. It is worth stressing again that Bentham, like Mill, denies that the greatest happiness principle, as a first principle, is susceptible of proof in the ordinary sense, and follows a dialectical strategy of showing how the supposed alternatives presuppose it, unless they are, e.g., ascetic.

128. Bentham, *An Introduction*, pp. 13–14. It is tempting to think that Bentham might thus be more the predecessor of such works as R. Pohl's *Cognitive Illusions: A Handbook on Fallacies and Biases in Thinking, Judgment, and Memory* (New York: Psychology Press, 2012) than of the old Chicago School of Economics.

129. Bentham, *Natural Religion*, p. 78.

130. Ibid., p. 33.

131. Bentham, *An Introduction*, pp. lxxxix–xc.

132. Ibid., p. 38.

133. See K. De Lazari-Radek and P. Singer, *The Point of View of the Universe: Sidgwick and Contemporary Ethics* (Oxford: Oxford University Press, 2014), chap. 9, and their "Doing Our Best for Hedonistic Utilitarianism," in *Etica & Politica* XVIII, No. 1 (Spring 2016), http://www2.units.it/etica/2016_1/SINGER-DE%20LAZARI%20RADEK.pdf. In a provocative move, these authors try to distance their hedonistic account of the good from their account of happiness, which follows Haybron's account in *The Pursuit of Unhappiness*. But as the following chapters will explain at greater length, despite renewed philosophical interest in defending hedonism, recent research has in some ways rendered the hedonistic accounts of pain and pleasure even more intractable; see, for example, Paul Bloom, *How Pleasure Works: The New Science of Why We Like What We Like* (New York: W. W. Norton and Co., 2010), which nicely explains the interpretive nature of pain/pleasure (how, as some research has it, protein bars "taste worse" to people if described to them as soy protein, orange juice "tastes better" if it is bright orange, etc.). Such problems were in fact anticipated by Bentham. For an excellent treatment of Bentham on hedonistic calculation and its complexities, see Michael Quinn, "Bentham on Mensuration: Calculation and Moral Reasoning," *Utilitas* 26/1 (March 2014), pp. 61–104, which underscores the interpretive dimensions of Bentham's hedonism.

134. Bentham, *An Introduction*, p. 42. Clearly, many different areas of research are relevant to working out an adequate account of hedonism, which still calls for new experiments in living. In addition to research in neurophysiology, work in cultural (and Foucauldian) studies—for instance, Constance Classen, *The Deepest Sense: A Cultural History of Touch* (Urbana: University of Illinois Press, 2012)—can illuminate how the cultural/interpretive frameworks for reporting sensory experiences and modalities shift and change at the deepest levels. Witness the growth of, for example, the new "pleasures" of shopping at Department stores, another nineteenth-century phenomenon. As she aptly notes, in her helpful discussion of Bentham on nonhuman animals, the "age of reason was also the age of sensibility—an age in which feelings, even those of animals, might merit respect" (p. 121). Indeed, some of Bentham's contemporaries argued that the pain of nonhuman animals might be felt even more strongly than the pain of human ones. Perhaps Foucault's work on the history of sexuality is more relevant to the reconstruction of Benthamism than his work on the Panopticon.

135. Quinn, "Bentham on Mensuration," pp. 92–93.

136. Crimmins, "Bentham and Utilitarianism in the Early Nineteenth Century," in Ben Eggleston and Dale E. Miller, eds., *The Cambridge Companion to Utilitarianism* (New York: Cambridge University Press, 2014), p. 41. See also the excellent entries in Crimmins,

ed., *The Bloomsbury Encyclopedia of Utilitarianism,* and the above-cited work by Quinn, which supports these points.

Chapter 3

1. By contrast with Foucault's uses of Bentham, critical theorist Jürgen Habermas's seminal work, *The Structural Transformation of the Public Sphere* (Cambridge, MA: MIT Press, 1991), used Mill's works to illustrate the idea of a genuine public sphere (albeit without noting their grounding in utilitarianism).

2. Mill, "Whewell on Moral Philosophy," CW X, p. 173. As will be noted more fully later in this chapter, Mill was scarcely fair to Whewell, who also held some progressive views about science and educational reform. But then, Whewell had scarcely been fair to Bentham.

3. Again, see J. Robson, ed., *The Collected Works of John Stuart Mill,* vols. I–XXXIII (Toronto: University of Toronto Press, 1963–99), herein referred to as CW.

4. John Skorupski, *The Domain of Reasons* (Oxford: Oxford University Press, 2010), pp. 337–38. In this section, Skorupski is trying to distinguish "pure utilitarianism" from "dominance utilitarianism," which is a weaker view that "does not deny the existence of practical reasons other than agent-neutral telic ones," though it still "shares the essential utilitarian spirit, namely, the very powerful teleological thought that nothing can ultimately beat the practical-normative force of Good." Skorupski defines a "telic reason" as follows: "If the fact that an action will promote a state of affairs is a complete reason to do it, that state of affairs is a *final end*. The fact that an action would promote a final end is a *telic* reason to do it" (p. 508). And his use of the Parfitian "agent relative" versus "agent neutral" distinction reflects, he claims, Nagel's original distinction between subjective and objective reasons in *The Possibility of Altruism*. Thus, "Consider the schema: (It's being the case) that Pa gives x reason to a . . . (i) If 'P' contains a free occurrence of 'x' then it is an agent-relative predicate. If it does not, it is an agent-neutral predicate. (ii) A reason for action which is expressible by an agent-neutral predicate is agent-neutral. A reason for action which is not so expressible is agent-relative" (pp. 63–64). As Michael Ridge explicates this, with a familiar example: "*ethical egoism* is an agent-relative theory (and hence concerns agent-relative reasons) while objective utilitarianism is an agent-neutral theory (and hence concerns agent-neutral reasons). For egoism holds that there is reason for a given agent to do something just in case his doing it would promote *his* welfare. Whereas objective *utilitarianism* . . . (on at least one version) holds that someone ought to do something just insofar as it promotes welfare, period (no matter whose it is)." Ridge, "Reasons for Action: Agent Neutral versus Agent Relative," *Stanford Encyclopedia of Philosophy* (December, 2011), http://plato.stanford.edu/entries/reasons-agent/#RelDis. But like the act/rule distinction, the agent neutral/agent relative distinction can become something of a straightjacket, blinkering or oversimplifying the interpretation of the original works.

5. For more on this, see the later sections of this chapter; also B. Schultz and G. Varouxakis, eds., *Utilitarianism and Empire* (Lanham, MD: Lexington Books, 2005) and B. Schultz, "Mill and Sidgwick, Imperialism and Racism," *Utilitas* 19 (March 2007), pp. 104–30 (parts of which are reproduced in the final sections of this chapter). L. Zastopil, *John Stuart Mill and India,* (Stanford: Stanford University Press, 1994) is a crucial work on a crucial topic. The influence of Edward Said's profoundly important works, *Orientalism* (New York: Vintage, 1979) and *Culture and Imperialism* (New York: Vintage, 1994), has too rarely been felt in Mill studies, despite their obvious relevance, though this may be changing. It is, however, heartening to see the expanding bandwidth of such recent Mill studies as the *Companion to Mill,* Christopher MacLeod and Dale Miller, eds., in the *Blackwell Companions* series (London: Wiley, 2016), even if much more work remains to be done.

6. Duncan Bell, *Reordering the World: Essays on Liberalism and Empire* (Princeton: Princeton University Press, 2016), p. 12. As Bell argues, the settler colonies afforded, for Mill, more opportunities for experiments in living. And as Bell rightly claims, both Mill junior and Mill senior took it as axiomatic that India was inferior and required British rule, even if "the primary duty of an imperial power was, through a combination of coercion and example-setting, to help educate subject populations until they were 'capable' of attaining responsible self-government" (p. 302). Bell's work, and that of his sometime collaborator Casper Sylvest, represent some of the best recent analyses of the "liberal imperialism" that both Mill and Sidgwick were entangled in, in invidious contrast to Bentham and Godwin.

7. See, for more details, the excellent entry on James Mill by Terence Ball in *The Stanford Encyclopedia of Philosophy*, available at http://plato.stanford.edu/entries /james-mill/.

8. Mill, *Autobiography*, CW I, pp. 69–70.

9. Mill, CW, XII: *The Earlier Letters Pt. 1, 1812-1848*, F. Mineka, ed., http://oll .libertyfund.org/titles/mill-the-collected-works-of-john-stuart-mill-volume-xii-the -earlier-letters-1812-1848-part-i.

10. Mill, *Autobiography*, CW I, p. 24. See also CW XI, *Essays on Philosophy and the Classics* to appreciate the full force of Mill's debt to the ancient Greeks. The review "Grote's Plato," in addition to conveying his respect for his fellow Philosophical Radical as a philosopher, conveys a good sense of Mill's view of the Socratic elenchus. T. H. Irwin's essay "Mill and the Classical World," in John Skorupski, ed., *The Cambridge Companion to Mill* (New York: Cambridge University Press, 1998, pp. 423–63) expertly compares Mill's appropriation of Plato to Grote's.

11. Ibid., p. 26.

12. Ibid., p. 35.

13. Ibid., p. 109.

14. Mill, The Early Letters of John Stuart Mill, 1812–1848, CW XIII, ed. F. Mineka, p. 601.

15. Mill, "Education," in W. H. Burston, ed., *James Mill on Education* (New York: Cambridge University Press, 1969), pp. 41, 46–47.

16. Ibid., p. 94.

17. "Introduction," in *James Mill on Education*, p. 17.

18. On this all-important topic, see the seminal works of Alan Ryan, especially *J. S. Mill* (London: Routledge and Kegan Paul, 1974). Also, John Skorupski, *John Stuart Mill* (London: Routledge, 1989), chap. 8. Bentham, for his part, would in 1789 write to a friend: "I don't care two straws about liberty and necessity at any time. I do not expect any new truths on the subject: and were I to see any lying at my feet, I should hardly think it worth while to stoop to pick them up. . . . I am sure you must have gone before me in regretting that a practical professional man should stand forth as an author upon subjects so purely speculative." Quoted in Blamires, *The French Revolution and the Creation of Benthamism*, p. 20 (again, a remarkable work that also makes it very clear just how much the younger Mill missed when it came to Benthamism).

19. Reeve, *John Stuart Mill: Victorian Firebrand* (London: Atlantic Books, 2007), p. 44. The three Johns, Roebuck, Graham and Mill, were known as the "Trijackia." The commitment to Malthus, whose views were discussed in the previous chapter, was one of the strongest and most enduring links between Mill and the Benthamites, though like Place he believed in birth control as a crucial aid to the progress of the working class. Mill was in fact arrested at a young age for distributing birth control literature—deemed "pornography"—in London, after he had directly witnessed the horrors of infanticide and child abandonment.

20. Mill, *Autobiography*, p. 139.

21. Mill, *Autobiography*, p. 141.

22. On this, see K. de Lazari-Radek and P. Singer, *The Point of View of the Universe*. As the next chapter and later sections of this one will suggest, Mill, like the other classical utilitarians, may have conceived his task in terms more akin to that of Singer's *How Are We to Live? Ethics in an Age of Self-Interest* (Amherst: Prometheus Books, 1995), in its attempt to achieve a convergence of egoism and rational benevolence via a kind of argumentative pincer movement. As Rosen argued with respect to Bentham, Mill's aggregative concern for the greatest happiness is never advanced without some form of distributivist regard for the happiness of each individual, albeit often in the language of egoism.

23. Mill, *Autobiography*, p. 145.

24. Mill, *Autobiography*, p. 149.

25. Although it is often noted that Sidgwick pointed to the conflation of egoism and utilitarianism as a confusion on the part of the earlier utilitarians, it is less often appreciated how his own favored resolutions to the "Dualism of the Practical Reason," or standoff between egoism and utilitarianism, invoked some such convergence between the two views, marking a point of continuity rather than contrast with his great predecessors. See the following chapter.

26. Mill, *Autobiography*, p. 147.

27. Indeed, Byron's bleak poem "Darkness" seemed designed to induce depression rather than cure it.

28. Ibid., p. 153.

29. Though, sadly, Sterling would die at the age of 38, a victim of the tuberculosis that would take so many during this era (and that Mill and Taylor Mill also suffered from). Also the author of works of poetry and the novel *Arthur Coningsby*, Sterling was, as Mill noted, very much a man of strong feeling, a needed counter to Mill the "reasoning machine." Sterling's long absence, for reasons of health, at the family sugar plantation on St. Vincent, in the early thirties, was hard on Mill, and his death in 1844 left Mill devastated.

30. For this remark and others of relevance, see Schultz, *Eye*, pp. 29–30. Some of the following paragraphs have been adapted from that work.

31. Ibid., p. 46.

32. Ibid., p. 45.

33. Named after George Grote's younger brother, John, an insightful critic of utilitarianism—see his 1870 work, *An Examination of the Utilitarian Philosophy*.

34. Schultz, *Eye*, p. 49.

35. Mill, *Autobiography*, p. 147.

36. Ibid., p. 147.

37. Donner, "Morality, Virtue, and Aesthetics in Mill's Art of Life," in Ben Eggleston and Dale Miller, eds., *John Stuart Mill and the Art of Life* (New York: Oxford University Press, 2011), pp. 155, 157, 154.

38. A classic treatment of these issues is Fred Berger's *Happiness, Justice, and Freedom: The Moral and Political Philosophy of John Stuart Mill* (Berkeley: University of California Press, 1984), which treats at length the issue of reconciling Mill's account of mental conditioning with his account of autonomy and valuing various ideal goods for their own sake. And as later sections will show, the Millian attempt to marry hedonism and perfectionism is highly controversial, and at the core of such recent works as David Brink's *Mill's Progressive Principles* (Oxford: The Clarendon Press at Oxford University Press, 2013). But as Berger, Skorupski, and Crisp show, a strong case can be made for the consistency of Mill's hedonism. See also John Skorupski's review of Brink, *Notre Dame Philosophical Reviews*, March 19, 2014, at http://ndpr.nd.edu/news/47034-mills-progressive-principles/.

39. Mill, *Utilitarianism*, CW X, p. 214.

40. Numerous recent works on happiness endorse some such view, albeit without the clerisy bit. See, for one of the better recent examples, Sissela Bok, *Exploring Happiness: From Aristotle to Brain Science* (New Haven: Yale University Press, 2011); also Haybron, *The Pursuit of Unhappiness*. Again, this line of argument suggests that Mill conceived of his task as an attempt to achieve a convergence of egoism and rational benevolence via a kind of argumentative pincer movement.

41. J. Carlisle, *John Stuart Mill and the Writing of Character* (Athens, GA: University of Georgia Press, 1991). This brilliant and provocative work is particularly good on the pervasive theme of "character" in Mill's work.

42. As is well known, one of the best ways to see what James Mill was about is to consider his famous—arguably, losing—exchange with Macaulay over the "Essay on Government." See J. Lively and J. Rees, eds., *Logic and Politics: James Mill's "Essay on Government", Macaulay's Critique and the Ensuing Debate* (Oxford: Oxford University Press, 1978). Macaulay charged Mill with being a modern day scholastic, which, in essence, meant with rigidly applying a narrow, economistic rational actor model of democracy no matter what the particular social and historical circumstances.

43. And he corresponded with everyone, notably Comte and Tocqueville; Carlyle was an early if difficult friend who had (wrongly) identified the young Mill as a potential disciple.

44. John Skorupski, *Why Read Mill Today?* (London: Routledge, 2006), pp. 9–10.

45. Carlisle, *John Stuart Mill and the Writing of Character*, pp. 165–66. Excerpt reprinted with permission of the University of Georgia.

46. Mill, *Autobiography*, p. 215.

47. Ibid., p. 211.

48. Mill, "Civilization," CW XVIII, p. 126.

49. Ibid., p. 133.

50. Ibid., p. 135.

51. Ibid., p. 136.

52. Ibid., p. 138.

53. Ibid., p. 139.

54. Ibid., pp. 139–40.

55. Ibid., pp. 140–41.

56. Ibid., p. 146. Perhaps the most eloquent and powerful expression of Mill's educational views came in his 1867 "Inaugural Address Delivered to the University of St. Andrews"—see CW XXI. But both early and late works reveal his conviction that one could and should have it all in education, that a many-sided liberal education was also deeply practical in the best sense. See Ryan, *Liberal Anxieties and Liberal Education* (New York: Hill and Wang, 1998).

57. D. Winch, *Wealth and Life: Essays on the Intellectual History of Political Economy in Britain, 1848–1914* (Cambridge: Cambridge University Press, 2009), pp. 34–35. In this excellent work, Winch notes that as the hopes for the Radicals collapsed, Mill's diagnosis was that "[w]e are entering upon times in which the progress of liberal opinions will again, as formerly, depend upon what is said and written, and no longer upon what is done, by their avowed friends." (p. 35). This was an attitude that would facilitate the completion of his *Logic*.

58. Ibid., p. 233.

59. For an overview of Whewell's philosophy, see my entry on him, and on "Late Modern British Ethics," in *The International Encyclopedia of Ethics*, ed. Hugh LaFollette, at http://onlinelibrary.wiley.com/doi/10.1002/9781444367072.wbiee309/abstract. Curiously enough, Whewell himself liked parts of Mill's *Logic*, explaining that "Mr. Mill appears

to me especially instructive in his discussion of the nature of the proof which is conveyed by the syllogism; and . . . his doctrine, that the force of the syllogism consists in an *inductive assertion, with an interpretation added to it,* solves very happily the difficulties which baffle the other theories of this subject" (quoted in CW XI, p. x, n. 13). Indeed, it must be admitted that Mill was scarcely fair to Whewell, who was himself, at least in his younger days, something of a progressive reformer, albeit a deeply religious one. For a more appreciative account of Whewell's progressive side, see Laura Snyder's *The Philosophical Breakfast Club* (New York: Broadway Books, 2012) and her entry on Whewell in the *Stanford Encyclopedia of Philosophy,* at http://plato.stanford.edu/entries/whewell/. Whewell in fact coined the term "scientist" and was a champion of expanding the role of science in the Cambridge curriculum and society in general. He also believed in progress, in moral theory and science, though he did seek to replace Paley with Butler, in the Cambridge curriculum.

60. Collini's engaging work on Mill has insightfully highlighted his role as a public moralist, in all its distinctiveness in the Victorian context; see his *Public Moralists: Political Thought and Intellectual Life in Britain 1850–1930* (Oxford: Oxford University Press, 1993).

61. Mill, *A System of Logic,* CW VII, "Introduction" by R. F. McRae, p. xlv.

62. Ibid., Chap. VIII.

63. John Skorupski, "Introduction," in Skorupski, ed., *The Cambridge Companion to John Stuart Mill* (New York: Cambridge University Press, 1998), pp. 5–6. Of course, inflating the realm of naturalism to encompass supposedly problematic entities has been a popular move from James and Dewey to Searle and Putnam.

64. Bertrand Russell, "John Stuart Mill," in his *Portraits from Memory* (New York: Simon and Schuster, 1969), pp. 123–24. For a remarkable, albeit controversial, defense of Mill on mathematics, see Philip Kitcher, "Mill, Mathematics, and the Naturalist Tradition," in Skorupski, ed., *Mill,* pp. 57–111.

65. On Mill in relation to such figures as John Dewey, see Alan Ryan, "The Point of View of the Universe: Mill to Dewey," in P. Bucolo, R. Crisp, and B. Schultz, eds., *Henry Sidgwick: Happiness and Religion* (Catania: Universita degli Studi di Catania, 2006), pp. 336–67. The recent history of philosophy has alas tended to overlook the striking continuities between Mill and the early pragmatists, though in many respects Dewey is a more obvious successor to Mill than Moore.

66. Fred Wilson, "Mill, John Stuart" *The Stanford Encyclopedia of Philosophy* (Summer 2015 Edition), Edward N. Zalta, ed., p. 14, http://plato.stanford.edu/archives/sum2015 /entries/mill/. This entry has since been archived.

67. Ibid., pp. 14–15. As noted previously, this very important clarification of Mill's argument has also been developed at length by Berger, in *Happiness, Justice, and Freedom.*

68. Skorupski, "Liberal Elitism," in his *Ethical Explorations* (Oxford: Oxford University Press, 1999), pp. 205–206. The challenge here is of course as alive as ever, as is evident from Skorupski's own magisterial *The Domain of Reasons* (Oxford: Oxford University Press, 2010) and Parfit's even more magisterial *On What Matters.*

69. Skorupski, *Why Read Mill?* p. 27.

70. See Schneewind, *Sidgwick's Ethics and Victorian Moral Philosophy,* especially chap. 5.

71. Mill, *Logic* II, p. 951. This is a point that, as the following chapter will show, Sidgwick took deeply to heart.

72. The collection by B. Eggleston, D. Miller and D. Weinstein, eds., *John Stuart Mill and the Art of Life* (Oxford: Oxford University Press, 2012) rightly emphasizes the importance and development of this section of the *Logic,* which, the editors stress, is crucial for making sense of such works as *Utilitarianism.* For Mill, the principle of utility played a role parallel to induction, but as the fundamental principle of all forms of conduct. And the domain of reasons (and feelings) was much wider than the domain of strictly moral

reasons (and feelings). The infatuation, in recent decades, with "Trolley" puzzle cases or moral dilemmas, as recounted in such works as Dave Edmonds's *Would You Kill the Fat Man?* (Princeton: Princeton University Press, 2014), has worked to obscure this larger playing field for Millian argument, which was actually more in line with Godwin's rethinking of his views on the Fénelon case.

73. Mill, *Logic*, p. 952.

74. Elizabeth Anderson, in "John Stuart Mill and Experiments in Living," *Ethics* 102, no. 1 (Oct., 1991), is surely correct in claiming that Mill regarded his own life as an example of the "experiments in living" that he called for in various works, including *On Liberty*.

75. Mill, "Diary," CW XXVI, p. 653.

76. D. Miller, "Mill, Harriet Taylor," *Stanford Encyclopedia of Philosophy* (Winter 2015 Edition), Edward N. Zalta, ed., https://plato.stanford.edu/archives/win2015/entries /harriet-mill/.

77. Ibid.

78. Jo Ellen Jacobs, *The Voice of Harriet Taylor Mill* (Bloomington, IN: Indiana University Press, 2002), pp. xxi-xxii. And even some supposedly more sympathetic writers can make their praise sound snarky: "You have to hand it to Harriet. She had a solid husband against whose placidity her own wit could shine all the more dazzlingly. Out of an uncomfortable marriage in which she felt sexually oppressed she had constructed a situation in which she had her husband's support, both emotional and financial, without paying the sexual debt she so much loathed. She had the luxury of thinking she was sacrificing her happiness for his. She had one of the most brilliant men in London as her intimate and devoted friend, and she had him convinced she was making a sacrifice for his sake, too. She had the love of her three children, who adored her, no doubt, for the same reasons Mill did—for her clarity and firmness, combined with warmth and spontaneity. She was an excellent mother and, throughout all these complicated domestic maneuvers, retained the reputation of being an excellent mother. Precariously, she even had her respectability. This was evidently a woman of extraordinary talents, as John Mill always said." Phyllis Rose, *Parallel Lives: Five Victorian Marriages* (New York: Vintage Books, 1984), pp. 113–14.

79. Jo Ellen Jacobs, ed., *The Complete Works of Harriet Taylor Mill* (Bloomington, IN: University of Indiana Press, 1998), p. xi.

80. Russell, "John Stuart Mill," pp. 122–23 and p. 128.

81. See Jo Ellen Jacobs, ed., *The Complete Works of Harriet Taylor Mill*.

82. Ibid., pp. xi-xii.

83. Capaldi, *John Stuart Mill: A Biography*, p. 102.

84. Reeve, *John Stuart Mill*, p. 83.

85. Ibid., pp. 83–84. John Taylor was an interesting figure in himself. Condemned by history as a competent but intellectually dull businessman, he did, despite some stock prejudices, somehow work his way around to largely accommodating Harriet's unusual requests.

86. See Jo Ellen Jacobs, ed., *The Complete Works of Harriet Taylor Mill*, sect. 1.

87. Quoted in Reeve, p. 89.

88. Mill, *On Liberty*, CW XVIII, p. 216.

89. M. St. John Packe, *The Life of John Stuart Mill* (London: Secker and Warburg, 1954), pp. 129–30.

90. Ibid., p. 130.

91. Jacobs, *Voice*, pp. 18–19.

92. Mill, *Diary*, CW XVII, p. 640.

93. Jacobs, *Voice*, pp. 28–29 and p. 49.

94. Mill, *Diary*, CW XVII, pp. 655–56.

95. Mill, *Autobiography*, CW I, p. 257.

96. Mill, *Autobiography*, pp. 254–57.

97. Jacobs, *The Voice of Harriet Taylor Mill*, p. 207.

98. Quoted in Winch, *Wealth and Life*, p. 53.

99. Mill, *The Principles of Political Economy*, CW III, p. 756.

100. Winch, *Wealth and Life*, p. 63. Winch nicely brings out the importance of nature to Mill personally: "Mill had been a keen amateur botanist since youth; he had acquired this hobby, along with a taste for mountain scenery, during his first visit to the Pyrenees as a fourteen-year-old. Later these tastes were moulded as much by necessity as pleasure. One of the palliatives he took for the tubercular condition he believed would kill him in the 1850s was extensive walking tours, during which botanizing was his chief activity, enabling him to become an amateur expert on the flora of Britain and several European countries. The hobby was chiefly pursued nearer to home in the Surrey hills, but one of the most important walking tours he undertook in Britain, undoubtedly, was the one that resulted in a visit to Wordsworth in the Lake District. . . . Memories of the visit left a small but significant mark on Mill's *Principles*. . . . The memory of his visit in 1831, when he had recorded that 'no penury' was visible among that peasantry, remained with him in the 1840s when marshalling evidence in favour of peasant proprietorship on a pan-European scale and against the background of his official, if second-hand, knowledge of peasant agriculture in India" (pp. 62–63).

101. Mill, *The Principles of Political Economy*, CW III, p. 758.

102. Ibid., pp. 762–63.

103. Mill, "Thornton on Labour and Its Claims," CW V, pp. 643–44. For an excellent discussion of Mill's views on poverty in comparison with those of Bentham and Malthus—a discussion that supports many points stressed in this book—see Michael Quinn, "Mill on Poverty, Population, and Poor Relief: Out of Bentham by Malthus?" *Revue d'études benthamiennes* 4 (2008), available at http://etudes-benthamiennes.revues.org/185?lang=en.

104. Ibid., pp. 657–58.

105. *Manual of Political Economy*, 2nd ed. (London: Macmillan, 1865), p. 277.

106. Ibid., pp. 283–84.

107. Ibid., pp. 117–18. The importance of this alternative would come to be treated more skeptically by Sidgwick, but it in fact remains a vital issue in economics; see Joseph R. Blasi, Richard B. Freeman, and Douglas L. Kruse, *The Citizen's Share: Reducing Inequality in the 21st Century* (New Haven: Yale University Press, 2013). As of course does the matter of challenging the obsession with economic growth—see CASSE, Center for the Advancement of the Steady State Economy, at http://steadystate.org/.

108. Mill, *The Principles of Political Economy*, CW III, p. 765.

109. Ibid., p. 769.

110. Ibid., p. 775. The emphasis on the co-operative movement increases in the later editions of the *Principles*, in response to political developments. The Mills expressed considerable sympathy, as well, with such democratic movements as Chartism, the working class movement for expanding the franchise, eliminating property requirements, etc., as described in "The People's Charter" of 1838.

111. Ibid., p. 939.

112. Ibid., pp. 936–71.

113. Winch, *Wealth and Life*, p. 54.

114. Quinn, "Mill on Poverty, Population and Poor Relief: Out of Bentham by Malthus?" p. 16. As Quinn recounts, "For Bentham, lack of education amongst the poor issued in ignorance and irrationality: 'The comparative weakness of their faculties, moral as well as intellectual, the result of the want of education, assimilates their condition in this particular, to that of *minors*.' In contrast, Bentham's industry house apprentices would be taught literacy and numeracy, while Bentham intended to make their education available

also to children and adults among the independent poor. Of course, the Bentham of the poor law writings, with his exaltation of the use of education as a tool of ensuring political quietude, makes Malthus look positively liberal, yet even Bahmueller, hardly an uncritical commentator, allows that, 'At long last pauper children would receive at least a modicum of systematic education'" (p. 24). Different as their strategies may have been, Bentham and Mill were at one on the need for pauper education.

115. Reeve, *John Stuart Mill*, p. 174.

116. Mill, *Principles*, p. 952.

117. Frank Podmore, *Robert Owen, A Biography*, vol. 1 (London: Hutchinson and Co., 1906), p. 78—79. For the grim realities of the situation, see *English Historical Documents, 1783-1832*, A. Aspinall and E. Anthony Smith, eds. (London: Eyre & Spottiswoode, 1959) and *English Historical Documents, 1833-1874*, G. M. Young, and W. D. Handcock, eds. (London: Eyre & Spottiswoode, 1956). Also, John Waller, *The Real Oliver Twist, Robert Blincoe: A Life that Illuminates a Violent Age* (Thriplow: Icon Books, 2006).

118. Mill, *Autobiography*, p. 161-62. Many of the Millian qualifications to democracy would of course be given extended consideration in *Considerations on Representative Government* (1861), the work that floated his ideas about proportional representation, giving greater weight to the votes of the educated, and the important educational effects of political participation. Like Godwin, Mill objected to the secret ballot. For a good brief overview of *Considerations* in connection with a (perfectionist) reading of Mill's other work, see David Brink's "Mill's Moral and Political Philosophy," *Stanford Encyclopedia of Philosophy* (August 2014), http://plato.stanford.edu/entries/mill-moral-political/.

119. Skorupski, *Why Read Mill Today?* p. 106.

120. Jacobs, ed., *The Complete Works*, pp. 103–104.

121. Ibid., *The Complete Works*, p. 131.

122. Ibid., p. xiii. Also, as Jacobs notes in *The Voice of Harriet Taylor Mill*: "During 1854, they spent only four and a half months together, and during 1855, only six months; the separations resulted from their illnesses. Harriet nearly died of a lung hemorrhage in 1853, and John was seriously ill with consumption in 1854–1855. Luckily, John's regime of walking twenty or more miles a day and sleeping in flea-ridden pallets in the hinterlands of Greece cured him sufficiently for him to resume his duties at India House in July 1855. From that time until Harriet's death three years later, they were rarely apart, and then only for short periods" (p. 168).

123. Ibid.

124. This is one of the main theses of Carlisle's *John Stuart Mill and the Writing of Character*. It is ironic that the work in hand should have to reassert as an academic novelty the very approach of the best-known of the classical utilitarians. They were certainly not ones to ignore persons, Rawls's famous critique of utilitarianism notwithstanding.

125. Reeve, *John Stuart Mill*, p. 214.

126. Mill, "Utility of Religion," CW X, p. 428.

127. Mill, *On Liberty*, CW XVIII, p. 293.

128. Ibid., p. 224.

129. Ibid., pp. 224–25.

130. The reference is of course to Singer's seminal 1972 essay "Famine, Affluence, and Morality," recently republished with a forward by Bill and Melinda Gates (New York: Oxford University Press, 2015). The case is spelled out much more fully in *The Life You Can Save*.

131. On these matters, especially the famous "harm principle," the works of Joel Feinberg and Joseph Raz still set the standard; see Feinberg, *The Moral Limits of the Criminal Law*, vols. 1–4 (New York: Oxford University Press, 1984–1988), and Raz, *The Morality of Freedom* (Oxford: Oxford University Press, 1986). But the literature is endless.

132. Mill, *On Liberty*, CW XVIII, pp. 235–36.

133. Ibid., p. 261.

134. Ibid., pp. 266–67. This practically defines the role of the clerisy.

135. Ibid., p. 267–68. Mill may have underestimated the role of positive peer pressure, the desire to belong, in social change—see Tina Rosenberg, *Join the Club: How Positive Peer Pressure Can Transform the World* (New York: W. W. Norton & Co., 2011).

136. Mill, *The Subjection of Women*, in A. P. Robson and J. Robson, eds., *Sexual Equality: Writings by John Stuart Mill, Harriet Taylor Mill, and Helen Taylor* (Toronto: University of Toronto Press, 1994), pp. 318–19. This work very helpfully collects together their chief published works on the subjection of women, including those of Helen Taylor, and thus serves as a complement to the *Complete Works* of Harriet Taylor Mill.

137. Ibid., pp. 324–25. As David Brink has noted, such passages should have kept Mill from thinking that there might be some natural division of labor between the sexes: "There is one significant blemish on Mill's feminist credentials. He sometimes assumed that a traditional sexual division of labor was natural in the sense that it was likely to emerge in a culture of equal opportunity for all." See Brink, *Mill's Progressive Principles* (Oxford: Clarendon Press at Oxford University Press, 2013), p. 276. Also his "Mill's Moral and Political Philosophy."

138. Martha Nussbaum, *Women and Human Development: The Capabilities Approach* (New York: Cambridge University Press, 2006) is of course a compelling development of this theme in connection with feminism. The capabilities approach overlaps at many points with the perfectionist interpretation of Mill.

139. Mill, "Chapters on Socialism," CW V, p. 753.

140. Mill, *Utilitarianism*, CW X, p. 232. Again, compare Singer, *How Are We To Live?* As stressed previously, this is a very familiar utilitarian line to work—namely, showing how apparently egoistic reasons can morph into or cohere with impartial utilitarian ones, and vice versa. And it is a line that Mill recognizes is there, at least in theory, in Bentham—see his "Remarks on Bentham's Philosophy," which explains how Bentham's notion of "interest" could have accommodated both the self-regarding and the sympathetic.

141. Ibid., p. 233.

142. Mill, "The Utility of Religion," CW X, p. 421.

143. Here again, the argument that Rosen made in connection with Bentham would appear to apply to Mill. And it should also be noted that this emphasis does lend support to the ties that Brink sees between Mill and such Idealists as T. H. Green, who resolutely tied individual good to common good. Brink correctly argues that Mill was not an egoist and that his language often sounded perfectionist notes. But clearly, like Godwin, Mill did not see his perfectionist side as at odds with utilitarianism.

144. Ibid., p. 234.

145. West, "Mill and Utilitarianism in the Mid-Nineteenth Century," in B. Eggleston and D. Miller, eds. *The Cambridge Companion to Utilitarianism*, p. 76.

146. Again, see Schneewind, *Sidgwick's Ethics*, chap. 5. But see also Bentham, *Introduction*, p. 13, where Bentham similarly denies that as a first principle the principle of utility could be "susceptible of any direct proof," or that such proof is needed, given the lack of alternative and the ways in which everyone, no matter how "stupid or perverse," defers to it.

147. Ibid., p. 211.

148. Skorupski, *Why Read Mill Today?* pp. 32–33.

149. Sturgeon, "Mill's Hedonism," *Boston University Law Review*, vol. 90 (2010), pp. 1716–17. For Crisp's detailed and slightly different and more reserved account, see his excellent *Routledge Philosophy Guidebook to Mill on Utilitarianism* (London: Routledge, 1997), especially Chap. 2.

150. De Lazari-Radek and Singer, *The Point of View of the Universe*, p. 253. As the next chapter will show, there are still many complications here, and de Lazari-Radek and Singer

have in fact revised their form of hedonism in light of Crisp's arguments: "As Crisp notes, in our book we approve of this 'heterogeneity objection,' and cite the work of the neuroscientists Kent Berridge and Morten Kringelbach in support of the view that pleasure is not a sensation, but rather is a kind of 'hedonic gloss' that our hedonic brain systems paint on certain sensations. Crisp thinks that it is better to interpret Berridge and Kringelbach as saying that pleasure is not merely a sensation, but allowing that the hedonic gloss may itself be a sensation, or a single type of feeling. We are now willing to concede that Crisp may be right on this point. If so, the heterogeneity objection can be met, to the extent that we can say that the hedonic systems of the brain put the same kind of hedonic gloss on various different sensations. The question is, however, whether this does not simply transfer the problem of saying what pleasure is to the problem of saying what the hedonic gloss is." See their "Doing Our Best for Hedonistic Utilitarianism," http://www2.units.it/etica/2016_1/SINGER-DE%20LAZARI%20RADEK.pdf. Of course, as noted at the end of the previous chapter, other modes of research are important for reconceptualizing hedonism, particularly given the social mediation of reports of pleasures and pains.

151. J. Dinwiddy, *Bentham: Selected Writings of John Dinwiddy*, ed. W. Twinning (Stanford: Stanford University Press, 2004), pp. 29–30.

152. Brink, *Mill's Progressive Principles*, pp. 28–29.

153. Sturgeon, "Mill's Hedonism," p. 1725.

154. Ibid., p. 1727.

155. And this, as the next chapter will show, notwithstanding Robert Nozick's famous "Experience Machine" counterargument to the effect that there must be more to value than conscious experience.

156. Again, for an excellent survey, see Crisp, *Mill on Utilitarianism*, and the same author's critical edition of *Utilitarianism* (Oxford: Oxford University Press, 1998). Also, Dale Miller, *J.S. Mill* (Malden, MA: Polity Press, 2010). Crisp is persuaded by the interpretation of Mill as an act utilitarian, but as his account also shows, Mill was scarcely forthcoming on the issue. His most explicit statement comes late in life, in an 1872 letter to John Venn: "I agree with you that the right way of testing actions by their consequences, is to test them by the natural consequences of the particular action, and not by those which would follow if every one did the same" (quoted in Crisp, *Mill on Utilitarianism*, p. 117). But this passage is too narrowly focused to address the concerns characteristic of, say, global utilitarians; see Julia Driver, "Global Utilitarianism," in *The Cambridge Companion to Utilitarianism*, pp. 166–176. As David Brink notes in his insightful chapter on the issue in *Mill's Progressive Principles*, even the better interpretations of Mill are not without "some interpretive strain" (p. 98). And as Dale Miller rightly observes, in *J.S. Mill*, "Mill never addressed the question of precisely what makes actions right or wrong directly, which means that interpreters are relegated to unearthing a moral theory that lies implicit in his writings" (p. 79). Miller opts for reading Mill as a "sophisticated rule-utilitarian." On rule utilitarianism in general, see the excellent work of Brad Hooker, *Ideal Code, Real World* (Oxford: Clarendon Press, 2000).

157. Mill, *Utilitarianism*, CW X, pp. 250–51.

158. Brink, *Mill's Progressive Principles*, p. 279.

159. Skorupski, "Review: David O. Brink, *Mill's Progressive Principles*," *Notre Dame Philosophical Reviews*, 2014.03.21, available at http://ndpr.nd.edu/news/47034-mills-progressive-principles/ See also, Skorupski, *John Stuart Mill*, p. 305: "The pleasure of a cold beer after a hot day's climbing is intense. The pleasure of listening to a Schubert sonata is not in that way intense. But I might still forgo the beer to get to a performance of the sonata by my favourite Schubert pianist. Nor is it anything other than *pleasure* that I expect—absorbing, even demanding, but still a pleasure, and its value lying therein. Mill wants to fend off the notion that utilitarianism, in philistine fashion, must measure the

value of pleasures only in terms of the former kind of intensity. Not only physical pleasures have that kind of intensity of course: so does reading a 'good bad book'. In both cases it is inherent in the kind of enjoyment involved that it is undemanding and releases one after effort. In contrast higher pleasures characteristically call for an active effort of attention and the deployment of absorbing skills; they call on our 'higher faculties'." Critics, as Roger Crisp has suggested to me, will simply say in response that then a utilitarian metaprinciple must be brought in to resolve the conflicts.

160. Reeve, *John Stuart Mill*, p. 387.

161. Martha Nussbaum, "Mill on Happiness: The Enduring Value of a Complex Critique," in *Utilitarianism and Empire*, Bart Schultz and Georgios Varouxakis, eds. (Lanham, Md., 2005), pp. 120–23.

162. Georgios Varouxakis, *Mill on Nationality* (London: Routledge, 2002), p. 116.

163. Martha Nussbaum, "An Interview with Martha Nussbaum," *The Dualist* (2004), p. 65. Nussbaum has developed and refined her position on cosmopolitanism and political emotions in such powerful works as *Political Emotions: Why Love Matters for Justice* (Cambridge, MA: Belknap Press, 2015). And as she makes clear, in for example the 2009 introduction to her work *The Therapy of Desire* (Princeton: Princeton University Press, 2009), she does not identify her approach to global justice with cosmopolitanism, which she does "not even accept . . . as a fully correct comprehensive ethical view, since . . . it gives too little space for a nonderivative loyalty to family, friends, loved ones, even nation." As she explains, "I have changed my mind on this point. Without such attachments, life becomes empty of urgency and personal meaning" (p. xvii). Moreover, Nussbaum's approach to justice, whether global or domestic, is a political liberal, not a comprehensive liberal, one. Following Rawls, she seeks an overlapping consensus, a "political doctrine that is fair to all the different ways in which citizens pursue the good, refusing to endorse one of them over the others" (p. xv). By contrast, Mill, like Kant, defended a comprehensive form of liberalism.

164. Anthony Kwame Appiah, *The Ethics of Identity* (Princeton: Princeton University Press, 2004), p. 144.

165. Ibid., pp. 145–46. The Catherine Hall versus Peter Mandler debate over the salience of the notion of race in the mid-Victorian context is important, but not addressed here. My sympathies are rather obviously with Hall (see Catherine Hall, *Civilizing Subjects* [Chicago: University of Chicago Press, 2002], p. 497, n. 127), though the theorizing about race (and racism) is in both cases somewhat sweeping. My own take on race follows David Theo Goldberg: "I am suggesting that race is a fluid, transforming, historically specific concept parasitic on theoretic and social discourses for the meaning it assumes at any given historical moment" (Goldberg, *Racist Culture* [Oxford: Oxford University Press, 1993], p. 74). See also Tommie Shelby, *We Who Are Dark: The Philosophical Foundations of Black Solidarity* (Cambridge, MA: Harvard University Press, 2005), Charles W. Mills, *Blackness Visible: Essays on Philosophy and Race* (Ithaca, NY: Cornell University Press, 1998), and Thomas Holt, *The Problem of Race in the Twenty-First Century* (Cambridge, MA: Harvard University Press, 2002).

166. Uday Mehta, *Liberalism and Empire: A Study in Nineteenth-Century British Liberal Thought* (Chicago: University of Chicago Press, 1999), pp. 195–96.

167. Ibid., p. 15.

168. Ibid., p. 214.

169. In the rest of this chapter, the focus will be chiefly on Mill in connection with the Jamaican blacks, though parallel arguments could and should be made about his views of the peoples of India, the Maori, Native Americans, and many others, including of course the Irish, about whom he was often quite disparaging (while also being more positive about their capitalistic potential; see volume XI of the *Collected Works: Essays on England, Ireland, and the Empire* [1982]). All too often, and at the least, Mill, and Sidgwick for that

matter, could sound astoundingly, preposterously naïve, as when he claimed that the "conduct of the United States towards the Indian tribes has been throughout not only just, but noble" (quoted in Miller, "Chairing the Jamaica Committee: J. S. Mill and the Limits of Colonial Authority," in *Utilitarianism and Empire*, Schultz and Varouxakis, eds., p. 178). The truth, as Roxanne Dunbar-Ortiz has so powerfully demonstrated in her book *An Indigenous Peoples' History of the United States* (Boston: Beacon Press, 2015), was obviously quite otherwise. Lynn Zastoupil's *John Stuart Mill and India* is especially helpful on Mill and India, on which subject there is now a considerable literature. England's Indian subjects were also often described in the most offensive terms, as "niggers," etc.

170. Goldberg, "Liberalism's Limits," pp. 133–34. Excerpt of essay republished with permission of Blackwell, from Julie K. Ward and Tommy L. Lott, eds., *Philosophers on Race: Critical Essays*, (London: Blackwell Publishers, 2002); permission conveyed through Copyright Clearance Center, Inc.

171. Carlyle, *The Nigger Question, Mill, The Negro Question*, ed. Eugene R. August (New York: Appleton-Century-Crofts, 1971). See also CW XXI, including the introduction by Stefan Collini. This episode can only make one wonder how Mill could have been such friends with Carlyle in the thirties, so much so that even the accidental burning of the manuscript of Carlyle's *French Revolution* by Mill's housekeeper was forgiven. Mill would always hold that there was much greatness in Carlyle, a view that Taylor Mill seems not to have shared.

172. Ibid., p. 40.

173. Goldberg, "Liberalism's Limits," p. 129.

174. J. Joseph Miller, "Chairing the Jamaica Committee," p. 163.

175. Goldberg, "Liberalism's Limits," p. 130.

176. Ibid., p. 134.

177. Anthony Bogues, "John Stuart Mill and 'the Negro Question': Race, Colonialism, and the Ladder of Civilization," in *Race and Racism in Modern Philosophy*, Andrew Valls, ed. (Ithaca, NY: Cornell University Press, 2005), p. 222.

178. Indeed, these lines would seem, alas, to have greater application to U.S. and British politics with every passing year.

179. Jennifer Pitts, *A Turn to Empire: The Rise of Imperial Liberalism in Britain and France* (Princeton: Princeton University Press, 2005), p. 160.

180. As Bogues helpfully summarizes it, when the rebellion (largely led by Bogle and his followers) reached its peak, involving some two thousand persons in the parish of St. Thomas, the "colonial government reacted by establishing a council of war. Arguing that this was but the tip of an island-wide conspiracy to overthrow the colonial government, and with the memory of the Haitian Revolution hovering over the colony, Governor Eyre organized a military force to brutally crush the rebellion. At the end of the day, Eyre unleashed severe repression—439 persons were killed, hundreds were brutally flogged, thousands of houses were burnt, and many of the leaders including Bogle were hanged. Eyre held Gordon responsible for the rebellion and duly executed him" (Bogues, "John Stuart Mill," p. 224). The best extended accounts of the rebellion are Hall, *Civilizing Subjects*; Bernard Semmel, *Jamaican Blood and Victorian Conscience: The Governor Eyre Controversy* (Westport, CT: Houghton Mifflin, 1962); and Gad Heuman, *The Killing Time: The Morant Bay Rebellion in Jamaica* (Knoxville, TN: University of Tennessee Press, 1994). Hall is particularly good on Eyre's background and character, though she has surprisingly little to say about Mill. But see the essay "Competing Masculinities: Thomas Carlyle, John Stuart Mill and the Case of Governor Eyre," in *White, Male, and Middle-Class: Explorations in Feminism and History*, Catherine Hall, ed. (Cambridge: Cambridge University Press, 1992), for some very illuminating remarks on the construction of both gender and race in this controversy. In developing a comparison between Mill's feminism and his views

on race, Hall allows that, on Mill's account, "whether there would be in the end, whatever the degree of education achieved by the blacks, a natural division of labor between the races, remains a problem," p. 288. See also Thomas Holt, *The Problem of Freedom: Race, Labor and Politics in Jamaica and Britain, 1832–1938* (Baltimore: Johns Hopkins University Press, 1991).

181. Pitts, *A Turn to Empire*, p. 161.

182. Ibid., p. 162.

183. Ibid. Pitts's argument here is primarily concerned with the limits of English and French liberal discourse, rather than with the overall cultural and historical limitations of the "times," which could muster a good deal more. A recent book, Michael W. Doyle's *The Question of Intervention: John Stuart Mill and the Responsibility to Protect* (New Haven: Yale University Press, 2015) is a curious work that is deeply admiring of Mill's thoughts on intervention, but very limited in its account of the colonialist project.

184. Ibid., p. 241.

185. John Robson, "Civilisation and Culture as Moral Concepts," *The Cambridge Companion to Mill*, J. Skorupski, p. 353. Robson also quotes from Mill's "Remarks on Bentham's Philosophy": "For a tribe of North American Indians, improvement means, taming down their proud and solitary self-dependence: for a body of emancipated negroes, it means accustoming them to be self-dependent, instead of being merely obedient to orders: for our semi-barbarous ancestors it would have meant softening them; for a race of enervated Asiatics it would mean hardening them" (p. 368). Robson's *The Improvement of Mankind* (Toronto: University of Toronto Press, 1968) remains one of the most enduringly valuable works on Mill's progressivism.

186. Georgios Varouxakis, "Empire, Race, Euro-centrism: John Stuart Mill and His Critics," in *Utilitarianism and Empire*, Schultz and Varouxakis, eds., p. 142.

187. Ibid., p. 144.

188. Ibid., p. 141.

189. H. S. Jones, "The Early Utilitarians, Race, and Empire: The State of the Argument," *Utilitarianism and Empire*, Schultz and Varouxakis, eds., p. 185.

190. Ibid.

191. Ibid., p. 186. Of course, that feminism has historically often had difficulties traveling, and finding forms of intersectionality, is a familiar theme, brilliantly set out in such work as Kathy Davis, *The Making of Our Bodies, Ourselves: How Feminism Travels Across Borders* (Durham, NC: Duke University Press, 2007).

192. The Varouxakis/Jones response does not recognize the cogency of Goldberg's construction of the interweaving of "race" and "ethnicity," for an extended treatment of which, see Goldberg (1993), which also includes an important critique of Appiah's biological conception of race. Cf. Shelby, *We Who Are Dark*, for an excellent account of biological essentialism versus anti-essentialism. Also, Eddie Glaude, *In a Shade of Blue: Pragmatism and the Politics of Black America* (Chicago: University of Chicago Press, 2008).

193. Of course, much valuable work (and activism) concerning race and racism has come to the fore in recent years. Paul Taylor's *Race: A Philosophical Introduction* provides a very helpful overview of the issues and recent literature, and Eddie Glaude's *Democracy in Black: How Race Still Enslaves* (New York: Crown Publishers, 2016) develops his critique in connection with recent political movements, such as Black Lives Matter. But on Mill's political context and racism, such generally excellent works as those of Duncan Bell, *Victorian Visions of Global Order* (Cambridge: Cambridge University Press, 2012) and Casper Sylvest, *British Liberal Internationalism, 1880–1939* (Manchester: Manchester University Press, 2009) simply concede (sometimes a bit grudgingly) all the crucial points argued above and in my previous works concerning Mill's racism, while hoping to sound a less indignant tone. On this issue, however, some indignation seems highly appropriate, for

the same reasons Frederick Douglass found it appropriate in his 1893 "Lecture on Haiti"; see http://faculty.webster.edu/corbetre/haiti/history/1844–1915/douglass.htm. The times really did allow for some compelling critique.

194.Anthony Kwame Appiah, "The Uncompleted Argument: DuBois and the Illusion of Race," in *The Idea of Race*, Robert Bernasconi and Tommy Lott, eds. (Indianapolis, IN: Hackett Publishing, 2000), pp. 126–27. And as Holt notes, "by the nineteenth century the term 'ethnic' is found in both English and French dictionaries coupled with 'race' as one of its synonyms" (Holt, *The Problem of Race in the 21ˢᵗ Century*, p. 17). As Hall points out, "these two discourses, that of cultural differentialism and that of biological racism, were, as Stuart Hall has argued, not two different systems, but "racism's two registers," and in many situations discourses of both were in play, the cultural slipping into the biological, and vice versa" (Hall, *Civilizing Subjects*, p. 17). Again, Goldberg (*Racist Culture*) takes a similar position.

195. And this is not to mention the publication, in 1885, of Antenor Firmin's remarkable anthropological work, *The Equality of the Human Races* (Chicago: University of Illinois Press, 2002), a striking piece of research supporting claims of racial equality. Or the still earlier and altogether amazing Comte de Volnay's *The Ruins of Empire*, available at http://knarf.english.upenn.edu/Volney/volney00.html. Volnay's work, which features a world congress of all peoples working on a basis of equality, was invoked in Mary Shelley's *Frankenstein*, and is suggestive of the positive anti-racism of the earlier utilitarians.

196. Philip Sherlock and Hazel Bennett, *The Story of the Jamaican People* (Kingston, Jamaica: Markus Wiener Publishing, 1998), pp. 247–48; see also Semmel, *Jamaican Blood and Victorian Conscience*. And Gad Heuman also compellingly demonstrates how the Morant Bay rebellion "was preceded by a long history of slave rebellions as well as a series of riots in the post-emancipation period. Many of the people involved in these riots continued to look to the rebellions as models of resistance," though after emancipation their agenda "included resisting any attempt at re-enslavement and regarded access to land as a measure of full freedom" (p. 42).

197. Holt, *The Problem of Race in the 21st Century*, p. 47. See also Holt, *The Problem of Freedom*, and Bogues, "John Stuart Mill," p. 223.

198. Mill, CW I, p. 305. It is instructive that Mill's close friend Sterling was himself in control of a West Indies sugar plantation.

199. Pitts, *A Turn to Empire*, p. 157.

200. On social constructions of whiteness and delusions of postracialism, see David Theo Goldberg, *Are We All Postracial Yet?* (New York: Polity, 2015) and Linda Martin Alcoff, *The Future of Whiteness* (New York: Polity, 2015).

201. George Fredrickson, *Racism: A Short History* (Princeton: Princeton University Press, 2002), p. 8.

202. Ibid., pp. 3–4.

203. Ibid., p. 108. Fredrickson is very careful on this score, allowing that "insofar as those relatively few individuals who assimilated Western civilization could actually gain such rights, the racist aspect was attenuated," and may not, as in the French case, always count as racism "strictly speaking" (p. 108). But clearly, on his account it does make very good sense to call some such colonial or imperial situations racist, when considering the functional or "polite" form of racism. And obviously, "something that can be legitimately described as racism existed well before the twentieth century or even the late nineteenth century" (p. 100).

204. Mill, CW XXVIII, p. 118.

205. CW XVI, p. 1206. There were of course others. In another 1866 letter to Urquhart, Mill laments the "sympathy of officials with officials & of the classes from whom officials are selected with officials of all sorts" and "the sympathy with authority & power, generated in our higher & upper middle classes by the feeling of being specially privileged to exercise

them, & by living in a constant dread of the encroachment of the class beneath which makes it one of their strongest feelings that resistance to authority must be put down per fas et nefas. . . . There is much in American politics that is regrettable enough, but I do not observe that there is a particle of the English upper class feeling that authority (meaning the person in authority) must be supported at all costs" (p. 1209).

206. Bruce L. Kinzer, Ann P. Robson, and John M. Robson, *A Moralist In and Out of Parliament: John Stuart Mill at Westminster, 1865–1868* (Toronto: University of Toronto Press, 1992), pp. 216–17.

207. Miller, "Chairing the Jamaica Committee," p. 172.

208. When the Grand Jury threw out the charges against Eyre, *Punch* celebrated the occasion with a singularly nasty poem, the first stanza of which runs, "Ye savages thirsting for bloodshed and plunder / Ye miscreants burning for rapine and prey, / By the fear of the lash and the gallows kept under, / Henceforth who shall venture to stand in your way? / Run riot, destroy, ravage, kill without pity, / Let any man how he molests you beware. / Beholding how hard the Jamaica Committee / To ruin are trying to hunt gallant EYRE." See *The White Man's Burden: An Anthology of British Poetry of the Empire*, Chris Brooks and Peter Faulkner, eds. (Exeter: University of Exeter Press, 1996), p. 206.

209. Duran, *Eight Women Philosophers* (Chicago: University of Illinois Press, 2006), p. 159.

Chapter 4

1. It is a shame that Foucault's late life fascination with *parrhesia* never led him to return to the consideration of utilitarianism. See his 1983 lectures on "Discourse and Truth: Parrhesia," *Foucault Audio Archive*, http://www.lib.berkeley.edu/MRC/foucault/parrhesia.html.

2. Sidgwick, "Autobiographical Fragment" dictated from his deathbed, in Schultz et al., *The Complete Works and Select Correspondence of Henry Sidgwick* (Charlottesville, VA: InteLex Corp., 1999). This chapter draws heavily on my previous publications on Sidgwick, especially *Henry Sidgwick, Eye of the Universe* (copyright © 2004 Bart Schultz, all excerpts reprinted with the permission of Cambridge University Press) and "A More Reasonable Ghost: Further Thoughts on Henry Sidgwick and the Irrationality of the Universe," *Rounded Globe* (February 2016), https://roundedglobe.com/html/34a3e7ff-778f-48d5-bca0-ed4e10132715/en/A%20More%20Reasonable%20Ghost:%20Further%20Reflections%20on%20Henry%20Sidgwick%20and%20the%20Irrationality%20of%20the%20Universe/.

3. Rawls, in *A Theory of Justice* and in his introduction to the Hackett edition of the *Methods*, celebrated Sidgwick for providing the best presentation of the classical utilitarian perspective, whereas Skorupski, as noted earlier, deemed Sidgwick the only one of the classical utilitarians who was not a pure utilitarian. As this chapter will show, both were correct, paradoxically enough.

4. Many important works appeared posthumously: *Lectures on the Ethics of T. H. Green, H. Spencer, and J. Martineau*, E. E. Constance Jones, ed. (London: Macmillan, 1902); *Philosophy, Its Scope and Relations: An Introductory Course of Lectures*, James Ward, ed. (London: Macmillan, 1902); *The Development of European Polity*, E. M. Sidgwick, ed. (London: Macmillan, 1903); *Miscellaneous Essays and Addresses*, E. M. Sidgwick and A. Sidgwick, eds. (London: Macmillan, 1904); and *Lectures on the Philosophy of Kant and Other Philosophical Lectures and Essays*, James Ward, ed. (London: Macmillan, 1905). For an excellent selection of Sidgwick's most important philosophical essays, see *Essays on Ethics and Method*, Marcus G. Singer, ed. (Oxford: Clarendon Press, 2000).

5. See the portrait of Sidgwick in Rayleigh, "Some Recollections of Henry Sidgwick," *Proceedings of the Society for Psychical Research* XLV (1938), pp. 162–73.

6. Sidgwick and Sidgwick, *Memoir*, p. 311.

7. Benson, "Henry Sidgwick," in his *The Leaves of the Tree: Studies in Biography* (London: The Knickerbocker Press, 1911), p. 91. As Benson notes, one "characteristic of him was his apparently invariable cheerfulness. He laughed often, a low, musical, rather lazy laugh, which gave a sense of great contentment. His diary is rather a melancholy record; but this was not at all the case with his talk, which was always light, humorous, and comfortable" (ibid., pp. 86–87).

8. See the monumental work, *The Letters of John Addington Symonds*, three vols., H. M. Schueller and R. L. Peters, eds. (Detroit: Wayne State University Press, 1967–69). Much of the best correspondence that was abridged in or deleted from E. M. Sidgwick and A. Sidgwick, *Henry Sidgwick, A Memoir* (London: Macmillan, 1906) can be found in *The Complete Works and Select Correspondence of Henry Sidgwick*, Bart Schultz et al., eds., (Charlottesville, VA: InteLex Corp., second edition 1999). See also Schultz, *Eye*, for an extensive discussion of Sidgwick and Symonds. The fluctuating social constructions of sexuality during this period, with the newly influential but often incoherent medicalization and psychiatric pathologizing of same-sex acts and identities, should recommend caution when using such terms as "homosexual" or "gay," and in any event, Sidgwick himself is difficult to classify by any standard. It was widely reported within his family that he was impotent, but he was certainly able to engage in the rhapsodic, passionate, Greek classics tinged, same-sex friendships that the Symonds circle celebrated. For an excellent survey of the changing discourse, see Linda Dowling, *Hellenism and Homosexuality in Victorian Oxford* (Ithaca, NY: Cornell University Press, 1997). Sidgwick's great niece, Anne Baer, the granddaughter of his brother Arthur, relayed to me the following passage from a letter her uncle Hugh had written to her father on the occasion of the birth of her brother Jeremy: "It is a dashed pity Uncle Henry and Aunt Nora never had any children. I suppose there was too much blooming intellect knocking about. But I daresay some characteristics are transmitted cross-wise. Ethel and I certainly got hay-fever from him, and I think at times that a certain calm spirit of scepticism has spread over us five from him. I think the normal betting in 1873 would have been on a family of idealists, disbelieving in the 39 articles but very little else in the world. Instead of which—well, dash it all, I think we are less easy to shock than any other family of five I know" (private communication).

9. Which is to say that in some respects the late Victorian context was more repressive than Bentham's.

10. As the concluding chapter of the *Outlines* shows, Sidgwick was well-versed in the pessimistic philosophies of von Hartmann and Schopenhauer. Indeed, many of Sidgwick's parapsychological interests can be found in earlier form in Schopenhauer's *Parerga und Paralipomena*.

11. An agnosticism that, like Mill's, could also take some perverse forms when it came to racial differences.

12. And yet, as Eleanor admitted, he was not quite as lugubrious and despondent as the *Memoir* tended to suggest.

13. *Memoir*, pp. 1–3. Henry later stated that his earliest memory was of picking up an enormous piece of chalk on the beach at Tenby, and he would later record that his uncle Robert was "meditating the problem of our genealogy; he gave me a copy of the stamp which the tobacconist at Leeds—believed to be 'Honest James' and my great-great-grandfather—used for his packets of Virginia. But we do not seem able to trace back the tobacconist to our ancestral hill-valley on the Cambrian border. So we must be content to *begin* with Tobacco. One might start from a worse thing." The allusion was to "a persistent

tradition in the family that they had originally migrated from Dent, a picturesque dale in the far north-west of the county" (ibid., p. 423).

14. W. H. Dawson, *History of Skipton . . . with Illustrations, etc.* (Skipton: Edmundson and Co., 1882), p. 280.

15. I would like to thank the current owner of Stone Gappe, Sir Richard McAlpine, for his generous hospitality and help during my visit to Stone Gappe in the summer of 2015.

16. For a colorful, rather sensationalistic account of Minnie's life, see Rodney Bolt, *Good as God, as Clever as the Devil: The Impossible Life of Mary Benson* (Atlantic Books, 2011). Simon Goldhill's *A Very Queer Family Indeed* (Chicago: University of Chicago Press, 2016) provides a delightful and candid history of the remarkably strange family that Minnie and the Archbishop produced. See also his talk, https://www.phf.upenn.edu/events /very-queer-family-indeed.

17. See Ian Lockwood, *Skipton 2000: The Millenium Walk* (Skipton: Skipton Millenium Task Force, 1999), p. 135.

18. Most of these dates are confirmed by Alexander W. D. Mitton's "Narrative Pedigree of the Family of Sidgwick of Dent, Leeds, Bingley, Skipton & Keighly," available at http://www.sedgwickuk.org/uk/places/yorkshire/dent%20and%20sedbergh/thomas1520 /sidgwick_narrative_pedigree.pdf.

19. See Sidgwick and Sidgwick, *Memoir*, p. 280.

20. See http://www.gutenberg.org/files/19011/19011-h/19011-h.htm.

21. Bart Schultz et al., eds., *The Collected Works and Select Correspondence of Henry Sidgwick*.

22. Ella Hatfield, *Skipton* (Skipton: Hedley Percival, 2005), p. 62.

23. Benson, *Life*, pp.15–17.

24. Ibid., p. 15.

25. Ibid., pp. 13–14.

26. Gibbons, *The Ancient Free Grammar School of Skipton in Craven: A Study in Local History* (London: Hodder & Stoughton and University Press of Liverpool, 1947), p. 99.

27. R. Geoffrey Rowley, *Old Skipton* (Clapham: Dalesman Publishing Company Ltd., 1969), p. 72.

28. E. F. Benson records how his grandfather, Edward White's father, had been under the tutelage of one Dr. Sollitt, who practiced astrology and various dark arts, until an attempt to raise Satan yielded alarming results and "he saw how potent was the power he evoked, and he made a solemn bonfire of his magical books, and practiced no more. My grandfather was of the same mind, and convinced that he too by means of astrology had acquired such knowledge as was not proper for me to attain to, burned his books and likewise devoted himself to more legitimate investigations into white lead instead of black magic." E. F. Benson, *As We Were: A Victorian Peep Show* (London: Longmans, Green, 1930), pp. 43–44. Such were the tales that filled the youth of both Sidgwicks and Bensons. "So with eyes round with pleasing terror, my father would steal up to his bed at Stonegappe or Skipton Castle, and when the holiday visits were over, returned to his mother's house at Birmingham Heath, from which every morning he walked to King Edward's school in the town, where he was now a day pupil and one who promised very well" (p. 45). This work also contains a priceless description of the elaborate toilette of Mary Sidgwick, Henry's mother.

29. Wilson, *Lothersdale*, p. 144. As Wilson also notes, in "1892, a private visit was paid to the church by the Archbishop of Canterbury, who pointed out the place on the south side of the church where, as a boy, he used to sit when spending holidays at Stone Gappe" (p. 147).

30. "'Should you imagine that children confined fourteen or fifteen hours a day in cotton mills would be so healthy as those who are only confined ten or twelve hours?' [Peel]

'Upon my word, I should think there would be no diminution of health; I do not see any reason to apprehend a diminution of health.' [Sidgwick]." See "Great Britain. Children employed in the Manufactories of the United Kingdom, 1816." *Report of the Minutes of evidence, taken before the Select Committee on the state of the Children employed in the Manufactories of the United Kingdom, 25 April-18 June, 1816. Ordered, by the House of Commons, to be printed, 28 May [and] 19 June 1816.* I would like to thank Roger Crisp for his help in locating the original source of this testimony at the Bodleian Library.

31. Speight, *Chronicles and Stories of Old Bingley*, p. 266.

32. Ibid., p. 287.

33. Ibid., p. 288.

34. Benson, *Leaves*, p. 86.

35. *Memoir*, p. 4.

36. Ibid., p. 6.

37. Bowen to Arthur Sidgwick, Sidgwick Papers, Wren Library, Cambridge University, Add.Ms.b.71.3.3–4.

38. Along with the remarkable Francis Martin, the bursar at Trinity College, who developed a close and very protective relationship with Benson.

39. Bolt, *As Good as God, as Clever as the Devil*, p. 26. Bolt's book manages to capture much of the detail of Minnie's life, with its very up ups and very down downs (that included an attempt on her life by her daughter Maggie). That she would become as much a sexual pioneer as Symonds has not often been remarked, and it is good to see that her relationship with Lucy Tait has at last been done some justice. Later in life, when Minnie was known as "Ben," she would live with Lucy in a remarkably open relationship, turning down an offer from Queen Victoria to live at Windsor Castle. See also *Eye*, pp. 73–74, n. 30. Again, Simon Goldhill's engaging and detailed work *A Very Queer Family* represents the best account to date of the Benson family and its obsessive self-recording. The story is indeed fascinating: "the thoroughly respectable and pious man who fell in love with an eleven-year-old girl; the loving mother who left her family in pursuit of another woman and came back to her authoritarian clergyman husband; the teacher who was erotically involved with his students; the Catholic priest terrified of being buried alive; the daughter whose madness was hating her mother . . . ." (p. 19).

40. Ibid., p. 36. "Etty" was Henrietta, Mrs. Sidgwick's spinster sister, and thus Henry's aunt.

41. B. Askwith, *Two Victorian Families* (London: Chatto and Windus, 1971), p. 109.

42. Sidgwick to Minnie Sidgwick, 1859, Sidgwick Papers, Wren Library, Cambridge University, Add.Ms.c.100.

43. Benson, *Leaves*, p. 77.

44. Ibid.

45. Sidgwick and Sidgwick, *Memoir*, pp. 34–35. The best works on the Apostles are Paul Levy, *G. E. Moore and the Cambridge Apostles* (London: Littlehampton Books, 1979), Richard Deacon, *The Cambridge Apostles: A History of Cambridge University's Elite Secret Intellectual Society* (New York: Farrar, Straus, Giroux, 1986), Peter Allen, *The Cambridge Apostles: The Early Years* (Cambridge: Cambridge University Press, 2010), and William Lubenow, *The Cambridge Apostles, 1820–1914: Liberalism, Imagination, and Friendship in British Intellectual and Professional Life* (Cambridge: Cambridge University Press, 1999). The same-sex attachments—the "higher sodomy"—that became so prominent with the Bloomsbury figures Lytton Strachey and John Maynard Keynes were in fact a gradual, longer term development that in some ways harked back to the idealized friendship celebrated in Tennyson's *In Memoriam*, a work that had a profound influence on Sidgwick.

46. Sidgwick, *Methods*, p. xvii.

47. Of the many excellent books on the Academic Liberals, see especially S. Rothblatt, *The Revolution of the Dons* (Cambridge: Cambridge University Press, 1968) and C. Harvie, *The Lights of Liberalism* (London: Lane, 1976).

48. Schultz et al., *Complete Works, Correspondence*.

49. See *Eye* for the fullest account of Sidgwick, one that stresses this side of him and his struggles with "the deepest problems of human life." Again, this chapter, like the previous one, adapts certain portions of *Eye* and "A More Reasonable Ghost"; also, my articles "Mill and Sidgwick, Imperialism and Racism" and "Sidgwick's Racism," as well as my entry on Sidgwick in the *Stanford Encyclopedia of Philosophy*, my Introduction to the *Complete Works*, my contribution to the *Oxford Handbook of Nineteenth Century Philosophy*, and my articles on "Sidgwick, Henry" and "Fawcett, Henry" in the *Palgrave Companion to Cambridge Economics*, Robert Cord, ed. (London: Palgrave Macmillan, 2016), reproduced with permission of Palgrave Macmillan.

50. Sidgwick and Sidgwick, *Memoir*, p. 226.

51. Sidgwick, "The Ethics of Conformity and Subscription," pp. 14–15.

52. Ibid., p. 15.

53. Ibid., pp. 30–31.

54. Ibid., pp. 11–12.

55. Ibid., pp. 33–34.

56. Sidgwick and Sidgwick, *Memoir*, pp. 200–201.

57. Ibid., p. 199.

58. Quoted in Schultz, *Eye*, p. 134.

59. Sidgwick and Sidgwick, *Memoir*, p. 38.

60. Broad, *Five Types of Ethical Theory* (London: Routledge and Kegan Paul, 1930), p. 143.

61. De Lazari-Radek and Singer, *Point of View*, p. 379.

62. Again, see also the symposium devoted to their book in *Etica & Politica* XVIII, No. 1 (Spring 2016), at http://www2.units.it/etica/.

63. The various slighting remarks of the Bloomsberries regarding Sidgwick are well known and too often repeated. See *Eye*, "Overture," for the usual litany, including the infamous crack by J. M. Keynes that Sidgwick "never did anything but wonder whether Christianity was true and prove it wasn't and hope that it was" (*Eye*, p. 4).

64. Hayward, "A Reply to E. E. Constance Jones," *International Journal of Ethics* 11 (2) (1900–1), p. 361.

65. In his magnum opus, *The Nature of Thought*, Blanshard went so far as to say that the best argument for hedonism was simply that Sidgwick believed in it; see *The Nature of Thought*, 2 vols. (New York: Macmillan, 1940), I, 391.

66. See Kenny, *What I Believe* (London: Bloomsbury Academic, 2007) and *Arthur Hugh Clough: A Poet's Life* (London: Bloomsbury Academic, 2007). The latter is a penetrating analysis of the poet who best captured Sidgwick's agnosticism.

67. As the rest of this section will show, Sidgwick's reduction of the number of methods to three is fraught with controversy, particularly in his treatments of Kantianism, perfectionism, and virtue ethics. The latter two appear to be broken up in some curious ways, partly subsumed under rational egoism, but mostly subsumed under the form of the duties set out as part of dogmatic intuitionism. For some superb recent discussions of Sidgwick's categorizations, see Crisp, *Cosmos* (especially chaps. 4–6), de Lazari-Radek and Singer, *Point of View* (especially chap. 1), and Hurka, *British Ethical Theories* (especially chaps. 7–8).

68. Although this form of intuitionism would seem to be the extreme particularism characteristic of some interpretations of Aristotle's notion of practical wisdom, or

phronesis, it is curious that, in a little known work, Reginald A. P. Rogers's *A Short History of Ethics: Greek and Modern* (London: Macmillan and Co., 1911), "aesthetic intuitionism" is instead identified with the views of such figures as Shaftesbury.

69. Sidgwick, *Methods*, p. 102.

70. Ibid., p. 421.

71. Ibid., p. 382. There is a great deal of controversy over Sidgwick's axioms, particularly the differences between his more exact and his less exact statements of them and the ethical theory he derives from them. See, for example, the classic treatment in Schneewind, *Sidgwick's Ethics*, pp. 286–311. See also Shaver, "Sidgwick's Axioms and Consequentialism," *Philosophical Review* 123 (2014), pp. 173–204; Skorupski, "Sidgwick and the Many-Sidedness of Ethics," available at http://www.henrysidgwick.com/8th-paper.1st.congress .cat.eng.html; Nakano-Okuno, "Universalizability, Impartiality, and the Expanding Circle," *Etica & Politica* XVIII, No. 1 (Spring 2016), at http://www2.units.it/etica/2016_1 /NAKANO.pdf ; and Crisp, *The Cosmos of Duty*, chap. 4.

72. But they have an admittedly difficult time defending their reconstruction while staying within the bounds of the text of the *Methods*.

73. Ibid., p. vi.

74. Sidgwick, "Professor Calderwood on Intuitionism in Morals," *Mind* 4 (1876), p. 564.

75. Schneewind, *Sidgwick's Ethics*, p. 192.

76. B. Blanshard, *Reason and Goodness* (New York: Macmillan, 1961), pp. 90–91.

77. See A. Donagan, *The Theory of Morality* (Chicago: University of Chicago Press, 1977).

78. *Methods*, pp. xvi–xvii. Or, as he had earlier put it to Dakyns: "You know I want intuitions for Morality; at least one (of Love) is required to supplement the utilitarian morality, and I do not see why, if we are to have one, we may not have others. I have worked away vigorously at the selfish morality, but I cannot persuade myself, except by trusting intuition, that Christian self-sacrifice is really a happier life than classical insouciance" (Sidgwick and Sidgwick, *Memoir*, p. 90). That Sidgwick missed much in his great utilitarian predecessors is also made clear by Schofield in "Sidgwick on Bentham: The Double Aspect of Utilitarianism," in Bucolo, Crisp, and Schultz, eds., *Ethics, Psychics, and Politics: Proceedings of the Second World Congress on Henry Sidgwick (Catania: University of Catania, 2011)*, pp. 412–69. Sidgwick's main essay on Bentham, "Bentham and Benthamism in Politics and Ethics," included in *Miscellaneous Essays*, is very witty, but based on a very limited menu of Bentham's texts. Bentham, for Sidgwick, was "eminently a representative" of his "stirring and vehement age: in his unreserved devotion to the grandest and most comprehensive aims, his high and sustained confidence in their attainability, and the buoyant, indefatigable industry with which he sought the means for their attainment—no less than in his exaggerated reliance on his own method, his ignorant contempt for the past, and his intolerant misinterpretation of all that opposed him in the present." But if Benthamism was "distinctly a child of its age," Sidgwick dryly adds, it "was not exactly a favourite child" (p. 137). And unlike Mill, Sidgwick allows "that there can be no doubt that Bowring has given us the genuine Bentham, and that the faithful historian must refuse to follow Mill in rejecting the *Deontology*" (p. 167).

79. Sidgwick, *Methods*, p. 338.

80. Ibid., p. 339.

81. Ibid., p. 341.

82. Ibid., pp. 341–42.

83. For a review of these controversies, see, in addition to the works cited earlier, Schultz, "Henry Sidgwick Today," in Schultz, ed., *Essays*. Also the exchanges between Anthony Skelton and John Deigh: Skelton, "On Sidgwick's Demise: A Reply to Professor

Deigh," *Utilitas* 22 (2010), pp. 70–77, and "Henry Sidgwick's Moral Epistemology," *Journal of the History of Philosophy* 48 (20110), pp. 491–519; Deigh, "Sidgwick's Epistemology," *Utilitas* 19 (2007), pp. 435–46; and "Some Further Thoughts on Sidgwick's Epistemology," *Utilitas* 22 (2010), pp. 78–89.

84. Sidgwick, *Methods*, p. 27.

85. Blanshard, *Reason and Goodness*, p. 23.

86. See Sidgwick, *Methods*, p. 111–12. But to say this is to side, against Rawls's *Theory*, with Broad, Frankena, Schneewind, Shaver, and Parfit. The best defense of the full-information alternative is in Crisp, *Cosmos*, who understands "Sidgwick to be suggesting the incorporation of the notion of harmony into the earlier [full-information] definition, rather than offering an independent alternative, though it remains unclear why he does not add a clause to that definition" (pp. 60–61). On irreducible normativity in general, however, Parfit's *On What Matters* is in many ways an extended, brilliant defense of Sidgwick on the irreducible normativity of ethical reasons. For a very discerning and compelling appreciation of this, see the sympathetic review of Parfit's work by Larmore, "Morals and Metaphysics: *On What Matters*," *European Journal of Philosophy* 21(4) (December 2013), pp. 665–75. Larmore also correctly identifies what both Parfit and Sidgwick miss in Kantianism—namely, the priority of rationality (or rational personhood) over reasons. See also Schultz, "Go Tell It on the Mountain," available at https://www.academia.edu /5609655/Parfit_Reviewfinalcorrected.

87. T. Hurka, "Moore in the Middle," *Ethics* 113 (2003), pp. 603–604. See also the more extensive discussion in his *British Ethical Theories from Sidgwick to Ewing* (New York: Oxford University Press, 2014). Hurka nicely identifies the issues that have led some, Roger Crisp for example, to think that Sidgwick avails himself of too many basic concepts, and should have limited his account to a concern with what one has most reason to do, dropping the "moral" reason qualification. See *The Cosmos of Duty*, p. ix. And on the specific claim about the fuzzy distinction between "ought" and "good," Crisp argues from the other side that "Sidgwick's point is that we cannot claim that attributions of ultimate goodness or bestness to actions imply a rational dictate to perform them because these actions may be impossible and hence such that they cannot be rationally required. Once we allow that rightness does involves a rational dictate, the idea that 'rightness implies can' seems plausible enough. But we might also want to claim that the idea of bestness implies a rational dictate to perform the action *if one can*. Further, the accounts of ultimate good Sidgwick has been discussing . . . have been limited in scope to what it is possible for me to seek. With that restriction in place, there is no contrast here between rightness and goodness" (Crisp, *Cosmos*, p. 63). Needless to say, however, the examination of the notion of "ought" is far from over, and such works as Matthew Chrisman's *The Meaning of 'Ought': Beyond Descriptivism and Expressivism in Metaethics* (New York: Oxford University Press, 2016) have raised new possibilities, treating the word as an intensional/modal operator, not a simple predicate.

88. Although there is a very rich literature on Sidgwick and reflective equilibrium—which has been a controversial topic ever since Rawls, in *A Theory of Justice*, claimed that he was following Sidgwick's approach, when practicing the method of reflective equilibrium—it has become increasingly difficult to say just what is at issue. Such Sidgwickians as Parfit freely claim to be deploying the method of reflective equilibrium, while others, such as Crisp, simply avoid this language, and still others, notably de Lazari-Radek and Singer, remain quite hostile to any such Rawlsian terminology, though they grudgingly admit that "[w]ithout knowing which moral theory is acceptable and whether there are philosophical arguments that reveal which moral judgments are objectively true, we cannot exclude the possibility that, once we have found the soundest moral theory and the best philosophical

arguments, we will be able to demonstrate that none, or virtually none, of our existing moral judgments are credible: and the strength of the reasoning in support of this theory may be such that we can confidently reject all, or virtually all, of our current moral judgments, and replace them with the judgments that follow from the moral theory. . . . In that case, the distinction between wide reflective equilibrium and foundationalism has narrowed to a vanishing point. It would then be true, but trivial, that when we do normative ethics, there is no alternative to the method of reflective equilibrium" (*Point of View*, p. 113).

89. Crisp, clearly a very sympathetic commentator, goes so far as to allow that "[a]lthough Sidgwick does not go on to state it, his view appears to be that if one lacks sufficient imagination, sympathy, and love of goodness, then it will make a difference to one's practical reasoning and action, whether one is a libertarian or a determinist. . . . Sidgwick is here somewhat complacent about the effects of utilitarian thinking on our moral and judicial practices. As he admits, retributive punishment in itself is a 'useless evil', and it is a question at least worth discussing whether utilitarian practices of deterrence and reform might not be considerably more humane than the system of prisons and other punishments standard in Sidgwick's and our own time. And he is complacent too about the utilitarian value of retributive notions themselves. . . . He could have omitted his chapter on free will entirely . . . and included a footnote to his chapter on utilitarianism and common-sense morality (4.3) on the unimportance to ethics—other than in highly unusual cases—of the outcome of the free will debate" (Crisp, *Cosmos*, pp. 54–56). Another, alternative Sidgwickian position would be that of Saul Smilansky, who has argued that the truth of determinism is better kept esoteric, since societal calamity would follow widespread belief in it. See Stephen Cave, "There's No Such Thing as Free Will," *The Atlantic* (June 2016), at http://www.theatlantic.com/magazine/archive/2016/06/theres-no-such-thing-as-free-will/480750/.

90. See T. H. Irwin, "Eminent Victorians and Greek Ethics: Sidgwick, Green, and Aristotle," in Schultz, ed., *A 'Fundamental Misunderstanding'?* *Utilitas* 19 (2007), pp. 78–90, and *The Development of Ethics* III (Oxford: Oxford University Press, 2009), especially chaps. 81–83.

91. R. Shaver, *Rational Egoism: A Selective and Critical History* (New York: Cambridge University Press, 1999), p. 270.

92. L. W. Sumner, *Welfare, Ethics & Happiness* (Oxford: Clarendon Press, 1996), p. 85.

93. Ibid.

94. Ibid., p. 87.

95. Ibid., p. 160.

96. Ibid., p. 86.

97. See "Sidgwick's Hedonism," in Bucolo, Crisp, and Schultz, eds., *Henry Sidgwick, Happiness and Religion: Proceedings of the World Congress on Henry Sidgwick* (Catania: University of Catania, 2007), p. 134. See also his *Reasons & the Good* (Oxford: Clarendon Press, 2006) and *The Cosmos of Duty*, chap. 3. Hurka, in such works as *British Ethical Theorists*, develops a line similar to Crisp's. And of course, Sumner's remarks scarcely seem to do justice to Bentham's hedonism as it was elaborated in chapter 2 above.

98. Crisp, *Cosmos*, p. 67. In fact, Sidgwick formulated objections that are as relevant as ever, for example against Kahneman's view that pleasure involves a conscious state that one seeks to prolong or continue.

99. Ibid., p. 70.

100. Ibid., p. 68.

101. Ibid. And as noted in the previous chapter, Crisp appears to get the better of de Lazari-Radek and Singer when it comes to the interpretation of the physiological evidence regarding pleasure: "Crisp thinks that it is better to interpret Berridge and Kringelbach as saying that pleasure is not merely a sensation, but allowing that the hedonic gloss may

itself be a sensation, or a single type of feeling. We are now willing to concede that Crisp may be right on this point. If so, the heterogeneity objection can be met, to the extent that we can say that the hedonic systems of the brain put the same kind of hedonic gloss on various different sensations. The question is, however, whether this does not simply transfer the problem of saying what pleasure is to the problem of saying what the hedonic gloss is." See "Doing Our Best for Hedonistic Utilitarianism," http://www2.units.it/etica/2016_1/SINGER-DE%20LAZARI%20RADEK.pdf.

102. Ibid. De Lazari-Radek and Singer cite new research by Adam Shriver on "the possibility of not desiring pleasure, understood as a particular feeling; see Adam Shriver, "The Asymmetrical Contributions of Pleasure and Pain to Subjective Well-Being," *The Review of Philosophy and Psychology* 5 (2014) 135–15, especially pp. 140–46."

103. Shaver, "Sidgwick on Pleasure," p. 907.

104. Ibid., p. 917, note 78.

105. Ibid., p. 928.

106. See Kahneman, *Thinking, Fast and Slow*, for his analysis of such phenomena as the "peak-end" judgments that reveal the disparities between a subject's moment to moment reports of pleasure/pain and remembered experiences of such, "experienced utility and decision utility" (see p. 378, and below). Shaver's account can also accommodate the evidence from neurophysiology, showing how subjects can be stimulated to want a state of consciousness to continue without finding it enjoyable. And this is not to mention the contextualist, relational, and interpretive dimensions of pleasure/pain that have come increasingly to the fore in recent research. Again, see Bloom, *How Pleasure Works*.

107. Haybron, "Happiness," *Stanford Encyclopedia of Philosophy* (July 2011), at http://plato.stanford.edu/entries/happiness/#Rel. For a fuller version of his theory, see his *The Pursuit of Unhappiness*. No doubt there is some strange irony in suggesting that the "Happiness Philosophers" should have been called the "Feeling Apprehended as Desirable Philosophers."

108. Though he rejects hedonism for failing to properly capture the centrality of the emotional structures and mood propensities going into happiness, being too responsive to trivial pleasures and pains: "Whereas the hedonist regards happiness merely as a state of one's consciousness, the emotional state view takes it to be a state of one's *being*. When you're happy, everything is different" (*Pursuit of Unhappiness*, p. 139).

109. De Lazari-Radek and Singer, *Point of View*, pp. 251–52. Unfortunately, the authors here miss another important component of Haybron's account: "mood propensity." But a concern with long-term character or personality structure would have been very congenial indeed to the great utilitarians.

110. In fact, Haybron himself allows that "[n]othing I have said thus far precludes a hedonistic account of well-being; my target has been hedonism about *happiness*. Hedonistic Utilitarians need not change the substance of their theories on the basis of the arguments given here; they need only grant that their views are not about happiness, in the psychological sense that concerns this book. Their Utilitarianism concerns not happiness, but pleasure" (ibid., p. 77). That there might, contra Sumner, be good reasons for utilitarians to abandon rather than embrace the notion of happiness and not their notions of pleasure/pain, is a line of argument for which support can be found in Davies, *The Happiness Industry*, which provides many telling examples of how "happiness" has lent itself to the manipulations of advertising and corporate management. Thus, "[o]ne of America's leading workplace happiness gurus, entrepreneur Tony Hsieh, argues that the most successful businesses are those which deliberately and strategically nurture happiness throughout their organizations. Businesses should employ chief happiness officers to ensure that nobody escapes workplace happiness. But if this sounds like a recipe for inclusive community, it isn't. Hsieh advises businesses to identify the 10 per cent of employees

who are least enthusiastic towards the happiness agenda, and then lay them off. Once this is done, the remaining 90 per cent will apparently become 'super-engaged', a finding which is open to more than one psychological interpretation" (p. 113). That some of the world's leading utilitarians have come to recognize the drawbacks of "Happiness Studies" is telling.

111. Again, Sumner's argument, in *Welfare, Ethics, and Happiness*, certainly marks a great advance over the crude measures of life satisfaction popularized in "Happiness Studies." One's reports of life satisfaction must, for Sumner, be informed and autonomous, not reflective of ignorance, manipulation, adaptive preferences, coercion, etc. Plausibly, this critical perspective can be adapted for hedonist purposes rather than tied to the deeply problematic notion of life satisfaction, which is an unreliable indicator of emotional well-being (see Haybron, op cit.). And it can be inflated in ways that Sumner does not recognize, as part of a larger critical theoretical perspective. Sumner also seeks a refined account of hedonism, linking it to "enjoyment" versus "suffering" rather than to the language of plea-sure/pain, which is too tightly linked to sensation.

112. Nozick's famous thought experiment, about a group of super advanced neurosci-entists able to hook one up to an Experience Machine that could simulate the experiences and lives of anyone, real or imagined, has been taken by many as decisively refuting the hedonist account of good, which according to Nozick was incapable of explaining why vir-tual or simulated experience was not as good as real world, veridical experience, since only the conscious experience mattered, whether it came from the world or you were "floating in a tank, with electrodes attached to your brain." (See Nozick, *Anarchy, State, and Utopia* [London: Blackwell, 1974], pp. 42–43, also his *The Examined Life* [New York: Simon & Schuster, 1989], pp. 104–108). This, as Crisp observes, is clearly a version of the objection that there are non-hedonic goods, and applies especially to internalist accounts of hedo-nism. But a plausible rejoinder, in line with Sumner's claims about authentic happiness, would be to urge the appropriation of any such machine for purposes of more societal experiment with the forms of pleasure and enjoyment, rather than supposing that either individuals or societies already know the best experiences to program. The subjects would somehow need to report, in an authentic way, on their experiences, judging whether con-scious feelings apprehended as desirable really were desirable.

113. Even some of the better works on happiness, such as Mathieu Ricard's *Altruism: The Power of Compassion to Change Yourself and the World* (New York: Little, Brown, and Company, 2015), fail to address the basic critical theoretical questions about the manipula-tive and ideologically suspect uses of mindfulness training.

114. Sidgwick, *Methods*, p. 501.

115. Blanshard, *Reason and Goodness*, p. 37.

116. T. H. Green, *Prolegomena to Ethics*, D. Brink, ed. (Oxford: Clarendon Press, 1883/2003), p. 470.

117. De Lazari-Radek and Singer, *Point of View*, p. 88. Given the difficulties with empiri-cal hedonism, the emphasis here should be on the expression "in principle." Alan Donagan put essentially the same point about Ross even more forcefully: "Unfortunately, the new intuitions did not suffice for moral guidance, as the precepts of the older intuitionism had done. When a man finds himself in a situation in which it would suit him to do something by which he would break his word, it is not enough for him to know that there is a consid-eration against doing that thing; what he wants to know is whether, in that situation, that consideration is decisive. . . . The most familiar objection to the newer intuitionism is moral: that it allows ordinarily respectable persons to do anything they are likely to choose, and to have a good conscience in doing it. . . . Philosophically, the chief objection must be that it is fraudulent to describe what the new intuitionists take to be a process of moral deliberation as one of 'weighing' or 'balancing' considerations. For that metaphor to be appropriate, there must be a procedure for ascertaining the weight of each consideration, either comparatively

or absolutely, a procedure analogous to that of putting objects on a balance or scale. . . . by repudiating anything that might order the various considerations it acknowledges, and accepting as 'weighing' or 'balancing' any process whatever in which a man, hesitating before alternatives supported by different considerations, without conscious insincerity overcomes his hesitation, the new intuitionism deprives the description of any definite sense. Hence, its laxist consequences" (Donagan, *The Theory of Morality*, pp. 22–24).

118. Hurka, *British Ethical Theorists*, pp. 162–63.

119. Ibid., p. 164.

120. Sidgwick, "Conformity and Subscription," p. 30. An anonymous reviewer of this manuscript objected that this was simply "biting the bullet": "The idea that one ought to promote the aggregate welfare seems vastly less compelling if understood as an all-things-considered requirement, i.e., one that necessarily overrides any competing consideration, than it is if instead understood as a pro tanto requirement, i.e., one that sits alongside other requirements and permissions and might be outweighed by them. Equally, though there is very much less dissent from the duties of commonsense morality if they are understood as pointing to pro tanto requirements than if they are understood as all-things-considered requirements. This is the main point of Hurka's: once we have the distinction between pro tanto and all-things-considered requirements, we see that commonsense morality is composed of pro tanto requirements. If that is granted, then Sidgwick's objection that commonsense morality's requirements can conflict seems hardly damning. Moreover, a requirement of benevolence is itself one whose intuitive grip and whose ability to attract consensus are hugely greater if the requirement is construed as a pro tanto requirement, rather than an all-things-considered one." Against this, it seems appropriate to point out that Donagan took himself to be largely following Whewell in his defense of a theory of morality and the absoluteness of its demands—Hurka's account of moral duties is a revisionist one, not the one that presented itself to both Mill and Sidgwick. The question is whether it is an improvement on the earlier form of intuitionism, as Hurka, Parfit, and Crisp maintain. On this, see the exchanges in the book symposium on *The Point of View of the Universe*, with de Lazari-Radek and Singer arguing, for example, that "Crisp does not discuss another reason why we think utilitarianism has an advantage over Rossian intuitionism. Ross starts by assuming that, as he puts it, 'the main moral convictions of the plain man' are 'not opinions which it is for philosophy to prove or disprove, but knowledge from the start.' As we have already indicated both in our book and in this response, we are skeptical about the validity of most of our moral intuitions. Debunking arguments, in other words, play a role here again in persuading us that utilitarianism is more defensible than Ross's intuitionism, whether the explanations of 'the main moral convictions of the plain man' are evolutionary or cultural." http://www2.units.it/etica/2016_1/SINGER-DE %20LAZARI%20RADEK.pdf. This line of objection can be extended, as noted previously, to reliance on intuitions about the Experience Machine in arguing against hedonism.

121. Crisp, *Cosmos*, p. 194. Crisp in some ways echoes the interpretations of Aristotelian judgment advanced by Gadamer, Irwin, and McDowell, linking it to aesthetic intuitionism and allowing that Sidgwick's interpretation of Aristotle seems to fail to do justice to both the role of judgment, or *phronesis*, and the way in which Aristotle incorporated "ought" (*dei*) as well as "good" in his system, which in turn suggests that Sidgwick's sharp distinction between ancient "attractive" visions of ethics and modern jural or "imperative" visions is untenable. See p. 193.

122. Parfit's famous Bk IV set out an agenda of problems that no ethical theory has yet successfully addressed. Even de Lazari-Radek and Singer, in *Point of View*, can only gesture in the direction of a defense to the effect that classical utilitarianism does not fail any more badly on this score than any other ethical theory. Still, that is something.

123. Sidgwick, *Methods*, pp. 489–90.

124. Williams, "The Point of View of the Universe: Sidgwick and the Ambitions of Ethics," *The Cambridge Review* 7 May (1982). The idea of an esoteric morality, or a self-effacing morality, is given a canonical treatment in Parfit's *Reasons and Persons*. But Williams, "The Point of View of the Universe," remains the best critique of, and one of the finest essays on, Sidgwick's approach. The Millian notion of a clerisy, or an elite of philosopher-poets, whether colonialist or not, might also serve Williams's purposes here, as might the "moral heroes" of philanthropy that the effective altruism movement seems to be fostering; see Larissa MacFarquhar, *Strangers Drowning: Grappling with Impossible Idealism, Drastic Choices, and the Overpowering Urge to Help* (New York: Penguin Press, 2015): "Do gooders are different from ordinary people because they are willing to weigh their lives and their families in a balance with the needs of strangers" (p. 299). And "some do-gooders are happy, some are not. The happy ones are happy for the same reasons anyone is happy—love, work, purpose. It's do-gooders' unhappiness that is different—a reaction not only to humiliation and lack of love and the other usual stuff, but also to knowing that the world is filled with misery, and that most people don't really notice or care, and that, try as they might, they cannot do much about either of those things. They lack that happy blindness that allows most people, most of the time, to shut their minds to what is unbearable" (p. 298). And importantly, "If everyone thought like a do-gooder, the world would not be our world any longer, and the new world that would take its place would be so utterly different as to be nearly unimaginable" (p. 300). The early Godwin could well agree.

125. De Lazari-Radek and Singer, "Secrecy in Consequentialism: A Defense of Esoteric Morality," *Ratio* 23 (2010), pp. 34–58. The point is also extensively developed in *Point of View*, chap. 10.

126. Sidgwick and Sidgwick, *Memoir*, p. 277.

127. Sidgwick, *Methods*, first edition, p. 473.

128. Sidgwick, "Some Fundamental Ethical Controversies," Mind 14 (1889), p. 483; reprinted in Singer, ed., 2000

129. Sidgwick, *Outlines*, p. 197n.

130. See Frankena, "Sidgwick and the History of Ethical Dualism," in Schultz, *Essays*, and "Sidgwick and the Dualism of Practical Reason," *The Monist* 58 (1974). For still longer perspective, see Schneewind's introduction to the first volume of his *Moral Philosophy from Montaigne to Kant: An Anthology*, 2 vols. (Cambridge: Cambridge University Press, 1990).

131. Sidgwick, *Methods*, p. xix.

132. See Schneewind, *Sidgwick's Ethics*, chap. 15.

133. See also Irwin, "Happiness, Virtue, and Morality," *Ethics* 105 (1) 1994, as well as his massive *Aristotle's First Principles* (Oxford: Clarendon Press, 1988) and *The Development of Ethics*, vol. 3, chaps. 81–83, which contain penetrating discussions of Sidgwick. The vitality of the ongoing debate over ancients versus moderns, as a question of rupture rather than continuity, is well attested. Along with many others, Charles Larmore also gives a very sympathetic and compelling defense of Sidgwick's account of ancient versus modern moral theory; see his *The Morals of Modernity* (New York: Cambridge University Press, 1996). However, again, Crisp has challenged this distinction by arguing that Aristotle himself deployed something like the modern "ought" in his account of the virtues; see note 120 above, and Crisp's introduction to his edition of Aristotle's *Nicomachean Ethics* (New York: Cambridge University Press, 2000).

134. Frankena, "Ethical Dualism," in Schultz, *Essays*, p. 177.

135. Ibid.

136. Darwall, *The British Moralists and the Internal 'Ought', 1640–1740* (New York: Cambridge University Press, 1995), p. 244, note 1.

137. Darwall, "Reason, Norm, and Value," in Schneewind, *Reason, Ethics, and Society: Themes from Kurt Baier, with His Responses* (Chicago: Open Court, 1996). Cumberland's *A Treatise of the Law of Nature* was counted, along with the books of Grotius and Pufendorf, as one of the three great seventeenth-century works of natural law. Cumberland holds that we can will to pursue the goods of others no less than we can our own. He accepts the traditional view of the will as invariably being of the good, but interprets this to mean that we can will anything we judge will promote the *good of any being*, oneself or others. Since, however, we can will either, we face a question which to pursue when they conflict" (pp. 29–30). Sidgwick was also fascinated and frustrated by Cumberland, but he found in him the first modern utilitarian rather than the first modern ethical dualist—an instructive difference.

138. Sidgwick, *Methods*, p. 509.

139. Ibid., p. 506.

140. D. Brink, *Perfectionism and the Common Good: Themes in the Philosophy of T. H. Green* (Oxford: Clarendon Press, 2003), pp. 122–23.

141. Sidgwick, *Lectures on the Ethics of T. H. Green, H. Spencer, and J. Martineau*, ed. E. E. Constance Jones (London: Macmillan, 1902), p. 78.

142. Parfit, *On What Matters*, vol. 1, p. 137. See also my review essay "Go Tell It on the Mountain," https://www.academia.edu/5609655/Parfit_Reviewfinalcorrected.

143. Quoted in Schultz, *Eye*, p. 329.

144. Sidgwick and Sidgwick, *Memoir*, p. 472.

145. In Schultz et al., *Complete Works, Correspondence*.

146. The *Methods* had in fact taken a very progressive stance on sexual morality—he found the notion of "purity" to be as vacuous as "natural," in common-sense morality. See Parfit, *On What Matters*, vol. 1, p. xxxviii, and Schultz, *Eye*, pp. 512–16. His views on this surely reflect the influence of Symonds's work on Greek pederasty.

147. Symonds, *Letters*, vol. III, pp. 206–207. Though Symonds was given to certain forms of mystical experience or cosmic consciousness, one instance of which made it into James's *The Varieties of Religious Experience*. Despite his distaste for the prospect of immortality, he shared various parapsychological interests.

148. Sidgwick and Sidgwick, *Memoir*, p. 471.

149. Gauld, *The Founders of Psychical Research* (London: Routledge and Kegan Paul, 1968) and Oppenheim, *The Other World* (New York: Cambridge University Press, 1985) are still the best treatments of the subject, but there is much research yet to be done. Many older works, such as Frank Podmore's *Newer Spiritualism* (London: T. Fisher Unwin, 1910) and Harry Price's *Fifty Years of Psychical Research* (London: Longmans, Green and Co., 1939) remain rich resources for research in this area. Despite the important work being done on the philosophical issues surrounding death and immortality—evident, for example, in Nussbaum's *The Therapy of Desire*—relatively few academic philosophers have ventured into this region, despite it figuring importantly in the work of Kant, Schopenhauer, Godwin, Sidgwick, Broad, and others.

150. James, "The Confidences of a Psychical Researcher," in *William James, Writings 1902–1910* (New York: Library of America, 1987), p. 1250.

151. Ellenberger, *The Discovery of the Unconscious* (New York: Basic Books, 1970), p. 314. See also, Samuel Hynes, *The Edwardian Turn of Mind* (London: Pimlico, 1968), especially p. 143. More recent works are cited in later notes.

152. Bruce, "The Ghost Society and What Came of It," *The Outlook* (1910), p. 462.

153. Myers, "Henry Sidgwick," in *Fragments of Prose and Poetry*, Eveleen Myers, ed. (London: Longman, 1904), pp. 98–99. Myers, like Symonds, deserves a chapter in himself. He had some of the flamboyance of Noel, or Oscar Browning, and much of their conceit, which made him a less than popular figure at Cambridge. Still, one of the richest sources

for understanding Sidgwick, after his correspondence with Symonds, is his correspondence with Myers, contained in the Myers and Sidgwick collections, Wren Library, Trinity College, Cambridge. Although Eleanor Mildred Sidgwick and Arthur Sidgwick made heavy use of this for their *Memoir*, the uncensored and unabridged versions are extremely revealing, and point up the remarkable affinities between Myers, Symonds, and Sidgwick. On the significance of Myers, see also my Introduction to the "Miscellaneous Letters," in Schultz et al., *Complete Works*.

154. Myers had had a doomed love affair with the married Annie Marshall, who committed suicide under tragic circumstances in 1876; his work in psychical research to his mind supported his claim that she had communicated with him after her death. See Schultz, *Eye*, pp. 300–301.

155. As early as 1864, Sidgwick had insisted that what was "required is psychological experiments in ethics and intuitive Theism: that is what on the whole the human race has got to do for some years." (Sidgwick and Sidgwick, *Memoir*, p. 124.) His work in psychical research was very largely just that, Mill's ethology or study of character with a new emphasis, another form of experiments in living.

156. Ibid., p. 100 and p. 101.

157. See Symonds, *A Problem in Greek Ethics* (privately printed, 1883) and *A Problem in Modern Ethics* (privately printed, 1891); the two volumes were printed together in a 1928 edition by AMS Press, New York. It is still not a widely known fact that Symonds contributed (among other things, a case study of himself) to Ellis's study of *Sexual Inversion*.

158. The passage from Ellis is quoted in Grosskurth, *John Addington Symonds, A Biography* (London: Longmans, 1964), p. 285; Grosskurth's observation about Whitman is on p. 286. In reference to Symonds's unusual attitude toward the possibility of an afterlife, Myers, in the revised but unpublished version of his "Fragments of Inner Life," wrote: "Such was J.A. Symonds, one of my most intimate friends, and a man whose deeply interesting character is not adequately represented by his books. With him, indeed, the indifference had another ground. It was not that he was unmindful of possible expansions of human fate, but his sadness, his weariness, his inward scepticism as to the cosmic meaning was such that he felt satiated in advance with all existences, and desired an endless rest." Myers Papers 18 (76–11), Wren Library, Trinity College, Cambridge.

159. Grosskurth does a good job of explaining Sidgwick's role in the Brown biography; see pp. 318–19. But see also Schultz, *Eye*, chaps. 6 and 8. Other works of vital importance for understanding Sidgwick's connection with Symonds are: *The Memoirs of John Addington Symonds: The Secret Homosexual Life of a Leading Nineteenth-Century Man of Letters*, edited by Phyllis Grosskurth (Chicago: University of Chicago Press, 1984), and *The Letters of John Addington Symonds*, three vols., which gives Symonds's side of the correspondence. Such letters from Sidgwick to Symonds as survive are singularly illuminating, and do powerfully suggest that he was drawn to the homoerotic ideal of fellowship promoted by Symonds, an ideal that in various respects was also to be found in earlier Apostolic infatuations, such as the idolizing of the Tennyson/Hallam relationship. For broader background on what Wilde represented, see Richard Ellman's magisterial *Oscar Wilde* (New York: Vintage Books, 1987).

160. Quoted in Schultz, *Eye*, p. 414.

161. Again, this comports well with his strategy of exploring the potential for a new, less egoistic human nature; like James, Sidgwick tended to look to psychology rather than social theory when thinking about fundamental social change.

162. Consider, for example, the concerns of "Is Prayer a Permanent Function of Humanity?" in "Unpublished Lectures," in Schultz et al., *Complete Works*, which explores the possibility of "symmetrical people," an interest that stayed with Sidgwick throughout his life, perhaps in part explaining his fascination with Symonds.

163. See Sprigge's insightful essay "Could Parapsychology Have Any Bearing on Religion?" *Parapsychology, Philosophy and the Mind: Essays Honoring John Beloff*, Fiona Steinkamp, ed., (Jefferson, NC: McFarland, 2002), pp. 127–45. Sprigge, like many Idealists, did not see why parapsychological evidence was necessary for the rejection of materialism—a cause Sidgwick shared—since a priori arguments could justify its rejection. But he did allow that it could help justify belief in the survival of physical death (a matter on which he remained agnostic). Also relevant here is Sprigge's masterful *James & Bradley: American Truth and British Reality* (LaSalle, IL: Open Court, 1993), which congenially argues that the two title figures, "usually considered diametrically opposed, share many main premises and some main conclusions, while the contrasts between their views are all the more interesting just because they share so much" (p. 573).

164. Quoted in Schultz, *Eye*, p. 441.

165. Though as noted previously, some, such as Saul Smilansky, might agree, at least if belief in free will, instead of a true deterministic view, were crucially dependent on religion; see http://www.theatlantic.com/magazine/archive/2016/06/theres-no-such-thing-as-free-will/480750/.

166. See Schultz, *Eye*, pp. 720–21.

167. Ethel Sidgwick, *Mrs. Henry Sidgwick, A Memoir* (London: Sidgwick and Jackson, 1938).

168. Quoted in Schultz, *Eye*, p. 299.

169. Gauld, *Founders*, p. 107.

170. Psychical research, Myers would suggest in the 1880s, could now claim "a certain amount of actual achievement," but as he recognized, it was not enough to satisfy Henry. See also Bruce, op cit.

171. See C. D. Broad, *Five Types of Ethical Theory* (London: Routledge and Kegan Paul, 1930), "Henry Sidgwick," in Broad, *Ethics and the History of Philosophy* (London: Routledge and Kegan Paul, 1938), and *Lectures on Psychical Research* (London: Routledge and Kegan Paul, 1966). This was a big and very troubling issue for Sidgwick, since he did think the case for telepathy was compelling, endorsing the statement by Myers that "We hold that we have proved by direct experiment, and corroborated by the narratives contained in this book, the possibility of communications between two minds, inexplicable by any recognised physical laws, but capable (under certain rare spontaneous conditions) of taking place when the persons concerned are at an indefinite distance from each other. And we claim further that by investigations of the higher phenomena of mesmerism, and of the automatic action of the mind, we have confirmed and expanded this view in various directions, and attained a standing-point from which certain even stranger alleged phenomena begin to assume an intelligible aspect, and to suggest further discoveries to come. Thus far the authors of this book, and also the main group of their fellow-workers, are substantially agreed." Myers et al. *Phantasms of the Living* (Hyde Park, NY, 1962), p. xx.

172. See also Gauld's superb short overview, "Henry Sidgwick, Theism, and Psychical Research," in Bucolo, Crisp, and Schultz, eds., *Henry Sidgwick: Happiness and Religion*.

173. For the fullest source material, see A. Roy, *The Eager Dead* (Sussex: Book Guild Publishing, 2008), and "An Interview with Professor Archie Roy, *The Searchlight*, http://www.aspsi.org/feat/life_after/tymn/a073mt-a-Prof_Archie_E_Roy_interview.php.

174. Ibid.

175. Roy, *The Eager Dead*.

176. Again, the "cross-correspondence" cases were cases in which different mediums would independently receive messages from 'the Other Side' that needed to be pieced together in order to make sense.

177. Quoted in Roy, *The Eager Dead*, pp. 446–48. Italicized words in the quoted passages are underlined in the original. "Phyllis" was the code name for Myers's lost love, Annie Marshall. "M.V." refers to Margaret Verrall, one of the "communicators." The references to the Palm Sunday case concern the supposed communications from Arthur Balfour's deceased true love, Mary Lyttleton, who died tragically on Palm Sunday 1875; her communications from "the Other Side," relating intimate details of her relationship with Arthur Balfour unknown to anyone else, went far to convince the psychical researchers of the reality of posthumous survival.

178. Ibid., p. 318. Interestingly, Henry Augustus was mentored at Cambridge by none other than Broad.

179. Gray, *The Immortalization Commission: Science and the Strange Quest to Cheat Death* (New York: Farrar, Straus and Giroux, 2011), p. 90.

180. Gray, *Immortalization*, p. 3. See also the engaging work by Stephen Cave, *Immortality: the Quest to Live Forever and How It Drives Civilization* (New York: Crown Publishers, 2012), which addresses some of the more recent schemes for overcoming death.

181. Ibid., pp. 235–36.

182. And as Warner aptly notes: "When poets and novelists project metamorphing personalities and destablilized identities, they have recourse to the venerable languages of ghost possession and the supernatural, and then attempt . . . to refashion them to appeal of contemporary readers and resonate with their experience." See her brilliant work *Phantasmagoria* (Oxford: Oxford University Press, 2006), p. 380.

183. Though it is difficult to resist the thought that they, the Sidgwicks included, longed to be headline news: "Scientists Prove There Is Life After Death." They would clearly have relished such works as Bernard d'Espagnat's *On Physics and Philosophy* (Princeton: Princeton University Press, rep. 2013) or Robert Lanza's *Biocentrism* (Dallas: BenBella Books, 2010).

184. Warner, *Phantasmagoria*, p. 239.

185. Sidgwick, *Methods*, pp. 418–19.

186. Myers, quoted in Gray, *Immortalization*, p. 100.

187. Quoted in Kelly and Kelly, *Irreducible Mind: Toward a Psychology for the 21st Century* (Lanham, MD: Rowman & Littlefield, 2007), p. 82. This massive volume in effect represents a reconstruction and defense of Myers's work.

188. James, *The Varieties of Religious Experience*, in *William James: Writings 1902–1910* (New York: Library of America, 1987), p. 457 and p. 217.

189. Sprigge, "Could Parapsychology," p. 143.

190. Myers, *Human Personality and Its Survival of Bodily Death*, 2 vols. (London: Longmans Green, 1903), II, p. 122.

191. In this, he would have been prescient, given the very fruitful uses of the language of different selves in current cognitive psychology, such as Daniel Kahneman's *Thinking Fast and Slow*, which suggests just such a wider range of conflicting selves, including very basic processes of cognition bearing on hedonistic calculation. In a famous experiment, alluded to earlier in this chapter, the "peak end" phenomenon illustrates how a retrospective hedonistic assessment of a colonoscopy can differ from a moment to moment one, rating a longer but otherwise similar process as less painful simply because the pain trailed off to a lower point by the end of the prolonged process (with a bigger difference between the pain at the peak and at the end). The self of memory does not add up pains or pleasures in the same way the presently reporting self does. It is for such reasons that John Gray had a point, when insisting on the philosophical relevance of Sidgwick's psychical research in his review of Peter Singer's *The Most Good You Can Do*. Singer replied: "Gray does refer to *The Point of View of the Universe*, but only to say that although the book discusses Sidgwick's

'dualism of practical reason,' the book barely mentions Sidgwick's interest in psychical research. Psychical research is of no relevance to the aims that Dr. Lazari-Radek and I had in writing our book, which, as we say in the preface, is not a study in the history of ideas, so it should not surprise Gray that we pay it scant attention." What this reply does not acknowledge is the potential ethical/philosophical relevance of Sidgwick's psychical research insofar as it was something of an early version of Parfit's explorations of the ethical/philosophical relevance of personal identity. That Parfit's work on personal identity is profoundly relevant to the viability of Sidgwickian utilitarianism would be difficult to deny. See Schultz, "Persons, Selves, and Utilitarianism," *Ethics* 96, No. 4 (July 1986), with a "Comment" by Derek Parfit. For the Gray/Singer exchange, see *The New York Review of Books*, May 21 and June 25 (2015), at http://www.nybooks.com/articles/2015/06/25 /whats-left-hanging/.

192. It should also be noted that Sidgwick was remarkably reticent, even in his philosophical writings, about the exact nature of Mind and Matter. He was impressed enough with the results of physiology, but also held, as Gauld has noted, that "the *prima facie* disparateness of mental facts and nervous changes, the apparently total absence of kinship between them, puts in the way of any materialistic synthesis an obstacle difficult to overleap" (see *Philosophy, Its Scope and Relations*, p. 54). On such a view, psychology, it seems, had at the least to deal with "double facts" and stay open to the possibility of purely mental causation, as in telepathy.

193. See for example, Sidgwick, *Lectures on the Ethics of T. H. Green, H. Spencer, and J. Martineau*, p. 3. Of course, the Idealist accounts of the self varied widely, especially depending on whether one was a personal or Absolute Idealist; for Bradley, the self was ultimately but part of the tissue of experiences forming the Absolute, not what it appeared to be in the world of appearances. And interestingly, as Sprigge has compellingly shown, Bradley was in many ways the critic of psychical research whose challenges James (and by extension Sidgwick) often seemed to be trying to meet. For Bradley, "we have no reason to believe anything that such spirits say, inasmuch as the normal conditions on which we can rely upon the testimony of others do not hold," and in truth "the very meaning of survival is unclear, for the main criterion of this, bodily identity, used in this life, cannot apply." But most importantly, in "all this Bradley is very much the 'refined' supernaturalist criticizing the crass supernaturalism of which James was the avowed champion. There may be a crass supernatural but what is spiritually significant is as present in this world as it could be in any other. In all equally there can be the expression of goodness, truth, and beauty, and all must equally play their role in constituting absolute experience" (Sprigge, *James and Bradley*, pp. 569–72).

194. As Mander, *British Idealism*, observes, the early Idealists often denied that "they were drawn beyond this world to some other," drawing instead "a division within this world, between the higher and the lower" (p. 6). But at the same time, "there ran a deep religious current through all of the idealist thinkers, and a common conviction that human reason had the power not only to reach the transcendent but to give it sufficient content to ground human hopes" (p. 138). And that there was a vein of mysticism in such figures as Bradley and McTaggart would be hard to deny.

195. Myers, *Human Personality*, II, p. 277.

196. Ibid., pp. 468–69.

197. Tennyson, *The Works of Alfred Lord Tennyson*, introduction by D. Hodder (London, 2008), p. 656. See also Sidgwick's touching essay, "Alfred Tennyson," *Journal of the Society for Psychical Research* 5 (1892), pp. 315–18.

198. Bradley, *A Commentary on Tennyson's In Memoriam* (London: Macmillan, 1923), pp. 81–82. Bradley was in fact the brother of F. H. Bradley.

199. See Schultz, *Eye*, especially p. 442. And he seems never to have entertained the provocative possibility, cogently explored by Tim Mulgan in his *Purpose in the Universe: the Moral and Metaphysical Case for Ananthropocentric Purposivism* (Oxford: Oxford University Press, 2015), that the cosmos does indeed have a purpose but humanity is irrelevant to it. At least, insofar as he did broach that line of thought, it terrified him.

200. Tennyson, *In Memoriam: A Norton Critical Edition*, E. Gray, ed., (New York: W. W. Norton, 2004), p. 5.

201. Ibid., p. 92.

202. See Parfit, *On What Matters*, p. 137, and D. Phillips, *Sidgwickian Ethics* (New York: Oxford University Press, 2011). Parfit's revision (and that of de Lazari-Radek and Singer) successfully avoids most of the problems with Sidgwick's framing of the dualism described by Skorupski in the *The Domain of Reasons*, where he states that when Sidgwick holds that egoism and utilitarianism are "individually self-evident" and then concludes "unless the egoist principle and the utilitarian principle taken individually always prescribe one and the same action there is a contradiction," he "completely understates the difficulty. The two positions just are contradictory, even if they never prescribe incompatible actions" (p. 349). But this just does miss the way in which Sidgwick's deeper anxieties concern the priority of the practical and the cosmic harmonization that would determine in a particular way how, in Skorupski's words, "the principles combine in generating practical conclusions about what a person should do." This is no mere logical difficulty.

203. And, admittedly, Sidgwick's views on cosmic justice go beyond his narrower accounts of equity, the axiom that what is right for one must be right for anyone similarly situated. His "debunking" of the rationality of the universe is a disheartening recognition that one may not matter to the cosmos despite being predisposed to think that one does.

204. De Lazari-Radek and Singer, *Point of View*, pp. 182–83.

205. See her "A Darwinian Dilemma for Realist Theories of Value," *Philosophical Studies* 127 (2006), pp. 109–66.

206. Ibid., p. 183. Of course, one could argue that Sidgwick's parapsychology provided him with a curious analogue to Kahneman's two selves, the self of memory v. the self of present introspection, the hedonistic calculations of which are incompatible. This is language that Sidgwick would have understood and complicated even further. And it is suggestive of how the "unity" of the package of reason may be profoundly compromised and conflicted, even if—or because—rational egoism is debunked.

207. On this, see the book symposium on *Point of View*, at http://www2.units.it/etica/.

208. Gauld, "Theism," p. 188.

209. Blanshard, *Four Reasonable Men*, p. 213.

210. My own sense is that a significant part of Sidgwick's larger concern was the familiar and powerful one voiced by, among many others, Martin Luther King, Jr., for example in his sermon on "The Death of Evil Upon the Seashore": "The death of the Egyptians upon the seashore is a vivid reminder that something in the very nature of the universe assists goodness in its perennial struggle with evil. . . . Something in this universe justifies Shakespeare in saying: 'There's a divinity that shapes our ends, / Rough-hew them how we will' and Lowell in saying: 'Though the cause of Evil prosper, / Yet 'tis Truth alone is strong' and Tennyson in saying: 'I can but trust the good shall fall, / At last—far off—at last, to all, / And every winter change to spring'" (in King, *Strength to Love* [Minneapolis: Fortress Press, 2010], p. 78.

211. Sidgwick's hopes revived in part because of the results with the American medium Leonora Piper. The Piper case converted James—who was no mere impartial observer in this business—to a belief in the personal survival of physical death, and Sidgwick, though more guarded, was also deeply impressed. See Gauld, "Theism," for a good summary account.

212. Schultz, *Eye*, p. 726.

213. Sidgwick and Sidgwick, *Memoir*, p. 357.

214. Ibid., p. 354.

215. Ibid., p. 358.

216. Ann Phillips, ed. *A Newnham Anthology* (Cambridge: Newnham College, 1988), p. 33.

217. Millicent Garrett Fawcett, *What I Remember*, pp. 72–73. In *The Works of Henry and Millicent Garrett Fawcett*, facsimile edition (Bristol: Thoemmes Continuum, 1995).

218. Quoted in Rita McWilliams Tullberg's classic *Women at Cambridge* (Cambridge: Cambridge University Press, 1975, 1998), p. 104. But on Newnham see also Gillian Sutherland, *Faith, Duty, and the Power of Mind: The Cloughs and Their Circle, 1820–1960* (Cambridge: Cambridge University Press, 2006). And for a nice account of Sidgwick's earlier work reforming Cambridge, Robert Todd, "Henry Sidgwick, Cambridge Classics, and the Study of Ancient Philosophy: The Decisive Years (1866–69)", in *Classics in Nineteenth and Twentieth Century Cambridge: Curriculum, Culture, and Community*, C. Stray, ed., *Proceedings of the Cambridge Philological Society, Supplement*, 24 (Cambridge, 1999). And *A Feminist Case Study in Transnational Migration: The Anne Jemima Clough Journals*, Mary Gallant, ed. (Newcastle upon Tyne: Cambridge Scholars, 2009) provides a rich vein of fascinating original source material on Newnham's first Principal.

219. E. M. Sidgwick, flysheet dated 12 February 1896, Newnham College Archives, reprinted in Ethel Sidgwick, *Mrs. Henry Sidgwick*.

220. Oppenheim, "A Mother's Role, a Daughter's Duty," p. 198.

221. E. M. Sidgwick, "University Education for Women" (Manchester, 1913), pp. 16, 20, and 7.

222. Sidgwick and Sidgwick, *Memoir*, p. 73.

223. Sidgwick and Sidgwick, eds., *Miscellaneous Essays and Addresses*, p. 121.

224. Mill, "Inaugural Address," p. 44.

225. Phillips, *A Newnham Anthology*, p. 46.

226. See the helpful summary at HerStoria, http://herstoria.com/?p=535.

227. Richard Symonds, *Inside the Citadel: Men and the Emancipation of Women, 1850–1920* (London: Macmillan, 1920), p. 97.

228. Sidgwick, "Review of J. F. Stephen's *Liberty, Equality, Fraternity*," *Academy* 1 (August 1873).

229. The gardens of Newnham are celebrated in Jane Brown's informative work, *Eminent Gardeners: Some People of Influence and Their Gardens, 1880–1980* (New York: Viking, 1990).

230. See R. Backhouse, "Sidgwick, Marshall, and the Cambridge School of Economics," *History of Political Economy* 38 (2006), pp. 15–44.

231. Sidgwick and Sidgwick, *Memoir*, pp. 394–96.

232. See especially P. Groenewegen, *A Soaring Eagle: Alfred Marshall, 1842–1924* (Aldershot, UK, and Brookfield, Mass.: Edward Elgar, 1995). See also Barbara Caine, "Feminism and Political Economy in Victorian England—or John Stuart Mill, Henry Fawcett and Henry Sidgwick Ponder the 'Woman Question'" in Peter Groenewagen, ed., *Feminism and Political Economy in Victorian England* (Aldershot, UK: Edward Elgar, 1994).

233. Sidgwick and Sidgwick, *Memoir*, p. 36.

234. Sidgwick, *Principles of Political Economy*, p. 33. But it must be confessed that he never went far enough in explaining how his ethical philosophy related to his work in politics and political economy, as the rest of this section will demonstrate. Beyond the larger problems swirling around the dualism of practical reason, there are the more tractable ones about, for example, the significance (or insignificance) of preference satisfaction.

Daniel Housman's excellent recent work, *Preference, Value, Choice, and Welfare* suggests the type of clarification of the limited value of preference satisfaction that Sidgwick plausibly should have offered.

235. Sidgwick, "The Scope and Method of Economic Science," Printed for the British Association (1885); reprinted in Sidgwick and Sidgwick, eds., *Miscellaneous Essays and Addresses*, p. 171.

236. Sidgwick, *Principles*, p. 48.

237. P. Deane, "Henry Sidgwick," in *The New Palgrave: A Dictionary of Economics*, J. Eatwell, M. Milgate, and P. Newman, eds., (London: Macmillan, 1987).

238. R. Howey, *The Rise of the Marginal Utility School* (New York: Columbia University Press, 1965).

239. G. Stigler, *The Economist as Preacher* (Chicago: University of Chicago Press, 1982), p. 41.

240. See S. Medema, *The Hesitant Hand: Taming Self-Interest in the History of Economic Ideas* (Princeton: Princeton University Press, 2009), "Sidgwick's Utilitarian Analysis of Law: A Bridge from Bentham to Becker?" *Social Science Research Network*, July 1, 2004, and "'Losing My Religion': Sidgwick, Theism, and the Struggle for Utilitarian Ethics in Economic Analysis," *History of Political Economy* 40 (2008), pp. 189–211. But it should be observed here that there are very different "utilitarian" approaches at work in what Richard Posner calls the "economic analysis of law" and what others call the "law and economics" approach. Thus, as Cass Sunstein has pointed out, the work of Guido Calabresi, *The Future of Law and Economics: Essays in Reform and Recollection* (New Haven: Yale University Press, 2016), is quite unlike Posner's Chicago School in viewing laws as "a precious repository of hard-won social wisdom" that economists should treat as such, as "products of insight and experience." For Calabresi, "we will be unable to understand some of the most important aspirations of the legal system if we do not see that people's preferences and values can be malleable—and are sometimes a product of the legal system itself," which can and should positively promote the pursuit of certain goods over others (see Sunstein, "Listen, Economists!" *New York Review of Books*, November 10, 2016, pp. 53–54). Calabresi identifies his approach with Millian utilitarianism, given its invocation of higher pleasures and effort to interpret and understand the meaning of various goods, including equality. But arguably, even Bentham would have been receptive to many of the subtle analyses of complex pleasures to be found in Calabresi's approach.

241. Sidgwick, *Principles*, p. 82.

242. A. C. Pigou, *Memorials to Alfred Marshall* (London: Macmillan, 1925).

243. See the lovingly edited *F. Y. Edgeworth's Mathematical Psychics and Further Papers on Political Economy*, Peter Newman, ed. (New York: Oxford University Press, 2003). Edgeworth is the formalizing link between Sidgwick's largely qualitative economics and recent figures such as Kahneman, though it cannot be said that he actually solved the problems with hedonism described in the previous section.

244. Sidgwick, *Elements of Politics*, p. 42.

245. Ibid., pp. 141–42.

246. See J. Bryce, and E. M. Sidgwick, eds., *National and International Right and Wrong: Two Essays by Henry Sidgwick* (London: George Allen and Unwin, 1919).

247. See also the excellent volume by Simon Cook, *The Intellectual Foundations of Alfred Marshall's Economic Science* (Cambridge: Cambridge University Press, 2009), which provides a wealth of important archival material on the early relationship between the two men, and how philosophically freighted it was.

248. Schultz et al., *Complete Works*.

249. Ibid.

250. Backhouse, "Sidgwick, Marshall, and the Cambridge School of Economics," pp. 15–44.

251. Medema, *Hesitant Hand*, pp. 28–29.

252. Ibid., p. 53.

253. Ibid., p. 49.

254. Sidgwick, *Principles*, p. 583.

255. Sidgwick, *Elements*, pp. 521–22.

256. Winch, *Wealth and Life*, pp. 226–27.

257. Sidgwick, *Principles*, p. 414.

258. Coase, *Essays*, p. 191. What Coase points to is actually a great plus in Sidgwick's political economy—namely, the way in which it avoids any reliance on crude notions of basic (especially negative) rights and the limits of government. This cannot be said of the work of Milton Friedman and various other figures in the Chicago School.

259. Sidgwick, *Miscellaneous Essays and Addresses*.

260. Medema, *Hesitant Hand*, pp. 23–24.

261. Sidgwick, *Principles*, p. 356.

262. Ibid., pp. 590–91.

263. In Schultz et al., *Complete Works*.

264. See Schultz, *Eye*, chap. 7, for the most comprehensive account, but also Schultz and Varouxakis, eds. *Utilitarianism and Empire*.

265. W. S. Jevons, *The Theory of Political Economy* (London: Macmillan, 1871), p. 177.

266. F. Y. Edgeworth, *F. Y. Edgeworth's Mathematical Psychics and Further Papers on Political Economy*, p. 78.

267. Sidgwick, *Elements*, pp. 213–14.

268. Again, see Tullberg, *Women at Cambridge*, and Sutherland, *Faith, Duty, and the Power of Mind: the Cloughs and Their Circle, 1820–1960*.

269. See A. Skelton, "Utilitarian Practical Ethics: Sidgwick and Singer," in Bucolo, Crisp, and Schultz, eds., *Henry Sidgwick, Ethics, Psychics, Politics*, pp. 592-633.

270. Sidgwick, *Elements*, 2nd ed. (London: Macmillan, 1897), pp. 327–28.

271. Ibid., p. 327.

272. Quoted in Geoffrey Dutton, *The Hero as Murderer: The Life of Edward John Eyre, Australian Explorer and Governor of Jamaica, 1815-1901* (Sydney and Melbourne, 1967), p. 250; Dutton's biography is quite sympathetic to Eyre and Carlyle, bringing out how the Carlyleans cast the governor as a "hero." Sidgwick, *Elements*, pp. 327–28.

273. Sidgwick to Mary Sidgwick, 21 Jan. 1867 (Sidgwick Papers, Trinity College Library, Cambridge University).

274. Mill, CW II, pp. 104–105. Again, many of Mill's remarks about "the state of mind of the negroes" betray (much) weaker versions of the same Carlylean stereotypes of blacks as "lazy," "docile," and "sensuous," etc.

275. Hall, *Civilizing Subjects*, p. 31. Hall's *Cultures of Empire* also gives a helpful conceptual clarification: "I use 'colonialism' to describe the European pattern of exploration and 'discovery,' of settlement, of dominance over geographically separate 'others,' which resulted in the uneven development of forms of capitalism across the world and the destruction and/or transformation of other forms of social organization and life. I use 'imperialism' to refer to the late nineteenth/early twentieth century moment when European empires reached their formal apogee" (p. 5). Sidgwick was very much within this trajectory from colonialism to imperialism. Hall also rightly stresses the importance of Sidgwick's friend and colleague, Sir John Seeley, a "founding father" of imperialism: "Empires, forgotten in the wake of decolonization as an embarrassment and source of guilt, re-emerge as it becomes clear that neo-colonialism is alive and well, and that imperial histories are playing

a part in postcolonial politics. . . . Seeley's categories—race, nation and empire—remain central to reconfiguring those histories in postcolonial terms" (p. 3).

276. Fredrickson, *Racism*, p. 91. And here Sidgwick's deep indebtedness to the Kantian tradition (as well as to the utilitarian one) might also raise troubling questions; Kant's views were extremely racist (see *The Idea of Race*, Bernasconi and Lott, eds.), and the colonialist and imperialist thinking inspired by them was capable of producing such figures as Alfred Milner. More broadly, P. Mandler's "'Race' and 'Nation' in Mid-Victorian Thought," in S. Collini, R. Whatmore, and B. Young, eds., *History, Religion, and Culture: British Intellectual History, 1750–1950* (Cambridge: Cambridge University Press, 2000), pp. 224–244) highlights some of the troubling features of mid-Victorian "Teutonism."

277. As noted in the last chapter, even the very informed and well-researched work of Duncan Bell (see *The Idea of Greater Britain: Empire and the Future of World Order, 1860–1900*) and his sometimes collaborator Casper Sylvest on late Victorian colonialism and imperialism seems to miss the point, when it comes to addressing late Victorian racism. Thus, Sylvest, quoting me, writes: "There is some truth in the statement that '[t]o gloss over the racism of the past is to perpetuate it', but to castigate Sidgwick for 'swimming in rather than examining the various prejudices of his times' seems too obvious an instance of the intellectual historian longing to be a time-travelling moralist." (*British Liberal Internationalism*, p. 136). Beyond the fact that Sylvest actually concedes all of my major points, and seems only to object to my "schoolmaster" tone, it is worth replying that my "time-travelling" involved nothing more than expressing objections that in substance might well have been made by Bentham and others in the relevant historical contexts (indeed, even by Whewell). In fact, after reading the works of DuBois, Sidgwick's much admired friend Bryce would come to regret and recant the racial prejudice found in his earlier writings. Racism was a recognized problem then, and it remains one now. Bell himself, Sylvest's frequent collaborator, writes of E. A. Freeman's "virulently racist" views (see p. 191), as well he should.

278. In Sidgwick, *Miscellaneous Essays and Addresses*, p. 219.

279. Pearson, *National Life and Character: A Forecast* (London: Macmillan, 1893), pp. 337–38.

280. Ibid., p. 342.

281. Ibid, pp. 343–44.

282. Ibid., p. 31. Interestingly, Pearson's claims about historical evolution bear some comparison to Kant's on cosmopolitan history—Kant, too, thought that history would inexorably work toward the triumph of his race. See Robert Bernasconi in the previously cited works and "Will the Real Kant Please Stand Up?" *Radical Philosophy*, 117 (Jan. Feb. 2003).

283. Ibid., pp. 84–85.

284. *Charles Henry Pearson: Memorials by Himself, His Wife, and His Friends*, W. Stebbing, ed. (London: Longmans Green, 1900), p. 186.

285. Ibid.

286. Sidgwick to Pearson, Feb. 8, 1893, Bodleian MS.Eng.Lett.d.190, 175.

287. Sidgwick, *Lectures on Green, Spencer, and Martineau*, pp. 236–37.

288. Balfour, "Decadence," in *The Mind of Arthur James Balfour*, ed. W. Short (New York: George H. Doran, 1918), p. 92. It seems obvious enough what Balfour would have considered a "superior" breed of humanity.

289. And much more could be said about this. For example, it is intriguing that, as Sir Guy Strutt reported to me, Sidgwick insisted on being buried in a wickerware coffin. This strongly suggests that Sidgwick had some sympathy with the "earth to earth" movement's call to resist cremation but still reform burial practices by deploying light perishable

coffins, such as wicker ones. See the fascinating account in Pat Jalland, *Death in the Victorian Family* (New York: Oxford University Press, 1996), p. 204. Having unconventional thoughts on death and burial was of course another familiar part of the utilitarian legacy.

290. Sidgwick, *Lectures on the Philosophy of Kant*, p. 264.

291. Sidgwick, *Elements*, pp. 213–14.

292. Sidgwick, *Practical Ethics: A Collection of Addresses and Essays* (London: Swan Sonnenschein, 1898), pp. 21–22.

Epilogue

1. See Sherry Turkle, *Reclaiming Conversation: The Power of Talk in the Digital Age* (New York: Penguin Press, 2015). Of course, to be fair, younger generations are surpassing older generations in recognizing the challenges confronting their world; see the GenForward surveys of the Black Youth Project, available at http://genforwardsurvey.com /assets/uploads/2016/07/GenForward-June-2016-Toplines-1.pdf.

2. The book by Robert Skidelsky and Edward Skidelsky, *How Much Is Enough? Money and the Good Life* (New York: Other Press, 2012) in fact provides a good overview of many of the critical concerns about consumerism, the quality of life, justice for future generations, etc., that the classical utilitarians would raise against current economic orthodoxy (if there is any such thing), but with an appropriate note of caution: "To go from the pursuit of growth to the pursuit of happiness is to turn from one false idol to another" (p. 123). The authors favor something closer to Brink's perfectionist or Nussbaum's capabilities reading of Mill. See also John Broome's concise review of the narrowing of the notion of utility over the course of the last two centuries, "Utility," *Economics and Philosophy* 7(1) (1991), pp. 1–12.

3. Braidotti and Gilroy, eds., *Conflicting Humanities*, pp. 2–3.

4. Eze, *On Reason: Rationality in a World of Cultural Conflict and Racism* (Durham: Duke University Press, 2008), p. 178.

5. See, in addition to the previously cited works, Norman Doidge, *The Brain's Way of Healing* (New York: Viking, 2015), which reviews the literature on such matters as acute versus chronic pain, with their very different neural circuitry. Even the notion of pain is a family resemblance one, with some pains involving complex interpretive feedback from a wide range of neural structures (see pp. 13–14). And as noted in previous chapters, Kahneman-style questions apply to research in both hedonism and happiness studies.

6. Eze, *On Reason*, p. 115.

A NOTE ON THE TYPE

THIS BOOK has been composed in Miller, a Scotch Roman typeface designed by Matthew Carter and first released by Font Bureau in 1997. It resembles Monticello, the typeface developed for The Papers of Thomas Jefferson in the 1940s by C. H. Griffith and P. J. Conkwright and reinterpreted in digital form by Carter in 2003.

Pleasant Jefferson ("P. J.") Conkwright (1905–1986) was Typographer at Princeton University Press from 1939 to 1970. He was an acclaimed book designer and AIGA Medalist.

The ornament used throughout this book was designed by Pierre Simon Fournier (1712–1768) and was a favorite of Conkwright's, used in his design of the *Princeton University Library Chronicle*.